THE
HISTORY OF
ADVERTISING
40
MAJOR BOOKS
IN FACSIMILE

Edited by
HENRY ASSAEL
C. SAMUEL CRAIG
New York University

A
GARLAND
SERIES

PRINCIPLES OF
ADVERTISING

DANIEL STARCH

GARLAND PUBLISHING, INC.
NEW YORK & LONDON
1985

659.1
S79p

For a complete list of the titles in this series
see the final pages of this volume.

This facsimile has been made from a copy in
the Yale University Library.

Library of Congress Cataloging in Publication Data

Starch, Daniel.
   Principles of advertising.
   (The History of advertising)
   Reprint. Originally published: Chicago : A.W. Shaw
Co., 1923.
   Includes index.
   1. Advertising. I. Title. II. Series.
HF5821.S74   1985   659.1   84-46041
ISBN 0-8240-6735-5 (alk. paper)

Design by Donna Montalbano ⑂

The volumes in this series are printed on
acid-free, 250-year-life paper.

Printed in the United States of America

PRINCIPLES
OF ADVERTISING

BY

DANIEL STARCH, Ph.D.

GRADUATE SCHOOL OF BUSINESS ADMINISTRATION
HARVARD UNIVERSITY

CHICAGO & NEW YORK

A. W. SHAW COMPANY

LONDON, A. W. SHAW COMPANY, LIMITED

1923

PREFACE

THIS treatise has been prepared with three aims in mind: (1) to make a broad and comprehensive analysis of the fundamental problems of advertising which would serve as a logical plan for the preparation of a book; (2) to develop, as far as practically feasible and possible at the present time, scientific methods in dealing with these problems; (3) to bring together as fully as possible all available material —practical business experience, scientific, experimental, and statistical data—which bear upon the problems outlined.

A thoroughgoing analysis of the broad problems was necessary at the outset in order to develop a consistent plan for correlating the various aspects of the subject, since no comprehensive plan covering all phases of advertising had been worked out before. The central conception of this book is that the primary function of advertising in business is to sell or to help sell. From this conception are derived the five fundamental problems or divisions of the book, namely, (1) To whom may the product be sold? (2) By what appeals may it be sold? (3) How may the appeals be presented most effectively? (4) By what mediums may the appeals be presented so as to reach the class of people to whom the product is to be sold? (5) What is a reasonable expenditure for promoting the sale of the product by means of printed sales efforts?

The most important idea which has been kept in mind in dealing with these problems has been the development of the scientific point of view and the application of corresponding methods. Waste is due largely to lack of information, to failure to use adequate means to secure the needed information, and to poor judgment in handling the practical problems as they arise from day to day. Much emphasis has therefore been placed upon the development of adequate methods for obtaining facts on which the business executive

iii

may base his decision. Some of these methods, particularly those discussed in Part III, in several chapters in Part IV, and to some extent those discussed in Part II, are new so far as general use is concerned.

This book has been planned as a companion volume for one on problems which is now under way. The problem book will serve as the basis of class discussion and instruction in educational institutions. The present work will serve to give the broader analytical background and supply an organized body of information to which the business man may turn in considering his immediate problems. It will also provide a treatise for students of advertising.

I take pleasure in acknowledging the assistance which I have received from several persons. I wish particularly to express my appreciation to Mr. Earl C. Norris, of Churchill-Hall, Inc., New York, who read the entire manuscript and made numerous useful suggestions; to Mr. Charles C. Eaton, Librarian of the Harvard Graduate School of Business Administration and formerly of the Publicity Department of the General Electric Company, who read a considerable portion of the manuscript and made many helpful suggestions; and especially to my secretary, Miss Perle M. Hopson, who carefully read both the manuscript and the proof and materially improved the phraseology and clarity of the text.

I also wish to mention the valuable personal contacts which I have had with Street and Finney, Inc., Joseph Richards Co., H. K. McCann Co., Frank Seaman, Inc., Lord and Thomas, Ruthrauff and Ryan, W. B. Snow and Staff, and J. Walter Thompson Co.

Finally I desire to make acknowledgment to *Printers' Ink* for the numerous quotations made in the text and to Scott, Foresman & Co., who published my earlier book on Advertising in 1914, for some material which has been included in the present volume.

Harvard University, April, 1923   D. S.

CONTENTS

PART I. INTRODUCTORY SECTION

PART II. THE HUMAN ASPECTS OF THE MARKET

PART III. THE APPEALS

v

PART IV.   THE PRESENTATION OF THE APPEALS

PART V.   MEDIUMS

CONTENTS

PRINCIPLES OF ADVERTISING

PART I

INTRODUCTORY SECTION

I

THE PROBLEMS AND SCOPE OF ADVERTISING

The functions of advertising. Definition of advertising. The five fundamental problems of advertising: 1. To whom may the commodity be sold?
2. By what appeals may the commodity be sold? 3. How may the appeals
be presented most effectively? 4. By what mediums may the advertisements be presented? 5. What is a reasonable expenditure for advertising
the commodity?

IN order to discuss systematically the chief aspects of
advertising, it is necessary to determine what its fundamental problems are. What these problems are will depend
necessarily upon our conception of what advertising is. It
is obvious that if our conception of advertising is of one
sort its chief problems will be in accordance therewith. If,
however, our conception of advertising is of another sort,
our analysis will reveal a different type of problem. Thus,
if we conceive the function of advertising to be primarily
that of publicity, that is of "making known," our fundamental problems will be distinctly different from the ones
which would result from the conception that the function
of advertising is to sell.

It is evident then that our definition will depend upon
our conception of the purpose and function of advertising.
There are two main points of view at the present time concerning its function in the distribution of goods. According
to one point of view the purpose of advertising is to make
a product known, but not to sell it. According to the
second point of view the purpose of advertising is not
only to make a product known but also to sell or help
sell it. The former is the initial conception, derived from
the original meaning of the Latin word advertere, *to turn
toward*.

Advertising at the present time means of course much

more than that; it means more than merely announcing, making known, or turning the attention of the public toward a certain product. Its ultimate purpose is to sell or to help sell. This is the prevailing notion today, and, in the last analysis, it is the real reason for its existence.

There are those who maintain that advertising never actually sells a commodity, that the sale is always made ultimately through personal contact. Undoubtedly that is true in a large majority of cases. However, that does not mean that advertising does not or may not play an important part in the complete selling process. Selling consists of very much more than merely the final exchange of an article for a piece of money.

It is true that a great deal of advertising, probably the greater share of it, does not actually sell in the limited sense of making the final step in the selling process. This may be the least important part of the sale. Take, for example, the advertising of an automobile, a phonograph, or a soap. The sale may be completed in person at the store, but half of the selling process may have been effected through the advertisements or through other influences before the customer came to the store. Thus, in buying a phonograph, the customer may have practically made up his mind, through reading advertising and other printed material, through observation and personal inquiry, and through the recommendation of friends, that he wishes to purchase a certain make of phonograph. He goes to the store to have the instrument exhibited and demonstrated before he finally makes the actual purchase. He may even visit a number of stores to have various makes demonstrated. Before he started, however, he may actually have had his mind made up to buy a particular make; and his visit to various stores may merely serve to substantiate his original decision.

If advertising serves any real purpose at all, it must play a part in the complete selling process. It must play a part in reducing sales resistance, by developing a readiness to accept a product, or by actually creating desire or demand for the commodity. Even if advertising only "made known," as it no doubt does, in many instances, that in itself is a very important part in the complete selling process. The goal of all sales and advertising efforts is to establish "consumer demand" for a product, and the influences that bring about "consumer acceptance" or even "consumer recognition" of a product play a highly important part. Advertising assists in all three, although its chief function may be in the last two. The complete buying-selling process includes all steps from zero knowledge of, and desire for, the product to the actual purchase and possession of it.

It is not likely that any sane business concern would continue over a period of years to spend money for advertising its products unless it knew, or believed for good reasons, that such efforts would sell or help to sell its products. It is evident then that the function of advertising in the complete selling process may vary all the way from merely making known the bare name of a product to completing, in some instances, the actual selling process to the point where the consumer will actually call for a given commodity.

DEFINITION OF ADVERTISING

The simplest definition of advertising, and one that will probably meet the test of critical examination, is that advertising is selling in print. Or to put it more completely, commercial advertising consists in presenting a commodity in print to the people in such a way that they may be induced to buy it. According to our conception, then, there are two types of selling: oral selling and printed selling. Many, if not all, of the fundamental processes of these two types of salesmanship are essentially the same. Oral salesmanship deals ordinarily with one person at a time; printed salesmanship deals with many people at one time. The former is individual selling, while the latter is mass selling.

In a broader sense, advertising includes somewhat more than commercial advertising, as, for example, the advertising done in connection with political campaigns, charitable organizations, churches, solicitation of funds, and the like. In this broader sense, advertising may be defined as the presentation of a proposition (usually in print) to the people in such a way that they may be induced to act upon it. This broader definition will include those forms of publicity which are used to influence people in other respects than in buying and selling, such as influencing public opinion, emphasizing the importance of public safety, sanitation, strike prevention, morale, and the like. On the borderline between advertising to sell and advertising to mold opinion are such forms of publicity as institutional and good-will advertising. A public service company, such as the American Telephone Company, may carry on an extensive advertising program to develop and maintain the good-will of the public; although indirectly it may help to extend or sell the service of the company.

In accordance with our conception that advertising is selling in print, five fundamental problems clearly present themselves:

1. To whom may the commodity be sold?
2. By what appeals may it be sold?
3. How may the appeals be presented most effectively?
4. By what mediums may the appeals or advertisements be presented?
5. What is a reasonable expenditure for advertising the commodity?

The *first* problem raises such questions as, Who are the users and buyers of this commodity? Where do they live? How many are there? How large is their need for this product? How do they now satisfy this need? In what ways? By what brands? What are their preferences, likes and dislikes, with reference to the various brands intended to fill this need?

The *second* problem may be analyzed further as follows: What are all the various possible appeals that may be used for the commodity? What is the relative value or effectiveness of these appeals? Which of the possible appeals shall actually be used? Which shall not be used? Upon which appeals should most emphasis be placed? By what methods may the relative value of these appeals be determined? Can their relative value be measured? Can it be measured in advance of their actual use?

The *third* problem deals with the specific principles and methods according to which advertisements are actually prepared.

The functions of an advertisement are fivefold: To attract attention (the advertisement must be seen); to arouse interest (the advertisement must be read); to create conviction (the advertisement must be believed); to produce a response (the advertisement must be acted upon); and to impress the memory (the advertisement in most instances must be remembered).

The specific question growing out of this analysis is, How may the appeals which are to be used be presented so that they will most effectively attract attention, arouse interest, create conviction, produce response and impress the memory?

It is obvious that this phase of our study will necessarily deal with the technique of layout, headline, illustration, color, typography, phraseology and statement of text, names and trade-marks, and means of establishing the memory and identification of products.

The *fourth* problem includes a detailed analysis and study of the various types of mediums, their circulation, relative values, and utility for specific commodities; their influence and standing with their readers; the distribution of a given medium throughout the particular buying population of a given commodity.

The *fifth* problem raises such questions as, How much

money should or may economically be spent for advertising? How may the appropriation be determined? What returns should be expected? May advertising be used economically for a given product and under given circumstances? Further analysis of these problems makes it evident that they are in part psychological and in part economical, perhaps in most instances primarily the former. Thus, for example, the first problem is psychological in so far as it deals with the human aspect of the market, that is, with the buyer, his desires, tastes, modes of living, habits of buying, his needs and demands, and the like. It is in part economic, in so far as it deals with the outlets and the distribution and economic values of products. It is evident from a simple analysis of this large problem—to whom may the product be sold?—into its subsidiary questions that the human aspect of the market is a very large and important one.

The second and third problems are almost entirely psychological in nature. The guiding principles in determining the appeals and in ascertaining the most effective modes of presenting these appeals are primarily based upon the consideration as to what will most effectively influence the mind of the buyer. Obviously the appeals to be selected and the manner in which they are to be presented will be determined on this basis. The many subsidiary problems that arise in connection with these two major questions are concerned chiefly with the mental processes of the prospective customer, with his likes and dislikes, his motives, instincts, habits, and attention processes.

Thus, it will readily be seen that the ultimate basis of many if not of most advertising processes—the "why" and the "how" of specific problems—rests on an understanding of human nature. All advertising problems are subsidiary, in the last analysis, to the one main question, namely: By what means and in what manner may the mind of the potential customer be influenced most effectively? Such questions as, What is the most appropriate headline? What is the most attractive form? What are the most appealing arguments and selling points? What is the most effective way of expressing them? What is the best style of type? What are the most suitable mediums? What will arouse attention to, and interest in, a given proposition? What will make the most convincing impression? What is most apt to secure response? and the like, find their ultimate answers in the light of how they will influence people, and, in particular, the class of people to be reached in any particular campaign. A sale is made not in a man's pocketbook but in a man's mind.

A large proportion of the principles of advertising, therefore, are based, either directly or indirectly, upon psychology. Broadly defined, psychology is the scientific study of human nature, of the laws and motives that control human behavior. Its central question is, How does the mind work? To know how to influence human beings, it is useful to understand the workings and laws of human behavior.

The fourth problem is in part psychological, in part sociological, and in part economic. It involves a study of the reading habits, likes and dislikes of the public and their attitude toward various mediums. From another angle it involves a study of the extent and distribution of the circulation and of the standing and influence of the various mediums among certain classes of people in the population at large.

In the practical preparation and execution of advertising plans the fifth problem is usually considered first, namely: What is a reasonable and economical expenditure for advertising a given commodity? This problem with its wider relations will be considered in Chapters III and IV.

A more detailed outline of problems may be of value at this point, as it will serve to give a panoramic view of the plan and logical interrelations of the various topics that will be considered in this book.

PART I (CHS. III AND IV). THE PLACE OF ADVERTISING
IN BUSINESS

PART II. THE HUMAN ASPECT OF THE MARKET: TO WHOM
MAY THE COMMODITY BE SOLD?

A. 1. Who are the users and buyers of the commodity?
    2. Where do they live?
    3. How many are there?
    4. How large is their need for this product and how
       much do they, and may they, buy?
    5. How do they at present satisfy this need?   In
       what ways?   By what brands?   From what
       sources?

B. 1. By what methods and from what sources may
       information be obtained to answer these ques-
       tions?
    2. The formulation and use of field questionnaires
       and the methods of obtaining the responses to
       questionnaires
    3. Statistical data, population, and census data
    4. Typical samples of investigations, data, and re-
       sults bearing on particular problems

PART III. THE APPEALS: BY WHAT APPEALS MAY THE
COMMODITY BE SOLD?

A. Analysis of the product to determine the appeals to
    be found in
    1. The raw material out of which the product is
       made
    2. The process of manufacture
    3. Uses and qualities of the finished product
    4. Price and value

B. Analysis of human nature—the psychology of de-
    sires, motives, and instincts involved in buying
    and selling

1. An inventory of desires and instincts
2. Their nature, relative strength, and importance
3. Desires and instincts concerned in the buying and selling of typical commodities

C. Methods of measuring the strength of appeals
   1. Laboratory and field tests
   2. Statistical methods in treating test results
   3. Use and interpretation of results
   4. Correlation of laboratory and field tests with actual returns from advertisements

D. Class and sex differences in the effectiveness of appeals

PART IV. PRESENTATION OF THE APPEALS: HOW MAY THE APPEALS BE PRESENTED MOST EFFECTIVELY?

A. It is assumed that the specific functions of an advertisement are as follows:
   1. To secure the attention of the reader
   2. To arouse his interest so that he will read and examine the advertisement
   3. To produce desire, conviction, and belief
   4. To produce a response, in most instances, either immediately or later
   5. To establish, in most instances, a memory and an identification of the product

B. How may the appeals be presented to accomplish these ends most effectively and economically?

C. Argumentative versus suggestive forms of appeals
   1. Analysis of argumentative, reasoned decisions in buying
   2. Analysis of suggestive decisions and responses
   3. When may either or both be used?

Note: The five functions, given under A above, may perhaps best be considered in the order in which they usually arise in the preparation of advertising plans rather than in the order in which they are enumerated under A above. Therefore we will consider them as follows:

  D. Producing interest, desire, conviction, belief
    1. The text—characteristics of convincing and appealing text
    2. Language and phraseology
    3. Truth and agencies for the betterment of advertising
    4. Interest incentives
    5. The headline
    6. The illustration
    7. The use of colors
    8. Laboratory methods of testing the interest factors of advertisements

  E. Securing attention
    1. The laws of attention-getting
    2. Space and the size of advertisements
    3. The layout—display features, balance and arrangement, typography
    4. Laboratory methods of testing the attention factors of advertisements

  F. Producing the response
    1. Methods of bringing about a response
    2. Methods of ascertaining the responses produced —keying systems

  G. Establishing memory and identification of advertisements and products
    1. Repetition of advertisements and cumulative effect
    2. Identification features of advertisements
    3. Trade-marks and names
        a. Their importance and value
        b. Characteristics of good trade-marks and names

4. Selection of mediums
5. The copy
6. Relation to personal sales campaign
7. Relation to retail advertising and dealer tie-up
8. The advertising agency
9. Analysis and preparation of campaigns

B. Retail advertising
   1. Policy
   2. The appropriation
   3. Daily and seasonal fluctuations
   4. Selection of mediums
   5. The copy
   6. Use and distribution of space
   7. Preparation of copy for specific commodities and stores
   8. Show windows

C. Mail-order advertising

D. Other special fields of advertising—such as foreign advertising, financial advertising, clothing advertising, automobile advertising, and so forth

The need of a thorough study of these problems is glaringly apparent. There is an urgent demand for the application of scientific methods to their solution, for the finding of facts and for the common sense utilization of these facts in the preparation and execution of plans. Money is expended without even an approximately complete knowledge of facts. Waste is inevitable under such conditions. If every printed piece of advertising material were made only 10% more effective it would effect a saving of $100,000,000 a year. That it could be made 10% more effective is not an idle wish when we realize that the average advertisement, even in our better grade mediums, has probably only half the effectiveness possessed by the few most effective advertisements in the same mediums. While such a statement is difficult to substantiate, it is, in view of the results presented in Chapter XIV, probably not far wrong. What we need are (1) adequate methods and facilities for obtaining facts, (2) initiative in obtaining the desired facts and (3) judicious application of the facts to the problems in question.

II

HISTORY AND DEVELOPMENT OF ADVERTISING

1. The pre-printing stage. 2. The early printing stage. First newspaper published, 1609. Early American newspapers. Typical 18th century and early 19th century advertisements. 3. The modern period. 4. The period of development of higher standards and practices in advertising. Characteristics of the past two periods, 1850-1911 and 1911 to the present: (a) Growth in quantity of advertising; (b) Growth in quality of advertising; (c) Increase in variety of uses. Present volume of advertising.

It may not be of great value to devote a large amount of space to analyzing and discussing the history of a subject when we are primarily interested in the practical problems of the present day. Nevertheless, a brief survey will give us a valuable background whereby we may judge more accurately the present status and development and understand somewhat more completely the problems which arise at the present time. Advertising as we know it today is a development substantially of the last 75 years, beginning about the middle of the 19th century. However, there has been advertising of one form or another as far back as there has been any method of recording ideas by means of visual symbols.

Speaking broadly, we may conveniently and logically trace the development of advertising through four stages of growth through which it has passed:

1. The pre-printing period prior to about 1450
2. The early printing period from 1450 to about 1850
3. The modern period of expansion from 1850 to 1911
4. The period of development of standards of practice and the introduction of research methods from 1911 to the present

I. THE PRE-PRINTING STAGE

Some form of advertising has probably existed since the time when men lived in communities and competed with one another for the necessities and luxuries of life. The first period covers such efforts as corresponded to the present forms of advertising, and embraces chronologically the period prior to 1450 A. D., when the modern process of printing by movable type was invented. Advertising on a large scale was of course impossible without a convenient, rapid method of reproducing visual symbols, such as was made possible by the invention of the printing press. Prior to that time there were forms of handwritten and inscribed announcements corresponding to advertisements. There were inscriptions on walls and announcements on sheets of papyrus. Perhaps the oldest known advertisement of this type is in the British Museum and was written on a sheet of papyrus found in the ruins of ancient Thebes, in Egypt. This announcement offered a reward for a runaway slave. It was written possibly about 3000 B.C.

In Rome, during the time of the Caesars, there were similar bulletins written by slaves and displayed on the boards erected for the purpose about the city. In both Greece and Rome, advertisements of gladiatorial exhibitions were posted, giving an appearance probably not unlike that of a present-day town when it is filled with circus posters. Another form of publicity used by the Greeks consisted in affixing to the statues of the infernal deities curses inscribed on sheets of lead, assigning the persons who had stolen goods or done other injury to the advertiser to the vengeance of these gods. The ruins of Herculaneum and Pompeii, buried on the morning of August 24, A.D. 79, show that the walls of buildings were covered with announcements painted in black or red. Baths were advertised—warm, sea, and fresh water baths—thus

THERMAE
M. CRASSI FRUGII
AQUA. MARINA. ET BALN.
AQUA. DULCI. JANUARIUS. L.

Houses, shops and apartments were advertised for sale or rent. Thus one such announcement in Pompeii, painted in red, was as follows: "On the estate of Julia Felix, daughter of Spurius Felix, are to let from the 1st to the 6th of the ides of August, on a lease of five years, a bath, a venereum, and ninety (?) shops, bowers, and upper apartments."

In both Greece and Rome it was customary to whiten a part of the wall of a house on which announcements pertaining to the affairs of the occupants were painted. Many such instances were found in Pompeii.

Likewise there was early interest in the development of trade-marks, in a very limited manner, however. These trade-marks were put on vases, pieces of crockery, and the like.

One form of attracting attention, in some respects a forerunner of advertising, was that employed by the Carthaginians who, when they arrived with a cargo of goods on the Phoenician shores, built a fire to attract the attention of the inhabitants who then gathered to examine and purchase the goods.

At first the merchant cried his wares on the streets, carrying them with him as he did so. Later when shops were established, the professional town-crier appeared on the scene. There were during the pre-printing period many town-criers in the various larger cities of Europe. While their method of announcing or selling was oral it was nevertheless a forerunner of present-day advertising in the sense of being mass selling.

The mediaeval crier used to carry a horn, by means of which he attracted the people's attention when about to make a proclamation or publication. Public criers appear to have formed a well-organized body in France as early as the twelfth century; for by a charter of Louis VII, granted in the year 1141 to the inhabitants of the province of Berry, the old custom of the country was confirmed, according to which there were to be only twelve criers, five of which should go about the taverns crying with their usual cry, and carrying with them samples of the wine they cried, in order that the people might taste. For the first time they blew the horn they were entitled to a penny, and the same for every time after, according to custom. These criers of wine were a French peculiarity, of which we find no parallel in the history of England. They perambulated the streets of Paris in troops, each with a large wooden measure of wine in his hand. from which to make the passers-by taste the wine they proclaimed, a mode of advertising which would be very agreeable in the present day, but which would, we fancy, be rather too successful for the advertiser.[1]

It is stated that in 1641 there were 400 town-criers in Paris. However, these town-criers were fairly definitely organized in groups or corporations and as early as in 1258 they obtained various regulations from the authorities, of which the following is typical:

Whosoever is a crier in Paris may go to any tavern he likes and cry its wine, provided they sell wine from the wood, and that there is no other crier employed for that tavern; and the tavern-keeper cannot prohibit him.

If a crier finds people drinking in a tavern, he may ask what they pay for the wine they drink; and he may go out and cry the wine at the prices they pay, whether the tavern-keeper wishes it or not, provided always that there be no other crier employed for that tavern.

If a tavern-keeper sells wine in Paris and employs no crier, and closes his door against criers, the crier may proclaim that tavern-keeper's wine at the same price as the king's wine (the current price), that is to say, if it be a good wine year, at seven denarii, and if it be a bad wine year, at twelve denarii.

Each crier to receive daily from the tavern for which he cries at least four denarii, and he is bound on his oath not to claim more.

The criers shall go about crying twice a day, except in Lent, on Sundays and Fridays, the eight days of Christmas, and the Vigils, when they shall cry only once. On the Friday of the

[1] Sampson, *History of Advertising*, p. 44.

Adoration of the Cross they shall cry not at all. Neither are
they to cry on the day on which the king, the queen, or any of
the children of the royal family happens to die.[1]

2. THE EARLY PRINTING STAGE

The second stage naturally arose when modern methods
of printing were invented. This made possible, of course,
the rapid and indefinite duplication of writing by means of
print which is the necessary medium of advertising. With
this development there then came about the publication of
newspapers and periodicals corresponding to our modern
magazines. It is said that the first newspaper was published in Strassburg in 1609. The *Frankfurter Journal* was
founded in 1615. In France probably the first newspaper
published was the *Journal Général d'Affiches*, or better
known as the *Petites Affiches*, first published on the 14th of
October, 1612. It was apparently started from the beginning with the purpose of carrying advertising. This journal
has been published under the same title continuously up to
the present time. Henry Sampson in his *History of Advertising*, published in 1874, tells us that "It is now the journal
of domestic wants of France; and servants seeking positions,
or persons wanting servants, advertise in it in preference
to all others. It is especially the medium for announcing
any public or private sales of property, real or personal;
and the publication of partnership deeds, articles of association of public companies, and other legal notices, are
required to be inserted in the *Journal des Petites Affiches*,
which is published in a small octavo form."

In London the *Weekly News* was published in 1622 and
the first advertisement appeared in this paper during that
year. It was an advertisement of a book.

In America the first newspaper was entitled *Publick Occurrences both Foreign and Domestick*, published in Boston in 1690. This was succeeded in 1704 by the *Boston*

[1] *Ibid.*, pp. 45-46.

News Letter, a weekly publication. The first issue of the *Boston News Letter,* published April 26, 1704, contained advertisements. The paper was written and edited by John Campbell, who at that time was postmaster of Boston. It was 40 years before this publication reached a circulation of 300 copies per issue.

In 1776 there were 13 newspapers in the Colonies. In 1788 the *Independent Gazette* of New York had 34 advertisements which were mostly announcements of runaway slaves, giving full descriptions of their defects and merits and offering rewards for their return. Sometimes notices of the sale of negro slaves were inserted. Thus one of them read: "Two very likely negro boys and also a quantity of very good lime juice to be sold cheap."

In this connection it will be of interest to note a number of sample advertisements, which appeared in the early printing period, collected and presented in a very interesting manner in Sampson's *History of Advertising.* Among the early advertisements of this period were those relating to beverages—coffee, tea, and chocolate.

Thomas Garway, a tobacconist and coffee-house keeper in Exchange Alley, the founder of Garraway's Coffee-house, was the first who sold and retailed tea, recommending it, as always has been, and always will be the case with new articles of diet, as a panacea for all disorders flesh is heir to. The following shop-bill, being more curious than any historical account we have of the early use of "The cup that cheers but not inebriates," will be found well worth reading:

Tea in England hath been sold in the leaf for 6, and sometimes for 10 the pound weight, and in respect of its former scarceness and dearness it hath been only used as a regalia in high treatments and entertainments, and presents made thereof to princes and grandees till the year 1657. The said Garway did purchase a quantity thereof, and first sold the said tea in leaf or drink, made according to the directions of the most knowing merchants into those Eastern countries. On the knowledge of the said Garway's continued care and industry in obtaining the best tea, and making drink thereof very many noblemen, physicians, merchants, etc., have ever since sent to him for the said leaf, and daily resort to his house to drink the drink thereof. He sells tea from 16s. to 50s. a pound.[1]

The opposition beverage, coffee—mention is made of the "copheehouse" in the "Tcha" advertisement—had been known in this country some years before, a Turkey merchant of London, of the name of Edwards, having brought the first bag of coffee to London, and his Greek servant, Pasqua Rosee, was the first to open a coffee-house in London. This was in 1652, the time of the Protectorate, and one Jacobs, a Jew, had opened a similar establishment in Oxford a year or two earlier. Pasqua Rosee's coffee-house was in St. Michael's Alley, Cornhill. One of his original handbills is preserved in the British Museum, and is a curious record of a remarkable social innovation. It is here reprinted:

THE VERTUE OF THE COFFEE DRINK
First made and publicly sold in England by
PASQUA ROSEE.

The grain or berry called coffee, groweth upon little trees only in the deserts of Arabia. It is brought from thence and drunk generally throughout all the Grand Seignour's dominions. It is a simple, innocent thing, composed into a drink, by being dried in an oven, and ground to powder, and boiled up with spring water, and about half a pint of it to be drunk fasting an hour before, and not eating an hour after, and to be taken as hot as can possibly be endured; the which will never fetch the skin of the mouth, or raise any blisters by reason of that heat.

The Turks' drink at meals and other times is usually water, and their diet consists much of fruit; the acidities whereof are very much corrected by this drink.

The quality of this drink is cold and dry; and though it be a drier; yet it neither heats nor inflames more than hot posset. It so incloseth the orifice of the stomach, and fortifies the heat within, that it is very good to help digestion; and therefore of great use to be taken about three or four o'clock afternoon, as well as in the morning. It much

[1] *Ibid.*, p. 67.

quickens the spirits, and makes the heart lightsome; it is good against sore eyes, and the better if you hold your head over it and take in the steam that way.   It suppresseth fumes exceedingly, and therefore is good against the headache, and will very much stop any defluxion of rheums that distil from the head upon the stomach, and so prevent and help consumptions and the cough of the lungs.

It is excellent to prevent and cure dropsy, gout, and scurvy. It is known by experience to be better than any other drying drink for people in years, or children that have any running humours upon them, as the king's evil, etc. It is a most excellent remedy against the spleen, hypochondriac winds, and the like. It will prevent drowsiness, and make one fit for business, if one have occasion to watch, and therefore you are not to drink of it after supper, unless you intend to be watchful, for it will hinder sleep for three or four hours.

It is observed that in Turkey, where this is generally drunk, that they are not troubled with the stone, gout, dropsy, or scurvy, and that their skins are exceedingly clear and white. It is neither laxative nor restringent.

Made and Sold in St. Michael's Alley, in Cornhill, by Pasqua Rosee, at the sign of his own head.[1]

In addition to tea and coffee, the introduction and acceptance of which had certainly a most marked influence on the progress of civilization, may be mentioned a third, which, though extensively used, never became quite so great a favourite as the others. Chocolate, the remaining member of the triad, was introduced into England much about the same period. It had been known in Germany as early as 1624, when Johan Frantz Rauch wrote a treatise against that beverage. In England, however, it seems to have been introduced much later, for in 1657 it was still advertised as a new drink. In the *Publick Advertiser* of Tuesday, June 16-22, 1657, we find the following:

In Bishopsgate Street, in Queen's Head Alley, at a Frenchman's house, is an excellent West India drink, called chocolate, to be sold, where you may have it ready at any time, and also unmade, at reasonable rates.[2]

[1] *Ibid.*, p. 68.   [2] *Ibid.*, p. 69.

In May, 1657, appeared a weekly paper under the title of *Publick Advertiser*. This consisted almost entirely of advertisements, including the announcements of arrivals and departures of ships, books to be sold, announcements of political items, runaway servants, fairs, cock fights, and so on.

What is considered by many to be the first bona fide and open advertisement ever published appears in a paper entitled *Several Proceedings in Parliament*, and is found under the date November 28-December 5, 1650. It runs thus:

> By the late tumult made the 27 of November, whereof you have the narration before; in the night time in Bexfield, in the county of Norfolk, about 12 Horses were stolen out of the town, whereof a bay-bald Gelding with three white feet, on the near buttock marked with R. F., 9 or 10 years old. A bay-bald Mare with a wall-eye and a red star in her face, the near hind foot white, 7 years old. A black brown Mare, trots all, 6 years old. Whomsoever brings certain intelligence where they are to Mr. Badcraft of Bexfield, in Norfolk, they shall have 20s. for each Horse.

The following number of the same paper, that for December 5-12, 1650, contains this:

> A bright Mare, 12 hands high, one white foot behind, a white patch below the saddle, near the side, a black main, a taile out, a natural ambler, about 10 li. price, stolen, Decemb. 3. neare Guilford. John Rylands, a butcher, tall and ruddy, flaxen haire, about 30 years of age is suspected. Mr. Brounloe, a stocking dier, near the Three Craynes, in Thame's Streets, will satisfy those who can make discovery.[1]

In 1659, also, we come upon an advertisement having reference to a work of the great blind bard, John Milton. It appears in the *Mercurius Politicus* of September, and is as follows:

> CONSIDERATIONS touching the likeliest means to remove Hirelings out of the Church; wherein is also discours'd of Tithes, Church Fees, Church Revenues, and whether any maintenance of Ministers can be settled by Law.

[1] *Ibid.*, p. 97.

The author, J. M. Sold by *Livewel Chapman,* at the Crown in Pope's Head Alley.[1]

Quack remedies and cure-alls were advertised as glowingly in the 17th century as they were in this country a quarter of a century ago. In the *Mercurius Politicus,* November, 1660, is the following:

> *Gentlemen,* you are desired to take notice, That Mr. *Theophilus Buckworth* doth at his house on Mile-end Green make and expose to sale, for the public good, those so famous *Lozenges* or *Pectorals,* approved for the cure of Consumption, Coughs, Catarrhs, Asthmas, Hoarseness, Strongness of Breath, Colds in general, Diseases incident to the Lungs, and a sovoraign Antidote against the Plague, and all other contagious Diseases, and obstructions of the Stomach; And for more convenience of the people, constantly leaveth them sealed up with his coat of arms on the papers, with Mr. *Rich. Lowndes* (as formerly), at the sign of the White Lion, near the little north door of *Pauls Church;* Mr. *Henry Seile,* over against S. Dunstan's Church in Fleet Street; Mr. *William Milward,* at *Westminster* Hall Gate; Mr. *John Place,* at *Furnivals Inn Gate* in Holborn; and Mr. *Robert Horn,* at the Turk's Head near the entrance of the Royal Exchange, Booksellers, and no others.

> This is published to prevent the designs of divers Pretenders, who counterfeit the said Lozenges, to the disparagement of the said Gentleman, and great abuse of the people.

Tooth paste is by no means a modern invention. Our modern advertisements are hardly improvements in their claims regarding the health- and beauty-giving properties of tooth paste. In the *Mercurius Politicus,* December, 1660, appeared the following:

> Most Excellent and Approved *Dentifrices* to scour and cleanse the Teeth, making them white as Ivory, preserves from the Toothach; so that, being constantly used, the parties using it are never troubled with the Toothach; it fastens

[1] *Ibid.,* pp. 102-103.

the Teeth, sweetens the Breath, and preserves the mouth
and gums from Cankers and Imposthumes. Made by *Robert
Turner*, Gentleman; and the right are only to be had at
Thomas Rookes, Stationer, at the Holy Lamb at the East
end of St. Pauls Church, near the School, in sealed papers,
at 12d. the paper.

The reader is desired to beware of counterfeits.[1]

Lotteries were commonly advertised in England. The
following is a sample of an advertisement of a lottery written by a Mr. T. Bish, who wrote numerous handbills. This
was the last state lottery drawn in England (1826):

THE AMBULATOR'S GUIDE
to the Land of Plenty

By Purchasing a TICKET
in the present Lottery

You may *reap* a golden *harvest* in *Cornhill*, and pick up
the *bullion* in *Silver*-street and have an interest in *Bank-
buildings*, possess a *Mansion-house* in *Golden-square*, and
an estate like a *Little Britain;* never be in a *Mungerford-
market*, but all your life continue a *Mayfair*.

By Purchasing a HALF,

You need never be confined within *London Wall*, but
become the proprietor of many a *Long Acre;* represent a
Borough or an *Aldermanbury*, and have a share in *Thread-
needle-street*.

By Purchasing a QUARTER,

Your affairs need never be in *Crooked-land*, nor your
legs in *Fetter-lane;* you may avoid *Paper-buildings*, steer
clear of the *King's Bench*, and defy the Marshalsea; if your
heart is in *Love-lane* you may soon get into *Sweeting's Alley*,
obtain your lover's consent for *Matrimony-place*, and always
live in *High-street*.

By Purchasing an EIGHTH,

You may secure plenty of provision for *Swallow-street;*
finger the *Cole* in *Coleman-street;* and may never be trou-

[1] *Ibid.*, pp. 108-109

bled with *Chancery-lane.* You may cast *anchor* in *Cable-street;* set up business in a *Fore-street;* and need never be confined within a *Narrow-wall.*

By Purchasing a SIXTEENTH,

You may live *frugal* in *Cheapside;* get merry in *Liquor-pond-street;* soak your hide in *Leather-lane;* be a *wet sole* in *Shoe-lane;* turn *maltster* in *Beer-lane,* or *hammer* away in *Smithfield.*

In short, life must indeed be a *Long-lane* if it's without a *turning.* Therefore, if you are wise, without *Mincing* the matter, go *Pall-mall* to *Cornhill* or *Charing-cross,* and enroll your name in the *Temple* of Fortune.[1]

BISH'S

In the *Daily Advertiser* of 1777 the following is discovered, and is noticeable for the horse-couping manner in which the young gentleman speaks of the future bride who is to assist him in setting up housekeeping. He must have had trouble in finding such a thoroughbred filly as he requires:

MATRIMONY

WANTED, by a young Gentleman just beginning House-keeping, a Lady, between eighteen and twenty-five years of Age, with a good education, and a Fortune not less than 5,000 li, sound Wind and Limb, Five Feet Four Inches without her Shoes; not fat, nor yet too lean; a clear Skin; sweet Breath, with a good Set of Teeth; no Pride, nor Affectation; not very talkative, nor one that is deemed no Scold; but of a Spirit to resent an Affront; of a charitable Disposition; not over fond of Dress, though always decent and clean; that will entertain her Husband's Friends with Affability and Cheerfulness, and prefer his Company to public Diversions and gadding about; one who can keep his Secrets, that he may open his Heart to her without reserve on all Occasions; that can extend domestic Expenses with Economy, as Prosperity advances without Ostentation; and retrench them with Cheerfulness, if Occasion should require.

Any Lady disposed to Matrimony, answering this De-

[1] *Ibid.,* pp. 466-467.

scription, is desired to direct for Y. Z. at the Baptist's Head Coffee-House, Aldermanbury.

N. B. None but Principals will be treated with, nor need any apply that are deficient in any one Particular; the Gentleman can make adequate Return, and is, in every Respect, deserving a Lady with the above Qualifications.[1]

In the early part of the 19th century, England imposed a tax of 3s. 6d. upon every advertisement irrespective of its length or subject matter. In 1830, this produced a revenue of 170,649 pounds. In that year it was reduced to 1s. 6d. for each advertisement. This rate continued until 1853 when the tax was abolished.

The levying of this tax required a record of the number of papers published and the number of advertisements appearing in each paper. The totals for Great Britain and Ireland in 1837 were as follows:

Number of papers	460
Number of advertisements	769,088
Amount of advertising duty	55,803 pounds

3. THE MODERN PERIOD

This period may be dated from 1850 to 1911. The reason for putting the dividing point between the second and third periods at 1850 is the rapid appearance of newspapers and magazines which made possible the development of modern advertising on a large scale. Advertising was impossible until printing developed and until people generally learned to read. One reason for the rapid increase in the number and distribution of advertising mediums at this time is probably to be found in the development of transportation systems—the railroads and the waterways. Prior to that time railroad lines were limited to restricted areas. There was no national transportation system as there is today. To illustrate to what extent transportation was dif-

[1] *Ibid.,* pp. 486-487.

ficult before that time, and even up to 1870 or 1875, we may quote the following announcement of the Kenosha (Wisconsin) *Telegraph*, in Rowell's Directory in 1869:

The town is renowned for the manufacture of wagons which find a market all the way to the Rocky Mountains and even to Oregon, being shipped by way of New York.

This shows to what extent it was difficult to distribute goods generally over the country. It is obvious, then, that without the possibility of transporting goods over the country there was no need of advertising mediums of wide circulation, and furthermore mediums could not develop a wide circulation because they could not be distributed conveniently or rapidly. During the middle and latter part of the 19th century the development of a national transportation system made possible the ready distribution of goods and publications.

Another reason for placing the dividing point between the second and third periods at 1850 is that about this time advertising agencies arose whose primary purpose was to serve as brokers of advertising space. They were very different in this respect from the present advertising agency which, in addition to contracting for space, is, in its best form, an organization giving expert counsel and service regarding advertising plans and methods.

During this period the number of magazines and newspapers grew very rapidly, so that in 1861 there were 5,203 magazines, papers, and periodicals of all kinds in the United States. Yet advertising was relatively limited as compared with the present day. *Harper's Magazine* had its first advertisement in 1864; *Scribners* in 1872. Magazine advertising on a large scale did not begin until about 1860 to 1870. It is stated that *Harper's Magazine* today has approximately as many pages of advertising in one year as it had in its first 24 years. At that time is was used chiefly as a medium for advertising the Harper publications. Advertising rates at that time began to assume real proportions. In

the early '70's it is said that Fletcher Harper refused $18,-
000 offered by the New Home Sewing Machine Company
for the back page for one year. *Harper's Weekly* was receiving $35 an inch for its back page in the '60's.
"In 1864 Jay Cooke, appointed by Lincoln to sell war
bonds, advertised in every good paper in the North. He sold
bonds to the amount of $1,240,000,000." [1] This was one of
the first national campaigns.

The first advertising agency was established in Philadelphia in 1840 by Volney B. Palmer. Later, offices were established in Boston and in New York. Rates and contracts
were unstandardized at that time. The agent contracted
for a certain amount of space with a publication and then
sold it for whatever he could, receiving sometimes as high
as 50% of the cost of the space as his commission. Among
the better-known early advertising agents were V. B.
Palmer, S. M. Pettingill and George P. Rowell. In 1864
J. Walter Thompson established an agency and is said to
have been the first to urge the use of magazines as advertising mediums.

4. THE PERIOD OF DEVELOPMENT OF HIGHER STANDARDS AND
PRACTICES IN ADVERTISING

The fourth period in the development of advertising may
be dated as beginning in 1911. It is since that time that
advertising has developed most rapidly as a standardized
business. The date 1911 is chosen here because it was in
that year that definite, organized steps were taken to forward the movement of truth in advertising. In 1911
counsel for *Printers' Ink* formulated what has become
known as "The Printers' Ink Model Statute," which has
been adopted in a large number of states up to the present
time. See chapter XX. At the same time, the Associated
Advertising Clubs of the World at their annual convention
established the Vigilance Committee, with the purpose of

[1] *Selling Forces,* Curtis Publishing Co., Ch. II.

forwarding higher standards of honesty and reliability in advertising. This committee organized, in connection with the various local clubs all over the country, local vigilance committees to eliminate objectionable, untruthful advertising. The activities of this movement will be discussed at greater length in Chapter XX.

About the same time, the Associated Advertising Clubs of the World undertook definite educational activity in outlining courses of study and discussions to be conducted by the various local clubs, for the purpose of studying advertising methods and of improving them. A distinct service has been rendered in this connection by the various educational activities of the different local organizations.

In 1914, there was organized The Audit Bureau of Circulations, which will be discussed more fully in Chapter XXIX. This, as will be seen, has become the leading agency for securing reliable information about advertising mediums and their selection for specific purposes. About 1913, there was organized the Association of National Advertisers, another important influence in the study and development of advertising practices. Likewise, during this period publishers have developed a distinct consciousness of censorship of advertising.

Finally, and perhaps most important, an increasing use of research methods has developed during this period. At least here and there these methods are beginning to be thoroughgoing in finding the facts on which advertising plans may be based.

In view of the developments which have taken place in recent years, and in view of what may still be done in developing better advertising methods, eliminating objectionable practices, and in reducing waste, it is interesting, if not surprising, to note the statement made by Dr. Samuel Johnson in 1759 in his *Weekly Idler* that "the trade of advertising is now so near to perfection that it is not easy to propose any improvements." [1]

¹ *Ibid.*, p. 13.

CHARACTERISTICS OF THE LAST TWO PERIODS—1850-1911
AND 1911 TO THE PRESENT

Considering the last two periods together, the chief developments in addition to those mentioned may be designated as follows:

(a) Growth in Quantity of Advertising. There has been a tremendous growth in the number of firms employing advertising in one form or another. The accompanying graph shows the number of firms using advertising in the *Century Magazine.* At the present time there are about 10,000 firms doing more or less national advertising. The directory of national advertisers prepared by The James McKittrick Company, Inc., contains slightly over 10,000 names. The report entitled *Leading Advertisers* prepared each year by The Curtis Publishing Company mentions 1,302 firms which spent $10,000 in 1921 in 36 leading national magazines. In this list there were 50 firms which spent $264,500 or more in 36 leading national publications in 1921.

There has been likewise an enormous growth in the number of mediums. In 1830, it is estimated that there were

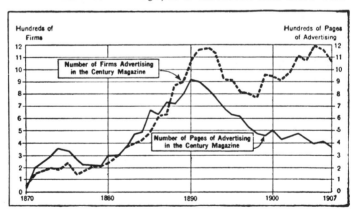

Figure 1:   Number of firms advertising and number of pages of advertising appearing in the *Century Magazine,* 1870-1907

approximately 800 newspapers in the United States, of which some 50 were daily publications. Their combined annual circulation was estimated at about 60 million copies, or a circulation of approximately 950,000 copies per issue. In 1830 the total population of the United States was 23,500,000.

In 1861 there were 5,203 papers and magazines for a population of approximately 30 million. See the accom-

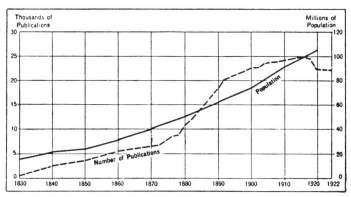

Figure 2: Increase in the number of publications and in population in the United States from 1830 to 1922

panying graph. In 1922 there were 22,353 magazines and newspapers in the United States. In other words, there has been an increase of magazines and newspapers since 1861 of approximately 5 times, whereas the population during the same period of time has increased approximately 3½ times. Since 1830 the population has increased approximately ly 4½ times; the number of magazines and newspapers has increased almost 30 times. However, a more striking increase has taken place in the total combined circulation. The estimated combined circulation per issue of the magazines is approximately 50 million copies and the total combined circulation of the newspapers is approximately 45 millions. Thus, since 1830 there has been a growth in total combined circulation of all magazines and newspapers from less than

one million to over 95 or 100 millions per issue. Besides
the marked increase in the number of mediums and in the
extent of their circulation, there has been an equally marked
increase in the amount of advertising carried in a given
issue of a publication. The author measured the advertising space in two newspapers—the *New York Tribune* and
the *Boston Transcript*—and found that in the former paper
the advertising space had increased fivefold from 1860 to
1918 and in the latter thirteen fold.

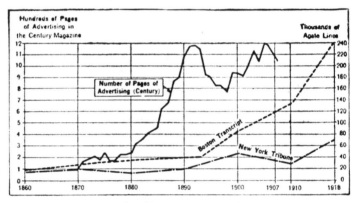

Figure 3: Growth of advertising space in a typical magazine from 1860
to 1908 and in two newspapers from 1860 to 1918

There has developed another form of advertising medium, namely, street-car cards, which did not come into general use until about 1890 when the change was made from
the horse-drawn cars to electric cars. With the introduction
of electricity the number of street cars increased and their
use for advertising display rapidly developed.

Another striking development during this period is the
growth of mail-order advertising. Not only have mail-order
houses sprung up in large numbers during this period but
also business firms of all kinds have developed a very extensive use of direct-mail material in the form of circulars,
catalogs, letters, and so on. Sears, Roebuck & Company
was established in 1892. The large mail-order houses com-

monly send out twice a year upwards of four million large catalogs in addition to the numerous smaller departmental catalogs issued.

(b) Growth in Quality of Advertising. During these two periods there has been a distinct growth in the quality of advertising. Methods of printing, typography, colored printing, art work, and the like, have been greatly improved. Besides the mechanical improvements there have been likewise very distinct advances in such qualities as accuracy in statement and descriptions, in reliability, and in truthfulness.

(c) Increase in Variety of Uses. There has been a marked increase in the variety of advertising used. Perhaps the dominating types of advertising which flourished originally, that is about the middle and latter half of the 19th century, were patent-medicine advertising, the circus bills, and in general much unreliable, dishonest, and objectionable advertising. Today there is hardly a business or type of commodity for which the printed word is not used as a means of selling. Banks and financial institutions of high grade are ready today to turn to advertising and find it profitable to employ in a dependable manner the methods which have been found so profitable by unreliable financial houses. Advertising has suffered because of the objectionable features which were so prominent in its earlier development. For this reason undoubtedly, high-grade financial houses, and to some extent other types of business, have been slow to take advantage of the possibilities which it offers. High-grade financial houses have a distinct responsibility to the community in guiding the savings of the people into the right channels. The unsound and unethical solicitor of investments has taken advantage of the use of the printed word and has mis-directed untold amounts into unsafe channels. It might be said that it is almost a duty of the high-grade house to use all legitimate sales methods equally

effectively and to help the community put its investments to proper uses. Churches, religious organizations, educational institutions, and governments are using advertising in various ways today. Advertising as we know it today is the development of the past 50 or 75 years. Procter and Gamble started in business in 1837. They did not advertise extensively until about 1880. At that time Ivory Soap was first being advertised. The fact that it was undertaken as an experiment to see to what extent it would be effective for a product of that sort illustrates the point of view then held regarding advertising.

As we shall see in a later chapter, the development of trade-marks is likewise a conspicuous characteristic of these last two periods, particularly of the past 30 years. A large proportion of the trade-marks known today throughout this country and all over the world have been developed during this time. Of the somewhat more than 150,300 valid trademarks registered in the United States patent office up to 1922 practically none were used prior to 1870 and only a small handful go back to 1885 or 1890. The development of national business has made trade-marks virtually a necessity and advertising has been an important means, perhaps the chief means, of making them known to the public.

PRESENT VOLUME OF ADVERTISING

Advertising today plays an important rôle in the operations of business. It has assumed such large proportions in recent years that it is difficult to estimate its magnitude and to calculate the exact place which it occupies in present commercial affairs. We may gain some notion of its immense proportions from the amount of money expended and from the amount of space used each year for printed advertising in America. It has been estimated that in the neighborhood of one billion dollars is spent annually for this purpose and that about 3,000 square miles of printed space are used each year in this country. Approximately half a million dollars is spent annually for advertising any one of a score or more of well-known commodities and as high as three and four million dollars is spent in exceptional cases. Or we may gain a concrete idea of the immensity of advertising from the cost of space for single advertisements in some of the leading mediums. Thus, for example, a page in the *Atlantic Monthly* in a single issue in 1923 cost $350 and the back outside cover cost $800. A page in the *Saturday Evening Post* in 1923 cost $7,000 and the back outside cover $12,000. A page in the large metropolitan newspapers costs as high as $1,400 to $1,600. From still another angle the immensity of advertising is indicated by the fact that from two-thirds to three-fourths of the cost of maintaining a newspaper or a magazine is derived from its advertising space.

The outsider naturally wonders whether advertising, with such high rates for space, can really be a profitable aid in selling; or whether it may not be an expensive luxury indulged in by large business concerns. The extent to which advertising plays a justifiable economic rôle in the distribution of goods is an important and intricate problem and will be discussed more fully in the succeeding chapters.

III

THE PLACE OF ADVERTISING IN BUSINESS

*Popular conceptions with regard to advertising. Wastes in advertising.
Chief arguments against advertising. The actual expenditure for advertising: (a) what people think is spent for advertising; examples of overestimation of cost of advertising by representative groups of persons; (b)
what is actually spent for advertising. Concrete examples of returns from
advertising: (a) from individual advertisements; (b) from campaigns.
Extent to which women read newspaper advertisements. The effect of
omitting advertising.*

Two common conceptions with regard to advertising
which are held by a considerable number of people are that
enormously large sums of money are expended for it, and
that much of this expenditure is an economic waste. Rumors
are spread about that a page in this magazine or in that
newspaper costs so many hundreds or thousands of dollars
for a single issue. Or it is learned that the manufacturer of
one's favorite breakfast food spends so many thousands
or possibly so many millions of dollars for advertising in
one year. The inference at once is that the consumer must
pay for it in the form of a considerably higher price than
the breakfast food or the soap or the suit of clothing would
otherwise cost. The small retailer quite often says to a
customer, "You had better buy this brand, because the company that makes it spends no money on advertising, so I can
sell it to you cheaper." At frequent intervals, commissions
and state and national legislatures conduct inquiries in connection with bills, with the implication that the money
spent for advertising is for the most part an economic waste.
These statements or impressions usually do not get at the
fundamental factors involved, nor do they as a rule analyze
the actual functions which advertising performs in the distribution of goods, or in the social fabric.

38

WASTES IN ADVERTISING

There are of course wastes in advertising, no doubt enormous wastes. No observer of current affairs would deny it. But there are wastes everywhere, in production, in distribution, in personal selling, in all forms of human intercourse. In spite of the long and persistent efforts in applying scientific methods in the production side of business there are still incredible wastes. Economy in the distribution side of business has no doubt lagged behind, but distinct advances have been made.

Probably the chief sources of waste in advertising are:

1. The lack of proper coordination between advertising and the other phases of a business—lack of coordination with distribution, personal sales plans, and production—advertising where there is no distribution, and the like.

2. The use of inefficient methods—weak, unconvincing and ineffective appeals, poor presentation, ineffective technique, the use of too large space or too small space—due to guessing instead of finding the facts on which to build and plan. In Chapter XIV it will be pointed out that if every piece of advertising material were made 10% more effective it would mean a saving of $100,000,000 to the business interests of this country. A 10% improvement is easily within the range of possibility.

3. The use of advertising for commodities in circumstances in which returns are highly uncertain or for business ventures which are too hazardous.

4. The excessive use of advertising in overly keen competition.

5. The failure to make all advertising literally truthful and dependable. Even if 96% or 97% of present advertising is in the main trustworthy and meritorious, the remaining 3% or 4% tend to weaken the effectiveness of the rest.

6. The use of advertising for illegitimate business, highly

speculative investments, financial frauds, or for commodities which are of doubtful value or actually injurious to mankind.

Improvements are being made in all these directions. Fundamentally, these sources of waste are not peculiar to advertising; they are ultimately due to the waste and inefficiency in business as a whole. Exactly the same sources of waste exist in oral selling. Oral selling is wasteful in making plans on guesses instead of on facts, in not being literally truthful and dependable in every instance, in a lack of proper coordination with other phases of a business, in the waste of time on the part of salesmen and in excessive personal expenditures. If every one of the 600,-000 traveling salesmen in the United States saved for his firm only 50 cents a day in his personal expense account it would be a total saving of $300,000 a day or $100,000,-000 a year. Furthermore, preliminary time studies show that the average salesman uses only about 15% to 50% of his working time in actual selling. There is waste in advertising that goes to persons who are not in a position to buy a given product; there is also a large waste in the case of salesmen calling on persons who are not in a position to buy. Personal salesmanship is used as much as advertising if not more so for illegitimate businesses, in excessive competition, in hazardous business ventures, and the like. Fundamentally these wastes in oral as well as in printed selling are not to be blamed upon these two aspects of business, but they are due to conditions in business as a whole, to mistaken judgment, to ignorance and moral weakness.

CHIEF ARGUMENTS AGAINST ADVERTISING

The chief criticisms of advertising are perhaps centered around four main arguments.

The first is that the actual total amount of money spent for advertising is enormously large. As pointed out in the preceding chapter, the probable amount spent in this country in one year is in the neighborhood of one billion dollars. The question is, Who pays for it, and how much different would the prices of commodities be if this expenditure were absolutely and entirely eliminated and in what way would the methods of distribution and the cost of distribution be different? The critic assumes that this money is an economic waste and that prices are higher because of it.

The second argument is that advertising has considerably increased the demand for, and the purchase of, luxuries and semiluxuries, such as cameras, beverages, automobiles, pianos, phonographs, vacuum cleaners, and so on. In the same connection it is also pointed out that advertising has stimulated a more rapid change in fashions and styles than would otherwise take place, and that this has led to extravagant expenditures.

The third argument is that advertising tends to create in part fictitious values and semimonopolies for specifically branded goods. On account of this, the manufacturer of such a commodity may charge a higher price than he otherwise could. It is pointed out that the constant reiteration of the qualities of a product tends to create a popular conception of higher value and quality than the commodity really possesses in relation to competing commodities of equal quality. This point may be illustrated by a piece of shaving soap which, let us say, originally sold for 10 cents. The manufacturer puts it up in a different form and sells it in a special container designed to be more convenient than the old-fashioned shaving mug. In this new form, the soap may sell for 25 cents. The manufacturer has added a certain amount of value in the form of a convenient container, and on that account is justified in charging a somewhat higher price. The argument, however, is that the increased price is considerably higher than it needs to be, but that it is charged because the commodity in this form is new, and that the advertising for it has created a semimonopolistic or fictitious value.

The fourth argument is that advertising has been responsible to a considerable extent for the increasing and wide-spread use of packages, cartons, wrappers, and labels for a large variety of products. Advertising has been responsible to a very large extent for the development of standardized brands and trade-marked articles. These wrappers and containers cost money which supposedly is not a part of the price paid for commodities bought in bulk. The argument is that all of this expenditure is added to the price of the product.

THE ACTUAL EXPENDITURE FOR ADVERTISING

With regard to the first argument, let us see first of all what the actual facts are. What is the actual expenditure for the advertising of specific commodities? Almost every person who makes a general statement that the prices of commodities are higher because of the advertising or that the money expended for advertising is wasted usually knows nothing about the actual facts of the *relative* amount of money expended for advertising a specific commodity.

(a) What People Think Is Spent for Advertising. Before we consider the actual figures of advertising expenditures for various commodities, let us determine what are the impressions of people in general concerning the proportion of the price of a commodity that is expended for advertising. The question is, What do people think they are paying for advertising? The emphasis here is on the word "think." The importance of this point is that the opinions of people in general, whether right or wrong, represent their attitude, and constitute the basis of their belief regarding the wisdom or wastefulness of the money expended for this purpose.

Casual comments by various persons indicate that people quite generally have a greatly exaggerated notion of the amount of money expended for printed advertising.

These comments led the writer, with the aid of C. W. Fernald, to make a somewhat more extended and detailed inquiry to ascertain what the actual opinions of people are.

Accordingly the following simple investigation was made. Thirteen articles which are well known and generally advertised were put into a list. After each article the current retail price was given. This list was then presented to a person, who was asked this question: How much of the price of each article do you estimate is probably expended for advertising? For example, "If you pay 10 cents for a can of Old Dutch Cleanser, how many cents or what part of a cent is probably expended for advertising? Or if a Hart, Schaffner & Marx suit sells for $50, how many cents or dollars do you suppose are expended for advertising?" In this manner, an estimate was obtained for each of the 13 articles listed in the table.

This inquiry was carried out individually with 75 persons. These persons were divided into three groups. One group was composed of 25 business men; the second was composed of 25 women; and the third was composed of 25 men students. The business men represented a variety of interests. Five of them were manufacturers; 5 were grocers; 5 were real estate men; 5 were retail cigar dealers; and 5 were professional men.

The results are set forth in Table 1. This table gives, in the first column after the names of the articles, the assumed retail price; in the second column, the highest amount estimated by any one individual in each group; in the third column, the lowest amount estimated by any one individual in each group; in the fourth column, the average estimate of each group.

The results in each column are given separately for each of the three groups of persons represented. The fifth column gives the actual expenditure for advertising for each article. This was computed from the percentage of sales appropriated for advertising. This percentage was obtained in most instances from published sources. In the remaining instances, it was either supplied by the firms concerned or estimated on the basis of the usual expenditure for advertising articles of that nature.

TABLE I

EXPENDITURES FOR ADVERTISING AS ESTIMATED BY CONSUMERS

Name of Product	Groups of Persons	Assumed Retail Price	Highest Estimate	Lowest Estimate	Average Estimate	Actual Expenditure for Advertising	Times Overestimated
Old Dutch Cleanser		$0.10					
	Business Men		5c	1/60c	$0.0154		
	Women		8c	1/4c	.0177		
	Men Students		4c	1./4c	.0212		
Average					$0.0181	$0.01	1.8
Ivory Soap		$0.07					
	Business Men		5c	1/10c	$0.0126		
	Women		3c	1/5c	.0141		
	Men Students		4c	1/4c	.0164		
Average					$0.0144	$0.002	7.2
Hart, Schaffner & Marx suit		$50.					
	Business Men		$25.	$0.05	$5.51		
	Women		25.	1.00	6.23		
	Men Students		12.50	.50	6.88		
Average					$6.21	$1.00	6.2
Arrow Collars		$0.25					
	Business Men		17c	1/10c	$0.0481		
	Women		12-1/2c	1./2c	.035		
	Men Students		15c	1c	.0476		
Average					$0.0436	$0.0087	5.0
Overland Automobile		$895.					
	Business Men		$350.	$1.00	$78.68		
	Women		448.	1.50	102.64		
	Men Students		100.	1.50	46.22		
Average					$75.85	$13.43	5.6

Name of Product / Groups of Persons	Assumed Retail Price	Highest Estimate	Lowest Estimate	Average Estimate	Actual Expenditure for Advertising	Times Overestimated
Shredded Wheat	$0.15					
Business Men		8c	1/10c	$0.02		
Women		8c	1/4c	.0252		
Men Students		7c	1/4c	.0249		
Average				$0.0234	$0.003	7.8
Wrigley's Spearmint Gum	$0.05					
Business Men		3c	1/100c	$0.0085		
Women		4c	1/5c	.0092		
Men Students		4c	1/4c	.0179		
Average				$0.0119	$0.005	2.4
Gold Medal Flour (bbl.)	$15.					
Business Men		$7.	1c	$1.86		
Women		6.	30c	1.88		
Men Students		4.	20c	1.78		
Average				$1.84	$0.45	4.1
Victrola	$100.					
Business Men		$50.	2c	$ 9.10		
Women		50.	50c	12.53		
Men Students		35.	75c	13.15		
Average				$11.59	$4.	2.9
Eastman Kodak	$15.					
Business Men		$10.	1c	$2.39		
Women		10.	25c	1.77		
Men Students		3.50	30c	2.98		
Average				$2.38	$0.45	5.2
Women's Dresses (Dept. Store)	$20.					
Business Men		$10.	1c	$1.94		
Women		10.	3c	2.52		
Men Students		3.50	5c	.65		
Average				$1.70	$0.50	3.4

Name of Product	Groups of Persons	Assumed Retail Price	Highest Estimate	Lowest Estimate	Average Estimate	Actual Expenditure for Advertising	Times Overestimated
Women's Special Suits		$18.					
	Business Men		$5.	1c	$1.36		
	Women		6.	7c	1.97		
	Men Students		8.	3c	1.29		
Average					$1.54	$0.47	3.3
Women's Gloves (Dept. Store)		$3.					
	Business Men		$1.	1/10c	$0.25		
	Women		1.	3c	.30		
	Men Students		.75	1/2c	.18		
Average					$0.24	$0.06	4.0
AVERAGE OVERESTIMATION							4.53

A study of this table shows an enormous overestimation, not only in the extreme individual cases, as given in the column of "Highest Estimates," but also in the column which gives the averages. Thus, the highest estimates by individuals indicate that these persons assume that from one-half to two-thirds of the purchase price of these commodities is expended for advertising.

For example, one person estimated that 5 cents of the 10 paid for a can of Old Dutch Cleanser goes for advertising, or that 5 cents of the 7 paid for a cake of Ivory soap goes for advertising, or that $350 out of $895 for an Overland automobile is expended for publicity. However, these are individual extremes.

The averages afford a fairer basis of comparison. But even these are surprisingly high. Thus, the average estimate for Old Dutch Cleanser is that $.0181 out of 10 cents is expended for advertising; and that for Ivory soap $.0144 out of 7 cents is expended for advertising; and that $6.20

is expended for advertising a $50 Hart, Schaffner & Marx suit.

The largest overestimations were made for Shredded Wheat, Ivory Soap, Hart, Schaffner & Marx clothes, and Eastman Kodaks. The lowest overestimations were made for Old Dutch Cleanser, Victrolas, and women's dresses.

Perhaps the most direct comparison of the amount of overestimation may be obtained from an inspection of the last column, which gives the ratio, or the number of times that the estimated expenditure is greater than the actual expenditure. Thus, the estimated expenditure for Shredded Wheat is 7.8 times as great as the actual expenditure; for Ivory soap 7.2 times as large as the actual expenditure; for Arrow Collars 5 times as great.

The average ratio is 4.53. That is, the average estimate by 75 persons for 13 products is 4.53 times as great as the actual expenditures for these products.

Another point of interest is the fact that if we consider only those persons whose average estimates are approximately correct, we find that only 20% of the 75 persons have an approximately correct conception of the amount of money expended for advertising. This is only one person in five.

Furthermore we find, if we compare the average estimates of the three groups of persons, that there is no essential difference among the groups. Even the business men had on the whole a no more accurate conception than did the women or the students.

The outstanding fact of this inquiry is that the average person has a greatly exaggerated notion of the amount of money spent for advertising. He believes that approximately five times as much money is expended for this purpose as is actually the case.

(b) What Is Actually Spent for Advertising. Let us take a variety of concrete instances to illustrate what the actual expenditures, in general, are. Let us take first the

case of a manufacturer and retailer of men's clothing. In the fall of 1920, Rogers Peet of New York prepared the following table:

TABLE 2

YOUR DOLLAR AND WHERE IT GOES WHEN SPENT
FOR ROGERS PEET CLOTHES

(Based on six months' actual experience)

Material—Cost, less cash discount		$0.2661
Labor—Wages for making, and salaries for selling		.4862
Rent		.0720
Taxes—Federal and State		.0362
Miscellaneous		
Money back	$0.0073	
Delivery and freight	.0072	
Postage, carfare, etc.	.0060	
Containers, twine, etc.	.0053	
Printing and stationery	.0050	
Fixture depreciation	.0029	
Building repairs	.0018	
Insurance	.0016	
Bad debts	.0012	
Telephone	.0008	
		.0391
Advertising		.0183
Profit of manufacturing, wholesale and retail combined—all that is left to pay dividends, and accumulate a surplus to insure our business future		.0821
		$1.00

The advertising expenditure is $.0183, or less than 2 cents per dollar of goods bought by the consumer. In other words, the advertising expenditure for a $50 suit of clothes would be 91 cents. It is evident that even if advertising played no part whatever in promoting the sale of Rogers Peet wares, the price of a suit of clothes would be substantially the same. Compared with various other items in

the table, the advertising expenditure is only a little over
three times that for containers and twine, or half as much as
that of federal and state taxes.

TABLE 3

PERCENTAGES OF SALES EXPENDED FOR ADVERTISING

Arrow Collars	3.5
Baker-Vawter System	3.5
Berry Brothers' Varnish	4
Cadillac Automobile	1
Champion Spark Plugs	7
Cloth craft Clothes	1.5
Colgate's Preparations	2
DePree Chemical Company	6
Evinrude Motors	8
Fatima Cigarettes	5
Globe-Wernicke Cabinets	3
Great Northern Railroad	1.83
Hudson Automobile	1.3
Ivory Soap	3
Kewanee Boilers	2.5
Kodaks	3
McCray Refrigerators	7.5
Markham Air Rifles	5
Northern Pacific Railroad	1.9
Old Dutch Cleanser	10
Packard Automobile	1.1
Phonographs	5
Reo Motor Cars	1
Ruud Heaters	2.5 to 3.5
Santa Fe Railroad	2.5
Saxon Automobile	2.6
Sears, Roebuck & Co.	10
Sherwin-Williams Paint	3.5
Stromberg Carburetors	3.5
Studebaker Automobiles	2
Union Pacific Railroad	2.5
Universal Portland Cement	2
Velvet Tobacco	6
Welch's Grape Juice	10
Wooltex Clothes	2

The median expenditure is 3%.

Let us take other instances. In 1919, the California Fruit Growers Exchange spent 2½ cents per box, or one-fifth of a cent per dozen, for advertising Sunkist oranges. For the year beginning November 1, 1921, the proposed expenditure was three-quarters of a million dollars, based on an estimated crop at the rate of 3⅓ cents per box for oranges, and 6 cents per box for lemons.

The California Associated Raisin Growers spent for the season of 1921 approximately $750,000 for advertising, or an expenditure at the rate of one-sixth of a cent per pound of raisins.

The walnut growers spent in 1920 approximately 1 cent per pound for advertising.

The advertising expenditure of the Fuller Brush Company amounts to a little over 1 cent per brush.

These illustrations represent specific instances. It will be more convincing, and representative of business generally if we take averages of expenditures for advertising by a considerable number of firms in various lines of business.

In 1916, Mac Martin found that the average advertising expenditure by 20 department stores was 2.5%. He also gives the percentages of gross sales spent for advertising by certain concerns as shown in Table 3.[1]

The Joseph Campbell Co. spent in 1922 approximately 3% of sales for advertising its soup.

An investigation of the knit-underwear industry by the United States Department of Commerce in 1915 showed that the average expenditure for advertising on the part of the 63 knit-underwear manufacturers investigated was 1.58%, based on net sales.[2]

Table 4, prepared by Wheeler Sammons[3] in 1915 and based on over 1,000 retail stores, shows the percentages of

---

[1] *Advertising Campaigns*, p. 48.

[2] Department of Commerce, *Miscellaneous Series* No. 32, 1915.

[3] Sammons, *Keeping Up with Rising Costs*, p. 78.

net sales expended for advertising of all types—letters, catalogs, window displays, newspaper space.

TABLE 4

PERCENTAGES OF NET SALES EXPENDED FOR ADVERTISING OF
ALL TYPES
(Based on over 1,000 retail stores)

Groceries	.83	Drugs	1.76
Hardware	1.12	Furniture	2.72
Vehicles and imple-		Jewelry	2.85
ments	1.22	Clothing	3.16
Variety goods	1.52	Department stores	4.01
Shoes	1.65	Mail-order houses	7.21
Dry goods	1.67		

A somewhat more detailed set of figures covering sales, gross profits, and advertising expenditures, as shown in Table 5, was obtained by Mac Martin covering the first six months of 1916.[1]

The average advertising expenditure in relation to gross sales in the case of these eight large stores is 4.27%. It will also be noted that so far as this group of stores is concerned the advertising expenditure tends relatively to be somewhat larger for the smaller stores.

Figures recently obtained by the Harvard Bureau of Business Research and based on a considerable number of stores in each case give in Table 6 the percentages of net sales expended for advertising for the years 1919 and 1920.

Commenting on the 1921 department store figures the report states: "The common figure for advertising was 2.4% of net sales. The highest figure for this item was 8.2% of net sales; nine other firms reported advertising expense over 5%. On the other hand, for a large group of firms, advertising expense was less than 2%, with a concentration around 1.7% standing out prominently." [1]

---

[1] *Printers' Ink,* Dec. 14, 1916, p. 54.

[2] *Bulletin No. 33,* Harvard Bureau of Business Research, "Operating Expenses in Department Stores in 1921," p. 18.

TABLE 5

FIGURES COVERING SALES, GROSS PROFITS AND ADVERTISING
EXPENDITURES—EIGHT RETAIL STORES

Stores	Sales	Gross Profits	Relation of Profits to Sales (Per Cent)	Advertising	Relation of Advertising to Sales (Per Cent)	Relation of Profits to Sales (Per Cent)
James McCreery & Co., New York	$4,546,550	$1,481,909	32.59	$171,169	3.76	11.55
Lord & Taylor, New York	4,302,617	1,545,448	35.91	149,891	3.48	9.69
Hahne & Co., Newark, N.J.	2,347,152	735,948	31.31	131,711	5.60	17.89
Powers Merc. Co., Minneapolis, Minn.	2,136,771	560,188	26.21	78,855	3.69	14.07
Adam, J. N. & Co., Buffalo, N. Y.	1,942,284	583,749	30.05	94,223	4.85	16.14
The Williams Hengerer Co., Buffalo, N.Y.	1,744,900	562,283	32.22	67,669	3.87	12.03
Stewart & Co., Baltimore, Md.	1,335,019	354,086	26.52	74,645	5.59	21.08
The Stewart, D. G. Co., Louisville, Ky.	972,725	281,580	28.94	58,720	6.03	20.85
	$19,328,018	$6,105,191	31.58	$826,883	4.27	13.54

These figures were obtained in a reliable manner and
probably represent fairly accurately the expenditures for
these types of stores. It will be noted that these figures

TABLE 6

PERCENTAGES OF NET SALES EXPENDED FOR ADVERTISING, 1919
AND 1920, IN RETAIL STORES

	Common Figure
General stores	0.2%
Retail groceries	0.2
187 Retail drug stores (1919)	0.7
130 Retail shoe stores (1919)	1.3
397 Retail shoe stores (1920)	1.9
182 Retail jewelry stores (1920)	2.0
190 Retail jewelry stores (1921)	2.5
266 Department stores (1920)	2.0
301 Department stores (1921)	2.4

are somewhat smaller than the ones for corresponding stores in the table just preceding.

It will be of interest to note the amounts of other items of expense in operating department stores. Table 7 gives the facts for the stores just mentioned, as obtained by the Harvard Bureau of Business Research.

TABLE 7
OPERATING EXPENSES IN DEPARTMENT STORES
(Net Sales = 100%)

Items	266 Stores in 1920 Common Figure	301 Stores in 1921 Common Figure
Salaries and Wages	13.9%	15.4%
Rentals	1.9	2.4
Advertising	2.0	2.4
Taxes (Except on Buildings, Income, and Profits)	.6	.6
Interest (On Capital—Borrowed and on Capital—Owned)	2.1	2.3
Supplies	.8	.8
Service Purchased (Heat, Light, Power, Delivery)	.6	.6
Unclassified	1.6	1.2
Traveling	.3	.5
Communication	.2	.2
Repairs	.3	.2
Insurance	.4	.4
Depreciation—Losses from Bad Debts	.2	.2
Other Depreciation	.5	.5
Professional Services	.1	.1
Total Expense	25.9%	27.8%
Gross Profit	27.8	
Net Profit	1.8	

Among department stores and men's clothing stores, the expenditure for advertising is larger for the larger stores. Thus the 301 department stores studied by the Harvard Bureau in 1921 (p. 25) showed the following percentages of net sales spent for advertising:

ADVERTISING EXPENDITURES IN 1921 ACCORDING TO VOLUME OF
SALES—301 DEPARTMENT STORES

Net Sales = 100%

	Less than $250,000	$250,000- 499,000	$500,000- 999,000	$1,000,000- 2,499,000	$2,500,000 and over
Number of Firms	81	66	47	61	46
Advertising	1.8%	2.1%	2.6%	2.9%	2.7%

In the case of retail jewelry stores, the Harvard Bureau found a similar relation between advertising expenditures and volume of sales.

ADVERTISING EXPENDITURES IN 1921 ACCORDING TO VOLUME OF
SALES—190 JEWELRY STORES

Net Sales = 100%

	Net Sales less than $20,000	$20,000- 49,000	$50,000 and over
Number of Firms	72	72	46
Advertising	2.2%	2.0%	3.3%

The men's clothing stores studied by the Northwestern University Bureau [1] showed the following percentages of net sales spent for advertising:

TABLE 8

RELATION OF ADVERTISING TO TOTAL NET SALES FOR STORES
OF DIFFERENT SIZES

Years	Classified Total Net Sales (in 000's)	Number of Store-Years	Advertising per $100 of Total Net Sales Average Amount
	Total	881	$2.07
1919, 1918, 1914, Combined	Under $40	264	$1.52
	$40 to $80	318	1.57
	$80 to $180	219	2.03
	$180 and over	80	2.57
	Total	192	$2.51
1914	Under $40	95	$1.85
	$40 to $80	61	2.25
	$80 to $180	31	2.86
	$180 and over	5	3.25

[1] *Series II, No. 3*, p. 8.

The Joint Commission of Agricultural Inquiry reported in 1922 its findings regarding the cost of marketing and distribution of commodities into which agricultural products primarily enter. The cost of advertising is listed separately in connection with two classes of food products, corn flakes and rolled oats. These two classes of food products are probably among those for which advertising expenditures are the highest. Tables 9 and 10 give the amounts of the various items for the years 1913, 1916, and 1921.[1]

TABLE 9

DISTRIBUTION OF DOLLAR CONSUMER PAYS FOR CORN FLAKES

	1913	1916	1921
Production	Cents	Cents	Cents
Producer receives	16.2	29.1	21.0
Transportation	2.9	3.5	5.9
Elevator margin and profit	4.5	3.9	1.6
Cost of manufacture	5.9	7.8	8.1
Total	29.5	44.3	36.6
Distribution			
Manufacturer's cost of selling	10.2	11.1	7.3
Advertising	11.1	5.6	4.5
Transportation	6.8	8.6	9.1
Taxes	2.8	2.2	7.0
Profit	4.9	.5	8.3
Wholesaler's operating expense	6.7	6.9	8.3
Profit	2.0	1.7	1.4
Retailer's operating expense	14.6	10.8	13.3
Profit	11.4	8.3	6.0
Total	70.5	55.7	63.4

The expenditure for advertising in the case of corn flakes in 1921 was 4.5 cents out of the consumer's dollar, as shown in Table 9, and 8.6 cents in the case of rolled oats, as shown in Table 10. In both instances the advertising expenditure decreased from 1913 to 1921.

[1] Pages 212 and 214 of the report. Part IV

TABLE 10

DISTRIBUTION OF DOLLAR CONSUMER PAYS FOR ROLLED OATS

	1913	1916	1921
Production	Cents	Cents	Cents
Producer receives	23.10	25.99	17.83
Transportation	1.32	1.33	2.04
Elevator margin and profit	.76	1.82	1.73
Cost of manufacture	7.82	9.02	8.92
Total	33.00	38.16	30.52
Distribution			
Manufacturer's cost of selling	5.69	5.06	6.73
Advertising	11.22	7.63	8.64
Transportation	4.68	5.20	8.13
Taxes	5.56	4.09	2.62
Profit	8.20	9.46	13.55
Wholesaler's operating expense	6.44	6.59	7.99
Profit	1.98	1.34	.74
Retailer's operating expense	14.84	15.48	15.68
Profit	8.39	6.99	5.40
Total	67.00	61.84	69.48

In general, we may say that the average expenditure for advertising on the part of manufacturers is approximately 3% or less. The figures given in the various tables are based more generally upon those concerns which do probably more extensive advertising and consequently an average based upon them would tend to be higher rather than lower for all manufacturers combined.

The average expenditure for advertising on the part of retailers is approximately 2% or less. It is true that certain types of stores, in particular department stores, expend over that amount. On the other hand, a very considerable proportion of retailers spend under that amount.

Taking these figures as a whole, it is probable that the expenditure for advertising as a whole, both on the part of manufacturers and on the part of retailers, is probably not over 4% to 5%. It is evident, therefore, that while the total expenditure for advertising the country over runs into large figures, nevertheless the relative expenditure in proportion to the cost of a commodity is small. In other words, if advertising played no part whatever in stimulating the sale of commodities, and if the cost of advertising were therefore directly added to the price of a commodity to the consumer, the price of an article would be almost inappreciably higher than it otherwise would be.

That is, an article which sells for $1 would have to be sold at $1.04 or $1.05, if advertising were purely a dead expenditure of money.

There is another angle from which we may obtain a rough estimate of the situation. The total income of the United States in 1921 was probably 50 to 55 billions. The estimate of total expenditures for all forms of advertising in 1921 was probably not over 1 billion (probably less). If 5 billions represented savings and if the remaining 50 billions of income were expended by the American people and half of this expenditure, or 25 billions, were paid for goods in connection with which advertising is done, then this 1 billion for advertising in proportion to the 25 billions would be 4%. This agrees fairly closely with the preceding figures.

The facts presented thus far show that the actual expenditure of money for advertising is relatively small in proportion to the price of commodities, and that the public has a greatly exaggerated notion regarding these expenditures. The public believes that approximately five times as much money is expended for advertising as is actually the case.

At this point we may note expenditures for other factors in the selling and distribution of goods. There are in the neighborhood of 600,000 salesmen in the United States. If we estimate the average salary and traveling expenses per man per year at $3,000 we find that the cost of salesmen alone to American business firms is about two billion dollars. Salaries and wages in retail stores are in the neighborhood of 10% to 15% of net sales.

We must, however, bear in mind that even though the actual expenditure for advertising is relatively small, even though it is probably not over 4% to 5% in the aggregate, nevertheless even this expenditure would be a serious waste if it produced no economic or social value. The 1% to 2% spent by retailers or the 2% to 3% spent by manufacturers would in many instances make the differences between success and failure.

CONCRETE EXAMPLES OF RETURNS FROM ADVERTISING

In considering these illustrations of the success attained or results produced by advertising we must bear in mind that there are failures and wastes. It would be unsound reasoning to select only the successes. More failures would have been presented here, since from an analytical point of view they are just as instructive as the successes, if it were not for the fact that failures are not as accessible and less frequently reported in print. On the whole, advertising has apparently been effective, otherwise it no doubt would have declined. There is always the danger of inferring too much or too little from individual instances. The following illustrations are presented with these considerations in mind.

(a) From Individual Advertisements. In 1911, Colgate & Co. placed in a few publications an advertisement which brought approximately 60,000 letters. It is true that this advertisement offered a series of prizes for the best letters setting forth the reasons for the preference for one of the two smaller advertisements contained in the advertisement. Nevertheless, the returns show the large number of people who read and notice advertisements. The 60,000 represents only those persons who took the trouble of writing a response. The number of persons who saw the advertisement was no doubt several times as large.

In February, 1921, Bedell's of New York City issued a full-page advertisement in color in one national woman's publication. This advertisement announced its spring catalog. This single advertisement brought over 80,000 requests for the catalog. "The only explanation we are able to make for this unusually large number of replies to one advertisement," said H. D. Stewart, advertising manager of the company, "is the merit of the goods, the reputation which the name of the company enjoys with the public, the fact that we are about 28 years old, and have been advertising consistently year after year." [1]

In the early spring of 1921, one of the Boston papers announced an Ad-Writing Contest, in which advertisements were to be submitted for 24 products. This contest ran for a period of 12 weeks. Weekly prizes were awarded, ranging from $100 in cash down to a considerable number of merchandise prizes. The first advertisement of the contest occupied less than a page, and appeared in a Sunday issue of the paper. During the first week, approximately 480,000 advertisements were submitted. During the entire period of the contest, nearly 3,000,000 individual pieces of copy were submitted. While most persons submitted several pieces of copy, nevertheless it represented a response from approximately 40,000 to 50,000 individuals each week. The point here is that the number of persons who notice advertisements and the amount of attention which they give to them are far greater than most of us realize.

The first advertisement of the Gillette razor appeared in February, 1904. It cost less than $200, and brought 187 orders for razors with $5 enclosed with each order, or a total of $935. In 1904, a total of 90,844 razors were sold. In the second year, 300,000 sets were sold. In 1914, the company did $7,500,000 worth of business. In 1920, it sold 2,090,616 razors, and 19,051,268 dozen blades. Early in 1921, the new improved Gillette was announced, and during the first six months, approximately half a million sets of razors were sold. Advertising has played a prominent and consistent part in the development of this business.[2]

[1] *Printers' Ink*, May 12, 1921, p. 142.   [2] *Associated Advertising*, 1915.

In 1895, Ostermoor & Co. inserted its first advertisement of half a page at a cost of $200. It produced orders amounting to approximately $1,000. Mr. Ames of Ostermoor & Co. sometime ago stated:

I had so little faith in advertising that it took this agent nearly three months to induce me to dig down in my jeans and produce the two hundred dollars. He had explained over and over again that I would be exploiting my mattress and necessarily creating a demand for it, but at that time I could not see the logic of it.

And when the agent showed me the copy and told me he intended spending all my money for a half-page in one magazine —well, what I thought of him wouldn't be esthetic publicity.

But my surprise can be imagined when in a few days the orders from that one advertisement amounted to nearly one thousand dollars. Naturally, I continued to increase my advertising appropriation until we were using some thirty national magazines.

When I tell merchants that my advertising appropriation has reached two hundred thousand dollars a year, and that my business has been built up through national magazine advertising, there is little need of anyone asking if I am a believer in national magazine advertising.

Our business has grown beyond our fondest expectations. As an example, I might state we did more business during the month of October, 1913, than we did during the entire year of 1896. And as the business was built entirely upon magazine advertising, we, naturally, feel indebted to the magazines.[1]

An automobile concern used a half-page in *Collier's*, April 11, 1914, which brought in 10 days, 1,000 inquiries which in turn led to 28 sales and to the establishment of 12 dealerships within a period of 6 weeks.[2]

A certain concern used two one-eighth pages in *McClure's Magazine* in 1914. The returns received led to sales amounting to $924.[3]

(b) From Campaigns. Kirsch Manufacturing Co. (Curtain Rods.) For the first seven years of its existence, the Kirsch Manufacturing Company did not advertise. For the past three years it has advertised. During the non-advertising period a

---

[1] *World's Work*, April, 1914.   [2] *Printers' Ink*, May 28, 1914, p. 41.
[3] *Ibid.*, April 9, 1914, p. 22.

business of about a quarter of a million dollars a year was built up. In the last three years, this volume has swelled to a figure approaching four times that figure.

The number of salesmen used in making the increased volume of sales is about a fourth more than that which produced the business of three years ago. The number of retail dealers handling Kirsch flat rods has been increased only some 25%. Yet the business has grown almost fourfold.

The first national campaign in February, March, April, and May issues of six women's publications in the spring of 1915 used space costing approximately $7,000.

In 1916 about double that amount was appropriated, while for the spring and fall campaigns of 1917 approximately $20,000 was put into advertising.

The space necessarily was modest in size at the outset—56 lines single column and 112 lines double column being the units used. The second and third year the space was increased and 112-line, single- and double-column ads were used.

The appeal in the advertising has been based each year upon the research and field work of the company's sales department. Thus it is kept in harmony with the latest information on the subject and is directed to overcome sales resistance in the most efficient manner.

The response to the advertising has been most generous. Over 10,000 inquiries were secured the first year, over 30,000 the second, and between 30,000 and 40,000 from the spring campaign of 1917. Most of the inquiries came from women who wanted the Kirsch Rod and Drapery Style Book. Some were from dealers.

Three years of advertising has cost under $50,000—it has been directly and indirectly responsible, in a measure, for a fourfold increase in the business—it has definitely interested several hundred thousand women in the story of what the flat rod does; it has made the company name practically synonymous with flat rod.[1]

Alexander Brothers (Belting). Seven years ago Alexander Brothers, of Philadelphia, set aside $1,200 for direct advertising. The following year the appropriation was increased to $1,800. In four years it was increased to $5,000. In 1916 it had risen to $35,000. This year it runs into six figures.

The first of the large advertisements appeared in February and in the six months since then there has been an increase of 60%

[1] *Ibid.,* Aug. 9, 1917, p. 8.

in a volume of sales which it took 50 years to build without advertising, and a 40% increase in distribution.

Throughout this preliminary period a radical change was being worked in distribution methods and more economic production methods were being evolved. The product of the business was being put out not merely as "good belting," but as "The Alexander Belt." The direct advertising methods were developed consistently in conformity with the distribution development.[1]

California Fruit Growers' Exchange. The various co-operative agricultural organizations have used advertising apparently to good advantage in developing the sale and consumption of farm products. The California Fruit Growers' Exchange was organized in 1905. About 1907 it faced the problem of a very greatly increased production of citrous fruits during the near future. The problem,

TABLE II

SHIPMENTS OF BOXES OF SUNKIST ORANGES, 1903-1921

Season Ended October 31	Boxes	
1903	8,094,720	
1904	10,246,656	
1905	10,225,908	
1906	8,973,342	
1907	10,290,729	Advertising begun
1908	10,742,944	
1909	13,441,016	
1910	11,187,792	
1911	15,645,168	
1912	13,680,612	
1913	6,346,692	Poor crop year
1914	17,986,482	
1915	15,857,856	
1916	15,490,399	
1917	20,167,846	
1918	7,862,757	Poor crop year
1919	18,066,368	
1920	16,658,525	
1921	22,116,776	

[1] *Ibid.*, Aug. 23, 1917, p. 49.

therefore, was to increase the consumption of these products. An advertising campaign was inaugurated in 1907-1908.

Table 11 shows the shipments of boxes of Sunkist oranges over a period of 19 years.

Twenty-seven years ago, when California shipped about 2,000,-000 boxes of oranges a year, the growers thought they were over-producing. The supply was so far in excess of the demand that at times the returns were less than the costs. By cooperation they reduced expenses, minimized decay, and increased the efficiency of their distributing machine until by 1906 they had pushed up their annual sales to 10,000,000 boxes. But in response to the stabilizing influence of organization thousands of new acres had been planted and with the big possibilities for making economies and increasing efficiency practically worked out, they faced the problem of overproduction once more. This time they turned to advertising to widen their basic market by educating the public to the delicious and healthful qualities of oranges and suggesting new ways to serve this fruit in the American home. In the 12 years since the first Sunkist campaign was launched in Iowa, the consumption of California oranges has doubled. The American consumer has been taught by cooperative advertising to eat nearly twice as many oranges as before.[1]

It would of course be false reasoning to say that the sale and consumption of oranges was doubled from 1907 to 1919 entirely because of the publicity carried out. The fact apparently was that fruit growers began to raise oranges in increasing numbers and something had to be done to sell the prospective crops in order to save the growers from financial disaster. The publicity effort made and the establishment of the brand-name "Sunkist" have no doubt played an important part as one potent factor. It may nevertheless be regarded as a distinctive achievement to have succeeded in selling the greatly increased crop and in developing the consumption of it.

A similar situation developed in the case of lemons, as shown by the following figures.

[1] Don Francisco, Advertising Manager, California Fruit Growers' Exchange, *Printers' Ink,* June 10, 1920, p. 33.

Sixteen years ago California supplied about one-fourth of all the lemons used in the United States and Canada. The balance came from Italy and Sicily. Today the relative importance of domestic and foreign lemons in the American market has been reversed. California furnishes not one-fourth, but three-fourths of the supply. Last year, to be exact, our share was 84.9%, as Table 12 shows:

TABLE 12
RELATIVE IMPORTANCE OF DOMESTIC AND FOREIGN LEMONS IN THE AMERICAN MARKET, 1903-1921

Year Ended June 30	California Shipments	Total Supply	Percentage California
1903	1,766	6,998	25.3
1904	2,168	7,786	27.8
1905	2,980	7,742	38.4
1906	3,362	8,112	41.4
1907	2,822	8,095	34.9
1908	3,618	9,730	37.2
1909	4,859	9,489	51.2
1910	4,511	10,010	45.1
1911	5,513	10,135	54.4
1912	4,326	10,314	51.6
1913	3,367	8,576	39.2
1914	2,556	10,039	25.5
1915	5,333	10,995	48.1 Advertising Started
1916	6,762	10,371	65.2
1917	7,814	10,977	71.2
1918	5,607	8,729	64.2
1919	9,836	11,583	84.9
1920	....	.....	70.3
1921	....	.....	83.7

Don't misunderstand me. I don't mean that advertising alone has brought us three-fourths of the domestic business. We set out to increase our share, and advertising was merely one of the tools employed. We have accomplished our purpose, and cooperative advertising deserves a part of the credit.

From the above table it appears that from 1903 to 1914 California's share was 39.2% on the average; from 1915 to 1921 it was 69.7%. The total supply of lemons increased approximately 10% in the latter period over the former period.

Sun-Maid Raisins. In 1913 the production and consumption record of the California Associated Raisin Company stood like this:

	Pounds
Produced	140,000,000
Consumed	110,000,000
Unsold	30,000,000

By 1917 the figures were quite different. The record was:

	Pounds
Produced	326,000,000
Consumed	326,000,000
Unsold	None

In four years the sale of California raisins was increased 216,000,000 pounds and the annual carry-over was wiped out, and the average consumer was eating 3.26 pounds of raisins a year instead of only 1.1 pounds as before. You are all familiar with the Sun-Maid raisin advertising that has helped make this increase possible.[1]

More complete figures are given in Table 13. It will be noted that the large increase in the consumption of raisins occurred before the advent of prohibition (January, 1919).

TABLE 13 *

PRODUCTION AND CONSUMPTION OF SUN-MAID RAISINS, 1913-1920

Year	Pounds Produced	Pounds Consumed	Pounds Per Capita	
1913	132,000,000	110,000,000	1.1	
1914	182,000,000	182,000,000	1.66	Advertising started
1915	256,000,000	256,000,000	2.6	
1916	264,000,000	264,000,000	2.64	
1917	326,000,000	326,000,000	3.26	
1918	334,000,000	334,000,000	3.17	
1919	365,000,000	365,000,000	3.41	
1920	347,000,000	347,000,000	3.28	

* *Judicious Advertising,* Sept., 1922, pp. 55-67.

[1] *Printers' Ink,* June 10, 1920, p. 33.

Walnut Growers' Association. Since the California Walnut Growers' Association was formed in 1913 the total annual consumption of walnuts in America has increased from 49,000,000 pounds to 85,000,000 pounds. (This includes domestic supply plus our imports.) The output of walnuts from California doubled during the period from 1914 to 1917 and almost doubled again from 1917 to 1919. In other words, the output is doubling about every three years; and cooperative advertising is doing its share to make the consumption of these great increases possible.[1]

Detailed figures on walnuts are shown in Table 14.

TABLE 14 *

PRODUCTION AND CONSUMPTION OF CALIFORNIA WALNUTS
1907-1921

Year	Walnuts from California, Pounds	California Plus Imports, Pounds	California's Share, Percentages	
1907	14,000,000	37,036,646	38.0	
1908	18,000,000	39,427,853	45.7	
1909	17,000,000	34,432,885	49.4	
1910	15,090,000	38,369,974	39.4	
1911	22,000,000	43,146,116	51.2	
1912	22,024,000	44,232,845	50.0	
1913	22,378,353	38,741,400	58.0	
1914	17,778,000	33,912,211	53.6	
1915	29,650,000	50,638,326	58.0	Advertising started
1916	29,200,000	51,810,418	56.8	
1917	33,000,000	50,177,992	66.0	
1918	40,230,680	43,534,683	93.0	
1919	56,496,000	77,731,078	72.7	
1920	39,954,000	56,026,807	70.0	
1921	41,638,000	87,208,618	47.0	

* *Judicious Advertising,* Sept., 1922, pp. 55-67.

Rice Millers' Association. The Rice Millers' Association and the Associated Rice Millers of America, the latter being the advertising organization, recently had their annual conventions at New Orleans. The president of the Associated Rice Millers of America, Frank A. Godchaux, declared that the short, intensive advertising campaign which had been undertaken a few months ago had tripled the consumption of rice in the United States.

[1] *Printers' Ink,* June 10, 1920, p. 33.

He also referred to a new campaign which is being planned. He said in part:

"Rice is being consumed in the United States at the rate of 7 pounds per capita, an increase of 4.53 pounds over the 2.46 pounds the average person ate during 1920.

"The advertising plan as carried out created a feeling and spirit of cooperation among the greatest number of jobbers and retailers throughout the country, and as a result rice has been placed on a proper cost-to-the-consumer basis." [1]

American Cranberry Exchange. In 1916 the production of cranberries in the United States totaled some 545,000 barrels. Production had increased nearly 200,000 barrels since 1906; there had been a continuous rise in the cost of production, and the consumption was small. The growers were up against it to meet expenses, much less a profit. Consumption must be increased— but how?

Twenty-three thousand dollars was appropriated to be spent on a cooperative advertising campaign in Chicago newspapers, street cars, printed bulletins and service work. This was largely an educational campaign. The American Cranberry Exchange, with a membership that now includes more than 65% of all the producing states of Wisconsin, Massachusetts, and New Jersey, had been organized in 1911, and had devoted most of its time to improving the quality of the product through uniform grading and packing. The association knew that the point was reached where uniform quality could be depended upon and that any increased demand could be properly met. In the campaign, emphasis was laid upon these factors. New methods of serving cranberries in an appetizing manner were suggested. There was a sugar shortage, and the public was instructed in ways of cooking cranberries with less than the usual quantity of sugar.

By the close of the season the Chicago sales had increased 47½% over those in 1915, 27½% over those in 1914, and 57% over those in 1913. At the same time New York, Boston, Philadelphia, Pittsburgh, Buffalo, and Cleveland, where no advertising had been done, showed decreases in sales ranging from 1% to 57%. Obviously advertising was the need of the cranberry industry.

In 1917 the crop was cut in half by a freeze in September and no advertising was done, although it is interesting to note that more money in the aggregate was received for the 1917 crop than

[1] *Ibid.,* Fall, 1921.

for a crop more than twice as large in 1914. But in 1918 the first national advertising campaign on cranberries was inaugurated, and beginning about October 15 in the United States and October 6 in Canada, $54,000 was spent for advertising in a 30-day period. It was the year of sugar regulation; everywhere in the United States the mild fall and winter weather was detrimental to the consumption of cranberries; the trade was apathetic, and it was felt that cranberries would be a drug on the market. To be sure, there was an advertising campaign on, but the growers were in the doldrums, and regarded other conditions as insurmountable.

Then lo! Cranberries began to sell in larger quantities than ever before and by January were bringing the record price of $22 a barrel. Those in charge of the campaign say that if no advertising had been done, the crop would have netted the growers not more than $6 a barrel, which was not considered a profitable price. But through advertising $8.89 a barrel net was realized—an estimated profit as a result of the campaign of more than $1,000,000.

The following year the cranberry growers were confronted with worse general conditions than ever before. The crop was 562,000 barrels, the third largest crop in the history of the industry. The sugar situation was acute, transportation was demoralized, and weather conditions were mild. Cranberries opened the season at $8.50 a barrel and by October dropped to $7.50. The advertising fund was $130,000. By November 15 the price rebounded to $8.50, where it remained until the last of January.

Of the advertising fund assessed in 1920, nearly $13,000 had to be returned to the growers because the demand created by the advertising already done was more than sufficient to consume all the berries produced.

Up to and including the 1920-21 season the growers had spent $300,000 for advertising, or an average assessment of 20 cents per barrel on all cranberries shipped cooperatively during the 5-year period ending with that season. Since 1917 the prices received by the grower have not only kept pace with production costs, but have meant a satisfactory profit. And the argument that prices of everything rose during the times does not apply. For the statistics show that cranberry prices did not rise during the war period in proportion to other prices; neither did they fall during the selling season of 1920-21 when the prices of practically all farm commodities declined. In a word, advertising has not only increased the consumption of cranberries, but through securing wider distribution of the crop has stabilized the price.[1]

---

[1] *Ibid.*, Oct. 13, 1921, p. 89.

California Pears. For a generation, fresh California deciduous fruits have been shipped East, delivered to auction houses or to wholesale jobbers, but unlike prunes or oranges or walnuts or raisins, the deciduous fruits have never been advertised nor merchandised.

If we could appeal to the consumer, we reasoned, by telling her when the pears arrived on the market; if we could arouse her interest in the health-giving and cooling qualities of the California pear during the eastern hot summer; if we could get retail cooperation in working for volume of sales at a moderate profit instead of limited sales at a wide margin; if we could make the month of August "California Pear month," then we would be doing something that had never been done before with a deciduous California fruit, and would succeed in breaking the hidebound precedents of 30 years.

We had difficulties to overcome; an appropriation limited to a nickel a box; markets thousands of miles away; no precedents to guide us; reduced buying power of consumers; a high freight rate; skepticism in the fruit trade; a short season; a late start and the need of fast work.

We attribute the success of the campaign to common sense "quick-shooting" methods, to splendid retail dealer cooperation secured mainly by personal interviews, to the dealer helps produced by the Advertising Service Department of the Schmidt Lithograph Company and to the newspaper copy prepared by Honig-Cooper Company.

Results are what count! We would have felt repaid if sales had increased 50% over those of the preceding year. But we were pleasantly surprised by the striking increase of 130% in sales in Boston and 102% in Philadelphia. The advertising sold 24,000,000 additional pears in one month.

Compared with other markets (for Boston and Philadelphia were the only two advertised markets), we have the following:

Out of increased arrivals of pears in all eastern markets— amounting in August, 1921, to 228 cars more than during the same period in 1920, Boston and Philadelphia absorbed 264 cars additional, or 90%. They became elastic enough to take up practically all the increase. In other words, they were the only two markets showing any gain over one year ago. They made enormous gain while all other markets showed decreased percentages.

The other markets were overburdened, and had not our advertised markets taken up the slack there would have been disastrous slumps in the other cities. Some of the fruit shippers estimate that the pear growers' campaign, costing less than $20,000, earned for the growers over $100,000 in maintenance of price.[1]

The consumption of cocoa has greatly increased during the past 30 years. The figures in Table 15 show the increase in imports of raw and prepared cocoa into the United Kingdom between 1889 and 1916.

TABLE 15
IMPORTS OF COCOA INTO THE UNITED KINGDOM

Year	Pounds of Raw Cocoa	Pounds Prepared Cocoa or Chocolate
1889	26,509,791	2,139,590
1890	28,112,210	2,473,423
1891	31,282,598	2,748,383
1892	30,839,525	2,538,460
1893	32,982,005	2,740,571
1894	39,115,963	2,852,104
1895	42,769,307	3,058,850
1896	38,281,803	3,846,025
1897	34,533,381	9,068,176
1898	42,833,993	8,127,191
1899	43,473,281	5,262,394
1900	52,647,318	7,860,966
1901	51,798,802	8,390,286
1902	58,137,364	8,748,353
1903	50,004,705	10,446,713
1904	60,908,784	10,619,652
1905	54,167,990	9,054,386
1906	51,670,321	9,173,580
1907	57,108,050	11,389,807
1908	66,833,413	10,765,503
1909	77,032,263	11,672,675
1910	70,650,300	15,118,208
1911	73,286,272	16,731,299
1912	75,276,704	23,670,640
1913	78,359,596	27,605,984
1914	93,511,294	22,969,296
1915	183,181,510	36,700,720
1916	198,938,768	29,874,880

[1] *Western Advertising*, November, 1921.

The total consumption of cocoa largely increased. The apprehensive advertisers actually profited by the expenditure into which they considered themselves forced. Bournville, the beautiful garden factory in which the enlightened benevolence of Mr. Cadbury is expressed, has been built since the new competitor arrived on the scene; Messrs. Rowntree of New York, and Fry at Bristol, are more famous and more prosperous than ever. Unless you are prepared to say that the sale of cocoa itself is an economic waste, you cannot say this of the cocoa advertisements.[1]

The consumption of various forms of tobacco has greatly increased in recent years. The figures in Table 16 show the consumption of pipe-tobacco and cigarettes in the United States between 1900 and 1917, and those in one of the tabulations on page 72, the consumption of cigars from 1906 to 1915. Of these three forms of tobacco, cigarettes have been advertised most extensively, especially

TABLE 16

CONSUMPTION OF TOBACCO AND OF CIGARETTES IN THE UNITED STATES, 1900 TO 1917*

Year	Pipe-Tobacco, Pounds	Cigarettes
1900	278,977,035	2,639,899,785
1901	294,101,715	2,277,069,818
1902	298,048,339	2,651,618,797
1903	310,667,865	3,043,030,604
1904	328,650,710	3,235,103,871
1905	334,849,110	3,376,633,673
1906	354,915,499	3,792,759,903
1907	369,186,288	5,166,941,756
1908	364,109,398	5,402,345,198
1909	388,756,941	6,105,424,173
1910	436,798,085	7,874,239,863
1911	380,794,673	9,254,351,722
1912	393,785,146	11,239,536,803
1913	404,362,620	14,294,895,471
1914	412,505,213	16,427,086,016
1915	402,474,245	16,756,179,973
1916	417,235,928	21,087,677,077
1917	445,763,206	30,529,193,538

* Thomas Russell, *Commercial Advertising*, p. 69.

[1] Thomas Russell, *Commercial Advertising*, p. 68.

during the last eight to ten years, pipe-tobacco next and cigars last.

From 1900 to 1917 the consumption of cigarettes has increased 11½ times; the consumption of pipe-tobacco has increased about 60%. The extraordinary gain in 1917 was no doubt due to a large extent to our entering into the World War, during which the American soldiers were generously supplied with cigarettes.

The consumption of cigars, on the other hand, has remained practically stationary.

From 1906 to 1915, the consumption of large cigars was as follows: [1]

1906	7,147,000,000	1908	6,488,000,000
1907	7,302,000,000	1909	6,667,000,000
1910	6,810,000,000	1913	7,571,000,000
1911	7,048,000,000	1914	7,174,000,000
1912	7,044,000,000	1915	7,096,000,000

Perhaps the best that can be said for the tobacco habit is that it is an economic waste—a thought in which most of us who use the weed will concur—and yet we must, as we review these statistics, take our hats off to the power of advertising.

The A. G. Gilbert Company. (Toys.) The sales of this enterprising toy manufacturer for the last nine years have been as follows:

1911	$ 37,272.66	1916	$1,182,236.20
1912	59,610.42	1917	771,802.11
1913	141,736.09	1918	1,053,843.47
1914	374,626.46	1919	1,710,086.23
1915	831,049.78		

Mr. Gilbert has been kind enough to supplement the foregoing information by letting *Printers' Ink* have his advertising investment figures for each year since he started to advertise in 1913. Here they are:

1913	$ 12,000.00	1917	$ 82,000.00
1914	47,000.00	1918	100,000.00
1915	110,000.00	1919	130,000.00
1916	124,000.00		

[1] *Associated Advertising*, Oct., 1916, p. 31.

The striking thing about these statistics is the relation that the sales figures bear to the advertising figures. Sales have been increasing in approximately the same relative proportions as have the advertising appropriations. In 1914 and 1915 the advertising increased more than the sales, but after the cumulative power of advertising had a chance to get in its work it will be noted that sales figures, especially for the years 1916, 1918, and 1919, climbed faster than the appropriation.

In 1917, it will be observed that sales dropped about 35%. It is significant that the decrease in the advertising appropriation for that year was about 34%.

The publication of these figures shows, as not anything else could, how sales are influenced by advertising. No doubt Mr. Gilbert could have sold his toys without advertising, but if he had tried it he would probably still be struggling with low volume and in the meantime there is no telling what the overhead would have done to the business. The value of constant advertising to a new business is that it quickly runs the sales up over the danger mark. Low volume is one of the gravest dangers a young business has to face. It is a danger that a wise investment in advertising, as Mr. Gilbert's experience indicates, can speedily overcome.[1]

TABLE 17

ADVERTISING APPROPRIATIONS AND SALES, SALADA TEA
COMPANY, 1892-1914

Year	Sales Pounds	Year	Sales Pounds
1892	12,658	1904	2,477,043
1893	28,312	1905	2,893,514
1894	69,301	1906	3,429,531
1895	149,408	1907	4,019,895
1896	273,710	1908	3,829,301
1897	509,230	1909	4,056,114
1898	712,005	1910	4,605,780
1899	965,917	1911	5,696,369
1900	1,220,752	1912	6,919,806
1901	1,496,432	1913	7,895,824
1902	1,694,996	1914	8,192,063 *
1903	2,244,310		

* *Printers' Ink,* June 21, 1917, p. 35.

[1] *Printers' Ink,* March 25, 1920, p. 199.

P. C. Larkin & Company. (Salada Tea). Starting to advertise over 24 years ago, P. C. Larkin & Company, with headquarters at Toronto, packers of tea, have kept it up ever since. In season and out of season, in good times and bad, and despite all obstacles, for a quarter of a century the advertising has been delivering its message unwaveringly. And the results? Take a look at the chart reproduced on page 35, showing the history of Salada sales since 1892. In that year sales were only 12,658 pounds, and in 1914, they were 8,192,063 pounds! Since 1914, though the business has been on a war basis, and regardless of the difficulty in getting the crop from primary markets, advertising has enabled the company to more than hold its position in the trade.

As national appropriations go these days, the $80,000 to $100,-000 which is invested in advertising Salada each year is not large, but nevertheless this appropriation makes the firm one of the largest advertisers of teas in America. It lays claim to being the pioneer advertiser of package teas and to the honor of being the most persistent user of advertising space in the field.

The Literary Digest Circulation Campaign. The *Literary Digest* has been engaged for some time in a campaign to increase circulation. For this purpose advertisements have been inserted weekly in a considerable number of newspapers. The copy for the most part has comprised a statement of the contents of each weekly number. These advertisements have usually appeared on the day of the week on which the *Digest* is issued.

The results of this effort are given as follows in an advertisement published May 9, 1921, in the *Boston Herald:*

> Circulation when the advertising began was 485,930.
> In nine months the circulation was 655,030.
> In eighteen months the circulation was 950,000.
> Today the circulation is 1,300,000.

The campaign involved the expenditure of about a million dollars a year.

Further Illustrations. A certain concern had developed during 73 years of its existence a volume of $3,000,000 worth of business without the use of advertising. Then advertising was introduced and in one year the business grew to $6,000,000. Nothing else was done differently. Another concern had made a product for nine years, and then they began to advertise it. The advertising resulted in a very considerable increase of business. No other essential changes were made.

EXTENT TO WHICH WOMEN READ NEWSPAPER ADVERTISEMENTS

Recently an investigation was made in connection with one of the large retail stores of Boston, under the direction of the author, with the aid of C. J. O'Connor, in which approximately 6,000 women were asked this question among others:

Do you read the newspaper advertisements before you go shopping?
Practically always - - Rarely - - Usually - - Never - -

This inquiry was made separately for customers in the basement section of the store and in the upstairs section of the store, since a different type of merchandise is handled in the two sections. The results were as follows:

UPSTAIRS STORE

	Always	Usually	Rarely	Never
Number	1,299	1,246	558	267
Per Cent	56.9	31.5	8.8	2.7

BASEMENT STORE

	Always	Usually	Rarely	Never
Number	719	397	112	34
Per Cent	56.9	31.5	8.8	2.7

It is evident that a decided majority of replies from the customers in both sections of the store indicates that newspaper advertising is used as a guide in shopping. Among the customers in the upstairs division, 75.5% always or usually read newspaper advertisements before going shopping, and only 7.9% state that they never do. In the basement section of the store, 88.4% of the customers stated that they always or usually read the advertisements before going shopping. The percentage is somewhat larger for the customers of the basement section, because the customers there are probably somewhat more interested in and attracted by special bargain sales of lower-priced merchandise.

This investigation was made among the customers who came into the store. In connection with a related investigation, made by interviewing 50 housewives in their homes, the same question was asked, with the following results:

HOUSEWIVES INTERVIEWED AT HOME

	Always	Usually	Rarely	Never
Number	26	16	7	1
Per Cent	52	32	14	2

While this particular inquiry was made among only 50 women, it is interesting to note that these results substantially agree with those obtained from the much larger number of customers in the store. Thus, 84% of the women interviewed in their homes stated that they always or usually read the newspaper advertisements before going shopping. This percentage corresponds quite closely to the ones previously mentioned.

For further data on this and allied problems concerning the extent to which the average person observes advertisements in magazines and newspapers the reader may turn to Chapter XVII.

THE EFFECT OF OMITTING ADVERTISING

A very interesting type of evidence regarding the effect of advertising may be obtained from instances of concerns which represent the reverse of the examples just cited, that is, concerns which have done a consistent amount of advertising for a considerable period of time, and then have abruptly discontinued it. Obviously it is difficult to obtain such illustrations, because it is rarely done voluntarily as an experiment, and in the instances in which it occurs usually other changes are made, which may in part account for the ensuing results. An interesting illustration in this connection is that of St. Jacob's Oil, which was a widely known product a generation ago.

A short time after the death of Charles Vogeler, of St. Jacob's Oil fame, his widow called in a banker to look over affairs. The banker, representing ideas of a former commercial epoch, toiled microscopically through the books, and was outraged at the items spent for advertising. He would mend that! See how much more money might have been made if there had been no advertising! He figured the publicity expenditures entirely as useless "expense," and he attempted to make the widow see it that way.

The widow had a lot of faith left in her husband, for she herself had seen millions of bottles sent away to uncounted buyers. Yet there were the awful figures "squandered" just for space in magazines or billboards, and besides, wasn't a banker an all-wise man whom one shouldn't dispute?

So it happened that St. Jacob's Oil came less and less frequently to the attention of the public. As the contracts ran out they were not renewed and before long St. Jacob's Oil, which had been known to nearly every man, woman, and child in America—yes, and the world—through the tremendous force of advertising, quietly effaced itself from American landscapes and from magazines and the newspapers. Within a year or so all advertising had practically ceased.

St. Jacob's Oil had a splendid distribution. It could be got anywhere. The banker had said that it would sell anyhow, because everybody had come to know it so well. But—as the advertising had nicely ceased to bother the expense columns of the ledgers, the demand slackened. Complaints reached headquarters from dealers that St. Jacob's wasn't going as it had. And so within another two or three years the golden stream of orders had shrunk to proportions that would have driven its former proprietor frantic. St. Jacob's had become a back number.[1]

A somewhat similar history has been related regarding Pearline.

Twenty years ago one of the best-known names in national

[1] *Printers' Ink*, March 9, 1910.

advertising was James Pyle's Pearline. The advertising had run continuously since 1873. In 1904, the appropriation for that year amounted to $500,000, which was a great deal of money in those days. In 1907, the concern having passed into the hands of an estate, the trustees saw an opportunity by which they thought they could save many hundreds of dollars by cutting out the advertising. In 1914, Pearline tried to "come back," and I understand that $150,000 was spent in advertising during that year. Now $150,000 even today would make a comfortable dent on the market for a new product. But Pearline was not a new product—it was a product trying to come back. The very next year, I understand, the company was sold to a competitor, a younger organization, but one whose policy was different. This concern got its biggest start and put forth its greatest sales effort in 1907. I understand that in 1915 Pearline was sold to the Procter & Gamble Co. for just the cost of the machinery as junk and the stock on hand as raw materials. I have heard that the price was $12,000.[1]

It is, of course, quite probable that the abrupt omission of advertising is not solely responsible for the decline of business in these two instances, since usually with a change of management other changes are made and other factors enter. It would be an interesting experiment, but probably a disastrous one, to discontinue abruptly the advertising of such a product as Ivory Soap, Cream of Wheat, Hart, Schaffner & Marx clothes, or Victrolas, without making any other essential changes. Probably no one would be more interested, not to say pleased, over such an experiment, than the leading competitors of each of these firms. The long, consistent printed sales activities which these and many other firms have carried on would probably deter any of them from making such an experiment, in view of the deeply entrenched positions which they hold.

[1] *Ibid.*, Feb. 24, 1921, p. 81.

IV

THE PLACE OF ADVERTISING IN BUSINESS
(*Continued*)

Effect of advertising on prices. Effect of advertising on selling cost. Effect of advertising on profits. The more general and indirect effects of advertising. Reduction of seasonal fluctuations. Standardization of products and quality. Progress in the level of living. The universal spread of newspapers and magazines. Interpretation and summary.

Effect of Advertising on Prices. *Printers' Ink* [1] made an inquiry among a group of firms by asking the following question: "Can you give us some definite figures proving that since you began advertising one of these three things is true:

"1. Prices of your goods have been reduced as a result of the larger output secured through advertising.

"2. Quality or intrinsic value of goods has been increased.

"3. If neither proposition can be proved, can you show that price and quality have remained staple in face of increased cost of raw material and workmanship?"

The responses obtained from 29 firms showed the following results:

Price reduced, quality remaining the same—5 products, as follows:

    Dioxogen (The Oakland Chemical Co.)
    Fish Flakes (Burnham & Morrill Co.)
    Borax (Pacific Coast Borax Co.)
    Grapejuice (Welch Grape Juice Co.)
    Soap (B. T. Babbitt Co.)

Price and quality the same—8 products, as follows:

    Underwood Deviled Ham
    Ingersoll Watches

[1] Jan. 22, 1914, p. 3.

Crabmeat (McMenamin & Co.)
Eskay's Food
Waterman Pens
Shoes (Roberts, Johnson & Rand)
Minute Tapioca
Indestructo Trunks

Price reduced and quality improved—5 products, as follows:

Eastman Kodaks   Munsingwear
Kellogg's Corn Flakes   Ansco Cameras
Williams' Shaving Soap

Price the same and quality improved—11 products, as follows:

Clothes (Hart, Schaffner & Marx)   Warner Corsets
Mallory Hats   Candies (National
Holeproof Hosiery   Candy Co.
Poroshknit Underwear   Stein-Bloch Clothes
Jello (Genesee Pure Food Co.)   Lyon's Dentifrice
Douglas Shoes   Whitman Chocolates

So far as the testimony of these firms goes, it would seem that the prices of none of these commodities were raised on account of the advertising, but rather, on the other hand, in the case of a large majority, either the price was reduced or the quality improved, or both.

It may be of interest to quote the statements of some of these firms.

Fish Flakes. B. & M. Fish Flakes is the product which we advertise most extensively. Our price to the wholesale grocery trade is 25% less than it was four years ago, advertising causing increased sales, and naturally increased production brought about this change.—W. J. Leonard, Vice-Pres. and Treas., Burnham & Morrill Company.

Underwood Deviled Ham. The largest increase in our sales, and also the largest increase in our trade discount, has been during the last four years, when we have spent more money for advertising. We feel absolutely confident that had it not been for the inauguration and systematic management of this advertising campaign, our business would be stationary or declining instead of gradually increasing, and that the tremendous cost of selling the product without advertising, combined with increased cost of the product, would have necessitated prices beyond the reach of a large percentage of the present consumers.—F. A. Harding, Wm. Underwood Co.

Candy. One great effect that advertising has upon our goods is the improvement in quality and package, and uniformity of both, as well as a decided stimulant to the liberal treatment of the trade and good service.

Advertising does nothing more nor less with us than to make known to the consumer our products, and, of course, in praising our products we have to be particularly careful that the product itself in quality and appearance comes up to all that we say about it.

I cannot in any way accede to the supposition that advertising increases the price to the consumer of the majority of advertised products.

The cost of advertising is in all cases equalized by a lower cost of production due to increased sales, and if advertising were not done, then in my judgment the cost of production would increase, and as a result the selling prices to the consumer would have to continue the same.

We find in our business that where unadvertised goods are substituted for advertised goods at a less price, that in all cases they are goods of an inferior quality.—V. L. Price, National Candy Co.

Hosiery. Our prices, both to the trade and to the consumer, are identically the same as they were in 1904, although the cost of raw material and workmanship have increased materially since that time. As a matter of fact, our goods that retail at 25 cents per pair cost us 20 cents per dozen more to produce today than they did in 1905; and it is, of course, due to the fact that we have steadily increased our volume of business by means of advertising that we are able to continue to market these goods at the same price to the consumer.—Edward Freschl, Holeproof Hosiery Company.

Corn Flakes. We can give definite evidence proving both:

1. That prices of our goods have been reduced as a result of the larger output secured through advertising.

2. Quality and intrinsic value of goods have been increased.

As to No. 1, when our product, then known as Sanitas Toasted Corn Flakes, was first placed on the market, the package was one-third smaller and sold for 15 cents. With the increased distribution resulting from national advertising, we have increased the size of the package 50% and decreased the price to the consumer 33-1/3%, so that the consumer today receives more than twice as much for his money as he did of the unadvertised product.—R. O. Eastman, Kellogg Toasted Corn Flake Co.

Shaving Soap. Twenty years ago we put out Williams' Shaving Stick in a metal leatherette-covered box with a slip cover, very simple and extremely inexpensive. Today the descendant of this leatherette shaving stick is being put out in a nickeled box with hinged cover, a container of very much greater value, convenience, and attractiveness. At the same time the net saving of the present shaving stick to the dealer is a fraction over 2% of the former leatherette-covered shaving stick, and with the additional advantage to the dealer that we are paying the freight on this and other products of our manufacture, which was not true until a few years ago.

A point of perhaps important significance in the present discussion is the fact that the consumer is getting 20% more soap in the nickeled box with hinged cover today than he got years ago in the plainer and less expensive box, so that to sum up the situation, the dealer is buying our shaving sticks at 2% less than the former price, he is getting the freight paid on his shipments, the consumer is getting 20% more for his money, besides having it packed in a much more durable and attractive container, and all this during a period when products in general were going upward in cost.—J. B. Williams Company.

Watches. As to exact figures, it is well known that our dollar watch has always sold at that price. We have not changed our price to the public or to the trade in 19 years. Our output has risen from a few hundred to fifteen thousand per day. Improved manufacturing facilities, inventiveness, and a constantly enlarged field cultivated by advertising which has kept people informed of our improvements has permitted us to progress in the manner I have herein described.—Wm. H. Ingersoll, Robt. H. Ingersoll & Bro.

Food. If there are 10-cent powders as good as his 25-cent article, the people will be told about them by somebody in some sort of advertising, and the people can take their choice. The statement that the high cost of living is in any way the result of great expenditure for advertising is entirely baseless.

To use our own product as an illustration: Fifteen years ago we spent a few hundred dollars a year advertising Jell-O; now we spend half a million, and all the time the price of Jell-O has remained the same, 10 cents a package, though thousands of dollars have been expended in increasing the quality of our product.—W. E. Humlbaugh, Genesee Pure Food Company.

Shoes. When Mr. Douglas first started in business in 1876, he did no advertising. Shoes were figured at that time probably like many other lines of goods; the items including cost of leather and other materials, labor, overhead, profit, but no margin for advertising.

In 1883, when Mr. Douglas first started to advertise, the same method of figuring our product was continued and is in use today, no item of advertising expense being included. It is a demonstrated fact that large manufacturers in the shoe business can purchase leather and materials in large lots cheaper than smaller manufacturers can. By taking advantage of market conditions, lots of leather can frequently be purchased at a more favorable price than later in the year when the demand is heavier. We take advantage of all these opportunities. Frequently contracts for sole leather, for instance, will involve $1,500,000.

We claim and can substantiate it that we give to the consumer all of these advantages, retaining only a small profit per pair, and are therefore enabled to produce and sell a better shoe at a standard price, $4.50, $4 and $3.50, than smaller manufacturers who are unable to buy in large quantities and take advantage of market conditions.

I repeat, we do not now figure nor have we ever figured our advertising as a part of the cost of a pair of shoes.—Frank L. Erskine, W. L. Douglas Shoe Company.

Fountain Pen. The selling prices to the public of Waterman's Ideal Fountain Pens are substantially the same today as they were at the time of their inception 30 years ago. This in the face of the fact that both labor and component materials of manufacture have nearly doubled in cost, taxes are higher, many items of selling expense are greatly increased and competition is keener.

The fact that we have been consistent, steady, and successful advertisers to the consuming world at large is the principal cause for the quality of merchandise that we supply and the service that we give the public at these same original and reasonable prices. The expense of advertising Waterman's Ideals enters into the cost of the pens, the same as taxes and import duties which we pay to support our Government, including the salaries of congressmen, judges, cabinet officers, and others who would be without a livelihood if the country were not big and prosperous enough to keep them in office.

The missionary work which must be done on behalf of our company can be handled more cheaply through intelligent advertising than by the employment of salesmen who must be paid a living wage. As this is an important element in the final cost of our product, we do not hesitate to state that the users of our pens would be paying a higher price today if we had not been able to develop our business with the help of judicious advertising.—F. P. Seymour, L. E. Waterman Company.

Shoes. First—the price of our shoes to the consumer has not been reduced as a result of the large output obtained through advertising. This is due to the fact that during the last five years leather has advanced in cost until it has reached the highest point ever known. The leather cost in a pair of men's shoes has advanced about 60 cents per pair during this period. There has been a large increase in the cost of other material used in shoes, and labor is higher today than it was five years ago.

Let me say, however, that our increased production, resulting from advertising, has kept the price down to a lower figure than would have been the case with a production of only half of what we are now turning out.—Roy B. Simpson, Roberts, Johnson & Rand.

Trunks. We are convinced that were we to discontinue our advertising, our business would fall off at least 50%, which would force us to distribute our overhead over about half the production which we are now getting. This would increase our cost per trunk very much more than the saving per trunk which we would make by discontinuing our advertising would amount to. —Charles R. Stevenson, Indestructo Trunks.

Soaps. Forty years ago, Babbitt's best soap sold for 10 cents a cake; it now sells everywhere at 6 for 25 cents. In all laundry soaps it can be proved that the large output obtained through advertising has enabled the manufacturer to cut manufacturing and selling cost to the very great advantage of the consumer.— B. T. Babbitt & Company.

Mr. J. F. Matteson states: "I recently asked 40 American manufacturers this question, 'Does advertising increase the price to the consumer?' The answer was, 'No, it does not!' " These manufacturers appropriated annually about $3,975,000 for advertising.[1]

The California Fruit Growers' Exchange. For fear some one might wish to credit cooperative advertising with creating such demand that oranges and lemons might be sold at exorbitant prices, I will show you our prices during the war. This chart happens to go back to the year we began advertising lemons, but our orange advertising started in 1907.

These charts show the increase or decrease in delivered prices of oranges and lemons compared:

First, with Bradstreet's Index of the wholesale prices on 96 commodities.

Second, with the Department of Agriculture's Index of articles which the farmers buy.

We take the 5-year pre-war average; that is, the average prices from 1909 to 1913, as 100%. Here are the facts:

Year	Bradstreet's Index	Articles Farmers Buy	Orange Prices	Lemon Prices
1914	99.8	103	40.0	95.5
1915	100.4	112	100.4	59.9
1916	132.6	125	111.3	96.6
1917	175.6	153	109.8	98.6
1918	210.0	189	213.6	134.2
1919	209.2	213	177.1	110.7

The charts and tables show that only once in the last six years have the prices of oranges and lemons exceeded, or equaled, the rise in price of 96 staple commodities, as reported by Bradstreet's, or the rise in the price of articles bought by farmers, as reported by the United States Department of Agriculture.

In 1918, due to the very short crop in California simultaneously with a short crop in Florida, the price of oranges slightly exceeded the rise in Bradstreet's Index and the Department of Agriculture's Index of the articles which farmers buy.[2]

The California Almond Growers' Exchange. This exchange was organized about 1909. It did no advertising during the first nine years of its existence.

"Does advertising increase the price of almonds?" is another question that is asked the Exchange. It is probably suggested

[1] *Printers' Ink,* May 10, 1917, p. 3.
[2] *Associated Advertising,* August, 1020. p. 11.

by the higher prices that each succeeding increased crop brings. The answer is that if money were not paid for advertising, it would have to be spent in still larger amounts to sell the crop. By speeding up turnover, the profits of each link in the chain of distribution are increased. So, as far as the middlemen are concerned, the advertising costs add to instead of taking from their profits.

As to the consumers—before the organization of the Exchange, consumers paid 35 cents a pound for the Nonpareil quality. At that price the growers were making no money. By improved marketing methods which the Exchange was able to supply, the price remained the same to the consumers for nine years, and the growers made enough from their crops so that the industry increased. During the last two years (since the Exchange has been advertising) the price has raised about 25% to consumers. One of the very good reasons for that increase in price is the fact that when the almonds were selling for 35 cents a pound, growers paid from $2 to $2.50 a day for board and labor. Last year one of the members was forced to employ Spaniards to do his harvesting on a tree basis and paid the equivalent of $16 a day for labor. That is just one of the reasons for an advance in the retail price. But this alone is convincing as to the necessity of a higher price.

This year the advertising cost will be the greatest yet expended and will amount to just 1 cent a pound. On nuts that are re-tailing at 45 to 50 cents a pound, that item is a small factor.[1]

A Breakfast Food Manufacturer. A large manufacturer of breakfast food sold in a recent year $123,000,000 worth of his product, and spent $1,000,000 in advertising. This is approximately three-fourths of one per cent of the business done. In other words, if the package sells for 25 cents, the cost for advertising would be approximately one-fifth of 1 cent per package.[2]

Advertising Tends to Steady Prices. While there are no extensive or conclusive figures available, it is probable that continuous advertising over a period of time, particularly in instances where the advertising has emphasized a uni-form price for a standard brand, has exercised a strong

---

[1] *Printers' Ink,* Oct. 14, 1920, p. 93.   [2] *Ibid.,* Oct. 16, 1919, p. 20.

influence in keeping the prices uniform when decided fluctuations otherwise occur. Particularly has this been the
case during the recent period of rapid price advances. The
concerns which for a long time had announced certain uniform prices were for the most part very reluctant to increase
these prices, and usually did so only when forced to do so
by the great increase in the cost of material and labor. It
is quite likely that figures would show that these increases
were made more reluctantly and more moderately in the
case of well-known advertised brands than in the case of
less well-known brands.[1]

The Oliver Typewriter Company. In 1917, the Oliver
Typewriter Company announced an abrupt change in its
policy. They decided to take off their entire sales force,
reduce the price of their machine, and attempt to sell entirely through advertising. The statement in their announcement was as follows:

Of each Oliver typewriter for which the user paid $100, more
than half has been spent for salaries, traveling expenses, and
commissions, to an army of salesmen and agents. Thousands
of dollars have been spent in maintaining expensive branch houses
and showrooms in many cities. Henceforth there will be no expensive sales force of 15,000 salesmen and agents, no high office
rents in 50 cities, no idle stock.

The price of the machine was reduced from $100 to $49.
Later when prices were generally raised, this price of $49
was raised to $64, and in 1922 it was lowered again to
$49.50. The campaign has been generally successful. The
sales have gone forward in a satisfactory manner. The new
sales policy has opened up a new market for machines, particularly among individual buyers such as professional men,
small retailers, teachers, clergymen, and farmers. It is perhaps a little early to say whether this experiment will be
entirely satisfactory in the long run. Recently it has been
stated that the company has found it necessary to employ

[1] *Ibid.,* Dec. 14, 1916, p. 133; Nov. 30, 1916, p. 72.

a comparatively small staff of men to supplement its advertising, particularly from the standpoint of service, repairs, and keeping machines in order.

The fundamental point from the standpoint of our present discussions is the fact that the introduction of extensive advertising has not raised the price, but rather lowered it, and that the maintenance of the sales force is a big item of cost in the distribution of goods which the superficial critic of advertising usually overlooks. The experiment of the Oliver Typewriter Company will probably also show that the most economical distribution of many types of goods consists of a proper proportion of printed and personal sales efforts, rather than the exclusive use of either.

EFFECT OF ADVERTISING ON SELLING COST

Maytag Washing Machine. In the early period of the marketing of this washing machine, it was found that a large number of service men as well as salesmen were required. The service men were needed in order to instruct housewives in the use of the machines, in operating them and in keeping them repaired. It is stated that of the first 4,500 machines sold, 4,100 were returned to the factory as unsatisfactory. Shortly after that, it was decided to use advertising and printed instructions to help avoid some of these difficulties. As an experiment, $23,000 was appropriated for advertising for a period of six months. This brought 55,000 inquiries, less than 5% of which came from the territory in which they had distribution.

"My idea was," says the manufacturer, "that if the machine were sold properly in the first instance, that there should be no need of service men. In some districts we had two service men for every salesman, and in every district we had at least as many service men as we had salesmen.

"The washer was a wonderful demonstrating proposition, so good, in fact, that about all the salesman had to do was to demonstrate it to the dealer and then take his order.

"The salesman did not sell the machine fully. He was conscious of the fact that the service man would be along behind him to take care of that. Consequently, the salesmen were not so careful to sell the machine so that it would stay sold, as they might have been had their sale rested entirely upon their own care and attention to details."

The manufacturer accordingly determined to remove his service men. The money which he saved by this move was equally divided between a national advertising campaign and a rebate in price to the purchaser.

This advertising campaign turned the light of publicity upon the weak point in the sales policy of the factory. It carried an educational appeal to the prospect which eliminated the dead wood in the old scheme.

By frank, straight-from-the-shoulder copy, the manufacturer told the prospect that she must renew her batteries at regular intervals or her machine would fail to give the utmost satisfaction; he educated her to the whims of the gas engine and he did it without the aid of the service men.

By removing the latter from the field, the salesmen naturally went after their business on a different basis. They were no longer order takers; they became salesmen, and they "sold" the machine along the correct lines.

National advertising has accomplished these tangible results for this manufacturer.

It has increased his business over 1,000% in just three years.

In the same length of time, it has decreased his selling cost just 7%.

During the first "flyer" campaign, the inquiry cost to this manufacturer was about $2 each. It should be remembered that no effort was made to secure direct inquiries, it being desired to maintain the dealer as the distributing agent.[1]

The Victor Talking Machine Company. The statement is frequently made by critics of advertising and particularly by retailers of competing instruments to the effect that the Victor Company has spent an enormous sum of money for advertising, and that therefore competing and less well-known instruments can be sold cheaper. It will be of interest in this connection to note the statement made by Mr. H. G. Brown of the Victor Company, apropos of a hearing before the Federal Trade Commission:

[1] *Ibid.,* Jan. 8, 1920, p. 154.

Mr. Brown declared that but for the force of Victor advertising the Victor Company would have to employ, in addition to its present force, not less than 2,000 salesmen, on an average salary of $2,000 and average annual expense accounts of $2,000 each. "The cost would have been double our advertising cost," he declared, "and the representation would not have been convincing." On this latter score, he pointed out that every Victor advertisement embodies not merely the ideas of the copy writer and the advertising manager, but the composite judgment of the whole roster of executives to whom it is submitted for suggestion and criticism. Herein was a tremendous advantage to the advertisement over oral solicitation. "We can't," said Mr. Brown, "make our traveling men say what we want them to say." [1]

If Mr. Brown's estimate is approximately correct, the total expenditure for 2,000 salesmen would be approximately $8,000,000, which is probably two or three times as much as the total expenditure for advertising at that time.

The California Fruit Growers' Exchange. Mr. Don Francisco, advertising manager of the California Fruit Growers' Exchange, points out that the cost of selling has decreased rather than increased in the period during which advertising was employed. His statement follows: [2]

The cost of selling oranges and lemons through the California Fruit Growers' Exchange is lower today than it was 10 years ago. Our percentage for sales and advertising expenses has gone down in the face of the recent rises in our cost of doing business. Last year our total selling expense, including advertising, amounted to only about 2% on our f.o.b. returns. The cost of advertising was approximately 1%. The cost of the Exchange marketing service, including advertising, is, I believe, the lowest known marketing cost of any perishable food product in America.

The figures given in Table 18 show graphically the relation of expense to volume of sales annually.

California Walnut Growers. Likewise, the California walnut growers, since organizing their association eight years ago, have reduced their cost of selling California walnuts from 6% to 3% of the f.o.b. value. The association's output in 1913 was only 5,000 tons, while today it markets over 20,000 tons in a normal year. [3]

[1] *Printers' Ink*, Dec. 6, 1917, p. 105.
[2] *Associated Advertising*, August, 1920, p. 11.   [3] *Idem.*

TABLE 18

RELATION OF EXPENSE TO VOLUME OF SALES, FRUIT GROWERS'
EXCHANGE, 1905-1922

Season Ended	Boxes Sold	F.O.B. Sales	Percentage of Adv. and Sell. Expense
1905	5,188,511	$ 7,124,377	3.28
1906	4,705,515	9,936,497	2.89
1907	6,149,708	12,268,752	2.65
1908	6,628,644	11,753,544	3.05
1909	8,710,828	13,958,990	3.44
1910	7,578,901	14,831,975	3.57
1911	10,842,831	20,708,000	3.25
1912	9,232,356	17,235,822	3.53
1913	4,940,068	13,640,091	2.62
1914	11,264,865	18,990,725	3.31
1915	11,893,201	19,526,397	3.72
1916	12,101,618	27,675,920	3.14
1917	15,492,340	33,478,139	3.01
1918	8,642,875	36,291,675	1.79
1919	14,862,000	54,627,000	2.05
1920	15,822,000	58,968,000	2.03
1921	18,326,000	56,905,000	2.25
1922	12,889,000	52,547,000	

Hart, Schaffner & Marx. When this house began advertising, the business amounted to about $1,500,000 a year; there were at that time a number of clothing concerns doing a larger business than that. Today our gross sales amount to more than $15,000,000; we are the largest clothing manufacturers in the country.

We believe our business would have grown without advertising. We do not think it would have reached anything like its present volume, nor that the growth would have been accomplished with anything like the same speed.

Volume alone would have enabled us to decrease the cost of the goods; but advertising has undoubtedly decreased also the cost of selling. It costs to sell our goods only half as much as it cost 15 years ago; we figure the advertising as part of the cost of selling.[1]

[1] *Printers' Ink*, Jan. 22, 1914, p. 3.

Mallory & Sons. Since starting to advertise in 1906 we have made a saving of 17% in the total cost of selling Mallory hats. This saving, which amounts to 7 cents on every hat we manufacture, more than pays our advertising appropriation. The saving in selling expenses has largely been brought about through the increasing demand for Mallory hats which our advertising has created, enabling our salesmen in many cases to sell double the amount of goods, with little or no increased traveling expenses.[1]

The Champion Spark Plug Company. Advertising has increased the number of our traveling representatives, because it has opened up to us markets that we did not before cover, but it has decreased the actual cost per plug as the volume of business from each territory has increased so tremendously that we have put on more sales representatives and the volume of business turned in by each man has increased several times in proportion to the increased cost of covering that territory. Our selling cost per plug has been decreased 70% in the past four years.

We have not, at any time, caused a raise in price to the consumer in connection with any advertising appropriation.[2]

Pepsodent. This new toothpaste was put upon the market and popularized solely through advertising. It is stated that the company has never employed salesmen for this product. Consumer demand was created through advertising. Within the period of a few years, this toothpaste has become one of the three or four leading brands in the country.

Postal Life Insurance Co. This company departed radically from the customary methods of selling life insurance. It undertook about 1905 to sell life insurance solely through advertising with the belief that it could be sold in this way more economically. Perhaps it is too early as yet to judge whether this point of view will be fully justified when carried out over a sufficiently long period of years. Nevertheless the experience of this company is interesting and has now extended over some 15 years.

In the year 1905, the Postal issued 205 policies, aggregating $347,000 of insurance, and spent $862.58 for advertising.

[1] *Idem.*   [2] *Idem.*

In 1908, 1,126 policies were issued, which is an increase of almost 500%. The amount of insurance was $1,976,522. The advertising cost $5,900.

In 1914, insurance was written to the amount of $2,577,720, the number of policies being 1,560. The advertising investment was $39,616.13. (The size of the appropriation grows at a steady gait, being based on the number of policyholders.) There are now 25,000 of these, and this year's appropriation will be about $40,000 or $1.60 for each policyholder.

The amount of money which may be spent each year for all expenses of operation of a participating company, including advertising, is limited by the laws of the State of New York, which declare that all such expenses must not be greater than a certain portion of the total annual premiums received. Thus, the smaller a company is, the smaller is the sum which the state permits it to spend in getting new business or retaining the old! The dilemma is exactly like that of the beginner in business: You can't get a job unless you have experience; and you can't get experience unless you can have a job! For life insurance companies it works out this way: You can't spend money unless you have policyholders, and you can't get policyholders unless you spend money.

Since the rigorous New York laws were passed, four other new companies, started about when the Postal Life did, have had to go out of business.

Nine companies have withdrawn from New York State, and are doing all their business elsewhere.

Two hundred new life insurance companies have been organized in other states of the Union. Not one has entered New York.

And not a single other company has been organized in New York!

And in the face of this record of disaster and withdrawal, the Postal Life has gone steadily ahead until it has $40,000,000 of insurance in force. Not all of this, to be sure, has been brought in by advertising. Several other companies have been "re-insured" by the Postal. However, a large enough proportion of the total business is the result of advertising to prove conclusively —to the Postal Life, at any rate—that this method of selling insurance is thoroughly sound.

"In a nutshell, here is the philosophy which lies behind the Postal," said Mr. Malone. "We believe that a life insurance company should grow from the ground up, and not from the top down. In other words, we think life insurance is such a fine thing that we would like to see all the people of America educated in regard to it until they appreciate it and will come and take it of their own free will. Our advertising is trying to accomplish that, and is succeeding quite as much as we have any right to hope.

"Sixty per cent of our policyholders already had insurance when they came into the Postal.

"Somewhere between 12% and 15% of those who answer our advertising become policyholders with us. We hope and believe that the other 85% take insurance somewhere else. We'd like to have them all insure in the Postal—of course! But we'd rather have them insure somewhere else than not at all."

How much it costs the average non-advertising life insurance company in agents' commissions to sell $1,000 of insurance is hard to say; but it is considerable. Of the first premium the agent is said to get about 45%; and he then gets about 7½% of the subsequent annual premium for a number of years.

And this, remember, is not an exorbitant rate of payment considering the work he does. For every call he makes which results in a purchase of insurance, he makes many others which meet with failure. The agent must eat; so the value of his time used in unfruitful calls has to be added to the value of the time used in really selling; and the whole is taken out of the premiums of the insured.

The non-advertising insurance company in some cases also has branch offices or agencies to maintain; moreover, it must pay fees and taxes in every state in which it does business; and these things mount up.

The Postal Life Company has found, after years of experience have put its theories to the acid test, that it can sell insurance by mail at about $10 a thousand. It has, of course, no agents' fees to pay. It has no branch offices, for all its business is done in New York State. A Supreme Court decision has sustained its contention that if a citizen of Kentucky, for instance, sends premiums to New York City, the company to which he remits is not thereby held to be doing business in Kentucky.

All told, the Postal believes its selling cost to be decidedly lower than that which is necessary under the agency system; though it is the contention of other insurance interests that this is not the case.

The saving which is effected by these economies is declared by the Postal Life to be approximately 9½%; and is the basis of the famous "annual dividend of nine and one-half per cent" which is guaranteed in every Postal Life policy.

Every State in the Union, of course, maintains the office of State Commissioner of Insurance (or some similar title). The duties which go with this office have to do with the collection of fees for the privilege of doing business, taxes on premiums collected in the state, and the like. The Postal, as we have already said, maintains no local agencies; and therefore pays no taxes in any state except New York, where its business is transacted.[1]

Community Silverware. In 1903 the Oneida Community, Ltd., began to brand and advertise one line of its silverware, a line it had been making for several years. Advertising began in a modest way, and in 1904 the total sales were $500,000. From that date to the present time advertising has been steadily and efficiently applied, with the result that this company, which had no trade standing as silverware manufacturers in 1903, and of whose goods the public was in total ignorance, has now a turnover of $4,000,000—just eight times as much as twelve years ago. This has been accomplished in the face of entrenched and nation-wide competition that in 1903 almost amounted to a monopoly.

In 1915 the sales expense of all kinds, including that of advertising, was three per cent lower than the average for the four previous years and showed a much greater reduction over all preceding years. During this whole period of rapid expansion production cost has rapidly declined, the result of increased turnover, due to efficient advertising coordinated with efficient trade salesmanship.[2]

Men's Clothing Stores. The Bureau of Business Research of Northwestern University made a study of the operating expenses of a considerable group of men's retail clothing stores covering the years 1914, 1918 and 1919. One of the problems studied was the relation between advertising and selling costs. These results are set forth in Table 19.

Referring to this table, the report says:

Two groups of stores are used, one in which sales in 1918 range between $40,000 and $60,000, and another in which stores of all sizes in 1914 available for study are included. In the first group, the stores are classified according to the amounts spent for advertising per $100 of sales in 1918. The chart indicates

[1] *Printers' Ink,* May 16, 1918, p. 4.   [2] *Ibid.,* Feb. 8, 1917, p. 111.

TABLE 19
RELATION OF ADVERTISING TO SALES AND TO EXPENSE REDUCTION

I

(Data based on stores with sales from $40,000 to $60,000 in 1918)

Advertising per $100 of Total Net Sales 1918	Number of Stores	Total Net Sales Per Cent Increase, 1919 over 1918	Selling Expense Per Cent Increase, 1919 over 1918	Selling Expense per $100 of Total Net Sales—Per Cent Decrease, 1919 from 1918
		Actual	Actual	Actual
Average	60	44.8	34.5	7.1
Under $1	23	45.2	41.0	3.0
$1 to $2	22	46.5	34.4	8.2
$2 and over	15	41.7	28.8	8.9

that the larger the amount spent for advertising in relation to sales in 1918, the greater the percentage of *decrease* in selling expense per hundred dollars of total net sales in 1919. For those which spent least, the decrease between the two years is 3.0%, while for those who spent most, it is 8.9%.

When all stores the records of which are available for 1914 are classified by the amounts spent for advertising per $100 of total net sales in that year, it is found that selling expenses expressed in sales decreased in 1919 over 1914 by 6.8%, for those which spent least for advertising, and by 13.7% for those which spent most for this purpose.

Without assigning a causal relationship between the decrease in selling expense and the increase in advertising expenditures, it is safe to conclude from the chart that a direct relationship obtains between these two factors. Obviously, there is a limit beyond which one can hope to reduce his selling expense through increasing his advertising. What this limit is the chart does not show. It does, however, indicate from the experience available an interesting association between selling expense and advertising and suggests to merchants the wisdom of closely scrutinizing their advertising expenditures and of observing in the light of these data their own experience from year to year.[1]

[1] Horace Secrist, Northwestern University Bureau of Business Research, *Series II, No. 3*, pp. 16-18.

TABLE 19 *(Continued)*
RELATION OF ADVERTISING TO SALES AND TO EXPENSE REDUCTION

II

(Data based on stores of all sizes)

Advertising per $100 of Total Net Sales 1914	Number of Stores	Total Net Sales Per Cent Increase, 1919 over 1914	Selling Expense Per Cent Increase, 1919 over 1914	Selling Expense per $100 of Total Net Sale Per Cent Decrease, 1919 from 1914
		Actual	Actual	Actual
Average	154	126.4	106.0	9.1
Under $1	27	98.1	84.4	6.8
$1 to $2	52	114.6	100.9	6.4
$2 to $3	36	112.7	93.1	9.3
$3 and over	39	151.9	117.6	13.7

EFFECT OF ADVERTISING ON PROFITS

The Knit Underwear Manufacturers. In 1915, the United States Department of Commerce reported an investigation of the knit underwear industry, covering such points as cost of manufacture, turnover, capital, wages, cost of selling and distribution, and so on. A comparison was also made with reference to profits between those manufacturers who advertised nationally to the consumer, and those who did not.

The investigation covered 63 establishments divided into five groups as follows:

Group I included 21 cotton knitting mills (20 in New York and 1 in Massachusetts).

Group II included 10 cotton knitting mills (9 in Pennsylvania and 1 in Ohio).

Group III included 3 cotton knitting mills (1 each in Maryland, North Carolina, and Tennessee).

Group IV included 13 mills knitting wools, worsted, merino, and cotton mixtures (3 in New York, 2 each in

Ohio, Michigan, and Wisconsin, and 1 each in Massachusetts, Connecticut, New Jersey, and Illinois).

Group V included 16 mills that spin all or some of their yarns (13 in New York and 1 each in New Hampshire, North Carolina, and Tennessee).

"Of these 63 establishments, 11 advertised nationally; that is, advertised in magazines and newspapers with a national circulation other than trade journals." Table 20 gives the comparison with reference to profits:

TABLE 20

COMPARISON OF PROFITS OF KNIT UNDERWEAR MANUFACTURERS
ADVERTISERS AND NON-ADVERTISERS

Firms	Per Cent Profit Based on Net Sales	Cost of Advertising Based on Net Sales Per Cent
Group I—21 establishments		
4 national advertisers	9.81	6.21
All 21 establishments	7.07	2.46
Group II—10 establishments		
2 national advertisers	.88	3.36
All 10 establishments	2.45	1.81
Group III contained no national advertisers		
Groups IV and V—29 establishments		
5 national advertisers	9.11	4.29
All 29 establishments	5.36	1.09
Average profit of all 63 establishments	5.73	

It will be noted that 9 of the 11 national advertisers made larger profits than the average for all put together in the respective groups. Two establishments which did national advertising made a smaller percentage of profit. It may be noted that these two spent less for advertising than the other groups did. However, the explanation probably lies partly in other directions. It should also be pointed out, of course, that the 52 firms which are treated here as non-advertisers did advertising in trade journals, the relative expenditure of which will be noted in the last column in the table.[1]

California Associated Raisin Company. It has been through the efforts of cooperative advertising that such agricultural interests as the raisin growers have been able to put themselves on a sound financial basis.

Since 1912, the returns to growers of the Associated Raisin Company have increased 99%, while the price to the consumer has increased only 30.4%. Cooperative advertising has brought relief to these industries without affecting the interests of the public, in ways we shall see in a minute or two. By the economic assistance which cooperative advertising has been able to render to those rural producers, it has effected a genuine social service.[2]

Mr. Holgate Thomas of the California Associated Raisin Company stated that:

"The success of the California Raisin Association is primarily an advertising success." Before the advent of the association, the raisin growers of the valley were all broke. During the last few years, they have become prosperous and have been able to take up the mortgage on their home and show a net profit every year that gave them the necessities of life.[3]

The Avery Company. The Avery Company of Peoria, Illinois, manufacturers of farm implements, sent out 100 letters to its dealers, to ascertain the extent to which they were doing local advertising. It received 91 replies, which gave the following facts. Eighty-one of the 91 dealers stated that they advertised more or less regularly.

> 81 dealers advertisers
>> Total goods sold—$848,508.71
>> Average goods sold per dealer—$10,475
>> Total expenditure for advertising—$11,746.76
>> Average expenditure for advertising per dealer—$140
>> Percentage of advertising to sales—1.38

[1] "The Knit Underwear Industry," Dept. of Commerce. *Misc. Series, No. 22*, 1915.

[2] *Associated Advertising*, Aug., 1920, p. 13.

[3] *Printers' Ink*, Dec. 2, 1920, p. 105.

10 dealers non-advertisers
Total goods sold—$8,000
Average goods sold per dealer—$800 [1]

A year later the Avery Company called for similar information from its dealers and obtained the following returns from 304 dealers:

268 dealers advertisers
Total goods sold $1,822,112
Average goods sold per dealer—$6,800

36 dealers non-advertisers
Total goods sold—$7,500
Average goods sold per dealer—$200 [2]

Department Stores. In connection with the study of operating expenses of 301 department stores in 1921, the Harvard Bureau of Business Research analyzed the relation of various items of operating cost such as salaries, advertising, and interest in relation to stock-turn and found the following situation:

TABLE 21

OPERATING EXPENSES, GROSS MARGIN, AND NET PROFIT OR LOSS IN 1921 ACCORDING TO RATE OF STOCK-TURN

(Net Sales = 100%)

	Stock-turn less than 2.5 times	2.5-3.4 times	3.5 times and over
Number of Firms	95	94	111
Salaries and Wages	16.2%	15.4%	14.7%
Rentals	2.3	2.4	2.5
Advertising	2.2	2.4	2.5
Interest	3.0	2.2	1.8
Total Expense	28.5	27.9	27.1
Gross Margin	27.7	28.9	29.4
Net Profit or Loss	Loss 0.8	Profit 1.0	Profit 2.3

So far as the item of advertising is concerned it was found

[1] *Building Trade with Farmers*, Sept., 1919.
[2] *Associated Advertising*, June, 1920.

that the 95 stores whose stock-turn was 2.5 times a year had an advertising expenditure of 2.2% with a net loss of 0.8% while the 111 stores whose stock-turn was 3.5 times or more had an advertising expenditure of 2.5% with a net profit of 2.3%. The bulletin (No. 33, p. 36) states:

The heavier advertising expense for the firms that had a high rate of stock-turn indicates one of the means by which these firms speeded up their stock-turn and thereby secured economies in other expenses that far more than offset the additional advertising expenses.

THE MORE GENERAL AND INDIRECT EFFECTS OF ADVERTISING

(a) Reduction of Seasonal Fluctuation. The reduction of seasonal fluctuation in the volume of business is in general desirable in most industries, since it reduces the cost of doing business. In many lines of business, decided efforts have been made through advertising and other types of printed sales material to iron out the peaks and valleys. As a result of efforts in this direction, the seasonal fluctuations, if not entirely eliminated, have been greatly reduced in certain fields of business. Thus, for example, the two seasons of buying men's clothing have been greatly extended. Formerly the sale of toys was largely confined to the holiday season. Now, while there is a holiday peak, toys are sold more or less throughout the entire year. The same is true of fountain pens, millinery, arms and ammunition, and so on.

Oranges and Lemons. The California Fruit Growers' Exchange has very considerably increased the consumption of lemons at seasons of the year other than the summer months and the consumption of oranges at seasons of the year other than the winter months.

Contrary to the experience of our orange growers, our lemon growers had trouble with their winter market. Lemon trees never rest. Some fruit is picked off each tree every 30 days and shipments must be kept going regularly. It is easy to sell lots of lemons when the weather is hot and people want lemonade, but during the cold months the demand has been relatively light. So we have concentrated our advertising in the winter months and featured winter or year-round uses, such as lemon pie, lemon in tea, lemon for garnishing, hair rinse, and so on.

During the last four years the sale of California lemons during the cold months, from December 1 to March 31, has increased 17.8% over the average sales for the same period during the previous ten years. During the balance of the year the sales have increased only 6.3%.

It is obvious that we have been making headway in straightening out our monthly sales curve, because we have increased our winter sales almost three times as fast as our summer sales.

There was a time when our own organization had few oranges to sell during the summer. Our oranges were chiefly navels, which mature from December to May. During the summer we took on outside accounts to keep busy.

But finally we developed a summer orange in California— the Valencia—which matures from May to November. Many people said the public wouldn't eat oranges while berries and other seasonal fruits were plentiful. But our people leaned on their old ally, cooperative advertising, and now we sell oranges the year round.

Last year we sold almost as many oranges in the summer as in the winter, as Table 22 well shows you.[1]

TABLE 22

SEASONAL SHIPMENTS (Carloads) ORANGES, CALIFORNIA FRUIT GROWERS' ASSOCIATION, 1909-1920

Season	Total	Nov.-April	May-Oct.	May-Oct.	
1909-10	28,252	18,532	9,720	34%	
1910-11	39,508	26,116	13,392	34	
1911-12	34,547	21,079	13,468	39	
1912-13	16,027	11,337	4,690	29	Poor crop
1913-14	45,306	26,635	18,671	41	
1914-15	39,617	26,179	13,438	34	
1915-16	37,897	23,764	14,133	37	
1916-17	46,591	26,330	20,261	44	
1917-18	17,119	11,006	6,113	36	Poor crop
1918-19	39,430	20,966	18,464	47	
1919-20		20,657			

[1] *Associated Advertising*, Aug., 1920, p. 11.

Walnuts. The sale of walnuts has likewise been spread out over a long season. While there is a peak in the fall and early winter, walnuts are sold more or less the year round.

Selling California walnuts after the holidays was once like try-ing to sell fire crackers after the Fourth of July. After Christ-mas the dealer would take the remainder of his walnuts to his warehouse or basement and leave them there in oblivion until the following Thanksgiving.

Largely due to the educational advertising of the California Walnut Growers' Association, walnuts have now become an all-year commodity. Their manager told me recently that he esti-mated that between 40% and 50% of the 1919 crop will be pur-chased by consumers between January and October of this year. These months were the "dead ones" a few years ago.[1]

Men's Hats. Since starting to advertise in 1906 our sales have increased 270%. This increased demand for Mallory hats which our advertising has created enables us to run our factory on full time the year round, making a great reduction in overhead charges. Formerly, in common with all manufacturers of non-advertised hats, we were able to run to full capacity just during the two hat-buying seasons of the year, with a long dull period between each season.[2]

(b) Standardization of Products and Quality. The es-tablishment of brand names and their association with uni-form quantities and qualities of various products has been undoubtedly greatly facilitated by information disseminated through the printed word. The success of advertising has been closely associated with the establishment of trade-names and trade-marks, in order that products and their qualities might be impressed upon the memory of people.

In the first place, standard package facilitates retailing. The establishment of standard packages has probably added to the cost of commodities to some extent; nevertheless we must remember that such standardization has rendered a real service to the public. We must also remember that the

[1] *Idem.*, p. 11.   [2] *Printers' Ink*, Jan. 22, 1914, p. 3.

cost of standard packages, which is probably very much less than the public supposes, is not entirely absent for a similar type of service in connection with the commodities sold in bulk. The retail selling of standard package goods is considerably simplified. A retail sales clerk is able to get standard packages into the hands of the consumer a great deal more rapidly than he can goods sold in bulk. The wrapping and weighing of bulk goods requires time. A brief and haphazard timing of the operations involved on the part of sales clerks in getting, weighing, and wrapping bulk commodities, shows that it requires approximately a minute to a minute and a half from the time when the order is given to the time when the goods are handed over in a wrapped package. This time of course is greatly shortened in package goods.

Secondly, in addition to facilitating the retailing process, decided progress has been made and a real service has been rendered in the more hygienic handling of goods, particularly foods. While many of the same products which are sold in packages are sold also in bulk, we find, nevertheless, that a large proportion of people prefer to buy them in standard packages. The quantity is accurate, the quality is uniform, and the handling of them is sanitary.

The third distinct advantage of the standardization and branding of commodities is the guarantee of uniform quality. Any one of the well-known standard brands is uniform throughout the country and throughout the world, wherever that product is sold. This is an advantage both to the manufacturer and to the consumer.

A pertinent illustration of this point is that of the poor crop season of Sunkist oranges in 1918. Mr. Don Francisco, advertising manager of the California Fruit Growers' Exchange, relates it as follows:

Two years ago the orange crop in California suffered quite a severe injury from frost. A slightly frosted orange is difficult to detect until several weeks after the damage has been done. Then it shows up dry and sometimes bitter.

In the old days the custom was to get the frosted fruit to market before the damage was apparent. Shippers who moved the damaged fruit promptly usually got good returns. Of course, it hurt the market later and did tremendous and permanent injury to the general reputation of California fruit. The consumer, perhaps not knowing the effect of frost, thought California oranges were not juicy and had poor flavor. The trade felt that they had been hoodwinked.

This happened in the early days. Now the point I want to make is this. Two years ago no frosted fruit was shipped under the Sunkist label. I say none, because it is difficult to detect. But, generally speaking, the handling of the situation was so successful that there was scarcely a complaint.

The growers had invested $2,000,000 in their Sunkist advertising and they were not going to lose that investment for any temporary advantage. In the Sunkist trade-mark they had a definite asset to protect.

I think it is clearly within the truth to say that cooperative advertising has given the public better and more dependable goods.[1]

Standardized packages and brands might have developed and no doubt would have developed quite apart from advertising. However, it is quite certainly true that this development has been much more rapid and far more widespread through the aid of printed publicity than it would otherwise have been. Advertising has probably been the chief factor in teaching the public brand-names and the qualities associated with them.

(c) Progress in the Level of Living. The noteworthy advances made in the general level of living, in public taste, in personal and domestic conveniences, in the general use of cultural agencies, must be attributed in part to the use of the printed word in the form of advertising. The general enjoyment and possession of these conveniences and advantages are in part due to this influence. We need only to mention such products as phonographs and the development in musical taste generally, vacuum cleaners, better-fitting clothes, better-constructed and designed houses,

---

[1] *Associated Advertising,* Aug., 1920, p. 11.

better-painted houses—to be convinced of the advancement which has been made.

We may appropriately ask, of course, whether we would not have all these things without advertising. There is no doubt that we would very likely have most if not all of these improvements and conveniences, but probably not nearly so many of us would have them or have them so soon. Printed publicity has no doubt helped to educate people to want more and better things in food, clothing, housing, personal comfort and enjoyment.

(d) The Universal Spread of Newspapers and Magazines. The well-nigh universal reading of magazines and newspapers has been made possible largely, if not solely, through advertising. Roughly, three-fourths of the income of a periodical is derived from its advertising space. In this sense, the newspaper or magazine is practically a by-product of advertising.

It would be a mere guess to estimate what the cost of an ordinary standard magazine would be at the present time if there were no advertising revenue. The average standard magazine contains as much text material as a good-sized book. The cost of it would probably be as great as that of a book of corresponding size, except for the somewhat cheaper binding of a magazine. In other words, it is not unlikely that if there were no revenue whatever from advertising, the average standard magazine could probably not be distributed at the present time for less than $1 to $2. That is, if this estimate is roughly correct, we would be paying $1 to $2 for a magazine instead of anywhere from 5 cents to 40 cents.

This would unquestionably have kept down the circulation very considerably and limited the reading of magazines to a very much smaller proportion of the population

A similar comparison for the average city newspaper would likewise show that the cost of the daily newspaper would be many times what it is today. The average city newspaper contains perhaps half as much text as the average book. The cost of production would possibly be proportional, except for the cheaper paper and the absence of binding. It is probable that if a newspaper received no return from advertising, the cost of it, instead of being 2 or 3 cents, might be anywhere from 10 to 20 times that amount. The advertising revenue, therefore, has largely made possible the large-scale production of newspapers and magazines, the social and educational value of which is beyond estimate.

Possibly there is no other single force which ties a country together and unifies it in its thought, action, and beliefs as the universal reading of the public press. It would perhaps not be too much to say that even if advertising served no justifiable economic function in the distribution of goods, the cost of it could well be borne for the sake of the social and educational uplift produced through the universal dissemination of information in our magazines and newspapers.

INTERPRETATION AND SUMMARY

1. In the first place, it is probably fair to say that there is no evidence that prices are higher or have ever been raised in order to advertise, or as a result of advertising. On the contrary, there is evidence to indicate that prices may actually be lower, that profits are probably greater, and that the selling cost is on the whole probably lower whenever printed forms of salesmanship are used in a sane and balanced manner. The emphasis at this point is of course upon the sane and properly balanced procedure in carrying out advertising and selling plans.

It has been shown that the public has a greatly exaggerated notion concerning the expenditure for advertising and that the actual expenditure for it is a relatively small item in the final cost of a commodity.

It seems quite reasonable to conclude that some products

may be sold most economically primarily through personal salesmanship, that some products may be sold to certain classes of people most economically primarily through printed salesmanship, but that probably the great majority of products may be distributed most economically by varied proportions of personal and printed selling. A great many critics of advertising forget that if the expenditure for advertising were eliminated, its place would be taken in most instances by some form of personal selling.

2. In the second place, aside from specific facts regarding the expenditures for advertising or its effect upon the cost of distribution or upon profits, perhaps the most important general argument for its place in the present business régime is the fact that it has survived as a part of business over so long a period of time. Advertising has now been for so long a time a part of the system of distribution, that if in the long run it were an uneconomical factor, it seems reasonable to suppose that it would have been gradually eliminated as a matter of the survival of the fittest. Instead, however, it has steadily increased in its use and scope of application, so that today it is playing relatively a larger rôle in the business world than it has at any time in the past.

There are numerous firms that have consistently and continuously used printed salesmanship over a long period of time. If one will examine the magazines and newspapers published in the '70's and '80's, one will find the advertisements of such well-known firms as Procter & Gamble, Colgate & Co., Cheney Bros., Waltham Watch Co., The Oliver Ditson Co., Mason & Hamlin Co., Packer Manufacturing Co., and many others.

If the advertiser could not compete successfully with the non-advertiser, then it would seem likely that the advertiser would have been eliminated, or that he would have abandoned his methods. If this theory were true, one would suppose that in general the non-advertisers would be the ones who would have survived and become the large concerns of today.

The tendency during the past 50 years has been in the direction of fewer and larger concerns in the respective types of industry. Printed salesmanship has played at least some part in bringing about wider distribution, and consequently larger scale production. It is, of course, obvious that other factors as well have operated in bringing about the concentration of business into fewer but larger firms. Table 23 shows the amount of concentration that has oc-

TABLE 23

CONCENTRATION IN TYPICAL INDUSTRIES IN THE UNITED STATES DURING PAST HALF-CENTURY

Industry	Year	Number of Establishments	Value of Product
Men's Clothing	1869	7,853	$148,660,000
	1914	4,830	458,211,000
Carpets and Rugs	1869	215	21,762,000
	1914	97	69,128,000
Automobiles	1904	121	26,645,000
	1914	300*	503,230,000
Agricultural Implements	1869	2,076	52,067,000
	1914	601	164,087,000
Boots and Shoes	1879	1,959	166,050,000
	1914	1,355	501,760,000
Soap	1904	436	68,275,000
	1914	371	127,942,000
Tobacco—Cigars and Cigarettes	1869	4,631	33,374,000
	1914	13,515†	314,884,000
Roofing Materials	1869	198	3,257,000
	1914	170	27,978,000
Watches	1869	37	2,819,000
	1914	15	14,275,000

* An increase, but with 12 companies doing 87% of the business. Furthermore, this period covers a decade in the growth of a new industry, during which naturally many new concerns enter the field.

† The manufacture of cigars is so largely a hand process that small units or factories are apparently able to compete successfully with larger concerns.

curred in typical industries in the last half-century in the United States: [1]

It is significant to note in this connection the parallel movement of business as represented by bank clearings and the volume of advertising done as indicated by the space used in magazines and newspapers. James I. Clarke, vice-president of the National Bank of Commerce, New York, published a study represented in Figure 4, on page 111, in which are shown graphically the fluctuation in the bank clearings outside of New York by months since 1910, and the parallel fluctuation in the lineage of newspaper and magazine advertising space during the same period of years.

The advertising lineage for magazines was derived from the monthly tables of lines of advertising carried by approximately 60 leading magazines, published by *Printers'* *Ink* for a considerable number of years. The lineage for newspapers was derived from a similar tabulation made for some years by the *New York Evening Post,* covering New York newspapers and in the more recent years covering approximately 100 leading newspapers in the larger cities over the country.

It will be noted that the volume of advertising as represented by these two criteria has had a steady movement, beginning to rise rather rapidly in 1918; it is accompanied at the same time by a rapid rise in bank clearings. The decline in bank clearings, beginning early in 1920, is accompanied by a decline in advertising lineage.

During the latter half of 1920 and the first months of the current year, business was again faced with a period of sudden and profound readjustment. Bank clearings outside of New York City, which reached a total of over $18,000,000,000 in October, 1920, fell to less than $13,000,000,000 in February, 1921. The volume of magazine advertising declined in accordance with the usual seasonal fluctuation during the fall of 1920 but much more precipitately than in previous years. It recovered somewhat in February, 1921, but the normal continuous increase in the total of March lineage over February became a slight de-

[1] Prepared by J. Walter Thompson Co., *Printers' Ink,* Feb. 5, 1920, p. 8.

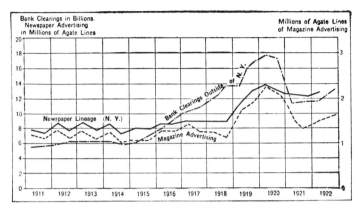

Figure 4: This chart, showing the fluctuation in bank clearings outside of New York and in newspaper (N. Y.) and magazine advertising, 1911–1922, is adopted from J. I. Clarke, but greatly modified and redrawn on a different scale and extended to include data for 1921 and 1922.

crease, although the spring gain recommenced with April. The volume of newspaper advertising, though somewhat below the totals of the corresponding months during the previous years, has followed the normal seasonal variations and has decreased proportionately less than bank clearings.

It thus appears that, apart from seasonal variations, the volume of advertising tends generally to move with general business activity but that on the whole the volume of advertising lineage possesses marked stability, rising less rapidly than business in seasons of extraordinary activity and falling less rapidly in periods of depression. Newspaper advertising appears to be more stable than magazine advertising.

There appears to be no reason to believe that the notable increase in periodical advertising during 1919 and 1920 was influenced to any great extent by Federal taxes, or was the result of any factor other than the stimulus of business activity.

The experience of the past 10 years and especially that of the periods of depression in 1914-15 and 1920-21 seems to demonstrate that the place of advertising in the present economic system is thoroughly well established, and it seems improbable that there can be any very considerable permanent curtailment of its volume.[1]

3. In the third place, the economic and social justification

[1] *Commerce Monthly*, July, 1921, p. 23.

of advertising ultimately rests (a) upon its service in increasing legitimate human wants and (b) upon its being an effective and fair agency of competition.

So long as we believe that human beings should continue to want more and better things which will in the long run contribute to their happiness and well-being—so long will we have individual effort and competition. If we believe in a philosophy of competition, then we must permit all means of fair and effective competition. If, on the other hand, there is to be no competition, then all agencies of competition should be eliminated.

This point of view may be illustrated by considering a commodity the consumption of which we may assume for the present to be absolutely limited and substantially at its maximum amount. Let us assume for the sake of our discussion that every man wears out two hats a year. If there are fifty million men in the United States, the consumption of hats would be a hundred million a year. It might be said that the advertising of hats serves no justifiable purpose whatever, since every man will buy two hats in one year in any event, and that the only thing which aggressive advertising might do for any individual maker would be to get more business of the total amount available, which would mean taking it away from someone else. In other words, it may be pointed out that all that advertising or any aggressive selling methods would do would be to shift demand from one brand to another, and that this would be a waste from the standpoint of society as a whole, since it would not mean any more business on the whole nor employ any more people, and the expenditure of money in shifting the demand from one brand to another would be largely a loss.

On the other hand, it must be remembered, however, that the shifting from one brand to another would mean ultimately greater concentration of business upon certain brands as a result of competition and that the competition thus stimulated would lead to the best individual effort both

in the production of high quality and in the most service-
able distribution. We may imagine the elimination of competitive effort to be justified only if we assume that each
maker of hats were to be allowed to produce only a certain
proportion of the total number of hats, that his sale of
these would be guaranteed, and that he must not attempt to
do anything better than any other manufacturer of hats.

Aside from shifting demand from one brand to another,
aggressive advertising and selling methods of course also
stimulate to a certain extent, perhaps to a considerable extent, the actual total demand, in so far as it stresses a desire
on the part of the average man to want to buy a new hat
more frequently, to obtain a more frequent variation of
style, or for some other reason. Again it results in more or
less of what we might call competition in personal appearance and all that is associated with it.

So long as we believe that competition is a desirable
factor in human welfare, just so long will competitive means
be used. Critics of advertising usually forget that if it were
eliminated or abolished, other methods would necessarily
be substituted for it. If you abolished the advertising of
hats, either by law or by common agreement, the same
manufacturers would resort to other methods of competition in personal salesmanship to a corresponding extent.
This might be and probably would be a still more costly
means to attain the same ends that are accomplished
through printed publicity. The probability is that a proper
balance between printed and oral salesmanship affords, in
most instances, the most economical form of competition
in the field of selling. One might as well argue that it is
highly wasteful for manufacturers to send out salesmen,
that ultimately men will buy so many hats in the course of a
year in any case, and that the expenditure for personal
salesmanship might as well be saved.

Apparently many critics of advertising have given most of
their thought and study to the economics of production, of

natural resources, and of mediums of exchange, and very little to the economics of distribution and service.

One further point may here be considered. The statement is sometimes made that more money is spent for advertising luxuries and semiluxuries than for the absolute necessities—more for pianos, phonographs, automobiles, toilet articles, household conveniences, clothing—than for bread and butter. In the same connection, it is also pointed out that advertising is responsible to a considerable extent for the widespread use of luxuries and semiluxuries.

In reply to this statement, it may be noted that it is also true that more personal sales efforts are expended in the distribution of luxuries and semiluxuries than in the distribution of bread and butter. And in the second place, it is not easy to say offhand that the striving for the possession of luxuries and semiluxuries is an evil. Undoubtedly, the striving for the possession of luxuries and semiluxuries serves as one of the most powerful incentives in human nature. One can therefore hardly condemn in an offhand manner the desire for and possession of luxuries. Rather the question resolves itself into a proper balance between one's personal income and the possession of luxuries. Progress no doubt consists in always wanting and getting something better, and anything that is better than the barest necessity is at some time a luxury or a semiluxury. It is quite conceivable that in the most primitive society a chair which consisted of nothing more than the barest device for supporting weight was a luxury, since one might as well sit upon the ground. As more and more elaborate chairs were developed, each one in its turn was no doubt regarded as a luxury for a time, until its use had become so common that it was regarded as a necessity. Instead of maintaining that the desire for and possession of semiluxuries are objectionable, one may possibly argue with reasonable sanity that people should strive to possess such luxuries as will contribute in the long run to their happiness and well-being, and for which they are honestly able to pay. If life consisted simply in getting enough plain raw food to keep from starving and of getting enough clothing and shelter to keep from freezing, there would probably be no civilization. If everyone saved absolutely all he could, and spent only for the barest necessities, there probably would be ultimately no place in which he might invest his savings. Again, the solution of the situation is undoubtedly a proper balance between resources and expenditures.

Advertising as the printed form of selling would seem therefore ultimately to be justified in so far as it serves as a means of increasing legitimate human wants, as an agency of fair and economic competition in the distribution of goods, and as a stimulant to social progress.

Through the search for facts and the application of scientific methods to business problems, wastes are being eliminated and improvements are steadily being made both in advertising as well as in other phases of business.

PRINCIPLES OF ADVERTISING

PART II

THE HUMAN ASPECT OF THE MARKET: TO WHOM MAY THE COMMODITY BE SOLD?

V

ANALYSIS OF PROBLEM

To whom may the product be sold? Essential subsidiary questions: Who are the users and buyers of this particular product? Where do they live? How many users and potential buyers are there? How large is the need of the class of users and buyers for this particular product, and how much may they be expected to buy? How do the actual or possible users of a commodity now satisfy the want which this commodity is intended to satisfy? What are the preferences, the likes and dislikes with reference to the needs which a given commodity supplies?

If we regard advertising as a form of selling, as pointed out in the first chapter, then the first question that logically arises is, To whom may the product be sold? The emphasis in this problem will be primarily upon the human side of the market rather than upon the more strictly economic side. All the economic factors must be considered and analyzed, but they must be examined primarily from the point of view of the human being to whom the commodity is to be sold. The economic factors are important. However, researches such as have been conducted thus far in dealing with advertising problems have for the most part been confined largely to the more strictly physical and economic phases—such as supply, manufacture, avenues of distribution, and the like—without a consideration of, and inquiry into, the habits, desires, modes of living, buying motives, of the groups of persons to whom a given product is to be sold.

Our next task is to analyze this large question—to whom may the product be sold—into its important subsidiary problems. If we had full, detailed, and accurate knowledge regarding the class of women who buy electric washing machines, or electric irons, or raisins, or any other product;

or if we had detailed and reliable information regarding the class of men who will buy an automobile of a certain price range, or shoes of a certain quality; or if we knew what classes of men and women will buy a certain food or a certain article of household convenience, we would have exceedingly valuable information for definitely planning our advertising efforts and we would not be in the dark and have to guess altogether about many of the problems that must be solved in order to carry out our plans intelligently.

What are the essential subsidiary questions in our large problem, concerning which we ought to have information?

The first question obviously is: Who are the users and buyers of this particular product? A distinction must be made in the case of many products between the users and buyers, since in many instances they are different. It should be determined, however, to what extent the users may influence the buyers. For example, in the case of most commodities used by children, the parents—chiefly the mothers—are the buyers. On the other hand, no doubt the children, particularly as they grow older, play an increasing part in determining the purchases. Or again, in the case of a vacuum cleaner, the husband may play a large part in the purchase, although the wife may be the chief user or supervisor of its use.

The second question is: Where do they live? This question may seem somewhat obvious and unnecessary. However, upon close examination, accurate information regarding it is highly important in directing the advertising efforts to the right places and to the right classes of people. Furthermore, this question is equally important both for the manufacturer and the retailer. As a matter of fact, very few retailers and likewise not all manufacturers know with any degree of accuracy where their actual or potential buyers and consumers are located. To illustrate the importance of this problem, we will take the case of a retailer in a moderate-sized city. Does he know from what section of the city or from what outlying territory his customers come? As a rule he does not know, except in so far as he has a general impression, which as a matter of fact may be quite erroneous, as will be shown later by concrete results.

The third question is: How many users and potential buyers are there? This question is of importance in so far as it is valuable to determine approximately the total demand or total possible market for that commodity. This again is a more important problem than appears at first glance. In most instances it would be quite instructive to know what proportion of the available business a given retailer or manufacturer is obtaining.

The fourth question is: How large is the need of the class of users and buyers for this particular product, and how much may they reasonably be expected to buy? What is the probable buying capacity—the economic, social, and educational status—of the users and buyers of the commodity under consideration? These questions, like the third one, are in part related to the larger problem of the amount of possible business that may be developed for a given product within a given territory, and the proportion of that business which a given concern may secure.

The fifth question is: How do the actual or possible users of a commodity now satisfy the want which this commodity is intended to satisfy? How have they satisfied and how are they likely to satisfy the need? In what way? By what brand or brands? And why? To what extent do they know the names of brands? To what extent do they buy by brand? What has influenced them to establish brand preferences or habits of buying a specific brand? All these queries are significant, and accurate reliable information regarding them is exceedingly valuable in making effective advertising and sales plans.

The sixth question is: What are the preferences, the likes and dislikes with reference to the need which a given commodity supplies, and with reference to the various methods and brands by which this need is supplied?

It needs no argument to show that if a manufacturer or a retailer had reasonably accurate and complete information on each of these questions, he would have a far more certain basis on which to determine his policies and methods for executing these policies. If he knew definitely the answer to the sixth question, he would have a fairly reliable guide concerning the method of approach and the appeals to use in his advertising campaign. Likewise, if he had a complete and reliable answer to the fifth question, he would know something definite regarding the severity of the competition, and how to meet it.

A superficial glance at the problems here raised would probably bring the response from many business concerns that they have rather definite ideas regarding the situation in their own business with reference to each of these questions. However, as will be shown later, this general impression is likely to be misleading in many instances, unless actual investigations have been made to ascertain the specific facts regarding these points. For example, in connection with one investigation a retailer of ready-made clothing had the impression that in a certain section of his city rather low-priced clothing was bought. The advertising had been carried out for that section of the city on that basis. When the investigation was completed, it was found that the retailer's impression was true so far as one class of buyers in that section of the city was concerned, but that it was entirely misleading so far as another and more important class in the same section was concerned.

At this point, the reader is quite apt to say, These questions are important, and conclusive answers are exactly what is needed; but are there any adequate, dependable, or possible methods of approach to them? Those familiar with the work of business concerns in this field will realize that many efforts are made to secure facts bearing either directly or indirectly on these points, but only rarely are adequate, thoroughgoing, impartial and complete data obtained. It is usually possible, at relatively small cost in relation to the financial considerations at stake, to obtain the facts desired. It is largely a matter of ingenuity and initiative in devising methods of inquiry and in applying them.

VI

METHODS OF INVESTIGATION: POPULATION
FACTS AND GENERAL STATISTICAL DATA

Census reports; government income returns; distribution of population; registration of automobiles, and so forth. Population facts; population density and distribution. Illiteracy. Incomes. The family budget. Application of general and population facts to a specific problem. Sample investigation of customer population of a retail clothing store.

IN general there are two sources of information or two methods of approach in attempting to answer the questions outlined in the preceding chapter. One method of approach is through the use of available published material for the purpose of gleaning any data or facts that bear upon the problems at hand. For example, it is possible to obtain at least indirect information from the census reports, government income returns, distribution of population, registration of automobiles, distribution of electric power stations, and so on. Very valuable information may often be secured from these sources. For the sake of convenience, we may call this library or desk research.

However, it is evident in many instances that such information, while interesting and relevant to a certain degree, as a rule does not conclusively answer the questions at hand. Hence, the second source of information or method of approach is through a direct first-hand investigation, for the purpose of getting specifically the information that is wanted, in so far as that is possible. This information may usually be obtained most directly, and if the inquiry is made properly, most reliably, from the particular classes of persons who constitute the actual or potential consumers of the product under consideration and to some extent from the persons who are directly associated with the distribution of the product. In other words, the method of approach consists of a systematic and sufficiently extensive inquiry, conducted usually by means of a well-prepared set of questions.

The solution of certain other important problems—such as those relating to copy, appeals, and the numerous elements in advertisements themselves—may be approached by means of definite tests which will be discussed in subsequent chapters. At the present moment, we shall confine our discussion to the questionnaire as a method of investigation. This we may call questionnaire-field research.

POPULATION FACTS

The first approach, then, to obtaining specific information on the various problems that arise in preparing for an advertising campaign is to obtain such facts and information as may be available in divers published sources. While these facts in many instances are not specific answers to the questions that are raised, they nevertheless furnish a desirable background of valuable basic facts which may be used in connection with more specific information obtained by the direct methods. In the first place, there are numerous problems which depend upon all sorts of facts about population, many of which may be answered by turning to various government publications, such as the census reports and bulletins on commerce, labor, and education. Other types of information may be obtained from other published sources, such as reports of investigations made by various private organizations or individuals. Industries in various fields undertake in many instances cooperative studies which are of value to the entire industry. Thus, for example, the trade publications interested in certain trades at times undertake investigations to determine facts pertinent to the entire trade. Examples of such investigations may be found in the electrical industry or the automotive industry.

POPULATION DENSITY AND DISTRIBUTION

While it is impossible here to present full and detailed facts about population which would be useful in connection with the multitudinous problems which are raised by the advertiser, it is nevertheless helpful to call attention to a number of the more important and common facts. First, according to the 1920 census, the total population of the United States is 105,710,620. The number of families is 24,351,676. That is, the average family is composed of 4.3 persons. This figure has been slowly reduced from one census to the next. In 1910 it was 4.5. The total number of negroes in the United States in 1920 was 10,464,013.

The density of population varies enormously by states. The average density is 35.5 per square mile. This ranges from as high as 566 per square mile in Rhode Island, 470 per square mile in Massachusetts, and 420 per square mile in New Jersey to as low as 3.8 per square mile in Montana, 2.9 per square mile in Arizona and New Mexico, 2.0 per square mile in Wyoming, and 0.7 per square mile in Nevada. The detailed figures regarding the density and distribution of population are shown in Table 24.

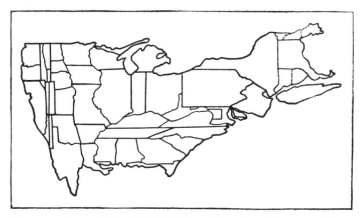

Figure 5: Map of the United States, with each state represented in proportion to its population

TABLE 24

DENSITY AND DISTRIBUTION OF POPULATION BY STATES

States	Population per Square Mile	Population by States	Per Cent of U. S. Population
Rhode Island	566.4	604,397	.6
Massachusetts	479.2	3,852,356	3.6
New Jersey	420.0	3,155,900	3.0
Connecticut	286.4	1,380,631	1.3
New York	217.9	10,385,227	9.8
Pennsylvania	194.5	8,720,017	8.3
Maryland	145.8	1,449,661	1.4
Ohio	141.4	5,759,394	5.4
Illinois	115.7	6,485,280	6.1
Delaware	113.5	223,003	.2
Indiana	81.3	2,930,390	2.8
Michigan	63.8	3,668,412	3.5
West Virginia	60.9	1,463,701	1.4
Kentucky	60.1	2,416,630	2.3
Virginia	57.4	2,309,187	2.2
Tennessee	56.1	2,339,885	2.2
South Carolina	55.2	1,683,724	1.6
North Carolina	52.5	2,559,123	2.4
Missouri	49.5	3,404,055	3.2
Georgia	49.3	2,895,832	2.7
New Hampshire	49.1	443,083	.4
Wisconsin	47.6	2,632,067	2.5
Alabama	45.8	2,348,174	2.2
Iowa	43.2	2,404,021	2.3
Louisiana	39.6	1,798,509	1.7
Mississippi	38.6	1,790,618	1.7
Vermont	38.6	352,428	.3
Arkansas	33.4	1,752,204	1.7
Minnesota	29.5	2,387,125	2.3
Oklahoma	29.2	2,028,283	1.9
Maine	25.7	768,014	.7
California	22.0	3,426,861	3.2
Kansas	21.6	1,769,257	1.7
Washington	20.3	1,356,621	1.3
Texas	17.8	4,663,228	4.4
Florida	17.7	968,470	.9
Nebraska	16.9	1,296,372	1.2

States	Population per Square Mile	Population by States	Per Cent of U. S Population
North Dakota	9.2	646,872	.6
Colorado	9.1	939,629	.9
South Dakota	8.3	639,547	6
Oregon	8.2	783,389	.7
Utah	5.5	449,396	.4
Idaho	5.2	431,866	.4
Montana	3.8	548,889	.5
Arizona	2.9	334,162	.3
New Mexico	2.9	360,350	.3
Wyoming	2.0	194,402	.2
Nevada	0.7	77,407	.1
District of Columbia	..	437,571	.4

The map reproduced on page 126 illustrates in a visual manner the variation in density of the various states in different sections of the country. Each state is shown in the size proportionate to the population which it contains.

The proportion of urban and rural population is divided as follows: 51.4% of the population is classified as urban and lives in towns and cities of 2,500 and over; 48.6% of the population is rural and lives on farms and in towns under 2,500. According to the 1920 census, there are 6,448,366 farms in the United States. Approximately 30% of the population actually lives on farms.

A large share of the population is obviously concentrated in the larger cities. The three largest cities in the country contain practically 10% (9.6%) of the population of the entire country, and 68 cities contain slightly over one-fourth (26.0%) of the total population of the country. The detailed figures are shown in Table 25.

The proportion of urban and rural population likewise varies enormously from state to state. The urban population is as high as 97.5% in Rhode Island and 94.8% in Massachusetts and as low as 13.6% in North Dakota and 13.4% in Mississippi.

TABLE 25

DISTRIBUTION OF POPULATION IN THE UNITED STATES

Population	Number of Cities	Per Cent of Population
1,000,000 or over	3	9.6
500,000 to 1,000,000	9	5.9
400,000 to 500,000	4	1.6
300,000 to 400,000	5	1.6
200,000 to 300,000	12	2.8
100,000 to 200,000	35	4.5
50,000 to 100,000	76	5.0
25,000 to 50,000	143	4.8
15,000 to 25,000	200	3.6
10,000 to 15,000	259	3.0
5,000 to 10,000	721	4.7
2,500 to 5,000	1,321	4.3
Total	2,788	51.4
Under 2,500 and on farms		48.6

Detailed proportions of urban and rural population by states according to the census of 1920 are shown in Table 26.

ILLITERACY

A general fact about population, which is of importance in connection with advertising plans, is the proportion of illiteracy in various sections of the country, in view of the fact that advertising depends upon the ability to read. According to the census of 1920, the proportion of illiterates is 6.0% for the country as a whole, considering all persons 10 years of age or over. This proportion likewise varies considerably by states, being as high as 21.9% in Louisiana, 18.1% in South Carolina, 17.2% in Mississippi, 16.1% in Alabama, and as low as 1.1% in Iowa, 1.4% in Nebraska, 1.5% in Oregon and Idaho, and 1.7% in Washington and South Dakota. The details by geographical divisions of the country as a whole are as follows:

New England	4.9%
Middle Atlantic	4.9
East North Central	2.9
West North Central	2.0
South Atlantic	11.5
East South Central	12.7
West South Central	10.0
Mountain	5.2
Pacific	2.7

Seven states have 15% or more illiterates, while 9 states have less than 2% illiterates.

Of the 60,861,000 native white population 10 years of age or over, 2.0% are illiterates. Of the 13,497,886 foreign-born white population 10 years of age or over, 13.1% are illiterates. Of the 8,053,225 negro population 10 years of age or over, 22.9% are illiterates.[1]

INCOMES

Several attempts have been made to determine the incomes of various amounts in relation to population. Such an undertaking is extremely difficult. However, probably the best attempt to arrive at as close an estimate as possible is that made by Mitchell, King, Macaulay and Knauth under the auspices of The National Bureau of Economic Research. According to this report, the total income of the United States in 1918 was placed at 61 billions. In 1920 it was probably about 66 billions. In 1921 and 1922

[1] A convenient digest of a considerable number of population facts is to be found in *Population and Its Distribution* by J. Walter Thompson Co., New York. This digest gives facts regarding the number of farms by states, number of post-offices by states, the miles of rural roads by states, the miles of improved roads by states, the miles of railroad lines, the number of automobiles and trucks by states, the number of telephones, the number of electric street cars, the number of electrically wired homes, and the number of central power stations. It also contains the Income Tax reports and amounts by states, and the subscriptions to the Liberty Loan by states and cities. It gives by states and cities the number of retail and wholesale firms in each of the following lines of business: automobile supplies, automobile garages and repair shops. boots and shoes, cigars, cigarettes and tobacco, confectionery, drugs, dry goods, electrical supplies, hardware, jewelry, men's furnishings, and sporting goods.

TABLE 26

PERCENTAGE OF URBAN AND RURAL POPULATION BY STATES, 1920

States	Urban Population	Rural Population	States	Urban Population	Rural Population
Rhode Island	97.5	2.5	Arizona	35.2	64.8
Massachusetts	94.8	5.2	Kansas	34.9	65.1
New York	82.7	17.3	Louisiana	34.9	65.1
New Jersey	78.4	21.6	Texas	32.4	67.6
California	68.0	32.0	Montana	31.3	68.7
Illinois	67.9	32.1	Nebraska	31.2	68.8
Connecticut	67.8	32.2	Vermont	31.2	68.8
Pennsylvania	64.3	35.7	Wyoming	29.5	70.5
Ohio	63.8	36.2	Virginia	29.2	70.8
New Hampshire	63.1	36.9	Idaho	27.6	72.4
Michigan	61.1	38.9	Oklahoma	26.6	73.4
Maryland	60.0	40.0	Kentucky	26.2	73.8
Washington	55.2	44.8	Tennessee	26.1	73.9
Delaware	54.2	45.8	West Virginia	25.2	74.8
Indiana	50.6	49.4	Georgia	25.1	74.9
Oregon	49.9	50.1	Alabama	21.7	78.3
Colorado	48.3	51.7	Nevada	19.7	80.3
Utah	48.0	52.0	North Carolina	19.1	80.9
Wisconsin	47.3	52.7	New Mexico	18.0	82.0
Missouri	46.7	53.3	South Carolina	17.5	82.5
Minnesota	44.1	55.9	Arkansas	16.6	83.4
Maine	39.0	61.0	South Dakota	16.0	84.0
Florida	36.8	63.2	North Dakota	13.6	86.4
Iowa	36.4	63.6	Mississippi	13.4	86.6

it had shrunk possibly to somewhere between 50 and 55 billions. According to these estimates, the per capita income in 1918 for the United States as a whole was $586. On a corresponding basis for 1921, the approximate per capita income was $476. The average family is composed of 4.3 persons, thus making on the 1921 basis approximately $2,046 of income per family. It is estimated that in 1918 the number of persons gainfully employed was approximately 37,569,060, exclusive of men in military and naval service. In 1920, the number of persons 10 years of age and over gainfully employed was 41,614,248. In other words, there were 1.7 earners per family. The average earnings per person gainfully employed were approximately $1,220. The distribution of incomes was approximately as shown in Table 27.

TABLE 27

DISTRIBUTION OF INCOMES, UNITED STATES, 1918

Approximately

152	persons or	.004%	had incomes of	$1,000,000 or over			
7,285	persons or	.02	had incomes from		100,000 to	$1,000,000
14,011	persons or	.03	had incomes from		50,000 to	100,000
41,119	persons or	.11	had incomes from		25,000 to	50,000
192,062	persons or	.51	had incomes from		10,000 to	25,000
587,824	persons or	1.56	had incomes from		5,000 to	10,000
1,383,167	persons or	3.68	had incomes from		3,000 to	5,000
3,065,024	persons or	8.17	had incomes from		2,000 to	3,000
5,222,067	persons or	13.92	had incomes from		1,500 to	2,000
12,428,120	persons or	33.14	had incomes from		1,000 to	1,500
12,531,570	persons or	34.44	had incomes from		500 to	1,000
1,827,554	persons or	4.87	had incomes from		0 to	500
200,000	persons or	.52	had incomes under		0	

Figures frequently given regarding the average earnings per person or per family have been quite misleading. This applies equally to the figures that have been based in a superficial way on the income tax returns. In view of the studies made by Mitchell, King, Macaulay and Knauth, and cited in the above table, we note that approximately one quarter of a million individuals in the United States have incomes of $10,000 or over. The income tax returns for 1918 showed that 4,425,114 persons reported to the Federal Government that they had an income of $1,000 or over.

In 1920 there were 7,259,944 federal income tax reports which were distributed according to sizes of incomes as shown in Table 28.

However, according to the careful estimates made by Mitchell and others, there were approximately 22,000,000 individuals in the United States with an income of $1,000 or over, and approximately 5,250,000 individuals with incomes of $2,000 or over.

TABLE 28

SIZE AND NUMBER OF INCOMES, UNITED STATES, 1920

(Taken from Income Tax Reports)

$ 1,000 to $ 2,000	2,671,950
2,000 to 3,000	2,569,316
3,000 to 4,000	894,559
4,000 to 5,000	442,557
5,000 to 10,000	445,442
10,000 to 15,000	103,570
15,000 to 20,000	44,531
20,000 to 25,000	23,729
25,000 to 30,000	14,471
30,000 to 40,000	15,808
40,000 to 50,000	8,269
50,000 to 100,000	12,093
100,000 to 150,000	2,191
150,000 to 200,000	590
200,000 to 250,000	307
250,000 to 300,000	166
300,000 to 400,000	169
400,000 to 500,000	70
500,000 to 1,000,000	123
1,000,000 and over	33
Total	7,259,944

THE FAMILY BUDGET

A further question of interest here is the distribution of the family income. From the advertiser's point of view, it is desirable to estimate the number of individuals or the number of families with sufficient income to be able to buy his particular product. Thus, for example, how many families are there in the United States who are able to buy a $50 vacuum cleaner, or a $160 ironing machine, or a $1,500 automobile, or a $3,500 automobile, or a $1,000 grand piano? In addition to the preceding table of incomes, some light will be thrown on the question by an analysis of family budgets.

The United States Department of Labor made a study of

the family incomes and expenditures of 12,094 families in 92 localities in the fall and winter of 1918 and 1919. These were all families of wage earners, 75% of whose income was secured by the chief earner of the family. The average percentages of expenditure for the various items were as shown in Table 29.[1]

TABLE 29

FAMILY EXPENDITURES OF 12,094 FAMILIES

Items	Per Cent
Food	38.2
Clothing	16.5
Shelter	13.4
Fuel and light	5.3
Furniture and house furnishings	5.1
Miscellaneous	21.3

The Federal Reserve Bank made an analysis of the family expenditure of those of its employees receiving less than $5,000 per annum. The distribution of expenditures for the various items and for the different sizes of incomes was as shown in Table 30.

Taking these two sources of data as a basis we may propose the following expenditures for the various items for a minimum family budget of $1,400 a year:

Food	$ 532	or 38. %
Clothing	231	or 16.5
Housing (including fuel and light)	266	or 19.
Furniture (including rugs, musical instruments, electrical appliances)	70	or 5.
Total Necessities	$1,099	
Savings	140	or 10.
Surplus, and miscellaneous, including automobiles, cameras, books, church, entertainment, school, tobacco, travel	161	or 11.5
Total	$1,400	

[1] *Monthly Labor Review*, May to August, 1919, and May, 1022, p. 85.

TABLE 30

FAMILY EXPENDITURES OF EMPLOYEES OF THE FEDERAL RESERVE
BANK OF NEW YORK RECEIVING SALARIES OF LESS
THAN $5,000 PER ANNUM *

Number of Families	26		68		95		166	
Food	$677	43.0%	$821	45.0%	$878	45.4%	$924	42.3%
Clothing	212	13.4	236	13.0	276	14.3	294	13.5
Housing	409	26.0	412	22.6	407	21.1	456	21.0
Furniture	31	1.9	111	6.1	92	4.8	147	6.7
Miscellaneous	248	15.7	244	13.4	283	14.6	362	16.6
Total	$1,577	100%	$1,824	100%	$1,936	100%	$2,183	100%

Number of Families	182		99		57		49	
Food	$960	39.4%	$1,035	40.1%	$1,206	39.9%	$1,177	37.4%
Clothing	369	15.1	398	15.4	516	17.1	534	16.9
Housing	520	21.3	547	21.1	571	19.0	618	19.6
Furniture	135	5.5	141	5.5	184	6.1	264	8.4
Miscellaneous	453	18.6	463	17.9	544	18.0	557	17.7
Total	$2,437	100%	$2,584	100%	$3,021	100%	$3,150	100%

Number of Families	20		18		32	
Food	$1,076	32.5%	$1,297	36.7%	$1,557	35.9%
Clothing	552	16.7	549	15.6	722	16.7
Housing	767	23.2	666	18.9	751	17.3
Furniture	159	4.8	129	3.7	215	5.0
Miscellaneous	757	22.9	891	25.2	1,091	25.2
Total	$3,311	100%	$3,532	100%	$4,336	100%

* Adapted from the table in the *Federal Reserve Bulletin*, December, 1920, p. 1294.

For larger family incomes, the percentage of expenditure for the various items may be regarded as practically constant with the exception of food for which the percentage becomes less as the income becomes larger. Table 31 gives the estimated distribution for typical incomes.

Commodities which are not absolute necessities or whose quality is above that of minimum necessity will in the long

TABLE 31

FAMILY BUDGETS OF INCOMES OF VARIOUS SIZES

Food	$532	38%	$700	35%	$930	31%
Clothing	231	16.5	330	16.5	495	16.5
Housing	266	19.	380	19.	570	19.
Furniture	70	5.	100	5.	150	5.
Savings	140	10.	200	10.	300	10.
Surplus & Misc.	161	11.5	290	14.5	555	18.5
Total	$1,400		$2,000		$3,000	
Food	$1,160	29%	$1,350	27%	$1,800	18%
Clothing	660	16.5	825	16.5	1,650	16.5
Housing	760	19.	950	19.	1,900	19.
Furniture	200	5.	250	5.	500	5.
Savings	400	10.	500	10.	1,000	10.
Surplus & Misc.	820	20.5	1,125	22.5	3,150	31.5
Total	$4,000		$5,000		$10,000	

run be bought only by those persons whose surplus permits this expenditure. Thus a $1,500 automobile cannot well be bought by a family unless its annual surplus is approximately that amount, or a $3,500 automobile cannot well be purchased unless the annual surplus is about $3,500. Or, the aggregate of semi-utilities and extras that may be bought cannot well exceed the amount of the annual surplus.

APPLICATION OF GENERAL AND POPULATION FACTS TO A SPECIFIC PROBLEM

Let us assume that the problem before us is to determine the possible sale and distribution of a household article operated by electricity, such as a vacuum cleaner, and suppose that in addition to this it were desired to determine the possible sale in certain states; that the manufacturer were in a position to distribute and sell his product in a certain number of states adjoining the state in which his product is manufactured—let us say the state of Ohio. Among the facts that should be obtained are the following: The number of wired homes in the different states, the percentage of wired homes, the density of population, and the income as indicated by various returns. Finally it would be necessary to consider the proximity of the various states to the one in which the manufacturer is located.

Considering for the moment the factor of the proportion of wired homes in the various states, we have the facts given in Table 32 which are based upon the electrical survey of July, 1920.

TABLE 32

PROPORTION OF WIRED HOMES BY STATES

State	Number of Families	Number of Wired Homes	Percentage of Wired Homes
Alabama	521,816	52,400	10.5
Arizona	74,258	12,920	17.3
Arkansas	389,379	48,200	12.6
California	761,525	561,000	73.8
Colorado	208,806	99,100	47.0
Connecticut	306,807	119,830	39.1
Delaware	49,556	9,270	18.7
Florida	215,216	67,000	31.
District of Columbia	97,238	21,800	22.
Georgia	643,518	80,700	12.
Idaho	95,970	38,160	40.
Illinois	1,441,173	626,000	43.5
Indiana	651,198	197,700	30.
Iowa	534,227	107,400	20.
Kansas	393,186	145,700	36.
Kentucky	735,029	90,200	12.
Louisiana	399,669	44,800	11.
Maine	170,700	77,700	45.
Maryland	322,147	50,000	15.
Massachusetts	856,079	338,500	39.6
Michigan	815,203	257,000	31.
Minnesota	536,472	188,000	35.
Mississippi	397,915	35,600	9.
Missouri	756,457	207,000	27.
Montana	121,975	51,300	42.

State	Number of Families	Number of Wired Homes	Percentage of Wired Homes
Nebraska	288,083	88,700	31.
Nevada	17,201	14,480	85.
New Hampshire	98,463	29,900	30.
New Jersey	701,311	218,000	30.
New Mexico	80,078	13,300	16.
New York	2,307,828	440,000	19.
North Carolina	568,694	49,200	9.
North Dakota	143,749	42,300	30.
Ohio	1,279,865	362,500	28.
Oklahoma	450,730	60,900	13.
Oregon	174,086	80,000	46.
Pennsylvania	1,937,782	365,500	18.7
Rhode Island	134,310	41,800	31.
South Carolina	374,161	51,000	13.
South Dakota	141,455	39,300	27.
Tennessee	519,530	54,500	15.
Texas	1,036,273	218,800	21.
Utah	99,866	68,600	69.
Vermont	78,317	26,320	33.
Virginia	513,152	90,300	17.
Washington	301,471	200,000	66.
West Virginia	325,267	37,200	11.
Wisconsin	584,904	147,700	25.2
Wyoming	43,200	13,580	31.
		Median	30.7 *

* J. Walter Thompson: *Population and its Distribution.*

From this table we learn that the largest percentages of wired homes are to be found in Nevada (85), California (73), Utah (69), Washington (66). However, the largest numbers of wired homes are to be found in Illinois (626,000), California (561,000), New York (440,000), Pennsylvania (365,000), Ohio (362,500). Considering next the question of proximity of states to Ohio, we note the following facts:

	Number of Wired Homes	Percentage of Wired Homes
Ohio	362,500	28
Pennsylvania	365,500	19

	Number of Wired Homes	Percentage of Wired Homes
Michigan	257,000	31
Indiana	197,700	30
Kentucky	90,200	12
West Virginia	37,200	11

A further question in this connection is, Which is more important from the standpoint of the possible sale of a vacuum cleaner, the absolute number of wired homes or the percentage of wired homes? Problems of a similar sort naturally arise with every product. Detailed facts for the solution of these problems must be ascertained from all available sources.

Of a similar nature but dependent upon different facts is the problem of the distribution of a certain farm implement, for example a machine used in connection with dairy farming, such as a cream separator. For this purpose it would be desirable to ascertain the number of dairy farmers in each state, the production of dairy products in each state, the number of cows owned by dairy farmers, and the like. In the case of a commodity to be used in connection with improving roads, as, for example, a product used in the construction of pavements, such facts as the proportion of improved and unimproved roads and the total miles of improved and unimproved roads would be desirable.

SAMPLE INVESTIGATION OF CUSTOMER POPULATION OF A
RETAIL CLOTHING STORE

The investigation [1] to be cited here pertains to the boys' clothing department of a store in a middle-western city of approximately 50,000 population, located in a rich agricultural area. This store is the leading one in its field in that city and compares very favorably with stores in larger cities. The purpose of the investigation, which was actually carried out, was to make a study of the boy population in the sur-

[1] This study was made by R. C. Armstrong, a former student in the author's classes.

rounding territory. The boys obviously are the customers of this department of the store. The aim was to determine the distribution and location of the customers and to analyze the advertising efforts that were being made in relation to the distribution of the boy population and the amount of business actually obtained from various sections of the territory, so that future advertising activities might be increased in portions of the territory where the business was relatively weak, and that the advertising plans might be directed more effectively. In a community of this type there are a considerable number of smaller towns surrounding the particular city in question, each of which has a local weekly newspaper. It is obviously important to determine the relative strength and weakness of a particular store in the various sections of its territory in order to know where its business ought to be strengthened and where more business may be expected.

In order to define the limits of what will be called the actual territorial market, the manager of the boys' department was asked to lay out upon a map the area from which the store was then drawing the bulk of its business. The contour of this area was verified and corrected by consultation with the other executives of the store, so far as was possible on the basis of general impression. Similarly, there was laid out beyond this area that territory which may be designated as the potential territorial market, including those portions in which no particular effort to secure business had been made but from which a considerable amount of trade might reasonably be drawn. These boundaries are indicated on the map reproduced in Figure 6, on page 141. The county areas are drawn in a diagrammatic manner and do not show the exact outline of the boundaries. The outlines are, however, essentially correct.

The next step in the investigation was to obtain as accurately as possible figures regarding the population of that class of customers in whom the department was interested, namely, boys under 20 or 21 years of age. Figures were

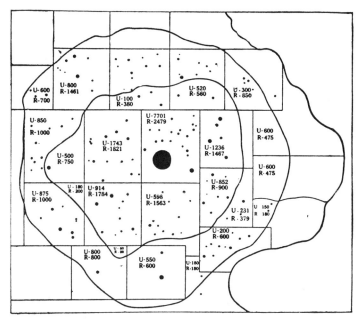

Figure 6: This map shows the distribution of the boy population within the area served by a certain men's and boys' clothing store. The rectangles represent counties; the heavy dot in the center the city in which the store is located. The smaller dots represent towns and villages. The figures indicate the number of urban and rural boys in the respective areas. The inner heavy circular line indicates the distribution of the present customers; the outer line indicates the potential customer area.

obtained from the report of the Department of Public Instruction, which makes a census of school population at regular intervals. The figures on page 142 give the number of boys between the ages of 5 and 21, distributed according to urban and rural area. For the sake of convenience, it was desirable further to determine the number of boys over 13 years of age. The reason for drawing the dividing line at this point is that boys usually pass from knee pants to long trousers at about this age. A table was prepared to show the urban and rural population, divided according to the age limits suggested, in 21 counties which were sufficiently adjacent to the city to constitute the actual or potential area. It will be unnecessary to give the complete details of this table, which showed the number of boys in each town or community and the number of urban and rural boys in each county as a whole. These figures are given in the diagrammatic map reproduced in Figure 6. The following is a brief summary:

	Present Business Area		Potential Business Area	
	Urban	Rural	Urban	Rural
Boys under 13 years	6,911	5,682	4,335	5,554
Boys over 13 years	7,795	6,407	4,889	6,263
Totals	14,706	12,089	9,224	11,817

This tabulation shows a total of 14,706 boys living in urban communities within the boundaries of the present market area and over 12,000 boys living in the rural districts of the same area. In those cases where the contour line indicating the boundary of the present market area cuts through a county, the proportion of the boy population within and without that line was estimated. It will be noted that in the present market area the greater proportion of boys were living in towns and cities, while in the potential market area there was a larger proportion living in rural areas. Hence, so far as developing business in the potential area was concerned, it was evident that special advertising would need to be used to reach the farmer boy and those who buy for him. It was also desirable to know the number of possible consumers of boys' merchandise in the more important towns, since the town customer presents a different problem from the rural customer. Accordingly, a table was prepared to indicate the number of boys in each of the 23 towns within its selling territory. It was found that approximately 24,000 boys were living in the urban communities of this territory and that approximately 75% resided in the 23 cities. This concentration of the boy population in a relatively small number of cities and towns was an important point which needed to be recognized in planning the advertising campaign.

The second step in this population analysis was to determine the territorial distribution of the actual customers. To accomplish this end, each salesman was required during a period of 11 days, including three Saturdays, to take the name and address of each cash customer. Analysis showed that the cash business constituted between 65% and 70% of the total sales. The results of this investigation are summarized as follows:

	Ratio of Out-of-Town Business to Total Business
First week average	46.7%
Second week average	53.4
First Saturday average	41.0
Second Saturday average	35.9
Third Saturday average	23.1
Average for week days, excluding Saturdays	33.0
Entire period average	50.1

This summary shows that the proportion of out-of-town cash business to the total cash business varied from 46% to 53%. Moreover, it became evident that the amount of out-of-town trade was consistently lower on Saturday than on other days of the week. Saturday apparently was the shopping day for the city trade. These facts are important in laying out the advertising schedule from the standpoint of choosing days on which city and out-of-town advertising should be used.

An analysis of the city customers showed that they were distributed as follows:

East side	58.1%
West side	37.9
South side	4.0

These results were surprising in view of the fact that the store had always considered itself equally strong on the east and the west side. It was also surprised at its weakness in the south side area.

In the next place, the geographical distribution of out-of-town customers by counties and towns was tabulated.

These results were then checked up against the actual boy population in each of these communities. This made it possible to determine community by community the relative strength or weakness of the business in each section of the territory. During this period of 11 days 737 cash customers were recorded, of whom 454 were from outside the city. Of this number, 377, or 83% came from the area designated as the present market area. The balance of 17% came from the area designated as the potential market area. A detailed analysis of the figures indicated certain important irregular distributions of out-of-town customers. In one community the patronage on the basis of population seemed high from three towns and particularly low from a fourth town which was easily accessible to the store and in which the store had always considered itself strong. Other data obtained later corroborated the same weakness. The same thing was true with regard to various other towns in the territory. Some towns which were less accessible brought relatively more customers in proportion to population than was the case in more accessible towns. The minute detail of these figures will not be necessary here, but it is evident that a careful tabulation of such facts, which are after all fairly easy to obtain, serves a very useful purpose in providing actual facts upon which advertising plans may be intelligently prepared. A further illustration of this point is found in the fact that there were only three customers from one town which had a population of 432 boys as compared with approximately four times as many from another town which had the same boy population. Both towns were about equally accessible.

An inspection of the detailed figures revealed the weak spots in the territory. For example, city M, with a boy population of 294 and a large surrounding rural area, had only two customers. While it is not as accessible as some other towns, the business there was not as large as it should be. Likewise, three counties sufficiently accessible to warrant business did not show a single customer during the

TABLE 33

(a) URBAN AND RURAL DISTRIBUTION OF STORE'S CUSTOMERS
AS SHOWN BY ANALYSIS

County	Total Boy Population Urban	Rural	Total Number of Customers During the 11-Day Test Period
B	1,743	1,821	108
C	1,083	1,279	63
Cl	4,606	1,764	3
D	1,314	1,403	5
F	2,479	2,050	3
G	856	1,419	7
I	914	1,784	19
J	1,598	2,063	24
Jn	1,236	1,467	31
K	1,679	1,633	2
L	7,701	2,479	136
T	1,349	1,852	7

(b) BOY POPULATION AND BOY CUSTOMERS BY CITIES

	City Boy Population	Boy Customers in 11-Day Test Period	Percentage
V	547	13	2.4
B	498	15	3.0
T	265	8	3.0
G	229	3	1.3
M	294	2	0.7
I	1,284	13	1.0
A	440	12	2.7
Mo	432	3	0.7
Ma	571	25	4.4
Mv	217	12	5.5

11-day test period. Special publicity efforts were planned accordingly.

Of the total of 737 cash customers whose addresses were reported during this 11-day period, 283, or 38.4%, came from the city in which the store was located. This group was further analyzed to ascertain the number and proportion of customers living in the six chief divisions of the city.

The city was divided for this purpose according to the general residential areas and the types of persons living in the various sections. A comparison of these results with the actual business coming from these sections indicated that there were very distinct differences between the actual number of customers and the potential customers available. These facts were significant, especially in view of the fact that the store had always considered that the number of customers coming from the more densely populated section was at least equal to the number coming from any other division of the city. This discrepancy had never been realized by the management until these facts were obtained. It was therefore found desirable to strengthen the advertising efforts in that particular area of the city in which the business was relatively weak.

VII

METHODS OF INVESTIGATION:
THE QUESTIONNAIRE

The questionnaire. Typical sets of questions that have been used: Raisin investigation. Toothpaste questionnaire. Fountain pen and propelling pencil questionnaire. Obtaining the responses: A. by mail; B. by personal interviews. The interview. How many returns are necessary? A check on the reliability of numbers.

In the preceding chapter, there were outlined methods of procedure for obtaining general statistical data bearing upon the questions connected with the human aspect of the market. It was pointed out that although such information is highly useful in supplying a background and in directly solving certain important points, there are many problems which relate directly to the consumer and to the uses of the product and its appeal to the consumer which must be approached by other methods.

After all, it is possible to determine specifically the consumer's preferences, likes and dislikes, habits of buying, brand preferences, habits of living, and so on, only by going directly to the consumer. For this purpose the questionnaire method is used.

THE QUESTIONNAIRE

Questionnaire investigations have been made recently in increasing numbers. There are, in certain quarters, rather severe objections to investigations made in this manner. The fact is, however, as will be shown by concrete examples, that information on many important questions can be gotten only in this manner, and that thoroughly reliable information may be obtained if the investigation is carried out according to acceptable scientific standards. The pronounced objections are due chiefly to the all too numerous investigations of this sort which are carried out in a haphazard, unscientific and prejudiced manner. In general, the following points should be observed in the preparation of a questionnaire:

First, the questions for the most part should be specific and definite, so that a clean-cut response may be obtained. Instead of asking "Do you buy many lemons in the winter time, and for what uses?" it is better to ask "At which season of the year do you buy most lemons, winter ———, spring ———, summer ———, autumn ———" or if the purpose of the question is to find out the relative purchase of lemons in the winter as compared with the summer, the question could better be put thus, "How does your purchase of lemons in the winter compare with the summer? Do you buy as many in winter ———, half as many ———, a third as many ———, a fourth ———, or other amount ———?"

Second, some questions of an indefinite nature should be inserted, so that the persons from whom the responses are obtained may be entirely at liberty to give an unhampered response in their own way. Two or three such questions scattered through a questionnaire in the proper sequence will serve as a useful check upon the information obtained in the more specific questions. They will also be valuable in supplying information which may not be obtained otherwise. For example, in a questionnaire survey of portable typewriters, an indefinite question such as "What do you like about the one you are now using?" is very useful in obtaining a person's spontaneous response. This may well be followed by a more specific question such as, "What do you consider most important about a typewriter? Number the following points from 1 to 8 in the order in which they seem important to you."

Visible writing	Easy action	Noiseless	Repair service
Standard keyboard	Light weight	Durable	Price

Third, leading questions which prejudice the response should obviously be avoided. A question which begins "Don't you think, etc." has an affirmative suggestion which warps the response. It is very much better to say, "What do you think, etc."

Fourth, the responses to a questionnaire will on the whole be most useful if they are obtained in such a manner that they will lend themselves to accurate statistical treatment and interpretation. This may be accomplished, usually, by exercising proper care in the way in which the questions are formulated. This point is illustrated in the question just cited regarding the order of importance of various points concerning a portable typewriter. Ranking them in the order indicated will yield results which may be treated statistically and will produce more usable data.

Fifth, the number of questions and the amount of detail that may be included depends obviously upon the manner in which the responses are to be obtained. If the responses are to be obtained by mail, the questions must necessarily be brief and few in number. If the responses, however, are to be obtained through personal interview, a surprisingly large amount of detail may be obtained and a considerable number of questions used.

These points may perhaps be best illustrated by examining some typical sets of questions that have been used. Three sample questionnaires are reproduced here: (1) a raisin questionnaire typical of one of medium length; (2) a toothpaste questionnaire, typical of a very brief one; and (3) a fountain pen questionnaire, designed to illustrate a rather long series of questions prepared in two forms, one for consumers and one for dealers.

The questionnaire in Figure 7 was prepared by the author in conference with his class, with the above ideas in mind, and with the purpose of actually using it in an investigation in which the responses were to be obtained by personally interviewing housewives. The purpose of the investigation was to obtain such facts and information as

Name   Address   **Date**
Number of persons in family
  1. Do you buy raisins in bulk   or package?
  2. If in package, what brand or brands?
  3. When you buy, do you call for them by name?   Yes   No
  4. How often do you buy raisins?   How many
       ibs.?   (In a year)
  5. Do you buy more at one time of year than at others?
       Yes   No   If so, when?
  6. In what ways do you use raisins?
       Eating uncooked In cake   In salad
       In pie   In puddings   Stewed
       In bread   On breakfast food
      Number in order of chief use 1, 2, 3, etc.
  7. Do you use raisins more at present than a year or two ago?
       Much more   More   Some more   Uncertain
  8. What do you like most about raisins?
       Taste good   High food value Relieve fatigue
       Contain iron   Good for health Easily digested
       Make delicious dishes A beauty food
      Number in order of preference 1, 2, 3 to 8.
  9. With what brands of raisins are you familiar?
 10. Which ones have you seen advertised?
 11. Where? Name magazines
              Name newspapers
              Name other mediums
 12. What do you remember about the ads?
                     a. About the pictures   b. About the text
 13. Do you think that you have been influenced toward buying
      raisins by the ads you have seen?   Very much
      Much   Some   Uncertain
 14. Have you bought Sun-Maid raisins because of the ads that
      you have seen? Yes   No
 15. What general magazines do you read regularly?
 16. Which one do you prefer most?
 17. What women's magazines do you read regularly?
 18. Which one do you prefer most?
 19. What newspaper(s) do you read regularly?

Figure 7: Questionnaire used in a raisin investigation

would be specifically useful in either critically examining the advertising done up to that time for a certain brand of raisins or in making new plans. This questionnaire was actually used by the students in the writer's class in the fall of 1921, and approximately 750 housewives were interviewed in and around Boston. It is not presented as a model of perfection but merely as a practical, usable basis for an investigation of this type.

The aim of this investigation was to obtain as far as possible definite answers to the questions outlined in the preceding chapter. In addition to these, however, there was an endeavor to obtain information on other points as well, since a personal interview provides opportunity for doing so—such as the impression created by advertising already done, the mediums read, and the standing of these mediums in the estimation of the consumers.

Questions 1, 2, 3, and 9 were inserted for the purposes of ascertaining some facts regarding competitive consumer preferences and brand familiarity. Questions 6 and 8 deal primarily with appeals. Questions 10, 11, 12, 13, 14, and to a less extent some of the other questions, deal chiefly with the effects of past advertising and its utility. Questions 11, 15 to 19 were inserted for the purpose of furnishing tangible evidence regarding the most suitable mediums.

It will be noted that for the most part the questions are specific and definite, and that the questions have been so formulated as to give entire freedom to the housewife in responding as she wishes. At the same time, the questions are so formulated that they allow of a gradation of answers in a fairly definite manner. This point is illustrated by Questions 6, 7, 8, and 13. For example, instead of having an answer of either Yes or No to Question 13, the question is so formulated that it does not necessarily prejudice the housewife to say Yes, any more than No, and at the same time, if her answer is Yes, it provides for an approximate gradation of a positive answer by the words Very Much ——, Much ——, Some ——, and Uncertain ——. Likewise, Questions 6 and 8 ask for a numbering of the points involved in each question in the order of importance. The housewife is entirely willing to do that, as it is not a complicated matter, and at the same time it secures much more accurate responses, which are capable of statistical treatment and interpretation. On the whole, this questionnaire is fairly detailed and covers the points of interest; and while it is fairly long, it is not too long. In actual use it proved to be quite satisfactory.

In preparing a questionnaire, it is usually desirable before it is actually used, to try it out on a limited number, say ten or a dozen persons, to determine whether there are any changes that ought to be made before it is finally used in the larger investigation. Frequently defects in the form of the questions are discovered. Perhaps the questions are not stated clearly; possibly some questions may be omitted, and others may be added, or their order should be changed.

The questionnaire shown in Figure 8 was used extensively in an investigation of toothpaste. It illustrates the brevity and simplicity ordinarily necessary in a questionnaire when the responses are sought by mail. The questions are well put, and call for definite answers as well as for entirely free unsuggested comments. The space required for the answers, between questions, is here omitted.

The two sets of questions, shown in Figure 9 and in Figure 10, relating to fountain pens and propelling pencils are examples of rather long detailed questionnaires and of the differentiation often made between consumers and dealers in securing information for the same products. They also illustrate the convenience of anticipating practically all varieties of answers to many of the questions and of printing them as a part of the questionnaire. The advantage of so doing lies in a saving of time in recording the answers, as in many instances only a check mark is required. When the anticipated classes of answers are printed in this manner, it is important to include the widest possible variety in order that the respondent may not be prejudiced. This is particularly important in connection with questions of opinion such as B. Consumer—General, No. 3, Reasons for changing.

These two questionnaires, particularly the one intended for dealers, are rather long, possibly too long. Some of the questions will not yield satisfactory or worthwhile responses, such as B., Nos. 29, 30, and 32 in the consumer list, and B, Nos. 6, 7, 8, and possibly 9 and 10 in the dealer

---

Date 19

Male or Female
(Please cross out one)

Will You Please Be Good Enough to Answer the Following Questions Briefly, and Mail Them in the Attached Self-addressed Stamped Envelope.

---

1. What brand of dentifrice do you use?
2. Why do you buy this particular dentifrice?
3. What is the most important factor to you in a dentifrice, and why?
4. How do you like Blank as compared with the dentifrice you are using? (Please check one.)
   1. Better.   2. Just as good.   3. Not as good.
5. What do you like about Blank?
6. What don't you like about Blank?
7. What magazine do you read most?

Figure 8: Questionnaire used in a toothpaste investigation

list. Several other questions in the dealer list could probably be omitted, particularly those which are merely a check in a less adequate manner on similar points in the consumer list.

Answers to the dealer questionnaire were obtained by personal interviews with 487 dealers and in the case of the consumer questionnaire answers were obtained by personal interviews with 270 consumers.

A. Identification

    1. Name of individual:

    2. Address: No.   Street   City   State

    3. Position of individual:

Professional	Clerical
Business executive	Salesman
Educator	Laborer
Labor executive	Farmer
Housewife	

    4. Sex of individual: Male   Female

    5. Approximate age of individual

        20 or under   21 to 30   31 to 40   40 or older

B. Consumer—General

    1. What make fountain pen does party use at present time:

Moore	Shaeffer	Waterman
Parker	Swan	Other make
Conklin	Tempoint (Boston)	None

    2. What other makes has party previously used:

Moore	Tempoint (Boston)
Parker	Waterman
Conklin	Other make
Shaeffer	None
Swan	Does not remember

    3. Reasons for changing:

        a. Unsatisfactory service   Would not write

          Leaked or blotted   Repair trouble

               Other reasons

        b. If unsatisfactory service, what was nature of service:

    4. What make of pen does party consider the best:

Moore	Shaeffer	Waterman
Parker	Swan	Other make
Conklin	Tempoint (Boston)	Does not know

    5. Why is this make preferred:

    6. What particular make pen has given longest satisfactory service, and how long:

        Pen   Time   Does not know

    7. What type of holder does party prefer:

        a. Regular   Safety   Self-filling   Does not know

b. Long   Thin   Gold
   Short   Chased   Silver
   Thick   Plain   Does not know

8. What style of nib does party like best:
   a. Extra fine   Coarse
      Fine   Stub
      Medium   Manifold
              Does not know
   b. Stiff   Flexible   Does not know

9. What type of self-filling device does party prefer:
   Lever   Button
   Crescent   Other make
              Does not know

10. Why is this type preferred: Does not know

11. In buying present pen, did party ask for pen by name:
    Yes   No   Does not remember

12. To what extent was party influenced by dealer in buying present pen:
    Very great extent   Some extent   Not at all

13. If party were to buy a new pen, would he ask for it by name:
    Yes   Perhaps   No   Uncertain

14. Would party insist on getting the make of pen asked for:
    Yes   Perhaps   No   Does not know

15. If dealer did not have make of pen desired, would party take dealer's recommendation for a different make:
    Yes   Perhaps   No   Does not know

16. Has party ever had pen in use at present time repaired by dealer:
    Yes   No   Does not remember

17. If yes, what kind of service rendered:
    Excellent   Good   Fair   Poor

18. Has party ever used a Blank pen:
    Yes   No   Does not remember

19. If yes, what kind of service did pen give:
    Unsatisfactory   Satisfactory   Does not remember

20. If unsatisfactory, in what way:

21. Has party ever used a cheap pen ($1.oo or thereabouts):
    Yes   No   Does not remember

22. Did pen give satisfaction: Yes   **No**

23. Has party any suggestions to offer as to how **Blank** pen can be improved: Yes   **No**

24. If yes, what are they:

25. Does party use a propelling pencil: **Yes**   No

26. If yes, what make used:
    Eversharp   Other make (give name)
    Sharppoint   Does not know

27. What make propelling pencil does party consider the best:
    Eversharp   Other make (give name)
    Sharppoint   Does not know

28. Why is this make preferred:

29. Is there any likelihood of fountain pen being adopted in the place of pencil by secretaries, stenographers, and other office assistants, for such purposes as taking notes, dictation, etc.:
    Yes   Perhaps   No   No opinion

30. In what order would you rank writing instruments as coming nearest to filling your daily writing requirements:
    Fountain pen   Propelling pencil
    Steel pen   Wood pencil
        No preference

31. What caused party to first use a fountain pen:

32. To what extent does party think that fountain pens are used by students:
    a. In graded school:
        Very great extent   Some extent
        Great extent   Does not know
    b. In High School:
        Very great extent   Some extent
        Great extent   Does not know
    c. In College:
        Very great extent   Some extent
        Great extent   Does not know

C. Advertising

    1. What makes of fountain pens can party name without suggestion:

Moore	Shaeffer	Waterman
Parker	Swan	Other make
Conklin	Tempoint (Boston)	None

2. What makes can party recall when list is read to him

Parker	Swan	Waterman
Conklin	Tempoint (Boston)	Other make
Moore	Shaeffer	None

3. What fountain pen does party recall having seen most extensively advertised: Does not remember:

4. What makes of pens has party recently seen advertised:

Moore	Shaeffer	Waterman
Parker	Swan	Other make
Conklin	Tempoint (Boston)	Does not remember

5. Where has such advertising been observed:

Magazines	Dealer's stores
Newspapers	Demonstration
Billboards	Booklets and literature
Street cars	Elsewhere
Movies	Does not remember
Dealer's windows	

6. What general magazines does party read regularly:

7. If party could have only one of these, which one would he prefer:
   Does not know

8. What women's magazines does party read regularly:
   None

9. If party could have only one of these, which one would he prefer:
   Does not know

10. What newspapers does party read regularly?
    None

11. If party could have only one of these, which one would he prefer:
    Does not know

D. Comments

Figure 9: Questionnaire used for investigation on fountain pens and propelling pencils among consumers

A. Identification
    1. Name of dealer:
    2. Name of individual interviewed:
    3. Address of dealer: No.   Street   City   State
    4. Position of Individual: Owner   Manager   Salesman
    5. Sex of Individual: Male   Female
    6. Approximate age of individual:
        20 or under   21 to 30   31 to 40   41 or older
    7. Kind of business:
        Drug store
        Jewelry store   Department store
        Book and Stationery store   News stands
        Commercial Stationery and   Cigar stores
            Office Supply store   Others
    8. Location of business:
        Central on main street   Outlying on main street
        Central on side street   Outlying on side street
    9. Is location considered:•   Good   Fair   Poor
    10. What kind of impression does inside of business establishment make:
        Excellent   Good   Fair   Poor
    11. What impression made by personnel:
        Excellent   Good   Fair   Poor
    12. Location of fountain pen display:
        Front center   Prominent
        Left center   Obscure
        Right center   None
        Back

B. Sales and Competition
    1. Does dealer handle:
        Fountain pens   Propelling pencils
        Steel pens   Wood pencils
    2. What make or makes of writing instruments does dealer handle:
        a. Fountain Pens:
            Moore   Shaeffer   Waterman
            Parker   Swan   Other makes
            Conklin   Tempoint (Boston)   None

   b. Steel Pens
      Estabrook   Spencerian   Other makes   None
   c. Propelling Pencils
      Eversharp   Sharppoint   Other makes   None
   d. Wood Pencils
      Dixon   Venus
      Eagle   Other makes
      Eberhard Faber   None

3. How do writing instruments compare in unit sales: (Number in order of importance)
   Fountain pens (units)   Propelling pencils (units)
   Steel pens (gross)   Wood pencils (dozen)
               Does not know

4. What is the order of importance in which writing instruments have gained in sales: (Number in order)
      Fountain pens   Propelling pencils
      Steel pens   Wood pencils
           Does not know

5. What has tendency been in the past several years with regard to use of writing instruments:
   a. Has fountain pen been making inroads on:
      Steel pens   Wood pencil
      Propelling pencil   Does not know
   b. Has propelling pencil been making inroads on:
      Fountain pen   Wood pencil
      Steel pen   Does not know

6. Do you find there is active competition in the sale of:
   a. Fountain pens: Yes   No   Does not know
   b. Propelling pencils:
               Yes   No   Does not know

7. If not, would such competition be welcomed:
   Yes   No

8. If yes, why:

9. How are various instruments selling at present:

a. Fountain pens:	Brisk	Normal	Dull
b. Steel pens:	Brisk	Normal	Dull
c. Propelling pencils:	Brisk	Normal	Dull
d. Wood pencils:	Brisk	Normal	Dull

10. If normal or dull, what reasons are given for this condition:

    a. Fountain pens: c. Propelling pencils:
        Does not know   Does not know

    b. Steel pens: d. Wood pencils:
        Does not know   Does not know

11. Approximately what percentage of dealer's business is done during:

    a. Fountain pens:
        December (Xmas trade)
        September (School trade)
        Vacation Trade
        Early Spring (Commencement)
        Does not know

    b. Propelling pencils:
        December (Xmas trade)
        September (School trade)
        Early Spring (Commencement)
        Vacation Trade
        Does not know

12. What percentage of dealer's business is represented by total and by each make of:

    a. Fountain pen:

Total	%	Total	%
Moore	%	Tempoint (Boston)	%
Parker	%	Waterman	%
Conklin	%	Others	%
Shaeffer	%	Does not know	
Swan	%		

    b. Propelling pencils:

Total	%	Total	%
Eversharp	%	Others	%
Sharppoint	%	Does not know	

13. What make does individual personally use:

    a. Fountain pen: None
    b. Propelling pencil: None

14. Why are these makes preferred:

    a. Fountain pen: Does not know
    b. Propelling pencil: Does not know

15. Does party recommend these brands to customers:
     Yes   No
16. What percentage of sales is represented in the follow-
     ing classes:
     a. Fountain pens:
                 Should total 100%
          $2.50 to $3.50   % $4.50 and up   %
           3.50 to   4.50   % Does not know
     b. Propelling pencils:
                 Should total 100%
          $1.00 and under   % $4.00 to $5.00   %
           1.00 to $2.00   %   5.00 and up   %
           2.00 to   3.00   % Does not know
           3.00 to   4.00   %
17. What types of fountain pen holders are selling best:
     a. Regular   Safety   Self-filling   Does not know
     b. Long   Thin   Gold
        Short   Chased   Silver
        Thick   Medium   Does not know
18. What styles of fountain pen nibs are selling best:
     a. Extra fine   Coarse   Stub
        Fine   Plain   Manifold
                    Does not know
     b. Stiff   Flexible   Does not know
19. What proportion of customers ask for fountain pens
     and propelling pencils by brand name:
     a. Fountain pens   %   b. Propelling pencils %
        Does not know   Does not know
20. Is tendency to ask for these writing instruments by
     name:
     a. Fountain pens:
             Increasing   No change
             Decreasing   Does not know
     b. Propelling pencils:
             Increasing   No change
             Decreasing   Does not know
21. Approximately how many writing instruments are sold
     by dealers in a year:
     a. Fountain pens (units)   Does not know
     b. Steel pens (gross)   Does not know

      c. Propelling pencils (units)   Does not know
      d. Wood pencils (dozens)   Does not know

22. How often does dealer turn over his stock:
      a. Fountain pens   c. Propelling pencils
         Does not know   Does not know
      b. Steel pens   d. Wood pencils
         Does not know   Does not know

23. What percentage have sales increased during past several years:
      a. Fountain pens   %   Does not know
      b. Steel pens   %   Does not know
      c. Propelling pencils %   Does not know
      d. Wood pencils   %   Does not know

24. What effect have cheap fountain pens ($1.00 or thereabouts) had on dealer's sales:
     Good   Bad   No change   Does not know

25. If good or bad, why:

26. Do many complaints result from the sale of cheap pens:
     Yes   No

27. If yes, what are the chief complaints in order of their importance:

28. What makes of standard fountain pens, propelling pencils are most complained about:
      a. Moore   Shaeffer   Waterman
        Parker   Swan   Other makes
        Conklin   Tempoint (Boston)   Does not know

29. What are the chief complaints of the brands mentioned:

30. What percentage of dealer's sales of
      a. Fountain pens are to:
         (Should equal 100%)
         Men   % Children   %
         Women   % Does not know
      b. Propelling pencils are to:
         (Should equal 100%)
         Men   % Children   %
         Women   % Does not know

31. What percentage of dealer's sales are to farmers: %
     Does not know

32. How would party rank the leading makes of pens:
    a. From standpoint of quality
       Moore   Swan
       Parker   Tempoint (Boston)
       Conklin   Waterman
       Shaeffer   Does not know
    b. From standpoint of popularity
       Moore   Swan
       Parker   Tempoint (Boston)
       Conklin   Waterman
       Shaeffer   Does not know

33. Are fountain pens sold by one or two particular persons in store, or by all: One or two   All

34. Would dealer be willing to make some one or two clerks responsible for this end of business:
    Yes   No

C. Service and Stock
    1. Does dealer render repair and adjustment service on:
       a. Fountain pens: Yes   No
       b. Propelling pencils: Yes   No
    2. What is the nature of this service:
       a. Fountain pens: b. Propelling pencils:
    3. On what brand or brands of fountain pens is service rendered:
       Moore   Shaeffer   Waterman
       Parker   Swan   Other makes
       Conklin   Tempoint (Boston)
    4. If dealer does not render a repair service, would he be willing to do so if properly equipped and instructed:
       Yes   No   Does not know
    5. In cases of repairs by manufacturer, which manufacturer renders:
       Best and promptest service:
       Most reasonable service:
    6. What stock of fountain pens does dealer carry: (In dozens)
       Moore   doz.   Swan   doz.
       Parker   doz.   Tempoint (Boston) doz.
       Conklin   doz.   Waterman   doz.
       Shaeffer   doz.   Other makes   doz.

7. Does dealer try to fit customer's hand and style of writing with size and style of fountain pen:
   Always   Sometimes   Seldom   Never
8. Would dealer find a chart of different writings and recommendations of different styles of fountain pens a help in this method of selling:
   Yes   No   Does not know

D. Advertising

1. What makes of fountain pens and propelling pencils has dealer seen advertised:
   a. Fountain pens:
Moore	Shaeffer	Waterman
Parker	Swan	Other makes
Conklin	Tempoint (Boston)	None
   b. Propelling pencils:
      Eversharp   Sharppoint   Other makes   None
2. What fountain pen has dealer seen most extensively advertised and what is his impression of this brand:
   Name   Excellent   Good   Fair   Poor
3. In what media has dealer seen fountain pens and propelling pencils advertised locally:
   N—newspapers   W—window displays
   M—movies   S—street cars
   a. Fountain pens:
Moore	Tempoint (Boston)
Parker	Waterman
Conklin	Does not remember
Schaeffer	None
Swan	
   b. Propelling pencils:
Eversharp	Does not remember
Sharppoint	Name
4. Does dealer do any local advertising of:
   a. Fountain pens: Yes   No
   b. Propelling pencils: Yes   No
5. If yes, what kinds:
   a. Fountain pens:
Newspapers	Street cars
Movies	Direct mail
Window displays	Other forms
Demonstration	

      b. Propelling pencils:

Newspapers	Street cars
Movies	Direct mail
Window displays	Other forms
Demonstration	

6. What advertising media would dealer recommend to promote sale of fountain pens and propelling pencils in his store: (Number in order of importance)

Magazines	Movies
Newspapers	Direct mail
Billboards	Other forms
Street cars	Does not know

7. Why are these methods preferred:

8. What general magazines does dealer read regularly:

9. If dealer could have only one of these, which one would he prefer:
   Does not know

10. What trade papers does dealer read:

11. If dealer could have only one of these, which one would he prefer:
    Does not know

12. Is dealer influenced by what he reads in trade papers:
    Yes   No

13. If yes, to what extent:
    Very great extent   Some extent   Very little extent

14. What newspapers does dealer read:

15. If dealer could have only one of these, which one would he prefer:
    Does not know

E. Discounts

    1. What trade discounts do different manufacturers allow:

      a. On fountain pens:

Moore	Swan
Parker	Tempoint (Boston)
Conklin	Waterman
Shaeffer	Would not state

      b. On propelling pencils:
        Eversharp   Sharppoint   Would not state

2. Do manufacturers ever exceed these open discounts:
  a. On fountain pens:
      Yes   No   Would not state
  b. On propelling pencils:
      Yes   No   Would not state
3. If yes, which manufacturers:
  a. Fountain pens:
      Moore   Shaeffer   Waterman
      Parker   Swan   Others
      Conklin Tempoint (Boston)   Would not state
  b. Propelling pencils:
      Eversharp   Other makes
      Sharppoint   Would not state
4. What do they offer:
  a. Fountain pens: Would not state
  b. Propelling pencils: Would not state

Figure 10:   Questionnaire used for investigation on fountain pens and pro-
             pelling pencils among dealers

OBTAINING THE RESPONSES

The method of obtaining the responses has a great deal
to do with the reliability of the results. There are two
general methods for obtaining responses.

A. By mail

**B. By personal interviews, which may be made in sev-
eral different ways**

(1) *By newspaper reporters.* Some agencies and advertisers arrange with the publishers of newspapers to have
the reporters obtain responses to a certain number of
questionnaires in their locality. This plan makes the investigation inexpensive, as the newspapers are usually willing to do this for little or no charge, because of the prospective possibility of carrying the advertising later on. It
has, however, the disadvantage of using a considerable
variety of persons who may not be carefully instructed in
the manner of obtaining answers. The results may there-

fore be biased or incomplete, and the temptation is also present of warping the responses to make them appear favorable to the particular locality or newspaper concerned.

(2) *Through correspondent investigators, located in various cities.* Advertising agencies and others, who customarily carry out investigations of this sort, may arrange with one or more persons in typical cities, upon whom they may call at any time, for making a questionnaire investigation, according to uniform and careful instructions. This method is used by a number of firms to carry out work of this kind.

(3) *Through investigators, employed on full time, and sent out from the home office of the organization in charge of the research.* This in most respects is probably the most certain way of securing reliable responses, as the investigators may be trained and carefully instructed in the method of carrying out the work. It is probably the most expensive method, however, of the four outlined. Methods B (2) and (3) are most certain of securing reliable results. and as a matter of fact several of the organizations which do worthwhile research use both plans, covering a part of the field by regularly employed investigators *routed* from the central office and covering other parts of the field, possibly the more distant sections, by correspondent investigators.

Securing responses by mail is no doubt the cheapest, but it is in many instances of questionable value, for the reason that the responses quite often do not represent a fair sampling of the total class of people to whom the commodity may be sold. In the first place, the relative number of responses obtained from among those to whom the questionnaire is sent is usually small. It may be from 1 or 2% to 10%. Even though as high as 20 or 25% of the persons addressed may respond, it is nevertheless obvious that this group of 20 or 25% represents a certain selected group who are not typical, nor do they represent a properly distributed sampling over the entire class to whom the product may be sold. The important point here is not the small number of returns received in proportion to the entire possible group of individuals who constitute the human market for a given product and from whom responses might be secured—in fact, even a relatively small number of returns will yield surprisingly accurate data if they are obtained by a fair, unselected chance sampling method—but the point is, that the returns obtained by mail usually constitute a selected group. The very fact that certain persons reply selects them for that very reason. The ones who do reply have for some reason sufficient interest in replying—they may be more intelligent, or more progressive, or be more conscientious, or more obliging or less busy, or have greater curiosity or what not than those who do not reply.

This point is well illustrated in the case of an automobile accessory investigation, carried out by mail, in which 5,000 automobile owners were addressed with a questionnaire. Somewhat over 900, or approximately 17%, replied. This is a large proportion of returns, as mail returns go. However, this group is a more or less select group and is not a fair sampling of the entire class of automobile owners. This is shown by the fact that of the total number of replies, 25% were owners of Fords, which means that Ford owners were not sufficiently fully represented in proportion to the total number of Ford owners, since approximately between 40% and 50% of all automobile owners were at the time of this investigation Ford owners. Furthermore, we do not know what particular class of Ford owners the 25% represented. All we know is that for some reason, these 25% took the trouble to fill out the questionnaire and return it. It is of course very probable that this element of selection may make very little or no difference on some points or in connection with some kinds of inquiries, but in many if not most instances it undoubtedly does make a distinct difference. Just what difference it may make is impossible to say. It is quite likely that the 25% of Ford owners who replied were above the average of their class in social standing, income, or intelligence, and that possibly they used a higher grade of tire, or other accessory, than the average, and consequently, their responses may have little significance for the others who did not reply.

Your Name   Address
Own or rent?   No. Acres
Do you take a daily paper?   Which one?
Do you take other farm papers?   Which ones?
Do you take any magazines?   Which ones?
In what town do you trade?   Distance from home?
What is the next larger town?   What distance from home?
To what extent do you trade there?
Do you buy by mail?   What articles?
To what extent?

Farm Equipment

Do you own any of the following?

Automobiles	Make	Motor trucks	Make
Tractors	Make	Manure spreader	Make
Roofing	Brand	Stock food	Brand
Veterinary remedies	Brand	Buy seeds from whom?	
Silos	Make	Portland cement	Make
Commercial fertilizer		Brand	

Figure 11: Questionnaire used in an investigation conducted by a farm paper

---

It is, on the whole, far more reliable to obtain a smaller number of responses, but to obtain them in person and from all individuals from whom a response is sought, than to obtain a selected group of responses by mail. The responses obtained in person will be more truly representative of the group of persons in whom we are interested; the responses obtained by mail may not be representative of the group at all. It has been shown in investigations conducted both by the author and by others with whose work he is familiar, that a surprisingly small number of personal responses, obtained with the observance of proper conditions, will give highly reliable results. Specific data on this point will be presented later.

A rather extensive investigation, in which the returns were obtained by mail, was conducted by a farm paper using the questionnaire shown in Figure 11.

In like manner, the questionnaire covered makes or brands of household equipment, miscellaneous articles, food products, and personal articles such as watches and clothing. This questionnaire was printed in an issue of the paper in the spring of 1920. A total of 6,115 farmers, constituting nearly 1% of the readers of the paper, filled out the questionnaire and returned it. While this is a large number of returns, and in fact larger even than would be necessary to ascertain a reliable index of the farmers of the United States, it is nevertheless doubtful to what extent these returns give a correct cross-section of farmers as a whole or even of the readers of this particular paper. The results are bound to be warped by the fact that they represent only those who replied, whatever the reason for their reply may have been. It is quite likely that they represent a predominance of the more progressive type of farmer. Responses to the same questionnaire obtained from 1,000 farmers, in which all grades and types of farmers were represented in proper proportion, would give a far more accurate indication of the commodities used and of brands preferred.

To illustrate this point, let us note the returns on the brands of men's clothing bought by these farmers. The results were as follows:

Hart, Schaffner & Marx	291
Styleplus	151
Tailor Made	115
Cloth Craft	47
Wooltex	27
Kuppenheimer	53
Royal Tailors	14
Society Brand	7

National	45
Chicago Tailoring	8
Miscellaneous	684
No Make	1,706
Total Replies	3,148

According to these results, 1,706, or 54%, stated that they had no brand preference, while 46% mentioned a brand preference. This proportion of brand preference is probably considerably higher than is the case with farmers generally, and higher even than is the case with the farmers who read this particular paper. This statement is based on the fact that in a carefully conducted questionnaire investigation in one of the best agricultural sections of the country, in which the returns were obtained by personal interview, brand knowledge and brand preferences were very much smaller. The returns showed that only 13% stated a definite brand familiarity or preference. Any returns in which the factor of selection plays a part, whatever it may be, whether it be the influence of neglecting to answer a mailed inquiry or some other factor, are necessarily warped or invalidated to the extent to which they represent a selected group.

The investigation in question here has of course a certain suggestive value with regard to various points, such as the relative standing of various brands, and so on, but the serious objection to any investigation in which a selective factor has operated, is that it is impossible to tell to what extent this selective factor may have warped the results. It is therefore extremely important, as a matter of scientific accuracy, to make sure that the returns are obtained from a fair and properly distributed series of samples.

The difference between the results obtained by these two methods may be further illustrated in the case of two investigations of dentifrice. One investigation was made by the personal interview method, in which 161 men and women were interviewed. The other investigation was carried out by mail, and questionnaires were sent to 2,000 men, of whom about 500 replied. One question in both inquiries related to the frequency of brushing the teeth. The returns were as follows:

	Mail Investigation	Personal Interview Investigation
Clean the teeth once a day	42.8%	21.9%
Clean the teeth twice a day	33.6	63.7
Clean the teeth 3 times a day	14.9	12.4
Clean the teeth more than 3 times	5.4	.6
Clean the teeth irregularly	3.3	1.4

Please answer these questions and mail in enclosed envelope:
1. Were you familiar with the name "Blank" before receiving this letter?
2. If so, what did "Blank" mean to you?
3. If you or any of your friends have ever worn "Blank" garments, what service and satisfaction did they give:
   Excellent   Good   Fair   Poor
4. Are you likely to purchase a new coat or suit this spring?
5. If so, which will you probably buy?   Coat   Suit
6. What color will you prefer?   What fabric?
7. About what price do you expect to pay?
8. At what store in Boston would you prefer to have an opportunity to see "Blank" tailor-mades and knockabouts?
   First choice   Second choice
   Please send copy of "Blank Booklet" to:

Figure 12:   Questionnaire used to secure information regarding a brand of ready-made women's coats and suits

While the cost of securing responses to questionnaires by mail may seem cheaper than by any other means, the difference in cost is not as large as it seems on first impressions. To send out 5,000 letters, each containing a questionnaire, a letter and a return stamped envelope, would cost probably not far from $350 to $450, including 2 cents postage for the return envelope. A total of 500 responses out of 5,000 would be a good percentage of returns. Personal interviews in research of this type may be obtained at the rate of 50 cents to $1 each. That is 500 returns obtained by personal interview would cost little more than the same number of actual returns received out of 5,000 questionnaires sent out by mail.

The results obtained by personal interview would not only be more accurate and represent a more proper distribution of samples, but would furnish more detailed and complete information.

Questionnaires sent through the mails must of necessity be brief in order to secure a satisfactory number of replies. To illustrate the brevity of mailed questionnaires, the samples reproduced in Figures 12, 13, and 14 are given.

From   To Mr. Conde Nast, Publisher of *Vogue*
Address   19 West 44th Street, New York City

To help determine whether the type of woman who reads *Vogue* directs and controls the purchase of food for her family, or whether she allows unregulated discretion to her servants, you will, as a *Vogue* subscriber, kindly answer the following questions:

1. Planning the Daily Menu
   a. Do you supervise the planning of the daily menu?
   b. Do you leave this to your chef or cook?

2. The Purchase of Food
   a. Do you direct the ordering of food?
   b. Do you give your servants discretion in purchasing?

3. Insistence on Quality
   a. Do you specify by name, or brand, the food you order—such as bacon, tinned soups and meat products, preserved vegetables and fruits—and insist upon receiving exactly what you ask for?
   b. Do you permit the tradesmen to substitute brands that are not known to you?

Figure 13: Questionnaire used by publisher in an investigation among his readers

We take advantage of the present opportunity to inform you that the "Hostess Department" of *Vogue* is to be enlarged, with the idea of affording even a better service to our readers. If *Vogue* had a fairly accurate idea of the actual family and household requirements of its readers, the "Hostess Department" would be doubly efficient. This usefulness could be approximately achieved if you would help by answering the following questions:

    1. How many are there in your family?

    2. How many servants do you employ?

    3. About how many guests do you entertain each week?

    4. How can the "Hostess Department" best serve you?

Answer to these questions will be sincerely appreciated. Your name will not be used in any way.

Figure 14:   Questionnaire used by the publisher of *Vogue* in the interest of the Hostess Department

Mail questionnaire investigations are not to be disparaged in toto or in every instance. For certain purposes and under certain circumstances they are undoubtedly useful and more feasible than personal interview investigations. The important point is to guard against conditions which give a selected, warped or distorted view of a situation.

THE INTERVIEW

To insure reliability of results, it is highly important to see that the interview for obtaining responses is properly conducted. The likelihood of securing reliable results in making the interview depends to quite an extent upon the manner in which the questionnaire itself is prepared. If this is properly prepared, the interviewer is much less likely to obtain replies of doubtful value.

Various methods are used by different organizations in making interviews. To begin with, there is the more or less indefinite interview, which has been the traditional way of making field investigations. The investigator, quite frequently a salesman, was instructed to sound out his customers regarding various points in which the house was interested. This is done more or less incidentally in connection with the salesman's regular calls upon his customers and usually without uniform or properly prepared questions. Quite often he has no specific instructions as to how to obtain the information desired. However, such results are apt to be nothing more than general impressions, which may be right or wrong, according to the preconceived notion of the person who makes the report.

When a carefully prepared questionnaire is used, the manner of its use varies quite distinctly among different organizations. For example, the majority of firms instruct their investigators to use the questionnaire and to follow it very closely. There are, however, exceptional cases in which organizations hold to the view that while a questionnaire has been carefully prepared, it must not be used, under any circumstances, in the presence of the person interviewed. The investigators are instructed to familiarize themselves thoroughly with the questionnaire, or preferably actually to commit it to memory, so that all of the points will be covered in the interview. The responses are then reported from memory on a questionnaire blank immediately after the interview. The belief on which this method is based is that the person being interviewed will be more reluctant to express himself freely if he sees the interviewer writing things down.

The drawback of this method is the greater possibility of error in remembering the responses actually obtained, in the variability in the way questions are presented, and in the more limited number of points that may be covered, as the interviewer is unable to retain as many details and as much information as may very easily be done when the responses are reported directly on a blank during the interview.

Furthermore, the objection sometimes given that the person being interviewed will be less inclined to talk freely if the questionnaire is used in his presence is minor and actually of little weight. Practical experience has shown that responses to a properly prepared questionnaire may be obtained in nearly every instance with the exercise of a moderate amount of tact.

The fundamental condition in research work is to carry it out without prejudice and without preconceived ideas to be proved.

In recent years publishers of magazines and newspapers have established research departments to make questionnaire-field surveys of their particular territories or classes of readers. While some of these surveys have obtained useful information, many of them are of limited value, as they are made too superficially, or with obvious bias to show advantage for the particular class of readers or the particular locality concerned.

The questions used in a survey of baking powder in a large city and the data thus obtained are typical of this class of investigations. The questionnaire used is illustrated in Figure 15.

Name

Type of Store   Party Interviewed

What brands of Baking Powder do you sell?   (List in order of popularity and price.)

What do you think is the reason for the leaders being the best sellers?

What percentage of your total baking powder business is on the leading brand?

How much baking powder do you sell a week?

What would you suggest a manufacturer to do to increase the sale of his baking powder in Blank City?

What percentage of your customers ask for baking powder by brand name?

Will you cooperate with the manufacturer of a baking powder if he advertises in Blank newspaper?

General Remarks:

Figure 15: Questionnaire used in a large city to secure information regarding baking powder

Seventy-five dealers were interviewed. The answers to some of the questions are undoubtedly valuable, but the data summarized for certain other questions are obviously worthless if not absurd, such as the following:

What do you think is the reason for the leaders being the best sellers?

Local newspaper advertising was the reason advanced by the majority of dealers for the large sale of the leader.

The summary of this question shows the following percentages:

Local newspaper advertising and quality	57%
Local newspaper advertising alone	33
Local newspaper advertising and coupons	3½
Quality	3½
Personal effort	3½

What would you suggest a manufacturer to do to increase the sale of his baking powder in Blank City?

Summarizing the suggestions received, the following is the result:

Participations in Blank newspaper Food Shows	47%
Newspaper advertising	30
Cooperate with dealer	7
Demonstrations	5
Coupons	5
Billboards	1
House-to-house personal work	1
Maintenance of quality	1
Price maintenance	1
Sampling	1
Special offer to customers	1

HOW MANY RETURNS ARE NECESSARY?

The number of responses that are necessary for a reliable set of data depends upon the territory that needs to be covered, and upon the number in any community necessary to give a reliable sampling of that community. When the investigation is carried out carefully, it is surprising how small a number of responses are necessary to give an adequate index of the status with regard to any given problem, either in a given community or in the country as a whole.

The actual number of returns obtained in typical investigations with which the writer is familiar varies anywhere from 100 to 2,000, and in exceptional instances to 5,000 or more, depending upon the circumstances involved and the purpose of the investigation. For example, in an investigation carried out by a large fish products concern, somewhat over 1,700 individual consumers were interviewed. In an automobile tire investigation, returns were received from not quite 1,000 individuals. In an investigation concerning the buying of investment securities in a middle-western state, an executive in each of slightly over 100 banks was interviewed with a definitely prepared questionnaire. In an investigation made by a retail clothing store, in a city somewhat under 50,000 in a middle-western state, 400 mothers were interviewed. In a study of certain advertising problems of a large department store in an eastern city, 50 housewives were interviewed in their homes, and over 5,000 customers were interviewed in the store.

The number of responses or interviews that are necessary to give a reliable representation of the answer to the problem may be determined statistically by ascertaining to what extent the data from various sizes of groups agree or disagree with one another. We may note in the first place the rather close agreement between the returns obtained from the two groups by the department store referred to.

One of the questions asked, both in the investigation conducted within the store and the interviews made with the women in their homes, was as follows:

Do you read the newspaper advertisements before you go shopping?

Practically always   Usually   Rarely   Never

The detailed tabulation of the responses to this question is given on page 75 in Chapter III. It will be noted that there is a difference between the returns from the customers in the upstairs section of the store as compared with the customers in the basement section of the store. There is probably a real cause for this difference in the type of customer more strongly predominating in the basement. However, if we group these two sets of data together, we will note that the returns from the 50 women interviewed in their homes correspond remarkably closely with the returns from the larger group of over 5,000 women. Thus, for example, 52% of the 50 women interviewed in their homes reported that they always examined the newspaper advertisements before going shopping, as compared with 47% of the 5,000 women who responded to the question in the same manner in the store. Similarly, 32% said that they usually read the newspaper advertisements before going shopping, as compared with 35% of the 5,000 women.

An examination of the data in Chapter VIII, concerning the investigation of raisins, will show to what extent the returns from various groups agree with one another. It will be noticed that the first two groups are composed of 50 persons each while the other groups are composed of 100 persons each. These different groups were made up entirely by chance. An examination of the results will show on the whole a remarkably close agreement between any two groups of 100, or even between either of the two groups of 50, and the final results of the entire 700 individuals. Thus, for example, in the first group of 50 homes, 7% of the housewives reported that they buy raisins in bulk, and 93% reported that they buy them in packages, as against 6.6% and 93.4% respectively for the total 700 women. Or, in the case of the second question regarding brands, it will be noted that 70% in the first group of 50 mention Sun-Maid, as against an average of 57.9% of the entire 700. Similar comparisons may be made throughout the entire report of the raisin investigation. On some points, the differences between the individual groups and the entire group are larger than in others. In general, however, it will be seen that either group of 50 or any group of 100 checks up, so far as the essential points are concerned, with the data for the entire 700, and that practically without exception, a group of either 50 or 100 in this case would give a sufficiently correct indication in this community of the status with regard to the problems here considered.

In the case of the fish product research referred to, the investigation was carried out in two sections. The first section covered a total of 539 interviews with housewives in six different cities, in as many different states. Approximately 100 housewives were interviewed in each city, with the exception of one in which 50 were interviewed. A little later, the same investigation was extended to cover 1,193 interviews with housewives in 16 different cities, located in 15 states.

One of the questions was "Do you like fish?" The responses showed that 87% in the first group replied Yes and 90% in the second group. A second question was "What kind of fish do you buy most frequently?" The answers to this showed that 29% of the first group preferred a certain kind, as against 40% of the second group; 13% of the first group preferred the next kind, against 10% of the second group; and 11% of the first group preferred a third kind most frequently, as against 9% of the second group. The next question was "Why do you buy this particular kind of fish?" The responses showed that 59% of the first group and 57% of the second group bought their particular preference because it appealed to their taste. Eleven per cent of the first group and 17% of the second group bought their particular preference because it was easily procured. Nine per cent of the first group and 3% of the second group preferred one particular kind because of the reasonable price. These comparisons are typical of the entire investigation, and demonstrate that nothing new was learned by carrying out the investigation with the second group of 1,193 housewives. It is obvious from a statistical comparison that the investigation might as well have stopped with the first group of 539. This, of course, was not known at that time, since there were no comparable data available on which to determine statistical reliability of this sort.

TABLE 34

SHOWING THE PERCENTAGE OF EACH GROUP OF CUSTOMERS OF A BOSTON STORE WHO READ THE VARIOUS PAPERS MENTIONED

No. of persons in each group	26	68	104	198	1,164	2,868	Total Group 27,668
Advertiser	4%	3%	13%	9%	5%	7%	9%
American	12	15	16	15	14	15	14
Christian Science Monitor	8	0	0	1	.5	.5	.6
Globe	26	21	18	21	27	24	24
Herald	4	10	3	6	5	6	6
Traveler	22	3	8	8	8	9	9
Jewish Advocate	0	6	1	2	2	1	1
Pilot	0	0	4	2	1	3	2
Post	20	24	22	23	26	24	24
Telegram	0	12	11	10	6	8	7
Transcript	4	0	4	3	3	2	3

The conclusion which seems to be justified by such data as are available is that approximately 50 returns obtained by personal interview and representing a properly distributed sampling of the class of persons in whom the investigator is interested is a sufficiently large number to give a fairly reliable index of that community. In the case of larger cities, the number might be extended to 100; and so far as the entire country is concerned, it is highly probable that 6 to 10 typical sections of the country sampled by means of 50 to 100 personal interviews each will, for most purposes, give as reliable a set of data as is ordinarily desirable.

As a further check on the reliability of various numbers of responses, the author found in an investigation conducted in connection with the advertising of milk in Boston, that returns from groups of 50 to 100 families showed substantially the same results as those obtained from the entire group of 367 families. It was also found that the average size of the families interviewed in this investigation was 4.9 persons. The census for 1910 showed that the average size of family in Boston was 4.8 persons. When samples of data are properly obtained and proportionately distributed, a surprisingly small number yields sufficiently reliable results for practical purposes.

Definite proof regarding the adequacy of various sizes of samples may be obtained by comparing samples of smaller and larger size with a very large group. Such a set of data is presented in Table 34. One of the larger Boston retail stores wanted to find out which of the newspapers were read most by its customers. A suitable record slip was printed and put into the hands of the sales persons in the store. After a customer had made a purchase the sales person asked whether she would mind telling which paper she reads regularly. A total of 27,668 customers were asked. Different sizes of groups were selected by chance from the entire group and are tabulated. The facts presented here have significance only for the store here in question and should not be interpreted as applying to other stores or to Boston in general. Each store would have to take a similar newspaper census of its own customers. An inspection of the different groups, as presented in the table, will show to what extent they agree with the total of 27,668 customers.

The small group of 26 customers agrees in the main with the total of 27,668, but there is a large discrepancy in the case of the Traveler, the Telegram and the Monitor. The large groups tend to agree more closely with the entire number. The group of 198 shows no important deviations from the total.

VIII

SAMPLE INVESTIGATION OF A NATIONALLY
DISTRIBUTED PRODUCT: RAISINS[1]

Actual manner of carrying out a questionnaire investigation of a nationally distributed food product. Results of a local investigation. Comments on the results. Bulk and package purchases. Competition among various brands. Purchases by brand-names, trade-marks. Amount of annual consumption of products per family. Seasonal buying. Various uses of product. Selling features of product. Effect of advertising and distribution method on consumption of product. Familiarity with different brands. Results of advertising brand-names. Part played by various mediums of advertising in creating familiarity with product. Effectiveness of pictures and text in advertisements. Influence of advertising toward buying products and on selection of particular brand. Conclusions and recommendations.

THE purpose of this chapter is to show in as complete detail as is feasible in a rather limited amount of space the actual manner of carrying out a questionnaire investigation of a nationally distributed food product. Facts obtained in this manner will serve as the groundwork for making plans for a new advertising campaign and for checking up the methods and results of the advertising carried out previously. It is only by obtaining definite facts in a reliable way and on a sufficiently extensive scale that it is possible to proceed without more or less blind guessing.

The investigation was conducted by means of the questionnaire presented in Figure 7, page 150. Approximately 750 housewives in the metropolitan area of Boston were personally interviewed. It is believed, therefore, that the results have a satisfactory amount of reliability and that they no doubt represent with a reasonable degree of ac-

---

[1] The investigations in this and the next two chapters are not presented in any sense as models but merely as brief samples of some actual cases In actual practice the results are presented and discussed much more fully than space permits here.

curacy the situation, at least in this territory. The chief difference in carrying out an investigation of this sort on a national scale and the present one would be twofold. In the first place, to make the results representative of conditions on a national scale, it would be necessary to make the same investigation in 6 to 10 typical sections of the country. In the second place, we know from the statistical consistency of our results that it would be unnecessary to obtain returns from as many as 700 housewives in any one community or section. A very much smaller number would be sufficient. In smaller cities, approximately 50 interviews would ordinarily be sufficient, and in larger cities the number might be extended to 100. One reason for making, in this raisin investigation, about 750 interviews in one general section was to compare the results from

TABLE 35

RESULTS OF RAISIN INVESTIGATION

(Summary of 700 Questionnaires)
(Returns obtained by personal interview)

Groups	I	II	III	IV	V	VI	VII	VIII	Average
Number of housewives in each group	50	50	100	100	100	100	100	100	

Question 1. Do you buy raisins in bulk or package?

	I	II	III	IV	V	VI	VII	VIII	Average
Bulk:	7%	4%	8%	6%	11%	8%	2%	7%	6.6%
Package:	93	96	92	94	89	92	98	93	93.4

Question 2. If in package, what brand or brands?

	I	II	III	IV	V	VI	VII	VIII	Average
Sun-Maid	70%	60%	45%	57%	63%	66%	56%	46%	57.9%
Not-a-seed	3	6	24	9		9	6	8	8.1
Epicure	3	6		3	1	3	1	6	2.9
Del Monte	3	4	5		3	4	1	2	2.7
Bonners Seedless	8			3	6	1			2.3
22 Miscellaneous brands									10.9
Blue Ribbon		6	2	2		5	3		2.3
Uncertain									12.9

Question 3. When you buy raisins, do you call for them by name?

	I	II	III	IV	V	VI	VII		Average
Yes	45%	48%	51%	56%	44%	52%	63%		51.0%
No	55	52	49	44	56	48	37		49.0

Question 4.   How often do you buy raisins?

Every week	23.0%
Every two weeks	16.0
Once a month	31.4
Once in 2 months	6.4
Once in 3 months	.6
Once in 6 months	2.2
About 3 times a month	1.2

Average number of pounds a year per family:

Groups	I	II	III	IV	V	VI	VII	VIII	Average
	34.7	34.1	24.3	23.5	29.6	20.1	16.0	21.3	25.5

Question 5.   Do you buy more at one time of the year than at another?

Yes	80%	75%	68%	73%	63%	68%	76%	49%	69 0%
No	15	25	32	27	37	31	24	30	27.6
Uncertain									3.4
When? Winter									39.
Fall									14.4
Holidays									13.5

Question 6.   In what way do you use raisins?

	Median Rank		Median Rank
In cake	1.4	In bread	4.4
In puddings	1.6	On breakfast food	6.3
In pie	3.0	In salad	6.9
Eating uncooked	4.4	Stewed	7.7

Note: The relative orders of frequency of use are practically identical for the different groups and hence are not given here.

Question 7.   Do you use more raisins now than a year or two ago?

Much more	5.6%	Uncertain	33.5%
More	10.5	No	31.0
Some more	19.4		

Question 8.   What do you like most about raisins?   (Number in order of preference—1, 2, 3, 8.)

	Median Rank		Median Rank
Taste good	1.5	Contain iron	5.1
Make delicious dishes	2.8	Easily digested	6.1
High food value	2.9	Relieve fatigue	6.3
Good for health	3.6	A beauty food	7.6

Note: The relative orders for these eight appeals are practically identical for the various groups.

Question 9. With what brands of raisins are you familiar?

Groups	I	II	III	IV	V	VI	VII	VIII	Average
Sun-Maid	88%	73%	68%	62%	69%	77%	69%	66%	71.5%
Not-a-seed	17	4	22	13	7	10	9	15	12.1
Blue Ribbon		4	5	5	4	7	19	2	5.8
Del Monte	3	8	5	4	5	6		3	4.3
Epicure (S. S. Pierce)	3	4		3	2	3	2	11	3.5
Bonners	8			3	3	2		4	2.5
36 Miscellaneous Brands									7.9

Question 10. Which ones have you seen advertised?

Groups	I	II	III	IV	V	VI	VII	VIII	Average
Sun-Maid	70%	69%	49%	48%	64%	70%	69%	70%	55.8%
Not-a-seed	5	4	14	8	7	2	5		5.0
Del Monte	3	4	2	5	1	5		9	3.6
Blue Ribbon			1	1	4	2	3	9	2.5
12 Miscellaneous Brands									4.5

Question 11. Where seen advertised?

a. Magazines

Saturday Evening Post	21.0%
Ladies' Home Journal	11.0
Good Housekeeping	10.3
Pictorial Review	3.3
American	3.0
Woman's Home Companion	2.0
McCall's	2.0
Modern Priscilla	.8
Cosmopolitan	.5
Delineator	.5
Hearst's	.33
Literary Digest	.33
Collier's	.16
Mother's Magazine	.16
Good Health	.16

b. Newspapers

Boston Globe	5.83%	Boston Transcript	1.0%
Boston Post	5.5	Boston American	.66
Boston Herald	3.5	New York Times	.16
Boston Traveler	1.16	Boston Telegram	.16

c. Other Mediums
   Street Cars   18.33%
   Stores   7.33
   Billboards   3.5
   News Stands   .16
   Lectures on Health   .16

Question 12. What do you remember about the ads?
Pictures
Pie	5.7%
Girl with sunbonnet	5.3
Girl	4.0
Delicious dishes	3.8
Bunches of grapes	2.3
Package of raisins	2.2
Picture	1.7
Girl with basket	1.5
General mention	1.3
Small boxes of raisins	1.3
Color	1.2
Using raisins in cereal	.7
"Appetizing"	.5
"Attractive"	.5
Confections	.33
Picture of process	.33
Sun	.33
Boy with mouth open	.16
Red color	.16
Trade-mark (not specified)	.16

Text

Recipes	7.3%	5-cent package	.33%
Contains iron	4.3	Real Man's pie	.33
Healthy	3.8	Spelled "maid"	.33
General mention	2.7	Sundried	.16
Food value	.7	California	.16
"Sun Maid"	.5	Tastes good	.16

Question 13. Do you think that you have been influenced toward buying raisins by the ads you have seen?

Very much	6.8%	Uncertain	31.5%
Much	7.0	None	31.2
Some	23.6		

Question 14. Have you bought Sun-Maid raisins because of ads you have seen?

Yes 30.0%   No 57.5%   Uncertain 12.5%

Question 15. What general magazines do you read regularly?

Saturday Evening Post	35.0%	Red Book	2.25%
American	19.3	Outlook	1.25
Literary Digest	16.9	Scribner's	1.5
Cosmopolitan	7.0	Country Gentleman	1.12
Atlantic Monthly	5.4	Review of Reviews	1.0
National Geographic	3.2	Asia	1.0
Collier's	3.1	Century	.87
New Republic	2.6	World's Work	.75
Harper's	2.3	Argosy	.5
Youths' Companion	.75	Railroad Magazine	.37
McClure's	.75	Travel	.37
Hearst's	.62	Leslie's	.37
Motion Picture	.62	Everybody's	.5
Harper's Bazaar	.62	20 Miscellaneous	
Vanity Fair	.62	Magazines	.19

Question 16. Which one do you prefer most?

Saturday Evening Post	19.2%	McClure's	.25%
American	7.4	Collier's	.25
Literary Digest	6.7	Life	.25
Cosmopolitan	2.6	Century	.12
Atlantic Monthly	2.3	Snappy Stories	.12
Outlook	1.0	Vanity Fair	.12
Harper's	.62	Nation	.12
National Geographic	.5	Everybody's	.12
Red Book	.5	Review of Reviews	.12
Country Gentleman	.37		

Question 17. What women's magazines do you read regularly?

Ladies' Home Journal	32.8%	Vogue	1.12%
Good Housekeeping	20.3	Needlecraft	.25
Pictorial Review	16.2	Elite	.13
Woman's Home Companion	15.2	Housewife	.13
McCall's	5.4	Woman Citizen	.13
Delineator	4.0	Mother's Magazine	.13
Modern Priscilla	2.5	Woman's Magazine	.13
Woman's World	1.88	Designer	.13

Question 18. Which one do you prefer most?

Ladies' Home Journal	25.9%	Modern Priscilla	.75%
Good Housekeeping	14.6	McCall's	1.4
Pictorial Review	7.0	Vogue	.37
Delineator	1.8	Woman's World	.37
Woman's Home Com-		Housewife	.12
panion	9.4	Designer	.12

Question 19. What newspapers do you read regularly?

Boston Globe	38.5%	Boston Traveler	17.0%
Boston Herald	35.3	Boston American	9.8
Boston Post	34.8	Boston Telegram	2.33
Boston Transcript	21.6	Boston Advertiser	1.16

various sizes of groups, so as to determine more precisely the maximum number of individual returns necessary to give a reliable cross-section of a given community.

COMMENTS ON THE RESULTS

Question 1. The returns on the first question show that the buying of raisins is done almost entirely in packages rather than in bulk. Only 6.6% of the housewives buy raisins in bulk. The significance of this fact obviously is that the selling of raisins becomes distinctly a problem of the right kind and size of package and of competition in package brands. The advertising should therefore be directed accordingly. The appearance of the package should be impressed upon the minds of consumers so that they will recognize it.

Question 2. The results of the second question show to what extent there is competition among various brands, and the relative standing of the various competing brands, in the New England territory. The Sun-Maid brand is the outstanding leader, being bought by approximately 58% of the housewives interviewed. There is a big drop to the second brand, Not-a-seed, which is bought by 8% of the housewives. The remaining brands are mentioned rather infrequently.

Question 3. The responses to Question 3 show that 51% or fully half of the housewives purchase by brand-name. This fact is interesting from two standpoints: In the first place it shows that various brand-names have been pretty well established in the minds of housewives. In the second place, it also shows that there is a considerable opportunity for the further establishment of specific brand-names and for more thoroughly impressing specific trade-marks on the minds of buyers, since about half of the housewives do not call for raisins by brand-name, in spite of the fact that they are familiar with various names. Thus, for example, 58% of the housewives buy Sun-Maid raisins, but only 51% of the housewives call for raisins by either this or some other trade-name.

Question 4 was designed simply to arrive at a rough estimate of the amount of raisins consumed by each family in a year. These results show that so far as such an estimate is reliable, approximately 25 pounds per year per family are bought. The returns on such a question as this are probably not as reliable as the responses to other questions, since they must necessarily be a rough estimate based on memory of recent purchases. Nevertheless this figure is probably not far from the correct amount. The total consumption of raisins in the United States is probably in the neighborhood of 250,000 tons. This would be 21 pounds per family, as there are somewhat over 24 million families in the United States. In view of the probability that the estimates on the part of the housewives are likely to err on the side of an overestimation rather than an under-estimation, the results are probably not far from correct.

Question 5 was designed to obtain some data regarding seasonal buying. The advertising of raisins has un-doubtedly had some influence in ironing out the seasonal fluctuation. Nevertheless, there is still a considerable amount of variation. Approximately two-thirds of the housewives state that they buy more raisins at one time of the year than another. Approximately 39% of the housewives buy more raisins during the winter months than at other times of the year.

Question 6. The purpose of this question was to obtain a more accurate notion of the various uses to which raisins are put, and of the relative predominance of various uses. The data on this point are obviously important, first from the standpoint of the types of uses which appeal most strongly and which therefore might be stressed, and secondly from the standpoint of developing new uses. It will be evident from an examination of the table that there are considerable differences in the proportions in which raisins are used for various purposes. The chief uses are in cake, puddings, and pies. On the other hand, raisins are used very little on breakfast foods, in stewed form, and on salads.

The purpose of *Question 7* was to ascertain from the housewives to what extent the recent advertising campaign for raisins and the accompanying distribution methods have increased the consumption of raisins. Thirty-one per cent of the housewives stated that their use of raisins had not increased during the past year or two, 35.5% of the housewives stated that they were using raisins anywhere from "Some more" to "Much more" than they had, and 33.5% of the responses were doubtful or uncertain. Evidently the consumption of raisins has noticeably increased within the last year or two.

The results of *Question 8* show that taste is the strongest appeal for raisins. "Make delicious dishes" and "High food value" are also strong and stand close to taste. The fatigue and beauty appeals are at the bottom of the list and therefore rather weak. There is a distinct break between the first four and the last four appeals. The drop from "Good for health" (3.6) to "Contain iron" (5.1) is considerable and larger than between any other two appeals

The results of *Question 9* may be interpreted in conjunction with Questions 2 and 3. The returns show that while 71.5% of the housewives are familiar with Sun-Maid raisins, 58% of the housewives buy them, and 51% call for this or some other brand by name. Likewise, while 12% of the housewives are familiar with Not-a-seed, 8% of the housewives buy them. The results as a whole on this question are interesting from the point of view of the advertising carried on for the various brands.

The purpose of *Question 10* was to determine to what extent housewives are consciously aware of having seen various brands of raisins advertised. It is interesting to note that approximately 56% of the housewives are consciously aware of having seen Sun-Maid raisins advertised. The other brands are mentioned much less frequently.

Question 11 was inserted for the purpose of ascertaining to what extent various mediums have been instrumental in bringing about familiarity with raisins. Taking the figures as a whole, the magazines apparently have played a much larger part than the newspapers. It is perhaps surprising to note the frequency with which street-car cards are mentioned as a source of information. At this point an interesting comparison may be made on the part of the distributer, between the amount of money spent in various types of mediums and the relative extent to which various mediums are responsible for acquainting the public with raisins. Such a comparison would be of value, or at least suggestive, in connection with the selection of mediums, that is in giving a rough index as to which mediums are most effective.

An analysis of the results obtained in response to *Question 12* will give some very interesting and suggestive points regarding the effectiveness of various elements in the past advertising of raisins. For example, it will be noted that pictures are recalled considerably more frequently than elements presented in the text. Nearly twice as many housewives recalled various pictures or items connected with pictures as those who recalled elements in the text. The feature recalled most frequently, whether picture or text, was the Sun-Maid trade-mark, the girl with the sunbonnet and the basket, which was mentioned by 10.8% of the housewives. The next item most strongly impressed upon the minds of housewives was the presentation of recipes. This was mentioned by 7.3% of the women. Evidently recipes are read by housewives and are interesting to them to a very considerable degree. The slogan that raisins contain iron was the next most commonly remembered element presented in the text (4.3%). The next most frequent pictures were those of the pie (5.7%), delicious dishes (3.8%), and bunches of grapes (3.8%).

The results of *Question 13* show the extent to which the housewives were consciously aware of having been influenced toward buying raisins by the advertisements they had seen. Specifically, only 31% stated that they had not been so influenced. Approximately 30% stated that they had been influenced, and approximately 31% were uncertain. It is obvious that the responses to this question are more likely to be understated than overstated, for the reason that most persons have seen advertisements and been influenced by them without being able specifically to recall when or where.

Question 14 shows to what extent women were influenced to buy the Sun-Maid brand. This brand has been most widely advertised and the responses show that 30% of the housewives stated that they had specifically been influenced by the advertisements of this particular brand. Twelve and five-tenths per cent were uncertain, and 57.5% said No. Again the responses to this question represent un-

doubtedly an underestimation rather than an overestimation of the influence of the Sun-Maid advertising.

CONCLUSIONS AND RECOMMENDATIONS

1. Raisins are bought by the housewife almost entirely
in package form (93.4%) and very rarely in bulk (6.6%).

2. Brand names are fairly well established. Six brands
constitute most of the purchases (76.2%). One brand
(Sun-Maid) constitutes nearly 60% of the purchases.

3. Approximately half (51%) of the housewives call
for raisins by brand name.

4. Approximately one-fourth (23%) of the housewives
buy raisins once a week, about one-third (31.4%) buy
raisins once a month and about one-sixth buy raisins once
in two weeks. The average family uses between 20 and
25 pounds of raisins a year.

5. There are still considerable seasonal differences in
the amount of raisins bought.

6. The three most frequent uses of raisins are in puddings, in cakes, and in pies. They are used very rarely
on breakfast food, in salads, or in stewed form.

7. Over one-third of the housewives (35.5%) used more
raisins than they did the year before.

8. Brand names of raisins are becoming well known to
housewives. Nearly all housewives (92.1%) are familiar
with one or more of seven brands, and over two-thirds of
the housewives (71.5%) are familiar with the Sun-Maid
brand.

9. The four strongest appeals in order are "Taste
good," "Make delicious dishes," "High food value," and
"Good for health." The four weakest appeals are "Contain iron," "Easily digested," "Relieve fatigue," and "A
beauty food."

10. Advertising has apparently played a large part in
familiarizing housewives with the various brands. About
two-thirds of the housewives (67.5%) are consciously

aware of having seen one or more of the four leading brands advertised. Over half of the housewives (55.8%) are aware of having seen Sun-Maid raisins advertised.

11. The advertising of raisins in the magazines has played by far the largest part in familiarizing the housewives with raisins. Over half of the housewives (55.6%) recall having seen raisins advertised in magazines, 18.0% in newspapers, and 18.3% in street cars.

12. The feature in the advertising most fully impressed on the minds of housewives is the picture of the Sun-Maid (girl with bonnet and basket). About 11% of the housewives recalled this feature. The other features of familiarity are recipes, recalled by 7.3% of the housewives, "Contain iron" (by 4.3%), pictures of delicious dishes (by 3.8%), and the health appeal (by 3.8%).

13. As further evidence regarding the effect of advertising, it was found that less than one-third of the housewives (31.2%) stated that they did not think they had been influenced toward buying raisins by the advertisements seen, over one-third (37.4%) felt that they had been so influenced, and 31.5% were uncertain about it.

14. Over 40% (42.5%) stated that they had bought the Sun-Maid brand because of the advertising they had seen.

15. The remaining data (Questions 15 to 19) obtained in this survey have a valuable bearing upon the selection of mediums.

16. Specific recommendations regarding future advertising plans and methods will not be made here. Definite recommendations would have to be made with reference to individual brands. While some of the suggestions would apply equally to all brands, many would necessarily vary with different brands.

IX

SAMPLE INVESTIGATION FOR A RETAIL STORE:
A BOYS' CLOTHING DEPARTMENT

Retail store problems that need investigation. Method of approach and manner in which results are interpreted. Questionnaire—boys' clothing. Typical sections allotted to each interviewer. Analysis of questionnaire. Results tabulated. Analysis of results. Should much emphasis be laid on makers' brands? Comparison of salesmen's estimates of buying power with results of consumer investigation. Most important appeals in the buying of boys' and children's clothing. Reasons for preference of a particular salesman. General conclusions and suggestions.

THE purpose of this chapter is to illustrate the sorts of problems that need to be investigated in connection with a retail store, the methods by which they may be approached, and the manner in which the results may be interpreted. The problems of a retail store are obviously different from those involved in the advertising of a nationally distributed product. In some respects, however, they are very similar.

The purpose of this study was to obtain fundamental facts regarding the past advertising as well as the proposed new plans for developing the boys' department of a retail clothing store. It was therefore decided to carry out a well-planned questionnaire inquiry in the territory from which the store actually obtained its business or might potentially expect to obtain business. This particular store was located in a city with a population somewhat under 50,000 in a rich agricultural section in the Middle West.

Some of the chief points regarding which it was thought desirable to obtain information were the following. It was decided to determine to what extent the father or the mother was the chief purchaser of the boy's clothing, to what extent the buying was done by brands, what prices were paid in various districts of the territory, what points of merit regarding boys' clothing appealed most strongly, approximately what was the cost of clothing a boy for a year, what particular mediums in the various parts of the territory most effectively reached the customers, and the like.

Accordingly, the questionnaire shown in Figure 16 was prepared, with the purpose of obtaining the answers from mothers by personal interviews.

Name   Address

1. How much of the boys' clothing do you buy?
    a. Boys under 13, % approximately
    b. Boys 13-18, % approximately
2. How much of the boys' clothing is bought by your husband?
    a. Boys under 13, % approximately
    b. Boys 13-18, % approximately
3. What brands of boys' and children's garments do you buy and why?
4. What prices approximately do you pay for your children's outer garments?

 a. Overcoats: b. Suits:
  Children under 13, $ Knee pant suits, $
  Boys 13-18, $ Long pant suits, $

5. What do you consider most important in buying boys' and children's clothing: (Rank in the order of importance)

Material	Comfort
Durability	"Wear Like Iron"
Union Made	Price
Style	Reputation of the Firm
Tailoring	Fit
"Satisfaction or Money	Maker's Guarantee
Back" guarantee	Merchant's Guarantee

6. Where do you buy your boys' and children's clothing and why?
7. Is there a particular salesman whom you prefer to have wait on you?
    a. If so, why do you prefer this particular salesman?

8. How many suits per year do you usually buy for each child?
   a. Knee pant suits   b. Long pant suits
9. What newspapers do you read most?
   a. Daily   b. Weekly
10. Are you interested in advertisements of boys' and children's
    clothing and announcements of special sales in these lines
    which you receive through the mails?   (Check one)
       Much interested   Slightly interested
       Interested   Not interested
11. What criticisms have you to offer of the firm's merchandise
    or service?
12. What suggestions have you as to how the firm can improve
    its service to its customers?

Figure 16:   Questionnaire used in investigation on boys' clothing

Responses were obtained by personal interviews from a
total of 400 mothers, located in the eight typical sections
into which the city and the surrounding territory were
divided.   Fifty mothers were interviewed in each of these
eight districts.

These eight districts may be described as follows:

District No. I was an urban section, in which foreigners
predominated, and in which a considerable number of the
lower classes of laboring men as well as a considerable
number of union labor men lived.

District No. II included largely the middle and upper
types of residential section, containing office workers, business and professional men.

District No. III contained for the most part the medium-
class families, including also a considerable number of union
and skilled workmen.

District No. IV was a nearby small college town.   Districts Nos. V, VI, VII, and VIII were rural sections, including small villages.

The results are tabulated in Table 36 by districts, for the purpose of showing the similarities or differences among these various sections.

Question 1. How much of the boys' clothing do you buy?
a. Boys under 13?   b. Boys 13 to 18?

Question 2. How much of the boys' clothing is bought by your husband?
a. Boys under 13?   b. Boys 13 to 18?

TABLE 36

RESULTS OF INVESTIGATION AMONG PARENTS ON BOYS' CLOTHING

District	Percentage of Clothing Bought by Mother		Percentage of Clothing Bought by Father	
	Boys Under 13	Boys Over 13	Boys Under 13	Boys Over 13
I (Urban—foreign laborers)	86.9%	86.6%	13.1%	13.3%
II (Urban—best)	86.7	50.0	13.2 (Boy buys 36.8%)	13.1
III (Urban—medium and union labor)	76.5	81.2	23.4	18.7
IV (Suburban)	98.5	50 0	1.5 (Boy buys 3.4%)	46.6
V (Rural)	76.5	51.5	23.5	48.5
VI (Rural)	83.3	78.1	16.6	21.8
VII (Town and Rural)	72.0	43.3	27.0 (Boy buys 17.0%)	56.0
VIII (Town and Rural)	54.0 (Boy buys 5.0%)	41.0	46.0 (Boy buys 15.0%)	39.0
Average	79.3%	60.2%	20.5%	32.1%

The table shows that the mothers buy by far the largest percentage of clothing for boys under 13 years of age, the average being 79.3%. This fact had been already recognized to some extent by the management of the store, but not to the degree which these facts would seem to warrant. In the first seven districts, the mother bought in no case less than 72% of the younger boy's clothing. The percentage

TABLE 37

RESULTS OF QUESTIONNAIRE ON BRANDS FOR BOYS' CLOTHING

District	Brands	Per Cent
I (Urban—foreign and labor classes)	Sampeck	6.0
	Kuppenheimer	3.0
	Widow Jones	3.0
	No preference	87.9
II (Urban—best)	Hart, Schaffner & Marx	13.2
	Sampeck	5.6
	Campus Togs	3.8
	Wooltex	3.8
	Xtragood	3.8
	Paul Jones	3.8
	No preference	71.4
III (Urban—medium and union labor)	Hart, Schaffner & Marx	1.7
	No preference	98.3
IV (Better class of suburban trade)	Society Brand	29.1
	Hirsch-Wickwire	27.0
	Sampeck	10.4
	Hart, Schaffner & Marx	10.4
	Kuppenheimer	10.4
	No preference	12.5
V (Medium—Rural)	Hart, Schaffner & Marx	3.9
	No preference	96.1
VI (Rural—Bohemian)	Hart, Schaffner & Marx	25.0
	Sampeck	6.6
	Society Brand	6.6
	Xtragood	6.6
	No preference	56.7
VII (Medium—Town and Rural)	Hart, Schaffner & Marx	6.0
	Sampeck	2.0
	No preference	92.0
VIII (Medium and Better, Town and Rural)	Hart, Schaffner & Marx	9.3
	Styleplus	3.1
	No preference	87.6

is as high as 86% for the first two districts (urban). The highest percentage bought by mothers was in the suburban college district, where the figure rose to 98.5%. For boys over 13, the average amount of the clothing expenditure made by the mother was 60.2%.

Boys under 13 years, according to the table, buy practically none of their own clothing; boys over 13 purchase an average of 6.7% of their own clothing. The amount bought by the father, in each case, is relatively small—an average of 20.5% for boys under 13 and 32.1% for boys over that age.

The management of the store concluded that these results should receive careful consideration in the future advertising procedure. That is, the bulk of the advertising of the boys' department should be directed to mothers. The copy should be prepared, and the mediums should be selected, with this in mind.

Question 3. What brands of boys' and children's garments do you buy and why?

In obtaining the data for Table 37, the interviewers were instructed to make no suggestions, but to leave the question of the brands known and bought entirely to the customer's memory and initiative.

The analysis shows that the mothers did not attach as much importance to the maker's brand, as is commonly supposed. Thus, in district No. III, the union labor district, 98% reported no preference. In the rural sections, districts Nos. V, VII, and VIII, 96%, 92%, and 87% respectively had no brand preference or knowledge of brands. The suburban college district, No. IV, showed a striking contrast to all the others, since only 12.5% of the mothers interviewed stated that they had no preference for some particular brand.

Society Brand Clothes had the highest preference of all in any one district, namely in the suburban college area, where this brand was preferred by 29.1% of the mothers.

For all districts taken as a whole, the Hart, Schaffner & Marx brand stood highest, receiving a 25% preference in rural district No. VI, 13.2% in urban district No. 11 (Best), 9.3% in rural district No. VIII (Medium and better), and 6% in rural district No. VII. With the exception of urban district No. II (Best), the chief preference for Hart, Schaffner & Marx clothes came from the rural areas. Moreover, it is probably true that this preference was not particularly for boys' garments, but for the brand in general.

Apparently it is only the brands that have been pushed with unusual persistency through national mediums which have penetrated appreciably into the consciousness of the average consumer. At least this is true as far as the mothers, the buyers of boys' clothing, are concerned. The store in question here had been consistently pushing the Hart, Schaffner & Marx name for years. This, of course, had been in the clothes for men. Thus, although this firm had been making boys' garments for only about one year prior to this investigation, it would seem nevertheless that the number of mothers indicating a preference for this line is comparatively small. Except for suburban district No. IV and rural district No. VI, the preference for other brands was almost inappreciable. The highest preference for Sampeck clothes was in the former section, where they were preferred by 10.4% of the mothers. The store had been advertising the Sampeck brand for a number of years.

In view of these facts, it is open to question to what extent, as a matter of policy, it is advisable for the retailer to emphasize makers' brands. Manufacturers of brands which have not been advertised nationally to any extent should not be given a prominent place in the general advertising copy of the retailer, since there is little good-will attaching to the name, except in so far as the dealer himself creates it. Instead of creating good-will for the maker, the retailer would prefer rather to use his advertising appropriation for pushing his own name among his customers. However, brands such as Hart, Schaffner & Marx, Sampeck, and Society Brand, which are familiar to the parents in this territory, would offer some advantage to the retailer. These brands have been advertised nationally to such an extent that the boys' department of the store would derive some advantage by using the names in its advertising copy. This retailer, however, was inclined to conclude in view of the data shown in the above table, that he should not stress the manufacturers' brands as extensively as he had in the past.

TABLE 38

QUALITY OF BOYS' GARMENTS WANTED, AS SHOWN BY PRICE

District	Prices of Overcoats		Prices of Suits	
	Under 13	Over 13	Knee Pant	Long Pant
I (Urban—foreign laborers)	$ 8.66	$23.75	$ 9.45	$29.71
II (Urban—best)	13.33	32.53	13.43	36.40
III (Urban—medium and union labor)	11.69	21.60	13.77	24.40
IV (Suburban)	11.76	27.03	13.50	34.82
V (Rural—medium)	9.53	13.71	13.00	24.06
VI (Rural—Bohemian)	9.00	26.00	11.97	39.62
VII (Medium—Town and Rural)	8.94	25.12	11.01	28.96
VIII (Medium and better, Town and Rural)	9.66	26.25	10.14	25.06

The only exception to this conclusion that he planned to make was in the suburban college district, where a considerable preference was shown for two brands. He decided to push these brands in this particular district, especially in view of the fact brought out by other parts of the present investigation, that the store was rather weak in this section.

Question 4. What prices approximately do you pay for your children's outer garments?

a. Overcoats: Children under 13; Boys 13-18.

b. Suits: Knee pant suits; Long pant suits.

The quality of merchandise wanted is fairly well indicated by the prices usually paid. For this reason Question 4 was included. The results in Table 38 must be interpreted in the light of conditions in 1919, as the investigation was made in the late fall and early winter of 1919-1920.

This table deserves careful study. First, it will be observed that the returns from the first four districts, the urban sections, agree quite closely. A similar agreement exists among the four rural communities. The range of prices of overcoats for boys under 13 years is very narrow, namely, from $8.66 for district No. I to $13.33 for district No. II, in the city sections, and from $8.94 to $9.66 for the rural communities. It is evident that the urban customer, on the whole, pays a higher price for children's overcoats than does the rural dweller.

The prices paid for the older boys' overcoats vary, in the urban sections, from $21.60 to $32.53. It should be noted that district No. I pays $23.75 for the older boys' overcoats, as against $21.60 paid by district No. III (Medium). Among the rural sections, there is little variation with respect to the older boys' outer garments, with the exception of district No. V, where the amount paid for this item is very low, namely $13.71. This may be due to the fact that in the middle and cheaper class rural communities the older boys more often wear mackinaws in place of the more expensive overcoats.

In suits for younger boys, district No. I (foreign and labor) pays less than any other section. On the other hand, an important fact to note is that it pays more even than district No. III in suits for older lads. Apparently the older boys in district No. I are in the market for better and high-grade merchandise. They earn their own money and are willing to spend it. The older boys in other districts attend high schools more generally and so probably do not have as much money for clothing. Furthermore, district No. I pays an average of $126.64, in outfitting its older boys (per year), as compared with $96.97 and $93.21 in the other districts. (See Table 39.) Table No. 38 shows that district No. VI, a rural section, where the foreign element is an important factor, pays as much or more for its older boys' suits than any other rural district. In overcoats for the same boys, this rural section ranks approximately with the better class rural community.

How Much Does It Cost to Completely Clothe a Boy for One Year (Under Prices Prevailing During the Last 12 Months)?

(Give your own individual experience)

I. Boys under 13 years:				II. Boys 13-18 years of age:			
Article	Number Per Yr.	Cost Each	Total Cost	Article	Number Per Yr.	Cost Each	Total Cost
Suits				Suits			
Overcoats				Overcoats			
(Mackinaws)				(Mackinaws)			
Hats Caps				Hats Caps			
Sweaters				Sweaters			
(Jerseys)				(Jerseys)			
Odd Trousers				Odd Trousers			
Underwear				Underwear			
Hose				Hose			
Supporters				Supporters			
Suspenders				Suspenders Belts			
Belts				Blouses			
Blouses				Ties Collars			
Ties Collars				Soft Collars			
Bathrobe				Bathrobe			
Raincoat				Raincoat			
Shoes				Shoes			
Miscellaneous				Miscellaneous			

Figure 17: Questionnaire used to secure information on the cost of clothing for a boy

On the other hand, the results show that, in both overcoats and suits for boys under 13, district No. I pays less than any other of the eight districts. The younger boys are entirely dependent upon their parents.

The store decided to embody these findings in a definite policy by consistently advertising to district No. I cheaper grade merchandise for the boys under 13 and high-class goods for the older boys. The store, as shown by other portions of the present investigation, was not especially strong in district No. I.

TABLE 39

RESULTS OF QUESTIONNAIRE SHOWING COST OF CLOTHING FOR A BOY

Article	Boys under 13	Boys 13-18
Suits	$19.46	$39.15
Overcoats (and mackinaws)	8.10	16.15
Hats	.50	1.38
Caps	2.16	4.11
Sweaters (and Jerseys)	2.07	3.15
Odd and extra trousers	4.22	6.39
Underwear	4.15	5.94
Hose	4.86	4.31
Supporters, suspenders, and belts	.96	1.09
Blouses and shirts	4.25	10.61
Ties	.94	3.44
Collars	.22	1.79
Bathrobes	.24	.37
Raincoats	.78	1.32
Shoes	11.68	17.19
Miscellaneous	.99	1.05
Totals	$65.81	$117.23
Totals (exclusive of shoes)	54.13	100.04

The store did not handle shoes.

Totals by districts:

District No. I (Urban—foreign laborers)	$56.61	$126.64
District No. Ia	66.50	96.97
District No. II (Urban—best)	78.40	152.09
District No. III (Urban—medium and union labor)	61.73	93.21

The figures shown here give a clue to the prices and hence the quality of the merchandise which should be advertised in each of the various districts.

In order to obtain further detailed information on the cost of clothing a boy, a special questionnaire sheet was prepared and 200 mothers in the four city districts (50 in each district) were interviewed. The mothers were told that no names or addresses were being recorded on the data sheets, so that they might give accurate and unbiased information as freely as possible.

The questionnaire sheet shown in Figure 17 was used.

The results were tabulated by districts. The averages for all districts are given in Table 39.

TABLE 40

COMPARISON OF EXPENDITURE FOR VARIOUS ITEMS OF CLOTHING
WITH TOTAL SALES OF THESE ITEMS BY THE STORE

Article	Percentage of Total Budget of Boys' Clothing	Percentage of Total Sales in Boys' Department
Suits	31.4	41.8
Overcoats and mackinaws	13.1	12.7
Hats and caps	4.4	6.2
Sweaters and jerseys	2.9	3.7
Odd trousers	6.0	5.5
Underwear	5.9	2.3
Hose	5.4	1.6
Supporters, snaps, etc.	1.2	.4
Blouses and shirts	7.8	5.3
Ties	2.2	.7
Collars	.9	.3
Bathrobes	.4	.9
Raincoats	1.2	1.1
Total	82.8	82.8

One of the uses made of the above figures was the comparison between the amount of expenditure for each item in a boy's budget and the actual sales of each item by the store. In this manner it was possible to determine whether the store was relatively strong or weak in the various items. For this purpose the figures for the boys under 13 and over 13 were combined and expressed in percentages of expenditure for each item in relation to the total budget. These figures are given in the first column of Table 40. The second column gives the percentage of sales of each item in relation to the total sales in the boys' department. It will be seen for example that the store was strong in suits, hats and caps, sweaters and jerseys but weak in underwear, hosiery, blouses and shirts.

These percentages do not total 100 because miscellaneous items (2.7%) and shoes (14.6%) are omitted as they were not sold by this store.

At this point a further comparison concerning expenditures for boys' clothing was made by having the salesmen in the boys' department of the store estimate the cost of the various items in completely outfitting a boy for one year. These estimates, as shown in Table 41, were made by the salesmen for boys in three urban districts as based on their general impression in selling boys' clothing.

TABLE 41

COMPARISON OF SALESMEN'S ESTIMATES OF BUYING POWER
WITH RESULTS OF CONSUMER INVESTIGATION

	Boys under 13		Boys over 13	
	Estimates by Salesmen	Consumer Results	Estimates by Salesmen	Consumer Results
Boy in District I (Urban-foreign laborers)	$ 66.87	$56.61	$ 83.82	$126.64
Boy in District II (Urban-best)	154.57	78.40	196.96	152.09
Boy in District III (Urban-medium and union labor)	121.70	61.73	147.67	93.21

In every instance except the first, there is a wide divergence between the salesmen's estimates and the results obtained in the investigation with the mothers. In the case of the boy under 13 years, the estimates of the salesmen for districts Nos. II and III were practically double the amounts actually expended. In the case of boys over 13, the salesmen overestimated about 50%.

In view of the fact that the same questionnaire was put into the hands of the salesmen as was submitted to the mothers, and that the salesmen were asked to use considerable care in making their estimates so that they would fairly represent the annual expenditure for the average boy in a given district, the danger of relying on such estimates, as a basis for an advertising campaign, becomes apparent. The salesmen and the executives of a store are so close to the business and their point of view is so much that of the seller that their estimates are likely to be untrustworthy. These divergencies emphasize the importance of getting information directly from the consumer rather than having someone guess about the consumer.

Question 5. What do you consider most important in buying boys' and children's clothing? (Rank in order of importance.)

Table 42 gives the median rank of each appeal as computed from the individual rankings made by the mothers interviewed in each district. In the second column for each district are given the ranks of these medians. Thus, in district No. I, "Material" had a median rank of 1.6, which is the smallest median and therefore is ranked first as the strongest appeal. If every mother had ranked it first, the median would have been 1., but some ranked it second or third or even fourth. The median of all these was 1.6.

"Material" stands in first place in each of the six districts as the most important consideration in the minds of the mothers in buying boys' clothing. While there is little variation on this appeal among the different sections, district No. IV places even more emphasis on this factor, the rating here being 1.3, as against 1.5 or above for each of the other areas.

The strong appeal of price in all but district No. II should be noted. This section contains the middle and well-to-do population of the city. Style was given a high rank and very nearly the same rank in all sections, its lowest position being in rural district No. V, where it stood fifth, and

TABLE 42

RELATIVE STRENGTH OF APPEALS FOR BOYS' CLOTHING

Districts	I		II		III		IV		V		VI		Average
Appeals	(Urban-foreign)		(Urban-best)		(Urban-medium & Union)		(Sub-urban)		(Rural-medium)		(Rural)		
	Median Rank		Median Rank		Median Rank		Median Rank		Median Rank		Median Rank		Average
Material	1.6	1	1.5	1	1.6	1	1.3	1	1.6	1	1.6	1	1.5
Durability	3.8	4	2.7	2	2.5	2	6.7	7	2.1	2	4.3	5	3.7
Style	3.6	3	5.8	4	2.9	3	4.2	3	4.9	5	3.3	2	4.2
Fit	5.4	6	5.5	3	2.9	4	4.6	4	4.5	4	3.8	4	4.4
Price	2.6	2	6.9	8	2.9	4	3.7	2	4.2	3	3.3	2	3.9
Comfort	5.6	5	6.8	7	3.1	11	6.4	6	5.0	6	5.9	6	5.5
Tailoring	6.3	7	7.1	9	3.1	9	7.6	10	6.5	7	6.8	7	6.2
Merchant's Guarantee	8.3	9	6.4	6	3.0	7	6.8	8	7.4	12	7.0	9	6.5
Reputation of Firm	7.3	8	6.4	5	3.1	9	8.7	11	7.4	11	7.6	8	6.7
Satisfaction or Money Back Guarantee	9.3	11	9.2	11	3.2	12	5.3	5	7.3	10	8.8	12	7.2
Maker's Guarantee	8.3	10	7.8	10	3.2	13	9.1	12	7.4	12	7.6	9	8.2
Wear Like Iron	11.0	13	9.7	12	2.9	6	6.8	9	7.1	8	7.8	11	7.5
Union Made	9.9	12	10.2	13	3.0	7	11.7	13	7.3	9	8.8	12	7.8

its highest rank in district No. VI, where it stood second. The importance attached to style is further evidence in support of the earlier statement that even the rural and laboring sections attach considerable importance to style and buy good grades of merchandise.

Maker's Guarantee, which has to do with the idea of branded merchandise and the fact that the manufacturer stands back of the goods, is apparently a relatively low appeal with these mothers and does not seem to carry as much weight as one would anticipate. This is in accord with the preceding data on the question of brand familiarity and preference. There is still considerable opportunity for manufacturers to develop brand knowledge. "Union

Made" ranked lowest in the various sections taken as a whole. It stood in thirteenth place in two districts—in No. II, a high class section, and in No. IV, the suburban college district. It stood near the bottom in all areas except in district No. III, union labor district, where it was ranked seventh. District No. III also attached the least importance to Maker's Brands, showing no preference in 98.5% of the cases. The appeal of Maker's Guarantee was given last place in this district.

In view of this attitude on the part of consumers, no emphasis should probably be placed on "Union Made" or "Maker's Guarantee" as selling points. In fact, there is hardly enough weight attached to them, except in one or two instances to warrant their use at all.

The ranking accorded Durability and Fit, averaging fifth and sixth places respectively, would justify the featuring of these appeals. The idea of fit had been neglected in the advertising of this store as will be pointed out later. Since consumers attach importance to this factor, it should be emphasized. Moreover, Comfort, receiving an average ranking of sixth, deserves attention. Apparently slogans such as "Satisfaction or Money Back," a Hart, Schaffner & Marx favorite, and "Wears Like Iron" do not have as much weight with consumers as is commonly supposed. It is also important to note that appeals having to do with the reputation of the firm, its size, its age, etc., are rated by consumers as weak. As between Merchant's Guarantee and Maker's Guarantee, it is to be noted that the former received an average ranking of eighth place, as compared with twelfth place for the latter.

Question No. 7. Is there a particular salesman whom you prefer to have wait on you? a. If so, why do you prefer this particular salesman?

A particular salesman was preferred by 23.4% of the customers.

Reason for Preference	Number of Cases	Reason for Preference	Number of Cases
Friend	13	Reliable	2
Acquainted	12	Accustomed to	1
Knows wants	10	Like him	1
Relative	5	On square	1
Pleases	3	Good service	1
Accommodating	3	Miscellaneous	4
Courteous	3	No reason	12
Pleasant	2		

The highest preference for some particular salesman (48%) was in district No. II, the best section of the city, and the next highest preferences were in district No. I (foreign and labor) (34%), and in a rural section (37%) in which there was a large proportion of foreigners. These results were called to the attention of the salesmen and special stress was placed upon the establishment of personal contact and acquaintances with customers.

Data on questions 6, 9, 10, and 11 are omitted as they have primarily a local significance. The returns to question 8 are omitted as they were not sufficiently complete or accurate to be satisfactory.

After an investigation has been completed, certain defects become obvious and improvements may be easily suggested. For example, it would probably have been desirable to obtain the results of boys according to three age groups, up to 6, 6 to 13, 13 to 18, since wash suits are worn considerably by the younger boys. It also would have been desirable to ascertain the brand familiarity and preference on the part of the fathers and on the part of the older boys.

GENERAL CONCLUSIONS AND SUGGESTIONS

1. Although the direct purpose of this investigation was to serve as a basis for planning the advertising in order to bring about an immediate increase in sales, the building of *permanent* good-will and the tying-in of the boys as life-

time customers should be the main objectives.   Hence a long-range policy should be followed.

2.   The advertising should be distributed in and among the present and potential population markets with four factors in mind: First, the total boy population; second, the character of the boy population, whether urban or rural, well-to-do or medium; third, the amount of business which the boys' department has been drawing from any particular area; and fourth, the distance from the city.

3.   In view of the fact that 60% of the urban boy population of the present and potential market population was found in 23 towns and that these towns are likely centers for an even larger rural population, the advertising should be concentrated accordingly.

4.   In distributing the advertising appropriation, the store should appreciate the fact that the city itself contains less than one-fifth of the boy population of the present market, and less than one-eighth of the total boy population for the present and the potential areas together.

5.   With reference to the present market, special advertising drives should be made in those towns and rural areas from which relatively small numbers of customers are coming as shown by the customer addresses obtained in the test records covering 11 business days.   With respect to the potential market, special advertising emphasis should likewise be placed on certain areas which seem to be weak.

6.   In view of present customer-distribution within the city itself, the boys' department should especially seek to strengthen its position in district No. I (foreign population) and in certain portions of district No. III.

7.   In view of present customer-distribution throughout the territory, that is, in regard to the classes of trade from which the department draws the bulk of its customers, it is evident that the store should concentrate its efforts on the upper 75% or 80% of the available business.   The advertising policy should be adjusted accordingly.

8. In allotting the advertising expenditure and in preparing the copy, the buying power of any particular district, both in total and for particular articles, as indicated by the results of the investigation, should be considered.

9. Since, according to buying power, the department was not getting its normal share of the business in 3 of the 13 counties, special advertising should be consistently applied in these counties.

10. There are substantial grounds for the theory that the foreign section, while buying low-class merchandise for the boys under 13 years, tends to buy the medium- and better-grade goods for the older boys. Since the strength of the department is considerably below normal with this class, a special advertising drive should be carried on with the above factors in mind.

11. The buying power of the market, the advantages to the department purely from an advertising standpoint, and the peculiarly favorable situation for selling would seem to warrant the establishment of a shoe section. (The store did not sell shoes.)

12. Since the greater part of the boys' clothing is bought by mothers, there should be a conscious direction of the bulk of the advertising to mothers. Copy should be framed and mediums should be selected with this in mind.

13. As a general policy, less emphasis should probably be placed on maker's brands.

14. The quality of clothing which is to be advertised in any particular district should, in general, be regulated by the prices paid as indicated by the results obtained in this portion of the investigation.

15. The average number of garments bought per boy per year, in other words, the number of times the customer comes into the store, should be considered in mapping out the advertising.

16. Since the results indicated the desirability of tying-up the customer to particular salesmen and that the cus-

tomer likes this personal interest, the department, as a matter of policy, should place emphasis on this factor.

17. The types of appeals used in the copy should be in accordance with their relative strength in the minds of consumers, as shown by the tests. The appeals of Price, Maker's Guarantee, and Reputation of the Firm, which have been used frequently in the advertising of the boys' department, should be reduced and a corresponding increase in emphasis should be placed on Material, Durability, Style, and Fit. The other appeals should be employed according to their values.

18. The failure of the estimates, even as made by experienced men in the department, with respect to the buying power of the population and the relative strength of appeals, to correlate with the actual returns from the field investigation shows that, as a matter of policy, the department should make its plans on the basis of the consumer investigations.

19. In order to build up trade on Monday, Tuesday, and Wednesday, the low days of the week, more advertising pressure should be applied on Saturday, Monday, and Tuesday, and possibly a plan of "Monday Specials" should be considered.

20. The choice of mediums should involve a consideration of the following factors: First, distribution of boy population; second, the buying power of particular sections of the population; third, present customer-distribution; fourth, the character and circulation of mediums with reference to particular classes and districts; fifth, the relative standing of the various mediums with consumers.

X

SAMPLE INVESTIGATION AMONG DEALERS
AND CONSUMERS: PAINT

Coordination of dealer and consumer investigations. Consumer investigation—questions used. Advertising arguments of most importance from the point of view of the consumer. Consumer's familiarity with brands. Relation between familiarity with brands and advertising of those brands. Memory value of appeals and illustrations in advertising. Percentage of consumers influenced more or less by advertisements. The dealer investigation. Most important qualities in the selection of a particular brand. Best advertising arguments from the dealer's point of view. Analysis of advertising campaigns of four large firms. Conclusion regarding individual campaigns.

THE purpose of this chapter is to illustrate the coordination of two sections of an investigation for the same product carried out among dealers and consumers, in which the responses were obtained in part by mail and in part by personal interview. Hence two sets of questions, one for dealers and one for consumers, were prepared, covering in part the same points and in part different points.

Aside from these questions of method, the purpose of the investigation was to make a study of advertising in the paint industry, and to suggest as a result of such a study possible ways of increasing its effectiveness. The results of the questionnaire inquiry were therefore compared with the methods employed in four paint advertising campaigns. A brief summary of the two sections of the inquiry, dealer and consumer, are presented in Figures 18 and 19.

Sixty-two persons, 56 men and 6 women, in metropolitan Boston were personally interviewed by means of this questionnaire. Practically all of these persons were owners of homes and represented a considerable variety of occupations.

Consumer's Name   Address   Male   Female

1. Do you buy paint by brands?
   Usually   Sometimes   Seldom
2. If yes, what brand or brands?
3. Why do you prefer the particular brand or brands mentioned? (Number in order of preference: 1 to 12, e.g. (a)—1, (g)—2, (c)—3, etc.)
   a. Variety of uses
   b. Durability
   c. Attractiveness of colors
   d. Ease of application
   e. Sets perfectly even
   f. Cheapness
   g. Dries quickly
   h. Dries hard
   i. Recommended by dealer
   j. Recommended by architect
4. Which of the following qualities do you consider to be of most importance? (Number in order of chief use: 1 to 11, e.g. (b)—1, (f)—2, etc.)
   a. Protects against wear
   b. Protects against disintegration
   c. Gives help to unemployed
   d. Civic pride
   e. Makes property easier to keep clean
   f. Increases the selling value
   g. Brightens the home
   h. Frees premises from infection
   i. Beautifies the property
5. Do you use more paint now than a year or so ago?
   Much more   More   Some more   Uncertain
6. With what brands of paint are you familiar?
7. Which ones have you seen advertised?
   Where?   Name magazines   Name other mediums
8. What do you remember about the advertisements?
   About the pictures?   About the text?
9. Do you think you have been influenced towards buying paint by the advertising you have seen?
   Very much   Much   Some   Uncertain
10. Has your attention been directed to the "Save the Surface" campaign now being conducted?   Yes   No

11. Where have you seen it advertised?
    Name magazines   Name other mediums
12. What do you remember about the advertisements?
    About the pictures?   About the text?
13. Do you think you have been influenced towards buying
    paint by the "Save the Surface" campaign?
    Very much   Much   Some   Uncertain
14. What general magazines do you read regularly?
    Which one do you prefer?

Figure 18:   Questionnaire used in consumer investigation

Question No. 2. If yes (i. e., buy by brands), what brand

	Per Cent
Usually	34
Sometimes	51
Seldom	14

Question No. 2. If yes (i. e., buy by brands), what brand
or brands?

TABLE 43

RESULTS OF INVESTIGATION ON USE OF PAINTS BY BRANDS

Brand	Per Cent of Total Replies	Brand	Per Cent of Total Replies
Lowe Brothers	20.3	Santa Cote	1.6
Sherwin-Williams	15.7	Mello Gloss	1.6
Devoe & Reynolds Co., Inc.	7.9	McMurtry	1.6
		*Kyanize	1.6
Bennett's	7.9	Gould & Cutler	1.6
Patton's	7.9	Witherall	1.6
Carpenter Morton	6.2	Dexter Brothers	1.6
*Valspar	6.2	Colonial	1.6
Acme	4.7	Buffalo	1.6
Pratt & Lambert	3.1	Murphy's	1.6
Seymour's	3.1	Fuller's	1.6
Wadsworth Howland	3.1	New Era	1.6
Watson Hallett	1.6	Lucas	1.6

* Indicates varnishes only.

Twenty-five different brands were mentioned. With the exception of two of them, practically every one is a nationally advertised brand. While Lowe Brothers heads the list with 20.3% of the total number, and Sherwin-Williams is second with 15.7%, the former figure was influenced somewhat by the fact that five or six questionnaires were filled out by customers of a store carrying Lowe Brothers' paints.

Question No. 3. Why do you prefer the particular brand or brands mentioned?

	Average Rank		Average Rank
Durability	2.2	Variety of uses	5.7
Ease of application	4.1	Dries hard	5.7+
Attractiveness of colors	4.8	Recommended by dealer	6.1
Sets perfectly even	4.9	Recommended by architect	6.1
Dries quickly	5.6	Cheapness	7.6

The above question was asked for the purpose of determining which of the advertising arguments for particular brands were considered of most importance from the point of view of the consumer.

It will be noted that the "Durability" appeal was considered by a large margin first in importance by the consumers. Probably the reason for this attitude is that it is generally felt that if a paint is durable, it usually will possess the other qualities which are desirable.

Another argument which has very strong weight is "Ease of application." It was ranked second. While it is admitted among dealers that, as a general rule, one paint is about as easy to apply as another, this argument stands sufficiently high to justify its rather extensive use in consumer advertising.

"Attractiveness of colors" was rated third. As a matter of fact this argument is similar to that of "Ease of application," inasmuch as the colors are considered to be almost equally good in most of the standard brands. But, since it appeals to the consuming public, it should be used to a considerable degree by the dealers in their advertisements.

"Sets perfectly even" was ranked fourth in importance. This point was ranked seventh by the dealers. (The reader may compare the data for corresponding questions with the dealer list discussed later in this chapter.) The reason for this difference of opinion is that the dealer has a more intimate knowledge of paint than has the average consumer. All dealers know that any good paint will "set perfectly even" if applied properly; hence they consider it a relatively unimportant selling point. That consumers do not possess this information, however, is evidenced by the fact that they place it so high on the list. It brings up the question of a choice between educating the public to its relative unimportance or taking advantage of this argument as a good selling point.

"Dries quickly" is ranked fifth by the consumers, as it was by the dealers. This comparatively high rating by the consumers may in part be due to the possibility that it is not very generally understood among them that drying too quickly may actually be a bad feature in paint.

"Variety of uses" was placed sixth by the consumers. This ranking indicates that a paint which has a variety of uses is very seldom expected to be the best one to employ for any specific purpose. This point was mentioned by the dealers when they were interviewed.

The "Dries hard" appeal was placed next to last by the consumers, probably because it has been their experience that all paints were about the same so far as this quality is concerned, and that any of them would become hard enough for the purposes to which it was put. Few of the consumers with whom the investigator talked considered this point at all important as an advertising argument.

The two appeals "Recommended by dealer" and "Recommended by architect" were included in the consumer questionnaire in order to make a comparison between these influences and other reasons why a consumer was influenced to buy a certain brand. The dealer's recommendation was ranked eighth, while the architect's recommendation was placed last in practically every instance. The average paint consumer seldom comes in contact with architects and this explains the fact that he places this argument last on the list. The consumer, however, must inevitably come in contact with the dealer on each occasion when a purchase is made. For this reason it is rather surprising that a larger percentage of consumers did not indicate influence by the dealer. On the other hand, however, this influence is likely to be more or less unconscious on the part of the consumer. He is, therefore, in many cases influenced to buy a particular brand, even though he may not realize it.

"Cheapness" was placed ninth on the list, probably because it is becoming more generally known to be poor economy to use a cheap grade of paint. The reason is that in most instances the cost of applying the paint is greater than the cost of the paint itself. Hence, it pays to apply the best wearing paint that can be obtained.

Question No. 4. Which of the following qualities do you consider to be of most importance?

Appeal	Average Rank
Protects against disintegration	3.1
Protects against wear	3.1+
Beautifies the property	3.7
Brightens the home	3.9
Increases the selling value	4.8
Makes property easier to keep clean	5.1
Frees premises from infection	6.3
Civic pride	6.6
Gives help to unemployed	8.2

These general advertising arguments were selected, as were those in question No. 3, from the campaigns of several national advertisers and from the "Save the Surface" campaign of 1922.

"Protection against wear" and "Protection against disintegration" were first in the list of arguments, as graded by the customers, both receiving an average of 3.1.

"Beautifies the property," which obviously is an important selling point for paint, was given third position.

Fourth in importance, from the consumer's point of view, is "Brightens the home or plant," because, as has been noted before, paint is now being used more extensively than ever before to lighten plants and to brighten homes and make them more cheerful.

"Increases the selling value" was placed fifth. Several consumers who were interviewed seemed to be very much impressed by an advertisement which suggested that a coat of paint—costing but little—would add very materially to the mortgage value of their property.

"Makes property easier to keep clean" was considered a fairly good appeal, although not as good as those mentioned before. It was graded sixth by the consumers as well as by both groups of dealers.

"Frees premises from infection," which received the rank of seven, was held to be unimportant because this usage for paint is very limited, in so far as the ordinary consumer is concerned.

"Civic pride" was also rated as a very weak argument. Consumer felt, generally, that if, by painting their property, they could thereby add to the beauty of the city, they would be pleased to do so; but to paint for this reason solely, they considered out of the question.

The same general line of reasoning was held by consumers with regard to the "Gives help to the unemployed" appeal. Here, too, they felt that if, when they decided to paint, they could thereby give some unemployed man work, that that was very desirable—but to paint for this motive only had little weight. Yet these appeals were being used in advertisements at the time of this study.

Question No. 5. Do you use more paint now than a year or so ago?

	Per Cent		Per Cent
Much more	12	Some more	15
More	15	Uncertain	56

As will be noticed, 42% of the consumers were buying at least some more paint than a year or so before, while 12% were buying much more. The reasons for this increase, as has been pointed out above, were: (1) lower costs; (2)

TABLE 44

RESULTS OF INVESTIGATION SHOWING FAMILIARITY OF BRANDS AMONG PAINT BUYERS

Brand	Per Cent of Total Replies	Brand	Per Cent of Total Replies
Sherwin-Williams	52.8	Santa Cote	1.9
Lowe Brothers	35.8	Rogers	1.9
Valspar	20.7	Masury	1.9
Acme	20.7	New Era	1.9
Bennett's	15.1	Witherall	1.9
Fuller's	13.2	Gould & Cutler	1.9
Devoe and Reynolds		Dexter Brothers	1.9
Co., Inc.	13.2	United States Navy	
Sun Proof	9.4	Deck Paint	1.9
McMurtry	7.5	Lincoln	1.9
Carpenter Morton	7.5	Bay State	1.9
Lucas	5.7	John's Asbestos Paint	1.9
Colonial	3.7	Seymour's	1.9
Mountain and Plain	3.7	Buffalo	1.9
Wadsworth Howland	3.7	Sears Roebuck	1.9
Patton's	3.7	Atlas	1.9
Moore's	3.7	Heath & Milligan	1.9
Watson Hallett	1.9	McPhee & McGinity	1.9
Aladdin	1.9	Pratt & Lambert	1.9
Berry Brothers	1.9		

increased building activities; (3) aggressive sales and advertising efforts; and (4) unemployment, giving the men more time in which to do the painting.

Question No. 6. With what brands are you familiar?

Thirty-eight different brands were mentioned, or an average of 1.3 brands per consumer. This figure indicates that the average consumer is not very familiar with brand names. There is evidently considerable room for impressing brands of paints on the minds of consumers. Except for the two or three local brands, the order of familiarity is in almost direct proportion to the amount of advertising done by the various firms.

Question No. 7. (a) Which ones (brands) have you seen advertised?

TABLE 45

RESULTS OF INVESTIGATION SHOWING EFFECTS OF ADVERTISING ON PAINT BUYERS

Brand	Per Cent of Persons	Brand	Per Cent of Persons
Sherwin-Williams	43.1	*Berry Brothers	1.7
Lowe Brothers	32.7	Santa Cote	1.7
Sun Proof (Patton's)	15.5	Certainteed	1.7
*Valspar	13.7	Mound	1.7
Acme	13.7	Glidden's	1.7
Bennett's	12.1	Gould & Cutler	1.7
Fuller's	10.4	Dexter Brothers	1.7
Lucas	10.4	Moore's	1.7
Devoe and Reynolds		John's Asbestos Paint	1.7
Co., Inc.	8.6	Colonial	1.7
McMurtry	6.9	Buffalo	1.7
Heath & Milligan	3.5	Sears Roebuck	1.7
Mountain and Plain	3.5	Carpenter Morton	1.7
Bay State	3.5	United States Navy	
Masury	3.5	Deck Paint	1.7
Rogers	3.5	*Kyanize	1.7
*Japalac	3.5	Pratt & Lambert	1.7
Watson & Hallett	1.7	McPhee & McGinity	1.7
Aladdin	1.7	New Era	1.7

* Indicates varnishes only.

Fifty-seven different brands were mentioned. They are ranked very closely in proportion to the amount of advertising done. It will be noted that 43.1% of the consumers remembered having seen Sherwin-Williams advertisements.

This firm is probably, by a considerable margin, the most extensive paint advertiser in the country.

The data on questions 7b, 7c, 11 and 14 will be omitted here, as they are similar to corresponding questions in Chapter VIII.

Question No. 8. What do you remember about the advertisements? (a) About the pictures?

In order to test the memory value of the appeals and illustrations used in paint advertising, the consumers were asked the above question. Thirty-four persons out of 64, it will be noted, remembered something about the pictures. The trade-mark of the Sherwin-Williams Company—a globe over which paint is being poured—was remembered by 30.0% of the total number of persons recalling pictures. Tied with it for first place was the illustration, used by many concerns, of a house in the process of being painted. Next in memory value (26.5%) was the "Valspar" advertisement of a woman pouring hot water on a table top. It is interesting to note that the "Save the Surface" brush was remembered only twice, although it is now generally used in paint advertisements, on stationery, etc.

PICTURES REMEMBERED (BY 34 OUT OF 64 PERSONS)

	Per Cent of Persons
Picture of paint on globe (Sherwin-Williams)	30.0
Man painting house	30.0
Pouring hot water on table (Valspar)	26.5
Painting interior of house	5.7
Women varnishing floor	5.7
"Save the Surface" brush	5.7
Home after being painted	5.7
Colonial doorway	2.9
Colonial man with brush (Wadsworth Howland)	2.9
Rain beating on varnished sill	2.9

Question No. 8. (b) What do you remember about the text?

TEXT REMEMBERED (BY 25 OUT OF 64 PERSONS)

	Per Cent of Persons
Protection against wear, etc.	40
"Save the Surface"	36
"Covers the Earth"	24
Makes for Cleanliness	12
Beautifies	12
Gives Prosperous Appearance	2
Civic Pride	2
Durability	2
Economy	2
Quality	2

Twenty-five persons remembered 10 different items. The idea of protection against wear and disintegration was first, that is, by 40% of those who remembered anything about the text, or by 27% of the total number. This figure strengthens the results of question No. 4. These qualities were considered most important both by dealers and by consumers.

"Save the Surface," which includes about the same idea as the argument just mentioned, was second, with 36%, or 25% of the total number.

Attention may be called to the fact that the qualities which were remembered here were in a general way graded high in the list of arguments in question No. 4.

Question No. 9. Do you think that you have been influenced towards buying paint by the advertisements you have seen?

	Per Cent of Total		Per Cent of Total
Very much	10.1	None	22.0
Much	5.0	Uncertain	18.6
Some	44.0		

About 60% of the consumers felt that they had been influenced more or less by the advertisements they had seen. About 10% stated that they had been very much influenced by them. The reaction to such a question is more likely to be an underestimation than an overestimation. People are influenced more or less unconsciously by impressions which they do not recall at the moment.

Question No. 10. Has your attention been directed to the "Save the Surface" campaign now being conducted?

	Per Cent of Total
Yes	72
No	28

It is interesting to note that a large percentage (72%) of the consumers have observed the advertising of the "Save the Surface" campaign.

Question No. 12. What do you remember about the advertisements in the "Save the Surface" campaign? (a) About the pictures?

Thirteen out of the 64 persons remembered five different pictures. The "Save the Surface" brush was remembered six times, or nearly as often as all the others put together. Rockwell's picture of a boy painting a doll house was second, with three recalls. This picture was used extensively, in a contest, in several mediums.

PICTURES USED IN THE "SAVE THE SURFACE" CAMPAIGN
REMEMBERED BY 13 CONSUMERS

	Per Cent of Total		Per Cent of Total
Brush stroke	46.1	Painted church (old)	7.6
Painting doll house	23.0	Industrial scene	7.6
Painted houses	15.3		

(b) What do you remember about the text?

TEXT USED IN THE "SAVE THE SURFACE" CAMPAIGN
REMEMBERED BY 21 CONSUMERS

	Per Cent of Total
Protection against wear, etc.	43
"Save the Surface and You Save All"	43
Beautifies the property	14
Gives prosperous appearance	9

	Per Cent of Total
Increases selling value	9
Makes for cleanliness	5
Quality	5
Civic Pride	5

Question No. 13. Do you think you have been influenced toward buying paint by the "Save the Surface" campaign?

	Per Cent of Total		Per Cent of Total
Very much	17	Some	30
Much	13	Uncertain	39

Here 60% of the consumers replied that they were at least somewhat influenced by the campaign. Apparently this cooperative campaign has exerted a distinct influence on the buying of paint.

THE DEALER INVESTIGATION

The questionnaire shown in Figure 19 was designed to include a part of the same points covered in the consumer inquiry in order to serve as a check on the results obtained from consumers and also to obtain the dealers' point of view on these points. In addition to such questions, others were included which could be answered only by dealers.

The responses to this questionnaire were obtained by personal interview from 25 dealers in metropolitan Boston and by mail from 75 dealers in the New England states and in New York state. To the latter group, 265 questionnaires were sent, of which 75, or 28.3% of usable returns, were received.

The results on questions No. 1 and No. 6 will be omitted because, while they would be of distinct interest to individual manufacturers of paint, they are not of general importance here.

Question No. 2. Do customers ask for a particular brand?

Dealer's Name   Address

1. What brand or brands of paint do you handle?

2. Do customers ask for a particular brand?
   Usually   Sometimes   Seldom

3. Which of the following qualities do you consider of most im
   portance in the selection of a particular brand?
   (Number in order of importance 1 up to 10, e. g. (b)—1
   (g)—2, (a)—3, etc.)

   a. Variety of uses
   b. Durability
   c. Attractiveness of colors
   d. Ease of application
   e. Sets perfectly even
   f. Cheapness
   g. Dries quickly
   h. Dries hard
   i. Demand created by advertising.

4. Which of the following advertising arguments do you consider most important?   (Number in order of importance,
   1 up to 9.)

   a. Protects against wear
   b. Protects against disintegration
   c. Gives help to unemployed
   d. Civic pride
   e. Makes property easier to keep clean
   f. Increases the selling value
   g. Brightens the home or plant
   h. Frees premises from infection
   i. Beautifies the property.

5. Do you sell more paint now than a year ago?
   Much more   More   Some more   Uncertain

6. What brand or brands, if any, have you advertised recently?

7. Do you think that your paint sales have been influenced by
   your advertisements?
   Very much   Much   Some   Uncertain

8. Do you think that your paint sales have been influenced by
   the "Save the Surface" campaign?
   Very much   Much   Some   Uncertain

Figure 19:   Questionnaire used in dealer investigation

	Mail Returns Per Cent of Total	Personal Interview Returns Per Cent of Total
Usually	30	44
Sometimes	60	29
Seldom	10	27

The data on this question should be compared with the data on question No. 1 in the consumer list. They agree roughly, although there is a considerable difference between the two sets of dealers. This may be due to a partial selection of the mail returns.

Question No. 3. Which of the following qualities do you consider of most importance in the selection of a particular brand?

	Mail Returns		Personal Interview	
	Average	Order	Average	Order
Durability	2.0	1	2.4	1
Attractiveness of colors	4.0	2	4.5	4
Demand created by advertising	4.1	3	3.9	2
Ease of application	4.2	4	4.4	3
Variety of uses	4.5	5	5.5	7
Dries quickly	5.7	6	5.2	5
Sets perfectly even	6.3	7	6.1	8
Dries hard	6.5	8	5.3	6
Cheapness	7.4	9	7.2	9

These two sets of results agree quite closely with each other and with those of question No. 3 in the consumer list.

Question No. 4. Which of the following advertising arguments do you consider most important?

	Mail Returns		Personal Interview	
	Average	Order	Average	Order
Protects against wear	2.3	1	2.0	1
Beautifies the property	3.5	2	4.5	5
Brightens the home or plant	3.8	3	4.0	3
Protects against disintegration	3.8+	4	2.8	2
Increases the selling value	3.9	5	4.1	4
Makes property easier to keep clean	5.6	6	4.8	6
Civic pride	6.5	7	7.5	8
Frees premises from infection	7.0	8	4.5	7
Gives help to unemployed	8.0	9	7.8	9

The purpose of this question is to determine which, from

the dealer's point of view, are the best advertising arguments for paint in general. These appeals were selected from paint advertisements in general, and specifically from the 1922 advertising campaigns of three national advertisers and from the "Save the Surface" campaign for that year. It will be noted that the set of appeals is the same as that used in the consumer investigation.

An appeal used quite extensively in 1922, especially in the "Save the Surface" campaign, was that paint "Gives help to the unemployed." Its actual effectiveness, however, is very doubtful, as it was rated last by both groups of dealers as well as by the consumers.

Question No. 5. Do you sell more paint now than a year ago?

	Mail Returns Per Cent of Total	Personal Interview Per Cent of Total
Much more	12	44
More	36	22
Some more	32	7
Uncertain	19	28

The next step in this study was to analyze the advertising campaign of each of four large firms. For this purpose a complete set of the advertisements in each campaign was examined in portfolio form. The appeals used in each campaign were analyzed and the approximate amount of space given to each appeal in terms of column inches was determined. The relative stress put upon each selling appeal was then compared with the relative importance of that particular selling appeal as indicated by the consumer and dealer results. Briefly the outcome of this comparison was as follows:

CONCLUSIONS REGARDING INDIVIDUAL CAMPAIGNS

A. *Wadsworth Howland Company*

1. This company placed too much stress upon "Variety of Uses" and "Dries hard" appeals.

2. It could profitably make use of "Ease of application," "Sets perfectly even," "Dries quickly," "Brightens the home," "Increases the selling value," and "Makes property easier to keep clean."

B. *Du Pont Company*
   1. This company should partially supplant "Dries quickly" by "Ease of application" and "Attractiveness of colors."
   2. "Dries hard" and "Beautifies the property" should receive less space.
   3. Considerably more space should be allotted to "Increases the selling value" and "Protection against wear" and "Protection against disintegration."

C. *Boston Varnish Company*
   1. It should greatly increase use of "Durability" appeal.
   2. It overstresses "Ease of application" and "Dries quickly."
   3. "Sets perfectly even" should receive appreciably more space.
   4. "Recommended by architect" appeal should be discontinued, or at least used very infrequently.
   5. More space should be given to "Increases the selling value" and "Brightens the home."

D. *"Save the Surface" campaign*
   1. It should give more emphasis to "Protection against wear" and "Beautifies the property."
   2. "Makes property easier to keep clean" and "Frees premises from infection" received too much space for their value as appeals.
   3. It should discontinue "Unemployment" appeal.

PRINCIPLES OF ADVERTISING

PART III

THE APPEALS: BY WHAT APPEALS MAY THE COMMODITY BE SOLD?

XI

ANALYSIS AND SELECTION OF APPEALS

Determining the appeals or selling arguments. A plan for analyzing the possible selling points for a community. Application of plan of analysis to concrete cases. Discovering uses of a product. Analysis of the advertisements of competitors. Analysis of 300 shoe advertisements. Summary of analysis. Analysis of appeals used by a retail store in advertising boys' clothing. Analysis of appeals used by Chicago stores in the advertising of boys' clothing.

THE next important step in analyzing our problem and in preparing the plan for advertising and selling a product is to determine the appeals or selling arguments by which the commodity may most effectively be sold. The first task in this analysis is to determine all the possible appeals which may be used in connection with the particular product concerned. The next task is the selection of the most effective appeals from this list of possible selling points.

Sample Analysis of Appeals for a Toothpaste. Let us assume that the product is a toothpaste put up in the form of a tube. We may examine the product, its qualities, its uses, its manufacturing process, its container, and prepare a long list of all possible selling points somewhat as follows:

Health
White, clean teeth
Taste
Counteracts film on teeth
Prevents acid in mouth
Dentists approve it
Has a wholesome effect on
   the gums
Prevents pyorrhea
Is safe and harmless
Price

Size of tube
Convenience of tube
Leaves pleasant feeling in
   the mouth
Contributes to beauty or
   good appearance
Urge frequent use
Contains no gritty substance
Urge habit of brushing teeth
   regularly
Purifies the breath

Paste is in concentrated form	Ingredients
	Method of manufacture
Large amount of research in the preparation of the paste	Is used widely
	Large manufacturing plant
	Used by well-known persons
Reputation of the firm	

This is a miscellaneous analysis and contains most of the possible selling arguments that might conceivably be used. No doubt the list could be extended still further. Not all of these appeals are of equal value. Some probably could not be used at all. However, before we attempt to select the appeals that might be most effective, or before discussing methods by which such a selection may be made, let us examine another sample analysis of appeals for a different product.

Sample Analysis of Appeals for a Vacuum Cleaner. Let us take as an illustration the possible arguments that might be used for an electric vacuum cleaner.

Simplicity of operation	Freshens colors of rugs
Its mechanical construction	Dealers' service
Contains a revolving brush	Guarantee
Has strong suction power	Prolongs life of rugs
Economy in use both as to time and labor	Removes grit and litter
Uses little electric current	Size of factory
Ease in using	Is used in beautiful homes
Sanitary in use	Straightens the nap of rugs
Keeps dust from spreading	Is recommended by rug importers
Health of family	
Does not injure rugs	Satisfied users
Has variety of uses	Reputation of manufacturer
Is thorough in cleaning	Age and experience of the firm
Is relatively noiseless and quiet	Where it may be bought
Is durable	Appearance
Is light in weight and portable	Takes little room
	Service and repairs
Price	Easy to clean
Method of payment	Free trial
	No furniture to move

Ordinarily we may list our possible selling appeals in a haphazard manner, as was done in the preceding analyses. However, it would be of considerable assistance if we had a plan according to which practically any given product might be analyzed. It is obviously important before any attempt is made at selection to examine all the possible selling points in order that none may be omitted that might prove effective. Therefore I wish to propose the following plan for analyzing a typical manufactured product for the purpose of ascertaining all its possible selling points.

A manufactured product may logically be analyzed from the following four points of view:

1. The raw material from which the product is made
   Source of the raw material
   History—origin
   Selection
   Quality

2. The process of manufacture
   How the commodity is produced
   Special process
   Special equipment—machinery
   Skilled workmanship
   Research in manufacture of article
   Sanitary conditions of manufacture
   Size of factory or business
   Age, experience, and reputation of firm as a sign of
     skill and reliability
   History of process
   Guaranteed quality and construction

3. The finished product—qualities and uses
   Special mechanical features of the finished product
   Its possible impression through the various senses
     The eye—appearance, shape, color, etc.
     The ear—sound
     Touch, taste, smell, motion, etc.
   Varieties of uses and specifications for uses
   Efficiency and thoroughness in accomplishing its uses

Wide usage
Frequency of use
Class of people using the product
Testimonials of users
Testimonials of authorities
Convenience in use
Ease of operation
Effects of using the article
Pleasure in using the article
Guarantee of satisfactory use
The package—its convenience and appearance
Repair service

4. Price and value of the finished product
Price compared with competing articles
Price in relation to quantity and quality of article
Economy in time, labor and convenience
Cheapness of operating the article
Durability

APPLICATION OF PLAN OF ANALYSIS TO CONCRETE CASES

Let us see how this plan of analysis would apply in specific instances. We may return to the two sample analyses of selling points. The samples as given in the preceding paragraphs gave a miscellaneous listing of various selling points. The above-proposed blanket plan for analyzing would be of distinct service in discovering or bringing to mind probably most of the important kinds of selling arguments. Let us now examine the list of selling points for a toothpaste.

First, with regard to raw material, it is possible to develop some valuable and effective selling points based on the source of the material from which the paste was made, the selection and quality of the material. In connection with some products, the history of the material affords a very interesting selling appeal.

With regard to the process of manufacture, the factor of special equipment might not be important in connection with a toothpaste, but it might be important in connection with the manufacture of a vacuum cleaner. The same is true in regard to the question of skilled workmanship. The special process of manufacture might make a very interesting point in connection with a toothpaste. Likewise the history of the process of manufacture may be utilized very effectively in certain connections. The history of the vacuum-cleaning process might be presented in a very attractive and appealing manner.

Sometime ago the Canners' Association ran a series of advertisements based upon the discovery and history of the process of canning foods—how, for example, it was employed in Napoleon's army, and the like. A distributer of butter based some very effective copy on the source of the butter, the history of the breed of milch cows, the sanitary process of producing the butter, and so on. Informative points about the origin of the raw materials and the production and manufacturing process of nearly all commodities afford a fertile source of interesting selling points.

The uses and qualities of the finished product usually afford a greater opportunity for the development of selling points than do probably the raw material or the process of manufacture. A strong appeal in practically every case is the use or the variety of uses to which a product may be put.

DISCOVERING USES OF A PRODUCT

A practical question in this connection is that of obtaining a list of the variety of uses to which a product may be put. The manufacturer many times is not able to anticipate all the uses made of his product. For this reason a profitable plan has been to obtain in some way directly from the users of the product what the various uses are which they make of it.

Probably the most direct and certain method of discovering the uses to which a product is put is by means of the questionnaire field investigations described in preceding chapters. Several questions may ordinarily be included on this subject.

A supplementary source of suggested or actual uses of a product is the letters received from users. Every concern accumulates in the course of time a considerable number of such communications. To make these conveniently available, the advertising department of one of the leading soap manufacturers keeps a complete, classified file of all uses or points obtained from all sources.

Another method quite commonly employed is to institute a contest among consumers and award prizes for the best lists of actual uses submitted. Thus, for example, in 1915 the Bon Ami Company carried on a contest in which it awarded $2,250 in prizes to housewives. The purpose of this contest was to learn to what different uses housewives put Bon Ami in cake form and in powder form. Bon Ami in cake form had been on the market for a considerable number of years, while the powder form was first offered for sale in the fall of 1913. Both forms were selling well, but the company did not know whether the powder was usurping the field held by the cake or whether new uses had been found for the powder which could not well be taken care of by the cake. The contest was announced in magazine advertisements in the spring of 1915. A total of 25,306 persons responded. Many different uses were submitted, both for the cake and for the powder. The winner of the first prize had a total of 706 uses which were allowed by the judges. The following report of the results of the contest indicates to some extent the value of such a contest:

The cake was the overwhelming favorite for mirrors, windows, nickel or stoves, automobiles and plumbing fixtures, silverware and white shoes. The powder was the big favorite for bath tubs, linoleum, tiles and all kinds of kitchen-ware except aluminum-ware, where it was closely tied with cake. Paint was a less important use than we supposed, and silverware was surprisingly big, although we had not advised or advertised Bon Ami for that purpose. Other favorite uses which we had overlooked in our advertising are enameled beds, wicker furniture and baby carriages, cut glass, piano keys, wooden-ware, lamp chimneys, refrigerators, rubber goods, false teeth, and straw hats.

The contest proved to our satisfaction that there is a distinct field for Bon Ami in powdered form, where it does not conflict with the cake. There will be persons, of course, who use one and not the other; we have polled 25,000 housewives, however, and find that a large proportion of them have both sorts on hand and seem to be quite particular which is employed for certain purposes. This is a sufficiently large number for us to base a logical conclusion upon, which we could not do with any information that was previously at our command.

More than this, some of the uses enumerated by the contestants show such a preponderating popularity, either of the old or new form of Bon Ami, that in the future we shall act on this evidence in illustrating our advertisements. For instance, if we picture a maid washing windows we will have her using the cake, and on the other hand, in illustrating a housekeeper in the act of cleaning the bath tub, we will have a can of the powder shown by her side. In the past it was always impossible to know which kind should be shown.

Another result of the contest that is of importance is found in the new uses of the product that have come to light. Some of them seem rather trivial, but it is of importance to us to know that Bon Ami is used quite generally, for instance, in polishing lamp chimneys and cleaning piano keys.

There are many concerns that have paid real money to discover new uses for their products. To the Bon Ami Company these have come as a matter incidental to one of chiefer importance. The big fact which the company wanted to determine was whether or not it was competing with itself, and this has been answered satisfactorily in the negative.[1]

At this juncture, the question arises, how can our blanket analysis plan be applied to a business whose output is service rather than some physical product, such as, for example, a bank. The outline was prepared primarily with a material product made by some process of manufacture in mind. However, it will not be difficult to see that the plan may be applied almost equally well to such a business as banking or investments. As in nearly all instances, certain portions of the outline are not pertinent, but a thor-

---

[1] *Printers' Ink*, Sept. 2, 1915, p. 24.

ough-going application of it will decidedly assist in discovering the points that are pertinent. Thus, under 1, Raw Material, few if any of the points would apply to a bank. However, the product or commodity of a bank is its service. This service is produced in many ways like a material product. What is the source and history of the material which produces this service? In a bank it is the personnel and the physical facilities. Under 2, Process of Manufacture, how is the service produced? Such points as special equipment—vaults, fixtures, expert employees or executives, age and experience of the firm, and the like would be directly pertinent. Under 3, The Finished Product—Qualities and Uses, such points as varieties of service, efficiency and thoroughness of service, wide and frequent use, i.e. numerous accounts or customers, class of customers, convenience of location, possibly testimonials from customers, and so on, would be possible appeals. In the same manner many points may be found under 4, Price and Value. Analysis with the assistance of such an outline plan will help to reveal numerous possible arguments or selling appeals.

ANALYSIS OF THE ADVERTISEMENTS OF COMPETITORS

In connection with the analysis of selling points for a given product it is usually quite instructive, as well as useful, to make an analysis of the appeals used by competitors. Such an analysis is instructive in showing what competitors are doing; it is useful in ascertaining what selling appeals are to be used and in deciding upon how to compete in the field with others.

The following analysis of shoe advertising does not give the facts for individual competitors separately, as this was not thought feasible here. It would, however, be desirable to make separate analyses in actually planning an advertising campaign, so that the particular appeals and methods of individual competitors might be clearly borne in mind. The following summary gives a detailed analysis of 300 advertisements and indicates pretty clearly the practice at that time (1920-1921) among shoe advertisers concerning the particular points investigated.

Analysis of 300 Shoe Advertisements. 150 advertisements of men's shoes and 150 advertisements of women's shoes. The purpose of this analysis was to answer such questions as the following:

    1. What differences, if any, are there in the methods generally employed in advertising women's shoes and men's shoes?

    2. How much text is used?

    3. What appeals or selling points are most generally used?

    4. How much of the space is given over to pictures and illustrations?

    5. What sorts of pictures are used? That is, are the shoes shown alone? or shown on the wearer's feet? Is the entire person shown?

The 300 advertisements here studied were taken from many different sources and represent, no doubt, the common practice in shoe advertising at the time. Each advertisement was carefully analyzed and tabulated with reference to the various points involved in the questions mentioned.

In the following summary of this analysis, Question 1 shows the number of times each appeal occurred in each of the two groups of 150 advertisements. The advertisements of men's and women's shoes were analyzed separately, in order to determine whether there are distinct differences in the manner in which shoes are advertised to men and to women.

It will be noted, from a detailed examination of the table, that, for example, the appeal of quality is used much more frequently in the advertisements of men's shoes than in women's, namely, 63 against 18. On the other hand, style is used much more frequently in the advertisements of women's shoes than in those of men's shoes. Similarly, there are noteworthy differences in the use of the appeals of wear, service, economy, and health.

With respect to the other questions, there are no very

striking differences in the advertisements for men's and women's shoes. Approximately the same amount of space is used for illustrations in each case, namely, about one-third. The length of the text, as indicated by the number of words, is approximately the same. The chief respect in which there is a difference is in Questions 4 and 6. In the advertisements of women's shoes, a picture of the person wearing the shoe is used considerably more frequently than in advertisements of men's shoes.

TABLE 46

APPEALS OR SELLING POINTS USED IN 300 SHOE ADVERTISEMENTS

150 Advertisements of Men's Shoes		150 Advertisements of Women's Shoes	
1. Quality	63	1. Style	69
2. Price	43	2. Price	49
3. Style	39	3. Comfort	38
4. Wear	26	4. Quality	18
5. Comfort	24	5. Health	13
6. Service	21	6. Economy	8
7. Economy	20	7. Fit	7
8. Fit	6	8. Beauty	7
9. Durability	5	9. Service	6
10. Workmanship	5	10. Wear	5
11. Appearance	4	11. Appearance	3
12. Value	4	12. Satisfaction	3
13. Prestige	4	13. Individuality	3
14. Material	3	14. Reputation of firm	3
15. Good looks	3	15. Distinction	3
16. Satisfaction	2	16. Workmanship	3
17. Distinction	2	17. Imported shoes	2
18. Health	2	18. Construction	2
19. Merit	2	19. Exclusiveness	2
20. Reputation of firm	2	20. Utility	2
21. World consumption	1	21. Reliability	2
22. Variety of sizes	1	22. Small feet	2
23. Security	1	23. Refinement	1
24. Individuality	1	24. Easy walking	1
25. Imported leather	1	25. Durability	1
26. Recommendation	1	26. Attractive	1
		27. Light weight	1

This analysis suggests further investigation of practically all of the points raised. It does not follow necessarily that quality is a stronger appeal with men than with women just because it is used more frequently in men's advertisements; nor does it follow that the element of comfort is a stronger appeal with women than with men.

The purpose of this analysis is merely to show what the existing practice is at the present time with respect to the various points raised. They rather emphasize the need of some carefully conducted investigations to determine in a scientific way the strength and value of the appeals to be used.

SUMMARY OF ANALYSIS

1. What appeals or selling points are used generally in shoe advertisements today? Table 46 shows the appeals used and the number of times they were used in the 150 advertisements of men's shoes and in the 150 advertisements of women's shoes.

2. How much of the space of shoe advertisements is used for picture or illustration?

In the men's shoe advertisements	36%
In the women's shoe advertisements	33%

3. How many advertisements use illustrations?

Men's shoe advertisements	91%
Women's shoe advertisements	89%

4. What proportion of advertisements show a picture of the shoe only?

Men's shoe advertisements	96%
Women's shoe advertisements	83%

5. What proportion of advertisements show the shoe on the foot only, not the entire person?

Men's shoe advertisements	0%
Women's shoe advertisements	6%

6. What proportion of advertisements show a picture of the entire person wearing the shoe?

Men's shoe advertisements	3%
Women's shoe advertisements	12%

7. How long on the average is the text in shoe advertisements?

Men's shoe advertisements	94 words
Women's shoe advertisements	92 words

ANALYSIS OF APPEALS USED BY A RETAIL STORE IN ADVERTISING BOYS' CLOTHING

The study here cited was an additional part of the investigation cited in Chapter IX. After all the statistical and questionnaire-field data had been brought together, it was found desirable to analyze the appeals used in the past advertising of the store as well as in the advertising of competitors or of stores in other cities.

In order to determine how the boys' department of the store in question might strengthen its advertising, an analysis was made of all the advertisements appearing in the three newspapers used over a period of eleven weeks (the first eleven weeks of 1920). Each advertisement was examined and the appeals used were classified under their respective heads.

Thus, in determining the frequency of the price appeal, the number of times specific prices were given was noted and to this was added the number of instances in which the idea of cheapness or price was set forth. For such an appeal as "All Wool," it was only necessary to count the number of times the specific word or its equivalent was employed.

The frequency of concepts related to "Material" was more difficult to define. Under this head, however, were included all cases in which the specific words "materials" or "fabrics" or their equivalents were used and all instances in which references dealt with quality of the goods not falling under other heads.

A similar method was followed in analyzing the appeals of Durability, Style, Tailoring, Fit, Fast Color. The "Two Pant" appeal consists, of course, of the idea that two pairs of knickerbockers come with each suit of clothes.

Under the head of "Reputation of the Firm" were grouped all references to the strength, age, sales, and high standing of the store. "Merchant's Guarantee" is closely associated with manufacturers' brands and refers to the presentation of the names of various makers, as argument for the value of the merchandise.

For each advertisement there was thus found the number of times each appeal was employed. The results are shown in Table 47. While there are difficulties in ascertaining the amount of space given to various appeals and in thus attempting to measure the relative stress put upon them by the advertiser, nevertheless an analysis by this method

TABLE 47

APPEALS USED BY THE BOYS' CLOTHING DEPARTMENT OF A STORE IN ITS NEWSPAPER ADVERTISING DURING THE FIRST ELEVEN WEEKS OF 1920

Appeals	Total Number of Times Used	Times Used per Advertisement
1. Price	845	32.5
2. Material	226	8.7
3. Style	90	3.5
4. Durability	38	1.46
5. Maker's Guarantee	22	.88
6. Two Pant	20	.77
7. All Wool	19	.73
8. Comfort	12	.46
9. Tailoring	12	.46
10. Fast Color	8	.31
11. Merchant's Guarantee	8	.31
12. Fit	6	.24
13. Satisfaction or Money Back	2	.08
14. Reputation of Firm	1	.04

shows in a fairly accurate way significant tendencies of vital importance in the preparation of advertising plans.

The outstanding feature of the advertising of the boys' department, according to the analysis made, was the prominence given to the price appeal. In practically every piece of copy, the factors of price, economy, savings and similar appeals gave the dominant note to the advertising. The table shows that the Price appeal was used on an average of 32.5 times per advertisement, as compared with Material, which was the next most frequent appeal, employed an average of only 8.7 times per advertisement. It was probably wise at that time of the study, when prices were soaring, to place considerable emphasis on the element of price and the economies which were to be attained by "buying now." However, when the price appeal is employed to the exclusion of nearly every other, the advertising is weakened.

On the other hand, the advertisements which the same store was running for its men's lines, did not, under ordinary circumstances and as a matter of policy, contain price quotations. Thus, the advertising of the boys' department went to the other extreme in the frequency with which the price appeal was utilized. The table on page 209 in Chapter IX shows that the consumer attaches first importance to the Material factor, while Durability, Style, Fit, and Price, in the order named, come next in weight. Hence, if the advertising is to have the maximum pulling power, it should probably place more emphasis on these latter factors and considerably less on the price appeal.

Maker's Guarantee stands fifth with respect to the frequency of its use in the advertising. In view of the fact that the consumer test reported in Chapter IX indicates that buyers of boys' clothing ranked this appeal in eleventh place, and that the test made with respect of Maker's Brands indicates clearly that relatively little importance was attached to the brand idea by the buyers of boys' merchandise, less emphasis, as a matter of policy, should be placed by the store on these points. On the other hand, the test showed that more emphasis might well be attached to the store's guarantee or the idea that it stands back of all the merchandise that it sells.

According to the table on page 209, consumers considered Fit as the fourth most important thing about boys' clothes. An examination of Table 47 shows that, in the advertising of the boys' department, this selling point was brought out on an average of less than once in four advertisements, .24 per advertisement. Considerably more attention should therefore be given to the idea of Fit. Moreover, greater emphasis should be given to the factors of All Wool, Comfort, and Tailoring.

In summary, the recommendations for strengthening the advertising of this store, based upon the analysis of the copy used and on the results reported in Chapter IX, would be as follows:

First, that the use of the Price appeal be reduced to about one-third to one-fourth of its present frequency and that a proportionate increase be made in the emphasis placed on Material, Durability, Style, and Fit.

Second, that the advertisements put more stress on Comfort, Tailoring, and Merchant's Guarantee.

Third, that in place of the price quotations, which now appear in bold type and occupy considerable space, more room be given to attractive illustrations and effective borders. This point was further emphasized by the analysis of the boys' clothing advertisements used by Chicago stores.

ANALYSIS OF APPEALS USED BY CHICAGO STORES IN THE
ADVERTISING OF BOYS' CLOTHING

In order to compare appeals used by other stores with those employed by the particular store here in question and to discover what appeals were considered of greatest

strength, an analysis was made, by days, of all the boys'
and children's clothing advertisements appearing in the
Chicago Tribune, during the course of six non-successive
months, in 1919. The analysis followed the same plan as
that used in analyzing the advertisements of the local store.
Each advertisement was gone over and the various types
of appeals were classified under their respective heads. The
appeals used and their relative frequency per advertisement
are shown in Table 48.

TABLE 48

APPEALS USED IN THE ADVERTISING OF CHICAGO FIRMS DURING
SIX NON-SUCCESSIVE MONTHS OF 1919; COMPARISON
WITH THE LOCAL STORE

Appeals	Average Frequency per Ad Chicago Stores	Average Frequency per Ad Local Store	Chicago Frequency Rank	Local Frequency Rank
Price	5.27	32.5	1	1
Material	.94	8.7	2	2
Style	.89	3.5	3	3
Durability	.66	1.46	4	4
Two Pants	.38	.77	5	6
Tailoring	.35	.46	6	8
Satisfaction or Money Back	.22	.08	7	13
All Wool	.18	.73	8	7
Reputation of Firm	.12	.04	9	14
Comfort	.06	.46	10	8
Merchant's Guarantee	.05	.31	11	10
Fit	.02	.24	12	12
Maker's Guarantee	.02	.88	12	5

The first column indicates the nature of the appeal; the
second column shows the average number of times per
advertisement any given appeal occurs; the third column
shows similarly the frequency of the same appeals in the
advertisements of the local store; columns four and five

show the frequency rank of each particular selling point in the advertisements of the Chicago firms and of the local store respectively.

The table indicates the same order of frequency for the first four appeals in the advertising of the Chicago retailers and of the local store. The former, however, did not give the preponderant weight to Price that was accorded to it by the local store. It must be noted that the average size of the Chicago advertisements was 15.26 inches, as compared with 64.12 inches for the local store. On this basis, had the former been as large as the local store's advertisements, the frequency of the Price appeal, in the Chicago copy, would have been only 21 times per advertisement, as compared with 32.5 times for the store's advertising.

The local store placed more emphasis on Material than did the Chicago retailers. The stress on Style was approximately the same. On the other hand, Chicago advertisements had considerably more to say about Durability, the "Two Pant" selling point, Tailoring, and the Satisfaction or Money Back Guarantee. With the exception of the last selling point, the local store should follow the example of the Chicago retailers in placing more emphasis on these appeals.

It has already been pointed out that the local store was concentrating most of its advertising around the Price appeal and secondarily around Material, Style, and Durability. This same tendency, only to a somewhat less extent, was observed in the Chicago advertising. In other words, it seemed that the bulk of the advertising of boys' clothes was on a price basis, with some little emphasis on the Material, Durability, and Style factors. This emphasis on price is usually found in connection with the sale of "convenience" goods, and its presence in the advertising of boys' and children's merchandise is probably an aftermath of the period when the cost of these goods was so relatively low that they might be classed as convenience goods. Today, however, as much care is put into the better classes of boys' garments as into those for men, hence, for the same reason that the Price appeal is not made the outstanding feature of men's clothing advertising, it is probably advisable that this appeal should not be made the main selling point for boys' merchandise.

Referring again to the last table, we will note that in the Chicago advertisements the factor of Maker's Guarantee occupied the lowest place, while in the local store's advertising, it ranked fifth in frequency. This policy of the Chicago firm bears out the theory already stated, that this appeal is not as strong with the buyers as has been assumed.

The detailed figures on which the preceding table is based bring out the fact that the price appeal is not emphasized with nearly as much frequency in the advertising of the largest Chicago retailers of boys' clothing, as it is in the advertising of smaller concerns and of department stores. On the other hand, in these high-grade stores, the appeals of Material, Durability, Style, the "Two Pant" selling point, Tailoring, and Comfort were brought out more frequently.

In this analysis of the advertising of Chicago retailers of boys' clothing, several features were noted which have a practical suggestion for the local store. First, in the advertising of the best concerns, instead of crowding in the copy for the boys' department at the bottom of the general advertisement for the store, separate space was used. The advertisement was thus made more effective. Secondly, it was found that the best advertisers used relatively large illustrations of the "action" type.

XII

DETERMINING THE VALUE OF APPEALS:
ANALYSIS OF HUMAN NATURE

Determining which ones of a list of appeals will be most effective. Analysis of human motives. Human desires and instincts. An inventory of desires and instincts. Chief characteristics of instincts. The potency of instincts. Why the fundamental desires and instinctive motives are potent. How selling appeals may be checked against the fundamental desires and motives of human nature. Evaluating appeals in relation to motives.

THE next problem is to examine our list of appeals for a toothpaste, or our list of possible selling arguments for a vacuum cleaner, in order to determine which of these appeals will be most effective and which ones should actually be used. On what basis or by what methods can we determine which of these appeals are likely to be most potent? Obviously, some of them are much less effective than others and some of them are probably rather impertinent and irrelevant if not actually negative or detrimental in their impression upon the buyer.

In the case of the vacuum cleaner, it might be doubtful to stress in minute detail the points based upon mechanical construction, since women play an important part in the purchase of vacuum cleaners. It is also questionable whether stress should be placed upon the point that it does not injure rugs, since it might raise the question in the minds of prospective buyers as to whether the vacuum cleaner in question may not actually injure rugs in spite of statements to the contrary. Is the size of the factory a point worth stressing? To what extent is a recommendation by a rug importer valuable?

Similar questions will arise with regard to the selling appeals of toothpaste. Is the health appeal strong? Is the taste appeal valuable? Is the statement that numerous dentists approve it effective? Is the emphasis upon the size of the tube effective or possibly even detrimental? Is the mention of gritty substances dangerous? May not the mentioning of gritty substance, even though it be to the effect that the particular toothpaste contains no gritty or harmful ingredients, arouse suspicion in the mind of the buyer? Obviously it is an extremely important problem to determine which appeals should actually be used for a given article at a given time.

Another important consideration in selecting the arguments to be used in advertising is the possibility that the most conspicuous feature about a product may not necessarily be the most effective argument for selling the product. The mechanical construction of the motor in an automobile or some portion of it may be the distinguishing feature but it may be questionable whether a detailed statement of it in an advertisement would be as effective as emphasis upon other aspects of the automobile. The human desire for outdoor life, social distinction, and enjoyment connected with the possession of an automobile might be far stronger as appeals. Years ago certain railroads advertised polite attendance, fast time, picturesque scenery, a great four-track line, and train schedules. More recently railroads have found it more effective to stress outdoor life, the appeal of a national park, a vacation trip, or golfing in the mountains, leaving the former points more or less as secondary. Which will be more effective—to stress in great detail the nutritive value of a food in terms of calories or in terms of health and vigor and taste?

The point in these questions is the fact that it is necessary, besides analyzing the product, to analyze the motives of human nature in order to determine what may appeal most strongly. This and the following chapters will set forth ways by which the relative value of appeals may in some measure be determined. This chapter will consider primarily the analysis of motives, desires and wants of human nature in relation to selling arguments. Suppose we knew all the fundamental desires and wants, the real driving motives of human behavior, and suppose we knew the relative potency of these motives with reference to specific ends—we would have a most helpful basis on which to determine which of our appeals for toothpaste or vacuum cleaners would be most effective.

ANALYSIS OF HUMAN MOTIVES

What are these motives? What are the fundamental desires and wants of human nature? Man will buy only what satisfies a real want or an inherent desire. Human nature is composed fundamentally of a large number of inherent wants accompanied by capacities or abilities to carry out the necessary behavior to satisfy these wants. The business of the advertiser or the seller is not to create fundamentally new desires. That is not necessary and really cannot be done. Man already has certain desires present from birth, which are a part of his fundamental make-up. All that a seller can do is to direct these desires in certain directions, or stimulate them to action, or show by what new ways an old desire may be satisfied.

The seller cannot create or implant the desire for personal adornment nor the instinct to satisfy this desire, and furthermore he does not need to, since it already is a powerful motive. All he needs to do and all he can do is to set forth how his particular product will satisfy this particular desire.

The fundamental make-up of human nature in this regard has probably not changed in any essential way, at least during the time of recorded history. The chief difference between the present and the past is that we today have created so many new and varied ways to satisfy the age-old desires and needs. The fundamental desires of primitive man were those of food, shelter, comfort, pleasure, and the like. Civilized man today has fundamentally these same desires with none added. The only difference between our complex civilized life today and that of primitive man consists in the number of ways in which we today may satisfy our desires for food, shelter, comfort, and pleasure. Instead of the raw foods such as nuts, fruits, vegetables, and meat, there are endless varieties of foods prepared by the ingenuity of man.

The fundamental law of human life known as the law of supply and demand is half a physical law and half a psychobiological law. The supply aspect of a product is primarily physical; the demand aspect is primarily psychological. The supply of a product is limited fundamentally by the natural resources available in the world for the manufacture of that product. The demand for it is determined primarily by the extent to which human nature desires it or may be stimulated to desire it. Demand, therefore, is dependent primarily upon the fundamental wants, needs, desires, and motives of human nature.

The problem before us at the present moment is to find out what the fundamental desires of human nature are, what their relative importance is, and then to match our proposed selling appeals for a given commodity against these fundamental desires to determine which appeals are likely to be most effective from the standpoint of stimulating the desire for or the purchase of that particular commodity.

HUMAN DESIRES AND INSTINCTS

The fundamental motives to action are the fundamental desires and needs of human nature. We may perhaps gain the clearest conception of the meaning and nature of these desires and instincts by going back for a moment to examine the behavior of the human infant. A child is born with certain desires necessary to maintain its individual existence. The most important of these are the feeling of hunger, accompanied by a desire for food and the feeling of pain resulting from bodily discomfort. Both of these desires are accompanied by various forms of behavior which the child is able to carry out for the purpose of satisfying these desires. He is able to satisfy his feeling of hunger and his desire for food by making his wants known through crying and either by sucking movements or by reaching and grasping things and putting them into his mouth. All of these desires as well as the forms of behavior to satisfy these desires are inborn in him. That is, he does not need to learn them. Later on these desires manifest themselves in various ways in addition to the ones exhibited in early infancy. At the same time also new and more complicated ways of satisfying these desires are developed. For example, the feeling of pain and the desire for comfort may be met first only by crying. Later on, after the child has acquired the capacity to walk he will use a much wider variety of responses or actions to satisfy the desire for bodily comfort.

The feeling of pain or hunger is accompanied by the desire for satisfying this feeling; it is also accompanied at the same time with a form of bodily movement or behavior to satisfy this desire. The former is the desire; the latter is known as instinct.

An instinct may be defined from the neurological side as an inborn neural connection between sense organ and muscle. It may be defined from the functional side as an inborn capacity to respond in definite ways under definite circumstances. These responses are prior to experience and training, and need not be learned. To close the eyes when an object suddenly approaches them, to get food when hungry, to strike when struck, to be afraid of thunder and to fondle infants, are illustrations of instinctive responses. The reflexive and instinctive responses are inherited in the sense that there is present in the nervous system, either at the time of birth or later on as a result of growth, a set of nervous connections already formed for the carrying out of a particular action in response to a given situation. If the child closes his eyes when an object suddenly approaches, it means that the motor impulses travel from the retina to the visual center of the brain, from there to the motor center which controls the movement of the eyelids, and from there out to the muscles of the eyelids to cause the contraction. In the case of inherited responses, the connection from the sensory to the motor centers is already present and ready to operate in carrying out the action. In the case of acquired responses, such as habits, these nervous connections must be formed as a result of effort and trial on the part of the individual.

The difference between reflexes and instincts is largely a difference of complexity. Both are inherited types of responses. Reflexes are simpler forms of reaction usually involving a limited set of muscles and occurring in response to precise stimuli. The contraction or expansion of the iris, the closing of the eyelids, the knee jerk, are illustrations of reflexes. Instincts are complex reactions involving the use of large groups of muscles or, in many instances, the entire muscular system of the body. They may be aroused either by external stimuli or situations or possibly by internal stimulation. To make movements in the direction of getting food when hungry, to seek shelter when cold, to offer resistance when hemmed in, to spit out what tastes bad, are instinctive reactions.

AN INVENTORY OF DESIRES AND INSTINCTS

Can we arrive at a satisfactory and fairly complete list of all the fundamental desires and instincts of human nature? A considerable number of attempts have been made by various students to do this. We may approach the problem either from the standpoint of desires, that is, feelings or wants, or from the standpoint of instincts, that is, modes of behavior to satisfy the desires.

From the standpoint of inborn modes of behavior, i. e. instincts, the following inventory may be suggested:

I. Food-getting and protective responses
   1. Eating—appetite, taste, hunger
   2. Reaching, grasping and putting objects into mouth
   3. Acquisition and possession
   4. Hunting—cruelty
   5. Collecting and hoarding
   6. Avoidance and repulsion
   7. Rivalry and cooperation
   8. Habitation—comfort
   9. Responses to confinement
   10. Migration and domesticity
   11. Fear—timidity, caution
   12. Fighting
   13. Anger

II. Responses to the behavior of other human beings
   14. Parental behavior
   15. Gregariousness—sociability, loneliness, hospitality
   16. Attention to other human beings
   17. Attention-getting
   18. Responses to approving and scornful behavior
   19. Responses by approving and scornful behavior
   20. Attempts at mastering and submissive behavior
   21. Display—ornamentation, beauty, pride in appearance
   22. Shyness—modesty, reserve
   23. Sex behavior
   24. Secretiveness and confession
   25. Rivalry—competition
   26. Cooperation—loyalty, faithfulness
   27. Suggestibility and opposition
   28. Envy any jealousy—cunning, intrigue
   29. Greed
   30. Kindliness—sympathy, sorrow, pity
   31. Teasing, tormenting, bullying
   32. Imitation

III. Miscellaneous
   33. Visual exploration
   34. Manipulation—constructiveness
   35. Cleanliness
   36. Curiosity
   37. Multiform mental activity
   38. Play—sport, joy, humor

These various instincts or modes of action occur in response to the desires, inborn feelings, or wants of man necessary to maintain his existence. We may therefore suggest the following fundamental desires or wants of human beings and the correlated appeals:

I. 1. Appetite—hunger
2. Taste
3. Cleanliness

II. 4. Bodily comfort
5. Warmth
6. Coolness
7. Rest—sleep
8. Health
9. Safety
10. Fear—caution

III. 11. Sex attraction
12. Personal appearance—beauty
13. Style
14. Shyness and modesty
15. Devotion to others

IV. 16. Parental affection
17. Love of offspring
18. Sympathy for others
19. Protection of others

V. 20. Domesticity—having a home
21. Home comfort
22. Hospitality

VI. 23. Possession—ownership
24. Efficiency—making things go well
25. Economy—saving of time, effort, material

VII. 26. Gregariousness — sociability — associating with other people
27. Social distinction
28. Approval by others—pride
29. Imitation of others
30. Group loyalty
31. Cooperation
32. Courtesy
33. Ambition
34. Competition—rivalry
35. Managing others

VIII. 36. Pleasure
  37. Play—sport
  38. Amusement
  39. Humor
  40. Teasing
IX. 41. Activity—mental and physical
  42. Constructiveness—wanting to build or make things
  43. Manipulation—wanting to handle things
X. 44. Curiosity—wanting to find out
XI. 45. Respect for or devotion to a superior power (Deity)

Hollingworth has proposed the following analysis of motives:[1]

1. Appetite—(Hunger, tastefulness, sense enjoyment)
2. Comfort
3. Sex—(Love, coquetry, parental affection)
4. Devotion—faithfulness, loyalty, affection
5. Play—playfulness, merriment, sport, joy, humor
6. Fear—(Timidity, anguish, caution)
7. Acquisitiveness (Propriety, selfishness, stinginess)
8. Hunting (Cruelty, eagerness)
9. Sociability (Loneliness, hospitality)
10. Competition (Emulation, jealousy, ambition)
11. Curiosity
12. Shyness (Modesty, reserve, bashfulness)
13. Ornamentation (Display, beauty, pride in appearance)
14. Cleanliness (Purity, decency, wholesomeness)
15. Constructiveness
16. Sympathy (Sorrow, pity)
17. Cunning (Secrecy, intrigue)

CHIEF CHARACTERISTICS OF INSTINCTS

The fundamental desires of human nature are probably centered primarily around two things: the preservation and comfort of the individual and the continuity and welfare of the human race. The instincts are likewise centered primarily around these two inborn modes of behavior designed to satisfy the fundamental desires of man.

[1] Tipper, Hotchkiss, Hollingworth, Parsons, *Advertising*, p. 80.

The chief characteristic then of instinctive behavior and responses is that they are inherited and therefore largely independent of experience and training, except in so far as they are incompletely developed and are subject to modification and training. Instinctive behavior, therefore, while it serves a purpose, does not involve foresight of the purpose or reason for the instinctive behavior. That is conspicuously true of the instincts of animals. It is likewise true of the instincts of infancy and early childhood, and to some extent it is even true of the instincts in adult life. The squirrel probably has no conception of the purpose of making a collection of nuts in the hollow of a tree, and a hen has probably no anticipation of what will happen to a nestful of eggs as a result of constantly sitting on them.

Another characteristic of instinctive action is that such action is not motivated by reason but rather it is motivated by the feelings and sensations that somehow it is more satisfying to carry out the action than not to carry it out. The desire is sufficient cause to want the desire satisfied, irrespective of reason or rational justification. This may well be illustrated by a simple experiment. The eye by instinct, or more specifically in this case by reflex action, closes upon the sudden and close approach of an object. If a plate of glass be held in front of the eye and a pellet of paper be thrown at the glass in front of the eye, it will suddenly and uniformly close, in spite of the conscious thought that the pellet cannot possibly hurt the eye. The neural mechanism in this case is so perfect that a large amount of training will be necessary to inhibit the closing of the eye.

William James has clearly stated this point in the following manner:

Now, why do the various animals do what seem to us such strange things, in the presence of such outlandish stimuli? Why does the hen, for example, submit herself to the tedium of incubating such a fearfully uninteresting set of objects as a nestful of eggs, unless she have some sort of a prophetic inkling of the result?   The only answer is *ad hominem*.   We can only interpret the instincts of brutes by what we know of instincts in ourselves. Why do men always lie down, when they can, on soft beds rather than on hard floors?   Why do they sit round the stove on a cold day?   Why, in a room, do they place themselves, ninety-nine times out of a hundred, with their faces towards its middle rather than to the wall?   Why do they prefer saddle of mutton and champagne to hard-tack and ditch-water?   Why does the maiden interest the youth so that everything about her seems more important and significant than anything else in the world? Nothing more can be said than that these are human ways, and that every creature *likes* its own ways, and takes to the following them as a matter of course.   Science may come and consider these ways, and find that most of them are useful.   But it is not for the sake of their utility that they are followed, but because at the moment of following them we feel that that is the only appropriate and natural thing to do.   Not one man in a billion, when taking his dinner, ever thinks of utility.   He eats because the food tastes good and makes him want more.   If you ask him *why* he should want to eat more of what tastes like that, instead of revering you as a philosopher he will probably laugh at you for a fool. . . .   It takes, in short, what Berkeley calls a mind debauched by learning to carry the process of making the natural seem strange, so far as to ask for the *why* of any instinctive human act.   To the metaphysician alone can such questions occur as: Why do we smile, when pleased, and not scowl?   Why are we unable to talk to a crowd as we talk to a single friend?   Why does a particular maiden turn our wits so upsidedown?   The common man can only say *"Of course* we smile, *of course* our heart palpitates at the sight of the crowd." . . .

And so, probably, does each animal feel about the particular things it tends to do in presence of particular objects. . . .   To the lion it is the lioness which is made to be loved; to the bear, the she-bear.   To the broody hen, the notion would probably seem monstrous that there should be a creature in the world to whom a nestful of eggs was not the utterly fascinating and precious and never-to-be-too-much-sat-upon object which it is to her.

Thus, we may be sure that, however mysterious some animals' instincts may appear to us, our instincts will appear no less mysterious to them.   And we may conclude that, to the animal which obeys it, every impulse and every step of every instinct shines with its own sufficient light, and seems at the moment the only eternally right and proper thing to do. It is done for its own sake exclusively.[1]

Furthermore, it is obvious that the fundamental desires and the accompanying instinctive responses are common to the entire race or species. All members of a given species of animals have the same instinctive characteristics. The strength of these instinctive responses may vary from one member to the next, but they are all present.

Habits differ from instincts in that the former are more or less automatic forms of action developed as the result of individual training and experience. Habits, therefore, are not common to all members of the race as instincts are. Furthermore, habits are in most instances developments of special forms of carrying out instinctive acts. My habits are my individual ways of automatic behavior based upon instinctive tendencies but developed as a result of my own efforts and experience, whereas the fundamental instincts are the same in all mankind.

THE POTENCY OF INSTINCTS

The fundamental inborn desires and instincts of human nature are the strongest motives to action that mankind possesses, if indeed they are not the only real motives to action. It takes very little observation and analysis to see how fully our behavior in all relations is dominated by the fundamental instincts. If we analyze our own behavior, it is obvious that the motive for any action, whether important or trivial, goes back in the last analysis to a fundamental instinct or desire. My choice of a career or an occupation will go back in the last analysis to the instinct and desire for personal welfare, self-expression, opportunities for satisfying the instinct of possession, social approval, and the like. In a similar way even so trivial a situation as my momentary anger over being unsuccessful in repeated efforts to pick up a pin on the floor will go back to the

[1] James, *Psychology; Briefer Course,* pp. 393-395.

fundamental instinct of not wanting to be thwarted by outside forces or circumstances.

Numerous examples might be given to illustrate how deep-seated the fundamental instincts are. Take, for instance, the inborn fear of the dark. Most people are not afraid of the dark by daytime, but it is very different at nighttime. Other things being equal, most men, no matter how courageous they may be, would probably just a little rather not go through a cemetery at night in the dark. Scott has pointed out that we are early at the bleachers but late at the pews. Writing to cousins and aunts is put off indefinitely, but a letter from a fiancée is answered by return mail.[1]

The instinct of acquisition and possession is one of the most deep-seated in human nature. In a certain store, a sale of rugs was contemplated by offering a reduction of 20% in price. Before this was carried out, someone conceived the notion of printing a facsimile dollar bill in the advertisement in the newspapers accompanied with the statement that this dollar coupon would be applied toward the purchase of a rug. The plan was very effective in disposing of the rugs with only a small reduction in price as compared with a 20% reduction. Somehow the facsimile of a dollar seems to have a more tangible value and to make a more realistic appeal to the instinct of possession than the more abstract conception of a 20% discount.

Some years ago a bakery in Chicago made a very effective appeal to the instinct of curiosity. The bakery inserted in the street cars a card which on the first day gave only the name of the baker. After that the cards were changed each day. The statement on the card was always brief. It did not state what the proposition was about, but in varying ways it referred to the original card or to preceding cards by such statements as "Did you see what Blank said yesterday?" "Watch for what will appear in this space tomorrow." This procedure was kept up for some time,

---

[1] Scott, W. D., *Psychology of Advertising.*

until finally a card appeared, telling that it all referred to a bakery and that the bread could be obtained at specified places. This plan had aroused a great deal of curiosity and interest, so that it became a common topic of conversation; even communications were written to the newspapers. This method brought about a very considerable increase in the sale of bread of this bakery, which kept up permanently at a very greatly increased volume.

The instinct of appetite, that is of eating what tastes good, is obviously very strong. In spite of all advice and reasoning to the contrary, people keep on eating what tastes good even though certain foods may not agree with them. The undisciplined child will reach for whatever is in sight to satisfy his appetite. It is only through persistent training that civilized, cultivated ways of eating are developed. The disciplined, controlled modes of behavior of the adult are largely a veneer on the outside, which rather easily crumbles away under strain or pressure. Men and women who are ladies and gentlemen under ordinary circumstances become fighting, scrambling beasts under extraordinary circumstances, in a panic or a fire, as evidenced by the many persons who are trampled under foot or crushed to death in theatre fires and similar catastrophes. In a crowded street car, the natural impulse for a person who is jammed or pushed is to push back.

The social, gregarious instinct likewise is an extremely potent motive in human life. "To be alone is one of the greatest evils for him (man). Solitary confinement is by many regarded as a mode of torture too cruel and unnatural for civilized countries to adopt."[1]

The instinct of possession, of obtaining things for little or nothing, is illustrated in a most striking way by spectacular occurrences almost every day. Note, for example, the large and small sums of money, totaling several million dollars, offered by people in all stations of life in the Ponzi affair in Boston in 1920, in which a return of 45% on the

[1] James, W., *Psychology*.

money within a short period of time was offered. Mr. Houston Thompson, Federal Trade Commissioner, estimated some time ago that the American people lose $500,000,000 annually in unsound, alluring investments.

Not long ago the Guardian Savings and Trust Company of Cleveland made the following experiment. A poster was placed in the window of the bank, setting forth the "perpetual motion" scheme for making money by means of a cat ranch. The card is reproduced in Figure 20.

GLORIOUS OPPORTUNITY TO GET RICH QUICK

Invest in

THE CALIFORNIA RANCHING COMPANY

Now being organized to start a cat ranch in California

We are starting a cat ranch in California with 100,000 cats. Each cat will average 12 kittens a year. The cat skins will sell for 30 cents each. One hundred men can skin 5,000 cats a day. We figure a daily net profit of over $10,000.

NOW WHAT SHALL WE FEED THE CATS?

We will start a rat ranch next door with 1,000,000 rats. The rats will breed twelve times faster than the cats. So, we'll have rats to feed each day to each cat. Now what shall we feed the rats? We will feed the rats the carcasses of the cats after they have been skinned.

NOW GET THIS

We feed the rats to the cats, and the cats to the rats, and get the cat skins for nothing. Shares are selling at 5 cents each, but the price will go up soon. Invest while opportunity knocks at your door.

THE CALIFORNIA RANCHING COMPANY

Figure 20: Poster used by the Guardian Savings and Trust Company of Cleveland in experiment

This poster was put up in the window of the bank with the following in large letters: "Some gullible people will try to buy this stock. It is a foolish fake, of course, but no more foolish than many "wild-cat" schemes being promoted today. Investigate before investing. Don't hand your money over to any unknown glib-tongued salesman."

Immense crowds gathered in front of the window. Numerous inquiries were made for the stock by mail and in person, asking about literature of the company. Inquiries were so numerous that they were obliged to take the card down.[1]

In 1916, when chain letters were circulated for various charitable purposes in connection with the war, some one started a chain letter stating that if the writer would send 10 cents to a certain address and transmit five copies of the letter to five other women, she would receive a new silk petticoat. When the office was raided on a Monday morning, there were 25,000 letters in the morning's mail, each containing a dime.

There is an old pedagogical maxim which stresses the potency of instinctive tendencies in children to the effect that teachers should work with nature, that is, human instinctive nature, rather than against it. The teacher will be able to influence the child more completely and the child will learn more rapidly if the natural inborn desires and instinctive responses are utilized and stimulated. The advertiser and seller may use the same principle to fully as great advantage. The most direct and effective way to influence the action of men and women is to appeal to their inborn desires and instincts. The fundamental instincts of men are the driving forces of human life that ultimately determine the motives and forms of behavior. They are so deep-seated in the human psycho-physical organism that we may say that to work apart from or against nature is a futile task. The skill of the seller and advertiser lies in studying and analyzing these fundamental desires and instincts, in determining which ones are most directly involved

[1] *American Magazine*, July, 1920, p. 60.

in a given situation and in devising means by which to stimulate them most effectively.

WHY THE FUNDAMENTAL DESIRES AND INSTINCTIVE MOTIVES ARE POTENT

The fundamental desires and their accompanying instinctive forms of behavior are the most potent forces in human life because they are most directly connected with the preservation and welfare of the individual as well as of the race. One might almost say that they constitute the central essence of the human being. Instinctive forms of behavior have developed in human life for the most part because in most instances the individual would not have time or be able to acquire the necessary forms of behavior in order to maintain his existence. To begin with, he must have ready at birth certain inborn actions for obtaining, getting, and swallowing food; later on, he must have certain inborn responses to react to his environment and to other human beings. It is necessary for him to live with other human beings, and consequently it is necessary for him to have more or less ready-made ways of responding to or cooperating with or competing with the behavior of his fellow men. Likewise, the instinctive behavior towards the opposite sex is necessary for the perpetuity and welfare of the race as a whole. To be sure, most of the instinctive responses beyond early childhood are not absolutely, mechanically fixed, as they are in the lower animals, but are more or less variable and modified by the particular environment under which the individual lives. Nevertheless, these tendencies towards specific responses are inherited.

The important point in our present consideration is the fact that these instinctive responses are there because they have been vital to the preservation of life. Only those individuals who possess these common instinctive capacities are the ones who are able to survive. By a process of natural selection, the ones who may not have possessed certain of these instinctive responses or who may not have possessed them in a sufficiently strong form have as a result become extinct. If the child were not born with certain instinctive forms of behavior to satisfy his necessary desires, he would not be able to acquire them by his own efforts and experience and would soon perish. Experience and training merely modify or direct the tendencies into specific channels or perfect them into certain habits as a result of repetition. Just as among animals the process of natural selection allows the individuals of a species to maintain their individual and race existence if they possess the inborn forms of behavior necessary to obtain food in the environment in which they must live; so among human beings, those who have possessed or inherited the necessary desires and instinctive modes of satisfying those desires have continued to exist.

HOW SELLING APPEALS MAY BE CHECKED AGAINST THE FUNDAMENTAL DESIRES AND MOTIVES

Man will buy that which satisfies a real want or inherent desire. The question at this point is, What is the order of strength of the various desires and instincts? Which are the strongest in general and which are the strongest specifically in connection with a particular commodity? Obviously the fundamental purpose of the human race from a biological point of view is the maintenance and preservation of the individual himself, and secondly, the maintenance and preservation of mankind as a whole. To grow, develop, produce seed, and pass away, is apparently the biological order of nature. Corn sprouts, grows, flourishes, produces seed and withers. Apparently, then, whatever contributes most directly towards these ends, fulfils the most fundamental wants.

Take as an illustration the instinct of appetite, that is, of eating what tastes good, and rejecting what tastes bad. Through countless generations, this instinct has been on the whole the safest guide in the selection of food. We eat to maintain our bodies, but we eat that which pleases our taste. Harmful things on the whole, taste disagreeable. It is evident, therefore, that a food which is presented with a strong appeal to the sense of appetite, appeals to one of the strongest instincts in human nature. The instinct of possession, of collecting and keeping things, of getting something for nothing, is extremely potent for the reason that from a biological point of view only those races or members of a race have been able to survive which have had a reasonable amount of providence in gathering food and shelter to tide them over periods when food and shelter could not be obtained at the moment or on the spot. Just as only those squirrels have been able to survive which had the instinct of gathering nuts in the hollow of a tree, so in the long run, only those human beings are able to survive who similarly have an instinct of providing for the lean seasons.

Why is the appeal of sleep, comfortable sleep, such a successful appeal in the advertising of beds? Man is first and by fundamental instinct desirous of comfortable rest when he is fatigued. If you can make the prospective buyer feel how delightful it will seem after a tiring day to lie down on a soft, comfortable bed, you will be appealing to a fundamental instinct in human nature. Man is not first and foremost interested in springs, mattresses, and posts; he is interested, first of all, in sleep. Then, if the mechanical construction of a bed may be shown to contribute toward greater comfort in sleeping, man will be interested in that phase. He will be interested in the price of a bed in so far as it appeals to his instinct of possession. of getting the most for what he can pay. He will be interested in beauty and design in so far as it appeals to his instinct of social approval and personal expression. This point is well put by the epigrammatic phrase attributed to Mr. Simmons of the Simmons Hardware Company: Don't sell the people augurs; sell them holes. They will then want to buy the augurs with which to make the holes.

Why is it that style is so strong an appeal in wearing apparel? Simply because one of the two fundamental reasons for wearing clothing is display and personal ornamentation —ornamentation for the purpose of securing the social approval and admiration of others, and perhaps particularly of being attractive to the opposite sex. The second fundamental reason for wearing clothing is bodily comfort and protection. Why is it that warmth and comfort are so strong as appeals for winter clothing? Why is it that comfort and coolness are so strong as appeals for summer clothing? The answer is that bodily comfort is one of the important and necessary fundamental wants of human nature. If you can get people to picture in their minds how attractive they will look and how comfortable they will feel in these particular clothes, you will be making one of the strongest appeals that it is possible to make.

In order to arrive at a somewhat more tangible evaluation of the various motives listed on page 260, a considerable number of persons were asked to express their personal reactions in accordance with the following instructions:

The following is a list of the most important motives for action in human life. Some are more potent than others in determining our actions and our behavior as a whole. Rate the following motives on a scale of 0 to 10.

Consider the strength and importance of these motives or incentives to action from the standpoint of your own personal life and behavior as a whole. Ask yourself in connection with each one how important it is in determining your own actions from day to day. Write 10 after the very strongest motives, and a number between 0 and 10 after the others, according to their relative strength or importance.

Ratings were thus obtained from 74 men and women. These ratings have been combined in Table 49. They are tentative and will be verified by reactions from additional persons. However, as they stand they will serve as an approximate guide for evaluating the possible appeals for a commodity.

TABLE 49

THE RELATIVE STRENGTH OF MOTIVES IN GENERAL

Motives	Per Cent	Motives	Per Cent
Appetite—hunger	9.2	Respect for Deity	7.1
Love of offspring	9.1	Sympathy for others	7.0
Health	9.0	Protection of others	7.0
Sex attraction	8.9	Domesticity	7.0
Parental affection	8.9	Social distinction	6.9
Ambition	8.6	Devotion to others	6.8
Pleasure	8.6	Hospitality	6.6
Bodily comfort	8.4	Warmth	6.5
Possession	8.4	Imitation	6.5
Approval by others	8.0	Courtesy	6.5
Gregariousness	7.9	Play—sport	6.5
Taste	7.8	Managing others	6.4
Personal appearance	7.8	Coolness	6.2
Safety	7.8	Fear—caution	6.2
Cleanliness	7.7	Physical activity	6.0
Rest—sleep	7.7	Manipulation	6.0
Home comfort	7.5	Construction	6.0
Economy	7.5	Style	5.8
Curiosity	7.5	Humor	5.8
Efficiency	7.3	Amusement	5.8
Competition	7.3	Shyness	4.2
Cooperation	7.1	Teasing	2.6

EVALUATING APPEALS IN RELATION TO MOTIVES

The primary purpose of the discussion in this chapter has been to show what the fundamental motives are, their relative strength and importance in human behavior and then to evaluate the advertising appeals that may be considered for any particular commodity in the light of these considerations. Concretely the question is, Which of the possible advertising points for a given commodity will appeal most strongly to the inherent motives and instincts of human beings? Let us consider the possible points for a fountain pen and turn to the table of motives or instincts on page 260. To which of these motives or desires does a fountain pen appeal? Evidently the following appeals could be used: cleanliness, in preventing ink from soiling fingers; safety, in protecting the pen point, or in not losing the pen itself; sex attraction, in neat writing to a young woman or a young man; parental affection, in the form of a gift to children; nearly all points under possession and economy; most of the points under gregariousness and sociability; pleasure in writing; and so on. A consideration of these appeals and of their relative strength as motives in human behavior will be distinctly useful in deciding which ones will be most effective in influencing persons to buy the article in question.

XIII

DETERMINING THE VALUE OF APPEALS:
LABORATORY-FIELD TESTS

Analysis of human nature in connection with the analysis of the product. Analysis of returns from past advertising. Tryout campaigns. Results from questionnaire investigation in determining the value of appeals. Illustration of a laboratory-field test. Statistical treatment of test results. Comparison of abstract appeals with completely phrased appeals.

THE analysis of human nature—in connection with the analysis of the product in determining possible selling points for it—is an extremely useful procedure in determining what selling appeals will probably be most effective in a given case. It will serve as a safeguard against making grotesque mistakes through the use of certain selling appeals or the overemphasis of others. However, useful as it is, the plan does not give us the final answer nor does it determine in a scientific way the effectiveness of specific appeals or of their particular form of statement or presentation. The plan of judging and analyzing appeals in the light of the fundamental motives and instincts is useful only as a general guide, and not as a specific and final measure of the strength of appeals.

We may assume that the appeal to taste is a strong one, possibly the strongest one for a food; however, much depends on the detailed statement of it, or on the particular manner in which the appeal is presented, either by word or by picture. To check possible appeals against the instinctive motives of human nature, is obviously very useful, but this is after all to a great extent a matter of individual judgment, not to say of individual guess or prejudice. I can determine individually how a given point or method of presentation appeals to me, and I can judge to some extent how it may appeal to others; but my own reaction, in the first place, may be peculiar or different from the majority of other people, and in the second place, my guess as to how it may appeal to others may be wrong. Our next problem, therefore, is to devise means whereby the effectiveness of an appeal may be gaged in a more accurate way with the least possible expenditure of time and money.

ANALYSIS OF RETURNS FROM PAST ADVERTISING

In case advertising has been carried on and in case there is any approximate measure of the results of various methods or appeals used, it is possible of course to analyze the results in relation to the appeals and methods used. The difficulty with this procedure is, first, that there are no accurate measures in many instances and, second, that if there are some reliable methods of measurement, such as returns, inquiries, or business done, the plan is obviously a costly one and represents learning by experience in its most costly form. The money has already been expended and if the plan was extensive, the error is serious and the loss is great. Nevertheless, of course, where no other means of analyzing the effectiveness of methods employed are available, the returns of a given plan should be analyzed, so far as possible in any case, and future plans should be made accordingly.

TRYOUT CAMPAIGNS

The next method of determining the effectiveness of appeals is to abbreviate the record of experience by making an experimental tryout of the proposed plan in a limited way. This method consists of making a relatively brief trial in a limited section of territory and of observing and evaluating as far as possible the results of the trial. For example, in 1909, when the California Fruit Growers' Exchange was planning a country-wide educational program for advertising Sunkist oranges, a tryout campaign was conducted in the state of Iowa.

This tryout campaign was carefully checked. The results proved to be highly successful and the plan was gradually extended to cover the entire country.

A somewhat different tryout plan was conducted by the Standard Oil Company in putting Nujol on the market. The particular purpose of this tryout was to determine the most effective appeals.

From the first, the product has received big and consistent advertising. . . . After its initial campaign, Nujol has done its best never to shoot at random, but to know exactly what it was aiming at and the sort of ammunition to use. All its copy has been "tested" copy. Every form of appeal used has been adopted as the result of tests.

Standard Oil is strong on tests. It never hesitates to spend money freely on any sort of investigation that is likely to produce useful knowledge. Here is how it tries out its advertising copy before using it in national campaigns.

A number of different types of copy, as many as 11 to 15, are run in as many different but typical sections of the country at the same time. Just before the advertising starts, the stock is again counted. This count in each case is deducted from the first count. The same procedure is gone through at the end of the advertising period. Some time before the advertising appears, Nujol men visit the dealers, ascertain how much of the product they have on hand and, if necessary, stock them up so that they will not run short nor have to buy during the test period.

In this matter, the company works much as do the United Cigar Stores and some other big advertisers, on the principle that an advertisement to be considered effective must produce immediate results. It is perhaps quite unnecessary to say that all the results obtained in the tests are carefully recorded, analyzed, charted and studied.

The type that produces the greatest percentage of increased sales is regarded as the best and is set aside for use in national campaigns. Those that fail to produce sufficient increase are thrown away entirely.

Checks of the results as to the form of appeal are made by publishing the different forms in varying classes of magazines. For instance, one of the seemingly most natural appeals is

"Health." Another is "Charm of Complexion." Others are "Babies," "Maternity," "Old People."

The tests have shown that "Health," as a matter of fact, does not appeal to all. It appeals a little more to men than to women, but men respond much more readily to "Strength," "Clear Head," "Vigorous Vitality." The Nujol habit is, however, largely a matter of education, and much of the advertising is devoted to that purpose.[1]

A slightly different method of conducting a tryout test is to prepare small advertisements of the ones to be used, to run them experimentally in typical mediums that are to be used, and to ascertain then by a proper keying method the inquiries brought by each particular piece of copy. The advertisements must contain something for which the reader may send, such as a booklet or a sample, or they may actually offer the article itself and thereby solicit orders. These small tryout advertisements may be used in quarter or eighth page or possibly smaller size. Mail order houses frequently try out their appeals in this way.

A well-known silverware company developed the "big idea" behind its advertising in this way: Two quarter-page ads based on its old type of appeal and two based upon a new appeal were run alternately in a weekly of large national circulation. In each a book was featured, the price of which was 20 cents. To every book sold by the old appeal something like *eight* were sold by the new. And this ratio held good on both insertions. The result was that this company knew in advance that it had a fundamentally sound "big idea," and magazine and newspaper advertisements, trade-paper advertisements, direct-mail literature, etc., could be prepared with the assurance that the money was being wisely invested, not merely spent. It was interesting to observe how the campaign almost formulated itself. Copy angles created themselves and vied with each other for attention! Illustrations—and even the name of the artists to do them—at once suggested themselves! Plans for booklets, trade-paper advertisements, counter and window display devices, etc., tumbled over themselves! All because the idea was so definite and the public itself had said, "Go ahead. You have the right idea." That campaign was launched, and has since been conducted against a

[1] *Printers' Ink*, July 14, 1921, p. 101.

background of absolute conviction such as few advertisers have never more than approximated.[1]

These tryout methods are very valuable and should be used wherever they can be applied in a reliable manner. The difficulty in many instances, however, is that many propositions do not lend themselves to a reliable test of this sort. A satisfactory tryout test can be made only where the returns can be checked accurately, either in terms of sales, or in terms of direct inquiries or orders.

A second difficulty lies in the fact that it is impossible to control fully all factors involved, such as the territory covered in the tryout, or the mediums used as compared with other mediums that will be used later, and so on.

A third difficulty, and in some respects the most serious one, is the fact that it is almost impossible to diagnose, in any detailed manner, what particular factors in the appeals or in the make-up of the advertisement are directly responsible for the results produced. For example, if the results are good from a given piece of copy, it may be due to an unusually good layout, or similar factors, when at the same time the appeal used may be relatively weak. Or the situation may be reversed; the appeal may be very strong, and other elements of the advertisement may be mediocre or weak.

The effectiveness of an advertisement depends upon numerous individual elements—the picture, headline, text, layout, color, typography, phraseology, and the like. It is practically impossible to determine by a tryout test of this sort which of these numerous elements are strong or weak and to which the success or failure of an advertisement is due. The ideal advertisement is one in which all elements are strong and the ideal testing method would be one by which all important elements could be accurately evaluated.

Probably the most direct way to determine the strength of the various elements is by means of carefully planned

[1] *Ibid.*, Dec. 29, 1921, p. 77.

and conducted laboratory-field tests, such as will be described presently. The chief doubt which most business men have concerning the proposed methods of testing is the question of reliability, that is, whether the conditions of the test approximate the real conditions under which an advertisement functions. This question will be deferred for the present, and a careful consideration and statement of the facts relative to it will be presented in a later chapter. At this point, let us consider the detail and technique by which such tests may be made.

Properly worded questions included in a first-hand questionnaire investigation will yield very valuable results and will give many helpful clues and suggestions for appeals and copy construction. For example, in Chapter VIII, Questions 6 and 8, particularly, yield many suggestive ideas for the determination of appeals. The same is true of Question 5 in Chapter IX.

As a further illustration of this approach to the problem, we may mention a relative ranking method applied to 21 abstract appeals for toothpaste. By abstract, here, is meant the statement of the appeal purely and simply in the form of a word or phrase. To illustrate, the following 21 appeals, stated only in the phrases as here given, were presented to a group of 46 men who were asked to rank them in the order in which they considered these selling points of importance. The numbers given after the various points in Table 50 are the median ranks for these points.

By means of such a test, a somewhat more extensive series of appeals may be evaluated than is ordinarily possible in connection with a questionnaire interview. Results of this sort are very suggestive and are a step in the right direction. The difficulty, however, with taking these results as final, is that the effectiveness of the particular

TABLE 50

RELATIVE EFFECTIVENESS OF APPEALS FOR TOOTHPASTE

Appeals	Median Ranks
White, clean teeth	2.3
Health	2.5
Film on teeth	4.3
Taste	**6.1**
Acid mouth	6.5
Effect on gums	6.7
Pyorrhea	7.2
Dentists' approval	8.5
Purifies breath	9.5
Pleasant feeling in mouth	10.5
Safe	12.0
Price	12.5
Convenience of tube and cap	13.5
Beauty	13.5
Size of tube	14.5
No grit	14.5
Frequency of use	15.5
Habit of brushing regularly	15.8
Research in preparation of paste	16.9
Concentrated paste	17.5
Reputation of firm	18.0

selling point depends to a considerable extent upon the manner in which it is formulated. Furthermore, each person is apt to have a somewhat different conception of the meaning and implication of the various points when considered only as phrases. When, however, each point is stated in the form in which it is to be used in the copy finally, all persons are reacting to the same identical argument.

A test such as this with the toothpaste appeals, or with the abstract appeals in the raisin or clothing investigations, serves as a useful basis and as a preliminary survey for the next step, which is to select the more effective appeals and then to phrase them in the form in which it is proposed to use them in the copy; and then submit them to a test such as is outlined in the next paragraphs.

ILLUSTRATION OF A LABORATORY-FIELD TEST

Let us assume that our problem for the moment is to determine which of the various possible selling arguments for a toothpaste should be selected. Each of the various selling points should be written out in the exact form in which it is proposed to use it. This was done with the following set of 24 arguments.[1]

A. Brushing the teeth with toothpaste or ordinary paste or dentifrice removes only the coarser particles of food. Microscopic particles remain to set up acid mouth, an injurious chemical condition. Acid mouth needs to be corrected by chemical means. Klenzo harmlessly brings about this chemical correction.

B. Klenzo meets the demand for a dentifrice that shall be safe. It keeps the mouth clean and healthy without employing scratchy substances and harmful drugs.

C. While the quality of a dentifrice is the main thing, yet quantity is distinctly a consideration. Klenzo comes in a package of generous size.

D. Pyorrhea loosens the gums and makes them bleed; lets the teeth drop out; allows bacteria from the infected gums to get into the system. It is a dangerous condition. Klenzo prevents Pyorrhea.

E. Persons of fashion and refinement use Klenzo, the dentifrice of quality. It belongs with all who exercise more than ordinary care in manners and appearance, and who choose their purchases with equal care. This is why they put Klenzo on the shopping list.

F. Klenzo leaves the mouth clean, cool and refreshed. There is none of the burning sensation which follows the use of some strongly chemical dentifrice.

G. An honest package of honest dentifrice for an honest price —that is what you get when you buy Klenzo. After all, what counts is not quantity or price, but value; and value is Klenzo's "Long suit."

H. If you use Klenzo you can smile. White and beautiful teeth will mark you as a clean, wholesome person, a person to know and like.

I. Klenzo, the right dentrifice, is sold at a right price. This gives you the maximum both of quantity and quality.

[1] The data bearing on this investigation and the illustration in Figure 25 are presented by permission of the United Drug Company of Boston.

J. Klenzo is not a medicine, a drug or a chemical. It does not profess to rectify abnormal or diseased conditions of the teeth. If you suffer from these, consult your dentist. Klenzo does the only thing a safe dentifrice can do or should be expected to do; it thoroughly cleanses the teeth.

K. Inadequate disinfection of the teeth and gums may lead to Pyorrhea, a dangerous condition. Do not wait for its symptoms to appear. Klenzo is an adequate disinfectant; prevents Pyorrhea.

L. Nature preserves the teeth of animals and of primitive man by keeping them perfectly clean and fit. Her method will preserve your teeth, too, if you will let it. Nature's method of preserving the teeth is the basis of Klenzo.

M. Klenzo is a harmless antiseptic dentifrice. Without employing injurious drugs, it keeps the teeth fit to resist deterioration and disease, and corrects threatening conditions of the mouth. All this it does with perfect safety.

N. The children like the taste of Klenzo. It solves the problem of getting them to brush their teeth regularly, and helps to form that valuable habit.

O. Klenzo was for years the subject of exhaustive experiment at the Clinic (devoted exclusively to the prevention and cure of diseases of the mouth and teeth). This research has proved to the dental profession the value of Klenzo as a dentifrice, and its superiority for general use as a dentifrice. Dentists recommend Klenzo.

P. When your gums are inflamed and tender, and bleed at brushing, beware of the gum decay which causes tooth decay. In the tiny openings in the diseased gums lodge insidious germs which attack the teeth, inflame the tonsils, and infect the nose and throat. Klenzo prevents these troubles at their source.

Q. Klenzo, by the sheer cleanness it creates, keeps germs and acids from developing in the mouth. All the mouth nerves testify that it has freed them from the stale secretions that made them feel hot and sticky. You can trust that cool Klenzo feeling.

R. The Klenzo taste whets your appetite for breakfast. That cool clean flavor is the best preparation for good food and good digestion.

S. That slimy film upon the teeth—the film that you feel with your tongue and that no ordinary treatment can remove—harbors millions of germs. There they breed; there they attack your teeth, your gums, your digestion. The film holds food substances which ferment into acids and corrode your teeth. The film covers the tartar, which causes decay. Klenzo removes that film.

T. Healthy teeth depend upon healthy gums. When your gums are solid and ruddy and hard, and hold your teeth firmly, your teeth simply must keep well. Start using Klenzo for the gums. It keeps them firm, hard and healthy, and helps guard the teeth.

U. Klenzo keeps the mouth free of the substances that foster germs, acid and decay. Its effect is so wholesome that you easily form the habit of using it and actually look forward to teeth-cleaning time.

V. Be guided by that wholesome Klenzo feeling. It means that your mouth is normal, your gums red and healthy, your teeth firm and clean.

W. Klenzo is prescribed by more dentists than any other dentifrice. An impartial investigation demonstrates:

    1. That Klenzo is the first choice of more dentists than any other dentifrice.

    2. That Klenzo is prescribed exclusively by more dentists than any other dentifrice.

X. The Klenzo flavor—cool and fresh—you may trust, for it is not merely a taste. It is evidence that your mouth is thoroughly pure and clean.

To determine which of these 24 selling arguments is the strongest, or which are the more effective ones, the test may be conducted as follows. Have a person read these statements carefully, and after he has done so, ask him to re-examine them and indicate which one influences him most fully in favor of wanting this particular toothpaste. Then ask him to number the 24 statements in the order in which they appeal to him as effective selling points for him individually, not as he would judge they might appeal to others. This rank order may be determined most conveniently by working from both ends; that is, by selecting the better ones on the one hand and likewise by numbering from the poorer end the ones that impress him least favorably. In this manner, he will gradually reduce the number of selling arguments which he is comparing and will be able to discriminate more accurately between the impression which the various appeals make upon him.

The procedure or test may be carried out with as many

individuals as seems desirable or necessary in order to obtain a sufficiently extensive set of results. Before considering the validity of such a procedure and its general practicability, it will be necessary to discuss the statistical methods for handling the test results.

STATISTICAL TREATMENT OF TEST RESULTS

Let us illustrate in the next place the manner in which a series of tests may be treated statistically so as to make the results usable and also to determine how reliable the results themselves may be. It is obvious that a test such as the one outlined for the 24 selling arguments for a toothpaste should be carried out with a sufficiently large number of persons to make the results representative of the consumers in question. For the present, we shall not discuss the question of the number of persons with whom a test should be made in order to yield valid data. This will be discussed later in this chapter. Let us notice first of all how the individual test results or rankings may be compiled and treated. The test with the 24 toothpaste appeals was carried out with 25 young men. These particular results are presented here primarily to illustrate the method of computation rather than the question of validity of the method.

Table 51 gives the order of the ranking made by the 25 young men. Thus, the first vertical column of letters gives the order of the various appeals as they impressed the first man. Argument T appealed to him as the strongest; argument S appealed to him next most strongly; argument L was third; and so on down the column, to argument E, which appealed to him as the weakest. Each of the other vertical columns gives the order as arranged by each of the other young men.

What we wish to know now is the average or final position which each of the appeals has with the 25 men as a group. Obviously the 25 men differ very considerably in the order in which they have arranged the 24 arguments.

TABLE 51

STRENGTH OF APPEALS FOR A TOOTHPASTE

1—T	A	D	S	S	H	A	H	X	S	H	O	W	H	V	X	J	J	S	H	H	J	R	H	A — 1
2—S	P	S	T	R	L	B	N	F	X	X	N	O	V	T	V	R	N	Q	Q	R	M	H	S	F — 2
3—L	W	P	P	Q	S	P	B	V	H	E	B	D	T	P	B	T	A	U	E	F	B	F	J	M— 3
4—N	E	T	A	H	N	T	V	J	F	B	K	K	N	U	R	B	W	B	O	U	A	X	Q	W— 4
5—A	X	L	Q	F	R	K	U	M	V	A	J	P	K	D	M	L	O	V	W	W	H	V	B	R — 5
6—M	H	H	J	X	Q	D	D	L	C	M	M	E	F	K	H	N	K	P	M	X	R	U	T	G — 6
7—H	R	J	K	B	F	S	M	B	O	W	T	N	X	A	A	F	B	T	A	N	F	B	B	B — 7
8—K	G	N	D	W	U	U	R	H	R	Q	D	H	Q	S	Q	P	S	R	F	D	X	T	W	V — 8
9—V	K	E	U	V	O	I	T	U	R	W	S	S	Q	T	A	T	M	U	M	L	E	A	P	P — 9
10—R	L	W	F	K	G	G	W	F	A	J	U	U	T	A	N	F	F	S	Q	U	Q	Q	U	E —10
11—Q	T	M	V	D	D	J	A	K	Q	G	P	J	J	H	U	V	V	U	X	D	E	Q	L	J —11
12—P	I	K	X	P	A	H	Q	D	P	C	S	B	P	L	N	O	O	Q	L	K	O	O	L	L —12
13—D	Q	O	B	T	T	E	W	P	K	I	A	A	U	F	J	M	D	N	P	G	W	W	R	R —13
14—U	O	F	W	U	E	N	G	S	D	N	L	L	M	X	W	U	V	H	T	T	G	A	N	Q —14
15—B	D	B	O	A	W	R	X	R	T	F	Q	M	D	R	O	Q	M	A	B	T	G	A	C	C —15
16—W	U	U	H	E	O	Q	P	O	M	V	F	G	B	J	P	C	F	W	L	I	I	M	F	H —16
17—G	M	Q	L	N	P	F	C	W	A	O	R	C	I	B	S	G	G	E	V	S	N	D	C	I —17
18—C	C	A	E	L	M	M	K	N	N	L	X	I	R	M	K	K	L	C	N	N	K	S	S	D —18
19—C	J	G	N	O	B	G	J	U	L	J	V	U	G	O	D	D	H	G	J	A	K	K	P	T —19
20—O	S	V	M	M	K	I	O	O	B	T	G	Q	L	W	L	W	X	J	X	C	P	T	N	U —20
21—I	N	R	G	J	C	X	E	C	G	S	H	V	E	I	I	E	O	R	R	P	T	N	D	K —21
22—J	V	X	C	G	I	L	T	G	E	K	I	R	O	I	G	H	R	K	I	L	V	C	K	X —22
23—X	B	C	I	I	J	V	S	E	W	D	E	F	W	G	C	E	C	D	G	B	P	G	V	S —23
24—E	F	I	R	C	X	C	L	I	I	P	C	X	C	C	E	S	I	I	C	J	E	I	O	N —24

We may determine the final position of each argument in one of two ways. Either we may determine the average rank of each appeal or the median rank. Let us illustrate the method of computation by taking the ranks of argument H. We will select this particular argument because it turns out to be the strongest one in our list of 24. If we follow the position of H across the table, we note that it is seventh in the first man's test, sixth in the second and third columns, sixteenth in the fourth, fourth in the fifth column, first in the sixth, and so on across the table. That is, argument H has the following positions in the rankings made by the 25 men: 7, 6, 6, 16, 4, 1, 12, 1, 8, 3, 1, 21, 8, 1, 11, 6, 22, 19, 14, 1, 1, 5, 2, 1, 16, or a total of 193.

These various ranks of argument H may be presented graphically as shown in Figure 21. In this figure it will be noticed that 7 of the 25 men ranked it highest, one ranked it second, one third, one fourth, and so on, over to one who ranked it twenty-second. We may now compute either the average rank or the median rank. The average would be computed in the usual manner of adding all of the ranks and dividing by 25; that is, 193 divided by 25. This gives us an average of 7.7. Or, we may compute the median. By definition, the median is the middle point of a series of measurements arranged in the order of increasing or decreasing size. That is, in the present illustration, the median point would be the thirteenth ranking as shown in the figure, since there are 25 persons who ranked these arguments. Counting from either end to the thirteenth, we find that it falls upon the middle one of the three over 6. In other words, the median is 6.[1]

Both the average and the median represent the central tendency of a series of measures. The difference is that the median is not affected by individual measures which

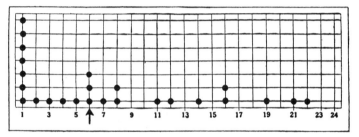

Figure 21: Selling argument H, ranked by 25 men students

depart very materially from the central tendency. The average, on the other hand, is distinctly influenced by erratic individual measures. This difference is illustrated in the data in Figure 21. The average is distinctly larger than the median; that is, 7.7 against 6.0. The explanation is that the three or four extreme individuals who ranked this selling argument as 19, 21, and 22 have a stronger effect in drawing the average in that direction than any three individuals who ranked this selling argument first.

A secondary advantage of the median is that it may be computed more quickly. By arranging the individual measures as illustrated in the figure, one obtains at the same

[1] For methods for computing the exact median, consult treatises on statistics.

time a visual representation of the distribution of the individual rankings.

An inspection of Figure 21 shows that while there is a considerable scattering among the individual rankings, there is nevertheless a very strong tendency for the rankings to be grouped around the left end of the distribution. More persons have given argument H the first rank than any other rank.

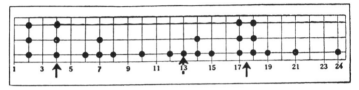

Figure 22: Selling argument N, "Children like the toothpaste," ranked by 25 men students. The distribution shows a tendency toward bimodality.

Another point of interest in connection with a distribution diagram is that it shows the manner in which the measures in a given case are scattered. Sometimes a given selling argument may appeal very effectively to some persons but be very weak with other persons. Usually, we find that most arguments show a distinct single central grouping area. Now and then, however, there is a decided tendency for the rankings to be scattered around two points. This is illustrated in Figure 22, which shows the distribution of the ranking of argument N. It will be noted that with approximately half of the 25 men this argument was very strong, while with the other half it was rather weak. There is a tendency in this distribution to have a grouping around 2 to 4 on the one end, and around 17 and 18 at the other end. Evidently the appeal that children like the taste of the toothpaste is a strong appeal with approximately half of the individuals and a very weak appeal with the other half.

To determine whether or not this tendency for people to be divided into two groups on this particular argument was merely a peculiarity of the group of the 25 young men whose results are here considered, the test data of an additional group of 51 men is combined with the 25 men in Figure 23. An inspection of this figure shows that the tendency is equally strong with the entire group of 76 persons. Two to 4 is the central point for the persons with whom this argument is strong, and 15 to 18 is the central point for the persons with whom this argument is weak.

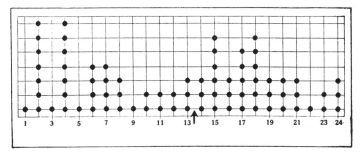

Figure 23: Selling argument N, "Children like the toothpaste," ranked by 76 men students. The distribution shows a distinct tendency toward bimodality, corroborating the ranking made by a smaller number of persons.

Table 52 gives the median ranks of each of the 24 arguments as based on the test made with the 25 young men. (For the sake of convenience merely a summary phrase is given in Table 52 for each of the selling arguments, instead of the lengthy wording actually used in the test.)

This table gives us the relative strength of the various selling arguments so far as this group of 25 young men is concerned. To assist us in visualizing the relative differences among these selling arguments, as ranked by this group of young men, we may represent the medians of the 24 arguments in graphic form as shown in Figure 24.

This graphic representation shows that H is distinctly the strongest argument with this group. The next three or four arguments are scattered along by small intervals from 7.4 to 9.5. Then there is a group of some 12 arguments which are very close together and are placed at about the

TABLE 52

RELATIVE EFFECTIVENESS OF A SERIES OF SELLING ARGUMENTS
FOR TOOTHPASTE

Selling Argument	Median Rank
H White, beautiful, clean teeth	5.8
B Clean, healthy mouth, safe dentifrice	7.4
T Healthy gums and teeth	8.7
R Taste—cool, clean flavor	9.0
A Correct acid mouth	9.5
S Slimy film, germs and decay	9.5
F Clean, cool mouth—no burning sensation	10.0
V Wholesome feeling and healthy mouth	10.0
Q Prevents germs and acids	10.5
U Prevents germs and acids	10.5
M Harmless, safe dentifrice	11.0
X Cool Klenzo flavor	11.0
J Not a medicine but a cleanser	12.0
P Prevents diseased gums	12.0
W Prescribed by more dentists than any other	12.0
L Klenzo like nature's method	12.4
K Prevents Pyorrhea	12.5
D Prevents Pyorrhea	12.7
N Children like it	13.0
O Klenzo based on research	14.0
E Persons of fashion and refinement use it	16.5
G Honest package and price	19.0
C A large package	21.0
I Maximum package and right price	21.3

middle of the scale, ranging numerically from 10.0 to 12.7. The next arguments are scattered along from 13 on down to C and I, which are distinctly the weakest appeals and stand very low numerically.

COMPARISON OF ABSTRACT APPEALS WITH COMPLETELY PHRASED APPEALS

A relative ranking of a series of six, ten, or a dozen abstract appeals as part of a questionnaire investigation (illustrated in Chapters VIII to X) or ranked in a special investigation made for the purpose (illustrated in the case of 21 abstract appeals on page 293) furnishes a very useful basis for the preparation of copy, but it is only a step in the right direction. In a thorough and complete succession of steps in building up the most effective appeals and plans,

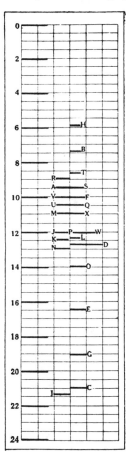

the results of the ranking of abstract appeals should be used for preparing the experimental copy, that is, copy or selling appeals fully worded as it is proposed to present them.

The importance of this is evident from the fact that certain mental images and meanings suggested by the phraseology may materially affect the strength or weakness of a given argument. This point is illustrated in Table 53, which gives in the first column the median ranks of the toothpaste appeals when they were fully stated as in the preceding experiment, and in the second column the median ranks when they were presented merely as abstract phrases.

(Mere summary phrases are used here for the appeals H, B, T, etc., instead of the lengthy wording actually used in the test. For the complete statement of the selling arguments represented by H, B, T, etc., see page 282.)

By comparing the ranks for the same appeal in the two columns, we note a decided difference in several of them. For example, S—Slimy film, germs and decay—stood much lower when thus fully stated (9.5)

Figure 24: Median ranks of the toothpaste selling arguments. *(See page 289)*

Figure 25: The advertisement which resulted from the investigation

TABLE 53

COMPARISON OF METHODS OF DETERMINING THE EFFECTIVENESS
OF APPEALS

Copy Completely Stated	Median Rank	Median Rank	Abstract Appeal
H White, beautiful clean teeth	5.8	2.3	White clean teeth
B Clean healthy mouth, safe dentifrice	7.4	2.5	Health
T Healthy gums and teeth	8.7	4.3	Film on teeth
R Taste—cool clean feeling	9.0	6.1	Taste
A Corrects acid mouth	9.5	6.5	Acid mouth
S Slimy film, germs and decay	9.5	6.7	Effect on gums
F Clean cool mouth—no burning sensation	10.0	7.2	Pyorrhea
V Wholesome feeling and healthy mouth	10.0	8.5	Dentists' Approval
Q Prevents germs and acids	10.5	9.5	Purifies breath
U Prevents germs and acids	10.5	10.5	Pleasant feeling in mouth
M Harmless, safe dentifrice	11.0	12.0	Safe
X Cool Klenzo flavor	11.0	12.5	Price
J Not a medicine but a cleanser	12.0	13.5	Convenient tube and cap
P Prevents diseased gums	12.0	13.5	Beauty
W Prescribed by more dentists	12.0	14.5	Size of tube
L Uses nature's method	12.4	14.5	No grit
K Prevents Pyorrhea	12.5	15.5	Frequency of use
D Prevents Pyorrhea	12.7	15.8	Regular habit of using
N Children like it	13.0	16.9	Research in preparation
O Based on research	14.0	17.5	Concentrated paste
E Persons of fashion and refinement use it	16.5	18.0	Reputation of firm
G Honest package and price	19.0		
C A large package	21.0		
I Maximum package and right price	21.3		

than it did when given merely as an abstract phrase, "Film on teeth" (4.3). Similar large differences will be observed in the case of "Prevents "Pyorrhea," 12.5 and 12.7 as against 7.2; "Prescribed by more dentists," 12.0 as against 8.5; "Honest package and price," 19.0 as against 12.5; "A large package," 21.0 as against 14.5; and so on. Clearly it is important to test the relative values of various appeals in fully stated form.

Objections Answered. From the practical point of view, the reader will have several objections to interpose at this point. In the first place, one objection to this method is that the person with whom the test is carried out is more fully conscious of what he is doing than when he merely glances over the advertisements in a casual way—that he is purposely attempting to state whether the various selling appeals impress him and how much. The objection is that under ordinary circumstances the observer of an advertisement does not make a conscious analysis of the situation, but that the impression is made upon him more or less in a semi-conscious manner. We shall not attempt to answer these objections fully at this point, but rather we will defer a detailed analysis to Chapter XIV. However, we may note, as a partial answer to this objection, that we *can* tell differences consciously and that we *do* have a distinct feeling that a better or worse impression is being made upon us by a given selling appeal; furthermore, that the average person is more conscious of his processes in noting and observing advertisements when he is doing it naively in the usual way than we are apt to suspect; and that when the reader is actually influenced by an advertisement he becomes quite aware mentally of the various points for or against a given proposition. Anyone who is in doubt about this point needs merely to look at a few advertisements and it will not require much introspection to see that he is affected very differently by them. However, this answer to the objection is purely analytical. The real answer will be found in the question, To what extent do the results of such tests as these check up with the actual returns obtained by the advertisements in which these same appeals are used under actual conditions?   Extensive data will be presented on this point in Chapter XIV.

A second objection that will readily occur to the reader is that such a test probably is no criterion of the effectiveness of a series of appeals since everyone is different.   Even though each given individual might be able to respond quite normally to the various selling points under consideration, the objection is made that people are so different that what may influence one person favorably may impress another one quite unfavorably.   This objection can be answered definitely and conclusively by conducting the test with a sufficiently large number of persons so that it will be possible to determine on a basis of fact to what extent individuals do differ or agree.   Data will be presented on this point later in this chapter.

In the third place, even though we should grant that the two preceding objections are not serious, nevertheless the objection is raised that this testing method does not give us a measure of the relative value of a series of selling points so far as their effect in making him want a given product is concerned.   What he likes may be no indication of what will really influence him to act upon the given proposition. The answer to this objection is that the test should be made specifically with the instructions to rank the appeals in the order in which they impress *him in favor of wanting the particular object involved*.   When that is done a highly reliable response is obtained from each individual, as will be shown by data presented later.

A fourth point that must be carefully borne in mind is that the test should be made with persons who are typical of the class of persons to whom the advertisements are ultimately intended to appeal.   Much of the testing work that has been published, not so much on this problem as on others (because little has been written on this specific problem) has been carried out by teachers with their students, chiefly because the student can easily be reached. The criticism is justly made that such tests are of lesser value on the ground that students are not always typical of the particular class concerned with a given commodity. It is evidently of the highest importance, therefore, that the tests should be made with persons who are typical of the class to whom the product is to be sold. If a product is to be sold to women, the tests should be made with women; or if the product is to be sold to business men of a certain class, the tests should be made with them; if the product is to be sold to skilled mechanics, the test should be made with them; or if the product is to be sold to owners of automobiles, the tests should be made with automobile owners, and so on. When this is done, the test results have a surprisingly high degree of reliability.

It should also be pointed out here that the particular test here discussed as a sample has dealt only with the test of one element of an advertisement. A complete series of tests of a set of advertisements must cover the other essential elements which may be even more important than the text, such as the headline, or the picture, or the attention-getting features of the layout. Tests covering these points will be discussed later.

How Many Tests Are Necessary? This question may be answered experimentally by making the same test with various groups of persons and by comparing these results in order to ascertain to what extent various groups agree with one another and to what extent various sizes of groups will agree with a rather large group made up of the combined results of a number of smaller groups. This was done with the present 24 toothpaste arguments. The results are shown in Table 54, which gives the median ranks of a group of 25 men students, 50 miscellaneous men (not students), 162 women (mostly housewives), 202 men (mostly business men), and finally the combined results of all of these groups, making a total of 389 persons (364 men and women plus 25 men students which are not included in the group of 202 men).

TABLE 54

COMPARISON OF TEST RESULTS FROM GROUPS OF DIFFERENT SIZES

Selling Arguments	25 Men Students, College Graduates	50 Miscellaneous Men	202 Men	162 Women	Total 364 Men and Women
H	6.5	8.6	8.2	8.4	9.2
T	9.2	10.9	8.6	9.2	9.5
J	11.8	7.0	10.0	9.5	10.3
B	7.7	10.1	9.4	10.8	10.9
F	10.4	10.7	10.6	11.8	11.3
S	9.7	10.4	10.3	11.0	11.3
K	12.7	9.6	10.4	11.2	11.5
W	13.1	13.3	10.1	11.3	11.5
D	13.7	11.5	11.4	10.3	11.6
A	9.7	11.2	10.9	12.2	11.7
Q	11.2	12.5	11.4	11.6	11.9
V	11.3	12.9	11.6	10.5	11.9
X	11.8	12.4	11.1	11.1	12.0
M	13.5	11.3	11.3	11.7	12.1
L	12.8	15.5	11.2	12.2	12.4
P	12.4	12.9	12.3	11.3	12.7
N	13.5	12.5	11.7	11.5	12.8
U	10.6	10.6	12.4	11.8	12.9
R	9.5	12.0	12.0	12.2	13.4
G	19.4	17.5	13.8	12.2	14.3
O	14.5	14.0	13.8	13.4	14.4
I	21.8	19.5	15.3	14.5	16.1
C	21.3	19.4	16.2	14.6	16.4
E	17.5	18.1	15.8	15.1	16.7

An examination of this table shows a close agreement among the various groups. Even the small group of 25 young men agrees remarkably well with any of the larger groups and with the total group. The surprising fact apparently is that a relatively small number of persons yields a fairly reliable set of results. In general, the same arguments are strong with all groups, and likewise, the same arguments respectively are weak with all groups.

Statistically, the most convenient as well as the most accurate method of expressing the amount of agreement between the results of various groups is by means of a coefficient of correlation.[1] In general, we may say that the coefficient of correlation expresses the amount of agreement between any two sets of measures. We may think of it as the percentage of agreement or disagreement between two sets of measures, since the maximum value which the coefficient of correlation may have is plus 1.00 and the minimum value is minus 1.00. A correlation between .0 and .25 indicates a slight tendency toward agreement, .25 to .50 indicates a moderate agreement, .50 to .75 indicates decided agreement and .75 to 1.00 means very close agreement.

In terms of the coefficient of correlation, the various

---

[1] Consult treatises on statistics for methods of computing the coefficient of correlation. One formula commonly used, known as Pearson's method of rank differences, is $r = 1 - \dfrac{6 \text{ Sum } d^2}{n(n^2-1)}$, in which d is the difference in rank between any two measures of the same item, or selling argument in this case, and n is the number of items or arguments.

To take a simple illustration let us take the first 10 appeals in Table 54 and show how this formula would be applied in computing the correlation between the 202 men and the 162 women.

	202 Men		162 Women			
	Medians	Ranks	Medians	Ranks	d	d²
H	8.2	1	8.4	1	0	0
T	8.6	2	9.2	2	0	0
J	10.0	4	9.5	3	1	1
B	9.4	3	10.8	5	2	4
F	10.6	8	11.8	9	1	1
S	10.3	6	11.0	6	0	0
K	10.4	7	11.2	7	0	0
W	10.1	5	11.3	8	3	9
D	11.4	10	10.3	4	6	36
A	10.9	9	12.2	10	1	1

Sum d² = 52

n = 10

Hence $r = 1 - \dfrac{6 \text{ Sum } d^2}{n(n^2-1)} = 1 - \dfrac{6 \times 52}{10(10^2-1)} = 1 - \dfrac{312}{990} = 1 - .30 = .70$

groups shown in the table have the following amounts of agreement:

Correlation between 25 men and total group (364)   .70
Correlation between 50 misc. men and total group   .79
Correlation between 162 women and total group   .83
Correlation between 202 men and total group   .95
Correlation between 202 men and 162 women   .76

To illustrate this point further with the test results obtained in a similar manner for selling arguments for various types of commodities, we may note in the next place the amount of agreement among four groups of men and women with whom a test of 12 appeals for a checkwriter was made.

TABLE 55

SELLING APPEALS FOR A CHECKWRITER

Selling Point		Group I 51 Business Men		Group II 54 Men Students New York C.		Group III 45 Men Students U. of Cal.		Group IV 38 Men Students U. of Wis.		Group V 30 Women Students U. of Pitts.		Total 218 Men and Women	
		Rank Order		Rank Order		Rank Order		Rank Order		Rank Order		Rank Order	
W	Protection	3.6	1	4.0	2	3.1	1	2.75	1	2.9	2	3.3	1
I	Legibility and Accuracy	4.7	2	3.5	1	4.5	3	3.41	2	5.0	4	4.2	2
J	Efficiency	5.3	3	4.8	4	4.4	2	4.75	3	6.0	5	5.0	3
X	Personality	5.6	4	4.4	3	5.7	4	5.75	4	2.6	1	4.8	4
C	Guarantee	6.9	7	6.1	5	6.1	5	6.31	5	7.2	8	6.5	6
G	Good Judgment —establishing credit	5.8	5	6.7	6	6.5	6	6.7	6	4.8	3	6.1	5
Q	Recommendation of large users	6.0	6	7.0	7	7.5	9	7.24	7	6.9	6	6.9	7
R	Light weight— compactness	8.6	9	8.2	11	7.8	10	7.83	8	8.4	10	8.1	9
V	Economy—capacity	9.4	11	7.7	10	7.3	8	8.64	9	8.1	9	8.2	10
Y	Quality and value	8.4	8	7.6	9	7.1	7	9.5	10	7.0	7	7.9	8
Z	Scientific construction	9.0	10	7.5	8	8.5	11	9.56	11	8.5	11	8.6	11
B	Reputation	10.0	12	10.3	12	9.6	12	12.15	12	10.6	12	10.9	12

In the tests the complete statement of the advertising arguments was used. The phrases in Table 55 merely indicate the chief point in each argument.

TABLE 56

CORRELATIONS OF RESULTS OF TESTS MADE WITH DIFFERENT GROUPS

Class	38 Men Students U. of Wis.	30 Women Students U. of Pitts.	51 Business Men	54 Men Students New York C	45 Men Students U. of Cal.
54 Men Students—New York City	.93				
45 Men Students—Univ. of Cal.	.91	.89			
38 Men Students—Univ. of Wis.	.95	.92	.93		
30 Women Students— Univ. of Pittsburgh	.90	.83	.83	.82	
Total—218 Men and Women	.08	.93	.95	.97	.89

The results from these different groups correlate very closely. The lowest correlation is between the group of women students and the other groups. The business men and the men students agree almost completely. With the possible exception of the women students, any single group of men would have been sufficiently large to give us an adequate measure of the relative value of these appeals.

Tables 57 and 58 give similar comparison between various sizes and types of groups with regard to the advertising arguments for candy and for automobile insurance respectively. In the case of the candy advertisements, the text was used in typewritten form apart from the advertisement. In the case of the automobile insurance tests, photostats of the actual advertisements themselves were used.

It is unnecessary to give any further detailed results concerning the extent of agreement when the tests are properly carried out between various groups of individuals. A series of tests was carried out with three sets of baking powder

TABLE 57
SELLING POINTS FOR A MINT CANDY

Advertisement	10 Business Women		17 Business Men		27 Women Students		20 Men Students		Total 74 Men and Women	
	Median Rank	Final Rank	Median Rank	Final Rank	Median Rank	Final Rank	Median Rank	Final Rank	Median Rank	Final Rank
A	7.3	9	7.5	9	7.3	9	6.5	9	7.1	9
B	4.1	3	3.1	1	6.1	8	5.9	6	4.8	4
C	6.5	8	5.7	5½	5.3	5	6.1	8	5.9	8
D	5.9	7	5.9	8	5.9	7	5.6	4	5.8	7
E	5.6	5	5.8	7	5.8	6	6.0	7	5.7	6
F	5.8	6	5.7	5½	5.1	4	5.7	5	5.6	5
G	2.7	1	4.0	2½	3.1	3	3.3	1	3.3	1
H	7.9	10	7.6	10	8.1	10	7.5	10	7.8	10
X	3.7	2	5.5	4	2.0	2	3.9	2	3.7	2
Z	5.5	4	4.0	2½	1.9	1	4.2	3	3.9	3

CORRELATIONS OF GROUPS

	10 Business Women	17 Business Men	27 Women Students	20 Men Students
17 Business Men	.85			
27 Women Students	.68	.64		
20 Men Students	.85	.67	.81	
74 Total	.97	.87	.80	.91

advertisements, six advertisements in each set. The first group of advertisements was tested with three groups of housewives, composed of 30, 30, and 48 housewives, respectively. The second set of six advertisements was tested with three groups, composed of 32, 25, and 47 housewives respectively. The third set of six advertisements was tested with 32, 30, and 46 housewives respectively. The results of these various groups correlate with each other and with the total group in each case in the neighborhood of .75 to 1.00. In other words, the correlations among these groups are approximately as high as those which have been cited in detail above.

Judging from the close agreement of various groups with one another, and considering the sizes of the various groups

TABLE 58

SIX AUTOMOBILE INSURANCE ADVERTISEMENTS

	Group I		Group II		Group III		Group IV		Group V		Total	
	20 Auto Owners		20 Auto Owners		30 Men Students		21 Auto Owners		40 Auto Owners		Total 131	
A	69%	3	68%	3	71%	3	73%	3	43%	4	62%	3
B	15%	6	17%	6	23%	6	17%	6	23%	6	20%	6
C	74%	2	81%	1	75%	2	75%	2	75%	1	76%	2
D	31%	4	26%	5	24%	5	37%	4	26%	5	28%	5
E	83%	1	80%	2	79%	1	80%	1	73%	2	79%	1
F	28%	5	28%	4	28%	4	18%	5	59%	3	35%	4

CORRELATIONS

Group   I 20 Auto Owners with total group of 131 persons   .94
Group   II 20 Auto Owners with total group of 131 persons   .94
Group III 30 Men Students with total group of 131 persons   .94
Group IV 21 Auto Owners with total group of 131 persons   .94
Group   V 40 Auto Owners with total group of 131 persons   .89

for which results have been presented, we may conclude that a test carried out with a minimum of 20 to 25 persons gives a remarkably reliable measure of the relative value of the given element being tested in a series of advertisements. An investigation intended to be the basis for a national campaign should undoubtedly cover various typical points over the country, possibly 5 to 10 typical localities. Statistically, it has been found that a minimum group of approximately 20 to 25 will give a sufficiently reliable index for an individual locality.

A complete series of tests of a set of advertisements usually requires several types of tests covering such elements of an advertisement as attention value, interest value, the headlines, the illustrations, convincingness of the text, and the like. In a complete program of tests of this sort, it is desirable, and in most instances necessary, to make each type of test with a different group of persons. Thus a total of 75 to 100 persons, using 20 to 25 for each type of test, will ordinarily give a sufficiently reliable measure for all practical purposes.

Perhaps the most outstanding feature noted is the remarkable uniformity of human nature in groups. While we realize that individuals differ enormously from one another as single individuals, it is evident from the facts presented that groups as a whole agree remarkably closely with one another. The array of statistical facts presented on this point furnishes undeniable proof that it is possible to measure the relative effectiveness of various selling appeals. The argument presented by sceptics, that individuals differ so enormously as to make any test of this sort invalid, obviously falls to the ground.

There is perhaps no more uncertain or variable factor in human life than the length of life. Yet, in the mass the proportion of individuals who will reach certain ages may be predicted with a high degree of mathematical precision. No one can predict how long any individual will live; yet, in the mass the probable length of life of various groups of certain ages may be foretold with remarkable accuracy. The extensive mortality tables of life insurance companies have made the life insurance business what it is today.

In this connection we may note the fact that even the average expert advertising man is quite incapable of determining by his own judgment the relative strength of various appeals with various classes of persons. H. L. Hollingworth made an experiment which is of interest in this connection. He determined the strength of a series of appeals with a group of 20 men and with a group of 20 women. Then he made the same test with 5 advertising men, asking them to rank these appeals (1) as they thought these points would appeal to men in general, and (2) as they thought they would appeal to women and (3) as they appealed to themselves. The results show the following correlations:

The 5 advertising men as they thought the arguments
would appeal to men, correlated with the actual test
with 20 men .65

The 5 advertising men as they thought the arguments

would appeal to women, correlated with the actual
test with 20 women .41

The 5 advertising men as the arguments appealed to
themselves correlated with the men and women combined .36

It is evident that even the consensus of five expert advertising men is not a very reliable index of the actual
effectiveness of a series of appeals with a group of women.
They succeed much better in estimating the probable
strength of appeals with men.

As further evidence on this point, we may refer to the
rankings of the list of 13 abstract appeals for boys' clothing
used in the questionnaire survey described in Chapter IX.
These appeals were ranked by 400 housewives interviewed
in the survey. They were also ranked by the salesmen in
the boys' clothing department of the store, as they thought
these selling points would appeal to customers. The median
ranks for the various appeals as ranked by the two groups
were as shown in Table 59.

TABLE 59

COMPARISON OF STRENGTH OF APPEALS AS TESTED WITH CON-
SUMERS AND AS ESTIMATED BY SALESMEN

Appeal	Salesmen Medians	House-wives Medians	Order According to Salesmen	Order According to Housewives
Material	2.6	1.22	1	1
Reputation of Firm	3.6	5.20	2	9
Durability	3.8	2.70	3	2
Style	3.8	3.40	3	3
Satisfaction or Money Back	5.0	5.48	5	10
Fit	5.8	3.60	6	4
Tailoring	6.4	4.90	7	7
Price	8.0	3.68	8	5
Merchant's Guarantee	8.0	4.98	8	8
Comfort	9.8	4.18	10	6
Wear Like Iron	10.4	5.84	11	12
Maker's Guarantee	11.0	5.65	12	11
Union Made	12.8	6.54	13	13

While the relative orders agree quite closely on most appeals, there are very large differences on several, as for example, Reputation of Firm, Satisfaction or Money Back. Both are ranked very much higher by the salesmen than by the housewives. On the other hand, the appeal of comfort is ranked distinctly higher by the housewives than by the salesmen. Obviously the tests must be made with, and the reaction must be obtained from, that particular class of persons who are the consumers of a given product.

XIV

THE VALIDITY OF LABORATORY-FIELD TESTS

The importance of ascertaining the actual effectiveness of any given advertisement. Tests of a series of life insurance advertisements. Tests of typewriter advertisements. Tests of advertisements for a book. Tests of encyclopedia advertisements. Lathe, piano, electric lamp, and soap advertisements. Objections to laboratory-field tests.

THE importance of this problem is very great, both from the standpoint of the economical expenditure of money for advertising, and from the standpoint of making advertising as a whole more effective and useful. Few business concerns fully realize the literally enormous differences in the effectiveness of the various advertisements in any given series or campaign. They are not aware of it because the great majority of businesses have no direct way of ascertaining the actual effectiveness or lack of effectiveness of any given advertisement or even of a series of advertisements.

To illustrate this point, let us note the following actual cases:

Of a series of fifteen advertisements for a player piano, the best one brought 258 replies, while the poorest one brought one reply. The other thirteen advertisements brought returns scattered all the way between these two extremes. All of these advertisements appeared in the same mediums.

Of a series of five lathe advertisements, the best one brought 40 times as many inquiries as the poorest one.

Of a series of eight advertisements of a book sold entirely by mail, the best advertisement sold three times as many copies as the poorest one, differences in seasons and mediums being considered.

306

Of a series of seven insurance advertisements, the best one sold three times as much insurance as the poorest. Allowance was made for the variation in the sizes of the advertisements and for the differences in the circulation of the various mediums used.

Of a series of fifteen typewriter advertisements, the best one was twice as effective as the poorest one.

Of a series of seven encyclopedia advertisements, the best one was over twice as effective as the poorest one.

Of eight advertisements for a calculating machine, the best one brought 380 inquiries and the poorest brought 92; of eight advertisements for a filing device, one brought 174 inquiries, while the poorest brought 62. In both cases allowance was made for differences in seasons. All advertisements were of the same size, and appeared in the same mediums. The differences are due therefore primarily to the copy and layout of the advertisements.

Examples might be multiplied indefinitely. The remarkable fact is that the differences in the effectiveness of the advertisements in any given typical series are astounding. The statement is true whether the results are measured by inquiries received or by actual sales resulting. As I shall show by later results, the average advertisement appearing in our better grade mediums has only approximately 50% of the effectiveness possessed by the 10% best advertisements in the same medium. A very large proportion of advertisements do not possess more than 25% to 30% of the effectiveness possessed by the 10% best advertisements.

These facts emphasize the fundamental importance of our problem, namely, Can we determine with an acceptable degree of reliability the effectiveness of advertisements before they are used and before money is expended upon them?

Returning once more to the series of fifteen player-piano advertisements, we find that if all fifteen advertisements had been as effective as the best one, they would have produced 3,870 replies instead of only 796.

Referring to the insurance advertisements, we find that if all seven had been as effective as the best one, the resulting sales would have been $105,000 instead of $74,000—a difference of $31,000. Similar comparisons would hold for the other cases cited.

It is evident then that the differences in the effectiveness of advertisements used by a firm for a given product are exceedingly great, and far greater than we are apt to realize without actual proof of this sort. The important practical problem is, Are there any methods by which we may eliminate the weak advertisements and substitute stronger ones in their places before any considerable amount of money is expended for space? The importance of this problem is further emphasized when we realize that in large national advertising campaigns the same identical advertisement is commonly inserted in a considerable number of mediums. For example, in the Sun-Maid raisin campaign in 1921 each of the chief advertisements was inserted in some 20 publications of which the total space occupied cost in the neighborhood of $75,000. When as much money is paid for the space used for a single advertisement as it would cost to build a small factory or business building, it is unnecessary to say that every essential element in the advertisement should be as effective as possible.

The considerable amount of experimental work that has recently been done on this problem has satisfactorily demonstrated that this method can be applied, and applied with a rather high degree of reliability. The problem resolves itself into an attempt to measure the extent to which a given advertisement or a series of advertisements fulfils the functions that it must fulfil in order to be successful.

In general, an advertisement to be effective must fulfil the following functions:

(1) It must attract attention
(2) It must arouse interest
(3) It must produce conviction

(4) It must impress the memory

(5) It must produce a response or action

Or, put somewhat differently, an advertisement, to be successful,

(1) Must be seen

(2) Must be read

(3) Must be believed

(4) Must be remembered

(5) Must be acted upon

The problem now resolves itself into the development of methods for testing these various functions.

A considerable variety of tests have been used for these purposes, and other methods of a similar nature may be devised. Each particular product or situation has problems of its own which require the development of new methods or the adaptation of old ones. However, the fundamental conception of the scientific nature of the procedure is essentially the same.

By adaptation of these methods the various elements of advertisements may be tested, depending upon the importance of these elements. Thus, for example, besides testing the value of the text and determining the strongest appeals to be used, it may be desirable, in the case of a given series of advertisements, to test the effectiveness of the headline, or the pleasingness of the colors to be used, or the relative efficacy of color versus black and white, or the interest and appealing value of the picture, or the relative importance of illustration and text, or to determine the value of various types of layout and arrangement.

The question which naturally arises at this point is, All this may be well and good as a matter of scientific interest and curiosity; but after all, will these tests really show what the actual effectiveness of a given series of advertisements is when they get to the people who are to be reached? These tests may be all right, as far as they go; but do they really indicate which of the proposed advertisements will actually be effective, and which will not?

I have been especially interested in this particular aspect of the problem, because the final proof of the validity of these methods is the important point. How will the results of these methods check up against the actual effectiveness of advertisements whenever that can be accurately measured by satisfactory records of inquiries, returns, or sales? As early as 1910, I advocated the use of methods of testing the relative values of advertisements, but there was no proof of the extent to which such tests would or would not measure the real effectiveness of advertisements in actual use.

In pursuit of this aim, I secured within the last few years, from firms in various lines of business, a considerable number of sets of advertisements for which records of actual returns or sales were available. Tests of the nature here mentioned were carried out. In most instances, it was not known what the returns secured by the various firms were until after the tests had been made. Then the results of the tests were compared with the actual returns or sales produced by the advertisements.

TESTS OF A SERIES OF LIFE INSURANCE ADVERTISEMENTS

Before showing to what extent the test results and the advertiser's returns did or did not check up, I wish to give in some detail the results of one group of tests made upon a set of seven insurance advertisements.

Three types of tests were carried out: one to test the attention value of the advertisements, the second to measure the value and appeal of the headline, and the third to measure the convincingness of the text.

The results are given in Table 60. The first column gives the letters by which the various advertisements are designated. The second column gives the median rank of each advertisement in the attention test. Thus, Ad A had a median rank of 2.2. With some persons it ranked first, with others second, with still others third, and so on. Its median rank was 2.2.

The third column gives the median test rank for the headlines of the various advertisements. The fourth column gives the median test rank for the convincingness of the text of each advertisement.

The fifth column gives the median of the three tests, and the sixth column numbers the various advertisements in order according to the median of column 5.

Column 6 shows that Ad A, according to the test, is the best one, Ad D is the second best, and so forth, and Ad C is the poorest.

How, now, do these results compare with the actual returns? The firm which had used these advertisements kindly sent me the number of inquiries brought by each advertisement, the amount of sales resulting from each one, the date on which each advertisement had appeared and also the name of the mediums in which each had appeared. From these data, it was possible to compute the returns for each advertisement in proportion to the size of the space used, the circulation of each medium, the probable effect of the season of the year, and the relative quality of the readers of each medium as indicated by the ratio of sales to inquiries.

The last column in Table 60 gives the order of the effectiveness of these seven advertisements as thus computed on the basis of the actual returns secured by the firm.

An inspection of Table 60 will show a close agreement between the final test ranks and the firm's ranks of returns. Ad A was the best one according to the tests; it was also first according to the returns. The only discrepancy is that Ad D is second according to the test and fourth according to the firm's returns, while Ad G is third according to the test and second according to the returns. Likewise, there is a slight difference on Ads B, E, and C.

TABLE 60

RESULTS OF TESTS OF SEVEN INSURANCE ADVERTISEMENTS

Advertisement	Attention Test		Headline Test		Test of Text		All Tests Combined	Final Rank According to Tests	Order According to Firm's Returns
	Median Rank	Order of Ranks	Median Rank	Order of Ranks	Median Rank	Order of Ranks			
A	2.2	2	2.3	1	2.2	1	2.2	1	1
D	1.9	1	3.5	3	3.3	3	2.9	2	4
G	4.0	4	3.2	2	3.1	2	3.4	3	2½
B	3.6	3	3.9	4	4.3	4	3.9	4	3
F	5.4	6	5.2	6	5.0	5½	5.2	5	5
E	5.3	5	4.2	5	6.0	7	5.3	6	7
C	6.6	7	6.8	7	5.0	5½	6.1	7	6

The exact amount of agreement may be expressed in statistical terms by what is known as a coefficient of correlation. For the sake of clearness, we may refer to the coefficient of correlation as the percentage of agreement between the two sets of ranks. This coefficient of correlation or percentage of agreement between the final test order and the firm's order, as computed by the usual statistical methods, is 86.

This is a very close agreement, which is of course evident from a direct comparison of the ranks. Obviously the results of the tests in this instance check up very closely with the actual effectiveness of the advertisements. It would have been a distinct advantage to this firm to have used advertisements of the type of A, D, and G, rather than of the type of F, E, and C. Considering size of space, circulation of mediums, and quality of readers, we find that Ad A brought three times as much business as Ad C.

Judging from this one experiment, we may say that it is possible to measure, with a rather high degree of reliability, the actual effectiveness of advertisements before they are used and before the money for space has been expended. However, one case is not sufficient to demonstrate the general validity of the methods proposed.

TESTS OF TYPEWRITER ADVERTISEMENTS

We tested next, therefore, a series of 15 advertisements for a typewriter. These advertisements were tested with respect to their attention value, interest value, and convincingness of the text. Table 61 gives in the first three columns the results for the various tests. In the fourth column the ranks as determined by all of the tests are given, and the last column gives the ranks as determined by the returns of the firm.

TABLE 61

RESULTS OF TESTS OF 15 TYPEWRITER ADVERTISEMENTS

Ad	Attention Test		Headline Test		Test of Text		Final Rank According to Tests (All Three)	Order According to Firm's Returns
	Median Rank	Order of Ranks	Median Rank	Order of Ranks	Median Rank	Order of Ranks		
L	3.7	1	6.2	3	5.2	1	1	1
N	6.5	5	5.9	2	6.7	3	2	3
A	7.1	6	5.7	1	7.3	4	3	4
D	5.8	3	7.5	7	8.3	6	4	5
E	4.5	2	9.9	12	6.1	2	5	12
H	7.9	7	7.2	6	7.5	5	6	7
I	8.7	8	6.95	5	8.7	8	7	2
O	6.3	4	8.2	8	8.8	9	8	9
K	9.3	9	6.0	4	8.9	10	9	13
M	9.7	11	8.0	9	9.8	11	10	6
J	11.8	13	12.9	15	8.5	7	11	10
B	11.0	12	10.5	13	10.3	12	12	11
G	9.5	10	12.0	14	10.8	13	13	14
C	13.5	15	9.2	10	10.9	14	14	15
F	13.0	14	9.7	11	12.2	15	15	8

Again the agreement is quite close, although not as close as in the case of the insurance advertisements. The percentage of agreement or coefficient of correlation is 71. The only discrepancies of importance are on Ad E, which is fifth according to the tests, and twelfth according to the returns; and on Ad F, which is fifteenth according to the tests, and eighth according to the returns.

It may be pointed out here that it often is very difficult to compute the relative order of returns brought by a series of advertisements so as to allow for differences in size of space, circulation of mediums, quality of readers, and so forth, even when careful records are kept of the inquiries and of the business resulting therefrom. A part of the discrepancy between the test results and the firm's rank according to returns is undoubtedly due to this factor.

TESTS OF ADVERTISEMENTS FOR A BOOK

The third case is that of a series of eight advertisements for a book which is sold entirely by mail. These advertisements were likewise tested with respect to their attention value, convincingness, and headline value. The results are given in Table 62.

TABLE 62
RESULTS OF TESTS OF EIGHT BOOK ADVERTISEMENTS

Ad	Attention Test Median Rank	Order of Ranks	Headline Test Median Rank	Order of Ranks	Test of Text Median Rank	Order of Ranks	Final Rank According to Tests	Order According to Firm's Returns
B	3.8	1	3.8	2	3.6	1	1	2
D	4.1	2	4.0	3	4.5	3	2	4
F	4.6	4	3.4	1	4.6	4	3	1
C	4.2	3	4.8	5	3.9	2	4	5
E	5.3	5	4.7	4	5.7	7	5	6
H	5.7	6	5.8	6	4.8	5	6	7
G	6.0	7	6.9	8	5.3	6	7	8
A	6.4	8	6.2	7	7.4	8	8	3

The correlation or percentage of agreement between the final test ranks and the order according to the firm's returns is 55. This again is a satisfactory agreement, although it is not as high as in the two cases mentioned. The only important discrepancy is on the last advertisement, which is eighth according to the tests, and third according to the publisher's returns. This discrepancy is explained in part by the difficulty of ascertaining in a completely reliable manner the relative returns so as to allow properly for variations due to seasons of the year, mediums, sizes of circulation, and so forth; and in part by the fact that some of the tests in this case were made with persons who were not entirely representative of the persons who buy this particular book.

Considering these factors, the results are quite satisfactory. In fact, I am inclined to believe that a series of carefully conducted tests gives a more reliable measure of the effectiveness of a set of advertisements than records of inquiries or sales, unless these are sufficiently extensive to iron out the influences due to such factors already mentioned as variations by season, sizes of space, circulation, quality of readers, and so on. Then, furthermore, a very important advantage of a series of laboratory-field tests is the diagnostic one of determining the relative strength or weakness of the various elements of an advertisement, such as text, headline, illustration, layout, and the like. It is practically impossible to determine the value of these individual elements by means of any set of returns, inquiries or sales.

TESTS OF ENCYCLOPEDIA ADVERTISEMENTS

The fourth case is that of a series of seven advertisements for an encyclopedia. Tests were made to measure the attention value of each advertisement as a whole, the convincingness of the text, and the values of the headlines.

The question may arise here in the mind of the reader, as to why the headlines were tested in the cases cited. The reason is that most of our tests have shown the headline to be a very important element in advertisements—an element probably more important than most persons realize.

The results of these tests as compared with the actual returns are given in Table 63. The publishers were good enough to supply the number of inquiries and the number

of orders brought by each advertisement, the dates on which
the advertisements appeared and the mediums in which
they appeared. In computing the relative ranks according
to the returns brought by the various advertisements, allowance was made as accurately as possible for the factors of
space, circulation of mediums, and seasonal fluctuations.

TABLE 63

RESULTS OF TESTS OF SEVEN ENCYCLOPEDIA ADVERTISEMENTS

Advertisement	Attention Test		Headline Test		Test of Text		Final Rank According to Tests		Order According to Firm's Returns
	Median Rank	Order of Ranks	Median Rank	Order of Ranks	Median Rank	Order of Ranks			
B	1.7	1	3.5	2	2.6	1	2.6	1	2
D	3.0	3	4.0	4	2.6	1	3.2	2	4
G	2.9	2	2.8	1	5.0	5½	3.3	3	1
E	3.3	4	5.0	7	3.0	3	3.8	4	3
A	5.4	5	3.8	3	4.7	4	4.6	5	6
C	6.8	7	4.5	6	5.0	5½	5.4	6	7
F	5.7	6	4.3	5	6.6	7	5.5	7	5

The correlation or percentage of agreement between the
order according to the tests and the order according to the
returns is 72. Evidently the tests give a very reliable index
of the relative effectiveness of these advertisements. The
advertisement which is the best according to the tests was
second according to the returns. The only two advertisements for which the difference is as much as two ranks
between the test order and the order according to the returns are Ads D and G.

In this manner the author has made numerous tests with
a total of 20 different sets of advertisements. In each case
the firms concerned supplied the data of actual returns;
with these the test results were compared. Table 64 contains a summary of the findings thus obtained, including
the results of the four sets of advertisements already described. The numbers in the four last columns are the
correlations of each one of the tests with the actual relative

TABLE 64

SUMMARY OF CORRELATION OF TESTS AND ACTUAL RETURN OF 20
SETS OF ADVERTISEMENTS

Business or Commodity	No. of Advertisements	Attention Value	Headline	Text on the Ads	All Tests Combined
Life Insurance	7	.68	.79	.88	.86
Encyclopedia	7	.90	.38	.30	.72
Typewriter	15	.48	.75	.46	.71
Book	8	.46	.75	.36	.58
Lumber	2	1.00	1.00	1.00	1.00
Spray Pump	3	.83	.00	.00	....
Toothpaste	4	.40	1.00	.20	.80
Water Heater	4	....	1.00	....	1.00
Filing Device	8	.81	....	.53	.72
Filing Device	8	.76	....	.55	.70
Filing Device	8	.88	....	.02	.65
Condensed Milk	2	1.00	1.00	.00	1.00
Coats and Suits	2	1.00	1.00	1.00	1.00
Health Exercise	5	.43	....	.78	.75
Correspondence Instruction	6	.59	.60	.71	.71
Correspondence Instruction	6	.49	.89	.34	.78
Addressing Machine	3	1.00	.75	.50	1.00
Duplicating Machine	6	.68	.90	.56	.87
Calculating Machine	4	.40	.40	.40	.40
Calculating Machine	5	.50	.45	.60	.80
Averages		.70	.78	.48	.79

effectiveness of the advertisements as measured by the returns brought.

Besides the attention value, the headline, and the text, several other elements were tested in some of the sets of advertisements mentioned, but it was found that in most instances these three factors are the most important. Other elements should be tested whenever it is probable that such other factors are of particular moment. It may be that it is the colors to be used, or the picture, or the text of the advertisement in separate form apart from the advertisement, or some other factor that should be tested. What particular elements need testing must be determined by the requirements of a given situation. Likewise the methods of testing must be adapted to the particular case in question.

From this table two important points appear:

First, the results demonstrate that it is possible by means of brief but carefully conducted tests to measure with a satisfactory degree of accuracy the relative value of advertisements as a whole and of the various elements in the advertisements. The average correlation between test results and business returns is approximately .80.

Second, the results show that certain elements in an advertisement are much more important than others. Specifically, the attention value and the headline are each nearly twice as important as the text of an advertisement. This is indicated by the fact that the correlations for these two elements are nearly twice as high as for the text.

The reader may ask why the correlations are not perfect, that is, 1.00. The reason is obvious. In the first place, the tests are not absolutely perfect measures. In the second place, the business results, such as inquiries or orders brought, are by no means perfect measures of the relative value of advertisements. The actual inquiries received are affected by such factors as class of readers of a given medium, seasonal fluctuation of business, different sizes of advertisements in a given series, size of circulation of different mediums in which the advertisements may appear, effect of preceding advertisements upon later ones for the same commodity, effect of other advertisements in the same medium, and so on. Of these factors it is relatively easy either to eliminate or to compute a proportionate adjustment for such factors as differences in size of advertisements, in circulation of mediums, and in seasonal fluctuation of business. Differences in classes of readers may be eliminated by using returns only from the same mediums. All of these factors were either eliminated or compensated for in proper ratios in the results on which Table 64 is based. It has not been possible thus far to eliminate or allow for the effect of preceding advertisements for a given commodity or of other advertisements in the same medium. In view of this it is almost surprising that the correlations are as high as they are. Furthermore, in view of these results and of the complexity of actually determining the relative pulling power of a series of advertisements, on the basis of inquiries or orders, it is probable that carefully applied tests give a more accurate measure of the relative value of a series of advertisements and of their elements than do the usual business returns themselves.

To illustrate the complexity of these factors and the difficulty of handling them and determining the part they play in the actual results produced by a series of advertisements, we may note how the element of seasonal fluctuation has been dealt with here. It is evident that in many types of business there is at certain seasons a distinct depression in the responses to the advertising or in the total business done. Thus, for example, an equally good advertisement may not bring nearly as many inquiries or orders during July or August as during January or February.

Table 65 gives the number of inquiries brought, month by month by advertisements of uniform size, for two office appliances in the same mediums.

It is evident that there is a distinct sag in these figures during the summer months. The inquiries in general are highest in January and gradually drop to a minimum in July and August, and then rise again to a maximum in December and January. The only exceptions to this general trend are the figures for the last months of 1920, during which the recovery was not as great as in the preceding years. This is probably due to the general business depression which began to be felt about that time. In averaging these figures and constructing a smoothened curve, we

TABLE 65

SEASONAL FLUCTUATION OF INQUIRIES FROM ADVERTISEMENTS

| | First Office Appliance | | | Second Office Appliance | | | | |
| | (Same Medium) | | | First Medium | Second Medium | Third Medium | Fourth Medium | Fifth Medium |
Month	1918	1919	1920	1920	1920	1920	1920	1920
January		264	347	215	67	67	12	11
February		260	297		80	87	14	13
March		179	261		73	56	13	14
April		112	203		80	55	19	4
May		108	146	75	60	65	12	6
June		126	166	23	19	56	9	3
July	88	132	157	19	40	55	4	3
August	108	166	126	67	52	40	7	8
September	100	149		41	30	18	3	6
October	98	173		32	37	28	5	
November	230	327		38	30	45	5	4
December		251		49	65	54	4	11

obtain the following relative expected values for the successive months of the year. Considering January as 100 we have:

January	100	May	47	September	45
February	85	June	43	October	60
March	70	July	40	November	75
April	55	August	40	December	95

By means of these relative values it was possible to determine whether an advertisement appearing, for example, in May or August brought as many inquiries as it should. Thus, if an advertisement in August brought 40% as many inquiries as the one in January, it probably was as good as the January advertisement in spite of its lower returns. The point is that the raw table of returns, such as inquiries, does not give at all a direct measure of the relative effectiveness of a series of advertisements. Proper allowance must be made for the various factors mentioned. The theoretical seasonal fluctuations here computed probably hold only for the type of commodity here considered. Other commodities no doubt have different fluctuations.

LATHE, PIANO, ELECTRIC LAMP, AND SOAP ADVERTISEMENTS

Besides the investigations here reported, similar comparisons between test results and actual returns have been made by Professor H. L. Hollingworth in the case of five lathe advertisements for which he found perfect agreement of 1.00; and in the case of fifteen player-piano advertisements, for which he found an agreement of .92. Professor E. K. Strong found a correlation of 1.00 between the tests of three electric lamp advertisements and the returns brought by them. Professor Strong also found an agreement of .92 for a set of eight Packer's Tar Soap advertisements between the test results and the general value of these advertisements as estimated by the firm and by the advertising agency. This last comparison, it will be noted, is not based upon actual returns; all others, however, are.

There is thus a considerable array of experimental evidence in support of the validity of the testing methods here proposed. The percentages of agreement in the cases cited range from .40 to 1.00 with an average of about .80. This evidence is sufficiently varied and convincing to demonstrate a very satisfactory degree of reliability in a carefully conducted series of tests for determining the relative effectiveness of advertisements.

OBJECTIONS

A criticism sometimes brought against testing methods of this sort by persons who have had little or no contact with investigational work of this type, is that it can't be done, that the situation of any test is artificial and that you cannot secure a reaction from a person under test conditions which is comparable to that secured in the usual every-day circumstances under which advertisements are observed.

However, in view of the considerable number of investigations made thus far and reported in the table in which the results of the tests have been checked against actual business returns, the answer is that it can be done and that whatever artificiality there may be in a test situation is inconsequential. If this were an important disturbing factor, the test results would not check up with business returns as closely as they do. It should further be borne in mind that the elimination of this factor depends very largely upon the manner in which the tests are conducted.

Another criticism sometimes urged is that a test made with a limited number of persons, even though it be several hundred, is no index of what the results would be for thousands or millions of people.

The answer to this point is that human nature in the mass is remarkably uniform, as shown by an abundance of psychological and statistical evidence. If a chemist wishes to analyze the water supply of a city, it is not necessary for him to analyze all the water in the reservoir or in the city mains. He needs only to test a few samples here and there. If he wishes to analyze a carload of iron, he needs only to chip off a few samples here and there, and analyze them.

Furthermore, these methods are not in any sense comparable to straw votes. There is as much difference between carefully conducted tests and the usual smoking-car straw votes on advertisements or on presidents as there is between a chemical analysis of food and a cook-book experiment.

Another point brought out by these tests is that the judgment even of expert advertising men is often wrong and that they are hardly better judges of what will appeal to the public at large than other observers of human nature. The fact that so many weak advertisements appear even in our best mediums and for products for which large sums of money are expended is ample proof of this statement.

The practical importance of developing and applying testing methods as a part of the program of preparing advertising plans hardly needs to be pointed out. The validity of the methods, when properly and scientifically applied, is, I believe, fully established.

Note, for example, how much greater would be the effectiveness of a series of advertisements if the weak ones were eliminated at the start and stronger ones were put in their places. If the player-piano advertiser had used advertisements of the type of the best ones of his series of fifteen, he probably would have secured five to six times as much business from the same expenditure for advertising space. If the typewriter advertiser had used only advertisements such as the more effective ones in his series, he would have secured between two and three times as much business from the same expenditure for space. The same is true of the other examples cited.

In view of the tests here cited, we find that *the average advertisement, even in high-grade mediums, has only about half the effectiveness possessed by the best advertisements in the same mediums and for the same products.*

Thus, a large national advertiser of shoes, whose advertisements were recently tested, would have made a 33% better and more effective impression if all his advertisements had been as effective as the best one in his campaign. The expenditure for space was $72,000. If all his advertisements had been as effective as his best one he would have made a $96,000 impression instead of a $72,000 impression, for the same expenditure of money.

The cost of a series of tests in connection with advertising plans of any importance whatever is trifling compared with the total expenditure for a season's or a year's advertising, or as compared with the greater effectiveness of the resulting advertisements.

The methods here proposed are not impractical theory;

they are simply the common-sense application of scientific methods to advertising problems.

Eight or ten years ago, a questionnaire-field investigation as the preliminary ground work for advertising plans was regarded as a novelty. Today such investigations are recognized as fundamentally important and are made quite commonly in connection with important advertising and sales projects. However, a questionnaire-field investigation, while basically important, furnishes only a part of the facts on which advertising plans are based. It is not sufficient merely to make such an investigation. Equally necessary is it to test the advertisements based upon the questionnaire investigation. The questionnaire investigation may show that taste or nutritive value is the strongest appeal for milk, or that style or wearing quality is the strongest point for shoes; but it will not show what the most effective presentation of the appeal may be. It will not show whether by picture or text or by what kind of picture or by what kind of phraseology the point may be presented most effectively.

This statement is fully borne out by several cases in which extensive questionnaire-field investigations were made, the results of which showed certain points to be plainly the outstanding features that should be emphasized in the sales appeals. Several copywriters and artists prepared advertisements which represented their best efforts to present these points. When these proposed advertisements were tested in proof form, they showed surprisingly large differences in effectiveness. A weak selling point presented in an effective manner will actually be more influential than a strong selling point presented poorly. By means of properly conducted tests, it is possible to arrive more closely at a correct answer to many of the numerous questions that arise; it *is* possible to determine which are the strongest appeals and which are the most effective presentations of these appeals.

The careful testing of the copy, text, illustration, layout, and other elements (which have been prepared on the basis of a questionnaire-field investigation) is a further important step in determining as fully as possible in advance the probable effectiveness of the proposed advertising plans. Thus, scientific testing methods, applied to the problems of advertising, promise to open a field of possibilities, making advertising more effective and putting it on a more economical level.

In view of the possibility and the reliability of these methods, no important advertising plan should be carried out without first making a careful test of the advertisements and of the essential elements in them.

XV

SAMPLE RESULTS OF A COMPLETE SERIES OF ADVERTISEMENT TESTS

Coordination of the different phases of research and testing work. Questionnaire investigation of automobile insurance company. Preparation of experimental advertisements. The tests: 1. The advertisement as a whole. 2. The picture. 3. The text. 4. Memory value. 5. The trade-mark. The campaign prepared.

At this point it will be useful to coordinate the different phases of research and testing work which have been discussed thus far in order to see how the various steps fit together. In a complete investigation, from the point at which the plans for an advertising campaign are begun to the point where the final advertisements are actually inserted in the mediums, we may briefly note the following steps:

1. Collection of all available information (a) from the business or firm in question and (b) from accessible published sources, libraries, government reports, and so forth.

2. First-hand questionnaire investigation, preferably by personal interview.

3. Preparation of advertisements for experimental purposes on the basis of the investigations made thus far.

4. Testing of the experimental advertisements together with advertisements of competitors, by means of laboratory-field tests.

5. Final preparation of the advertisements on the basis of these tests.

Let us illustrate the method of procedure in connection with the preparation and the carrying out of the advertising program of an automobile accident insurance company.

Questionnaire Investigation of Automobile Insurance Company. This part of the investigation will not be described here in detail, since this phase of research work has been discussed in sufficient detail in earlier chapters. It will suffice, therefore, simply to say that a carefully conducted questionnaire investigation was carried out, in which over 1,000 owners of automobiles were interviewed.[1] This investigation showed that, so far as the appeals were concerned, the chief selling arguments should be centered around three points:

Financial soundness and reliability of the company
Quickness and liberality of claim settlement
Cost of insurance

PREPARATION OF EXPERIMENTAL ADVERTISEMENTS

On the basis of the findings of the questionnaire investigation, six advertisements were prepared, in which these three selling arguments were presented in various ways. These experimental advertisements were prepared with the idea of using them in full-page space in newspapers.

The layout of these six advertisements, which will be referred to by letters as A, B, C, D, E, and F, was similar. Each advertisement contained a picture or a series of pictures occupying one-half to two-thirds of the space. Each one had a trade-mark at the top. On the right-hand side, in a narrow panel extending the full length of the space, was given a list of the directors of the company and their business connections. Advertisements A, C, and E contained each a different picture of an automobile accident. Advertisement B contained a picture of a dragon attacking a primitive man and his wife at the entrance to the cave. The man was defending himself with a long spear. Advertisement F showed a series of 12 small pictures of an auto-

---

[1] The data in this chapter are presented by permission of The Liberty Mutual Insurance Company of Boston.

mobile entitled "Wonder What an Insured Automobile Thinks About." Advertisement D contained a picture of a Quaker realizing that he had been paying too much for his insurance in the past.

THE TESTS

Five series of tests were made with these six advertisements. The first set of tests was designed to give a measure of the relative value of these advertisements, based on a casual inspection of the advertisements.

The second set of tests was designed to give a measure of the value and appropriateness of the illustrations used.

The third was designed to test the relative strength of the pieces of text used in the six advertisements.

The fourth was designed to measure the relative memory value of both the illustration and the text.

The fifth test was designed to determine which of the six variations of the trade-mark was the most suitable.

We shall not describe in detail the manner in which each of these tests was carried out, as the technique of such testing work will be discussed in the proper connection in ensuing chapters. It will suffice to say at this point that the first test was carried out with 131 persons, the second with 20 persons, the third with 73 persons, the fourth with 50 persons, and the fifth with 93 persons. All of these persons, with the exception of one group of 30 students, were typical owners of automobiles, including high-, medium-, and low-priced cars. They further represented 52 different occupations, including bankers, plumbers, clergymen, business men, and so on.

Test I—The Advertisement as a Whole. The purpose of the first test was to determine the effectiveness of the advertisement as a whole. The question which this test endeavored to answer was, Which advertisement would influence you most toward wanting Blank automobile insurance?   The test was carried out by the ranking method.   The six advertisements were spread in chance order before the person being tested.   He was asked to read the text and to observe the other elements, to examine the advertisements carefully as a whole.   After he had done so, he was asked to arrange the advertisements in the order in which they impressed him most favorably.   The investigator then recorded the order of the advertisements from one to six.   The person tested was then asked to give his general impressions and his reasons for ranking the advertisements as he did.

In this manner the test was carried out with 131 persons.   All of these persons were typical automobile owners with the exception of a group of 30 men students, of whom a few were also owners of cars.

The rankings thus obtained were then scored as follows: An advertisement which had been ranked first was given a score of six points, since there were six advertisements in the series.   An advertisement which had been ranked as second was given a score of five points.   Rank three was given four points, and so on, while an advertisement ranked six was given one point.   The total number of points scored by each advertisement was thus computed and the scores were then transmuted into percentages by considering the highest possible score that any advertisement could obtain as 100%, and the lowest possible score as 0.   The results are given in the first column of the table on page 334.   It will be noted that the six advertisements fall into two groups.   E, C, and A were near the top and F, D, and B were near the bottom.   Advertisement E stood highest in the test and Advertisement C was a very close second.   E, C, and A contained a picture of an automobile accident, while F, D, and B did not.   Apparently the "accident" advertisements made a stronger and more favorable impression.

The comments of the persons tested showed that E was first because of the simple understandable illustration and the catchy slogan. The illustration attracted attention and the advertisement as a whole "got over" to the reader a clear, definite idea of automobile insurance. Advertisement A, which also showed a picture of an accident, did not stand as high in the test as E and C, evidently because the picture was not as clear and as easy to comprehend.

F, D, and B did not present ideas as closely related to insurance as did the other three. F, the cartoon advertisement, was ranked low because it took too long to discover what it was all about. The few persons who ranked it high did so because it appealed to them as being unusual and clever. The great majority of persons ranked it low.

The Quaker advertisement, D, was ranked low because it did not get the attention and interest of the persons with whom the test was made, and because the illustration was not closely related to automobile insurance. The dragon advertisement, B, attracted attention on account of its uniqueness, but it was ranked low because the picture and the idea in the advertisement as a whole did not produce a strong impression in favor of wanting automobile insurance.

The outcome of this test evidently is that the most effective advertisement is one which shows an automobile accident and which presents ideas directly related to the thing advertised, namely, automobile insurance. Advertisement E is the one which succeeded best in getting the idea over in the most direct and effective manner.

Test II—The Picture. This test was designed to measure the relative value of the illustration as such, from the standpoint of interesting the casual reader, getting him to read the advertisement and examine it as a whole. The test was made by placing the six advertisements in chance order before the person being tested and asking him to look at them in a more or less casual way as he would if he saw them in a magazine or newspaper. Then he was asked "Which picture influences you most toward reading the advertisement?" The six pictures were then ranked in order accordingly. This test was made with 20 persons. It helped to measure the initial attention and interest value of the advertisements.

The results were scored in the same manner as were those of Test I, and are presented in the second column of the table and of the chart, Figure 26. The results of the test coincide very closely with those of Test I. Advertisements E, C, and A ranked high and F, D, and B ranked low. The difference between the best and the poorest in this test is very pronounced, a difference of 69 points. The close coincidence of the results of Tests I and II indicates that the picture is probably the chief determining factor in the relative effectiveness of these particular advertisements.

Test III—The Text. The purpose of the next test was to ascertain the relative value of the various pieces of text used in the six advertisements. The test was carried out in two ways. In one case it was made with the text on the advertisement. In the other case it was made with the text off the advertisement, that is, in typewritten form. It is quite likely that the impression which a piece of text makes is influenced by the surroundings of the rest of the advertisement, such as the picture, the layout, typography, and the like. To obtain a measure of the relative effectiveness of the text as such, the test should obviously be made with the text apart from the advertisement, either in typewritten or printed form.

In the present case, the test was made in both ways for the purpose of comparison. The test with the text on the advertisements was made with 32 persons, while the test with the text in typewritten form was made with 40 persons. In both instances, the persons were asked to read the various pieces of text carefully and to rank them in the order of convincingness. The question was asked, "Which of these six arguments or statements influences you most toward wanting Blank insurance?"

The rankings were computed in the same manner as were those of Tests I and II and the results are shown in the third and fourth columns of Table 66.

An examination of Table 66 and of the corresponding portions of Figure 26 will reveal some interesting differences. While in general the same piece of text stood high or low in both tests, there is a very large difference in the ranges between the highest and the lowest. In the test with the text on the advertisements, E was the highest with a score of 80, while F was the lowest with a score of 11. In the test with the text in typewritten form, C was the highest, with a score of 58, while B was the lowest with a score of 38. The reason for this difference is that the presence of the picture helps to accentuate the differences that are present in the text. This fact corroborates further the point already made in connection with Test II, that the picture is possibly the most important feature in this particular set of advertisements.

The chief discrepancy between the results of these two ways of making the test is in the case of advertisement F. In the test with the text on the advertisements, F stood at the bottom of the scale, considerably below the next to the lowest one, while in the test with the text in typewritten form, it was fourth in order and stood about the middle of the scale. The explanation of this discrepancy is probably that since this was the cartoon advertisement, it was necessary to state in making the test with the text in typewritten form that this text would be used with a cartoon of a well-known artist. This statement no doubt had an effect of enhancing the possibilities and impressiveness of this particular piece of text.

So far as the method of testing is concerned, unless the text is directly dependent upon the picture, it is possible to obtain a more reliable measure of the value of the text as such if the test is made with the text in typewritten or printed form entirely apart from the remainder of the advertisement.

Test IV—Memory Value. The purpose of this test was to determine the relative memory value of the six advertisements. The test was made by returning to 50 of the persons with whom some of the tests had been made and asking them to state which of the advertisements they remembered and what they remembered about these advertisements. The investigator did not state in connection with the first test that he would return at a later time for this purpose. An interval of three days elapsed between the two tests.

The results were tabulated to show in one instance what was remembered of the illustrations and in the second instance which of the advertisements as a whole were remembered. The investigator recorded what each of the 50 persons remembered, both with regard to the picture and the text. The results are shown in terms of percentages in the last two columns of Table 66. The percentages indicate the proportion of persons who were able to recall each advertisement or picture.

Perhaps the most striking fact in the results is that Advertisement B, containing the picture of the dragon, had the highest memory value; but on the other hand it stood either lowest or next to the lowest in all the preceding tests, so that in spite of its memory value, it would not be as effective as the other advertisements, since persons would be impressed with the picture without tying it up with the proposition advertised. It is also interesting to note that Advertisement E, which had been at the top or near the top in the preceding tests, was almost as high in memory value as the dragon advertisement. The cartoon advertisement, F, was next in memory value, which is explained undoubtedly by its uniqueness; but for the same reasons as those which advise against using the dragon advertisement, this advertisement would not be effective, since it would impress the cartoon upon the memory without tying it up with insurance.

The particular points, phrases and items which were remembered in the texts of the various advertisements were very suggestive with regard to their appropriateness and value.

TABLE 66

SUMMARY TABLE OF TEST RESULTS

Advertisement	Test of Entire Ad (131 Persons)		Test of Illustration (20 Persons)		Test of Text on the Ad (33 Persons)		Test of Text Alone (40 Persons)		Test of Memory Value of Illustration (30 Persons)		Test of Memory Value of Entire Ad (20 Persons)	
E	79%	1	90%	1	80%	1	53%	2	63%	3	75%	2
C	76	2	70	2	79	2	58	1	76	2	52	4
A	62	3	59	3	61	3	52	4	28	6	42	5
F	35	4	30	4½	11	6	54	3	60	4	65	3
D	28	5	30	4½	36	4	45	5	40	5	40	6
B	20	6	21	6	35	5	38	6	76.5	1	80	1

Test V—The Trade-Mark. The final test carried out in connection with this series of advertisements was for the purpose of determining which of six different variations of the trade-mark was most pleasing and suitable. Accordingly, two series of tests were made. In the one case the trade-marks were shown on the advertisements, while in the second case the trade-marks were shown separately, that is, off the advertisements.

The test was conducted by asking a person to examine the various forms of the trade-mark, and then asking him to rank them in the order of preference or appropriateness. The test with the trade-marks on the advertisements was made with 53 persons. The test with the trade-marks off the advertisements was made with 40 persons.

The results were expressed in terms of percentage value, obtained in a manner similar to that described in connection with the preceding tests. The values are shown in Table 67.

Note here the narrow range of values in the test "On the Advertisement." This is probably due to the fact that in seeing the trade-mark as a part of the advertisement it

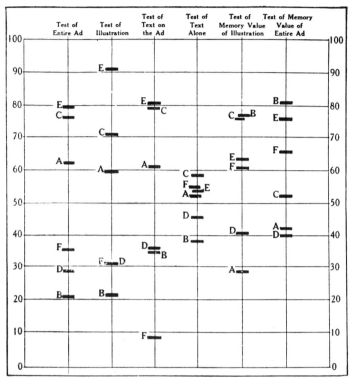

Figure 26:   Graphic representation of results shown in Table 66
(See page 334)

looked less important than when seen separately, and furthermore the other elements of the advertisement, particularly the picture, influenced the observer's impression.
Trade-mark F, with a slight modification, was the one used.

THE CAMPAIGN PREPARED

On the basis of these test results a campaign was pre-
pared in which the advertisements were all patterned after
Advertisement E, the one that stood highest in the tests.
All advertisements were laid out in the same manner.   They

Figure 27: A typical advertisement prepared as the result of the investigations cited in the text

were varied practically only in respect to the particular contents of the picture and the descriptive text accompanying it. The same type of picture, namely an automobile accident, was used for all advertisements. A full-page newspaper advertisement thus constructed appeared each month in one paper in each of three cities. The results of the campaign have been very satisfactory. It has been the

TABLE 67

TEST OF THE TRADE-MARK

Ad	On the Advertisements	Off the Advertisements
F	53%	73%
E	55	53
D	47	51
B	44	51
C	54	41
A	47	31

most effective advertising this company has done. Within one year the business increased 77%. Each advertisement brought many inquiries and direct leads for the salesmen, who found the impression produced by the advertisements a distinct advantage.

An investigation such as this demonstrates (a) the costliness of experience, either proceeding on a trial and error basis or relying on individual judgment albeit that of a supposed expert; and (b) the economy of methods of inquiry, research and testing, the cost of which is almost negligible beside the total expenditure for ordinary advertising plans.

This point is further illustrated by the fact that the advertisement which the tests showed to be the poorest was suggested by an advertising expert of considerable experience. In fact, all of the six experimental advertisements were prepared or suggested by persons of wide experience, and all attempted to present the same selling points in the most effective manner. Yet three of them were far below the value of the others.

XVI

SEX AND CLASS DIFFERENCES

1. Sex differences. Amount of purchasing for the home done by housewives. Sex differences assumed by business executives and others. Popular *vs.* scientific view of sex differences. Scientific ways of comparing mental traits of groups of persons. Scientific facts on mental sex differences in general. Comparisons in general intelligence. Comparisons in thinking processes. Comparison in accuracy of observation. Comparison of selling appeals to men and to women as determined by tests. Summary and interpretation of results. 2. Class differences.

WOMEN have assumed a very important place as buyers, not only of commodities for their own personal use, but also of commodities for the home, and even to quite an extent of commodities used exclusively by men. Very pronounced and important sex differences in the instincts and motives and in the habits of buying are assumed by sales and advertising managers. It is therefore highly important from a practical standpoint to determine to what extent actual and pronounced differences exist between the two sexes in the buying activities and in the influences that control buying activities.

In 1913, Professor H. L. Hollingworth reported a preliminary study of the amount of purchasing for the home which is done by housewives. This brief study was made by means of an investigation with a group of 25 New York City families. Members of the family were requested to report "with respect to 80 commonly used articles, whether each article was purchased (a) by the men of the household alone, or (b) solely by the women, or (c) by either or both in consultation." Of the 25 families studied, 72% lived in apartments, and 60% of them possessed neither vehicles nor conveyance, pets, nor musical instruments. The annual incomes ranged from $2,000 to $5,000.

Table 68 gives the results summarized under 12 classes of articles:

TABLE 68

MEN AND WOMEN AS PURCHASERS

Class of Article	Number of Specifications	Percentage by Men Alone	Percentage by Women Alone	Percentage by Both	Percentage by Neither
Men's clothing	11	65	11	23	1
Women's clothing	11	1	87	12	0
Druggist's articles	6	10	48	41	1
Kitchenware	6	2	89	8	1
Pets	3	19	5	15	61
Dry Goods	4	0	96	4	0
Vehicles	3	23	1	15	61
House furnishings	8	4	48	46	2
Musical instruments	5	13	7	20	60
Raw and market foods	6	0	87	13	0
Package foods	5	3	79	14	4
Miscellaneous	12	6	22	68	4
Totals	80	146	580	279	195
Averages	..	12.2	48.3	23.2	16.2

1. The only article of clothing bought by men exclusively is their own collars. Only 80% buy their own shoes and hats. In over 50% of the cases the men's jewelry, handkerchiefs, socks and underwear are purchased either by the women alone or in consultation with them. In one-third of the cases the women help buy the men's shirts. One-third of the men buy their own handkerchiefs.

2. On the other hand, the men participate but little in the purchase of the women's apparel. Women buy men's things exclusively 11 times as often as the men buy women's things exclusively. Women cooperate with men twice as much as men cooperate with women, in the purchase of their respective apparel.

3. In 100% of the cases women are sole purchasers of their own underwear, lace, thread, and cooking utensils. In 80% of the cases they are the sole purchasers of dresses, cloaks, foot-

wear, hats, parasols, gloves, fans, handkerchiefs, clothes lines, chafing dishes, kitchen tables, ribbon, cloth, flour, vegetables, eggs, butter, bread, cereals, water and canned goods. In over 50% of the cases they are the sole purchasers of curtains, mattresses, meats, ranges, talcums and perfumes. Women buy 83% of the food, but less than 50% of the house furnishings, exclusively.

4. Women buy more of the magazines, men more of the newspapers. Women buy many wedding presents exclusively, but men participate more largely in the purchase of Christmas gifts, birthday gifts, and children's toys. Only 5% of the pets are bought by women alone, 20% by men alone.[1]

Recently an investigation was conducted by the Bureau of Advertising of the American Newspaper Publishers Association for the purpose of ascertaining the amount of men's underwear bought by women. Two questions relative to this point were asked in an interview covering 22 department stores and 38 men's furnishing stores in cities in Alabama, California, Pennsylvania, Connecticut, Illinois, Kansas, Kentucky, New York, North Carolina, Texas, and Wisconsin. The two questions were:

1. What proportion of men's summer underwear do you sell to women?

2. What proportion of men's fall and winter underwear do you sell to women?

The returns showed the same results for both questions as follows:

Questions 1 and 2—In 22 department stores, Median Percentage bought by women—50.

In 38 men's stores, Median Percentage bought by women —25.

These figures are obviously subject to a considerable amount of uncertainty, since they were based primarily upon the general impression of persons in these various stores. Their estimates varied considerably from as low

---

[1] Hollingworth, *Advertising and Selling*, pp. 290-292.

as 10% to as high as 70% in men's furnishing stores, and from as low as 33% to as high as 90% in department stores.

The important thing to determine, in so far as the amount of buying done by women is concerned, is the part that women play in the purchase of specific commodities. While it is interesting to note how much of the family budget in general is expended by women, it is more specifically to the point for each manufacturer or distributer to know how large a factor are women or men in the purchase of his particular product. For example, it is important for the manufacturer of a vacuum cleaner to know how large a share women have in deciding upon the particular make of cleaner to be bought. Wherever that question is important, reliable facts should be obtained. This can be done quite readily by means of a questionnaire investigation, as illustrated in the case of the purchase of boys' ready-made clothing, reported in Chapter IX. It was found in that instance that the mothers in the case of 79% of the boys under 13 and in the case of 60% of the boys over 13 were the determining factors in the purchase of their clothing.

In view of these considerations, it is obviously important to ascertain what fundamental psychological differences may actually exist. The purpose of the present chapter is to bring together the scientifically established facts regarding the problem.

SEX DIFFERENCES ASSUMED BY BUSINESS EXECUTIVES AND OTHERS

Striking differences are assumed by advertisers and others engaged in the selling of products to men and women, as shown by the following statements:

Men's Clothing—Now a manufacturer is about to come out with a national campaign for men's clothes, where the appeal is directed wholly to women. The concern is Michaels-Stern & Company of Rochester, New York. The entire product has been called "Value-First Clothes," the name being based on the theory that men buy by appearance only, but that women can be sold solely on value. Heretofore, men have considered style more than quality in their clothing purchases, but through the women this manufacturer hopes to educate them along the line of value.

Women always think into the future.

Will the suit wear well?

Will it look well after a little time?

Will it hold its shape?

Based on the belief that men buy their clothes to please women —as women buy theirs to please men, the copy will appeal to women as judges of value and to their interest in wanting to see the men of their household well groomed.

When a man goes into the subject of clothes-buying he does it because he needs something, while a woman often buys what she does not need because it attracts her and she knows she can use it.[1]

The whole plan is based on knowledge of how men and women shop. The average man purchases largely through habits. He waits till the last minute when he needs clothes, then he rushes into the store he is used to and buys. If he gets fairly good service he sticks to that one firm for the chief articles of clothing. He may see a scarf or a tie in some other store that pleased him and go in and buy, but nine times out of ten he doesn't consider buying suits and coats that way.

With women it is different. Women look about and shop carefully. They compare fabrics. They are keener in their judgment of good tailoring, careful workmanship in all the little things than men. They pay attention to the matchings of linings. They notice whether or not the buttons are the exact color of the suit. Then, too, a woman knows what becomes a man better than he knows himself. She has a more critical eye for style, fit, and color.[2]

Shoes.—In the· advertising of men's shoes, we feel that the masculine psychology is far different from the feminine psychology in its reaction to creative publicity. One of the principal differences is this: That the masculine mind conceives of dress and apparel as secondary to other considerations, whereas, the feminine instinct is thoroughly centered on apparel. For this reason most of our advertisements of men's shoes have a single motif: That

---

[1] Helen A. Bullard, *Printers' Ink,* July 3, 1919, p. 101.

[2] Ibid., Feb. 27, 1919, p. 3.

is, we feature only one style with plenty of display and white space, with a snappy illustration, and a human interest and quality appeal. Most men have single-track minds when it comes to reading advertisements.

. . . . The third is an advertisement of women's shoes in a style similar to that used by us regularly. In presenting numerous styles—somewhat "catalogy," true—we are adhering to the point made in the first paragraph that feminine instinct is very strong for style, and that the average woman will wade through specifications of a number of shoes with less boredom than the average man reading an advertisement of a single shoe.[1]

General Statements—What are the reasons that influence women to buy? First on the list I should put "Beauty."

The second reason why women buy is "To Save." To save labor, save time, save money.

I have saved the most important reason until last. It is "Because Women Love to Spend."

Women are more easily appealed to in advertising through their feelings than through their reason—and in this respect they are no different from men.

Be specific. Women are always getting down to cases. To make your story vivid, make the personal application wherever you can.

An easy recipe for advertising that will sell women is to use pictures. Women are naturally observant.[2]

An expert on sales letters makes the following statement regarding differences between men and women: "Women are more interested in adjectives, appreciate more personal touches, are more subject to flattery, and harder to sell. Therefore, an iron-clad guarantee or a testimonial is very effective."

As a woman consumer, I am frank to say that it is men and not women who are appealed to by the pretty girl as she is universally exploited in our current advertisement. Do pretty women appeal to women? Do women admire the "chicken" type of girl in advertising? I answer NO—there is no antagonism so pronounced as the antagonism of the great average common-sense type of women for the artificial doll type, for

[1] *Western Advertising*, Feb., 1920, p. 11.
[2] Dorothy R. Entwistle, Advertising Department, Wm. Filene's Sons Co., Nov., 1920, p. 25.

whom you men, in your gross ignorance and uncritical susceptibility, so commonly fall.[1]

In general, to appeal to women, you must be personal. An abstract word means nothing to the average woman. She cares very little about things in general. She is always thinking about I—Me—My—Ours. A woman wants something special. She buys more conscientiously than a man does. She feels that she is the trustee of the family's money, and she wants to prove her efficiency as a buyer.[2]

In a recent pair of companion articles on the question of men and women, the following differences were stated or assumed to exist by the two writers.[3]

The article discussing the characteristics of women stated that

1. Women naturally blockade passageways in public buildings upon meeting an acquaintance and stopping to talk to her. Men, meeting under the same circumstances, would invariably step aside so as to leave the passageway free.

2. A woman gets into the street car but fails to see the empty seat at the front of the car and so hangs on to a strap at the rear.

3. The conductor comes to collect the fare, but the woman does not have the fare ready for him.

4. She fails to signal for her stop on time and so is carried to the next stop.

5. She gets off the car the wrong way, facing toward the rear. Man always and instinctively gets off the right way.

6. She wants economic equality but refuses to be treated the same as men by her employer. She weeps and flies into a temper. Woman cannot divorce social relations from economic relations, as indicated by her dress.

7. Women as business associates make confidantes of one another. Men do not, hence women fall out with each other. A woman, 99 times out of 100, is more a creature of one idea.

The article discussing the characteristics of men states that

[1] Mrs. Christine Frederick, Director Applecroft, Experiment Station, Greenlawn, L. I., *Marketing*, Nov. 1, 1921, p. 742.

[2] H. N. Casson, Marketing, April 1, 1922, p. 306.

[3] *American Magazine*, October, 1919.

1. Men cannot stand jokes on themselves. Women can.

2. Women are less conventional in matters of dress and etiquette.

3. Women think straighter, but not so fast.

4. Men are always only grown-up boys. They have to be taken care of; they must be told to get their hair cut, or to go to the tailor.

5. Men hang on to their old garments more persistently. Men are like cats; women like dogs, despite popular notions to the contrary.

6. Men stand together, as witnessed by the strength of labor unions. Women do not, because of "their terrible alikeness."

7. Women play bridge to fill in time. Men play it to beat the other fellow.

8. Women work longer and harder than men.

9. Men are the slaves of fashion, women are not. The evidence of this is the dress suit.

It is interesting in this connection to note the practice in current advertising with regard to the differences in the manner in which advertising is carried out. The reader may at this point refer to the data presented in Chapter XI, with reference to the differences in the advertising of men's and women's shoes.

A similar analysis made of 283 advertisements of men's clothing and 150 advertisements of women's clothing, which appeared in 1919, showed the following similarities or differences:

	283 Ads of Men's Ready-made Clothing	150 Ads of Women's Ready-made Clothing
Average size of advertisement	⅝ page	½ page
Percentage of advertisement occupied by text	47%	53%
Percentage of advertisement occupied by illustration	53%	47%
Average number of words of text	112	122

POPULAR VS. SCIENTIFIC VIEW OF SEX DIFFERENCES

Probably more fallacious psychology of sex has been spread abroad by novelists and journalists than has been disseminated on any other psychological question of popular interest. Occasional and extreme differences in individuals of either sex have been seized upon and exaggerated by descriptive phraseology and represented as though they were the normal divergences between men and women. Up to less than two decades ago, there was practically no scientific knowledge of the nature of mental sex differences available.

Such popular beliefs have been in part justified by the probability that there are many obvious differences which are due to the different work and the resulting variation in experience and environment of women as contrasted with that of men. Thus men know more about business, politics, current events and machines because their occupations bring them much more in contact with these things; but it does not follow that women could not, or would not, know as much about them if their occupations were as much concerned with them. Women know more about cooking, social events, and household utensils because their occupations bring them much more in contact with them; but it does not follow that men could not, or would not, acquire as much knowledge or skill in these directions if their occupations required it.

The differences between the sexes are probably quantitative rather than qualitative. Both men and women have the same reflexes, instincts, and capacities with the exception of certain aspects of the sex instinct. These are probably similar in the main and differ chiefly in their manner of expression. The differences in occupations and experiences will account for many of the superficially observable differences between men and women.

What are the differences that have been scientifically measured and compared? In order to produce a complete picture of mental differences between men and women it would be necessary to measure each trait in a very large number of persons and to compare the measurements with regard to both the averages of the traits and the manner of the distribution of each trait. This has been done in part only with a few traits and only with small groups of persons.

SCIENTIFIC WAYS OF COMPARING MENTAL TRAITS OF GROUPS OF PERSONS

There are two methods by which abilities of two groups may be compared. Either we may state the actual average or median of each group, or we may state how many members of one group reach or exceed the average or median of the other group. The latter method is preferable in many respects to the former in that it makes possible a comparison of groups of various sizes and indicates the relative differences more nearly true to fact. The two methods may be illustrated in the case of a memory test consisting of the oral presentation of ten words at the rate of one word per second. The subjects were asked to record immediately the number of words remembered. We may then state that the number of words remembered on the average by men was 6.9 and by women 7.2. Or we may state that 43.6% of men reached or exceeded the median of the women. The latter method of comparison represents probably more true to life the amount and kind of difference or similarity that actually exist. The differences, hastily inferred from a comparison of averages only, would lead to the conclusion that in regard to memory women are distinctly superior to men. The implication would be that all women have a memory superior to that of men, whereas the fact is that the number of women having a memory superior to that of men is really small and that, in these few women, memory is better only by a very small shade. If 43% of men reach or exceed the median of women, it means that if the 7% of women having a slightly superior memory were omitted, the remaining 93% of the women would have a memory ability identical with that of the men. A difference of 7% in the distributions between two groups

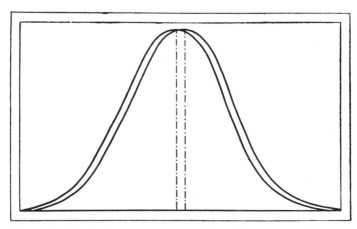

Figure 28:　Distribution curves representing a difference of 7% between
the medians of the two groups

is represented by the curves in Figure 28. The difference
is so small that the groups could hardly be distinguished.

By the method of amounts of overlapping in the distribution of one group over the other, the following results
were obtained by the author from students in the University
of Wisconsin, in a series of tests on memory, on perception,
on motor ability, and on mental addition. The memory test
was conducted according to the method above described;
the perception test was conducted by asking the subjects to
cancel as many figures of a certain kind of geometrical figure as possible within one minute; the motor ability test
was conducted by having the subject tap with a pencil upon
a card as rapidly as possible for 30 seconds.

In the interpretation of these percentages of overlapping
it must be remembered that if 50% of one group reaches or

PERCENTAGE OF MEN REACHING OR EXCEEDING
THE MEDIAN OF WOMEN

Perception of geometrical forms	193 men	200 women	54.5%
Memory of words	55 men	77 women	43.6
Motor ability	25 men	50 women	72.0
Mental addition	21 men	46 women	66.7

exceeds the median of the other, it means of course that the two groups are identical in ability and distribution. If the percentage of men reaching or exceeding the median of the women is over 50% it means that the men are superior by the number exceeding 50%. These facts are presented here to illustrate the method of properly comparing groups with respect to mental characteristics. Proper comparison is fundamental to correct interpretation of sex differences.

SCIENTIFIC FACTS ON MENTAL SEX DIFFERENCES IN GENERAL

Helen Thompson Woolley made a series of tests, as indicated in Table 69, upon 25 men and women at the University of Chicago, on the basis of which Thorndike has computed the following percentages of men reaching or exceeding the median of women.

TABLE 69
PERCENTAGES OF MEN REACHING OR EXCEEDING THE MEDIAN OF THE WOMEN *

Reaction time	68%	
Tapping	81	
Sorting cards, speed	14	
Sorting cards, accuracy	44	
Thrusting at target	60	
Drawing lines	72	
Threshold of pain	46	
Threshold of taste	34	(22)
Threshold of smell	43	
Lifting of weights	66	
Two-point determination	18	(43)
Memory (syllables and learning)	32	(46)
Ingenuity	63	

* After Woolley, as computed by Thorndike, *Educational Psychology*, III, p. 178.

In a similar comparison made by Gilbert on 100 boys and 100 girls, the percentage of boys reaching or exceeding the median of girls was as given in Table 70.

TABLE 70

PERCENTAGES OF BOYS REACHING OR EXCEEDING THE MEDIAN OF GIRLS *

	to 14 years	15 to 17 years
Discrimination of weights	48%	58%
Discrimination of colors	39	58
Reaction time	57	76
Resistance to size-weight illusion	55	68
Rate of tapping	64	73

* After Gilbert '94, as computed by Thorndike, *Educational Psychology*, III, p. 182.

Thorndike [1] reports a comparison of the percentages of boys reaching or exceeding the median of girls, for persons 8 to 14 years old, as follows:

Associative tests, opposites, addition, multiplication, etc.	48%
Perception, A-test, etc.	33
Memory of words	40

The author has made comparisons in the case of school subjects on the basis of abilities measured by means of tests and scales. Speed of writing was measured in terms of letters written per minute. Quality was rated by the Thorndike scale. Attainments in the remaining subjects were measured by the author's tests in these fields. The following percentages of boys reaching or exceeding the median of the girls were obtained:

Speed of handwriting,	about 1,100 boys and 1,100 girls	47%
Quality of handwriting,	about 1,100 boys and 1,100 girls	39
Arithmetical reasoning,	about 1,250 boys and 1,250 girls	60
History,	about 429 boys and 526 girls	72
Geography,	about 447 boys and 472 girls	48

Figures of a similar sort computed by Thorndike [2] on the basis of teachers' marks showed the following percentages of boys reaching or exceeding the median of girls:

[1] *Educational Psychology*, III, p. 183   [2] *Idem.*

	High School Pupils
English	41%
Mathematics	57
Latin	57
History	60

	College Students
English	35%
Mathematics	45
History and economics	56
Natural sciences	50
Modern languages	40

The difficulty with many of the measurements is that they are based on too small a number of persons. Comparisons based on 25 persons from either sex may be indicative but not final. Summarizing, we may say that women and girls are superior in sensibility, in memory, in most forms of perception, in quality of handwriting, and in linguistic fluency. It is interesting to note in this connection that in the survey of mental-test results in Whipple's *Manual of Mental and Physical Tests* the women excel in 12 out of 14 tests which depend chiefly upon linguistic fluency. Thus the females excel in speed of reading, both oral and silent, in amount of information given in describing an object or in making a report, in the genus-species test, in the number of words thought of and written per minute, in the part-whole test, in the opposites test, in memory span for words, in memory for logical verbal material, in the word-building test and in the Ebbinghaus completion test; while the males excel in the rate of association and in the sentence-building test. Apparently the popular belief in the greater linguistic fluency of women is not without foundation. Men and boys are superior in motor capacities, such as tapping, quickness of reaction, in arithmetical reasoning, and in resistance to suggestions as indicated by the size-weight illusion and the use of suggestive questions in testimony. The two sexes seem to be approximately equal in associative processes and in most school subjects.

The amounts of difference, however, are very small. This is particularly true of all the traits that have been measured in a sufficiently large number of persons to make the comparisons safe. Any differences lying between 40% and 60% of the number of either sex reaching or exceeding the median of the other sex are practically negligible. If 60% of one sex reach or exceed the median of the other, it means that 10 persons in 100 of the one sex are by a small amount superior to the other sex. Differences larger than this have been established with a fair degree of certainty practically only in the case of one large field of capacities, namely, that of motor abilities. Differences in nearly all other respects in which comparisons have been made on large numbers of persons are almost entirely within the limits of 40% and 60%.

COMPARISONS IN GENERAL INTELLIGENCE

Terman found, in measuring the general intelligence of nearly 1,000 boys and girls by means of his revision of the Binet-Simon tests, that for the ages of 5 to 14 girls tend to be very slightly superior to boys and that after 14 they are practically equal. His results are set forth in Figure 29.

It seems a likely interpretation that motor superiority has been carried over to imply intellectual superiority as well. For centuries women have been considered intellectually inferior to men. They were thought to be incapable of acquiring anything more than an elementary education. It has been only since the middle of the 19th century that co-education and women's colleges have been generally established. Intellectual inferiority has probably been inferred chiefly from motor and muscular inferiority and from the conditions of a narrower environment and dependency due to the bearing and rearing of children. The inference and belief of intellectual inferiority is apparently unfounded. This conclusion may be fairly drawn both from the specific psychological tests that have been cited and

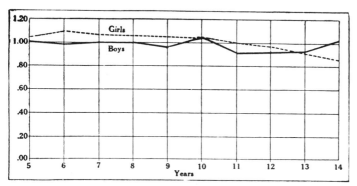

Figure 29: Comparison of general intelligence of boys and girls as measured by the Stanford revision of the Binet-Simon tests.* The numbers along the vertical axis are intelligence quotients. *(See page 352)*

*After Terman, *The Measurement of Intelligence,* p. 72.

also from the recent successes of women in the acquisition of higher education.

The rapid development of intelligence tests in recent years has made it possible to make specific comparisons between the sexes so far as general ability is concerned. The test known as the Alpha Test, prepared for use in the army during the war, has been given since the close of the war to a considerable number of students in colleges and high schools. It will therefore be of interest to note some typical comparisons.

The following figures show the comparison of boys and girls in the McCall School, Philadelphia. The scores on the Army Alpha Test run from 0 to a maximum of 212. These figures give the median scores for boys and girls of ages 9 to 15.

Age	Boys	Girls
9	107.5	101.7
10	118.5	108.4
11	129.2	126.3
12	143.1	137.5
13	151.6	141.1
14	155	148
15	148	125

In similar manner, the Army Alpha Test was given to the students in three Omaha high schools. The results were as follows:

	Boys	Girls
Freshmen	98	93
Sophomores	110	110
Juniors	120	115
Seniors	127	117

The Alpha Test is composed of eight groups of tests, each of which is designed to measure a different type of mental processes. Some of the groups emphasize particularly reasoning ability, others practical judgment, and so on. It will therefore be of interest to note the comparison of boys and girls with respect to these eight types of tests. The following tabulation gives the scores for each test separately.

	Boys	Girls
1. Directions test	8.7	7.5
2. Arithmetical problems	11.5	9
3. Practical judgment	9.5	9.7
4. Synonyms-antonyms	14.7	14
5. Disarranged sentences	10.5	11.5
6. Completion of number series	9.7	9.0
7. Analogies	16.5	16.2
8. Information	22.2	19.3

An examination of these figures will show that in general the boys made a somewhat higher score than the girls. The difference, however, is not very great. The advantage of the boys may in part be due to the fact that the test included certain items which as a result of environment are somewhat more familiar to boys.

A study of the last tabulation, giving the comparisons by types of tests, indicates that boys have a higher score in Test No. 1, Directions; Test No. 2, Arithmetical Reasoning; Test No. 6, Completion of Number Series; and Test No. 8, Information. The girls have a notably higher score in Test No. 5, Disarranged Sentences, which is primarily a linguistic test, and a slightly higher score in Test No. 3.

The Army Alpha Test has been given to a considerable number of university students. Typical results are as follows:

	Men	Women
Freshmen	130	129
Sophomores	138	134
Juniors	142	135
Seniors	145	142
Graduates	159	156

A test made with a standardized examination in geometry, prepared by the author, showed the following comparisons between boys and girls in the four parts of the test:

	Definitions	Reasoning	Problems	Constructions
Boys	12	25	3	1.5
Girls	12	27	3	1.2

The differences are practically insignificant and are probably within the limit of chance.

COMPARISONS IN THINKING PROCESSES

A further investigation was carried out by Miss Katherine Tierney under the direction of the author. The object of this study was to ascertain to what extent there may be a difference between men and women in their thinking processes. For the purposes of this experiment the answers to a question given in a final examination in elementary psychology were used. The question selected allowed of considerable individual liberty in thought and discussion. Answers written to this question by 10 men and 10 women students were copied in typewritten form and submitted to a group of 30 judges. They were used in typewritten form in order that differences in handwriting might be eliminated. Each of the 30 judges was asked to read the 20 answers which were given to him in chance order. After he had read a given answer, he was asked to state whether it had been written by a man or by a woman. Four of the 30 judges were instructors who were accustomed to reading examinations of this type.

The results showed that the average percentage of correct judgments for the 30 judges with respect to the 20 answers was 52.8%. It is evident that 50% of the answers would be correct by pure chance for the reason that a judge was asked to say whether a given answer was written by a man or by a woman. In other words, he could give only one of two answers which in the long run would produce as a matter of chance 50% correct answers. It is evident, therefore, that these judges, on the whole, were unable to determine from the nature of the thought processes or the language involved in these answers, whether an answer was written by a man or by a woman. Apparently the thinking processes, at least so far as this type of thinking is concerned, are not essentially different.

After each person had given his decision in connection with each paper, he was asked to state, so far as he was consciously aware, what was the basis of his judgment. The reasons thus given were as follows:

1. That men use shorter sentences and answer more concisely was mentioned by fifteen judges.

2. That women use longer answers was mentioned by six judges.

3. That men use slang was mentioned by six judges.

4. That men are more logical was mentioned by four judges.

5. That women were more literary was mentioned by two judges.

6. That the scientific and long words are more common among women was mentioned by two judges, and that they were thought to be more common among men was mentioned by four judges.

These reasons were checked up, and the actual examination of the answers showed the following: With reference to the length of sentences and answers, it was found that of the seven shortest answers, four had been written by women, and three had been written by men. The three longest answers had been written by men. Hence the question of length of answer was purely a fictitious assumption. With reference to the use of slang, it was found that it occurred in two answers, both of which had been written by men. One of the two answers which contained slang included the word "bosh" and "fake." This paper was judged correctly most frequently, namely 83.3. In this case the element of slang was the determining indication.

It may be of interest to add further that the four instructors who were accustomed to reading examination papers of this type succeeded practically no better than did the others in guessing whether a given answer was written by a man or by a woman. The general inference from this experiment is that the thinking processes of men and women are not sufficiently different to be readily distinguished.

COMPARISON IN ACCURACY OF OBSERVATION

The statement is frequently made that women observe detail more accurately than do men. Several opinions quoted from business men and women at the beginning of this chapter assume such a difference. In recent years, some experimental work has been done on the question of accuracy and fidelity of observation. Such experiments are usually carried out by exhibiting to a person a picture for a brief interval of time. He is told to observe it as attentively as possible, and then to give either a voluntary report of what he saw or to answer questions with regard to the picture. In some instances such experiments have been carried out by means of acts dramatized in person before observers.

Three investigators have reported somewhat contradictory results due probably largely to different methods employed and to the limited number of persons on whom the experiments were made. Stern made tests with pictures, events, and with estimations of time and distances and found that the reports of men were more accurate by 20% to 33% but were less extended than those of women. He found a similar sex difference in his tests with school children. Wreschner and Miss Borst found women superior to men in accuracy as well as in range of observation. Miss Borst found that the range of the men was from 76% to 83% of that of the women, while the accuracy of the men was approximately 96% of that of the women. More extensive experiments would probably show no very marked differences between the sexes in range and accuracy of observation.[1]

COMPARISON OF SELLING APPEALS TO MEN AND TO WOMEN AS DETERMINED BY TESTS

Appeals for various types of commodities have been tested with groups of men and women. Results of such tests will show rather specifically the similarities or differences in the strength which various selling points have with the two sexes.

The 24 selling appeals for toothpaste mentioned in Chapter XIII were tested with 202 men and 162 women. The results expressed in terms of the coefficient of correlation showed a correlation of .77. No important difference existed on any particular selling appeal. The largest difference was found in the case of F, which emphasizes feeling. This had a median rank of 10.6 with the men and of 11.8 with the women, which is after all a negligible difference.

Nine clothing appeals were tested with 110 men and 15 women. The correlation in this case was .73. The largest difference existed in the appeal of cheapness, which had a median rank of 6.8 with the men, and of 4.7 with the women. Apparently it was slightly stronger with the women.

---

[1] Stern, L. W., *Zeits. j. d. ges. Strafrechtwissenschaft*, 22, 1902; Wreschner, A., *Archiv j. d. ges. Psychologie*, 1, 1905, 148-183; Borst, Marie, *Archives de Psychologie*, 3, 1904, 233-314.

Ten appeals for shoes were tested with 50 men and 58 women. The correlation in this case was .06. This, on the face of it, would mean a complete absence of any relationship. However, as a matter of fact, the two sexes agreed quite closely on all appeals except one, namely, "make and material." This had a median rank of 2.4 with the men and 7.0 with the women. There was also a considerable difference on the general appeal, emphasizing in an abstract way "a good shoe." This was weaker with the men than with the women. It had a median rank of 7.2 with the men, and of 4.4 with the women.

Twelve appeals for a checkwriter were tested with 38 men and 30 women. The correlation was .82. There was no significant difference in regard to any selling point.

Ten appeals for a mint candy were tested with 37 men and 37 women. The correlation was .90. There was likewise in this case no significant difference on any appeal.

Professor E. K. Strong tested 20 appeals for soap with 101 men and 95 women. See Table 71 on page 364. There was a correlation of .91. The largest difference was on the appeal of beauty, which had an average rank of 10.7 with the men and 8.1 with the women. The next largest difference was on the appeal of "reliable firm," which had an average rank of 9.4 with the men and 10.1 with the women. Neither of these differences is significant.

Professors H. L. Hollingworth and H. F. Adams report a test made with 50 abstract appeals. This test was carried out with 60 men and 40 women. The correlation was .77. Hollingworth further reports a test made with 15 appeals for a player piano, with a group of men and a group of women. The correlation in this case was only .28. This is unusually low and is due primarily to the difference which was found in the case of two appeals.

Tests of 15 typewriter advertisements and of 8 advertisements of a book, made with a group of 26 men and 25 women, showed the following correlations between the men and the women.

	Typewriter Ads	Book Ads
Attention value of Ads	.70	.05
Headlines	.82	.93
Text	.64	.39

SUMMARY AND INTERPRETATION OF RESULTS

1. Perhaps the first and most important outstanding feature is that mental sex differences are much exaggerated in popular thought, and that a good deal of difference made in actual practice is probably without foundation. In most intellectual traits, the two sexes are very much alike. The surprising thing is their similarity rather than their differences.

(a) Man's greater physical strength has unconsciously been taken to imply mental superiority and greater power of thought.

(b) Women's ignorance of things with which men commonly deal, such as business, machines, places, and events, is likewise taken to imply women's intellectual inferiority. We are inclined to forget that men are equally ignorant about the things with which women deal, such as domestic, family, and social matters. These differences are occupational and environmental, rather than fundamental.

(c) Each sex judges the other mainly by the more strictly sex behavior toward the other. That is, the judgment is based primarily on a behavior resulting from a combination of efforts at attraction and evasion. These characteristics are paraded before our eyes in literature, drama, and journalism, and so represent to many people the complete exposition of sex differences or similarities.

2. The differences that do exist and are of importance are the ones connected more or less directly with sex behavior and the sex instinct in the more limited sense. The difference is not so much in the sex behavior itself as in the fact that the behavior is directed toward the opposite sex.

That is, the sex behavior of boys and girls or of men and women is more nearly alike than is usually supposed. Both sexes try to attract, please, or interest the other sex. Both try in each other's presence to appear at their best. Boys and girls seem to be very much alike when they are apart; but very unlike when they are together.

The adolescent girl makes herself attractive, but so does also the adolescent boy. It happens that at the present time women pay particular attention to dress, display and personal adornment. We should, however, remember that a century or more ago men dressed in silks and velvets almost as much as women. The appeals directly connected with the instinct of display and attraction are probably stronger at the present time with women than with men.

3. From the practical standpoint, the most important thing for the advertiser to do is to find out, whenever a question of sex difference is involved, whether there really

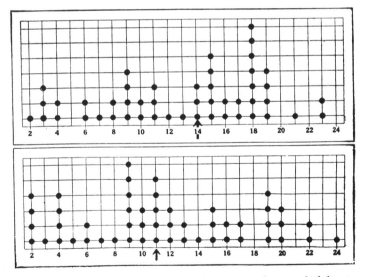

Figure 30: Above: selling argument F (*see page 282*), as ranked by 50 women; below: selling argument F, as ranked by 50 men

is a difference, and if so, how large and important it is, rather than to assume on the basis of purely personal impressions (which may be prejudiced or superficial), that such and such a difference exists and then to build plans on it. It is of some value to know, in general, that the differences are in the large majority of instances not as great as they are usually assumed to be. This has been shown by the experimental and statistical data presented in this chapter. It is of more value, however, to determine by means of questionnaire-field inquiries and then by means of tests of the proposed advertisements themselves, what differences exist in each specific case, if any, and how large they may be.

2. CLASS DIFFERENCES

An important problem in determining appeals to be used is the possible difference that may exist between various classes of persons. The common impression is that such differences are very considerable. For example, many persons assume that the differences between North and South or East and West, between farmer and city dweller, between laborer and capitalist, between various social strata of society, are very large.

There is a meager amount of scientific information available on this question. Some pertinent facts will be found in the rating of the appeals for boys' ready-made clothing, as found in the study reported in Chapter IX. The 13 appeals were ranked in the order of strength by approximately 50 mothers in each of six districts. An examination of Table 42 will show that the various districts agree on the whole quite closely. There are, however, certain striking and important exceptions. Probably the most important difference will be found in the third group designated as District No. III, composed primarily of union skilled and unskilled laboring groups. The most striking feature of the results obtained from this group is the fact that the 13 selling points seemed to have practically the same strength of appeal. It will be noted that the range between the strongest and the weakest appeal is only from 1.6 to 3.2, whereas the range in most of the other groups is in the neighborhood of 8 to 10 points. Thus, for example, in the second column, which contains the results from the best residential section of the city, the range is from 1.5 to 10.2, and the range in the first column is from 1.6 to 11.0.

By an examination of the last two columns, which represent two rural communities, it will be noted that, while the difference between the strongest and the weakest appeals is considerably wider than in case of the third column, the range is nevertheless not quite as wide as in the case of the first, second, and fourth columns. This point is borne out to some extent by the results in the table on soap appeals, presented below.

Another point of interest in column 3 is the fact that the appeal "Union Made" is somewhat stronger with the laboring group than it is with other groups. It is either 12th or 13th in the other groups, whereas it is 7th in the union labor group. This, however, is not particularly important, in view of the small difference in the entire list of appeals. The explanation apparently is that with the group in column 3, one appeal is practically as good as any other appeal. The discrimination is not as keen, and consequently the appeals seem to be practically of equal value.

Professor E. K. Strong made an investigation of the relative value of 20 selling arguments for a soap. He tested these 20 selling points with four groups of persons, as shown in Table 71. These results show somewhat the same general tendency so far as group comparisons go. The men and the women and the student group show in general the same relative ranks for the various appeals. The group of 97 farmers, however, differs quite distinctly from the other three groups, and in general in the same manner as the union labor group differed from the other groups. To a less extent the rural groups differed from the other groups in the boys' clothing investigation just mentioned.

TABLE 71

SOAP APPEALS

Appeal	50 Students Median Rank	101 Men Median Rank	95 Women Median Rank	97 Farmers Median Rank
Pure and clean	3.8	3.9	2.7	11.7
Doesn't irritate the skin	5.0	6.0	4.1	10.4
Health	6.3	6.5	5.3	10.7
Expensive	8.3	8.6	6.4	11.3
Shampoo and bath	8.5	6.4	8.3	11.4
Carnegie Institute	8.5	12.1	11.6	10.2
Dr.'s recommendation	9.0	9.5	9.7	10.7
Guaranteed	9.0	9.6	9.4	11.6
Baby	9.5	9.6	9.8	9.7
Exhilaration in bath	10.5	8.6	8.4	11.4
At our expense	10.7	10.1	10.1	11.6
Beauty	10.8	10.7	8.1	10.8
Reliable firm	10.8	9.4	10.1	9.4
Cheap	12.7	14.8	15.1	7.1
Sold everywhere	13.0	13.1	12.6	8.7
Roosevelt recommendation	13.5	12.1	13.7	13.1
Royalty recommendation	13.5	11.1	14.5	10.6
For particular people	15.8	12.3	15.4	9.6
Large factory	16.1	16.5	16.6	9.7
Souvenir free	18.3	18.8	19.1	8.2

In the first place, the difference between the strongest and the weakest appeal with the group of farmers is very small. The strongest appeal, that of cheapness, has an average rank of 7.1, while the weakest appeal, Roosevelt's recommendation, has an average rank of 13.1. In other words, the range is only about 6 points, whereas in the other three groups, the range is approximately 15 to 17 points. The explanation, apparently, again is, that this particular farmer group did not discriminate as accurately as did the other groups, and that one selling argument seemed to be almost as strong or as weak as any other. It ought to be mentioned that this point probably depends not so much on the fact that the group was composed of farmers, but rather on the amount of general education and information possessed by a given group. There are farmers and farmers just as there are different types of city dwellers. This point is borne out by the fact that the farmer groups in the clothing investigation were taken from one of the more progressive and prosperous farming areas and it will be noted that the various appeals had very nearly the same values with them as with the better city groups. It will be of interest here to turn to the data presented in Chapter XIII, to see how closely on the whole the test results from various classes agree, as the data from business men and students in various sections of the country.

So far as we may generalize on the question of class differences, two statements may be made. The first is that differences do exist, but that the differences are probably inversely proportional to the amount of general education, enlightenment and intelligence possessed by given groups. That is, differences in information, general education and progressiveness are probably more important than differences in occupation or geographical location.

TABLE 72

REASONS FOR BUYING READY-MADE CLOTHES IN RELATION TO AGE

Reasons	Business Men Over 30	Business Men Under 30	Students	Total
General reasons	27%	27%	26%	27%
Material (wear)	24	23	20	23
Style or cut (appearance)	11	19	22	16
Fit	11	10	9	10
Price	7	7	6	7
Workmanship	5	5	6	5
Other reasons	15	9	11	12

The second point of importance is that class differences should not be blindly assumed to exist and plans made accordingly, but that some reliable form of investigation should be undertaken to discover whether differences do exist and to what extent, and the nature of the differences.

There are often secondary differences existing between various sections of the country due to climatic condition, local historical facts or events, which may be tied up with advertising. There are no doubt also differences due to the age of persons. Older persons may not be as much influenced by factors of style and other elements as are younger persons. Definite facts should in each case be obtained before plans are made. Such facts can usually be obtained as a part of a properly planned questionnaire survey and as a part of the laboratory-field tests of the advertisements themselves.

Thus, for example, one of the questions in a field survey made by a manufacturer of high-grade, hand-tailored clothes was, If you wear a particular brand of ready-made clothes, why do you wear that brand? The answers obtained by personal interview with over 1,200 men showed the results as given in Table 72, analyzed from the standpoint of age.

The only difference of any importance at all is with regard to style. It is mentioned more frequently by the business men under 30 and by the students than by the business men over thirty.

The common tendency is to exaggerate age, sex, or class differences. The important point is that accurate facts should be discovered and used as a basis of action.

PRINCIPLES OF ADVERTISING

PART IV

THE PRESENTATION OF THE APPEALS: HOW
MAY THE APPEALS BE PRESENTED
MOST EFFECTIVELY?

XVII

ANALYSIS OF PROBLEMS

Factors that determine the most effective presentation of the appeals determined upon. Argumentative *vs.* suggestive methods. Elements in the problem. Application of analysis.

THE central problem of this part is an analysis and a study of the factors that determine the most effective presentation of the appeals which have been determined upon according to the plans thus far discussed. The problem presents itself clearly in the following manner. Suppose we have determined that an appeal of taste or healthfulness or of nourishing food value is the one that should be most widely used. The practical question that still remains is: How, in concrete detail, may any one of these appeals be presented? In other words, the problem raises the many minute details regarding the technical preparation and execution of advertising plans.

Specifically, the problem would resolve itself into a study of the most effective manner in which each of the five main functions of an advertisement may be accomplished. As pointed out in Chapter XIV these five functions are:

1. To secure attention
2. To arouse interest
3. To bring about conviction
4. To produce action
5. To impress the memory

The problem in its practical execution is: How may the appeal of nourishing food value, for example, be presented so as to accomplish each of these five purposes most effectively?

ARGUMENTATIVE VERSUS SUGGESTIVE METHODS

Before these five functions of an advertisement may be considered specifically, we must raise the fundamental question as to whether a given appeal should be presented primarily in argumentative or in suggestive form, or to what extent it may be presented by a varying combination of these two methods in proper proportion. Thus, the appeal of nourishing food value might be presented primarily in textual, argumentative form, by discussing and presenting facts, such as the comparative food value as determined by scientific tests and expressed in terms of calories or other units. On the other hand, the appeal of high nutritive value of a food might be presented primarily by means of the illustrative, suggestive form, by showing a picture of a strong, healthy, active person enjoying himself in outdoor activities, or eating the food with apparent delight. The difference between these two methods of presentation is represented by the colloquial phrases, "reason why" copy and "pictorial" copy.

We must determine what are the relative proportions of these two methods which may be combined most effectively before it is possible to consider the technical details involved in the actual preparation of the layout, the size of space, the arrangement of features, and the like.

Elements in the Problem. What are the factors on the basis of which this question may be determined? The question as to whether argumentative or suggestive advertising, or a combination of both, is to be used will depend upon the following chief factors:

1. The buying process. It will depend upon the nature of the buying process involved in purchasing a given commodity; that is, whether the buying of the commodity in question is done in a deliberate, thoughtful manner, or whether it is done in an impulsive, spur-of-the-moment manner.

2. Frequency of purchase. It will depend upon the frequency with which the commodity is purchased—whether the buyer buys from habit or whether each individual purchase is the result of considerable deliberation and choice.

3. Familiarity. It will depend upon the familiarity of the public with the article. If it is well known, the reminding, pictorial, suggestive appeal is likely to be effective; whereas, if the commodity is new, the use of a considerable amount of text and informational material will be necessary.

4. Price. It will depend upon the price of the article; that is, whether the price is low enough so that ordinarily a minimum of deliberation is involved, or whether the price is high so that it is a matter of more or less careful consideration.

5. Competition. It may depend upon the severity of the competition. If the field is hard fought, argumentative copy may be the more effective.

6. Copy used by competitors. It will depend upon whether competitors uniformly use the one or the other type of advertising. In such a case the opposite type of presentation would have considerable attention value. If everyone used largely argumentative presentation, the pictorial method, used by a single firm, would attract much attention.

7. Complexity of the article or proposition. If the commodity is technical and intricate or if the situation is complex, the argumentative type may be the more effective; while if the commodity is simple or the proposition easily understood, the suggestive type may be more suitable.

8. Class of people. It may depend to some extent upon the class of people to be reached, whether they are likely to read advertisements extensively or not.

9. Mediums. It will depend upon the mediums that are to be used. Obviously, the poster, reminding type of ad-

vertising must be used on street-car cards, billboards, and similar mediums.

10. Sentiment. It depends to some extent upon whether the commodity is one that is surrounded with personal sentiment rather than necessary utility. The suggestive type of appeal possibly lends itself somewhat more readily to the development of sentiment and artistic atmosphere.

11. Purpose. It depends in part upon the purpose which the advertiser wishes to accomplish. If he wishes to produce direct sales, or to accomplish a great deal of the selling process through his advertisements, argumentative presentation will probably be needed. If, on the other hand, he wishes to do only a part of the selling, such as making the name known or stimulating further inquiry or inspection of the article, the suggestive presentation may perhaps be the more effective.

12. Finally, it depends upon the effectiveness of influencing the actions of people by means of suggestion as against reasoning. The question is, To what extent is suggestion in general, and specifically in relation to a particular commodity, a more or a less effective way of bringing about the desired action than an appeal to reasoning may be? These various factors have been stated here with the qualification of "perhaps" or "possibly" for the reason that the importance of each factor depends upon the particular commodity and its immediately surrounding conditions. The most certain way of determining whether argumentative presentation, or suggestive presentation, and how much of either, or what particular combination of the two, may be most effective, is by means of a well-planned and properly conducted series of tests, such as have been outlined in preceding chapters..

Tipper, Hotchkiss, Hollingworth, and Parsons [1] have suggested that human interest copy is suitable for the following classes of commodities:

[1] *Advertising*, p. 208.

1. Articles for personal use, especially for adornment or the improvement of one's appearance, such as toilet articles, jewelry, clothing accessories, etc.

2. Articles for family use that contribute to the enjoyment of life, such as musical instruments, toys, and the like.

3. Articles that contribute to the personal safety or longer life of the individual or members of his family, such as insurance, safety devices, revolvers, etc.

4. Most foods and smoking materials, especially those bought for enjoyment rather than for nourishment, such as candy, ginger ale, grape juice, tobacco and cigarettes, also beer and liquors.

5. Articles bought frequently as gifts, such as silverware, books, and flowers.

No doubt this classification has some value, but it cannot be followed directly as each particular commodity must be analyzed more fully from the standpoint of the factors which have been enumerated. In almost any concrete instance, any one of these factors may outweigh the fact that a given commodity may belong to any of these five classes. This one factor might make it advisable to use argumentative rather than human interest appeals.

APPLICATION OF ANALYSIS

Let us now apply our analysis of the factors determining the relative amount of argumentative or suggestive advertising to be used to some concrete cases in which one form or another has been used quite exclusively.

In 1921 and 1922, the Dodge automobile was being advertised by means of a unique method which was primarily of the suggestive type. A typical advertisement in this series consisted of a full-page space which contained nothing more than a phrase or a sentence with the name Dodge Brothers at the bottom, or possibly a picture of the car. Some of these phrases were, "What will your car be worth a year from today?" "Low operating cost," "Dependable," "A good name," and so on.

Let us now ask the question, What factors tend to justify this method? We may mention the following:

1. The car is well known, and therefore would not require a detailed amount of text such as a new automobile in the field would require.

2. The advertisements have high attention value because of the large amount of white space. They will be readily noticed, not only as compared with advertisements in general, but also as compared with automobile advertisements in particular.

3. The phrases and sentences used relate to some important point. The brevity of these statements makes them stand out and probably impresses them more fully upon the mind of the reader than the same idea would be impressed if it were contained as a part of longer text. The reader cannot help but see the phrase "Low operating cost" if he sees the advertisement at all. The phrase will be impressed upon his memory and his reaction to it is likely to be somewhat along this line: "Oh, yes! I have heard it said that the Dodge car has a low operating expense, and has a high resale value."

On the other side, in answer to the question, What factors are opposed to the method here used, we may point out the following:

1. An automobile costs a large sum o. money, and is not bought without a considerable amount of deliberation and comparison. Consequently, argumentative copy ought to be used.

2. Automobiles are bought infrequently, ordinarily only once in several years, and consequently the buying is not done from habit, but is a matter of careful consideration at the time.

3. The phrases stimulate questions, but do not provide a definite answer. As such they encourage comparison with other cars without providing definite information regarding the Dodge car. They are, however, applied in such a way that the answer to the question would be apt to be favorable as far as this car is concerned.

The conclusion to be arrived at on the basis of a comparison of the factors on both sides will depend, obviously, upon the relative weight which is assigned to each factor. The conclusion which it would seem reasonable to draw is that since the car is well known, the appearance of the advertisements very unusual, and since each advertisement stimulates thought along some specific line, it would seem that these factors have a great deal of weight and might, therefore, justify the method employed.

We may make a similar comparison in the case of current shoe advertisements. The W. L. Douglas shoe has been advertised uniformly and consistently by the use of both picture and text, but with a strong predominance of the text element. The Beacon shoe, on the other hand, has been advertised very largely by the suggestive method, the picture greatly predominating and the text consisting of typical phrases, such as "Beacon Shoes—There are no better."

Analyzing the factors involved in these two instances, we may point out with reference to the Douglas plan, the following points in its favor:

1. Even though shoes are bought frequently, and therefore more or less from habit, and in accordance with certain brand preferences, they are bought, nevertheless, rather deliberately, because of the fitting which is necessary. Therefore a considerable amount of text material would be justifiable.

2. In the Douglas shoes, the price is one of the strong appeals, and style, while mentioned, is perhaps more secondary. Hence, the suggestive, sentimental appeals which could be stressed by use of a picture are not quite so important.

On the other side of the problem, we may mention the following points:

1. The public is very familiar with the name Douglas.

2. Shoes are probably bought often enough to establish fairly definite habit and brand preferences.

So far as the Beacon shoe advertising is concerned, the suggestive method employed is somewhat more justifiable perhaps than it would be in the case of the Douglas shoe. Style and appearance are prominent appeals in the case of the Beacon shoe. However, the Beacon shoe is possibly not as well known as the Douglas.

The conclusions that might be drawn are that the Douglas advertising might continue its general method, but change its text from time to time, stressing somewhat more the suggestive element by the use of more attractive typography, and thus making the appearance of the advertisement less crowded and more inviting to read. The superlative statements should be eliminated or changed.

The Beacon advertisements should no doubt stress the suggestive side through style, appearance, and refinement, but should probably contain more convincing textual material in place of the general superlative statements now used.

Let us take one more illustration, that of Kuppenheimer clothes. The kind of advertising used has been largely of the suggestive, pictorial type. In favor of this method, we may mention the following points:

1. The importance of style and appearance for a commodity of this sort;

2. The fact that the name is well known;

3. The importance of sentiment and personal adornment in clothing.

On the other side, we may mention the following:

1. A suit of clothes is bought with considerable deliberation, particularly because of the fitting involved.

2. Such factors as material and tailoring are very important elements in arriving at a decision.

3. Competition in the clothing field is very keen.

4. At the present time, there is a great deal of similarity in the type of advertising employed by several leading manufacturers of clothing. One would almost think that each one tried to make his advertising as much like that of his competitors as possible.

The conclusion that might be suggested would be that the pictorial, suggestive element should remain prominent, but that more argumentative, textual material should be introduced to give the reader an impression of difference between one maker and another and to meet the factor of competition.

Two very important elements in the decision as to which mode of appeal, or what combination of the two methods, is the most effective are: first, to what extent people at the present time are willing to or do read the text portions of advertisements; second, to what extent people in general are actually influenced favorably by one or the other method. The latter question, particularly, is difficult to approach by tangible methods of investigation. We know quite obviously that mere familiarity with the name of a commodity creates a strong predisposition in the mind of the buyer in favor of that commodity, irrespective of any specific information or impression regarding it.

In the attempt to arrive at somewhat more tangible facts regarding these two questions, the author made the following investigation. Five questions were asked in a personal interview with 603 persons in Boston and its immediate environment, as follows:

1. When you receive a new magazine do you purposely look through it to look at the advertisements? Always—usually—occasionally—or do you see them only incidentally as you read articles in the magazine?

2. The same for newspapers: Always—usually—occasionally—only incidentally as you read the paper.

3. To what extent do you read individual advertisements entirely through? About how many on the average in one copy of a magazine—In one copy of a newspaper?

4. What advertisements that you have seen recently did you read pretty completely? Name the article or the firm. Name the magazine or newspaper, and its approximate date.

5. How did you happen to read this advertisement (or these advertisements)?

The 603 persons interviewed included 195 business men, 174 housewives, and 234 men students. The responses obtained to the first two questions are shown in Table 73 separately for these three groups. The numbers in the tables are the percentages of persons who responded in the manner indicated.

TABLE 73

EXTENT TO WHICH ADVERTISEMENTS ARE READ

	195 Men	174 Women	234 Men Students
Purposely looking at advertisements in a magazine			
Always	35.7%	33.2%	37.6%
Usually	22.5	22.3	30.0
Occasionally	22.3	23.2	18.8
Incidentally	20.2	21.5	13.7
Purposely looking at advertisements in a newspaper			
Always	7.1%	18.0%	3.9%
Usually	7.7	18.9	13.8
Occasionally	30.7	26.1	18.6
Incidentally	54.4	37.5	63.6

This table shows that approximately one-third of the men and women, according to their own statement, *always* look through a magazine when they first get it, to see what advertisements it contains. Not quite one-fourth *usually* do so, and likewise not quite one-fourth *occasionally* do so. Approximately one-fifth of the readers see the advertisements *only incidentally* as they read articles in the magazines. This is a larger proportion of persons who always or usually look through a magazine to see the advertisements than

TABLE 74

EXTENT TO WHICH ADVERTISEMENTS ARE READ

	195 Men	174 Women	234 Men Students
Average number of advertisements in a given issue of a magazine read entirely through, per person	3	3	3
Percentage of persons who state that they do not read any m a g a z i n e advertisements entirely through	28.8%	27.8%	16.7%
Percentage of persons who read in a given issue of a magazine 10 or more advertisements entirely through	14.4%	12.2%	12.8%
Average number of advertisements in a given issue of a newspaper read entirely through, per person	2	2.5	1.5
Percentage of persons who state that they do not read any newspaper advertisements entirely through	38.5%	32.0%	36.3%
Percentage of persons who read in a given issue of a newspaper 10 or more advertisements entirely through	10.2%	11.0%	2.1%

most of us would anticipate. It is further interesting to note that the proportion of persons in the various groups is approximately the same in the case of the business men, the women, and the students.

The situation is somewhat different in the case of newspapers. A very much smaller proportion of persons either always or usually look purposely at the advertisements it contains. The great proportion of men (54.4%) see advertisements in a newspaper only incidentally, or look for them occasionally (30.7%). Only approximately 7%

always look for the advertisements, and another 7.7%
usually look for them. In the case of newspapers there is
a noticeable difference between men and women in their
habits of reading the advertisements. The proportion of
women who purposely look for the advertisements either
always (18.0%), or usually (18.9%), is about 2½ times
as great as the corresponding proportion of men.

The results obtained in response to Question 3 are shown
in Table 74.

These results also show rather close agreement among
the three groups. A somewhat larger number of magazine
advertisements are read entirely through than newspaper
advertisements. In the case of the men, it is 3 against 2;
and in the case of the women, it is 3 against 2½. This, however, is probably about the same proportion of advertisements, since the average magazine contains somewhat more
advertisements than an average newspaper. It should be
borne in mind that the newspapers here considered are
those published in Boston, and are therefore typical of the
larger metropolitan papers.

The inferences from these data are that people in general
are developing the habit of looking at the advertisements in
magazines, that nearly 60% do so with regularity, but that
a relatively small proportion of advertisements are read entirely, or nearly, through.

The data obtained in response to questions 4 and 5 are
summarized in Table 75.

The predominating element causing people to read advertisements nearly, or entirely, through is attention value and
the factors that heighten the attention value. These factors
were mentioned 216 times. The second most important element causing people to read advertisements through is
interest in the product advertised. This was mentioned 194
times. The interest value of the text was mentioned 88
times. "Considered buying" was mentioned 75 times; "Interest in the appeal used" 51 times; the "attention and interest value of the headline" 32 times, and so on.

TABLE 75

REASONS WHY ADVERTISEMENTS WERE READ THROUGH BY

(195 business men who had read 245 advertisements)
(234 men students who had read 371 advertisements)
(174 women who had read 250 advertisements)

Reasons for Reading	Business Men			
	Men	Students	Women	Totals
1. Attention value of ad, layout, unusualness, size, etc.				
Attractive ad	9	20	20	49
Attention value of ad	16	12	8	36
Colors	4	14	13	31
Unusual, striking, novel ad	5	20	2	27
Brevity of ad	2	14	1	17
Attracted by arrangement	5	7	4	16
Liked ad	5	..	3	8
High quality of advertisement	..	4	2	6
Interesting ad	..	3	..	3
Double-page ad	..	2	..	2
White space in ad	..	2	..	2
Easy to read	..	3	..	3
Large size of ad	3	2	..	5
Full-page ad	2	..	..	2
A new ad	2	2	..	4
General appearance of advertisement	2	..	..	2
Large type	1	1	1	3
Totals	56	106	54	216
2. Interested in product advertised	71	74	49	194
3. Attention and interest value of illustration				
Attractive illustration	12	63	46	121
Unusual illustration	5	4	..	9
Picture of pretty girl	1	3	..	4
Picture of child in ad	..	..	1	1
Totals	18	70	47	135
4. Interest value of text				
Interesting text	12	18	6	36

Reasons for Reading	Business Men	Men Students	Women	Totals
Historical material in text	3	3	. .	6
Amusing ad	2	5	2	9
Human interest copy	1	. .	. .	1
Explanatory copy	1	4	1	6
French words in ad	1	1	. .	2
Story type of ad	3	2	3	8
Jingles in ad	2	1	2	5
Odd text	1	7	. .	8
Well written	. .	2	. .	2
Dialect in ad	. .	1	. .	1
Dialogue in ad	. .	2	. .	2
Attracted by slogan	. .	. .	1	1
Quaint	. .	. .	1	1
Totals	26	46	16	88
5. Considered buying	18	20	37	75
6. Interest in the appeal used				
Appeals used in ad	3	. .	. .	3
Appetizing	3	3	4	10
Guarantee	2	1	. .	3
Price reduction	2	7	. .	9
Price given	1	2	1	4
Prize offered in ad	1	. .	. .	1
Health	1	. .	2	3
Recipes	. .	. .	6	6
Looking for style suggestions	. .	. .	5	5
Looking for bargains	. .	. .	6	6
Complexion and beauty	. .	. .	2	2
Free trial offer	. .	. .	1	1
Totals	13	11	27	51
7. Attention and interest value of the headline	14	13	5	32
8. Interest in certain ads				
Ad seen so frequently	5	1	. .	6
Ad seen so frequently	5	1	. .	6
Interested in series of ads	2	. .	. .	2
Totals	8	1	0	9

Reasons for Reading	Business Men	Men Students	Women	Totals
9. Position of ad on cover or front page, etc.	4	4	1	9
10. Miscellaneous				
A new product	4	7	..	11
Interested in advertising	4	9	7	20
Interested in magazine	2	..	..	2
Looking through the ads	3	1	7	11
Nothing else to do in subway	2	4	..	6
Curiosity	2	8	3	13
Like particular style of advertisement	1	2	..	3
Interest in the firm	1	17	3	21
By chance	1	6	1	8
Attracted by name of product	..	1	..	1
Antagonism toward product	..	2	..	2
Music described in ad	..	1	1	2
Does not know	..	..	2	2
Totals	20	58	24	102

Our results indicate that the average reader reads three advertisements in a magazine entirely through. The magazines most frequently mentioned here had roughly about 100 advertisements per issue. In other words, an average of 3 advertisements in 100 are read entirely through or nearly so. In the case of 97 out of 100 only the more conspicuous features are read or observed in a relatively brief glance. The generalization here suggested is that probably the most effective advertisement is the one that imparts something worth while to both classes of readers, namely, to those who glance hastily and to those who read carefully.

XVIII

SUGGESTIVE ADVERTISING

Four types of suggestive advertisements: 1. Display of the name only. 2. Quality suggested by elegant surroundings. 3. Quality suggested by use. 4. The direct command. Effectiveness of suggestive advertising. Purpose of suggestive advertising. Principles underlying suggestive advertising. The ideo-motor principle. Tendency in the use of suggestive advertising. Methods of making suggestive advertising effective. 1. Attention test. 2. Persuasion test.

WE may distinguish four types of suggestive advertisements, according to the degree of definiteness of the suggestion.

1. *Display of the Name Only.* The most extreme form of suggestive copy consists of a simple presentation of the name without comment of any sort. An example of this class is shown in Figure 31. The entire advertisement is so constructed that it directs attention to the name "Cream of Wheat" and its trade "character." There is no argument or description. All that you see is a matter of inference based on your past acquaintance with this product. The sole purpose of this advertisement is to remind you of the name. The other parts of the advertisement simply add an atmosphere of interest. The words "A Dainty Breakfast—A Delicious Dessert" give the only hint of the nature or use of the article.

2. *Quality Suggested by Elegant Surroundings.* The second type, besides giving the name, goes one step further by suggesting or implying directly the high value of the article. This is accomplished by presenting the product in elegant surroundings, or by implying a wide use of it, particularly by the better classes of society. A recent advertisement showed a Victrola artistically placed in one of the rooms

384

Figure 31: Specimen advertisement showing one form of suggestive copy
—that is, display of the name only *(See page 384)*

of the White House.   This is a form of suggestion which is indirect but nevertheless powerful in stimulating a desire to possess and enjoy the product in question.

3. *Quality Suggested by Use.*   The third type not only gives the name and represents the commodity in attractive

Figure 32:   An example of suggestive copy where quality is suggested by elegant surroundings

surroundings, but goes still another step by exhibiting the article in actual use and thus suggesting its value and desirability. A typical illustration of this class is presented in Figure 33, which exhibits the maid in a neat,

Figure 33: Specimen advertisement showing suggestive copy where quality is suggested by use

orderly kitchen, applying the cleanser to a frying pan. Another recent advertisement showed a family happily gathered in their beautiful home enjoying the music of a Victrola.

The psychological strength of this type of advertising lies in its potent appeal to the imitative tendency in human nature. We like to follow the lead of others, particularly if social superiority and prestige are thereby attainable.

4. *The Direct Command.* The fourth type takes the final step in suggestion by giving a definite suggestion or command to use the article or to do a definite act toward obtaining it. This command may be stated directly, as in a recent camera advertisement, "Take a Kodak with you" (Figure 34); or indirectly, as in the well-known soap advertisements, "Good morning, have you used Pears' soap?" Each form has a certain advantage, according to the particular conditions under which it is used.

EFFECTIVENESS OF SUGGESTIVE ADVERTISING

Our next question is: What evidence do we have to show that suggestive advertising is really effective? There are those who believe that pure publicity advertising is poor publicity and that the only style of advertising worth while is the argumentative style.

In the first place, the argument that suggestive advertising is effective under certain circumstances is given weight by the fact that its use has tended to increase in the last three or four decades. Many firms whose products are widely known resort very largely to this type of copy. They have experimented with suggestive advertising for a sufficient time to be convinced that it brings results. Notable examples of firms or commodities which have been advertised through suggestive copy are the Kodak, Cream of Wheat, Gold Medal Flour, Old Dutch Cleanser, Pears' Soap, Royal Typewriters, Kellogg's Corn Flakes, Tiffany and Co.

Suggestive advertising, either in its pure form or in its various combinations with argumentative elements, has come more and more into general use in recent years. This increase is undoubtedly due in part to its real effectiveness; it is also due in part to better methods of reproducing illustrations and to more numerous drawings and paintings

Figure 34: Specimen advertisement using suggestive copy with the direct command *(See page 388)*

available for commercial purposes; and it is due in part to the wide reputation of certain commodities for which argumentative copy may no longer be essential and may possibly be even less effective than suggestive copy.

In the second place, human nature is influenced in everyday action perhaps as much by suggestion and imitation as by reason and deliberation. Imitation is usually the chief factor in determining the spread of fashion, custom, manners and social usages, pronunciation, slang, and the like. We may refer here to the contest conducted in the fall of 1909 by Colgate & Company in which an advertisement was published containing smaller reproductions of two advertisements of dental cream. The one was largely argumentative and the other primarily suggestive. A similar advertisement for their Talc Powder was also published. These two contest advertisements appeared in the *Ladies' Home Journal*, *Woman's Home Companion*, and the Butterick trio. Colgate & Company desired to make a test campaign to determine the relative value of suggestive and argumentative copy. They therefore offered prizes for the best brief essays telling which of the two advertisements shown was considered the better, and why. Approximately 60,000 letters were received. These fell, curiously enough, into two almost equal groups. About one-half of the correspondents considered the argumentative advertisement better and the rest considered the suggestive advertisement better. Hence the latter apparently stands in as high favor with the consumer as the former.

In the third place, the results of some tests may be cited which show that the chief impression created through advertising is the remembrance of the name of the product. The author requested a class of students to make a list of all commodities with which they were familiar, through use, advertising, or any other means, and then to state what particular features they remembered about them. A typical record follows:

Cream of Wheat	Lack of reading matter
Spearmint gum	The arrow pictures
Overland automobiles	The red borders of advertisements
Goodyear tires	Novel photographs in the ads
Ford automobiles	Statistics connected with the Ford
Oliver typewriter	17 cents a week
Ivory soap	99% pure
Angelus players	Odd pictures
Columbia phonograph	Large type and pictures
Prince Albert tobacco	Cool
Indian motorcycles	Red print
Arrow collars	Inhuman men in pictures
Pears' soap	Picture of soap
Fairy soap	The little girl
Gold Dust	The twins
Omar cigarettes	Good illustration

From the various lists obtained, it is evident that the item most commonly remembered is the name, and that more rarely is a definite argument or selling point remembered. In not more than 20% of the commodities listed was a specific selling argument mentioned. Most of the features mentioned relate to attention or interest elements or to the structure of the advertisements. The significant point to notice here is that the retention of the name of the commodity in the minds of the people is the chief accomplishment of the advertisement. And for many commodities the suggestive, human interest advertisement can secure this name-retention more effectively than the lengthy argumentative advertisement.

PURPOSE OF SUGGESTIVE ADVERTISING

The purpose of the suggestive method of advertising is to accomplish three things:

1. To secure favorable attention and interest in a commodity

2. To develop a fringe or atmosphere of favorable associations

3. To lead to action directly by frequent repetition

Recalling the five functions which an advertisement aims to accomplish, mentioned in Chapter XVII, we note that suggestive advertising aims to jump directly from securing attention and interest to the production of action, without developing particularly the element of conviction. In other words, the suggestive method attempts to eliminate entirely or largely the element of deliberation and comparison involved in a deliberate argumentative purchase. The entire effort of the suggestive method is therefore confined to the elements of attention and interest and the element of producing action. This results in impressing the memory so thoroughly that when occasion arises for buying an article of a given class, the purchaser will at once recall one or another particular brand which he has seen advertised, and call for it. Whether it is soap, or toothpaste, or some other product, he will recall instantly some particular brand; he will recall whatever brand has been impressed upon his memory. He will not necessarily recall any definite reasons in favor of the particular brand that he calls for, but the one particular brand-name dominates his mind, and as a result of it, he proceeds to purchase this brand.

PRINCIPLES UNDERLYING SUGGESTIVE ADVERTISING

What is the fundamental cause of the forcefulness of suggestion in determining human behavior? To begin with, we must realize that our actions are determined far more by suggestions and imitation than we commonly believe. The human being is as much superior to lower animals in his tendency to imitate as he is in any other trait. The generally accepted belief in the imitativeness of apes has been proved by recent investigations to be utterly erroneous. The human being is far more imitative than any animal. It is this trait which makes him more educable.

The Ideo-Motor Principle. At the bottom of suggestion and imitation lies the basic law of human nature that ideas tend toward action. Normally every idea, sensation, impression, or suggestion tends to produce its appropriate response. The entire organization of mental life and its neural mechanism is constructed on this basis. Incoming nerve currents from the sense-organs are redirected outward to the muscles. The meaning of the ideo-motor law is that impression normally leads to expression without intervening deliberation or voluntary decision. The idea, impression, or stimulus alone is sufficient to cause action. Numerous examples in daily life can be observed by everyone. If you are reading and a fly alights on your hand, the touch alone is sufficient to cause you to move your hand without the intervention of will. Or, if you see only indirectly out of the "corner of your eye" some particles of dust on your coat sleeve, the visual impression of it causes the other hand to brush it away—all possibly without the slightest interruption in the reading.

The author [1] made an experiment in which he attempted to measure the unconscious effect of different models of writing upon the normal writing of adults. Four samples of writing were obtained from each of 106 university students. In order to avoid any suggestion of imitation, written rather than oral directions were given, instructing the students to produce samples of their writing by proceeding at once to write the passages presented without further thought or questions. The four passages put before each person consisted of (1) a typewritten selection, (2) an extreme vertical model, (3) an extreme slanting model, and (4) a large model with many flourishes. The purpose of the typewritten passage was to obtain at the outset a sample of the normal writing of each person. The other three models were taken from school copy books.

After the experiment was finished, each person was asked whether he had tried purposely to imitate the various models. Three persons stated that they had intentionally modified their styles of writing. Their records were thrown

[1] Starch, D. *Psychological Review, 18,* 1911, pp. 223-228.

out. The samples produced by the remaining 103 persons were carefully measured to ascertain their slant and size. Slant was measured by means of a specially prepared, transparent device with ruled lines for determining the angle of inclination of certain tall letters, such as l, f, and p, with the base line on which the words were written. Size was measured by determining the horizontal width of letters by measuring the length of words and dividing by the number of letters in the word.

These measurements showed that the average tendency for this group of persons was to make the letters distinctly more vertical when the vertical model was before them and more slanting when the slanting model was before them as compared with their normal styles of writing. They also tended to write slightly larger when the large model was before them. The amounts of these changes were as follows:

Average inclination of l in the normal writing	65.1 degrees
Average inclination of l written from vertical copy	68.8 degrees
Average inclination of l written from slanting copy	61.5 degrees
Change from normal to vertical	3.7 degrees
Change from normal to slant	3.6 degrees
Total range of change	7.3 degrees
Average width of letters in normal writing	4.33 mm.
Average width of letters written from large model	4.85 mm.

When we realize that the handwriting of adults is a pretty firmly fixed habit, we see that the amount of unconscious imitation is considerable—a total of 7.3 degrees in slant and of .52 millimeters in width.

Another example of the ideo-motor principle is the universal experience of so-called inner speech which accompanies thinking or reading. The vocal organs make miniature movements in pronouncing the words that express the thought processes in the mind. The ideas in the mind tend to produce motor responses.

Many additional illustrations might be given to demonstrate the force of this principle as it operates in muscle reading, the planchette, the psychology of the crowd, imitation in fashions, and the like.

The application of this principle to suggestive copy is evident. An idea impressed by an advertisement will tend to produce a response, just as in other forms of human behavior. The repeated seeing and hearing of the name of an article will tend to produce a desire for procuring it. Similarly, the constant seeing of commodities displayed in shop windows will tend to make the spectator buy. If a clerk presents two or three brands of the same kind of food the customer will, other things being equal, buy the brand of which he knows the name, or with which he has some acquaintance.

Suggestive copy, then, is based upon the ideo-motor principle. It aims to impress the name and to surround it with an atmosphere of worth and desirability. The repetition of the name and the display of the commodity in various advertisements will increase the momentum of the ideo-motor impulse until it finally takes effect. This is the answer to the question, Why is the suggestive, "name-before-the-public" type of advertising effective?

TENDENCY IN THE USE OF SUGGESTIVE ADVERTISING

There has been a decided increase in the use of the suggestive element in advertising. This is indicated particularly by the increase in the use of illustrations. While a picture is not necessarily of the suggestive type, and may in instances actually be argumentative, nevertheless, its prime function is to operate according to the suggestive method. It will be of interest at this point to turn to Chapter XXII to notice the graphs which indicate tendencies in the use of illustrations. For example, Figure 47 shows the remarkable increase which has taken place in the proportion of advertising space occupied by illustrated advertisements. Thus, for example, in 1860, 6% of the advertising space in *Harper's Weekly* was occupied by illustrated advertisements. In 1885, this had risen to 60%, and in 1910 to 1915, it was approximately 75% to 80%.

Figure 49 shows the proportion of illustrated advertisements in which the picture is primarily illustrative or primarily attention-getting. There has been a very distinct tendency toward an increase in the latter function and a decrease in the former function. This is particularly significant in relation to our present problem. The attention- and interest-getting quality employs to a greater extent the suggestive element even than is the case with pictures which are used primarily for illustrative purposes.

A tabulation made of 283 men's clothing advertisements and 150 women's clothing advertisements showed, as stated in Chapter XVI, that approximately half of the space occupied in these advertisements was occupied by illustrations. This is typical of practically all present magazine advertisements. A tabulation of the advertisements in two recent issues of magazines indicated that 56% of the space in one and 52% of the space in the other was occupied by pictures. Figure 48 in Chapter XXII shows that in *Harper's Weekly* during the period from 1860 to 1915 approximately 40% to 45% of the space in illustrated advertisements was occupied by illustrations. In the case of a newspaper, it is of course somewhat less. The figures for the *New York Tribune*, as shown in Figure 48, indicate that approximately 30% of the space occupied by illustrated advertisements was occupied by pictures.

EFFECTIVENESS OF ILLUSTRATIONS

Generally speaking, there are two opposing camps of advertising men. The one group believes that "reason why," or logic, is the one fundamental consideration in the preparation of copy. The other believes that attractive pictures, unconscious impressions, artistic decorations, and high-class art work are the main forces in advertising. But a complete analysis of the principles underlying the practice of advertising and a careful observation of human nature must convince one that both features are important. To be sure, the one set of factors is relatively more potent for some commodities, while the other set may be more effective for other commodities or in other circumstances. We act from reason as well as from suggestion.

Hollingworth has shown by an investigation that there are two fairly distinct types of persons: those who are more attracted by straightforward description or argument, and those who are less imaginative and therefore require pictures to assist in forming clear ideas of objects. In studying a group of expert engineers with respect to the persuasiveness of different sorts of machinery advertisements, Professor Hollingworth says, "The men broke into two sharply defined groups. Members of one group seemed to think in terms of visual pictures. They did not need an illustration of the machine, for the words themselves called

TABLE 76

EFFECT OF ILLUSTRATIONS ON DIFFERENT CLASSES OF PERSONS
GROUP A, WITH GOOD PICTORIAL IMAGINATION

1	2	3	4	5	6	7	8	9	10
All Text	All Text	½ Cut	¾ Text	½ Cut	½ Text	¾ Cut	¾ Text	¾ Cut	All Text
—4.2	—2.6	—0.1	+0.2	+0.7	+0.4	+1.3	—1.0	—1.0	+1.0

GROUP B, WITH POOR PICTORIAL IMAGINATION

1	2	3	4	5	6	7	8	9	10
All Text	All Text	½ Cut	¾ Text	½ Cut	½ Text	¾ Cut	¾ Text	¾ Cut	All Text
+3.1	—2.9	+0.1	—0.2	—0.3	+1.0	—1.1	+0.9	+0.5	—0.3

up vivid mental pictures of the parts and the advantages described. To these men, the presence of a cut was not necessary—they wanted all the text they could get and placed copy advertisements above illustrations.

"But for the men in the other group, the words called

up no mental pictures. They thought in terms of sound and movements, and had to have a complete cut of the machine before they could perfectly comprehend its advantages. For such men advertisements with clear cuts were more persuasive than those with only reading matter."

Strong made a similar investigation with 30 women, using 10 soap advertisements. His results, as shown in Table 76, corroborate the conclusions of Hollingworth.

The plus signs indicate that the advertisements were preferred, and the minus signs indicate that they were not preferred. The numbers indicate the extent of preference or prejudice. Group A, quite uniformly, placed the text advertisements high and the cut advertisements low, while for group B the reverse holds. "The inference is, then, that the ideal advertisement should contain, other things being equal, both cut and reading matter."

METHODS OF MAKING SUGGESTIVE ADVERTISING EFFECTIVE

A great many different specific rules or statements might be given to make the suggestive method effective.

1. The product should be suggested in a favorable, and at the same time, clean-cut, definite and forceful manner.

2. Avoid the suggestion of competing ideas or obstacles which would interfere with obtaining or desiring the commodity.

3. Avoid any suspicion, doubt, or comparison regarding the commodity.

Since the purpose of the suggestive method is to develop a high degree of attention and interest in the commodity which may lead directly to action, any statement or implication which tends to encourage comparison should be avoided.

The potency of the suggestion will be considerably enhanced by the implication of reliable authority or mass approval behind the product. The first may be brought about by the picture of a reliable, authoritative person, not necessarily an actual person, but a picture of the type of person who would convey an air of authority and confidence. Another method is to use a "character" such as the Cream of Wheat chef or Aunt Jemima. Such characters lend a human touch and interest even though they are purely fictitious. The second principle may be carried out by suggesting or implying that many people are using or approving the product. Such an implication must, however, be carefully presented so that it will not give the impression that the statement is purely imaginary or possibly untruthful.

The more interesting the picture and the briefer the text, the more effective will suggestive advertising be. Thus the name of the commodity will be most permanently impressed upon the mind. The illustrations in Figures 31, 32, 33, and 34 accomplish this very effectively. They are almost sure to arrest every reader's eye, for they strike chords of interest in every human being.

In order to pursue this question further to obtain more extensive data, a series of tests was made with two sets of advertisements. The purpose of these tests was to determine somewhat more accurately to what extent people in general are influenced by suggestive, as against argumentative types of advertisements. Consequently each set of advertisements included one which was primarily suggestive, one which was primarily argumentative, and four which were partly suggestive and partly argumentative in varying proportions. One set was a series of food advertisements and the other a series of automobile advertisements. See the accompanying reproductions, Figure 35, 36, 37, and 38.

The specifications for the tests were as follows:

1. *Attention Test*: Spread the six advertisements before the person being tested. After the person has had a general, brief glance at them without carefully reading any of them, ask: "Which of these advertisements gets your attention

Figure 35: Advertisements used in attention and persuasion tests
(*See page 399*)

Figure 36: Advertisements used in attention and persuasion tests
(*See page 399*)

Figure 37:   Advertisements used in attention and persuasion tests
(*See page 399*)

Figure 38: Advertisements used in attention and persuasion tests
(*See page 399*)

first? next?" and so on. Ask the person to rank them all in order.

2. *Persuasion Test*: After the person has examined and read the advertisements more carefully ask: "Which influences you most in favor of the commodity advertised? which

TABLE 77
FOOD ADVERTISEMENTS

	Attention Test				Persuasion Test				
	61 Business Men	68 Men Students	63 Women Students	Average	61 Business Men	68 Men Students	63 Women Students		Average
D—Cream of Wheat	1.80	1.68	2.14	1.87	3.77	3.30	3.12	3.40	2.38
B—Beech-Nut	2.29	2.28	1.76	2.11	3.08	3.50	2.60	3.06	2.43
A—Aunt Jemima	3.10	3.30	3.38	3.26	2.19	3.03	2.37	2.54	3.02
C—Campbell's	4.10	3.73	4.27	4.03	3.93	3.58	3.50	3.67	3.91
E—Penick's	4.60	4.85	4.33	4.60	4.14	4.25	4.41	4.27	4.49
F—Fleischman's	5.25	5.10	4.58	5.31	4.67	5.32	5.20	5.06	5.23

TABLE 78
AUTOMOBILE ADVERTISEMENTS

	Attention Test				Persuasion Test				Aver. Atten. Persuas. Tests
	57 Business Men	92 Men Students	43 Women Students	Average	57 Business Men	92 Men Students	43 Women Students	Average	
D—Haynes	2.37	2.11	2.25	2.24	3.00	2.76	3.00	2.92	2.47
F—Earl (Picture Ad.)	2.38	1.94	1.90	2.07	3.92	4.17	4.33	4.14	2.76
A—Cadillac	3.00	3.08	4.00	3.36	2.86	2.07	2.62	2.52	3.08
C—Maxwell	3.10	3.26	3.30	3.22	3.17	3.25	3.37	3.26	3.20
B—Hupmobile	4.60	4.86	4.17	4.54	3.93	4.39	3.40	3.91	4.33
E—Earl (all text)	5.60	5.81	5.59	5.67	4.83	5.17	5.21	5.07	6.14

next?" etc. Have them all ranked in order. The emphasis in this test is on the favorableness of the impression of the advertisement as a whole toward making a person *want* the particular commodity.

These two particular tests were made because they represent the two chief distinguishing elements between argumentative and suggestive types of advertisements. The one type of advertisement attempts primarily to convince in a logical way; the other attempts mainly to secure attention and interest. The results are set forth in Tables 77 and 78 which give the median ranks of the advertisements for each of the groups of persons with whom the tests were made.

The averages for the two tests given in the last columns are weighted averages in which double weight is given to the attention test and single weight to the persuasion test. This was done in view of the findings in Chapter XIV which indicated that the attention-getting function is approximately twice as important as the convincing functions of the text in the actual returns brought by an advertisement. There is, however, little difference between these weighted averages and simple averages.

These results indicate that the suggestive pictorial advertisements—such as D and B in the food series and D and F in the automobile series have distinctly greater attention value than the all-text or primarily text advertisements. The Cream of Wheat advertisement is first in the attention test and third in the persuasion test; but when both elements are combined it is first. It is however practically tied for first place by the Beech-Nut advertisement. A detailed study of this table in relation to the advertisements themselves here reproduced will reveal some interesting points regarding suggestive and argumentative elements.

XIX

ARGUMENTATIVE ADVERTISING

Analysis of the mental processes involved in arriving at a deliberate decision in carrying out an act. Steps in a deliberate purchase. How comparisons may be made. What makes an argumentative advertisement convincing? By what criteria may the convincingness of an advertisement be determined? The coupons or method of keying. The language and phraseology of argumentative advertisements. Criteria for effective phraseology. Description and descriptive phrases. Concreteness of mental pictures. Rules for the use of descriptive phrases.

THE most direct approach to a study of argumentative advertising is through an analysis of the mental processes involved in arriving at a deliberate decision in carrying out an action. Fundamentally, the processes involved in any deliberate action are the same, whether they relate to buying or to any other form of choice. An analysis of these processes and steps will be useful, since it will help us to isolate and recognize the elements involved and thereby make it possible for us to see what may be done to facilitate each of the various steps. If a deliberate buying process is similar to any other form of deliberation, then the advertiser's problem consists of making it possible for the buyer to take each one of the steps as readily as possible.

What are the steps in a deliberate decision? Let us take the situation of an important decision. Let us assume that a young man is deciding upon a college education. When he finally arrives at a decision, he will probably have gone through the following four steps:

1. Recognition of the desirability of training such as a college provides.

2. A comparison of various ways by which a college education may be obtained.

3. A comparison of the ways in which the particular college training may be obtained.

4. After all comparisons and deliberations have been made, there follows the final step, the actual decision which closes the whole process.

STEPS IN A DELIBERATE PURCHASE

A deliberate purchase involves a similar series of steps, which may be enumerated as follows: (Let us assume that the purchase is that of an automobile.)

1. The desirability of, or the need for, that kind of an article
2. A comparison of competing brands
3. The means of securing the article
4. The final decision

The first stage consists of a realization of the desire to possess and use an automobile. It involves the various elements that make one realize and picture how desirable it would be to have an automobile to use. After that desire is fairly strong, the next step consists in making a comparison among the various competing automobiles which come approximately within the class for which the purchaser is able to pay. This will involve a comparison of the various advantages and disadvantages possessed by each make of automobile. In the third place, after the comparison of competing articles has been carried to a fairly complete point, there follows a realization of the various means by which finally one or another automobile may be obtained. How and where may it be purchased? What will it cost? On what terms may it be bought? Finally the fourth step is the actual decision which is made after all comparisons have been finished, and which terminates the deliberating process.

Scott has presented a somewhat different analysis of the processes of deliberate action. Fundamentally, however, these steps are similar to the ones we have outlined. His analysis is as follows:

Voluntary action may be analyzed into (a) an idea of two or more attainable ends, (b) an idea of the means to attain these ends, (c) a feeling of the value or worthiness of the different ends, (d) a comparison of the values of the different ends and of the difficulties of the means, and finally (e) a choosing of one of the ends and striving to attain it.[1]

Tipper, Hotchkiss, Hollingworth, and Parsons have proposed the following analysis of steps.[2]

(1) The mind must recognize a need.
(2) It must see that the article advertised will supply it.
(3) It must recognize its superiority over competing articles.
(4) It must make a decision.

Scott's analysis makes a somewhat more detailed enumeration of steps. Nevertheless, a comparison of these three analyses will indicate the fundamental similarity of the processes involved. The analysis proposed by the author describes the steps involved in the buying process perhaps as fully as is practicably useful. Even in this analysis, steps 2 and 3 are rather closely connected and in most instances actually merge into the one general process of making comparisons of the merits of competing brands and of the ways of securing the article, so that it might possibly be even more desirable to state that the process of a deliberate purchase consists of three general steps, namely (a) recognition of the desirability of that class of commodity, (b) comparisons of competing articles in that class, and (c) the final decision after comparisons have been made.

The analysis of this process is obviously schematic and not all of these steps may occur at one time, nor need all these steps be presented at one time. Probably in many instances it would not be advisable to emphasize each of these steps. Nevertheless it requires little analysis of

[1] *Psychology of Advertising*, p. 94.   [2] Page 188.

various concrete deliberation processes to indicate that these are substantially the steps through which the mind passes in arriving at a deliberate purchase or a deliberate choice of any sort.

Not every argumentative advertisement needs to cover all these steps. Separate steps may be emphasized in different advertisements, but all of them must undoubtedly be impressed upon the customer's mind in one form or another before he finally makes a deliberate purchase. The mind naturally goes through these processes in the course of reaching a reasoned decision.

An examination of typical argumentative advertisements will reveal the fact that several of these steps are stressed in each one and all three or four are stressed in a considerable number. To illustrate this point, we may examine the Hoosier Kitchen Cabinet advertisement in Figure 39. The first paragraph and the fifth paragraph emphasize the general desirability of a kitchen cabinet, as follows:

There is nothing you can give a woman that is so *personal* as the one thing that will lighten her burden the whole year round. And that one thing is the Hoosier Kitchen Cabinet. It works for her and with her every day of the year—easing the strain of her housework, shortening the time she must spend in the kitchen, turning drudgery into happiness.

Through all the years, the Hoosier you give this Christmas will stand as a monument to your loving thoughtfulness. Through all the years, it will minister to the health and happiness of the woman who means more to you than all the world—it will save her miles of steps each day, cut out the needless lifting and stooping of kitchen work, and increase the hours that may be spent in happy recreation.

While the name Hoosier is mentioned in these two paragraphs, the statements made, however, would apply to any kitchen cabinet, and serve to emphasize simply the general desirability of possessing a kitchen cabinet. The second step, that of comparison, is stressed in paragraphs 2, 3, and 4, as follows:

But do not think that because the Hoosier will do all this, "just any old cabinet" will function as well.

There is only one Hoosier—and it is built not out of imaginations of men as to what will help make housework lighter—but out of actual experiences of the women themselves.

These women—Hoosier owners—have contributed to us their ideas of what it takes to make a perfect Kitchen Cabinet. These

Figure 39: Typical argumentative advertisement *(See page 409)*

ideas we have actually tried out on the Hoosier. The best have been accepted—the rest rejected. And today, the Hoosier is America's cabinet of proved improvements, the greatest household help that womankind has ever received at the hands of science.

In this particular advertisement, steps 3 and 4 are combined in the last short paragraph, as follows:

Go to your Hoosier store for a demonstration—at once. Have a Hoosier reserved for Christmas delivery. Make this the happiest Christmas your home has ever known.

A recent Vivomint Toothpaste advertisement may be analyzed in a similar manner. Step 1, the desirability of toothpastes in general, is emphasized in the first three paragraphs, as follows:

Exercise keeps the body healthy and strong, but only constant and intelligent care can prevent the teeth going bad.
The New Way to Have Perfect Teeth Is to Keep the Entire Mouth Hygienically Clean.
Brushing the teeth is not enough to keep them clean. Three or four brushings daily would not suffice. The entire mouth must be kept clean.

The second step, that of making comparisons and pointing out the advantage of Vivomint, is stressed in the next four paragraphs as follows:

Vivomint was made by expert dental chemists to meet just such a need. It is more than a mere dentifrice. It does double duty—cleanses and purifies the whole mouth while whitening the teeth.
One of the ingredients of Vivomint is a remarkable antiseptic— a germ destroyer that no tooth-destroying agent can withstand.
This antiseptic is not added to Vivomint to give it a pleasant taste. It is put into this new dentifrice solely to destroy the germs in the mouth, little microscopical germs that hide in every interdental crevice and in the tiny folds of mouth membrane. These are what cause tartar and decay.
When you use Vivomint you will note in the Vivomint taste an agent of cleanliness.

Step 3 is in many instances combined either with step 2

or step 4. In this instance, it is combined primarily with step 4, which is stressed as follows:

Send for a Free Trial Tube. Try Vivomint at our expense without delay. We are sure you will prefer it. Fill out the coupon below and mail it to us and a generous trial-size tube will be sent you.

The foregoing analysis of the processes involved in a deliberate decision shows that these steps are actually necessary to bring about a deliberate decision to buy a product. It is evident that all three or four steps are actually found in a great many typical argumentative advertisements.

The next practical question is, When and in what way may each of these steps be emphasized, either in a given advertisement or in a series which constitute a campaign? In general, we may point out that step 1, developing desirability for a given type or class of product, must ordinarily be emphasized when a given product is new in its field. For example, when dictating machines were first manufactured, it was necessary to use so-called educational advertising, designed to inform the prospective buyers of the possible desirability of using a device of this sort. As soon as competitors came into the field, it was necessary to emphasize steps 2 and 3 somewhat more. When there are several competing products from among which to choose, the customer makes comparisons and consequently it is necessary to stress the comparison phase of the copy. This does not mean, necessarily, that it should be made in a direct manner, but rather that it should be made in a way whereby the customer may see the comparative advantages of the particular make concerned.

When Neolin was first introduced, it was quite necessary to stress the general desirability of this type of product, that is, to emphasize step 1. The same is true of practically every new product that comes into the market. In other words, we may conceive of products in a given field as developing or passing through these three stages, namely: first, the "educational" or general desirability phase of that class of product; second, the comparison or competitive phase; and third, the decision or action phase. No doubt all these aspects must be stressed more or less at all times. Nevertheless, in a broad way, it will be observed that the general, informational stage comes when a product is new. The competitive, comparison stage comes as soon as competition becomes keen, and the action stage is present practically all the time, but probably may be stressed primarily after a product is well known and when competition is more or less in hand. Most products remain in the competitive and action stages and may for the most part, after they are well known, give a minimum of stress to stage 1.

HOW COMPARISONS MAY BE MADE

A very difficult question in the preparation of argumentative copy is, How may the comparison or competitive aspects be handled most effectively? It is not only in bad taste, but poor selling practice as well, to stress in a direct way comparisons with competing articles, and to point out specific differences between particular brands in a manner disparaging to competitors.

Comparisons may be made in two ways, either directly or indirectly; that is, either by stating in so many words that A is better than B, or by merely pointing out the advantages of A without any reference to B. The one makes comparison by direct reference, the other by implication. The latter method is undoubtedly the better and more effective one. A considerable advance has been made in recent years in the more skilful as well as more effective handling of the comparison phase of advertisements. In other words, "knocking" in advertisements as well as in the better types of salesmanship has tended to grow less and less in recent years. In fact, advertisements that may be described as "knocking" are relatively rare at the present time, at least among high-grade mediums and high-grade concerns. Up to

15 years ago, it was not so uncommon to find advertisements which struck at competitors in a crude and obvious way, so that it was evident from the statements which particular competitor was meant.

About 1906, an advertisement of Fairy's Soap contained the following text:

NOT MERELY PURE

Some soap makers claim Purity as the greatest thing ever.

And then they even give the percentage of Purity their soaps contain, as though Purity alone is all that soap requires to make it proper as a cleansing agent for the skin.

Now, soaps are made from animal fats and vegetable oils, balanced or neutralized by an alkali—usually soda.

A soapmaker can make his soaps from pure refuse fats and pure soda, and claim, with absolute truth, that his soap is 100 per cent Pure.

But if that soap is not colored artificially, nor perfumed, it will be yellowish in color and smell like axle grease, or worse.

That, good people, is the way many so-called pure soaps are made.

And that, in very truth, is not the sort of thing to put on that vital organ of yours, your skin, with its 28 miles of minutely fine glands to keep clean from the tiny flakes of dead matter, grease, etc., which constantly collect and which tend to impede its function. In absolute health at least two pounds of waste should be removed from your body every day—in the form of vapory moisture.

Soap made from such cheap material stops up the gland mouths (pores) or irritates them and sets up a disorder that will surely make itself felt throughout the entire body.

You should take care of your skin by using soaps in which the materials are not *merely pure,* but which are absolutely the *highest grade* and the most expensive that money can buy, and which are made from fats such as you buy from your butcher to eat and pure cocoanut oil such as Milady uses for her delicate complexion—all properly balanced so that there is absolutely no excess alkali to injure the most delicate skin. Certain of these kinds of soaps retail at from 25 to 50 cents a cake—because of the needlessly expensive perfumes they contain. One of them retails at only 5 cents a cake.

An Egg-O-See advertisement contained a picture of a man eating breakfast and being served apparently with meat. The text was as follows:

TAKE THAT MEAT AWAY

We will have no more meat or heavy, hard-to-digest foods on our breakfast table this Summer. We never felt so well in our lives as we did last Summer, when we made EGG-O-SEE the foundation of every meal.

If you do not use EGG-O-SEE for EVERY meal, you should at least make it the LAW OF YOUR BREAKFAST TABLE, and insure Summer Health and vigorous happiness for your entire household.

EGG-O-SEE is Nature's own food—the whole wheat in its most tempting, delicious and sustaining form.

More EGG-O-SEE is eaten each day than all other similar foods combined.

This is the strongest endorsement ever accorded any food by the American people.

Costs no more than the ordinary kinds—large package 10 cents.

The following type of reference to competitors is injurious to the entire industry.

Old "Dr. Goose" is a Great Friend of the Tailor.

The Flat-iron is the "dope" of the clothing business.

With the hot pressing Iron a slack section of cloth can be SHRUNKEN in a minute, to any desired degree.

Or a tight section may be *stretched* to any given degree in the same manner, at trifling cost compared to the sincere hand-needle work required to produce a similar result in a *permanent* manner.

Now practically 80% of all clothes are *faked* into shape in the making, by Old Dr. Goose, the hot Flat-iron.

And, any garment that owes its shape to the *Flat-iron* will need the *constant* use of the same Flat-iron to *keep it* in shape.

That's a big thing to remember, Reader.

We are telling you about this vital point of Style-insurance, and Economy in Shape-retention, because we are makers of the "Sincerity Clothes."

And every "Sincerity" Garment is faithfully shaped to a finish by the needle instead of by a faky Flat-iron.

Every defect in the workmanship of Sincerity Clothes is investigated, and when found, is permanently corrected by Sincere hand-needlework, instead of by the quick, easy, and tricky Flat-iron.

That's practical Shape-insurance, isn't it?

And, a coat so made, inspected, and revised (if necessary) will hang well, look square shouldered without excessive padding, and *keep* its shape with one-third the "Pressing" that a Coat *faked into* shape by the Flat-iron would need.

To men who would dress well on a moderate outlay this fact is mighty important.

Now, if Shape-insurance and Style-retention are *worth* anything to you, Mr. Reader, look for the label of the "Sincerity Clothes" on your next Coat or Overcoat.

To this advertisement a competitor "came back" thus:

"I've sampled all the 'say so' and 'printers' ink talk' I care for," says this fictitious personage.

"I've heard all the stories of 'exclusive patterns' and 'costly hand-work.'

"I've read the advertisements.

"And I've worn the clothes.

"I've made a caricature of myself in 'fancy priced duds' and I've bought cheap stuff that made me look like the low comedian in a 10 cent show.

"So *now* I say—'Guaranteed Clothes' for me!"

A manufacturer of ice-cream freezers in Cincinnati used the following statement in his advertisements:

The *only* way to be sure that ice-cream is fit for the home table is to *make* it at home.

An advertisement of baked beans was as follows:

When a Snider salesman goes to a Grocer to sell him Snider Beans, he doesn't *talk,* he just *acts.*

He buys a tin each of the best kind of Pork and Beans that the Grocer sells, opens them up on the counter, and asks the Grocer himself to *look* at them, and *taste* them.

Then he opens up a tin of SNIDER Pork and Beans beside them, and asks the Grocer to compare and taste these also.

This selling method almost *never* fails.

Because the Beans in every tin of SNIDER'S are found whole, white, and dainty to the eye, as shown in the lower photograph herewith.

Other Beans are often (and many kinds are always) found (as in two upper tins) split, squashed, soupy, discolored, and of "beany" instead of "fine" flavor.

Comparisons made in an obvious and direct way, particularly when they approach the "knocking" spirit, are poor advertising because such attacks on competitors tend to reduce confidence, not only in the particular concern making them, but in the whole industry concerned with that class of goods. "Knocking" is apt to create a suspicion that something is wrong all along the line. In the second place, in many instances, it tends to emphasize unessential aspects. In the third place, direct reference to competitors usually advertises the competitors as much as yourself; and in the fourth place, it tends to accentuate and prolong comparisons, which are apt to delay the final choice. Customers do a great deal of comparing in any event, so that an accentuation, particularly of undesirable comparisons, is apt to prolong the buying process.

A recent (1921) form of reference to competitors is open to question in spite of its frankness:

EVERY DAY IT'S GETTING HARDER TO JUDGE CARS
FROM THE ADVERTISEMENTS

I tell you it would puzzle a man that had been in the automobile business twenty years to pick a car from the advertisements today.

Now, just for instance, you can get "a new and joyous thrill in motoring" for less than fifteen hundred dollars, but if you want a "new and glorious zest in motoring" it will cost you almost three thousand dollars more. The question is, is it worth it?

Or, you can find in the average automobile section a dozen advertisements, each of which comes right out flat-footed and says that there was never before such a tremendous value offered at any price.

And, when you come to the inclosed stuff, it sure has you

guessing. They start out by calling them "magnificent equipages" and work up from that.

They even advertise "luxurious appointments" with them. It seems to me that something ought to be done about that.

It makes it awfully hard to write advertisements, too. You see, all we are really after is to ask people to ride in the Packard Single Six and drive it themselves on a trip long enough so that they can really size up the car.

When people take that sort of a ride in the Single Six they usually buy one because there ARE a lot of likable things about the car.

But it doesn't sound exciting at all when you write that kind of advertisement and put it alongside of the rest of the bunch.

There's a whole lot of people who would gladly pay $2,690 for a Packard Single Six if they just knew how good a car it is. The Packard itself can tell them just how it stacks up with other cars they have driven.

If we tried to tell you, we wouldn't know how to go about it.

We wouldn't want to say less than the other boys have said in their advertisements around the edge of this one—it wouldn't do us any good to say the same thing—and we don't know how to say more than they have said.

All we can do is hope you'll come in and let the Packard tell you its own story in its own way.

The following copy used in 1921 by a large retailer of men's clothing is likely to produce a reaction unfavorable to the retailers and manufacturers alike:

From Silk Shirts to Shoddy!

From one extreme to another. How typically American. So that today you find the clothing market flooded with the poorest quality of clothing known for a generation, and actually nearing a shortage of high-grade suits and overcoats. For when the "Don't Buy" propaganda started the avalanche of cancelations that closed the mills, it was the best merchandise that was canceled and today there are hardly enough fine goods to go around.

Our orders were placed for the best clothes the market produces—to meet the needs of the richest and most prosperous people on earth—and we accepted every dollar's worth. These are the clothes we are selling at YOUR PRICE—to dispose of them soon and help start the mills.

WHAT MAKES AN ARGUMENTATIVE ADVERTISEMENT CONVINCING?

By What Criteria May the Convincingness of an Advertisement be Determined? The purpose of argumentative advertising, as distinguished from suggestive advertising, is to produce action by persuasion instead of suggestion. How may an advertisement be made convincing? How does a convincing advertisement differ from one that is not?

Let us begin our analysis by examining a few specimens to see how they differ.

Specimen No. 1

The Same High Mileage in Every McGraw

Recall the mileages you have received from tires of the same make—three, five, even ten thousand miles. There is no uniformity because the tires are not equally perfect. Some have wrinkled, pinched or buckled fabric—body flaws invisible to the naked eye but a menace to tire service.

A perfect tire will yield all the mileage of which the materials in it are capable, abuse excepted.

This is precisely the merit of McGraw Tires. Tread and tire-body, united by the McGraw Duplex Method of Vulcanization, are formed into a casing structurally sound.

What the Duplex Method *Is* and Does.

This is a McGraw process of vulcanization which prevents fabric buckles and mold pinches—the worst menace to tire life. It consists in deferring compression of the tire in the vulcanizing molds until the rubber becomes heated and plastic. Then, when hydraulic pressure is applied to vulcanize the tire, the rubber "flow" is not stiff enough to pull the fabric out of place. The fabric layers "set" smooth and even. No creases can form. Pinches and buckles are avoided. The tire is a perfect structure.

In McGraw Tires you receive the full mileage inherent in high quality materials.

Cord Tires 8,000 Miles   Fabric Tires 6,000 Miles

Specimen No. 2

The Doctor, Too, Needs the Efficiency of the Continental-Powered Car

When the doctor buys a car, he looks first to the motor.

He cannot risk experiments—he must have a motor that has already proved its worth. Only by the record which the years have shown, by what the motor *has* done, can he be certain what it *will* do.

Judge a motor by the test of time—and your choice too will be the Red Seal Continental Motor.

The Red Seal Continental has stood the test of time, and service —during more than fifteen years. It represents nothing untried, nothing experimental. Rather, it represents the coordinated thought of the foremost motor engineers, for more than a generation.

It is a *proved certainty*. It is America's Standard.

Today more than 165 successful manufacturers of automobiles and trucks, by equipping their output with the Red Seal Continental Motor, vouch for its integrity.

Upward of 16,000 dealers base their business prosperity, their business future, upon Continental-motored cars.

Hundreds of thousands of satisfied owners are living testimonials that the judgment of these manufacturers and dealers is *right*.

When you buy an automobile or truck, choose a motor that TIME has proved—and identify it by the Continental Red Seal.

Specimen No. 3

Paige—The Most Beautiful Car in America

In less than thirty days our new five-passenger "Glenbrook" model has established itself as one of the most popular cars on the American market.

From every section of the nation comes the same hearty word of endorsement and an unending stream of orders.

Just as we predicted, the "Glenbrook" has taken its place as the ideal five-passenger motor car.

It is appealing to the discriminating public as a really great achievement in automotive engineering and a superb example of the designer's art.

It now merely remains to pledge ourselves that this latest of Paige Models shall continue to deserve the high regard and confidence which it has so quickly won.

Back of the power plant, chassis and every detail of construction are three years of patient experimental work and testing. We have spared neither time nor expense in a definite effort to produce the most efficient of all light sixes.

The "Glenbrook" is a distinctive creation—conceived by Paige engineers and built in the Paige shops by Paige mechanics.

It is a strictly modern development and, as such, we feel that it merits the serious consideration of every man who owns or who contemplates owning, a motor car.

If you will communicate with our dealer he will be very glad to arrange for a demonstration.

Specimen No. 4

"EVER-READY" SAFETY RAZOR

There never was and never will be a neater, handier, more efficient article for a man to own than "The Little Barber in a Box." Costs $1.00—Lasts a lifetime. Sold the world over.

Extra Radio Blades 6 for 40 cents.

American Safety Razor Corporation

Makers of the famous Ever-Ready Shaving Brushes.

These advertisements obviously differ in several respects. The first two are specific, contain facts which are stated accurately and for the most part moderately, and for that reason they are believable. The last two advertisements are less convincing. They lack in definiteness, they overstate, and give an impression of being not quite true or believable. The reader is likely to react as follows: "Oh, well, this is stated in an advertisement, and must be taken with a grain of salt!" One reacts just as he does to the statements of the over-enthusiastic salesman. The thought is "That's salesman's talk!"

It is difficult to discover what characteristics are uniformly present in advertisements which are convincing, or uniformly absent in advertisements that are not convincing. For the sake of obtaining some tangible statement we may suggest the following at least tentative criteria. To be convincing, an advertisement ought to have the following characteristics:

1. It ought to have a strong selling point or points.

2. It ought to be specific, rather than general, in the statement of facts or events.

3. The statements should be relevant and to the point. Avoid far-fetched, uninteresting analogies.

4. It ought to be absolutely true and ought to give the impression of being absolutely true. Avoid exaggeration and overstatement.

If an advertisement measures up to these criteria, it is pretty sure to be convincing. We need not discuss the first criterion, since we have discussed, at considerable length in earlier chapters, the methods for obtaining and determining strong selling arguments. The second requirement, that the advertisement be specific, may be met by observing in general three points:

(a) By using real, concrete facts which many times may be actually numerical in character. An excellent example of this type of presentation is the following:

200 KEWANEE UNIONS ON THE WORLD'S MOST POWERFUL LOCOMOTIVE

In any piping that must withstand extremes of temperature and high pressure, and where frequent disconnection is necessary, the Walworth Kewanee Union is standard.

The American Locomotive shown above hauled 17,600 tons—by far the heaviest load ever pulled by one locomotive—over a long grade in the Blue Ridge. It operates with superheated steam at 215-lb. pressure, and a temperature of 650 degrees F. Its 200 Walworth Kewanee Unions make leak-proof steam and air connections.

The Kewanee Union's five distinctive points of advantage are—

(1) Brass to steel ball seat—no gasket
(2) Brass to iron thread connection—no corrosion
(3) Compressed-air test under water—no defective unions

(4) Solid three-piece construction—no inserted parts

(5) Easily connected and disconnected—no force required

We are sending ¾-inch Kewanee Unions for 24 cents to engineers—as the quickest way to make a demonstration.

WALWORTH MANUFACTURING COMPANY, BOSTON, MASS., AND KEWANEE, ILLINOIS

(b) By using specific human interests, experiences or incidents.

This principle is well illustrated by the specific, human interest events of the following advertisement:

JOHN MCCORMACK'S FIRST AUDIENCE

The Irish lad who ran away to be a minstrel and grew up to be a world-famed artist.

A boy nine years old stood at a street corner on a "fair day" in Athlone and listened to an old fiddler and ballad singer. The first thrill of romance surged in the boy's veins. When the wandering minstrel struck out for the next town, the lad trudged blissfully by his side, with boyish indifference to the home folks beside the river Shannon. Two days later the boy's frantic parents overtook him at Mullingar. He got no "licking"—only a mother's blessing and the tears of those who heard him sing "Molly Brannigan," the first ballad he ever learned.

Thus did John McCormack take his first journey on the highroad to Fame. Today the minstrel-boy has grown into a world-famed artist, a singer renowned in every land. His first wayside audience of country folks has swelled to vast audiences filling the great auditoriums in the capitals of the world and to that still mightier host who knows and loves him through his Victor Records.

John McCormack makes records for the Victor exclusively. With the artist's instinct, he knows and appreciates Victor Supremacy.

Hear the McCormack records at the nearest Victor store.

VICTOR TALKING MACHINE CO., CAMDEN, N. J., U. S. A.

VICTOR SUPREMACY

Victor Trade-mark "His Master's Voice."

(c) By giving specific evidence or reasons for general statements and assertions. Avoid making general unsupported claims.

The third criterion, that of avoiding irrelevant statements and far-fetched analogies, is illustrated by the following:

INTELLIGENCE

If a horse entangles his foot in a barbed wire, he will cripple himself for life;

While a cow will take her foot out unharmed the way she got it in.

Such intelligence cannot fail to increase man's regard for his invaluable friend, the cow—

A regard already great among those who have enjoyed the rich, creamy milk served at Child's.

The fourth characteristic is perhaps the most important. The common tendency toward overstatement, the use of superlatives and the like prevents many an advertisement from being as convincing as the product in itself would otherwise be. Avoid the use of statements which may be literally true but which are so strong that they do not have the appearance of being true.

Some years ago Mr. John Lee Mahin proposed for use in his organization the following 10 questions by which an advertisement should be judged.[1]

1. Is it institutional? i. e. class appeal
2. Is it natural?
3. Is it specific?
4. Is it timely?
5. Is it pertinent?
6. Is it consistent?
7. Is it persistent?
8. Is it authoritative?
9. Is it plausible?
10. Is it sincere?

General and meaningless statements are all too prevalent in current advertising and unquestionably weaken very materially much argumentative text. An examination of 84 advertisements in a recent issue of a magazine showed that no less than 20 full-page advertisements contained, to a

[1] *Advertising,* "Selling the Consumer," p. 81.

greater or less degree, either weak generalization or questionable overstatement. One automobile advertisement stated:

Only in cars costing hundreds of dollars in excess of the Blank will you find bodies to compare in quality of construction and exquisite finish. All body members are sawed to shape from selected hardwood stock—screwed together and glued in a wonderfully accurate manner.

Another one said:

Never in our history was a car the center of such interest and admiration as the New Blank in the authoritative style at the several shows just concluded.

A truck "actually does better hauling at less cost."

Still another car was described as "the best car of its class in the world."

A certain tire gives "most miles per dollar." Another tire advertisement states "With Blank tires on your car, you have surety that you are getting the best in tires that human devotion to ideals and workmanship can produce or that money can buy."

The attempt to avoid the use of superlatives has apparently led many copywriters to use the comparative form in such a way that it virtually implies a superlative meaning, thus: "The name Blank on your shoes is a definite guarantee of full value and longer wear"; "Blank Shoes— There are No Better"; Blank Almond Bars "give you more almonds and better chocolate at no greater cost"; Blank's Saws represent "the greatest development in saw and tool making" and "insure a standard of better material and finer workmanship resulting in easier and quicker work, increased output and greater service"; "Blank for 1920 represents the highest developments in storage-battery history."

Here are further examples of attempts at making big impressions with high-sounding statements.

From the incoming host of new ideas of lighting, ... Service selects for the makers of . . . . Lamps only those developments in design, material, and methods that will improve the light you enjoy.

Scientific investigations and progressive development have brought the .... to the premier position which it now occupies. Designed and manufactured only after the most thorough study of the theory and practice of ignition, it is right on every count—and yet it costs no more than ordinary plugs.

After a man tries out a ...., his new tires thereafter will almost invariably be .... That motorist has sailed through the stormy sea of doubt and anchored safe in the harbor of decision. There is no question in his mind now. When you ask him which are the best tires, he will say without hesitation "............, of course." He may change cars. There are many types and many prices of cars, and what is best for him today may not be tomorrow. But for him there is only one tire for every car.

In the .... machinery industry, the makers of the .... have been real trail-makers. They have blazed the way time after time with new ideas, new ways and new methods. They are the sum of all that is best in knowledge, materials and method in the .... field. Wherever found, they uphold in all ways the integrity of intention and effort behind them.

A tire manufacturer states the following:

What tubes are best for your car? Ask your dealer and he will tell you .... tubes. What casings are best for your car? Ask your dealer and he will tell you .... casings. For a new degree of tire satisfaction, use .... casings and tubes.

By contrast, note the effectiveness of specific statement and fact. Sometime ago an automobile manufacturer stated this specific fact:

"$65,000,000 of motor cars bearing the stamp of Studebaker."

The advertisement of Rand-McNally maps, in Figure 40, is full of specific human incident as well as definite statements and facts. The whole advertisement is both interesting and convincing. A definite point is asked in a manner in which it may naturally arise in a family. The advertisement does not make the superlative statement that it is the leader in spending the largest sum of money to maintain accuracy, but rather it states that several hundred

"Say, Pop! Where is Czecho-Slovakia?"

Children have a way of asking embarrassing questions. In this particular case we are very much afraid little Johnnie will be requested to "run along and not bother Papa."

For despite the fact that the name Czecho-Slovakia has been appearing in the public prints for nearly three years, there are comparatively few men and women who could sit down tonight and definitely fix its position on the map.

We believe you will agree with us that few people use maps as frequently as they should. Yet never was the intelligent use of maps as necessary and as important as today. Recent world events have wrought many changes.

The efficiency of an atlas or a map depends on its accuracy. In the maintenance of a reputation for accuracy, built up through half a century, RAND McNALLY & COMPANY spend several hundred thousand dollars yearly. The very size of this expenditure—and the necessity for it—show why it is always best to deal with *Map Headquarters.*

No small map maker could ever hope to approximate the accuracy, completeness and dependability that have been characteristic of RAND McNALLY ATLASES AND MAPS for more than half a century.

When you buy a new atlas or map—and this year every family should have a new atlas—make sure that it bears the name RAND McNALLY.

There is a
RAND McNALLY ATLAS
for every purpose

Here are a few of them. Others in preparation.

For the home and library

INTERNATIONAL ATLAS

For the desk

HANDY ATLAS OF THE WORLD

For pocket reference

POCKET ATLAS OF THE WORLD

RAND McNALLY & COMPANY
Map Headquarters

536 S. CLARK STREET, CHICAGO   42 E. 22ND STREET, NEW YORK

RAND McNALLY ATLASES ARE FOR SALE AT ALL BOOKSHOPS

Figure 40: Specimen advertisement illustrating effectiveness of specific statement and fact (*See page 426*)

thousand dollars are spent yearly in keeping maps accurate and up-to-date.

The effect of specific statement is shown in the following experience:

A young man put up a large garage, featuring the mechanical department, the overhauling of cars, etc.

He sent out a neat form letter to a list of names, telling that the new garage was open for business and that competent mechanics were ready to do any sort of repairing. It was quite the usual thing couched in the usual language.

Not ten letters were received in reply. As far as actual results were concerned, it was a dismal failure.

An advertising man happened to keep his car in the garage and offered to write another letter. He made this odd proposal in the letter:

"We make an interesting offer. When repairing your car we invite you to come around and see how it is done. Allow us to explain some of the mysteries of the inside of that power plant.

"There are parts of your car that you know little about. There are intricacies that mean trouble on the road. We will gladly explain these points to you and initiate you into some of the little-known engine problems."

That letter brought 70% of replies and the shop has more work booked for the winter than it can handle.

It seems too bad to weaken the reputation of a good name and a good product with flabby generalities, as is done so many times. Why not say something specific, concrete, something that will really get into the reader's mind and stir up definite ideas and images. Luckily for many of our advertisements, the text is often not read. Most of the advertisements of the type quoted will do some good by impressing the name and the picture, but luckily for many of them the text will not be read to depreciate the impression thus made. We sometimes speak of $10 a word copy. A word does not need to be in very large type to occupy $10 worth of space in our high-priced mediums. Many advertisers squander their money by putting worthless verbiage into high-priced space.

The most important principle to follow is to analyze all

pertinent points and then to use the essential, the most direct facts. Too much emphasis cannot be laid upon the use of definite, undeniable facts in the preparation of copy. Many advertisements are vague and general. Actual facts go incomparably farther than superlative exaggerations toward convincing anyone of the truthfulness of a proposition.

The schoolmaster, not so very long ago, had occasion to test the comparative value of mere enthusiastic assertions as compared with statements of actual happenings. The first advertisement cited no case, but assured the reader that such-and-such was the case and that so-and-so would happen, and this was all told in a gingery way—the snappy, crackling, spark-emitting copy that many are fond of. The other advertisement related actual circumstances that proved the claims made for the product, and the headline was a "news" headline. Maybe the result should not be taken as an invariable rule, but in this particular case the second piece of copy pulled twice as well as the first.[1]

THE COUPON AND METHODS OF KEYING

The return coupon came into more common use about 1900 and since then has been used with increasing frequency until today it is used very generally. It serves two purposes, namely, to identify or "key" the advertisement which brought the response and to make it easy to respond.

There is no question that the presence of a return coupon, other things being equal, considerably increases the number of responses brought by an advertisement.

According to the postal regulations the coupon must be only an incidental feature in an advertisement.

Coupons, order forms, and other matter intended for detachment and subsequent use may be included in permanently attached advertisements, or elsewhere, in newspapers and periodicals, provided they constitute only an incidental feature of such publications and are not of such character, or used to such extent, as to destroy the statutory characteristics of second-class publications, or to bring them within the prohibitions "designed primarily

[1] *Printers' Ink,* June 5, 1913, p. 84.

for advertising purposes," or to give them the characteristics of books or other third-class matter.[1]

The phrase "incidental feature" is interpreted in general practice as meaning not to exceed one-fourth of the area occupied by the advertisement.

A "key" is a means of identifying the advertisement which brought a particular response. When a large number of publications is used it is desirable to have a flexible system of keying to identify each advertisement in each publication. When a coupon is used the usual key consists of the initials of the publication and the date printed inconspicuously on some part of the coupon as W. H. C. 5 '23.[2]

When no coupon is used, the key usually is included in the address, as "Write for booklet K" or "Address department N." When the number of insertions and of publications is large, the key usually consists of a number which may.be varied almost indefinitely, as "Dept. 615," "Dept. 616," "Dept. 617," etc.

THE LANGUAGE AND PHRASEOLOGY OF ARGUMENTATIVE ADVERTISEMENTS

It is difficult to treat separately the language and the ideas conveyed thereby. The language is an important element. Strictly speaking it is not correct to say that the same thought is expressed in different words. Using different words usually makes a different thought out of it. The ideas and the words are really opposite sides of the same shield.

What we wish to determine, from the practical point of view, is what constitutes effective language and phraseology. By what criteria may we judge it? What characteristics does effective language possess as contrasted with ineffective language?

Let us begin our analysis by citing some concrete in-

---

[1] Section 441 of U. S. Postal Laws and Regulations, paragraph 6.

[2] *Woman's Home Companion*, May, 1923.

stances. The following are examples of the complete texts of recent advertisements:

.... in a .... disposes of all doubt about its quality. You take nothing on faith; you know that .... is right or the name would not be there.

.... prices are reasonable; .... quality is unusual.

Another illustration follows:

Thought adds value to your gift. Care in selecting the proper package of .... to fit the occasion wins golden opinions. Get acquainted with the individual merits of .... and others. Inspect them at the store that shows the .... sign and sells the .... line.

There is nothing to suggest in these two pieces of text what either one is about. Neither one stimulates any particular thought in the mind of the reader; neither one creates any picture of the product in the reader's mind. Advertising is replete with vague generalities, such as "the swellest furniture," "the smile of satisfaction," "the best breakfast food in the world," "latest, greatest, cheapest," and many more to be found in current advertisements. Descriptions are often nothing more than a mass of dead verbiage that would apply to one commodity as well, or as poorly, as to any other. If the name of the article were omitted from the text of such advertisements, one could not possibly guess what it was about. What is the explanation? Obviously the reason is that the statements are general rather than concrete.

CRITERIA FOR EFFECTIVE PHRASEOLOGY

There are obviously many differences between effective and ineffective phraseology. One necessarily hesitates in proposing definite criteria by which to judge the effectiveness of language or to state what the characteristics of effective language are. Nevertheless, in order to improve the phraseology of text and become at least consciously aware of certain aims that should be striven for, some advantage will be found in establishing tangible criteria. We may propose the following two general criteria with certain corollaries under each one. Good, effective language should probably have in general the following characteristics:

1. It should be concrete rather than abstract or vague.
   (a) Words and phrases should arouse concrete mental pictures and ideas.
   (b) The ideas conveyed should tie up readily with the ideas in the reader's mind and should cause him to think.
   (c) Short and meaningful words are to be preferred to long and meaningless words.

2. It should be appropriate to the proposition or commodity.
   (a) It should be dignified where dignity is required.
   (b) It may be colloquial where familiarity is called for.
   (c) It should be elegant where refinement is desired. It should never be over-flowery.
   (d) It should be pleasing, never degrading to the product to which it is applied.

To illustrate these points, note the following expressions: "Big Ben," "The Prudential has the Strength of Gibraltar." Underwear is described in one advertisement as follows:

You'll be mighty thankful for Hanes' winter underwear when you have to shiver out of the sheet those nippy mornings this winter, but when you pull that warm cottony fabric up around your legs, it will thaw the chills right out of you. It snugs firm and close without the least trace of bind.

An advertisement of hams and bacon uses the following text:

Premium ham, because of the delicacy of its flavor, the fine texture of its tender meat, has long been the choice of those who appreciate the best.

For enjoying to the full its rare, delightful flavor, many new ways of serving it have been devised. Of these, one of the most delicious and original is the special pride of a New York epicure—with a hobby for working out unusual dishes. By baking it with maple syrup, he adds a unique, subtle flavor to the always appetizing savoriness of Premium Ham.

Appropriate colloquial style is illustrated in the following advertisement of an easy chair:

"Ah," says the tired *home-from-business man*, as, lighting his fragrant Havana, he prepares for peaceful rest—in his . . . . A thoughtful wife has drawn out the Leg Rest. The chair is waiting. He drops himself into its luxuriously inviting depths. He pushes the button—the back reclines—and now for solid, head-to-heel comfort. Imagine a more *ideal holiday gift!*

On the other hand a good example of appropriate, dignified style is the following:

NEW ENGLAND PROSPERITY AND THE SHOE INDUSTRY

The prosperity of present-day New England is due in no small measure to the continuance of the old spirit of the bootmakers of Boston. The policy of "good work and pride in it" has been the cornerstone of success for Lynn and Brockton, for Haverhill and Boston, for Manchester, Auburn and Lewiston. So that today over half the nation is shod by New England.

The magnitude of this industry and the rôle it plays in New England life may be appreciated when it is stated that the annual output is between 5,000,000 and 6,000,000 cases of shoes, valued at $400,000,000. In all there are over one hundred leading communities in which some phase of the craft is plied, giving employment to more than 100,000 workers. Indeed, so highly developed and specialized is it, that whole cities are given over to the making of different kinds of footgear. Brockton leads in men's shoes, Lynn in women's, while Haverhill sets the fashion in slipper and low-cut styles.

As a reservoir of skilled labor New England offers exceptional advantages—not only in the shoe industry, where the character of the old Boston cobblers has indelibly left its mark, but in other lines as well. In fact, one of the chief contributions to the stability and success of New England manufacturers has been the co-operation of skilled and intelligent labor. Otherwise New England goods could never have achieved their present standard of quality and value.

Add to all this the tremendous waterpower resources of New England and the unexcelled railroad and shipping facilities she enjoys, and it is plain that her present title is also her future destiny —"The Workshop of the Nation."

New England is planning to celebrate the Tercentenary of the Pilgrims' Landing—its own 300th birthday. To commemorate this event fittingly, it extends to all—North, South, and West— a cordial invitation to visit its historical landmarks and its vacation grounds by lake, sea and mountain. View again its old shrines—Plymouth, Provincetown, Boston, Salem, Providence, Portsmouth—and while in New England make the office of this Company your headquarters.

Write for our booklet "The Spirit of America—as shown by her great documents, 1620-1920," voicing the fundamental principles of American liberty.

OLD COLONY TRUST COMPANY, BOSTON

DESCRIPTION AND DESCRIPTIVE PHRASES

The worthiness and the desirability of an article depend, among other factors, upon a clear, distinct idea of what the article is like; and a clear idea of the nature of the object depends upon the illustration and the descriptive phrases used concerning it. The most vivid idea of an article can be obtained by seeing, hearing, tasting, smelling, touching, or handling the article itself. In advertising, the article can be represented only by proxy. The best substitute for the article is a good picture of it. The next best substitute is a good, brief, vivid description of it.

A vivid description should produce mental pictures of the object in the mind of the reader. By a mental picture or image is meant the recalling in the mind of just how the object looks, or feels, or tastes, or smells, or sounds, depending upon which sense or senses are stimulated by it. We have as many different kinds of mental images as we have sense organs. Thus you may recall in your mind's eye how your mother looks. This picture may be so vivid that you can almost see her stand before you. Likewise, you may recall exactly how her voice sounds so that you can almost hear her speak. You may recall the odor of the coffee that she used to cook for breakfast, so vividly that you can almost taste it. Or, you may recall the touch of velvet so distinctly that you can almost feel it. These are mental images. They are the most realistic representatives of objects when the objects themselves are not present.

Concreteness of Mental Pictures. This particular phase of the advertiser's work requires the use of much thought and ingenuity. Concreteness and definiteness in phrases are always preferable to glittering generalities. An apple might be described as "The Michigan Apple, the finest in the world." Or, it might be described as a beautiful red apple with a delicious flavor. The latter description, carried out more fully, arouses a picture in one's mind of the appearance and the taste of the apple. It appeals to the same sense as the apple itself does. The former description is vague and exaggerated. Someone has said that an advertisement of food is not good unless it makes your "mouth water." It should appeal in a most lively manner to the sense of taste.

RULES FOR THE USE OF DESCRIPTIVE PHRASES

In the writing of copy, two rules should be borne in mind: (1) Use words and phrases which will arouse concrete mental images in the minds of the readers. (2) For articles which appeal primarily to a certain sense, use words and phrases that will emphasize the images of that particular sense. For example, descriptions of foods should arouse taste images; descriptions of musical instruments should call up sound pictures. Advertisements of clothing may make strong points of appearance and style. Advertisements of shoes may emphasize touch and comfort to the feet. Each advertisement should appeal to the sense or senses to which the commodity itself appeals. In the case of direct, personal salesmanship, the article itself can be seen, heard, touched, tasted, or smelled, according to the nature of the article. The customer knows exactly what it is like. In salesmanship through print, the advertisement must stimulate the customer's imagination so that in his mind he can see, hear, touch, taste, or smell the article.

The best writers are those who are able to create through simple language rich and everchanging thought-pictures in the minds of the readers. The writings which are enjoyed most and live the longest are the writings of the great masters of simple image-bearing words which recreate in the minds of others the thoughts of the writer. Job's statement[1] has here a new and significant meaning: "How forcible are right words!"

---

[1] Job, 6:24, 25.

XX

TRUTH IN ADVERTISING

The greatest requisite for making an advertisement convincing. Types of objectionable advertising: Exaggeration. Comparative prices. Misleading names. Misleading labels. Testimonials. Proprietary remedies and patent medicines. Investments offering high rate of returns. Certain forms of educational and self-improvement advertising. "Free" advertising. "Blind" advertisements. Fictitious cases of pseudo-scientific evidence. Agencies for improving advertising. (a) Better Business Methods and Standards. (b) Publishers and mediums. (c) Legal methods: *The Printers' Ink Statute*. (d) The National Vigilance Committee. (e) The Better Business Commissions.

IN the preceding chapter, we proposed four requisites to make an advertisement convincing. The greatest of these four is truthfulness.

Honesty is the foundation of confidence; and confidence is the greatest asset that any business can possess. Advertising, as well as all other forms of business transactions, should be absolutely trustworthy, for two reasons: First, for the general moral reason that all forms of human intercourse should be honest and dependable; and, secondly, for business reasons, that lying and cheating in advertising, in the long run, are commercial suicide. Dishonesty in advertising destroys not only confidence in advertising, but also in the medium which carries the dishonest advertisement. It hurts not only the particular business and the particular medium, but it indirectly harms the buying public. No one can be ill in a community without endangering others; no advertiser can be dishonest without casting suspicion upon others.

Mr. Richard Lee, for several years counsel for the National Vigilance Committee of the Associated Advertising Clubs, stated that according to his observation 97% of all advertising was fundamentally truthful and dependable.

The author conducted an investigation to determine what percentage of the advertising in newspapers is of an objectionable or questionable nature. Four large metropolitan newspapers were used as the basis of this investigation. Six issues of each, appearing at intervals of about a week, were carefully examined. Three types of objectionable or questionable advertising were classified: (1) Distinctly objectionable, (2) Doubtful or borderline cases, and (3) advertising in which a phrase or a sentence was questionable. All the advertising space was measured in terms of column inches and the proportions of the various classes were then computed and found to be as follows:

	Distinctly Objectionable	Doubtful Borderline	Phrase or Sentence Objectionable
1st Paper	7.7%	7.4	2.9
2nd Paper	4.6	4.0	1.9
3rd Paper	3.2	5.1	...
4th Paper	3.0	4.9	.1
Average	4.6	5.3	1.2

TYPES OF OBJECTIONABLE ADVERTISING

Exaggeration. Examples of exaggeration can be found in almost any advertising medium. The use of the superlative is altogether too prevalent. "The finest," "the best," "the greatest," "the purest," "the most economical," and so on *ad infinitum,* are hurled at the public everywhere. Surely not all products of the same class can be the best or the finest. Thus in one magazine we find that ". . . . . Tires are America's Highest Grade Automobile Tires." Likewise, in the same medium one typewriter manufacturer claims to have "every improvement that 20 years of thought and study could suggest." Near by, another typewriter manufacturer claims to have "the greatest advance in typewriter construction."

To show how frequent are the superlatives in current

advertisements, here is a list taken from one magazine: "The best seven-jewel watch." ". . . . . . Cement, none just as good." ". . . . . . Pork and Beans are the best that money will buy." ". . . . . . Ketchup, Our product is recognized as the best and purest of its kind." ". . . . . . System of re-inforced concrete means the lowest cost of fireproof construction." "Not only is the . . . . . . better, but it sells for less than any other vacuum bottle." ". . . . . . Stove Polish lasts longest." "Perfect fit and comfort of . . . . . . quarter sizes, together with their custom style and quality, combine to make . . . . . . shoes the greatest shoe value in the world." "These paints are selected because they are the most durable."

". . . . . . Buggies are the best made, best grade, and easiest riding buggies on earth for the money."

". . . . . . Motor Boats—superior to all others for safety, comfort, durability, and speed."

". . . . . . Boats, the only one offering the combination of speed with comfort and safety."

"A perfect shoe lace is here at last."

"A perfect dentifrice and a perfect package."

"We believe them the finest chocolates in the world."

". . . . . . Stoves and Ranges, the best in the world."

"The best business card is the . . . . . . card."

"We believe this new . . . . . . to be the best car in the world."

"The most admired of time pieces."

Such exaggerations have been so common that the public takes them with a grain of salt and partly excuses them as being due to the advertiser's license of self-assertiveness. Nevertheless, the fact remains that superlative generalities are weak arguments and far less convincing than a statement of facts. Much advertising copy would be improved immensely by doing away with brag and substituting actual facts about the merits of the article. Thus, instead of saying that So-and-So's is the best flour on earth, it would be far more illuminating to state some simple fact about its

manufacture or about the grain from which it is made, or
its nutritive value, or anything else that really means high
quality. Here are two motor boat advertisements: One
says: "Superior to all others for Safety, Comfort, Durability, and Speed." The other says:

A stock boat entered last September in the Championship Race,
New York to Poughkeepsie and return, maintained an average
speed of 22.57 miles for the entire distance.

It is quite obvious which of these two is the more convincing. One simply makes a big claim, while the other
gives an actual test which anyone could verify as a matter
of record.

Exaggeration and superlatives have in recent years tended
to disappear, although they still appear all too frequently.
Such exaggerations would disappear even more rapidly if
the occurrence in the recent suit against the Shaker Salt
Company were more frequently duplicated.

The suit was brought by the Diamond Crystal Co. to enjoin
the Worcester Co. from the use of the words "Shaker Salt," and
from the use of a red carton to hold its salt. Judge Hand upheld
the contentions of the plaintiff, but refused relief, because of certain statements in the plaintiff's advertising which, though not particularly harmful, were still misleading.[1]

COMPARATIVE PRICES

A much abused method of advertising is the quotation
of comparative prices. The appeal of comparative price
has been used freely particularly in the past two or three
years (1919-1922) during the period of the adjustment or
lowering of prices. Through it all, however, there has been
a distinct tendency on the part of retailers to use comparative prices less frequently, and a considerable number of
high-grade retailers follow the policy of not using comparative prices at all.

The objection to comparative prices lies in the fact that

[1] *Printers' Ink*, Jan. 15, 1914.

so many times they are not strictly true, and frequently when they are literally true they are not true in spirit. High-grade business houses have refrained from using direct comparative prices because of the abuse and untruthfulness back of them in so many instances. Furthermore, fluctuation of prices quite frequently makes it difficult to state correct changes in prices.

Comparative prices themselves are not objectionable. They are objectionable primarily because the public as a rule has no way of knowing when and to what extent comparative prices are literally true. When they are literally true and actually believed, comparative prices are entirely legitimate and constitute unquestionably one of the strongest appeals that a retailer can use.

To avoid the use of direct comparative prices, a retailer may resort to other methods of showing that a price reduction has been made; for example, he can state it in such a way that customers are inclined to believe what he says. The activities of the national as well as of the local vigilance committees, and more recently of the Better Business Commissions, have shown to what extent comparative prices are abused or untrue. In some instances, the committee found that prices were not reduced at all, notwithstanding the advertisements which had been issued; and in other instances, the prices had actually been raised. An article selling at 25 cents was quoted at a special sale at 29 cents, with an implied impression that it had been reduced from 50 cents. One of the most striking and extensive investigations made was that carried out in connection with a special annual sale by one of the large Metropolitan department stores in 1916. The investigation was carried out by purchasing typical articles advertised in this sale and by comparing their values with corresponding articles sold by other stores, not advertised as special reductions, or by having expert buyers evaluate the articles. The sale was announced as follows:

$6,000,000 stocks of fine, new merchandise, bought months in advance at prices which in many cases are lower than present wholesale prices, will be placed on sale during October.

"Iceland Fox" was advertised at a special sale at $4.45 for a scarf. The impression given was that this was real fox fur, whereas as a matter of fact, it was lamb and at that price was approximately a fair charge.

"Men's suits at $14.75, formerly $22.50 to $27.50." They were advertised with the words "ordinarily you would pay $22.50 to $27.50 for these suits." "$22.50 to $27.50 values. Standard . . . . . . clothes. The suits are smart, new models, the pick of the best clothes made in America, and must not be confused with average clothes selling around their present prices. We unreservedly pronounce this the best offer . . . . . . has made this year."

An expert appraiser examining one of the suits, estimated that it should sell at $12.50 retail. Another estimated it at $13.50.

Men's hats were advertised as "regular $3 and more" for $1.85. The salesmen stated that the lowest-priced hat in the lot had been $24 per dozen wholesale. If this were true a fair retail price would have been $3. An investigator purchased one of these hats and found that the wholesale price had been $16.50 and $17 per dozen. A normal retail price would have been $2 to $2.25.

Women's dresses were advertised as follows:

A Thousand Silk Dresses at $9.75
Street and Afternoon Dresses That, Bought
in the Regular Way, Would Sell at
$15 to $19.75.

These dresses were advertised also as containing "40 Styles to Choose from, the Season's Newest and Best." The investigators bought a dress at $9.75. Inspection showed that it was not the season's newest and would hardly be considered as the season's best. An expert appraiser valued it at from $6 to $7 retail.

In the linen department, Madeira-embroidered napkins were advertised "regularly $7.50 a Doz. Price $5.75." At another store napkins of practically the same quality were bought at the regular price of $5.25 per dozen, except that these latter napkins were actually superior in quality to the ones sold at the special price of $5.75!

In the blanket department, blankets were advertised as "$8.75 pr. Regularly $12." At another store blankets were bought at $10.50, which were markedly superior to the supposedly "regular $12" blankets mentioned above. The investigators bought blankets at $8.50 regular price at another store which were practically of the same quality as the ones being sold at . . . . . . for $8.75 on sale, "Regularly $12." Comforters which . . . . . . were advertising at $6, "Regularly $7," were found, on comparing them with comforters bought elsewhere, to be practically the same value as comforters bought at $5.19, regular price.

In the furniture department, the advertisements read "Stickley Craftsman Furniture at Half Price." Although the furniture was supposed to be marked at half price, it was found by the investigators that this was not true. The chairs, one of which was bought, were marked originally at $39 and now reduced to $23.50. The 50% reduction did not seem to be in evidence. In one case it was found that a 50% reduction had supposedly been made. A china closet of a pattern discontinued but formerly catalogued by Gustav Stickley at $54 retail, was marked at $30, sales price. Thirty dollars is not a 50% reduction from $54, so in order to make it a 50% reduction, ... marked the original price of the china closet on the ticket up to $60 and then marked the reduction price $30!

Portieres were marked "Value $25 per pair; Sale Price $18.75." It was found on comparison with portieres bought at regular prices at another store, that the actual value of these portieres was not $25, but $16.89, actually less than the sale price set upon them.

A Salz Bros. fountain pen No. 4 was advertised thus:

"Fountain Pen, $1; sold regularly for $2.50." However, it was found upon inquiry at other stores that this fountain pen was selling regularly at $1.

Sweaters were advertised as "Men's All-Wool Sweaters, $4.95 and $6.45; Values $6.50 to $10.50." The salesman, when asked, said that they had no $10.50 sweaters but handed the investigator one which he said was a "$9.50 value," selling at $6.45. This sweater was purchased and compared with sweaters at other stores, and was found to be about the same quality as one selling at a regular price of $5.95 at another store. The only difference was that this $5.95 sweater was actually a trifle superior in quality to the $6.45 sweater, "Value $9.50."

Women's suits, advertised as the season's best $19.75 to $29.75 suits for only $15, were next examined. Two suits purchased for $15 apiece from this lot were described by the appraisers as follows: One was a last spring's regular $15 model, and the other "among the poorest of the regular $15 models on the market."

At a preliminary sale before the big sale, the clothing department came out with an advertisement as follows:

One $7.50 Suit for $7.50—Two $7.50 Suits for $8.50.

These $7.50 suits were found to be sold elsewhere at the regular price of $4. After it had been shown that they were selling $4 suits at a raised price, all purchasers of the "two for $8.50" suits were told that they might return them and have their money refunded. The advertisement read as follows:

Due to a mistake in our Stock rooms, a quantity of Suits which our Buyer had rejected as not being up to .... Standard, were inadvertently sent down and included in the Sale instead of being returned to the manufacturer.

Objectionable practices are often connected with so-called one-cent sales, in which two articles may be bought for a certain sum which is supposedly one cent more than the price of one article.

The Quaker Valley Manufacturing Company, a supposedly reputable mail order house located at Aurora, Illinois, recently circulated through the mails a postal card on which an offer of all wool army blankets was made, as follows:

An All Wool Army Blanket for a Cent

That's precisely what we mean!
On condition that you order one of these blankets at the sale price of $7.85 we will send you one more for one cent. And permit me to give you my assurance that this second blanket is practically a gift.[1]

The case of the elimination of comparative prices is well stated by Horace E. Ryan as follows:

When I heard George M. Husser, secretary of the National Vigilance Committee of the Associated Advertising Clubs, say recently that the average saving in advertising appropriations in a number of stores which had eliminated comparative prices in their advertising had been .9%, I was struck by the fact that this has been exactly the reduction the L. S. Ayres & Co. store has been able to make.

Since we eliminated the use of comparative prices, our advertising costs have steadily decreased and our gains in business have just as steadily increased.

During 1916, our advertising expenditure dropped from 3.1% to 2.2%, and sales increased at more than the normal rate.

If you will think for a moment what .9% of the sales of a department store amount to, you will realize that the saving through the adoption of the new policy has been an important item—$9,000 on every million dollars' worth of business done.

In the meantime, we expect to be able to make a further reduction, so that our advertising will average around 2% of our sales during the next year, and it will readily be seen what a difference this will make in the service we can give our customers, either by giving increased values or better service, or both.

A few years ago department stores in this city believed that 4% was about the proper advertising appropriation, and some of them are reported still to employ that much.

When we adopted the new policy, we believed this would eventually increase public confidence in our advertising, and at

[1] *Associated Advertising*, April, 1921, p. 22.

the same time, have a tendency to make our advertising more interesting and therefore more productive from being more generally read.

One of the biggest advantages which comes from eliminating comparative price statements, I believe, comes from the fact the advertisements are more interesting. When the advertising writer cannot fall back on price, and yet must write "Copy" that will sell goods, he must *describe the goods*. Department managers and others who supply information for advertisements are confronted with the same necessity, for they realize their department sales depend upon getting into the advertisements facts which will make people want the *merchandise*.

We must tell the color, the thickness and the nature of the goods. We must describe the quality of the thing we are offering for sale. That sharpens our wits. It opens our eyes to selling points.

In this same connection is the interesting fact that the use of more descriptive advertising statements also has a tendency to instruct the salespeople in the use of real selling points in presenting goods to the customer.

One of the real needs in retail selling is to teach the man or woman behind the counter that the customer is likely to be a good deal more interested in other things than price.

When the salesperson reads the advertisements of a store which does not rely on the comparative price appeal, he or she finds descriptions and selling points which become the basis for effective selling arguments.

These things, and especially the fact that our advertising is apparently more interesting and more generally believed, have overcome the disadvantages of the change in policy, for it does, at times, seem to have some drawbacks. For example, when we have a few articles of a given kind which are greatly reduced in price, it would often be possible to move them off the shelves much more quickly if we could quote comparative prices.

Some time ago, we had half a dozen dresses which had been $75 and which were being cleared at $25. A statement that we had six such dresses would have brought women flocking to the store. As it was, it required a bit of descriptive effort to make the reader realize that this was a rare opportunity.

However, there is an advantage in getting the customer into the store, then showing her that the opportunity was even better than she imagined from reading the advertisements.

This was brought forcibly to my attention, recently, when a young woman I know very well, after reading of a clearance sale in silverware, went to another store to buy because the other store had quoted exceptional reductions, using comparative prices.

After she had bought what she wanted there, she came to our store and found that she could have done better here than at the store where she made the purchases, and she said she wished I had told her about our bargains. Eventually we sold her several pieces.

I believe she will be more interested in our advertisements when we say in the future that prices have been reduced in this or in other departments.

While our advertisements have brought much more business for each agate line of advertising space used, another element in the saving has come from the fact that we have been following the policy of using only such space as is actually necessary to tell our story.

By employing concise descriptions, we have been able, often, to use smaller spaces than in former times, and these smaller spaces have brought more business than the larger spaces we formerly used. This, I believe, is because the advertisements, with better descriptions, have been more interesting, as well as because more readers apparently believe all statements made.

We have concluded that the most economical thing is to buy the space we need to tell the story, rather than to plan to make a certain "showing." We tell the story and stop.

We would not go back to the former policy because the new method has paid us so well, and we feel that we will reap bigger and bigger benefits as the years pass.

There is a world of difference between making sales and making customers. A selling policy which inspires confidence and brings people into a store because they believe in the merchandise the store handles, will build for the future—will win customers who will not go off to some other store the moment it quotes what seem to be lower prices.

We have less trouble. We have fewer discontented customers, for they know more about the *merchandise*. They are thinking more about the goods they buy and less about the price, and appreciate the goods more.

The policy pays in all respects.[1]

Misleading Names. The next form of objectionable practice is the use of misleading trade-names, such as Iceland Fox for lamb; Brook Mink, Hudson Seal, or Arctic Seal for

[1] *Ibid.*, Sept., 1917.

dyed muskrat; Laskin, Baltic, Hudson Bay, Baffin seals for dyed rabbit; Hudson Lynx for French Coney; Boston Leather for an imitation leather, or sterling leather for an imitation product; Parisian ivory for celluloid products; Empire Brussels for rugs which have no relation to the Brussels carpets commonly known; and furniture finished in stains to imitate various types of wood without actually being that particular wood. The name Castile soap is often used for soap that is not Castile.

There are numerous trade-names containing the word silk which are applied to fabrics which are only part silk —such names as lining silk, Aledo silk, Tussah, Tezzo, Seco and silk muslin. Fiber silk is not silk at all but is a wood pulp product. The word silk should therefore not be used in conjunction with fiber. Fiber materials such as Tricolette, Baronette, Kumsi Kumsa, Mignonette, Deluskuit, Monnette, Fan-ti-si, Minor Chene, Dew Kist, and the like, are usually regarded by the public as silk.

A similar confusion or deception occurs in the use of various expressions which use the word wool. Wool or All Wool means 100% wool. Cashmere is often applied to a fabric which is part cotton. According to the ruling of the Federal Trade Commission, a material should not be called cashmere unless it is all wool.

The Supreme Court, in the case brought by the Federal Trade Commission against the Winsted Hosiery Company relative to the use of the term "Merino" in connection with knit goods, decided (1922) that trade-names and labels used by manufacturers must not convey to the purchasing public an inaccurate description of the materials or ingredients of the products.

Some of these names are not as misleading as others because their real meaning has become well known. Thus, for example, it is pretty well known by many customers that Hudson Seal is not seal but dyed muskrat. Nevertheless, these names are in a great many instances misleading, particularly to persons who are not well informed regarding qualities and materials of such products. The objectionable point lies in the fact that these terms imply—to the uncritical or uninformed—that the product is something which it is not. It is customary for many high-grade retailers to put in parentheses after the trade-names what the product really is. Even where a given trade-name is generally known to apply to an article that is not the genuine commodity, there are nevertheless many other people who do not know the real facts and for them such names are misleading. Furthermore the use of such names by reputable merchants opens the door to more objectionable practices on the part of less scrupulous merchants.

Misleading Labels. Another very common practice closely allied to the use of misleading trade-names is the use of labels which imply that the product has been imported, or obtained from sources from which it did not come. In 1915, the *New York Tribune* made an investigation of the use of labels in men's hats which implied that the hats were imported from foreign countries.

At the store of ...... a hat having the following label in it was purchased: "Clayton & Co., Denton, England, Imported by ......, U. S. A." When the *Tribune* investigator turned up the sweatband, however, there was a U. S. union label underneath it, showing that the hat had really been made in the United States, but that a foreign label had been put into it, in order to fool the public into believing that it was purchasing imported headgear.

At another store, hats were advertised as follows: "$5 Velour Hats for $2.75; Special Sale." When one of these hats was shown to the investigator, it was found to contain the following label inside: "Felix—Budapest, Austria—Imported for ...." However, upon turning up the sweatband, the U. S. union label appeared, as in the other case mentioned.

For $1.50, the investigator purchased a warranted English derby, marked, in the crown: "Briggs & Co.—English

Make." The union label of a U. S. union was found underneath the sweatband in this hat also, however.

At still another store, a hat containing the following label was purchased. "Made in England—Bannock Bros., Ltd.— Imported by ...." Inside the sweatband, the American union label was found, as in the other cases.

Testimonials have a legitimate place in meritorious advertising and often are very effective. They have, however, been greatly misused, particularly in connection with products which of themselves are open to question. Perhaps the most objectionable use of testimonials is the custom of quoting the endorsement of some person who is well known and who stands high in the public estimation or some person who is quoted as belonging to a profession such as law or medicine, or again a person who stands high in a church. In other instances, the names of prominent actors and actresses or athletes are used. In most instances, there is no inherent objection to an endorsement, but the objectionable element usually inheres in the manner in which the endorsement is used, or in the product for which it is used, and in the fact that the person whose testimonial is quoted cannot possibly be in a position to state in an authoritative manner the particular things which he states.

A great deal of effectiveness is often lent to such objectionable testimonials by a bold statement that these testimonials are genuine and that a reward of some considerable sum of money is offered to anyone who can prove that the testimonials in question are not genuine. What this usually means is that the testimonial was subscribed to by some real person, not that the things which are attributed to the product may actually have brought about the results claimed. In many instances the person giving the testimonial may be quite sincere in his beliefs about the product.

Testimonials for patent medicines are objectionable in most instances in spite of the fact that the person who gives the testimonial may quite sincerely believe that the particular remedy has produced the cure claimed. The situation often is this: Nearly all persons who are in the habit of buying patent remedies for any and all sorts of temporary or chronic ailments will at some time or other improve in their health at least for the time being. The particular remedy which is being taken at that time is the one that receives the credit, and a very glowing testimonial is then willingly given by the patient. The testimonial is the "long suit" of remedy advertising of this kind. Statements may be put into the mouths of patients and quoted in the form of testimonials which could possibly otherwise not be made, and which thereby actually become more effective with the unwary victim than a direct statement by the manufacturer would be.

A surprising fact in connection with testimonials for remedies is the element of belief that a certain remedy has produced a cure. An investigation made by the Vigilance Committee for the State of Michigan revealed the fact that certain persons had given testimonials, apparently quite sincerely, for having been cured of certain ailments by a device known as an Oxydoner. The presumed basis of this method of curing ailments is that of increasing the supply of oxygen in the human system. Whether or not the introduction of oxygen in the human system has a curative effect is itself open to question. That oxygen may be introduced into the human system by this particular method is certainly open to question. A testimonial had been given by a mother to the effect that her little boy had been cured of cross-eyedness. When the investigator called upon the family, the little boy was as cross-eyed as he apparently had ever been even though his mother denied it.

A woman was reported to have undergone a series of operations and, after all had failed, she was reported to have been cured by Oxydoner. She died within a month after the Oxydoner cure was supposedly effected. The same was reported regarding a capitalist, who died within a few weeks after the supposed cure. The autopsy showed that the diseased organs had not been affected by the Oxydoner cure.

Another variety of the testimonial advertisement is the so-called prescription advertisement. It is set up after the fashion of ordinary news-matter in the paper. To all outward appearances, some well-known person, possibly an actress, conducts a column of advice regarding beauty hints. The advertisement reads for the most part like a news-item and like personal advice. However, toward the end of the advertisement, there is mentioned some particular remedy or product which may be obtained at such and such a place and which this prominent person highly recommends. It is quite probable that in many instances the person quoted has little or nothing to do with the preparation of these statements, except to lend his or her name to them. The effectiveness of this type of advertising has been somewhat reduced by the fact that such material must, according to law, be labeled "advertisement."

The case of a testimonial for a patent medicine given by a prominent person is illustrated by the following statement made by a well-known artist:

I have used Sanatogen from the first of the year and find it a wonderful tonic. I am recommending it to my overworked friends.

Mr. S. H. Adams, in the *New York Tribune*,[1] remarks concerning this testimonial thus:

Now if he (the artist) had written, "I obtained the pretty pink color which lends the flush of youth to the cheek of beauty in my pictures by mixing Sanatogen with my paint," that would be something to the purpose. For nobody paints more prettily or more pinkly than Mr. . . . . But when it comes to a question of nerve-strain and overwork, which is the purport of the advertisement embodying the letter, somehow I fail to be convinced that Mr. . . . . 's opinion on this, one of the most difficult and obscure problems in medical science, contributes greatly to the sum total of human knowledge.

[1] Feb. 2, 1915.

Another advertisement for the same product states:

Over twenty-one thousand physicians have written letters, telling how they had watched Sanatogen reconstruct cell and tissue, enrich the blood, recall keener appetite and better slumber, and infuse the whole system with a new vigor.

Mr. S. H. Adams comments concerning this as follows:

There is a blanket testimonial for you! Its principal weakness is that it isn't true. That valiant twenty-one thousand haven't "watched Sanatogen reconstruct cell and tissue—enrich the blood —" or perform any other wild impossibilities, nor have they said that they did. From the selected letters which the Sanatogen people themselves furnished to me, it appears that a large majority of the medical indorsers refer to the preparation as a good invalid food *and nothing else.* Similarly, in its reply to my former criticism, the Sanatogen concern defends itself as being a "standard food tonic" and quite properly quotes the eminent von Noorden as terming it an "excellent albuminous preparation." Granted with all my heart! But no "standard food tonic" nor "excellent albuminous preparation" will perform the miracles of reconstruction of brain and nerve implied in the Sanatogen advertisements. Nothing could, short of an elixir of life!

An illustration of the use of the name of a prominent athlete is an advertisement featuring Jack Dempsey, immediately after his combat with Carpentier in 1921. A copy of the advertisement carrying his testimonial is reproduced in Figure 41.

An illustration of the use of a testimonial from a person proclaimed as having had a long experience in the practice of medicine is the following endorsement of Tanlac, by a Dr. Elder.

ILLINOIS DOCTOR PRESCRIBES IT

Says He Has Never Known Medicine to Produce Results Like Tanlac

B. H. Elder, M. D., with offices at 410 Schradzi Building, Peoria, Illinois, comes out with his unqualified endorsement of Tanlac.

Dr. Elder graduated from Butler University of Indianapolis,

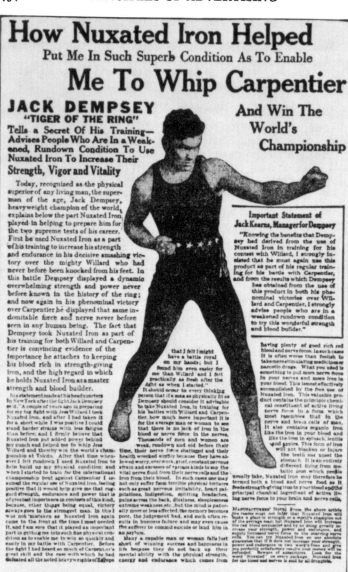

Figure 41: Illustration of an advertisement using the name of a prominent man as a testimonial *(See page 453)*

Ind., later took a post-graduate course at Rush Medical College, Chicago, and has also studied abroad.

He has been in active practice over 40 years—25 years in Peoria—and is one of the best-known physicians of that city.

"So far as my knowledge goes," said Dr. Elder, in an interview recently, "medical science has never produced a medicine that brings results like Tanlac. It is altogether too good to keep from suffering humanity and I have been prescribing it in my practice for some time with remarkable results."

The testimonial continues at considerable length in the same vein.

Proprietary Remedies and Patent Medicines. Closely allied to objectionable testimonial advertising is a considerable amount of advertising of proprietary remedies. In spite of the remarkable advance made in recent years in the elimination of the objectionable advertisements of this class from our better-grade mediums, there is still a surprisingly large number appearing in the mediums which exercise less discrimination. The better-grade magazines have almost entirely eliminated advertising of this sort. A considerable number of the larger and well-edited newspapers also have eliminated such advertising. Nevertheless there is a regrettable number of even the larger city papers which carry distinctly objectionable advertising of this class. The advertising of questionable remedies is even now appearing in some of our largest city newspapers.

Investments Offering High Rate of Returns. In spite of the many safeguards and legal regulations, advertising of this class continues to appear. In recent years a great deal of fraudulent advertising has been carried on in connection with oil fields and oil wells. A few years before there was a large amount of advertising of worthless mining stock. Fortunately it is becoming. more and more difficult for operators of this type to get a foothold and to carry out their plans without being discovered before they are very far advanced. Much of the material presented in advertisements of this sort is misleading to the unwary. Thus a recent advertisement states:

This advertisement will appear in a large number of metropolitan daily papers in the very near future.

Note the price, $2 per share.

Then note the special pre-organization offer outlined in our letter herewith.

$6,794,000,000

was the value of the 1906 farm products. (From Annual Report of Secretary of Agriculture Wilson.) There is an opportunity for you to participate in these splendid profits.

$750,000,000

was the increase in valuation of farms in one state from 1900 to 1906. Here is an opportunity for you to share in these tremendous increases in value, etc.

These figures are quoted from government reports and are no doubt true and correct but they have little to do with the proposition offered in the body of the advertisement. To the uncritical they lend an air of authority and reliability to a questionable investment.

Certain Forms of Educational and Self-Improvement Advertising. A great deal of advertising of long distance educational plans has appeared in recent years. A large number of correspondence and extension institutions have arisen. Some of these organizations undoubtedly do legitimate educational work, carried out by proper methods. However, a great deal of the advertising of a few of them is open to severe criticism. The criticism centers chiefly around the offer of large returns and the raising of hopes far beyond reasonable possibility.

"Free" Advertising. The use of the word "free" is often a trap for catching the unwary. Something is apparently offered free but it is quite probable that a purchase of something is required later.

"Blind" Advertisements. To this class belong advertisements usually appearing in the classified sections of newspapers and in some of the less discriminating magazines. The advertisement does not state the proposition involved at all, but conceals the real point under an offer of employment or work for one's spare hours, or some other guise. When the reader sends an inquiry about this advertisement, he finds that it is really an attempt to sell a product or samples of it. He is told, in reply, that if he sends in $15 he will receive "a full and complete outfit" of the ironing board appliance or whatever the product happens to be.

Fictitious Cases or Pseudo-Scientific Evidence. Advertising which purports to be based upon scientific facts or investigations, or which relates experiences that are purely fictitious but apparently real, is in many instances objectionable and misleading. Cases in point are the vitamines in certain foods, or iron in others, or brain-building elements in still others. The point here is not that such arguments are not justifiable where scientific research has demonstrated their presence or value, but that such arguments are often either abused or overemphasized. Recent biological research has called attention to the value of vitamines.

Certain foods do contain vitamines in larger quantities than others. Such advertising arguments are therefore in just that degree justified. However, the harm lies in the fact that scores of food advertisers seize upon the fact that their particular food contains this or that vital or body-building element and incorporate in their advertisements exaggerated statements about its abundance and value. The particular food championed, for instance, may contain a large amount of vitamines, but it may contain absolutely no more than many other kinds of food. Yet such advertising *implies* that the particular food in question contains more vitamines than does any other food.

In the midst of this regrettable situation the hopeful sign is that very substantial progress has been made during the past 10 or 15 years in the betterment of advertising and in the elimination of its objectionable forms. Indeed the progress that has been made along this line represents one of the most important developments, in fact in some respects the most important development, in advertising that has taken place in its entire history. If a comparison were made between conditions as they were prior to 1910 or 1905 and the situation as it exists today, one would be very forcibly impressed with the progress which has been made. A number of forces have been at work during the past decade to bring about better conditions. The more important are the following:

   a. Better Business Methods and Standards
   b. Publishers and Mediums
   c. Legal Methods: The Printers' Ink Statute
   d. The National Vigilance Committee
   e. The Better Business Commissions

   a. Better Business Methods and Standards. The incident is related that some years ago Mr. John A. Wanamaker asked Mr. Powers, "Tell me something new to do in advertising." It is said that Mr. Powers replied, "Be honest; it has never been tried before." The general improvement in standards of doing business, which has taken place in the past two or three decades, has undoubtedly furnished a background for the parallel development in the advertising field. Advertising is a part of business and as such is probably no better and no worse than business in general. It is probably true that advertising is criticised as frequently as any phase of business, but this is largely due to the fact that advertising is in printed form. It is seen and open to public inspection perhaps more than any other aspect of business. It is tangible and accessible and consequently the public is quite ready to point its finger at any fault or failing which it sees. Objectionable and unethical methods in other phases of business are not exposed to public view; in fact the public frequently knows nothing about them, and consequently they escape criticism. Thus, it is not unlikely that the methods and standards of advertising are on a par if not actually in advance of other business transactions, which are not as open to inspection.

The statement attributed to Marshall Field, "The customer is always right," or the phrase "Satisfaction or Money Back," and similar phrases are typical of the policies of the better business houses of the present day. The wide-spread adoption of this point of view is indicative of real progress in the ethical standards of business.

The mail-order houses which have developed to enormous proportions within the past two decades have been able to acquire such a large volume of business largely because of their policy of literal truthfulness and dependability. This has necessitated absolutely accurate description of the goods so that the customer at a distance may be able to picture as accurately as possible the goods that he orders. All this has been necessary in order to build up confidence in the mail-order business and to avoid the difficulties connected with the return of goods. At the present time most of the large, dependable concerns of this class have eliminated the use of the word "Free" in prominent type. The description of goods has been made so accurate that one of the largest mail-order houses reports that the goods returned constitutes less than one-tenth of 1%. Many houses in this field of business, and most high-grade retailers, require that the garment or the article must be before the copywriter or the artist so that he may describe or represent it with complete fidelity.

Advertisers, and particularly persons who write and prepare advertisements, are just beginning to realize that

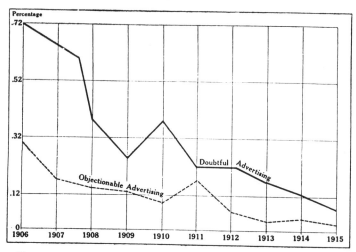

Figure 42: Percentage of doubtful or objectionable advertisements in newspapers, showing decrease *(See page 465)*

the most effective appeal is the one that is absolutely and literally true, put in such a form that it gives an impression of complete sincerity. This point, however, is only just beginning to be realized in its absolutely literal sense by a relatively small number of business concerns. When one realizes how effective the literal and sincere truth is, one wonders why every business house does not make this its unvarying policy. In support of this contention the following experiences of the effectiveness of truth and believable sincerity will not be amiss.

What a Perfectly Frank Statement Did

A Michigan department store has found that it pays to take the public into its confidence and give the precise reason for reduced prices on merchandise.

As an example, it had in stock some parasols which were giving trouble because the handles were prone to break easily.

The price was reduced from $1.50 to 95 cents, and a small space announcing the reduction was used in one newspaper. The advertisement simply presented the fact the store had a few parasols that had been $1.50 which had been reduced to 95 cents. The advertisement sold three parasols, and one of them came back the next day with a broken handle.

Four days later, the parasols were featured again, in a similar space in the same newspaper, but this time, it was stated that the reduction was made because the handles were inclined to break easily, but that, with care, they should last as long as any parasol. The price, 95 cents, was the same as before.

When people saw that there was a reason for the reduction, the remaining 17 were taken out of the store by early afternoon and many more could have been sold had they been in stock. Moreover, people who took them on the strength of the second advertisement had been informed of their possible fault and whether any was broken or not, none was returned to the store on this account.[1]

A Successful Sale of Rotten Raincoats—How It Was Put Over

Here's a new true tale, with a point and a moral for dealers and advertising writers, told by Frank Armstrong, secretary of the Better Business Bureau, of Iowa.

It concerns a well-known department store proprietor, noted for his bluntness of speech and his peppery temper, who walked into the office of his advertising manager one day to give orders regarding an advertisement in the next morning's dailies. The advertising manager was ill, and his new assistant, a young college man, was doing his best to keep things going.

"Young man," said the merchant, "I want you to stir up some interest in the waterproof garment department. The fact is, we have a lot of rotten raincoats we've got to get rid of. They are shopworn, and some of them are cracked, and we'll sell them for little or nothing. Now we've got to get the people here to buy 'em. There are some good ones in the lot, but if we can't sell 'em we might as well dump 'em in the river."

The young man assured "the Boss" he knew exactly how to do it. Then the storm broke.

The next morning when the merchant opened his paper to read his store's advertisement for that day, he came pretty near having a fit, for on the page opposite the editorials was the raincoat advertisement, away across the page in bold black-face type, and it read this way:

---

[1] *Associated Advertising*, Dec., 1916, p. 31.

"To tell the truth, we have a lot of rotten raincoats we've got to get rid of. They are shopworn, and some of them are cracked, and we will sell them for little or nothing."

Down went his fist on the table, rattling the dishes and spilling the coffee. He read on:

"There are some good ones in the lot, but if we can't sell them, we might as well dump them into the river."

Agreeably Surprised.

Without waiting to eat breakfast, he jammed his hat close to his ears and started off down town an hour ahead of his usual time, to discharge the youth who had written the advertisement. Red in the face, he headed straight for the advertising manager's office. His partner met him on the way, and asked:

"Do you know about the raincoats?"

"Do I know? Yes! I'm on my way to kick that fool out of this store."

"Then you don't know!" said his partner. "There was the biggest crowd in the raincoat department we ever had. Every garment was sold out thirty minutes after we opened this morning. That advertisement was a wonder. Seemed to please the people by its absolute frankness."

The merchant paused, and then turned his steps toward his office. He sent for the advertising man.

"Young man," he said, "how did it happen that you used my exact words in that advertisement this morning?"

"You told the truth so simply and directly that I couldn't improve on your way of saying it," was the answer.

"Well," said the merchant. "But you were right and I was wrong. You may run the advertising department in your own way from now on."

This house, says Mr. Armstrong, by way of comment, has ever since been known for the simplicity, frankness, and truthfulness of its advertising.[1]

Advertising a Real Bargain Sale of Clothing

Reasons for Low Prices Were Obviously True and Sales Were Five Times Greater Than on Any Previous Day

Hart, Schaffner & Marx

Chicago, Feb. 28, 19—

Editor of *Printers' Ink:* We are sending you a copy of an advertisement which brought remarkable results for one of our

---

[1] *Ibid.*, April, 1919, p. 31.

customers, together with a little story on the accompanying sheet, which tells about it.

We know that you often make use of articles of this kind, and believe that this one will be of interest to your readers.

Hart, Schaffner & Marx

Here's an advertisement that sold 100 suits in one day in a very small clothing store whose previous high record for a single day's business had been nineteen garments.

In addition it was used as an object lesson in honest advertising in the School of Commerce of Northwestern University, and proved so convincing that a number of students and even an instructor or two took advantage of the sale to replenish their wardrobes.

The store is located on a residence street in Evanston, Ill., nationally known as the "classic" or "highbrow" suburb of Chicago.

The clothes which it was desired to sell were the left-overs of several seasons, in colors, styles and materials which had not proved popular with discriminating buyers.

"You couldn't give those clothes away in Evanston," said the manager of the store. "Our trade is the most fastidious in the country."

You know every merchant, no matter where located, thinks he has a particular kind of trade, or some special situation which makes his problem different from all the others.

The advertising department of Hart, Schaffner & Marx, however, thought that human nature in Evanston was very much the same as anywhere else, and persuaded the manager to run the advertisement.

It appeared Thursday and Friday afternoons.

There was a crowd in front of the store when it opened on Saturday.

When it closed that evening just two of the suits remained— one so small no one could get into it, and one which seemed to have been designed for a fat man in a circus.

At least 250 men had applied for the suits during the day, and as a number of the early comers bought more than one suit, the great majority necessarily was disappointed.

One result of the advertisement was that since it appeared sales of higher-priced clothes have been much larger than before.

$20

Beginning Saturday, February 19

We'll be frank about this.

These suits have been in stock for two or three seasons.
They are not in the very latest styles.
Some are in colors and patterns that have not proven most popular.
Some seem to be just as attractive as any we have, but for reasons we can't explain, haven't sold well.
But—
 Every one is all wool
 Every one is well tailored
 Every one is in perfect condition
You see men—well dressed men, too—wearing suits just like them every day, suits they've had for a season or two.
Why not get one or two of these suits now when you can get them at one-third or one-fourth of the original price?
Sale opens Saturday morning, February 19.
It won't last long.[1]

b. Publishers and Mediums. A considerable number of publishers of advertising mediums have taken a definite stand with regard to the advertising which they will or will not accept. The announced or stated policy may not be fully lived up to in practice in all instances; but again the best evidence of the actual progress made in this regard lies in a comparison of the present issues of leading magazines and newspapers with issues of a decade or two ago. It will be noted that the improvement is very marked.

Figure 42, on page 460, illustrates the progress made during a period of 10 years on the part of one of the largest city dailies in the country. The total advertising space in this paper was measured to determine the relative amount of either distinctly objectionable or questionable border-line advertising carried. The drop in the two graphs is very decided, indicating a marked decrease in these two classes of advertising. Objectionable or questionable advertising has almost entirely disappeared from this paper. The same is now true of an increasing number of other high-grade newspapers.

[1] *Printers' Ink,* March 10, 1921, p. 33.

Kitson [1] reported an analysis of the advertisements in three mediums, namely, the *Indianapolis News*, the *Cosmopolitan* magazine and the *House Beautiful* magazine. He analyzed the advertisements appearing in these three mediums from 1900 to 1919 for the purpose of determining the proportion of advertisements in which superlative expressions were used. In 1900 the average of the three ranged from 15% to 21%. In 1919 the average was approximately 2%. This shows in a concrete way the very decided tendency towards the improvement of copy and the reduction of exaggerated overstatements.

The following is a typical statement of policies adopted by leading newspapers and magazines.

GENERAL RULES GOVERNING ACCEPTANCE OR REJECTION OF MEDICAL ADVERTISING

"A" The *Chicago Tribune accepts* advertisements of:

1. Approved medical books and periodicals
2. Approved procedures and proposals for preventive medicine
3. Sanitary appliances
4. Disinfectants, soaps and other cleansing agents
5. Ventilating and heating devices
6. Mineral waters
7. Health foods and curative remedies the worth of which is generally recognized by the medical profession, having the U. S. Government approval as to the alcoholic content for internal remedies which present no claims of extravagant results for the treatment of specific ailments, but which are, in the judgment of the *Chicago Tribune,* advertised for those purposes which will not tend to diminish in the minds of readers the necessity of proper medical attention, and subject to the following limitations which apply especially, but not entirely, to curative medicines.

"B" The *Tribune* does *not* accept advertisements of:

1. Physicians, surgeons and specialists in medicines
2. Treatments of venereal diseases. Treatments of so-called diseases of men and women.
3. Abortionists, remedies to produce abortion, instruments to produce abortion; remedies, instruments and appliances to prevent conception.

[1] Kitson, H. D., *The Mind of the Buyer.*

4. Remedies, drugs, appliances and methods the proprietors of which have been convicted by the federal, or any state, or municipal, government of violation of the Federal Food and Drug Act, the Sherley Law, or any state of municipal law of the same general character and intent as the above laws.

5. Remedies, drugs, appliances and methods which have been brought into public disrepute by wide-spread charges brought by any federal, state, municipal, health or food department, by the American Medical Association, National Retail Druggists' Association, the National Dental Society, or any other well-established, reputable organization, or by any considerable section of the public press.

6. Internal remedies containing cocaine, morphine, heroin, or any other habit-forming drug.

7. Internal remedies except laxatives and purgatives and those acceptable under rule "A-7."

8. Local applications, sprays, inhalations, lotions, liniments, ointments, dyes, and other local applications which contain wood alcohol, lead, cocaine, or any other substance that is poisonous or liable to do harm.

9. Hidden advertisements (prescriptions.)

10. Remedies, drugs, appliances and methods for which extravagant and obviously impossible claims are made, such claims as are against the letter or the spirit of the Sherley Law. This applies if the claims appear on the label, in a circular or booklet, or in any advertising whatsoever.

11. Dental advertising.[1]

In addition to the elimination of objectionable and doubtful advertising, a considerable number of mediums have gone a step further by guaranteeing the advertising which they carry; that is, guaranteeing it in the sense that they will either themselves make good on any misrepresentation or deception which may have appeared in connection with their advertising, or will see that the advertiser in question makes good. A typical illustration of this policy is the guarantee published regularly in *Good Housekeeping*.

Every article advertised in *Good Housekeeping* is covered by a money-back guarantee. This money-back guarantee is made possible because all household appliances, food products, and toilet preparations have been tested and approved by the Department

---

[1] *The Chicago Tribune Book of Facts*, 1921.

of Household Engineering or the Bureau of Foods, Sanitation, and Health, maintained by *Good Housekeeping*. These are marked with a star (*). The examinations are technical and practical, the tests being made under the supervision of experts.

Every article advertised which cannot, by its nature, be tested, bears the same money-back guarantee if the advertisement appears in *Good Housekeeping*.

With most of the high-grade mediums a policy of guaranteeing is substantially implied, and is almost unnecessary in view of the commendable care which is exercised in rejecting questionable commodities or irresponsible business houses.

A similar policy of guaranteeing was announced by the *New York Tribune* some years ago. The same plan has been adopted by a substantial number of the leading publications.

As an example of a publisher making good, the following may be cited:

How large a part of the confidence of the public in magazine advertising is due to the careful advertising policy of publishers is not appreciated by all advertisers. A large national advertiser said the other day that if the advertising pages of the publications he used carried one-half of the advertising that most magazines carried eight or ten years ago, he would seriously consider withdrawing altogether from advertising his product. He could not afford to appear anywhere in juxtaposition to objectionable advertising.

(Mr. S. K. Evans says the following for the *Woman's Home Companion*): "I want our readers to feel that the *Woman's Home Companion* will go shopping with them through the advertising pages, and will guarantee to make good every advertiser's representations. No reader can have much purchasing security by any other method of shopping, and I want to keep that faith inviolate.

"We have had several interesting cases in which we were given an opportunity to prove our principles. A woman bought a bird from one of our advertisers some time ago, and when it arrived it was a dead bird. She wrote to the concern, but it made no effort to satisfy her. Then she wrote to us. It was a small matter to have reimbursed the woman, but we were after the principle, and kept after the advertiser until he finally made good to the woman. She had done her part, doing exactly what the advertiser asked her to do, and had sent her money. If she had been given no satisfaction, her entire faith in advertising might have been shattered.

"Another case was that of a southern man who had bought an automobile which would not auto. It is possible that it was his own fault, since he knew little of machinery, but that was not the point at all. He desired the prerogative of a purchaser to get his money back, and when he came to us to help him get it we investigated the matter and gave it to him. If that man had been unable to get satisfaction from either ourselves or our advertiser, he would have been a living signboard to the end of his days against advertising columns."

One of the few magazines, if not the only one, however, which has actually put an advertiser behind the bars is *Success Magazine*. A Buffalo man advertised houses, and many people sent him money. He promised to deliver them, but kept sending promises only. He had a splendid suite of offices, but no discoverable factory. After making an investigation and giving him until a certain time to raise money to put on deposit against his obligations to those who answered his advertisements, *Success Magazine* finally decided to prosecute, and he is now serving a sentence.

c. Legal Methods: The Printers' Ink Statute. Perhaps the most important achievement has been the adoption of legislation against fraudulent advertising. In 1911, *Printers' Ink* caused a statute to be prepared which makes dishonest advertising a misdemeanor. This statute has been made a law, practically in the form devised by the counsel of *Printers' Ink,* in about three-fourths of the states. The text of this statute is as follows:

Any person, firm, corporation, or association, who with intent to sell or in any wise dispose of merchandise, securities, service, or anything offered by such person, firm, corporation, or association, directly or indirectly, to the public for sale or distribution, or with intent to increase the consumption thereof, or to induce the public in any manner to enter into any obligation relating thereto, or to acquire title thereto, or an interest therein, makes, publishes, disseminates, circulates, or places before the public, or causes, directly or indirectly, to be made, published, disseminated, circulated or placed before the public, in this state, in a newspaper or other publication, or in the form of a book, notice, handbill, poster, bill, circular, pamphlet, or letter, or in any other way, an advertisement of any sort regarding merchandise, securities, service, or anything so offered to the public, which advertisement contains assertions, representation, or statement of fact which is untrue, deceptive or misleading shall be guilty of a misdemeanor.

This statute (a) places the responsibility for deception upon the advertiser, (b) deals with questions of facts about goods rather than opinions, and (c) designates the making of untruthful, deceptive, or misleading statements a misdemeanor. Up to November, 1921, this statute had been adopted in 22 states in substantially the form in which it was originally prepared by counsel for *Printers' Ink,* and in 15 states in modified form. The 22 states in which it was adopted in substantially the above form are as follows:

Colorado	Kentucky	Nebraska	Ohio
Idaho	Louisiana	Nevada	Oklahoma
Indiana	Michigan	New Jersey	Oregon
Iowa	Minnesota	New York	Rhode Island
Kansas	Missouri	North Dakota	Washington
	West Virginia	Wyoming	

The 15 states in which it was adopted in modified form are as follows:

Arizona	Illinois	North Carolina	Utah
Alabama	Maryland	Pennsylvania	Texas
California	Massachusetts	South Dakota	Wisconsin
Connecticut	Montana	Tennessee	

In these 15 states the modification which has been made in the statute consists for the most part of the insertion of the words: "knowingly" or "with fraudulent intent." It is obvious that this change very considerably weakens the forcefulness of the statute. Nevertheless, the adoption of this statute has been a powerful force in bringing deception, misrepresentation, and dishonesty in advertising under legal control.

Figure 43 shows a map of the United States on which the states are represented in different ways. The white states are the 22 in which the statute was adopted in unmodified form; the shaded states are the 15 in which it was adopted in modified form; and the black states are the ones in which no legislation has been adopted with reference to this matter.

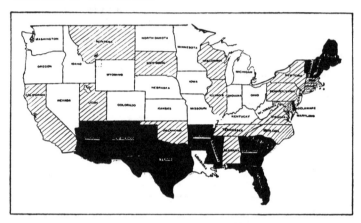

Figure 43: Map showing adoption by states of the "Printers' Ink Statute" against dishonest advertising

The Associated Advertising Clubs of the World, the national and local advertising clubs and other organizations have been active in pushing the adoption of this or similar legislation. This has been a powerful influence towards the remedy of objectionable practices in advertising by legal procedure.

In addition to state legislation a number of larger cities have ordinances covering certain undesirable advertising practices.

d. The National Vigilance Committee. About 1912 the Associated Advertising Clubs of the World adopted the motto, "Truth in Advertising" and established a National Vigilance Committee whose function it was to take active measures toward eliminating objectionable and dishonest advertising and to promote the establishment of a higher ethical standard.

The work of the National Vigilance Committee, the activities of local vigilance committees, the cooperation of the Better Business Bureaus more recently established at the instigation of the National Vigilance Committee, and the leverage afforded by the statutes recently adopted—these factors taken together have undoubtedly been the most potent forces in advancing the movement toward the betterment of advertising.

Numerous cases, large and small, have been handled by the Vigilance Committee. Probably the two largest and most invidious cases handled by the Committee are the Pandolfo Motor Case and the Bidwell Automobile Tire Case. A brief statement of these will illustrate the difficulties involved, the shrewdness with which the parties concerned laid their plans, and the task involved in successfully combating them.

The story of the Pandolfo case may perhaps best be stated by quoting an account of it up to its successful termination, as follows:

The Pandolfo Case. One of the most conspicuous frauds perpetrated in recent years is the Pandolfo case, which was successfully terminated by the activities of the Vigilance Committee of the Associated Advertising Clubs of the World. Very briefly, the history of the Pandolfo case was as follows:

S. C. Pandolfo conceived the idea of organizing a company for manufacturing automobiles to be known as the Pan Motor Company. The evident purpose in the organization, however, was not to produce automobiles, but to sell stock in the organization whether there were automobiles to sell or not. After various attempts at selling the stock in' New Mexico, Wyoming, and Colorado, he came to Chicago and announced that he had sold stock to approximately 800 individuals. In January, 1917, he incorporated the company and sent out announcements regarding the plan for the purpose of receiving invitations from various cities to come and locate there. Finally an invitation was accepted from the Commercial Club of St. Cloud, Minnesota. He presented his plan in person to the representatives of St. Cloud, stating in glowing terms that he would construct a car which would have a high clearance, as he had observed that the mountains in New Mexico and Texas were higher and that ruts were deep and the centers of the road were high. The car would have a special compartment, a tank for extra oil, gas, food, and refreshments, he said, and it would contain a folding bed, and so on. He also pointed out that every $100 originally invested in the Ford Motor Company had returned approximately $250,000. He planned to issue one million shares of stock at a par value of $5 each, but they were to be sold at $10 each so that a sufficient amount of capital would be provided. One of the chief features in his whole plan was the manner in which he succeeded in getting the endorsements of bankers and prominent business men, not only in St. Cloud, Minnesota, but in practically all sections of the country. To begin with he chose eight of the leading business men of St. Cloud as directors of his company and he referred to them in his printed matter as representing $20,000,000 of assets. His sales activities were carried on west of the Mississippi River because the Emerson Motors Company had just then been put out of business by the United States Government in the eastern part of the country. One of the chief methods employed by Pandolfo was the use of letters of recommendation. Many of these he wrote himself and submitted them merely for the signatures of various persons. He presented a number of his letters to the St. Cloud Commercial Club, some of which were repudiated by their writers. It is said that one man offered money to Pandolfo to get his letter back. Attorneys for Pandolfo wrote letters endorsing Pandolfo and his scheme and stated that they were stockholders in the company and expected to buy more as soon as they were able to. They did not state, however, that they were directors in the company and that their holdings amounted to only $50.

He promised to manufacture 100,000 cars in the first year and set definite dates for the beginning of deliveries; he printed earnings of various automobile companies in his announcements. As soon as opposition began to develop on the part of various interests, such as the Post Office Department and Federal Trade Commission, the Capital Issues Committee and the Vigilance Committee of the Associated Advertising Clubs, Pandolfo began to criticize these as enemies, conspirators, "forked-tongued scorpions," "rattlesnakes" and the like, the Vigilance Committee being regarded as the "chief conspirator."

Another scheme which he used very widely was to insert extensive stories and recommendations about himself and his company in several sheets and publications which apparently exist for the sole purpose of selling their space in this manner. For example, in Chicago a publication called "Banker" and another called "Banker, Merchant and Manufacturer" printed elaborate stories. In connection with the trial, the editor of the latter publication was put into jail under a $10,000 bond. Pandolfo was likewise extensively written up in a paper called the "Daily News," in Grand Junction, Colorado. He purchased hundreds of thousands of copies of these papers and circulated them broadcast in the mails and through his agents.

Along with this printed material one favorite plan was to go to a city and get in touch with a prominent citizen who was well known to a great many people. He would secure this citizen's endorsement of the stock and of himself personally and would give him a percentage on all the stock sales made in the particular town. In company with him he would then call upon the prospects and sell the stock. After a city had been sufficiently started in this direction he would leave the town in the hands of this individual and go on to another city.

He likewise interested bankers in various cities. He

would organize a Bankers' Advisory Board and promise to pay them a commission of 10% on all cars sold in their territory after the company was established and in operation. Their names in the meantime were used very effectively in selling stock.

A plant was actually built on a 50-acre site. One part of the plant, equipped with drop forge machinery was kept in operation by doing some work on outside contracts. The plant lost $350,000 in the short period during which it was in operation. After the buildings were up and a part of the plant in operation the next step was to have committees from surrounding cities come to see the plant in operation. These visits of inspection were written up in glowing terms in the newspapers and used to good advantage in selling stock.

As opposition from various sources became active he then referred to these various sources as giant conspiracies and brought suit against the Better Business Bureau of Minneapolis for $1,000,000; against the Arizona Bankers Association for $1,000,000; against the *World's Work* for $500,000; against the *Financial World* for $500,000; against the Durango, Colorado, *Democrat* for $500,000; against E. T. Taylor for $250,000 and against Richard H. Lee, special counsel of the Associated Advertising Clubs, for $100,000. None of these cases were ever tried.

The Vigilance Committee, through its special counsel, pursued the matter and finally brought the case to a successful termination on December 16, 1919, when the Federal Court in Chicago sentenced Pandolfo to 10 years in prison and imposed a fine of $4,000 for the use of the mails to defraud.

During the trial it was testified that approximately $9,500,000 worth of stock of the company had been sold to some 70,000 persons. Under Pandolfo's original plan the first 50% received from the sale of the stock was to go to him personally. Approximately $7,500,000 was collected from the sales. Some $2,000,000, most of which belonged to the 50% to go to the company, remained uncollected.

The total production of the Pan Motor Company was less than 300 automobiles.

The abuse of advertising was directly responsible for Pandolfo's conviction. The indictment charged misrepresentation in letters and literature mailed to prospective stockholders.

Of next importance to the elimination of one fraudulent advertiser by this trial, Mr. Lee believes is the fear which has been thrown into publishers of "write-up" journals and publishers who undoubtedly allow fake advertising to appear in the columns of their publications. Mr. Lee gives as his reason for this belief the fact that Judge Landis sent to jail under $10,000 bail the editor of a journal that "pulled the high sounding name of *Banker, Merchant and Manufacturer*," when at the trial it was disclosed that a paid endorsement had been given the Pan Motor Company in its editorial columns.[1]

A fuller account of this case is given in *Associated Advertising*, January, 1920.

Bidwell's International Automobile League. About 10 years ago, Mr. A. C. Bidwell organized one of the most fraudulent companies that has ever been called to the attention of the Vigilance Committee. Bidwell, through this company—which was called the International Automobile League, defrauded thousands of people and amassed a large fortune. No one knows how much money he made, for most of the records were never found. However, one record that was not destroyed proved that he had received more than a half-million dollars from the International Automobile Tire Company of Buffalo, which was one of his subsidiaries.

The International Automobile League was supposed to be a cooperative buying association through which the members might purchase standard tires and other automobile accessories at prices substantially below the market. His false price quotations on well-known automobile tires and

---

[1] *Printers' Ink*, Dec. 25, 1919, p. 59.

supplies were advertised merely as "bait" to obtain a $10 annual fee from members. These membership fees must have amounted to millions of dollars, and it was from this source that Bidwell obtained his real income. Furthermore, the members had to send cash for whatever accessories they desired, and this increased Bidwell's revenue—for he almost invariably sent them inferior goods in filling their orders.

A prospective member was given an attractive catalog in which most of the standard accessories were listed at ridiculously low prices. The reasons given were so plausible and the prices quoted so attractive, that it was almost an impossibility for anyone interested in the buying of automobile accessories to refuse to become a member. Hence, the prospective member, eager to join the League, filled out the application, not even taking time to read the fine print on the sheet.

Then the new member, desiring to partake of the benefits of the League, and at the same time to recover the cost of joining, ordered a set of Hood or Goodyear tires or some other standard brand. Soon afterwards he received a letter from Bidwell thanking him for the order, and stating that the tires would arrive at his garage within the next few days. After a day or two, the tires did arrive; but when they were unwrapped the buyer was astounded to find that the tires were not the kind that he had ordered. He had sent for Hood or Goodyear tires, and the tires which he received were stamped "National"—being manufactured by the International Automobile Tire Company of Buffalo.

Needless to say, the new member became very angry, for he suspected that he had been made a victim of a fraudulent scheme. A letter was immediately sent to Bidwell, demanding an explanation for the sending of these unheard of tires. In reply, Bidwell politely called his attention to a provision in the application which stated that, if the requested accessories were not on hand, he (Bidwell) had the privilege of forwarding an equally good substitute. Besides, he was referred to the prices in the catalog which quoted National Tires at a much higher price than those which had been specified. But, of course, Bidwell did not demand the difference in price.

Further argument was futile; and the best thing that the provoked member could do was to forget all about this affair, and charge the loss to experience.

After three or five years had passed, a letter was received for $30 or $40 dues, depending on the length of time which had elapsed. After the unpleasant experience with the tires a member would be doubly incensed at receiving a request for dues for several years. Bidwell, however, in answering, again referred the member to an unnoticed section in the application, which stated that unless a member filed his resignation by registered mail 60 days before the expiration of the year's membership, he continued to be a member. The latter also contained a prepared clipping, supposedly from some newspaper, which informed the enraged member of a similar case where a member refusing to pay his dues was brought to court and found guilty. So the disgusted member, desiring to avoid the cost of fighting the case in court, and also not wishing to bring any disgrace on his family, forwarded the money along with his resignation.

At this point the National Vigilance Committee was requested to investigate the doings of this company. Mr. Richard H. Lee, special counsel for the Committee, was instructed to gather the facts. When the desired information was acquired, Mr. Lee brought evidence of Bidwell's dishonest operations to the attention of the Post Office Department, and requested that a fraud order be issued. The summoning of Bidwell for a hearing marked the beginning of one of the biggest and longest cases ever recorded in that Department. Bidwell, sparing no expense, was defended by one of the ablest lawyers in the United States. Besides, many prominent men from all sections of the country appeared at the hearing to assist him.

Fortunately, this was not the first time that Bidwell had

been called upon to defend his questionable enterprise; and these previous cases proved of great assistance to the Committee in drawing up its plans. The Committee saw that Bidwell had always received the support of many reputable citizens, and it was this factor more than anything else that had influenced the court in its decisions.

In investigating the evidence for the defense Mr. Lee made some interesting discoveries. It was learned that Bidwell's agents had been using reputable and prominent citizens as decoys to help attract other members to the League. For instance, an agent would interview a prominent physician and persuade him to become a member. Then, the agent would suggest that the doctor order a set of tires, in order that he might experience the great advantages to be derived from membership in the League. The doctor acted on the suggestion by ordering a set of high-grade tires. In due time the tires were delivered and carefully fitted on his car.

In about a month the agent would return and ask the doctor how the tires were wearing. Of course, he was informed that they were very satisfactory, for how could high-grade tires be otherwise in such a short time? But the agent, being scrupulously interested in the welfare of the doctor, would insist on going to the garage to examine the tires. On seeing the tires, he became greatly alarmed, and told the doctor that the tires were in a very unsatisfactory condition. There was only one thing to do, and that was to get another set of tires. So, before the doctor had a chance to say anything, the agent hurried off for the new tires. In about an hour he would return, and put on the brand new set of tires in place of the practically new tires that were on the car. Then, carelessly throwing the "old" tires into the corner, he would tell the doctor to give them to his chauffeur.

Of course, the doctor was very much surprised, and highly pleased with this splendid service, since he had received two new sets of high-grade tires for less than the price of one set. Being in this grateful mood, he thanked the agent and told him that the International Automobile League was certainly a wonderful association. The agent, in return, suggested that if that was the way he felt about it, he (the doctor) ought to write a letter to the president, for Bidwell would be delighted to know that his methods were appreciated. The doctor acted on the suggestion, and thereafter his letter was used to influence prospective members to join the League. It was this scheme that brought prominent professional and business men to testify in behalf of Bidwell and his League—and they were honest in their friendliness.

The Vigilance Committee had discovered these things, and was prepared to offset such testimony, as Mr. Lee had collected evidence from thousands of members and former members, who had not received the same special treatment as the doctor referred to. Then, when Bidwell's counsel offered to present the testimony of reputable citizens in behalf of the League, Mr. Lee declared that he had such a mass of testimony from people who had been mistreated by the League, that he would produce one hundred such depositions for every favorable witness the defendant presented. Bidwell's counsel, unable to accept this challenge, rested the case right there.

The fraud order was issued, and within the next few days five more fraud orders were issued against new concerns that Bidwell tried to start one after another under the names of employees and relatives. Bidwell was then indicted by a Federal grand jury; he pleaded guilty to the charge, and was sentenced to the penitentiary. This ended one of the most interesting cases of misrepresentation and fraud that the country has ever known.

Gasoline Economizers. Another instance of deceptive advertising uncovered by the Vigilance Committee is that of various forms of gasoline economizers. As in other cases, a questionable product was put upon the market and advertised in glaring and extravagant terms. A number of these have been investigated by the National Vigilance Committee and the products in many instances have been tested by the United States Bureau of Standards; all of them have been shown to contain no elements which could in any way increase the normal energy of gasoline. Some of the typical products of this class that have recently appeared are Famo, Gas Aid, Muscle Motor Gas, Powerene, Carbocide, Ovee Ball Gas, Carbonvoid, Ogasovim, Mormiles, and Nitrolene. Statements regarding some of these products made in the advertising are as follows:

Nitrolene is a chemical discovery that attacks and softens the skin or covering on the globules of gas, causing them to dissolve the mixture quickly and releasing the imprisoned gas, thus becoming more explosive and more powerful, giving a faster and more even combustion.

To the unwary this statement may sound like convincing "scientific" argument. The United States Bureau of Standards, after examining a number of these products, made the following statement:

The natural conclusion from the tests so far performed is that nearly, if not quite all, the seeming improvement in engine operation when these elixirs, etc., are added to the gasoline is due to the reduction in the proportion of gasoline used, caused by readjustment in the carburetor, which is nearly always recommended to be made when the new fuel "dope" is added. It is, of course, a well-known fact that many engines are habitually operated on too rich a mixture, mainly for the sake of ease of starting and satisfactory operation when first started, and that the reduction in the proportion of gasoline to air will often produce all the desirable results claimed for these "tonics," etc., without the addition of any foreign material whatever. Very conclusive tests of a number of materials have shown that there is no measurable difference between the power produced by gasoline with, and the same gasoline without, the added material.

And yet the distributers of such products advertised that their use would increase the efficiency of gasoline from 15% to 100% and that power equal to that obtained from a gallon of gasoline could be obtained at a cost of only 2 to 5 cents.

Chemical analysis has shown that these "elixirs" are composed of the same constituents as moth balls; namely, naphthalene. The advertising usually states that there is no camphor in these products, which is true. There is likewise none in moth balls.

e. The Better Business Commissions. During the last few years organizations known at first as Better Business Bureaus and now as Commissions have been established at the instigation of the National Vigilance Committee, now the National Better Business Commission. The purpose of these commissions has been to carry on locally in each city active efforts, similar to those of the National Commission, toward the elimination of dishonest and objectionable advertising and related business methods. Up to the present time (1923) such commissions have been established in 38 cities, including Boston, Chicago, St. Louis, Cleveland, Indianapolis, Kansas City, Des Moines, Minneapolis, St. Paul, Spokane, Portland (Oregon), and New York City.

A commission can do the work more effectively than it can be carried out by other means. It is neither easy nor effective for one merchant to call upon his competitor and tell him that he does not believe that the statements in his advertising are true. Such a complaint would be received with the feeling that the complainant was making it out of selfish motives, and furthermore, it would be received with the attitude that it was none of his business. On the other hand, an independent organization such as a Better Business Commission, which is independently organized and supported by all types of business in a community, is able to undertake the investigation of complaints without the knowledge of the person or firm against whom the complaint is lodged as to where the complaint came from. In this way there can be no objection on the ground that the complaint was made from selfish or unjustified motives.

In most of the cities the support for a Better Business Commission is usually derived from all types of business concerns in the community. In the case of one bureau, support is derived from the Retail Shoe Merchants Association, the printing trade, furriers, the music trade, milk dealers, the engraving industry, importers, manufacturers, and advertising agencies. In most cities the newspapers take an active part in the support of the work of the commission not only in a financial way, but through direct cooperation in the suppression of objectionable advertising.

The operation of a commission is usually as follows: Anyone may submit a complaint; or the bureau itself may be active in locating cases of objectionable advertising. In either case, the source of the complaint is always confidential. The bureau then sends an investigator to the firm against which the complaint is brought; or a letter may be sent to the firm, calling attention to the nature of the complaint and asking for a statement to indicate whether or not the complaint is a justified one and what the explanation of the case may be. This statement is usually accompanied by printed information regarding the nature and work of the commission and its organization. In many instances undesirable practices are eliminated or corrected by this method. However, when this does not adjust the situation, further action is necessary. In some instances legal procedure is required. As a matter of fact, however, a large majority of cases are adjusted by calling the attention of the defendant to the complaint and by pointing out the efforts that are being made in the community to eliminate such practices. To illustrate the extent and nature of the work of a bureau, the activities of the Boston Better Business Bureau from September, 1920, to February, 1921, may be cited. During this period the Boston Bureau handled 61 cases, either upon complaint made directly to the Bureau, or referred to it by the Retail Trade Board of the Chamber of Commerce, by publications, or by other agencies.

Twenty-nine of these were cases of advertisements in daily papers which were claimed to be untruthful or misleading. Of these, eight were of a financial nature and twenty-one were mercantile.

In eight cases the advertisements were excluded from the newspapers at the instance of the Bureau. In ten cases the advertiser changed the form of the advertisement and eliminated the objectionable matter by agreement with the Bureau. In two instances the advertiser justified himself. In two instances the advertiser continued his objectionable advertisements because of the Bureau's lack of shopping funds and facilities to obtain sufficient proof with regard to them. Two cases were dealt with by the National Vigilance Committee, and three cases were still pending.

There were eight cases of adjustment between merchant and customer. Through the action of the Bureau, in seven of these adjustment was made satisfactorily to both parties. In one case the firm in question referred the matter to its attorney and the case was still pending.

Five cases of stock selling by literature sent through the mail were investigated.

Five cases were investigated for the National Vigilance Committee and for other Bureaus.

Four cases of alleged questionable and fraudulent business methods were investigated.

Two large outside store signs of objectionable and misleading character were removed at the instance of the Bureau. One case of misbranding of merchandise was examined.

In one case a retailer was forced to abandon his objectionable misuse of the United States flag.

One warning was issued to Boston newspapers against a fraudulent classified advertiser.

One investigation was made of the use of the word "velvet" as applied to certain fabrics.

One case of misleading tire advertising was bulletined at the request of the National Vigilance Committee.

A case of misleading foreign advertising was investigated.

One case was the sale of cheap jewelry as valuable goods at a jewelry auction sale.

The merchandising or retail division of a Better Business Commission operates by scrutinizing daily the advertisements and by sending shoppers to purchase merchandise regarding which there is doubt. A report is then rendered to the store whether the suspicion was confirmed or shown to be unfounded. If an objectionable practice is discovered, the matter is then taken up with the merchant.

XXI

HEADLINES

PROBABLY the most important words of an advertisement are the words of the headline. In the first place, the headline is the only part of many advertisements which the very large majority, perhaps 90%, of all readers ever catch. To this statement the objection may be urged that those persons who read no more than the headline are not the sort of persons who are apt to buy the commodity advertised because they have no need of it, no desire for it, and no interest in it. The reply to this objection is, however, that even casual impressions, when repeated often, have an unconscious effect which in the course of time acquire much weight, so that later on when the reader is actually in need of the commodity, he is decidedly influenced by these impressions in favor of the particular brand. The headline is, therefore, exceedingly important, since it is the only means whereby a selling point or favorable impression concerning the article is made upon thousands of possible buyers.

In the second place, the headline determines whether the reader will read on further into the text of the advertisement. Headlines are the guide-posts of advertisements. If the headline is sufficiently interesting and gripping, the reader will naturally read further. It is obvious that no matter how interesting or convincing the body of the text may be, it will arouse no interest and produce no conviction if it is not read. The headline, therefore, has the difficult function of putting the rest of the copy "across." It is the attention- and the interest-getter. This is particularly true when no picture is used, or when only an insignificant one is used. For example, the headline "What Does Multi-cutting Mean to You?" is more likely to arouse the curiosity of the reader to read more about the commodity than is the headline "Vertical Turret Lathes." In the first instance his curiosity is aroused to find the answer to the question. Both headlines were used in advertisements for the same machine, and as shown in Table 81, on page 490, the former headline was not only the more interesting and stimulating but the advertisement which contained this headline was the one which brought the greater returns of the two.

The processes of a personal sale are sometimes said to be as follows: the introduction; the appeal of the proposition; and the closing of the deal. In an advertisement, the headline is the introduction; it is the first point of contact. But its function is probably more difficult as well as more important than the introduction or the entrance of the salesman. It is more difficult because the salesman, even though he makes a poor beginning, cannot so easily be turned out of doors; whereas the eyes of the reader may easily move on, or the page may readily be turned over if the headline makes no impression, if it has no appeal to stimulate further consideration of what the advertisement has to present. The task of the headline is more important than is the introduction in personal salesmanship, because the function of the headline is not only to get an entrance but also to impress upon the mind of the reader some favorable or essential point about the commodity.

In the third place, the interest and selling strength of the headline determine to a large extent the selling strength of the text as a whole. They determine the results of the advertisement probably to a much greater extent than most people, even advertisers, commonly realize. To ascertain the extent to which the general strength of the text of an advertisement is determined or represented by the headline, the following experiments were made.

Twenty advertisements recently used by the Savage Arms Company were obtained. These advertisements were very similar in all essential respects. They were all half-page spaces; they all contained a cut of the revolver of the same general appearance, put in practically the same position in the advertisement; and they all had the name of the firm at the bottom. The chief differences among the 20 advertisements were the text and the display line at the top.

Two tests were made on the basis of these advertisements. In the first one the headlines were taken by themselves and presented to a group of 114 persons with the request that they were to read them carefully and to rate them according to their strength, interest, or "gripping" qualities. They were asked to give number one to the most appealing headline, number two to the next most appealing, and so on down to the twentieth one with the least appeal.

The results show a considerable amount of uniformity and agreement among the various persons with whom the experiment was made. In spite of the belief held by some persons that each headline might appeal very differently to each person and that the most appealing headline to one person might be very uninteresting to another person, the rankings were found to agree to a remarkable extent. After these judgments had been obtained, the advertisements as a whole were presented both to the original group of persons who had rated the headlines and to a second group of persons who had never seen the headlines or advertisements before. This second experiment was made after an interval of several months so that the persons who had seen the headlines before had entirely forgotten them. These groups of persons carefully compared the 20 advertisements as a whole and numbered them in the order of persuasiveness, giving number one to the most persuasive advertisement, number two to the next most persuasive, and so on to the least persuasive one. The results of these tests are given in Table 79.

From this table it appears that there is a remarkably close agreement between the strength of the headline alone and the persuasiveness of the text of each advertisement as a whole. Thus, headline Number 1, "A Match for Any Burglar," was ranked first, and the persuasiveness of the text of this advertisement was ranked fifth. As we follow down the numbers of the two columns we notice that with few exceptions the two agree very closely. Apparently the strength

TABLE 79

COMPARISON OF EFFECTIVENESS OF HEADLINES AND TEXT

Headlines	Rank of Headlines Separately	Rank of Texts as a Whole
1. A Match for Any Burglar	1	5
2. Shoot the First Shots	2	6
3. Banishes Night Fear	3	14
4. The Only Gun a Burglar Fears	4	3
5. Detective Burns Applauds It	5	2
6. Cold Steel *vs.* Cold Sweat	6	8
7. That Finger Will Save Your Life	7	1
8. Only the Burglar Need Be Afraid	8	9
9. No Wild Shots from This Gun	9	7
10. 3,000 Burglars Loose	10	12
11. Fights for Her Life Like a Fiend	11	4
12. Must a Burglar First Come?	12	17
13. There He Is—The Burglar	13	16
14. Woman's Turn Has Come	14	15
15. Why Live in a Haunted House?	15	13
16. Chain Your Bedroom Doors	16	18
17. In the Hands of a Frightened Woman	17	10
18. Dr. Carver Banishes Burglar Fear	18	20
19. Is Yours an Egg-Shell Home?	19	19
20. Mrs. Dock—a Novice—Fires on Burglar and Tips Him	20	11
	Correlation .67	

and interest of the headline are a very significant index of the strength of the text as a whole.

A similar test was carried out with a series of eight Packer's Tar Soap advertisements. The eight headlines were rated separately according to their strength and interest. These ratings are given in Table 80 where they are compared with the actual effectiveness of the advertisement as a whole, as judged by the advertising department of the Packer's Tar Soap concern and by three members of the advertising agency which prepared these advertisements.

TABLE 80

COMPARISON OF EFFECTIVENESS OF HEADLINES WITH RETURNS
FROM THE ADVERTISEMENTS

Headlines	Rank of Headlines Separately	Effectiveness of the Advertisements
1. Real Satisfaction—Packer's Tar Soap	1	4
2. A Refreshing Shampoo with Packer's Tar Soap	2	$2\frac{1}{2}$
3. Packer's Tar Soap for Baby's Bath	3	5
4. The Standard for Hair and Skin	4	6
5. Conservation—Packer's Tar Soap	5	$2\frac{1}{2}$
6. No Woman Is Beautiful	6	7
7. Packer's Tar Soap	7	8
8. With Packer's Tar Soap	8	1
	Correlation .12	

The agreement between the strength of the headline and the effectiveness of the advertisement is on the whole again quite close with the exception of Number 8. This headline "With Packer's Tar Soap" was considered the weakest one, but the advertisement to which it belonged was the most effective one. The explanation of this discrepancy is to be found in the picture. This advertisement had a very interesting and dominating picture which gave it the strength that it had. The headline was entirely secondary.

A third test was made with a series of five Turret Lathe advertisements. The headlines were tested separately with reference to their strength and interest. The most interesting point here is their comparison with the actual "pulling power" of the advertisements as indicated by the results produced. The comparisons are shown in Table 81.

TABLE 81

COMPARISON OF EFFECTIVENESS OF HEADLINES WITH RETURNS FROM THE ADVERTISEMENTS

Headlines	Rank of Headlines Separately	Rank of Advertisements According to Results Produced
1. What Does Multi-cutting Mean to You?	1	1
2. Is Centralized Control of a Machine a Good Point?	2	2
3. The Modern Descendants of Two Good Machines	3	4
4. Study the Vertical Turret Lathe	4	5
5. Vertical Turret Lathes	5	3
		Correlation .70

The agreement between the strength of the headline and the actual results brought by these advertisements is very close. The strongest headline belonged to the advertisement which brought the largest returns. The next strongest headline was a part of the advertisement which brought the second largest returns. There are slight shifts on the others.

These investigations serve to emphasize in a new and convincing way the importance of headlines and the care and skill with which they ought to be prepared.

It was shown by means of the various tests described in Chapter XIV that the headline has approximately twice as great an influence upon the final effectiveness of an advertisement as the text itself has. The correlation between the value of the headline and the final returns brought by the advertisement (.78) was nearly twice as close as was the correlation between the value of the text and the final returns (.48).

The importance of the question, What's in a headline? is well illustrated in the recent experience of Armour and Company. Two recipe booklets entitled "Pastry Wrinkles" and "Sixty Ways of Serving Ham" were given approximately equal publicity. The company received about 50 times as many calls for the latter as for the former.

CRITERIA FOR JUDGING HEADLINES

It may be useful here to set down specific criteria by which a headline may be evaluated, at least so far as individual judgment can do so. A headline has two important aspects, the mechanical aspect and the meaning aspect. By the mechanical aspect is meant type and its arrangement. The meaning aspect refers to the content of the statement. Accordingly we may set down the following criteria:

I. *Mechanical Aspects*
1. The type should be large enough to set it off and secure the attention of the reader.
2. The headline should have as few words as possible so that it may be read as quickly as possible.
3. The type and the arrangement of the words should make the reading as easy as possible.
4. The headline should be located where it will be seen to the best advantage.

II. *Meaning Aspects*
5. The headline should say something worth while about the article or the message of the advertisement.

    a. It should be relevant rather than blind.

    b. It should state the vital or central point of the advertisement.

    c. It must be truthful, sincere and believable.

    d. It should be easy to grasp, unless otherwise sufficiently interesting to hold the reader's interest so that he will find out what it is about.

    e. It should be pleasing, not repulsive.

6. The headline should stimulate the reader to read more. It may do so

    a. By presenting news and appealing to the instinct of curiosity.

    b. By tying up with what is prominent in the minds of the class of persons to be reached.

    c. By appealing to fundamental instincts and human interests.

Tipper, Hotchkiss, Hollingworth and Parsons point out that a headline should be short, specific, apt, original and interesting. Not every characteristic is absolutely necessary in every individual headline. For certain purposes a headline may be longer or shorter; it may be more specific in some cases or more general in others, and so on. Brevity is undoubtedly an important feature. What is known in psychological terminology as the principle of counter-attraction or isolation (see chapter XXV) has an important application here. According to this principle the amount of attention given to an object or a series of objects depends upon the absence of counter-attraction or the extent to which the objects are isolated from other objects. It has been shown by psychological tests that the number of objects or words which can be grasped simultaneously by the eye is, for the average person, four or five. On this basis, the headline, which ought to be capable of being read instantaneously or nearly so, should be as short as possible.

Let us now consider more fully the criteria for evaluating headlines and their application in concrete cases.

Size of Type for Headlines. A brief discussion bearing on this point may be found in the chapter on Layout, Chapter XXV.

Length of Headline. One of the psychological principles of securing attention is known as the law of isolation or counter-attraction, and may be stated in the following general terms: *Other things being equal the amount and duration of attention* depend upon the absence of counter-attraction. That is, the fewer the number of objects, the greater are the chances that any given object will attract attention. A single person going by your window is more certain of being noticed than the same person in a crowd. One conspicuous feature on a printed page or on a billboard is more certain of being noticed than a dozen.

Experimental Demonstration of the Law. The law of counter-attraction was demonstrated experimentally as follows: To each of 10 persons a set of cards was exposed for a brief interval of time. The first card contained 5 words, the second 10, and the third 25. Immediately after the exposure of a card each person wrote down the words he had noticed.

Number of words exposed	5	10	25
Average number of words noticed by each person	5	4.9	4.8

The average number of words noticed was 5 and this number was practically constant, no matter how many words were exposed. The test shows that the greater the number of words, the smaller are the chances that any particular word will be noticed. Thus, when only 5 words were shown, each word was certain of being noticed; when 10 words were shown, the chances were one in two that a given word would be seen; and when 25 words were exposed, the chances were one in five that any particular word would be noticed.

The basis of this law is the fact that the grasp of the attention is limited, a fact which holds not only for visual impressions, but also for auditory and tactual impressions. Thus, in a rapid succession of sounds no more than five or six can be recognized at a single impression. The same is true of touch. If you place your finger upon a group of raised points you can recognize at a single impression not more than five or six. This fact is observed in the construction of the alphabet for the blind, in which the maximum number of raised points for a letter is six.

This principle has a significant bearing upon the structure of the display line. In the usual habit of glancing over advertisements the time given to any one feature is almost momentary. It is obvious that if the reader is to derive anything from this snapshot impression which may further interest him in the advertisement, the headline must contain no more than the mind can grasp instantaneously or at least quickly. We have demonstrated that this limit is approximately four or five words for the average person. It would follow that unless there are definite reasons to the contrary, which is rarely the case, a good headline ought to be limited to the fewest number of words possible—not more than four or five, and preferably less. A larger number of words should be used only when there are special circumstances which demand it. Note the difference in quickness and ease with which the two headings in Figure 44 can be grasped. If a prominent illustration is used, the structure of the headline is not quite so important a matter.

INCREASE IN USE OF SHORT HEADLINES

It is significant to note here that the number of headlines containing five words or less has gradually increased as advertising has improved, so that today the large majority of high-grade advertisements have short headings. The long,

> # Campbell's Tomato Soup
>
> # America's biggest maker of yarns tells how to wash knitted things

Figure 44: Showing the difference in quickness and ease with which a long and short heading may be grasped *(See page 494)*

wordy headline has gradually tended to disappear. Observation and experience have proved the short, terse headline to be the best, because it can be grasped more quickly and therefore has greater attention-value.

The figures below, compiled from the advertising sections of standard magazines, show for several years the percentage of full-page advertisements containing short headlines, that is, headlines of five words or less.

1881	37%	1890	59%
1885	57%	1909	87%

Thus it appears that in the standard mediums all but a small percentage of the full-page advertisements have short headings. The proportion has grown in the last 25 or 30 years from 37% to 87%. Good judgment and wide experience have proved the short heading to be the more effective.

The Magazine Test. This fact is further borne out by the results of our magazine test. In this test a person was asked to look through the advertising section of a magazine for 20 minutes. Then he was asked to write down the advertisements he remembered having seen. This test was made with 374 persons and is described more fully in Chapter XXIII. If we consider the advertisements in which the headline is the chief means of arresting attention, we find that the advertisements with the short display lines were noticed and remembered much oftener than the advertisements with the long display lines, as the tabulation below indicates. There were ten full-page advertisements and seven half-page advertisements which had either no cut at all or else an entirely insignificant one. In this division the advertisements whose display line contained five words or less were mentioned between two and three times as frequently as the ones whose display line contained six words or more. It is self-evident that for this comparison advertisements without illustrations only could be used, because in advertisements which have a prominent illustration the display line is of less importance as an attention feature, and in fact should ordinarily be less conspicuous.

FULL-PAGE ADVERTISEMENTS

	Headline Five Words or Less	Headline Six Words or More
Number of advertisements	5	5
Number of mentions	33.6	13

HALF-PAGE ADVERTISEMENTS

	Headline Five Words or Less	Headline Six Words or More
Number of advertisements	3	4
Number of mentions	5.3	2.2

These results indicate that in the case of full-page advertisements the ones which had short headlines (5 words or less) were recalled about 2½ times as often as were the ones which had long headlines (6 words or more). Practically the same ratio held for the half-page advertisements.

Form of Heading. Since the function of the heading is to present at a glance the gist of the advertisement, its form should be such that it can be read at a glance. The heading should therefore be concise and to the point. As has been pointed out, the number of words should not, as a rule, exceed five—in fact, a smaller number is preferable. Short words are preferable to long words. A one-line or "single-deck" heading is ordinarily better for advertisements than a heading with two or three "decks." Several forms are shown in Figure 45. When a heading must be long it should be arranged so as to make it as legible as possible.

Location of Headline. This point belongs more appropriately in the chapter on Layout where a brief discussion will be found. The chief consideration to be borne in mind is that the headline should be placed where it will be seen most readily or lead most directly to further reading, or connect immediately with the text or illustration to which it relates.

STATING THE VITAL POINT OF THE ADVERTISEMENT

This requires a great deal of keen analysis on the part of the copywriter. He must pick out the most dynamic idea in the whole advertisement and then state it tersely. For example, "Spare Time Money" is an excellent heading for an advertisement of the Curtis Publishing Company to secure canvassers for its publications. It strikes the nail on the head, and appeals exactly to the persons who are likely to be interested in this sort of work.

An advertisement in a college publication, designed to secure students for the purpose of selling aluminum ware during the summer vacation, might use any one of the following headlines, some of which have been actually used:

How
hundreds
of women
double
their
VACATION
ALLOWANCES!

**The advice of
your home banker
helps other business men**

The Secret of Greater
Power and Speed

Not Mere Oats

Figure 45: A heading should ordinarily be confined to one or two decks. The first one has too many decks. The third and fourth are good examples of a single- and double-deck headline. *(See page 497)*

It Pays   Make Money
Aluminum Ware   A Paying Proposition
Earn Your College Expenses

There is a quite obvious difference in the relevancy and selective nature of these headings. The first is blind and could be used for advertising anything from a thumb-tack to an adding machine. It is general and indefinite, and relates only indirectly to the essential points of the text. The second is stereotyped and relatively uninteresting. The rest have perhaps an ascending degree of definiteness and interest-value. The young man who makes his own way through college is practically the only one interested in the proposition, and therefore the last two headings would be more to the point.

The headline should give the gist of the advertisement, so that it may attract just that class of individuals who are likely customers. It should act as a sort of sieve for sifting out only the potential customers. "The Car for the Business Woman" will secure the interest of this particular class of possible buyers of automobiles.

A Chicago medical house was having considerable difficulty some years ago with its advertising. It apparently was producing only mediocre results. The headline was "Cold Feet" in black Gothic type. It was planned along logical lines. The ad meant to attract people who were bothered with cold feet.

Somehow that copy didn't attract very well. An agency man suggested changing the word "cold" to "warm." It was done as an experiment. Not another word in the advertisement was changed.

In a twinkling the copy began landing the orders. To people with cold feet there was a lure in the words "warm feet," and the advertisement so headed brought back their orders. The same copy with the same headline is running today.[1]

BLIND HEADINGS

So far as the irrelevant or blind heading is concerned,

---

[1] *Printers' Ink,* Jan. 4, 1921, p. 17.

there is little by way of commendation that can be said for
it. In the early days of patent medicine advertising it was
considered the height of skilful advertising to shout
"Murder" in a bold headline and then tell a cruel tale of
assassination and finally refer at the end to So-and-So's
pills or bitters. Clean advertising today looks with disap-
proval upon such methods. The present tendency has been
very distinctly away from irrelevant material in advertisements and toward a straight-forward presentation of the
proposition. Statistics show that in 1890 and earlier, about
15% of the full- and half-page advertisements contained
either irrelevant headings or irrelevant illustrations; about
5% used both. Today less than half as many advertisements
use irrelevant material. The opinions of nearly all advertising experts are against the use of blind headings and cuts.

Objections to Blind Headings. The chief objections to
irrelevant displays are: 1. An irrelevant headline or cut
gives absolutely no information about the article or about
the proposition. Its only excuse can be to arrest the momentary attention of the reader. But relevant material will
do that just as well and, in addition, will impart some facts
or qualities about the goods. It is no less absurd than it
would be for a salesman to spend most of his time talking to
his customers about events in distant parts of the world and
at the end of his conversation to refer incidentally to his
line of goods. As a matter of fact, the salesman in this
case would have a certain efficiency, because he would
finally get in a word about his goods, whereas one seldom
reads the irrelevant advertisement far enough to learn even
the name of the article advertised.

2. Blind and misleading headings often give the reader a
feeling of being deceived and trapped into reading something in which he is not in the least interested. This is
particularly true of advertisements set up so as to resemble
the regular reading matter of a newspaper. In such in-

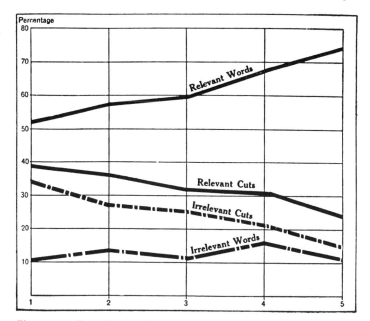

Figure 46: Chart showing the permanent attention and interest value of relevant and irrelevant cuts and words when used as headlines

stances the blind heading becomes a blind trap and it makes the reader a permanent enemy.

3. Irrelevant material does not have as much permanent attention and interest value as does relevant copy. Gale [1] made some experiments to determine the interest value of relevant words, relevant cuts, irrelevant words, and irrelevant cuts as headlines. He used actual advertisements in which each of these features was prominent and tested them by means of the rapid exposure method in five successive trials. His findings are set forth in the curves of Figure 46. These curves show that relevant words rank the highest for attention value and that they tend to increase in interest in the successive trials. Next in value come relevant cuts, then irrelevant cuts, and last irrelevant words. These last

[1] Gale, *Psychology of Advertising*, p. 50.

tend to decrease in interest in successive exposures. By these repeated exposures Gale approximated the condition of a reader seeing the advertisement in different mediums or repeatedly in the same medium. The results indicate that as soon as the novelty of the irrelevant material has worn off the advertisement loses in interest, whereas the strictly relevant material maintains interest because it actually furnishes something for further consideration.

4. The memory value of irrelevant material is usually less. Thus in the magazine test referred to earlier in this chapter it was found that many of the irrelevant display lines or cuts were remembered, but that the persons did not recall what the advertisement was about. Several recalled seeing a picture of a "woman and a snake," or "a man plowing dollars," or "a girl driving," but they did not remember that the first was an advertisement of books, the second of a railroad, and the third of a soap. Shryer, in his table of results, page 566, shows that the irrelevant blind copy used in the 36-line space brought many inquiries, but they were of an undesirable kind. It "caught" many curiosity seekers who inquired for the sake of inquiring. The result was that while the cost per inquiry was low the cash return per dollar of advertising cost was less than the cash returns of any other space except the 20-line space. The 20-line space was ineffective because of the absence of illustrations.

There are no doubt rare exceptions in which irrelevant matter is justified and possibly more effective than relevant matter. When such exceptional instances turn out well it is usually because they are very skilful appeals to curiosity.

STIMULATING READING OF THE TEXT

The effective headline must lead the casual observer to read the text.

Using the News Factor. A headline may arouse interest by stating some significant, live news element relative to the goods advertised. News always appeals to the sense of curiosity.

The following are typical examples of advertisements which employ the news element in their headings:

New Speed in Billing (Typewriter advertisement).

The Trained Man Has Money (International Correspondence School).

Every Grocery Store a Pure Milk Station (Borden Co.).

In Front of the White House (Tarvia).

Appealing to Human Instincts. Interest may always be stimulated by appealing to some fundamental human need or instinct. This applies not only to the headline, but to the advertisement as a whole. The advertiser constantly demands "Put human interest into your copy." Psychologically, this simply means an appeal to the deep-seated human desires and instincts, such as curiosity, personal pride and ambition, social distinction, economy, comfort, pleasure, and so on, which were discussed in Chapter XII.

Many of the advertisements of the International Correspondence School appeal to the personal ambition of the young man by such headings as, "Here Is the Job—Now Produce," "Big Pay If You Can Do It," "Opportunities for Government Positions," "The Talk That Made Bill and Broke Jim."

Much of the advertising of the Royal Tailors appeals to the instinct of social superiority by headlines such as these: "When You Become a Royal Tailored Man," "It's Funny What a Difference a Few Clothes Make."

Appeals to such desires, deeply ingrained in human nature, are the most pulling incentives to interest and action that can be applied.

An inducement to further reading may often be successfully brought about by the statement of something in the headline which relates to an unusual event, uppermost in the minds of people. The excavation in 1923 of the tomb of the Egyptian king, Tutankhamen, was widely utilized by retailers, who named styles after costumes discovered in the tomb or referred to the event in other ways. The work of excavating and examining the findings was one of the leading news items of the day for a considerable period of time.

It seems rather hopeless to attempt any systematic classification of the bewildering variety of headlines used in current advertising; however, a little analysis shows that they fall into a rather small number of fairly distinct classes, according to the purpose which each one attempts to accomplish.

(a) The name of the firm or article. Examples of this are: Victor-Victrola, Community Silver, The House of Kuppenheimer, or the Willys-Overland Company.

(b) The statement of a selling point, such as "Starts, Ignites, Lights" (used by the Remy Electric Company); "Men's Shirts $3" (used by the Life-Long Silk Company); or "Cooks Better" (used by the Kalamazoo Stove Company).

(c) The indirect or suggestive heading. This is closely allied to the preceding class and differs from it mainly in that the value or utility of the article is stated or suggested somewhat indirectly, such as "Your Home and Your Neighbor's" (used for paint by the Lowe Brothers Company); "When You Build" (used by the Hydraulic Press Brick Company) or "If You Manifold" (used by L. C. Smith Bros. Typewriter).

(d) Irrelevant or blind headings, such as "Burglars" (used for a breakfast food), "We want," "Here it is," and so forth.

Each one of these classes except the first may be subdivided according to the grammatical form of the statement, as a direct declarative statement, a question, or a command. Hence we often speak of declarative, interrogatory, or imperative headings. For example, the heading of the Kalamazoo Stove Company may be "Cooks better," or "Do you want to cook better?" or simply "Cook better!" Each form has a certain advantage for certain purposes.

RELATIVE MERITS OF DIFFERENT CLASSES OF HEADINGS

The use of the name of the firm or of the goods is in general a good, conservative, dignified form of headline. It reveals at once whose advertisement it is. The name of the article is, as a rule, better than the name of the firm. It is usually shorter and states just what is being presented. The name "Tiffany & Co." is used regularly by this firm as the display line. There are many readers who have seen this name frequently, but who could not say what the firm makes or sells. The display "Community Silver" is much more to the point. It combines the trade-name with the class of goods advertised. The advertiser should realize that, no matter how well he may be known, there is always a certain percentage of the readers who do not know the firm, and as a rule they are the ones to be sought after as the field for new trade. The mere displaying of the firm name is effective, but it requires a longer time and more frequent presentation of the advertisement. It is desirable, therefore, when possible to combine the firm name with the commodity.

A Selling Point as Heading. The statement of a selling point in the headline is more apt to arouse interest than is the simple statement of the name. It gives opportunity to employ in original and forceful ways the news factor and thereby stimulates curiosity and a feeling of inquiry. It furthermore gives some definite point in favor of the goods. The heading "Men's Shirts $3" not only states the article but also the fact that it is a high-grade shirt. The heading "$1,250 for Husbands," used by the Curtis Publishing Company in a recent advertisement, contains a stirring news element which is quite sure to arouse interest in further reading.

The following experience is an illustration of the result of a change in copy based chiefly upon the news element in the headline:

Years ago an advertising solicitor went to the maker of a device for deaf persons. The solicitor was to furnish a new piece of mail-order copy for this advertiser. If the copy brought results, there was a large piece of business in it for him. Former copy had been pulling fairly well, but it was not entirely satisfactory to the ambitious advertiser. He wanted inquiries under a dollar each.

The solicitor went back to his agency and put the best man in the place at work on this problem. The copywriter dug, dug, dug for three weeks. Several hundred pieces of copy were torn up before he was satisfied he had the right one.

It was presented to the advertiser, who o.k.'d it without comment. It was tried out in a few mediums first. It pulled consistently. Inquiry cost dropped to 34 cents. At once it went into the concern's entire list. Its size was only three inches. Within a year it had quadrupled the business of the manufacturer. The headline was the basis for the entire copy. It was: "The Deaf Now Hear Whispers."

In the first place, the headline is short enough to be taken in at a glance of the eye. It was arranged in two lines—a stephead. You know that the eye grasps but four words at a single glance. There were three short words on one line, and two on the other.

In the second place, the headline is news. Third, it attracts the natural market at which it is aimed—the deaf people. The word "deaf" does that.[1]

The effect of a statement of the vital selling point in the headline is well illustrated in the following example:

There are a number of manufacturers of "knock-down" houses who are securing excellent results from their advertising.

One of them, several years ago, was selling his output at an advertising cost of less than $2,100, this amount being expended

---

[1] *Printers' Ink*, January 4, 1912, p. 17.

in small copy run several times in a very few mediums. The copy was usually only about two inches double column in size. Sometimes it ran to three inches double column.

. . . . Such headlines as "The Ideal Knock-Down House," "Your Summer Home $———," "Build Your Own Summer Home," were used to advantage. They pulled the inquiries, and with an ordinary follow-up system landed enough orders to dispose, each year, of an output slightly larger than the year previous.

. . . . He (the agency copywriter) remembered having once erected one of the houses in less than two hours. The thought struck him that this would make an excellent topic for one of the advertisements in the campaign. It happened that, instead of writing an entire advertisement on the subject, he was compelled to take an advertisement very similar to one utilized the year previous, and he merely scratched out a somewhat platitudinous headline and wrote this for the headline: "Build Your Own House in Two Hours."

. . . . The entire advertisement was two and a half inches double column. . . . Along in May or June of a year or so ago this advertisement—the first of the campaign—appeared in one of the well-known national weeklies . . . . The week the advertisement appeared the manufacturer received 1,000 inquiries from this five-inch piece of copy. To him, that in itself was extraordinary. Before the advertisement ceased pulling it brought 3,000 inquiries and it was scarcely a month later when the year's output was sold. This advertisement had pulled more than six times the number of inquiries of any previous advertisement— solely as a result of a changed headline. A correctly gaged headline effected the sale of the entire year's output. The remainder of the space was canceled.[1]

The Question and the Command. The interrogatory form of heading tends to arouse curiosity. A question naturally stimulates a response as a matter of habit. Likewise, the command is a forceful form of caption. It is particularly useful in advertisements aiming to secure immediate action, because the immediate impulse in response to a command is to obey it. This fact is based upon the subtle power of suggestion and habit.

There are numerous instances of successful command headings.

[1] *Ibid*, February 28, 1912, p. 28.

The Pompeian Massage Cream People know that their headline, "Don't Envy a Good Complexion: Use Pompeian and Have One," has probably sold more of their product for them than any other headline that has ever been used as a caption for their advertisements.[1]

Others of the same type that have pulled effectively are, "Don't be a Pump, Buy One," used by the Fuller & Johnson Company; later, "Don't be an Adding Machine, Buy One!" was used by an adding machine manufacturer, and Dickson's "Stop Forgetting" has brought large returns. The Pompeian heading is rather long, but it is exceptionally "catchy" and suggestive.

RELATIVE FREQUENCY OF USE OF DIFFERENT KINDS OF HEADINGS

In this connection it is interesting to notice the relative frequency with which the different classes of display lines are used in current mediums. A tabulation of the 325 ad-

TABLE 82

FREQUENCY WITH WHICH DIFFERENT KINDS OF HEADLINES ARE USED

Kinds of Headings	Full-Page	Half-Page	Quarter-Page	Smaller Spaces
Name of article	60%	65%	68%	28%
Name of firm	4	4	3	0
Selling point	16	5	13	25
Indirect heading	10	16	10	19
Blind heading	4	0	0	5
Command	3	8	3	19
Question	3	2	3	4

vertisements appearing in an issue of *Everybody's Magazine* (in 1912) showed the percentage given in Table 82 for each class of heading and for each size of advertisement.

The name of the goods is used as the caption by approxi-

[1] *Ibid.*, January 4, 1912, p. 17.

mately two-thirds of all advertisements except the very small ones. The next largest class is the statement of a selling point either stated directly or suggested indirectly. These selling-point headlines comprise about one-fourth of all headings. Another significant fact is that the very small advertisements use the command and the statement of some selling point far more frequently than do the larger spaces. This is no doubt to be explained by the fact that the users of small space are seeking for immediate returns more generally than the users of large space. And possibly under the pressure of using small space they are forced to make their proposition just as interesting, forceful, and concentrated as possible. Hence the command and the selling argument are uppermost in the mind of the copywriter.

CATCH PHRASES AND SLOGANS

Catch phrases such as "Ivory soap, it floats," are elements in advertising which are closely related to headlines. They are designed primarily to popularize and impress upon the minds of the people some significant point about a commodity or a proposition. Many national advertisers have developed such phrases and popularized them very successfully. Psychologically they are simply an aid to memory.

The requisites for a good catch phrase are that it should be short, euphonious, rhythmical, alliterative. Not all of these features are necessary for a successful slogan, but they may all contribute in one instance or another. The words of a slogan should rhyme or at least have a pleasing sound so that they may be easy to remember, easy to speak, and "catchy," so as to induce repetition, for that is just the purpose of the slogan. A phrase with rhyming words and poetical cadence is retained in mind more easily, as has been shown by experimental studies. In school, various things that have to be committed to memory, such as the months of the year, the number of days of the different months, grammatical forms, and the like, are frequently taught to children by constructing them into rhymes. The following are some of the popularized slogans:

Works without waste (Sapolio).
Ivory soap, it floats.
Have you a little fairy in your home? (Fairy soap).
Hasn't scratched yet (Bon Ami).
There's a reason (Postum Company).
Costs more—worth it (Occident Flour).
Ask the man who owns one (Packard automobile).
The machine you will eventually buy (Underwood typewriter).
You can pay more but you can't buy more (Royal typewriter).
From Kalamazoo direct to you (Kalamazoo Stove).
His Master's Voice (Victor phonograph).
Don't travel—telephone (Bell Telephone Company).
The Ham what am (Armour & Co.).
Hammer the hammer (Iver Johnson revolver).
The road of a thousand wonders (Southern Pacific).
The watch that made the dollar famous (Ingersoll watch).
Who's your tailor? (E. V. Price & Co.).
Eventually—why not now? (Gold Medal).

Most of the preceding phrases are constructed on the correct principles. Particularly good are "From Kalamazoo direct to you" or "Ask the man who owns one." They are suggestive of worth and convenience. The latter contains an implied challenge, laying the record and efficiency of the commodity open to the best possible test, namely, the test of experience on the part of the user. Such a challenge carries with it greater power of conviction.

On the other hand, such a phrase as "Who's Your Tailor?" is meaningless and devoid of any suggestive worth. The phrase is not apt to be associated more readily with one tailor than with another. "For school life and life's school" is too difficult to speak and lacks rythmical swing. It reminds one of the phrase "She sells sea-shells." "The watch that's made for the majority" also is weak in rhythm and "catchiness." It would seem obvious that the advertiser wastes money when he spends large sums in the effort to popularize his products by phrases totally lacking in meaning and "catchiness."

HOW TO TEST HEADLINES

After the best judgment and skill have been exercised in preparing headlines, the surest method of determining the value and appropriateness of various possible headlines for a given product is to submit them to a brief but adequate series of tests. Two types of tests may be conveniently conducted: One for the purpose of ascertaining the relative values of the mechanical aspects; the other for measuring the relative values of the meaning aspects.

For measuring the mechanical aspects, a convenient procedure is to use what is known as the rapid exposure method. The headlines should be set up exactly in the form in which they are to appear in the advertisement. These headlines should then be shown one at a time in brief exposure to the observer. He should be asked to write down, after each headline is shown, what he has seen or grasped. By repeating this test with a number of persons a fairly accurate measure will be obtained of the relative legibility of the various headlines and the extent to which the reader is able to grasp each one in a short interval of time. Variations of this method may be devised for various purposes.

To measure the meaning aspect, a useful procedure is to apply the ranking method previously discussed. That is, a series of headlines may be submitted to a person with the request that he rank them in the order in which they impress him in favor of the product, and arouse his interest so as to cause him to read more of the advertisement. These are the two chief meaning functions of a headline. That the headline can be evaluated with a satisfactory degree of accuracy by this method has been demonstrated by tests

TABLE 83

RELATIVE EFFECTIVENESS OF HEADLINES COMPARED WITH THE
EFFECTIVENESS OF THE ADVERTISEMENTS

Ads	Text of Headlines	Median Rank	Final Rank
G	Save $43 by being your own salesman. Try the Oliver for five days at our expense	5.72	1
N	Was $100—now $57—A finer typewriter at a fair price—Buy direct via coupon —Save $43	5.94	2
K	Free trial—a finer typewriter at a fair price—Send no money	6.25	3
B	Over $700,000 sold—A $100 Oliver for $57	6.90	4
E	Oliver economy in your office—Save $43 on each machine	6.95	5
D	A stenographer's advice on typewriter buying—How to save $43	7.25	6
I	Free trial—Keep it for $3 per month or return it at our expense	7.56	7
F	A finer typewriter at a fair price—Only $3 a month after free trial	8.25	8
L	Via coupon—Save $43. This Oliver is shipped from the factory to you for free trial	8.92	9
A	Save $43 now—The guarantee of a $2,000,000 concern is back of every Oliver typewriter	9.25	10
O	Two ways of selling the Oliver typewriter —Old indirect and new direct. The new way saves you $43	9.75	11
C	Save $43 now—No need now to pay $100 for a new Oliver typewriter — latest model	9.92	12
J	Brand new Oliver No. 9—Save $43— Be your own salesman	10.56	13
H	The greatest typewriter buy—And our new self-selling plan	12.05	14
M	Big business welcomes the Oliver plan	12.95	15

conducted in this manner, reported in Chapter XIV. The correlation between the relative values of the headlines of a series of advertisements, as measured by the ranking method, and the actual effectiveness of the advertisements as a whole as indicated by the returns brought, is in the neighborhood of .75. This indicates that our method of measuring the relative effectiveness of headlines is valid and fairly accurate and also that the headline is an exceedingly important feature of an advertisement.

To illustrate concretely the results of a typical series of tests on a group of headlines the following data are presented in Table 83. Fifteen headlines used in Oliver typewriter advertisements were ranked by 85 persons, mostly business men and women. The numbers in the first column at the right give the median ranks of the respective headlines and the last column gives the final ranks, that is, the ranks of the medians.

The tests showed that the best headline is G, "Save $43 by being your own salesman. Try the Oliver for five days at our expense." The poorest one is M, "Big business welcomes the Oliver plan." It is easy to see why the former is the best and the latter the poorest when we have the results of the test before us, but it would be a highly difficult undertaking for any given individual—even though he were an expert copywriter—to tell which of these would be the best and which the poorest and how the others would stand between these extremes. The correlation between the test ranking of these headlines and the actual returns brought by the advertisements containing the headlines was .75.

XXII

ILLUSTRATIONS

The part played by pictures in conveying ideas to the mind of the reader. Increase in the use of pictures. The functions of an illustration. Criteria for judging an illustration. 1. Attention and interest value. 2. Illustrative value. 3. Artistic value.

PICTURES play a highly important part in conveying ideas to the mind of the reader and observer. The statement has been made that a good picture is worth a million dollars. Mankind has a natural interest in pictures, because pictures are the most realistic substitutes for the objects portrayed. Pictures speak a universal language. Before the development of methods of writing by means of letters and words, primitive people drew pictures of objects, and of animals and their actions. An illustration can represent at a glance what would require paragraphs to describe. A picture, therefore, helps to impart the message more easily, more quickly, and more completely. The importance of the picture is indicated by various phases of the tests with advertisements reported in several of the chapters in Part III. The attention value of an advertisement as a whole depends to quite an extent upon its pictorial features. The attention value of the advertisement, as shown by these tests, is approximately twice as important as the convincingness of the text itself. The attention value of advertisements correlates almost twice as closely as does the convincingness of the text, with the ultimate effectiveness of the advertisement as a whole.

In Chapter XXIV a detailed table is presented to show the returns brought by a series of 12 letters which were printed on various colored papers. A part of these letters contained cuts and a part did not. One thousand copies of each of these 12 letters were sent out to different addresses. These 12,000 names were chosen from a list of 30,000 dealers. The same letter was sent to all. The variation consisted only in color of paper and the use or absence of a cut. A tabulation of the returns with reference to the comparison of letters with cuts and without cuts is given in Table 84.

TABLE 84

RESPONSES TO LETTERS WITH AND WITHOUT ILLUSTRATIONS

Letter No.	Color	Cut Omitted	Cut Used
1	White	9%	
2	White	12%	
3	White		18%
4	White		22%
5	Corn	14%	
6	Corn		26%
7	Green	16%	
8	Green		28%
9	Gold	21%	
10	Gold		34%
11	Pink	26%	
12	Pink		48%
	Average	16.3%	29.3%

From these comparisons we note that when the factor of color is either eliminated or when it occurs equally often with a cut and without one, the letters which contained a cut produced nearly twice as many replies as those which did not contain an illustration, average percentages being 29.3 against 16.3.

Generally speaking, there are two opposing camps of advertising men. The one group believes that "reason why," or logic, is all that is worth considering in the preparation of copy. The other believes that attractive pictures, artistic decorations, high-class art work, and suggestive, indirect appeals are more effective; but a complete analysis of the principles underlying the practice of advertising and a careful observation of human nature must convince one that both features are important. To be sure, the one set of factors is relatively more potent for some commodities and under certain conditions, while the other set may be more effective for other commodities and under certain other circumstances. As already pointed out we act both from reason and from suggestion. The reader may here turn to Chapter XVIII to recall the relative interest which people have in the picture and in the text of an advertisement.

To compare further the actual pulling power of advertisements with pictures as compared with those without pictures we may examine the table on page 566. In the column giving cost per inquiry it will be noticed that the 20-line copy brought the most expensive returns, namely $1.47 per inquiry, which is over twice as high as the average cost per inquiry of the others ($0.68). This 20-line copy is the only one in which no illustration was used, except the classified advertisements. Such a record as this compiled by Shryer furnishes tangible data concerning the actual attention and interest value of illustrations.

Another example of the value of illustrations is given in the following campaign:

Thomas Cort, Inc., of Newark, N. J., is now doing considerable advertising of a high-grade line of ready-to-wear, custom-made shoes. The copy is being run in the highest grade publications, usually in preferred position. The Cort shoes are made to sell for from $8 to $14 per pair. The advertiser started in February of this year. According to Mr. Tonkin, an official of the concern, the reason why no illustrations have been used in connection with his series of advertisements is the fact that it is perfectly possible to prepare cuts which will make a $3.50 pair of shoes look just as good as a pair of $14 Cort-made. . . . Although but one lone dealer inquiry has been received in four months, Mr. Tonkin explains that he is not overanxious about returns upon his advertising before December at the earliest, inasmuch as he believes that it will naturally take that long to attain its efficiency. . . .

Whether all this aversion to illustration is squeamishness, or is founded on real fact, is a matter that does not seem to be settled. The majority of indications seem to point toward the illustration of the goods wherever possible. The logic of the matter is unassailable, and only for goods of radical exclusiveness does there seem to be even a gleam of justification for refusal to show what the goods look like. Even these might improve their results if they employed art work in keeping with their pretensions. . . .

Perhaps no better illustration, by way of comparison between the illustrated advertisement and the non-illustrated advertisement, and one, by the way, bearing directly upon the Thomas Cort experiment, is at hand than the case of a certain other dealer in high-grade shoes who recently took space in *Vogue*. He preferred not to use illustrations in spite of the fact that practically every competitor, such as William Bernstein, Andrew Alexander, and J. & J. Slater, was using high-grade illustrations freely. The dealer was urged to use at least one illustration, but persistently refused, preparing carefully hand-lettered copy. The results were naturally awaited with great interest. Where the advertisers who used illustrations had excellent returns, the dealer who preferred to run solid talk found practically no return for the money he had spent.[1]

INCREASE IN THE USE OF PICTURES

Illustrations have come more and more into general use in advertising during the past 50 years. A detailed study of this problem was made under the direction of the author by one of his former students, W. L. White. The method of this investigation consisted of a careful examination of the advertisements appearing in two mediums, a newspaper and a weekly magazine, namely, the *New York Tribune* and *Harper's Weekly*, respectively. It was not necessary nor desirable to examine all of the advertisements in every issue of these two publications. Consequently a cross-section was taken at certain regular intervals. In the *New York Tribune* the advertisements appearing during four typical weeks of every fifth year from 1865 to 1915 were examined. The weeks chosen were the second week in January, May,

---

[1] *Printers' Ink,* June 23, 1910, p. 33.

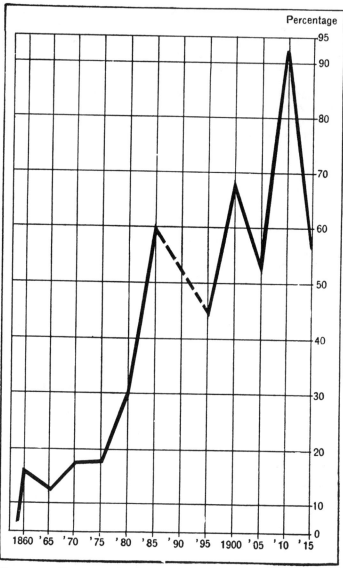

Figure 47: Percentage of total advertising area occupied by illustrated advertisements in *Harper's Weekly (See page 519)*

August, and December. The first illustration found during
this period in the *New York Tribune* was a three-inch,
single-column advertisement of Linderman & Sons, manufacturers of pianos, in the issue of May 23, 1865.

This study was undertaken to determine to what extent
illustrations were being used and for what purposes, and
what the trend in their use has been. The results are
shown in the accompanying graphs. Figure 47 shows the
percentage of advertising space occupied by illustrated advertisements. Thus, for example, in *Harper's Weekly* in
1860, 6% of the total advertising space was occupied by
illustrated advertisements. This rose to 60% in 1885 and
to 93% in 1910. It dropped in 1915 to 58%, which is
probably due to the business situation and to the decline
in relative standing of this magazine.

Figure 48 shows the percentage of area occupied by the
illustration in illustrated advertisements. Thus, in 1860,
26% of the area of illustrated advertisements was occupied by the illustration. In 1915 it was 30%. In the *New
York Tribune* it was 22% in 1865 and 25% in 1915. Evidently the proportion of the space occupied by the illustration in illustrated advertisements has not materially

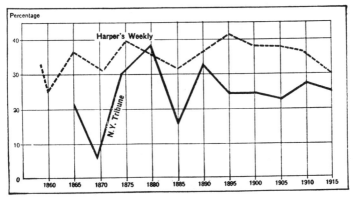

Figure 48:   Percentage of the space occupied by illustrations in illustrated
advertisements

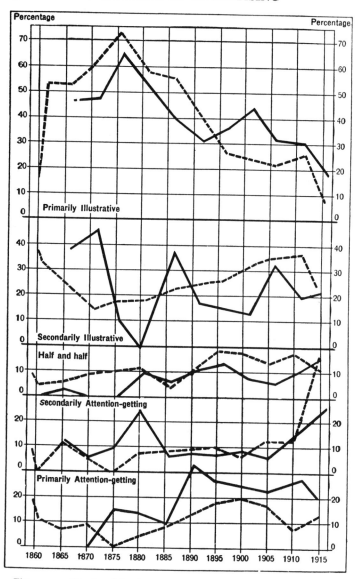

Figure 49: The trend in the purpose for which illustrations are used
(See page 521)

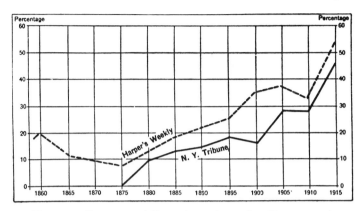

Figure 50:   Percentage of illustrations using action *(See page 522)*

changed.   However, the curve in the preceding figure shows
a very marked increase in the proportion of advertisements
which use illustrations.

Figure 49 shows the results of the analysis of the purpose
for which illustrations are used.   The two chief purposes
are (a) primarily for illustrative functions and (b) primarily for getting the attention of the reader.   In most
advertisements the two functions are combined in various
ways.   In some advertisements one or the other of these
two functions appears alone.

For the purpose of making this study concrete these two
functions were analyzed in the following five different combinations:

1. Entirely illustrative
2. Primarily illustrative and partly attention-getting
3. Equally illustrative and attention-getting
4. Primarily attention-getting and secondarily illustrative
5. Entirely attention-getting

An examination of the graphs will show that there has
been a distinct change in the use of illustrations for these

purposes. The chief changes are that the primarily illustrative function has tended to decline and the entirely attention-getting function has tended greatly to increase.

Figure 50 shows the tendency with regard to one type of illustration-appeal, namely the representation of action. The graphs show a very marked increase in the use of action pictures. In the case of *Harper's Weekly* it rose from 11% in 1865 to 56% in 1915.

A similar study dealing with the growth in the use of illustrations, covering a shorter period of time, has been reported by Dr. H. D. Kitson. The mediums examined were two weekly magazines, *Collier's* and the *Literary Digest*, and two newspapers, the *Indianapolis News* and the *Bloomington (Indiana) World*. Measurements of the advertising space were made at four-year intervals from 1895 to 1919. The years 1903 and 1911 were missing in the newspaper files. The results are presented in Figure 51. They show• that the proportion of illustrated advertisements in the magazines rose from about 70% to around 90% in the period from 1907 to 1919; and that in the newspapers the proportion rose from about 25% in 1895 to over 90% in 1919 for one paper and to about 70% for the other paper.

Kitson reported also a study of the trend in the use of particular art forms or types of illustration used. The illustrations were classified as follows: pen and ink, wash-drawing, photograph, pencil, charcoal and combination (any one of these combined with another or with color). The advertisements examined were those in two weekly publications, the *Literary Digest* and *Harper's Weekly*. Since the latter discontinued publication in 1916, *Collier's* was substituted after that date. All of the advertisements in these magazines, with the exception of the cover pages, were examined at five-year intervals from 1895 to 1920. The results are given in Figure 52. They show that the use of pen and ink illustrations has greatly decreased, dropping from 91% in 1895 to 21% in 1920. On the other hand, wash-drawings, photographs and combinations increased

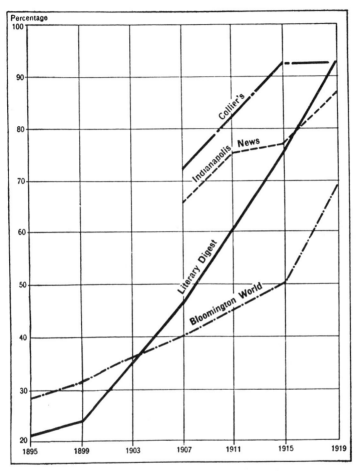

Figure 51: Percentage of advertisements containing illustrations
(See page 522)

considerably and at about the same rate. A quarter of a century ago nearly all illustrations were made by means of pen and ink. While this type has greatly decreased it is still used about as much as any one of the other three types shown in the graph.

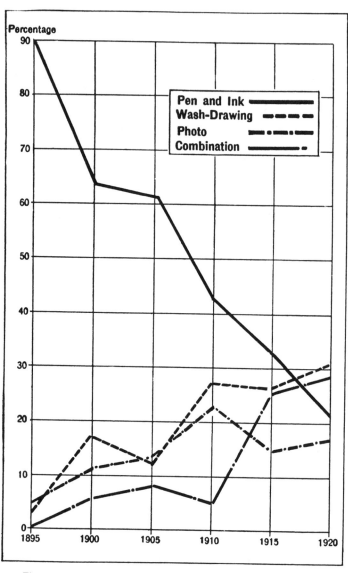

Figure 52: Tendency in the use of art forms in advertisements
(See page 522)

THE FUNCTIONS OF AN ILLUSTRATION

The primary purposes of an illustration are (1) to attract attention, (2) to make the advertisement easier to comprehend by portraying the article or illustrating some relevant point, and (3) to make the advertisement artistically pleasing, and attractive to look at. When a cut is designed to illustrate, it should really illustrate. There are, of course, advertisements in which the cut serves other purposes, but if a cut is used for the purposes of illustration, it should really exhibit the goods. It may illustrate (a) the appearance and construction of the article, or (b) the article in use, and the convenience derived therefrom, or (c) some good quality or selling point about the article. For example, a suit of clothes may be exhibited on a hanger, but a cut of a young man wearing the suit adds a touch of realism.

Illustrations may be used to give an advertisement an artistic tone or atmosphere which cannot be produced in any other way.

In the more exceptional advertisements the cuts may add to the trustworthiness of the proposition. A bank may illustrate its location and building, or the deposit vaults. A portrait, particularly in mail-order advertising, often increases confidence in the advertisement.

The portrayal of action in an illustration heightens the interest and vividness. An object in action appeals more to our interest than the same object in a stable, inactive condition. The graph in Figure 50 shows that action pictures are used far more frequently today than in the earlier history of advertising. Today, whenever human beings are portrayed in illustrations they are as often as possible represented in action.

One point, however, requires special notice here, namely, that whenever a human being or an animal is represented in action it should be shown in one of the natural resting positions of that action. That is, a picture of a man walking

WHILE passing through a wood one day
A train was wrecked and, strange to say
Some IVORY SOAP consigned to town
Was scattered through the forest brown
Then wolves and foxes, bears and all
Soon gathered round a water-fall
Said they "We often heard it said,

'It has no equal in the trade';
While men of science and of art
Pronounced it pure in every part.
But here, at last, we found an hour
To prove indeed its cleansing power
And while the IVORY SOAP we find,
Be sure we'll use no other kind!"

The cakes of Ivory Soap are so shaped that they may
be used entire for general purposes, or divided with a stout
thread into two perfectly formed cakes for Toilet Use.

Figure 53: How Ivory Soap was advertised in the early '80s

should not show him with one foot on the ground and
the other in mid-air, but both feet should be on the ground
just as he has completed a step and is ready to take the

Figure 54: How it is advertised today—an excellent example of good
taste in advertising

New charm for your
windows—at little cost

with shades of beautiful Brenlin

A well-known decorator, writing of windows, asserts that "to look upon the shades merely as 'shades' is a mistake. They can do so much to make or mar the charm of the window effect—and indeed of the whole room!"

Are you getting the most in artistic possibilities from your window shades? Are they in perfect color harmony with their surroundings? And what is their condition? Are they faded or discolored, or unsightly with cracks and pinholes? For surprisingly little money, you can literally transform the appearance of your windows with shades of beautiful Brenlin. You will notice the difference at once.

Brenlin is lovely. Among its many soft colors you will find one that blends harmoniously with your color scheme. The fabric is supple, not stiff, and always hangs straight and smooth.

What is more, Brenlin wears—two or three times as long as the ordinary shade. Brenlin fabric is a fine, closely woven material, and requires none of the brittle

clay or chalk filling that in ordinary window shades so soon falls out, causing cracks and pinholes. Experts finish Brenlin by hand and apply with the utmost care the beautiful colors that resist fading by the sun and defy stains by water. If you wish a different color on each side, get Brenlin Duplex for perfect color harmony.

Look for the name Brenlin perforated or embossed on the edge. If you don't know where to get this long-wearing shade material, write us; we'll see that you are supplied.

How to Shade and Decorate Your Windows Correctly—Free

We have your copy of this very readable and instructive booklet on how to increase the beauty of your home with correct shading and decoration of your windows. Send for it. Actual samples of Brenlin in several colors will come with it.

For windows of less importance Camargo or Empire shades give you best value in shades made the ordinary way.

THE CHAS W BRENEMAN COMPANY INC CINCINNATI OHIO
The oldest window shade house in America

Factories Cincinnati Ohio, and Camden, N. J. Branches New York City, Philadelphia, Dallas, Texas, and Portland, Ore.
Owner of the good will and trade marks of the J C. Wemaga Co

Brenlin
HAND MADE
the long-wearing
WINDOW SHADE *material*

Figure 55: Specimen of advertisement portraying the article in use

next one. Unless this is done the figure appears awkward and stilted. The chief reason for this fact is that unless a figure is represented in one of the several resting positions it appears unstable and lacking in sufficient support. Another reason is that the eyes do not see an object distinctly while they are in motion, but they stop momentarily and obtain successive glimpses of a moving object. Consequently we do not associate the unpoised positions with movement as readily as the naturally poised positions.

CRITERIA FOR JUDGING AN ILLUSTRATION

As in the case of headlines, it will be useful, in evaluating an illustration, to set down specific criteria by which a picture may be judged. Bearing in mind the functions which the illustration or picture is intended to serve in an advertisement, we may judge its value by the extent to which it serves the following purposes:

1. Does it secure attention?

Figure 56:   Example of advertisement effectively linking attention value with relevancy

2. Does it illustrate either the commodity or something connected with it?

3. Is it pleasing?

An illustration may be good even if it is not strong in all three respects, providing it is particularly strong in some one of the three important characteristics or functions. Thus, for example, a picture may not illustrate the commodity directly, but it still may be a very effective picture, provided it has a very high attention and interest value. On the whole that picture which satisfies most fully these three requirements will be the most effective one.

On the basis of the functions served by illustrations in advertisements, we may suggest the following criteria for evaluating an illustration:

1. *Attention and Interest Value*—To help secure attention and interest. The means by which this may be accomplished are in principle the same as those which apply in the case of the headline (see page 492), namely:

> a. By appealing to fundamental instincts and human interests.
> b. By presenting that which is new and appealing to curiosity.
> c. By tying up with things prominent in the minds of the persons to be reached.

2. *Illustrative Value*—To help convey the message of the advertisement

> a. It should illustrate the article or something closely related to it.
> b. Its meaning should be easy to grasp. The only exception should be a picture which is so interesting that thereby it will cause the reader to decipher the meaning.
> c. It should contain nothing unnecessary.
> d. It should be relevant rather than blind or irrelevant.

3. *Artistic Value*—To be pleasing

> a. From an artistic point of view.
> b. From the standpoint of its meaning.
> c. It should be in accord with the nature of the product and the purpose of the advertisement.

METHODS OF TESTING ILLUSTRATIONS

In accordance with the above criteria for evaluating a picture we may proceed to devise a technique for testing or measuring the relative values of pictures. To illustrate

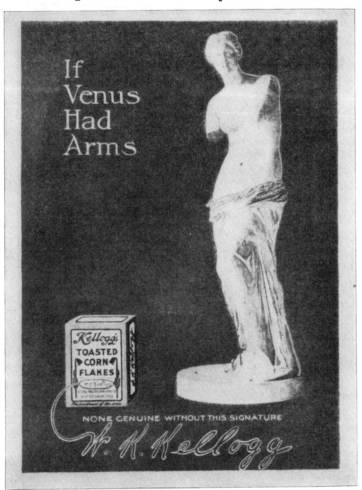

Figure 57: The illustration in this advertisement brought widely varying responses in the test for relevancy *(See page 535)*

the method, the tests made with 21 illustrated advertisements will be described briefly. The three tests were as follows:

1. *Attention Value.* Instead of using the ranking method in this instance the observers were instructed to use a percentage scale in which 100 was to be regarded as a picture

Figure 58: Specimen of advertisement that is weak in illustrative value
(See page 534)

which ideally had the highest possible attention value so that it could not be missed whenever it was brought before the observer, and o was to designate a picture which had no appeal or would probably not be noticed at all.

2. *Illustrative Value.* This quality was tested by means of what is known in psychological technique as the free association method. That is, the picture from an advertisement, without the text or name, was exposed to the observer for a period of five seconds, after which he was asked to state what the picture suggested to him or what he thought it advertised. The numbers under illustrative value in Table 85 are the percentages of persons to whom the picture suggested the article advertised or something relevant to it.

3. *Artistic Value or Pleasingness of the Picture.* This test was carried out after the plan of the attention test; that is, 100 was arbitrarily assumed to designate a picture which had the highest value of pleasingness, o to designate an indifferent picture, neither pleasing nor displeasing, and values under o were used to designate a displeasing or disagreeable picture.

TABLE 85

RESULTS OF TESTS OF ILLUSTRATIONS

Advertisement	Attention Value	Illustrative Value	Artistic Value	Average
A—Hart, Schaffner & Marx, picture of coach and horses	70%	33%	65%	56%
B—Ivory Soap, streets and snow	50	24	75	50
C—Shredded Wheat, girl and dog	75	24	35	45
D—Hart, Schaffner & Marx, two men and a horse standing	50	95	50	65

Advertisement	Attention Value	Illustrative Value	Artistic Value	Average
E—Grapenuts, dog and girl walking to school	65%	43%	65%	58%
F—Ivory Soap, automobile and men cleaning windshield	50	62	50	54
G—Ivory Soap, mother and child reading	45	19	40	35
H—Kellogg's Corn Flakes, statue of Venus	85	0	80	55
I—Kellogg's Corn Flakes, child yawning	75	33	55	54
J—Hinds Cream, child and sleigh	85	24	80	63
K—Ivory Soap, mother putting stocking on child	45	48	40	44
L—Luxite Hosiery, man and two women	80	43	65	63
M—Hart, Schaffner & Marx, Mardigras	40	19	30	30
N—Postum, woman drinking	60	100	60	73
O—Hart, Schaffner & Marx, man in foreground	40	100	15	52
P—Gold Medal Flour, city in darkness	70	0	80	50
Q—Cream of Wheat, child in a box	70		75	
R—Cream of Wheat, Rastus art gallery	75		80	
S—Pompeian Cream, woman's head	75		60	
T—Kellogg's Corn Flakes, girl spilling basket	75		40	
U—Kellogg's Corn Flakes, boy eating corn flakes	85	100	70	85
V—Prince Albert Tobacco, old man smoking	80	100	65	82

These three tests were carried out with a group of 20 men. The results are given in Table 85. The last column gives the averages for the three tests.

These results show remarkable differences among the rankings of each of these three characteristics. Thus, for example, in illustrative value or relevancy the results vary from 0 to 100. Advertisement H, Kellogg's Corn Flakes, and Advertisement P, Gold Medal Flour, never suggested to anyone the kind of product which it was intended to advertise. The artistic value or pleasingness ranges all the way from 80% in the case of several advertisements, down to as low as 15% in the case of Advertisement O—Hart, Schaffner & Marx. The combined value represented in the average will give a fairly reliable measure of the relative usefulness of these pictures.

Advertisement H, Kellogg's Corn Flakes, which showed a large picture of the statue of Venus, brought widely varying responses in the test for relevancy or association. It suggested the following commodities to the 20 persons with whom the test was made: underwear, 2; face cream, 2; soap, 2; silk, 1; pencils, 2; gymnasium, 1; architect, 1. It suggested nothing to 8 persons.

Advertisement P, Gold Medal Flour, showing a panoramic picture of a city at night in the dark, produced the following reactions in this test: men's clothing, 2; insurance, 2; talcum powder, 1; Pennsylvania Railroad, 1; construction company, 1; women's clothing, 1; soap, 1; cigarettes, 1; weed tire chains, 1; nothing, 8.

It is obvious that an advertisement containing a picture which suggests nothing relative to the commodity advertised has a heavy momentum to overcome in presenting its message.

XXIII

THE SIZE OF ADVERTISEMENTS

The problem of size of space and frequency of repetition or insertion. Tendencies in the use of space. Experimental data on the value of space. Conclusions based on experiments. Results of business experience. "Mortality rate" of advertisers. Experience of advertisers. Factors in the use of space. Conclusion.

THE problem of the size of advertisements, coupled with the problem of the frequency of insertion, is an extremely important one, both from the point of view of the economic expenditure of a given advertising appropriation and also from the point of view of the public, which often raises the criticism that the use of large space is an uneconomical expenditure of money. The critic feels that a full-page or a two-page advertisement says no more than a half-page or a quarter-page advertisement, and therefore it must represent a waste of money and paper. However, the problem is an intricate one, and cannot be disposed of with a superficial consideration of this sort. Concretely, the problem comes down to the question, What is the most effective expenditure of a given amount of money? Assuming a certain fixed expenditure for advertising, the ultimate problem is, will it be more effective to use space in large units less frequently or in small units more frequently, or possibly an alternation of large and small units in varying succession? That this problem has always been considered important is indicated by the following interesting encouragement given in early Colonial days by a Boston paper to its small advertisers: "Keep on advertising. Don't fear to have a small advertisement by the side of a larger competing one. The big one can't eat it up." [1]

[1] Sampson, *History of Advertising*, p. 570.

536

The practical importance of the problems of size of space and frequency of repetition or insertion is emphasized when we note the actual plans followed in typical instances. On the one hand, Palm Olive Soap was advertised in a double-page spread every four weeks in a leading weekly publication. The same was true of Wrigley's Gum. Would it be more effective and economical to use a page every two weeks or possibly a half-page every week? At the other extreme, we find the National Life Insurance Company of Vermont using less than a column inch at the bottom of the front page of the *Boston Transcript* every day, year in and year out. See Figure 59. It is said that this company has done so for some thirty-five years. Would it be more economical and effective to use the six column inches once a week or possibly twelve inches once in two weeks or twenty-four inches once a month? Between these extremes there are such firms as The Florsheim Shoe Company, which uses a quarter of a page every week in a leading weekly magazine or The Selz Shoe Company, which uses a full-page every four weeks in the same publication.

Two practical questions must be examined at this point. First: Is pure attention value directly proportional to the size of the space? That is, other things being equal, does a full-page advertisement have twice as much attention value as a half-page advertisement or four times as much as a quarter-page advertisement? Or, stated in different terms, Will a full-page advertisement be seen by twice as many people as a half-page advertisement, or by four times as many people as a quarter-page advertisement? Or from still another angle we may ask, Will a full-page advertisement be looked at twice as long as a half-page or four times as long as a quarter-page advertisement by the same number of people? Possibly the real situation is that a full-page advertisement is seen by more people, but not by twice as many as a half-page one, and longer by the persons who do see it but not twice as long. Second: What are the various factors that must be considered in determining

Figure 59:   Example of small advertisement run consistently by one company *(See page 537)*

the size of a single advertisement, or of the advertisements of a series for a given campaign and the interval between the successive advertisements in a series?

In considering the first question we must clearly distinguish between the various problems involved. Whether it is better to use small space rather than large space for advertising a fountain pen, or whether it is better to use large space rather than small space for advertising a typewriter, are questions which involve many other elements besides the attention value of the space. These factors will be considered a little later. But in order to get at the ultimate facts of the problem we must single out the separate elements and deal with them in turn. Aside from secondary considerations, such as the illustrations, extensive explanatory text, complexity of proposition, funds available, and so on, the prime factor in determining the amount of space for a given advertisement is the relative attention value of the different sizes of space and the importance of the frequency of repetition.

TENDENCIES IN THE USE OF SPACE

Whatever the true answer to the question may be, the first significant fact is that, since the beginning of adver-

tising in America until within the last decade, there has
been a steady and continuous tendency toward the use of
larger space.

Professor Scott made an investigation to determine the
average size of the advertisements appearing in the *Cen-*

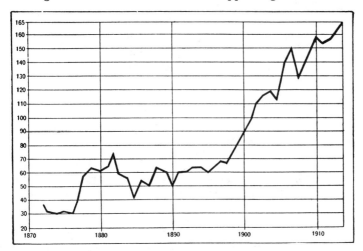

Figure 60:   Average size of the advertisements appearing in the *Century
Magazine* since 1872

tury Magazine since 1872.   In Table 86 are given the average number of agate lines per advertisement.   In 1872, the
average number of lines per advertisement was 38, whereas
in 1913 the average number of lines was 169.   According to this investigation, therefore, the average magazine advertisement today is four times as large as it was half
a century ago.

This point is further corroborated by the appearance
and common use of double-page advertisements during the
last decade and by the tremendous increase in the use of
full-page advertisements.   Up to 1890 only about one-fifth
of the total advertising space in magazines consisted of
full-page advertisements.   Today the ratio is about three-
fourths.   Conversely, there has been a decrease in the fre-

TABLE 86

AVERAGE NUMBER OF AGATE LINES IN EACH ADVERTISEMENT
APPEARING IN THE "CENTURY MAGAZINE" FOR THE
YEARS INDICATED *

Date		Date	
1872	38	1907	151
1875	31	1908	131
1880	61	1909	145
1885	43	1910	159
1890	50	1911	154
1895	61	1912	157
1900	88	1913	169
1905	114		

* Abbreviated from the table on p. 183, *Psychology of Advertising*, W. D. Scott. The figures since 1907 have been added by the author.

quency of using small space. In 1880 half-page spaces were used about two and a half times as often as full-page spaces; in 1890 less than twice as often; and today about one-third as often.

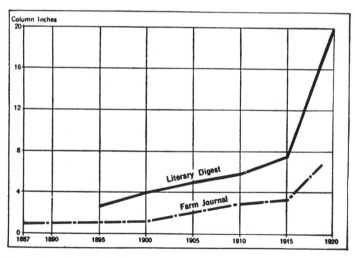

Figure 61: Increase in the average size of advertisements in two publications since 1887 and 1895 *(See page 541)*

The author made a tabulation of the amount of advertising space used and the number of individual advertisements appearing in the *Literary Digest* during a period of nearly 30 years. These results show a very remarkable increase in the average size of advertisements. See Figure 61.

A similar tabulation made with the advertisements in the *Farm Journal,* an agricultural publication of wide circulation, gave substantially similar results. A tabulation was likewise made with the advertisements appearing in the *New York Tribune* and in the *Boston Transcript* at five-year intervals since 1860. The results show a very striking increase in the size of the average advertisement. See Figure 62.

A similar tendency is shown in the proportion of full-page advertisements appearing in such publications as the *Saturday Evening Post,* the *Ladies' Home Journal,* and other publications. The graphs in Figure 63 illustrate the percentage of total advertising space occupied by full-page advertisements in two publications.

What is the explanation of this enormous increase in the

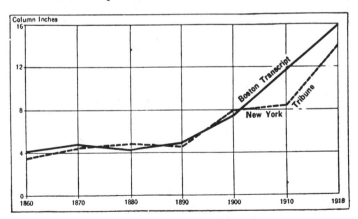

Figure 62: Increase in the average size of advertisements in two metropolitan newspapers since 1860

size of the average advertisement, which increase is one of the outstanding features in the development of advertising since 1850?   Four reasons may be assigned:

1. Competition and imitation.   If an advertiser wished to dominate the space when quarter-pages were the common unit, he proceeded to use a half-page.   Others followed suit.   When half-pages became common he would proceed

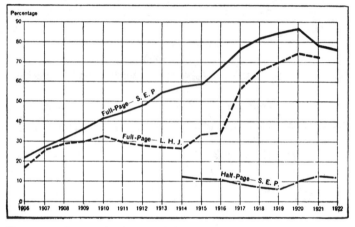

Figure 63:   Increase in the use of full pages in the advertising space of the *Saturday Evening Post* and the *Ladies' Home Journal,* and tendency in the use of half-pages in the *Saturday Evening Post (See page 541)*

to use a full-page and when full pages became common he began to use double-page spreads.

2. Possibly large space may be more effective.   If a certain total amount of space is to be used in a year or in a season, it may be more effective to use it in large units than in small units.   However, actual facts need to be gathered to determine whether or not and to what extent such a plan is wasteful competition.

3. Perhaps today there are more commodities which require the use of larger space.   There is, for example, the automobile which perhaps can be advertised more effectively in large space.

4. There are more large business concerns which are in a position to use large space advantageously.

EXPERIMENTAL DATA ON THE VALUE OF SPACE

There is obviously a difference in attention value between large and small advertising space. Just how large that difference is and to what extent it is proportional to the space is a difficult problem. However, a number of experimental and statistical investigations have been made in the attempt to solve this problem. The number of factors that enter are so many that few if any of these researches have been successful in obtaining clean-cut facts regarding the problem. However, in view of the psychological and economic importance of this problem, any serious attempt to throw light on it is worthy of consideration. We shall briefly review these experimental efforts.

The first experiment endeavoring to determine the relative attention value of various sizes of advertisements was conducted by W. D. Scott, and reported in 1908. In this experiment 40 students were asked to look through a current issue of the *Century Magazine* in the ordinary manner, but were asked not to read any of the articles in the reading section. At the end of 10 minutes each person was asked to put aside the magazine and write down all the advertisements that he remembered having seen. This experiment was then repeated in the same manner with some 500 young people between the ages of 10 and 30 years, living in various parts of the country.

In tabulating the results the advertisements dealing with books and periodicals were listed separately.

The tabulated results for all advertisements other than those of books and periodicals are given in Table 87.

The tabulated results for advertisements of books and periodicals were as given in Table 88.

The investigation was further carried out with 50 adults in the same general manner. In this case a specially pre-

TABLE 87

SIZE OF ADVERTISEMENTS

Details of Test and Results	Full-Page	Half-Page	Quarter-Page	Small
Number of advertisements	27	39	67	98
Pages occupied	27	18.5	16.75	6
Total number out of 500 persons who mentioned them	530	358	223	65
Average number of mentions for each advertisement	19.6	9.2	3	.64
Average number of mentions for each page occupied	19.6	18.3	13	10

pared dummy magazine containing 100 pages of advertisements and a section of current reading matter was used. This dummy was carefully made up so that it appeared like an ordinary magazine.

Table 89 gives the tabulated results secured from the 50 adults for all miscellaneous advertisements.

Tabulated results for all advertisements of books and

TABLE 88

SIZE OF ADVERTISEMENTS

Details of Test and Results	Full-Page	Half-Page	Quarter-Page	Small
Number of advertisements	64	8	3	Less than a single quarter-page of small advertisements of books and periodicals. Hence they are not tabulated.
Pages occupied	64	4	.75	
Total number out of 500 persons who mentioned them	606	16	2	
Average number of mentions for each advertisement	9.2	2	.67	
Average number of mentions for each page occupied	9.2	4	2.67	

TABLE 89

SIZE OF ADVERTISEMENTS

Details of Test and Results	Full-Page	Half-Page	Quarter-Page	Small
Number of advertisements	43	15	36	93
Pages occupied	43	7.5	9	5.5
Total number of mentions	281	41	39	14
Average number of mentions for each advertisement	6.5	2.2	1.1	.16
Average number of mentions for each page occupied	6.5	5.5	4.33	2.5
Total (additional) number of recognitions	544	118	122	34
Average number of recognitions for each advertisement	12.7	7.8	3.4	.36
Average number of recognitions for each page occupied	12.7	15.7	13.5	6.2

periodicals secured from the 50 adults were as given in Table 90.

These results tend to indicate that the attention value of an advertisement increases more rapidly than the size of the advertisement. "The full-page advertisement was more than twice as effective as a half-page advertisement; a half-page advertisement was more than twice as effective as a quarter-page and a quarter-page was more effective than a quarter-page of small advertisements." [1]

The author made a similar test as follows:

A copy of a magazine (*Cosmopolitan*, April, 1910, or *Everybody's*, March, 1909) was placed in the hands of each of 374 persons to allow examination of its advertising section. Fifteen minutes were allowed for this purpose, after which each one was asked to write down all the ad-

[1] Scott, p. 172.

TABLE 90

SIZE OF ADVERTISEMENTS

Details of Test and Results	Full-Page	Half-Page	Quarter-Page	Small
Number of advertisements	31	4	6	7
Pages occupied	31	2	1.5	.5
Total number who mentioned them	85	1	3	1
Average number of mentions for each advertisement	2.7	.25	.5	.14
Average number of mentions for each page occupied	2.7	.5	2	1
Total (additional) number of recognitions	276	24	11	2
Average number of recognitions for each advertisement	8.9	6	1.8	.3
Average number of recognitions for each page occupied	8.9	12	7.3	4

vertisements he remembered having seen. In the test 284 persons were given the *Cosmopolitan* and 90 were given *Everybody's*. A table was then prepared to show the number of times each advertisement had been mentioned.

Several points of criticism of this method of testing the attention value of advertisements should be noted here. An advertisement, aside from its attractiveness, might have been mentioned by many because it was familiar, because it was located on the outside cover, or because it had a special interest. To eliminate the advantage of location, none of the advertisements in preferred positions were included in the present tabulation. To eliminate the force of familiarity, each participant in the test was asked at another time to write down all brands of articles with which he was acquainted, through advertising, use, or otherwise. The number of times each commodity was thus mentioned

TABLE 91

ATTENTION VALUE OF SIZE

Size of Ads	Number of Ads	Mentions per Ad	Number of Pages Occupied	Mentions per Page Occupied	Mentions per Page Occupied Minus Familiarity
2 pp.	3	13.4	6	67.	42.3
1 p.	69	48.4	69	48.4	33.0
¾ p.	10	36.1	7.5	48.1	35.5
½ p.	58	10.7	29	21.4	17.0
¼ p.	56	2.4	14	9.0	9.6

was deducted from the number of times it was mentioned in the "magazine test." For example, the Old Dutch Cleanser advertisement was mentioned 219 times in the test and 88 times in the enumeration for familiarity, which left 131 mentions due chiefly to its attention value. The results appear in Table 91.

The seven full-page advertisements in preferred positions were not included in this tabulation.

From this table it can be seen that the double-page advertisements were recalled more than twice as often as one-page advertisements; whole pages were recalled more than twice as often as half-page advertisements; and half-pages were recalled more than twice as often as quarter-page advertisements. If small advertisements had as much attention value as large advertisements in proportion to the space occupied, the figures in the last column should all be alike, but instead there is a rapid decrease from the larger to the smaller spaces. Considered in relation to size, the double-page advertisements were mentioned about four and one-half times as often as the quarter-page advertisements, the full- and the three-quarter-page about three and one-half times, and the half-page nearly twice, as often as the quarter-page advertisements.

A similar investigation was carried out by the author with nine different issues of the *Saturday Evening Post* appearing in the latter part of 1914. The experiment was made in essentially the manner described above. The test was made with 80 persons. The results are presented in Table 92. In this table the number of recalls is tabulated in relation to the size of the advertisements, beginning with the two-page advertisements.

The last two columns give the space or size ratios of the advertisements and the recall ratios as shown by the test. If we let the size of the full page equal 100 then the other sizes obviously are as indicated. Likewise if we let the number of times the full-page advertisements were recalled by the 80 persons equal 100, then the numbers of recalls for the other sizes were in the ratios indicated. A comparison of the two columns of ratios shows that they decrease or increase in approximately a parallel manner, the chief exception being that the two-page spaces did not have double the number of recalls as the one-page spaces.

The author likewise made a similar experiment with the *Chicago Tribune* and the *Chicago Herald* in 1915, and with the *Boston Post* and the *Boston Herald* in 1922. The experiment was carried out by asking a person to look through a given paper, instructing him to examine what interested him and to pass over what did not interest him. He was, however, requested to turn every page of the paper. Then he was told to lay the paper aside and record the advertisements he was able to recall. After he had done so he was

TABLE 92

ATTENTION VALUE OF SIZE

Size of Advertisement	Number of Advertisements	Average Recalls per Advertisement	Space Ratios	Recall Ratios
2 pages	21	5.9	200	131
1 page	122	4.5	100	100
½ page	70	2.5	50	55
¼ page	160	1.4	25	31
6 to 8 inches	71	.5	14	11
3 to 5 inches	94	.5	8	11
½ to 2 inches	246	.14	3	3

asked to take the paper again and look through it to record the advertisements he had not been able to recall but which he could recognize as he saw them again. The latter data are given in the table under "recognitions."

Table 93 gives the results obtained for the *Boston Post* and *Boston Herald* combined. The results for the *Chicago Tribune* and *Chicago Herald* were tabulated in the same manner.

TABLE 93
ATTENTION VALUE OF SIZE

Range of Size of Ads in Column Inches	Number of Ads	Average Size of Ads	Recalls per Ad	Recall Ratios	Recognitions per Ad	Recognition Ratios	Space Ratios
51 or more	4	87.	15.7	150	18.0	116	234
26-50	9	32.9	10.5	100	16.4	100	100
11-25	22	15.5	4.3	41	8.2	50	47
6-10	24	6.9	1.55	15	3.13	19	21
2.6-5	50	3.8	.68	6	1.0	6	12
0-2.5	99	1.69	.31	3	.49	3	5

These results are shown graphically in Figure 64, in which the size ratios, the recall ratios, and the recognition ratios are plotted. From the standpoint of attention value apparently the more economical space, at least as indicated by this test, is the size 26-50 column inches. Smaller sizes tend to fall below the corresponding size ratios. Thus, for example, size 11-25, considering the two graphs together, falls a very small shade below the actual size value. The larger size, above 50 inches, may be affected by the fact that the number of advertisements of that size in the particular issues used in this test was too small—only four advertisements—to give valid results.

Münsterberg reported an experiment conducted for the purpose of determining the value of size and repetition. The experiment was conducted by preparing 60 pages of advertisements obtained from the *Saturday Evening Post* and the *Ladies' Home Journal.* These pages contained 6 full-page advertisements, 12 half-page advertisements, and a group of one-fourth-page advertisements, one-eighth-page advertisements, and one-sixteenth-page advertisements.

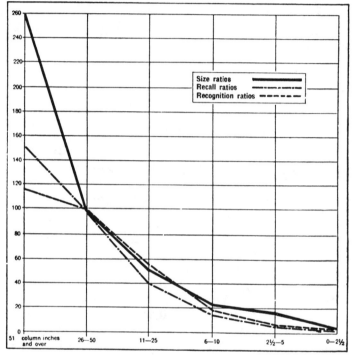

Figure 64: Test with two Boston newspapers *(See page 549)*

These advertisements were mounted in various combinations on each page.

A test was made with 30 persons. Each person was permitted to observe each page for 20 seconds, with an interval of 3 seconds between succeeding pages. Immediately after all of the 60 pages had been seen, each person recorded the advertisements he remembered having seen. These results were then tabulated to indicate the average number of times each advertisement was recalled per person. The figures are as given in Table 94.

TABLE 94

MEMORY VALUE OF SIZE AND REPETITION (Münsterberg)

1 -page ads were remembered	.33 times per page per person
½-page ads repeated 2 times were remembered	.30 times per page per person
¼-page ads repeated 4 times were remembered	.49 times per page per person
⅛-page ads repeated 8 times were remembered	.44 times per page per person
¹⁄₁₂-page ads repeated 12 times were remembered	.47 times per page per person

Münsterberg concludes as follows: "Hence we come to the result that the 4 times repeated fourth-page advertisement has 1½ times stronger memory value than one offering of a full page, or the two times repeated half-page, but that this relation does not grow with further reduction of space." [1]

The conclusion therefore arrived at by Professor Münsterberg was that small space repeated sufficiently often to aggregate the same amount of larger space is more economical. In other words, a quarter-page inserted four times is worth approximately 50% more than a single full-page advertisement. It is questionable whether this is true, whether it will hold for advertisements seen under the usual every-day conditions. In the first place, the attention given to these 60 pages of advertisements was voluntary rather than spontaneous; that is, each person was required to look at each page. In the second place, the length of time during which each page was observed was uniformly 20 seconds. This is certain to give an advantage to the smaller spaces as compared with the case when they are seen under the ordinary conditions of spontaneous attention. In the third place, instead of the smaller spaces being seen at in-

[1] Münsterberg, H., Psychology and Industrial Efficiency, pp. 258-270.

tervals—one week apart, for example—as advertisements appear under actual conditions in magazines, they were exhibited by Professor Münsterberg within a few minutes of one another. In actual conditions, a quarter-page advertisement is seen all alone, instead of four of them being seen practically together. The experimental conditions were not sufficiently close to normal conditions under which advertisements are seen and observed, to make this investigation conclusive.

In 1913, Dr. E. K. Strong conducted an investigation bearing on this problem under the auspices of the Association of National Advertisers. Dr. Strong prepared four dummy magazines in which 288 advertisements from 144 firms were used. These advertisements were of three sizes, full-page, half-page, and quarter-page. They were mounted in various combinations on separate sheets. Advertisements of well-known firms were not included.

The tests were made in two ways: to some of the persons with whom the experiment was carried out, each page of advertisements was shown for one second; in the case of the other group of persons each individual turned the sheets and observed each advertisement as long or as short a time as he cared to. Twenty-one persons were tested by the first method and 18 persons were tested by the second method. The four sets of advertisements were shown one month apart. After an interval of one month the persons concerned were tested by the recognition method; that is, the advertisements originally shown a month previous and an equal number of other advertisements shuffled with them were presented to the person and he was asked to select the ones he had seen. Typical results obtained by these methods are given in the following paragraphs.

Consider the question, How should a half-page be used in four months? Is it better to use a half-page once during the four months or two quarter-pages separated by an interval of two months?

January	¼	½
February		
March	¼	
April		
Efficiency	1.22	1.45

¼ page once in 4 months is taken as the basic value of 1.00

These results would indicate that two quarter-pages used in this manner during a period of four months are only 22% more valuable than one quarter-page used during the same period of time. On the other hand, a half-page used once in four months is 45% more valuable than two quarters used during the same interval. Similar comparisons of space are given in Tables 95, 96, 97, and 98.

According to these results two full pages used in four months are more effective than four half-pages used in four months.

TABLE 95

How Different Sizes Compare When Used with the Same Frequency

Months	Size of Advertisement			Ratios in Terms of ¼ Page		
January	¼ p.	½ p.	1 p.			
February						
March						
April						
Efficiency	1.00	1.45	2.20	1.00	1.45	2.20
January	¼	½	1			
February						
March	¼	½	1			
April						
Efficiency	1.22	1.83	2.73	1.00	1.50	2.24
January	¼	½	1			
February	¼	½	1			
March	¼	½	1			
April	¼	½	1			
Efficiency	1.73	2.22	3.47	1.00	1.28	2.00
			Average	1.00	1.4	2.15

TABLE 96

How Should Two Pages Be Used in Four Months?

January	½	I
February	½	
March	½	I
April	½	
Efficiency	2.22	2.73

Proposition XI is better than X and if a big impression with some readers is to be made XII is better than XI or X. Large space is better than small space when a large impression is to be made upon the reader.

Table 98 is adapted from Strong's data with the purpose of bringing together all his results obtained by the two methods of experimentation and all sizes of space and frequencies of repetition:

TABLE 97

How Should Four Pages Be Used in Four Months?

	Proposition X				Proposition XI				Proposition XII
	A	B	C	D	A	B	C	D	A
January	¼	¼	¼	¼	I	I	I	I	I
February	¼	¼	¼	¼					I
March	¼	¼	¼	¼					I
April	¼	¼	¼	¼					I
Proposition X			1.73 x 4		6.92				
Proposition XI			2.20 x 4		8.80				
Proposition XII					3.47				

This table reads thus: 1.7% of the quarter-page ads were recognized when they had been seen for one second but once in four months, 2.3% of the half-page ads were recognized, etc.; 3.8% of the quarter-page ads were recognized when they had been seen once in four months but as long as the reader desired, etc. Sections II to IV of the table give these percentages in various ratios. The table must be studied carefully in order to note its meaning.

Various combinations of size of ads and frequency of repetition may be made. Thus, for example, one full page in four months (3.6% and 8.7%) is better than two half-pages in four months (3.1% and 7.0%) and these in turn are better than four quarter-pages in four months (3.0% and 6.5%). Section III of the table gives the ratios for these percentages.

From these experimental data Dr. Strong drew the following more fully stated conclusions:

When IMMEDIATE RETURNS from the advertisement are desired small space is more efficient than large space.

These results agree with the consensus of opinion among advertising men, for nearly all agree that small space is more profitable than large space in mail-order business. (The mail-order advertisement is built to secure immediate returns from each advertisement. Moreover, accumulative effect is not aimed at in such advertising.)

When PERMANENCY OF EFFECT is desired, i. e., when immediate returns are not so much looked for, but a cumulative, educational campaign is planned for, small space is not so economical as large space.

When considerable impression per reader is necessary, as in auto advertising, Proposition XII is most efficient. When less impression per reader is needed (but more than can be obtained through one advertisement) then Proposition XI is best. When little impression per reader is needed, as in mail-order advertising, the smallest space which can give that impression will be found to be most efficient.

In the case of special interest to us, repeated presentations do not have proportionate efficiency. One, two, and four presentations do not have ratios of efficiency of 1.00 - 2.00 - 4.00 - but rather ratios of efficiency of 1.00 - 1.25 - 1.62. (These ratios are approximately equal to the cube roots of the number of presentations, i. e., V 1 - V 2 - V 4 equals 1.00 - 1.26 - 1.59.)

To the extent in an advertising campaign that each advertisement is a unit in itself, that is, not dependent on the other advertisements in the series, Geo. S. Parker's statement that "Small space in many media is better than large space in few media," is correct. This is the general situation in mail-order advertising.

But to the extent in an advertising campaign that each adver-

TABLE 98

RESULTS OBTAINED BY THE TWO METHODS OF EXPERIMENTATION OF DR. STRONG AS ADAPTED FROM HIS DATA

Frequency in 4 Months	Method of Exposure	Section I Percentage of Firms Recognized 1 Month After Last Exposure			Section II Size Ratios		
		Sizes of Ads			Sizes of Ads		
		¼ p.	½ p.	1 p.	¼ p.	½ p.	1 p.
1	1 per second	1.7%	2.3%	3.6%	1.00	1.35	2.12
	Leisure of reader	3.8	5.9	8.7	1.00	1.55	2.20
					1.00	1.45	2.20
2	1 per second	2.2	3.1	4.6	1.29	1.82	2.70
	Leisure of reader	4.4	7.0	10.5	1.16	2 05	2.76
					1.22	1.93	2.73
4	1 per second	3.0	3.9	6.0	1.76	2.29	3.53
	Leisure of reader	6.5	8.2	13.0	1.71	2.15	3.42
					1.73	2.22	3.47

tisement is not a unit in itself, or in other words, that a cumulative, educational, general effect is desired from an entire series of advertisements, Parker's statement is incorrect. The practical experience of auto advertisers, whose campaigns are typical of this situation, agrees with our results. In such campaigns cumulative effect is obtained more efficiently from large space than from small space more frequently used.[1]

Practically all of the experimental work that has been conducted thus far is open to two serious objections which leave the results open to question. First, practically all of the experiments reported were made under conditions in which the attention of the observer was voluntary. That is, he was requested to look at certain advertisements and then to report what he had observed. This condition is different from that which occurs in the average every-day observation of advertisements. The attention, in the usual observation of advertisements, is spontaneous; the reader

[1] Strong, E. K., *Size and Frequency of Advertisements.*

TABLE 98 *(Continued)*

RESULTS OBTAINED BY THE TWO METHODS OF EXPERIMENTATION
OF DR. STRONG AS ADAPTED FROM HIS DATA

Frequency in 4 Months	Method of Exposure	Section III Size Ratios Sizes of Ads			Section IV Size Ratios Sizes of Ads			Average
		¼ p.	½ p.	1 p.	¼ p.	½ p.	1 p.	
1	1 per second	1.00	1.35	2.12	1.00	1.00	1.00	
	Leisure of reader	1.00	1.55	2.29	1.00	1.00	1.00	
		1.00	1.45	2.21	1.00	1.00	1.00	1.00
2	1 per second	1.00	1.41	2.09	1.29	1.35	1.28	
	Leisure of reader	1.00	1.59	2.39	1.16	1.19	1.21	
		1.00	1.50	2.24	1.22	1.27	1.24	1.25
4	1 per second	1.00	1.30	2.00	1.76	1.70	1.67	
	Leisure or reader	1.00	1.26	2.00	1.71	1.39	1.49	
		1.00	1.28	2.00	1.73	1.54	1.58	1.62
	Average	1.00	1.41	2.15				

notices whatever engages his interest. The only exceptions to this are in the case of classified advertising or in the case of a deliberate examination of the advertisements of a new issue of a magazine or newspaper. In this case, however, while the attention is more or less voluntary the situation is, nevertheless, different, since he is not conscious of any experiment being made with him nor does he have the thought that he is likely to be asked to report or to remember any of the advertisements.

The second criticism, though it is possibly not a serious one, is that most of the experiments have been carried out with students who may or may not be typical of the habits of the average reader, and in some instances the material used in the advertisements was rather familiar to many of the observers.

In view of these conditions, the author undertook an experiment to determine the relative attention value of various sizes of advertisements under the usual every-day conditions for the observation of advertisements, without the consciousness that an experiment was being made. Accordingly an investigation was conducted and persons were interviewed after the plan shown in Figure 65.

Briefly, according to this plan a person was simply asked to state what advertisements he remembered having ob-

---

We wish to find out to what extent people generally remember ads. Will you please help us find out by answering the following questions:

Please put here the date   Sex   Occupation

1. Name of one magazine which you read regularly.

2. What is the date of the last issue of this magazine which you have read?

3. Write in the following space the names of as many ads in this particular issue as you can recall. Do this without looking at the magazine again.

Put a question mark (?) after any of which you are not sure.

1._____

2._____

3._____

Etc.

4. Next take this particular issue of the magazine. Look through it and write in the following space the names of all the ads that you recognize having seen in this particular issue. Put a question mark if you are not sure. Put after each one the size of the ad—that is, whether it is a 2-page, ½-page, ¼-page, or less than ¼-page. Please indicate whether it is a colored ad. Simply write "colored" if it is. In the last column indicate in each case whether you have ever seen this article advertised before, so far as you can remember. If you have never seen it advertised before, write the word "new" after it.

Ad   Size   Colored   New

1._____

2._____

3._____

Etc.

Figure 65: Data on remembering advertisements

served in the last or a recent issue of a particular magazine which he had read in his usual manner. After he had done so he was asked to take the copy of this particular issue and go through it page by page to record those advertisements which he now recognized having seen in this particular issue before. The conditions of this procedure, therefore, eliminated (during the period of observation of advertisements) any consciousness that an experiment was being made. This experiment made it possible to determine to what extent individual advertisements make an impression in their usual way, under conditions of attention typical and customary.

The results are set forth in Table 99. The investigation covered a total of 17 different magazines read and reported by 142 persons. These persons were men and women of the average type of intelligent reader and business man.

TABLE 99

PERCENTAGE OF PERSONS WHO RECALLED ADVERTISEMENTS OF VARIOUS SIZES

Magazine Advertisements	Two Pages Color	Two Pages B. & W.	One Page Color	One Page B. & W.	Two-thirds Page	One-half Page	One-third Page	One-quarter Page	Less Than Quarter
Per cent recalled	20.5	12.1	14.1	7.5	3.4	0.73	1.7	1.3	.3
Recall Ratios considering one page B. & W. as 100	273	161	194	100	45	9	23	17	4
Space Ratios	200	200	100	100	67	50	33	25	12.5

These results are shown graphically in Figure 66. Regarding a page in black and white as 100 and graphing the results both for the test and for the space ratios accordingly, we observe that the results—both for the advertisements recalled outright and for the advertisements recognized when the magazine was again examined—agree in all important respects; that is, the highest attention value in relation to the space occupied is the full-page advertisement. The graph both for the recall ratios and for the

TABLE 100

PERCENTAGE OF PERSONS WHO RECOGNIZED ADVERTISEMENTS OF VARIOUS SIZES. THE ONES RECALLED AND TABULATED IN THE PRECEDING TABLE ARE NOT INCLUDED

Magazine Advertisements	Two Pages Color	Two Pages B. & W.	One Page Color	One Page B. & W.	Two-thirds Page	One-half Page	One-third Page	One-quarter Page	Less Than Quarter
Average per cent recognized	48.7	36.2	42.7	23.3	15.8	7.1	7.1	5.0	0.9
Recognition Ratios	209	155	184	100	68	30	30	21	4
Space Ratios	200	200	100	100	67	50	33	25	12.5

recognition ratios shows a drop at nearly all points below the graph for space ratios; that is, a one-half-page, instead of having 50% of the attention value of a full page, has only 35% of the attention value of a full page; a quarter-page, instead of having 25% of the attention value of a full page, has only 15% of the attention value of a full page. On the other side, the double-page advertisement, instead of having 200%, or twice the attention value of the full page, has only 158% of the attention value of the full page. We note also that the color pages are recalled 94% more frequently and recognized 84% more frequently than the black and white pages. In the case of the two-page spaces the advantage of color is also considerable.

In a certain sense the process by which the name of a product and its merits are impressed upon the minds of people through advertising is a process of learning and forgetting. Extensive experimental work has shown that the rate of learning and its opposite the rate of forgetting follow certain fairly definite laws. Figure 67 shows the rate of forgetting in the case of syllables, prose and poetry which had been committed to memory. The significant feature of these curves is that the rate of forgetting is much more rapid at the beginning. In the case of nonsense syllables, Ebbinghaus found that a person forgets as much in the first hour as in the next 30 days and in the case of meaningful material (poetry or prose), a person forgets as much in the first 24 hours as in the next 30 days.

These facts probably should be considered in planning the frequency of insertions when a new product is first being advertised. To counteract the rapid rate of forgetting, the insertions or repetitions should come much more frequently at the beginning than later on.

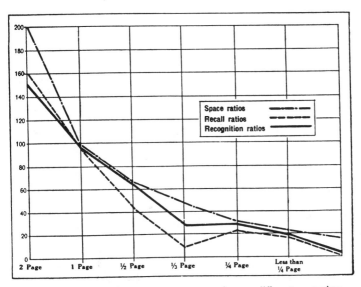

Figure 66: Report from 142 persons covering 14 different magazines
(See page 559)

In this connection it is interesting to note that there has been a marked increase in the size of the individual space unit in mail-order catalogs. Mail-order houses are in an excellent position to determine accurately the results produced by various advertisements and various sizes of space. Experience there has shown that featuring certain articles in large space has produced better results in proportion to the space occupied. However, the same article cannot profitably be featured, as a rule, continuously in successive issues of the catalog. The tendency, in other words, in mail-order catalogs has been to advertise fewer items in a given amount of space, but to use larger display. Until within the last few years double pages devoted to a single article in a mail-order catalog were unknown. They are not uncommon at the present time. Thus, for example, a

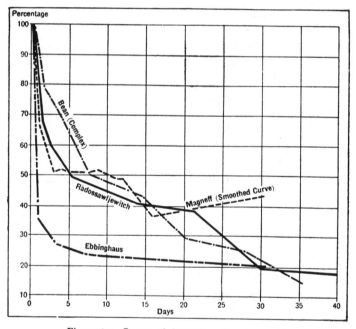

Figure 67: Curves of forgetting *(See page 560)*

recent mail-order catalog of a large house featured a work shoe in a double-page space. It also featured a better grade shoe in a full-page space. It showed overalls in a one-page space, and a sewing machine, a piano, and a phonograph were featured in one-page inserts each. A stove was displayed in a full-page space.

The cost of space is carefully computed so that if an article fails to bring returns in proportion to the space allotted for it in the catalog, the space is modified or eliminated.

CONCLUSIONS BASED ON EXPERIMENTS

The general inference which I think may be fairly drawn from all of the experimental work thus far conducted is that, other things being equal, for general display advertising, where the attention is spontaneous rather than voluntary, the full-page unit is apparently the most economical space to use. It is evidently more economical than the smaller spaces and also more economical than double-page units. Due consideration here should of course be given to the qualifying phrase "other things being equal." Other factors, such as the nature of the product or the business, may make it advisable to use larger or smaller space than the full-page unit, or than the unit which according to the general rule would be most economical.

The conclusion suggested by some of the experimental investigators, that the attention value of space increases more slowly than space itself, that, in other words, small space is more economical in proportion to the area occupied than large space, is true apparently only in the case of advertisements of the classified type. And this is true only of certain types of classified advertising,—for example, mail-order advertising—in which the attention is voluntary and the customer or reader is definitely interested in searching for a certain commodity and hence looks through all of the advertisements with great care. Small space apparently under such circumstances is more economical. The conclusion drawn by Hollingworth and others, that the number of inquiries or orders tends to increase as the square root of the amount of space used, would apparently hold only for this type of advertising and for the attention conditions here mentioned.

RESULTS OF BUSINESS EXPERIENCE

The evidence presented thus far has all been derived from the laboratory type of investigation. It will be of value now to study the available evidence derived from actual business experience.

"Mortality Rate" of Advertisers. Professor Scott has shown that the "mortality rate" of advertisers is very much greater among the users of small space than among the users of large space. He made a tabulation of all the firms located west of Buffalo which advertised in the *Ladies' Home Journal* during eight years.

TABLE 101

"MORTALITY" OF ADVERTISERS

Number of Years the Firms Continue to Advertise	Average Number of Lines Used Annually by Each Firm
1 year	56 lines
2 years	116 lines
3 years	168 lines
4 years	194 lines
5 years	192 lines
6 years	262 lines
7 years	218 lines
8 years	600 lines

"This would seem to indicate," says Professor Scott, "that in general, if a firm uses 56 lines annually in the *Ladies' Home Journal,* the results will be so unsatisfactory that it will not try it again. If it uses 116 lines annually it will be encouraged to attempt it the second year, but will then drop out. If, on the other hand, it uses 600 lines annually, the results will be so satisfactory that it will continue to use the same magazine indefinitely." [1]

A. H. Kuhlman made a study of the relation between the number of sales of pure-bred cattle and the amount of

[1] *Psychology of Advertising,* p. 163.

TABLE 102

SIZE OF ADVERTISEMENTS IN RELATION TO SALES

Year	January to June Advertising	Sales	July to December Advertising	Sales	Totals Advertising	Sales	Column Inches for One Sale
1900	118.0	63	245.0	30	363.0	93	3.9
1901	246.0	48	262.2	25	508.2	73	6.9
1902	326.0	97	292.0	105	618.0	202	3.1
1903	326.0	82	327.0	108	653.0	190	3.4
1904	347.0	107	390.0	90	737.0	197	3.7
1905	599.5	171	397.5	188	997.0	359	2.8
1906	427.5	161	361.0	137	788.0	298	2.6
1907	537.0	254	492.0	195	1,029.0	449	2.3

* Shryer, W. A., *Analytical Advertising*, p. 171.

space used in the agricultural papers in advertising them. This study is particularly important because it was possible to tabulate not only the amount of advertising space used, but also the exact number of sales made. The latter was determined from the registers and transfers of pure-bred stock. The results are set forth in a table which shows the number of column inches of advertising used and the number of sales made during each six months from 1900 to 1907: [1]

The interesting facts brought out by a study of this table are that the number of column inches per sale decreased as the advertising space increased, and that the sales and the advertising space as shown in the curves of Figure 68 have a close parallel fluctuation. With an increase of space there is a relatively greater increase in the number of sales. Or, in other words, the larger amounts of space were slightly more profitable. It will be observed that these curves run practically parallel. When the advertising space was increased the sales generally in-

[1] From an unpublished thesis in the library of the University of Wisconsin.

creased, and when the advertising space decreased the sales decreased. The increase in space was not due to the use of more mediums, but to the use of larger space in the same mediums.

A series of advertisements for a school, inserted in 51 college publications, were run in two sizes. One size was 12 column inches (2 columns by 6 inches), the other was 4 inches, single column. These advertisements were alike in other respects and appeared alternately in successive weeks. The larger size brought one inquiry per 30 inches of space whereas the smaller size brought one inquiry per 42 inches of space.

The returns tabulated from the advertising of the American Collection Service by Mr. W. A. Shryer point in the same direction. The figures in Table 103 indicate that the cash return per dollar of advertising cost is greater for the full- and half-page spaces than for the smaller spaces.

TABLE 103

RELATIVE VALUES OF SMALL AND LARGE COPY *

Size of Advertisement	Number of Mediums	Number of Insertions	Inquiries	Advertising Cost	Cash Returns	Cost per Inquiry	Returns per Dollar Adv. Cost
5 lines classified	66	721	13,374	$4,441	$20,222	$0.30	$4.50
7 lines	50	84	911	484	921	.53	1.90
16 lines	55	126	3,643	2,549	5,476	.70	2.10
20 lines	12	12	127	185	114	1.47	.60
36 lines	15	18	1,078	476	827	.45	1.70
¼ page	42	99	2,766	2,109	3,730	.76	1.80
½ page	21	60	2,458	2,246	6,095	.92	2.70
1 page	18	69	4,296	4,774	10,772	1.11	2.30

* Shryer, W. A., *Analytical Advertising*, p. 171.

Mr. Shryer presents these results to show that the large spaces were less profitable than the small spaces. That is

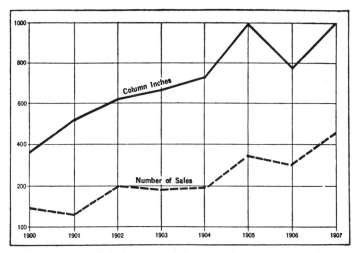

Figure 68: Chart showing relation of number of sales to number of column inches of space used in advertising *(See page 564)*

true if the cost per inquiry alone is considered. The cheapest inquiries were brought by the five-line classified advertisements, and the most expensive inquiries were brought by the larger advertisements. But it is quite obvious that not all inquiries are of equal value. The author has therefore computed the number of dollars of business brought per dollar invested in advertising, as shown in the last column—which is the ultimate test of the efficiency of advertising. It will be seen that the most profitable space was the small five-line insertion. It brought $4.50 worth of business for every dollar spent for advertising. The returns, however, for this classified advertisement must be omitted from the present consideration because the problem of attracting attention by classified matter is very different from the problem of attracting attention by general publicity advertising. Attention in the former case is largely of the voluntary type, whereas in the latter it is largely of the involuntary type.

The large space would probably have shown even greater

relative value if it had not been for the fact that much of the larger space had been arranged for as "trade deals" with mediums which might not otherwise have been selected. The full- and half-page spaces brought the most profitable returns. The 20-line space proved to be the least satisfactory because the text of the advertisement was very poor. It had no illustration—all other advertisements had; the headline was small, and the body type was small. It would be very helpful to the development of a science of advertising if other firms would follow the excellent example of Mr. Shryer, namely, keep accurate returns, whenever possible, and make these results available for analysis.

EXPERIENCE OF ADVERTISERS

Recently an inquiry was made by *Printers' Ink* to determine whether "small space in many media is better than large space in few media." The inquiry was addressed to large advertisers and attempted to ascertain what their experiences and actual results were. Replies from the 26 advertisers who responded fell into the following groups. Seven were in doubt and said that it depended on the particular conditions involved. Three firms favored small space in many media. These were the makers of the Parker Fountain Pen, Three-in-One Oil, and Onyx Hosiery. Sixteen firms, or about two-thirds of the entire number, favored large space in fewer media. Some interesting and significant statements were as follows:

E. Mapes (Cream of Wheat Company): "Personally, I believe in the use of large spaces and preferred positions for a product like ours."

C. W. Nears (Winton Motor Car Company): "We have tried the small-space-in-many-publications idea, and, so far as we could learn, we created practically no impression whatever. On the other hand, we have abundant evidence of having created an impression by means of large space in few publications."

E. St. E. Lewis (Burroughs Adding Machine Company): "Speaking from the standpoint of the Burroughs Adding Machine

Company, we believe that a big space in a few media is better than a little space in many media, because we must tell a story."

T. A. DeWeese (Shredded Wheat Company): "In the last three years we have completely changed our methods of newspaper advertising, going from 80-line space to 440-line space. In that time the sales of Shredded Wheat Biscuit have more than doubled and we have not added a dollar to the original advertising appropriation."

B. D'Emo (William Wrigley, Jr., Company): " . . . . spent several thousand dollars in small space without creating a ripple . . . . then shifted to space twice the size used the same number of times, creating thereby a large and profitable business within slightly over a year."

W. L. Taylor states that the Wilbur Stock Company, in keeping a careful record of the cost per inquiry, found that "a full-page advertisement once a month in a weekly publication was found to produce larger returns at lower cost per inquiry than the regular insertion of small copy in each issue. To be definite, a full-page once a month in a weekly publication produced better than quarter-pages in each of four consecutive issues." [1]

Numerous examples might be quoted to show the experiences and policies of national advertisers regarding the use of space. The recent change of policy of Montgomery Ward & Co. is interesting and instructive.[2]

A year ago Montgomery Ward & Co. made a radical change in the advertising policy, which in the opinion of the house is thoroughly justifying itself.

The old type of advertising was of a piece with the advertising of all other mail-order houses, and might often have been considered a model in its way; but it was growing less and less effective. For two years the cost of getting inquiries had been increasing with this house, as it had with all others. The day of the 10-cent inquiries was long past. The average had climbed, first up to 15, then to 20, 25, and at last even to 30 cents.

The argument for economy had been all along with the mail-order houses, but certain practices of less reputable concerns in the field had been having a deleterious effect on public confidence. The increase of cost in getting replies was the measure of the

[1] *Printers' Ink,* October 5, 1911, p. 3.

[2] *Ibid.,* January 4, 1912, p. 81.

harm done. This was the reason why the bargain offer, "This chair for $7.98," or "Send now for our catalog and save money," lost a great deal of its original effectiveness.

Montgomery Ward & Co. became convinced that the bargain idea was the wrong one to put forward. The real need was for a *restoration of confidence*. They decided to attempt this on their own part by giving the public a new conception of Montgomery Ward & Co., one that should impress it with a sense of the quality of its merchandise and service, the consistency of its prices and the integrity and generosity of its policy.

And they have carried it out, or sought to carry it out, by engaging 15 of the leading American artists in black-and-white to symbolize the business in allegorical and other designs, and then presenting their work to the public in large space in the leading mail-order mediums.

This conception and the method of its execution were, it is hardly necessary to say, somewhat revolutionary. They were not adopted by the directors without the most serious consideration. Up to this time there had been practically only one kind of mail-order copy in use. Some few copywriters had managed to break away from the standard and achieved excellent results for a while with large space and reason-why copy, but always at last they had been driven back in the old rut. . . .

The first copy did not begin to run until September. It went into a list of papers about one-third the previous list and ran on an average of 672 lines or about 12 inches across 4 columns, occasionally deeper. The contracts were for an average of 28 insertions during the year. The old copy was seldom over 6 inches, single column, and most of the time 4 or 5 inches.

When the copy began to run, the advertising world was amazed.

"Our good friends came in to tell us that we were making the biggest mistake of all, pleasing ourselves instead of the public, and 'shooting over the heads of our customers,' " said Mr. Lynn.

"In other quarters, there must have been a lot of quiet chuckling. Our worthy competitors did not pay us the compliment of imitation—I do not suppose they were waiting for results before experimenting themselves; they had simply set the campaign down as a mistake."

The critics were only less mistaken than Montgomery Ward & Co. were, no more than Ward had been before. Instead of going far over the heads of the farmers and small-town dwellers it proved the very thing they had been waiting for. No urban population could have shown more appreciation—the response was almost instantaneous. Not only did Ward begin to hear from them, but many of them took the trouble to write in to the publishers and tell them that they were a credit to the latter, and that they hoped they were going to see more of them, a wish in which the publishers were not too disinclined to unite, because some of them forwarded the letters to Ward & Co.

And striking results were shown in the actual dollars-and-cents returns. The campaign started in September and there was, therefore, only about an average of two insertions per month, in the list, about one-third of the year. But traceable returns in that time cost only 25 cents per inquiry. As traceable returns are seldom more than one-half of the total number, this signified a real cost of not more than *twelve and one-half cents* per inquiry, which would take us almost to the palmiest days of mail order!

It was too much to expect that this would be kept up after the novelty began to wear off. It was natural for the feeling to dull after the first impression. But it showed how strong that first impression was. All are confident now that they have touched the spring of the situation and that slowly, perhaps, but certainly, the business will expand until the full cumulative force of the advertising becomes effective and acts with a mighty urge. Because such advertising as this must not only stimulate those who have previously done business with them, but also those who from prejudice or indifference have never bought goods by mail, it is dignifying and elevating the whole mail-order field.

The plans and results of the advertising of several other firms, as recently described, have a bearing upon the problem of space.

The Liquid Carbonic Company, of Chicago, about 10 or 12 years ago began the manufacture of soda fountains, in a small way. The company previous to that time had been a maker of carbonic acid gas, machinery for carbonating water. The company's advent into the soda fountain field was at a time when a company commonly known as the Soda Fountain Trust was supposed to have everything its own way. The Liquid Carbonic Company began at once using two- and four-page inserts of extraordinary beauty in all the leading druggists' and confectioners' journals, setting a pace that revolutionized methods of advertising in that industry. This bold, aggressive manner of advertising has been carried on continuously ever since. Today the Liquid Carbonic Company builds and sells twice as many fountains as any other firm in the business and has just completed a new 20-acre plant costing over $1,000,000.

Of course, advertising did not do it all, by any means, but big space and good copy did in a few years what small space could not have done in centuries.

The Inland Steel Company, of Chicago, had been attempting for some years to build up a trade on galvanized sheet steel, and though that company made an excellent grade of steel it found difficulty in getting as high a price for it as a well-advertised brand made in the Pittsburgh district. The company had been using standing cards in many trade papers for a long time.

I went to them and told them that I believed they could make a name for themselves and convince the buying public of the high standard of their product by a full-page quality campaign in all the leading papers that reached their trade.

A campaign was begun a year ago, and though the past year has been an extremely dull one for the sheet steel world, with most mills running half time, the Inland Company not only sold its full output, but more than doubled its output, and, on top of it all, is getting a higher price compared with other brands than it ever got before.

Dealers, jobbers, and wholesale consumers all responded to this advertising, and many manufacturers of galvanized steel products now make a special point in their own advertising matter of the fact that their products are made from Inland Open Hearth Sheets.

In one year's time this comparative newcomer in the galvanized sheet steel field has made an impression equaled by few firms that have been in the business for a generation.

The management of the Hawley Down-Draft Company, an old established Chicago concern, fell into the hands of the young son of a man who had been proprietor of the business for a number of years. The young man had courage and believed in advertising. The old standing cards that the company had used were therefore abandoned and in their place full-page copy of the most unique and catchy kind was used in the leading mediums to reach the three classes of purchasers of their product—steam engineers, iron and steel manufacturers, and brass and metal workers. The expenditure would have made some of the older men turn in their graves, but at that the cost of this advertising campaign is not over one-tenth as large as the public commonly believes.

The result of this campaign has been such a flood of inquiries and such an increase in business that the company has been forced to abandon its present quarters and erect a large plant in Chicago.

The Cleveland Crane & Engineering Co., of Euclid, Ohio, had been using one-eighth pages in 21 magazines, with little, if any, results. A new policy changed this to 6 or 7 magazines, with full-page copy. In three months this advertising brought more returns than all the advertising in 21 papers in 8 years.

Burton W. Mudge & Co., of Chicago, makers of railway specialties, had been using very small spaces—one-sixteenth and one-eighth pages—in railway papers, without results. They finally took out a contract for a full-page run in the *Railway Age Gazette,* and it was only very shortly after this campaign began that a railroad official tore out one of these page advertisements and attached it to an order for ventilator equipment for 100 passenger coaches, the profit on which would probably pay for a full-page campaign for several years, and this was only the beginning of a marked increase in business due directly to advertising.

The Marion Steam Shovel Company had been using two-inch spaces in the trade papers for nine years. It was induced to increase its space to one-quarter pages and after four months the representative of the *Mining and Scientific Press* was asked to call. He went, fearful that these people intended to cancel the advertisement. Instead of that, they voluntarily increased to one-half page, stating that they never knew what advertising results were until they increased to the one-quarter page, and now they were going to try one-half pages or larger.

The Janesville Pump Company, of Hazelton, Pa., accomplished a phenomenal increase in their business by using four-page colored inserts in one paper called "Mines and Minerals" for one year. Their advertising before this had been perfunctory and unproductive, but this four-page insert got the business.

At the end of the first year's campaign the Janesville Pump Company mentioned in their advertisement that they had prepared a convenient binder for binding up the 12 inserts just printed and would be glad to send one upon request. They received 1,400 requests for this binder, which was something like 15% of the whole circulation of the paper.

The Imperial Brass Manufacturing Company, of Chicago, started advertising in the *American Architect* by using one-quarter pages, alternating with one-sixteenth pages. About a year ago they increased their quarter-pages to full pages, frequently using coupons on the full pages. While the smaller spaces had brought but indifferent returns, J. J. Rockwell, who handles their copy so ably, testifies that the returns from the full-page advertisements were so spontaneous and so prolific in direct orders that it would be hard to find a stronger proof of the superior efficiency of the large space.

Chauncey B. Williams, the western manager of the *Architectural Record*, some time ago made a study of the files of his magazine for the last 20 years and he discovered that, without exception, all firms who persisted in their advertising campaigns from the first to the last issue of his paper were those who used big spaces.

Mr. Lampman, of the *American Exporter*, tells of an experience of a Buffalo firm who had been using one-eighth page space in his paper for six years, without results. The firm increased its space to one page and only a week or two after the first issue was out received a cablegram costing $15 for a bill of goods the profits on which would pay for a year's full-page campaign.

Instances of this kind might be cited till night, and then again tomorrow, and then the recital would only be begun. My references have been wholly to technical and trade journals, but the same thing applies to the popular magazines like the *Saturday Evening Post*—hence the popularity of the double spread. I honestly believe that the first man who bought a double spread in the *Saturday Evening Post* got 10 times the value that he would have gotten out of a single page, and a thousand times the value that he would have gotten out of a 100-line-single-column advertisement.

The same tendency is true in bill-posting. A man was telling me the other day about a friend of his who was using a 24-sheet poster in Chicago. A 24-sheet poster is a pretty big affair, as you know, and people would come to him and say, "Mercy, man, you must be using thousands of these posters. I see them wherever I go."

As a matter of fact, this advertiser was using only 112 stands.

The same principle applies to window dressing.

Mr. Clough, of the Abbot Alkaloidal Company, of Chicago, told of a little instance that came to his own attention.

It was one of those little corner stores opposite the schoolhouse where the children go to buy pens, pencils, writing-pads, marbles, toys, and knick-knacks of every kind—the things that children love, including school necessities. But in the center of the window was a pail of chocolate creams, tilted downward so that the candies were spread out in heaping measure before the youthful gaze. The woman in the store told Mr. Clough that she sold more chocolate creams than all the other things in the window.

That was an instance of a big advertisement surrounded by a lot of little ones.

This homely illustration brings up another fact, and that is that *concentration of attention* is vital in order to make an advertisement effective. The pail of chocolate creams was so overpoweringly attractive that the children concentrated their attention on them instead of allowing their gaze to wander over the balance of the window display.

The man who has a one-eighth-page advertisement alongside of seven others of the same size gets only one-eighth of the attention, and that confused, and if the one-eighth be on the same page with a one-half and three other eighths he can be sure that the one-half page gets at least three times the attention of all the small spaces combined.

The man who will use large spaces and put the right kind of copy into those spaces not only gets larger actual returns far out of proportion to the actual expenditure, but he gets the reputation of being a wholesale advertiser; if he uses 5 papers, people think he uses 25, and if he uses 10 they think he uses 100, while he might use little card spaces in a hundred papers and never be known as an advertiser at all.

Right or wrong, just or unjust, this is the day of the big space and the striking copy. If I were to solicit for a trade and technical journal and ran across a man who had a good proposition, but not enough money to advertise it properly, I would advise him to do one of two things; either to borrow money to do the advertising right, or spend as large a sum as he could afford on classified advertising.

Classified advertising is the only small-space advertising that is worth what it costs, and it is worth what it costs because it gets the full value of what is called voluntary attention. In other words, because of the fact that it is classified under its heading it is sought out by people who are interested in exactly the kind of proposition named under the heading.

The advertisement that receives the voluntary attention of the reader is like the store sign. It simply tells the prospective buyer the place and number, the line of goods carried, and if he is looking for that line of goods he may or may not enter the store, according to the way he is impressed by the make-up and surroundings of it, the latter being, of course, an appeal to the involuntary as well as the voluntary attention. People are either interested, indifferent, or uninterested in your product. If they are interested they may go to the trouble of hunting out a small advertisement; if they are indifferent they may be caught involuntarily, and held for a time by a big, powerful advertisement. And this is the function of the big advertisement—changing indifference to interest. The big advertisement also has an educational function in seizing hold of the uninterested, because in these changing conditions of business efforts a man who is uninterested in your proposition today may be interested tomorrow; and when the occasion arises that does awaken his interest, the advertisement that has most forcibly struck him in the past is the one that he will search out and answer.

There is just one more feature about the big advertisement, and that is its effect on, and helpfulness to, the traveling salesman. Nearly all advertising in trade and technical journals is done for the purpose of eliciting inquiries, or in other words, making it easier for the salesman to close the deal. You may run one-eighth pages and quarter-pages in 40 journals, and there is not a salesman on your force who will take the trouble to look for the advertisements or refer to them in his conference with a merchant or manufacturer. But begin a full-page campaign and you not only stiffen the spine of your salesmen, but you make them so proud of your efforts that they make it a point to show the advertisements to their prospective customers. And this is true not only of the salesmen on the road, but of every one in your whole business organization. A high-class, full-page campaign, run in the right kind of media, if it is a quality campaign, appeals to the pride and loyalty of every employee, and makes him feel like doing everything in his own individual power to measure up to the standard described in the advertising.

This fact I demonstrated strikingly in the case of the Inland Steel Company, whose product, through pure force of interest of every man in the company, has become better and better as the "Quality" advertising campaign progressed. It was good at the start, but every little means for improvement that was discoverable was discovered.

In its last analysis, the big space and the good copy is *advertising,* and the small space and the standing card is not advertising.

Advertising pays.

The other thing does not pay.

A few good advertisements pay in proportion to their cost. Hundreds of little advertisements do not pay in proportion to their cost, because they are not advertising.

I am speaking particularly of the trade and technical press. The same principle applies to all other media in a greater or less extent.[1]

FACTORS IN THE USE OF SPACE

Among the more important factors that must be considered in deciding what may be the best distribution of the space to be used, we may mention the following:

1. How big an impression must be made to accomplish the aim sought?
2. How much is it necessary to say?
3. The nature of the article. Automobiles and thumbtacks may require different space.
4. The extent of the possible market.
5. The newness of the commodity. A new product may perhaps be introduced most effectively by using larger space at first and smaller space later.
6. The seasons of the year. Large space may be desirable during the active season.
7. The number of mediums. If it is necessary to use a large number of mediums the smaller units must be used.
8. The size of space used by competitors.

CONCLUSION

It is difficult to formulate any generalization because of the numerous factors and conditions involved in various industries and sales plans. Yet the available facts, both from experimental investigations and from business experience, indicate pretty definitely that, other conditions being equal, for display advertising where the attention of the reader must be attracted, large space used less frequently

[1] Shuman, R. R. *Advertising and Selling*, January, 1911, p. 51.

is more effective than small space used more frequently. In making this general statement we must place due emphasis upon the modifying phrase, "other conditions being equal." By this we mean that where other conditions would permit just as well the use of either large or small space, the large space apparently is more effective.

On the other hand, for classified advertising or advertising to which the reader gives voluntary attention, small space is apparently more economical than large space. In other words when the advertisement seeks the reader large space is apparently more economical; when the reader seeks the advertisement small space is apparently more economical. Concretely, we may infer that a quarter-page once a week would probably not be as effective as a half-page every two weeks, and the latter would probably not be as effective as one page every month.

What are the reasons for this? In the first place, large space makes a more intense impression by its sheer magnitude. Second, it has less competition with other advertisements for the reader's attention. A full page has no counter-attracting features on the same page, and so is able to secure the reader's attention more exclusively. A one-eighth page advertisement must compete with the other seven on the same page. Third, large space permits of more adequate presentation of the proposition, such as larger and better illustrations, more complete text, better and more readable type. Fourth, large space tends to create an impression of the greater importance and reliability of the firm which is advertised.

The recent movement unquestionably has been in the direction of intensive, concentrated advertising and away from extensive, diffused advertising. Nevertheless, our conclusion must stand as a more or less tentative one which must remain open to revision in accordance with reliable experimental and business findings that may be made available in the future.

XXIV

COLOR

Extent of the use of color pages in magazines, newspapers and catalogs. Evidence regarding effectiveness of color in advertising. "Pulling power" of color. Opinions of advertisers. Use of color. Artistic value of different colors. Attention value of colors. Illustrative value of colors. Tests to determine (a) the relative values of colors and (b) the colors to be used for a specific purpose. Color theory. The Munsell system of color notation. Tests to determine the validity of this theory. Methods of the investigation.

UNTIL about 1915 color in magazine advertising was confined very largely to the cover positions. Recently, however, there has been a very marked increase in the use of color in advertisements in the body of magazines and in Sunday newspapers. Closely allied to color is the introduction of rotogravure sections in newspapers. Definite figures are presented in Table 104, which gives the total number of full pages in the *Saturday Evening Post* year by year since 1907 and the number of full-page advertisements printed in colors other than those on the cover pages.

From this table we observe that the number of color pages increased very little from 1907 to 1912. From 1912 on, the number grew more rapidly and in fact very rapidly after 1915.

A similar tabulation was made by K. S. Boardman at the suggestion of the author for the large catalog issued twice a year by Sears Roebuck & Co. Table 105 gives the total number of pages in each catalog, the number of pages in color and the percentage of pages in color.

This table shows an increase in the proportion of color pages closely parallel to that in the preceding table. In 1909 very little color was used, while in 1922 nearly 10% of the pages were in color.

H. D. Kitson made a tabulation of the number of color pages in the *American Magazine, Collier's*, the *Ladies' Home Journal* and *Country Life*, from 1905 to 1920. The results are shown in the graph of Figure 69. In 1905 the four magazines had 1.1% of their full-page advertisements in color and in 1920 they had 20.2% in color.[1]

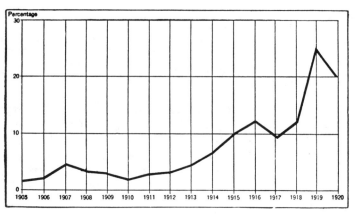

Figure 69:   Percentage of colored advertisements in four magazines, 1905-1920.   (*American, Collier's, Ladies' Home Journal*, and *Country Life*)
(*See page 581*)

Color inserts have become very common in the high-grade magazines such as the "Quality Group" and other high-grade magazines.   It is therefore highly important to analyze carefully the factors that determine the use of color and to ascertain the scientific basis upon which color may be made effective and suitable for various uses.

EVIDENCE REGARDING EFFECTIVENESS OF COLOR IN ADVERTISING

It is evident that colors have a certain amount of contrast value and attraction by virtue of which a colored advertisement stands out among the rest and its general effectiveness

[1] *Journal of Applied Psychology*, March, 1922, p. 65.

TABLE 104

TABLE SHOWING TOTAL NUMBER OF FULL-PAGE ADVERTISEMENTS
AND THE NUMBER AND PERCENTAGE OF COLORED
ADVERTISEMENTS—1907-1922

Year	Total	Color	Per Cent
1907	179	1	.5
1908	268	5	1.9
1909	467	4	.9
1910	672	2	.3
1911	731	3	.4
1912	837	20	2.4
1913	927	17	1.8
1914	1,008	10	1.0
1915	1,000	23	2.3
1916	1,607	95	5.9
1917	2,377	203	8.6
1918	2,585	380	14.6
1919	5,388	868	16.1
1920	4,903	1,344	27.4
1921	2,705	793	28.1
1922	2,907	813	28.0

is probably to a certain extent increased. Since the increase
in the use of colors, comparisons have been made by advertisers, particularly those in the mail-order field, who are in
a position to make tabulations of returns and thus to compare the use of color with black and white. Several typical
instances will be of interest. For example, one mail-order
house which sends out several million catalogs each year
printed one page in color in half the catalogs and in black
and white in the other half. The catalogs were sent out
without any regard to this point so that the distribution
was a matter of chance and the two types of catalogs
reached in general similar classes of persons. The returns
from the color page were 15 times as large as those
from the black-and-white page. A different order number
was used in the two instances as a key. In another case
a shoe was printed on a colored background instead of
black and white. The text of the advertisement and the

TABLE 105

INCREASE IN USE OF COLOR IN MAIL-ORDER CATALOGS

	Spring Catalog			Fall Catalog		
Year	Total Pages	Color Pages	Per Cent of Color Pages	Total Pages	Color Pages	Per Cent of Color Pages
1909	....	..	..	1,183	29	2.5%
1910	1,183	36	3.0%	1,349	40	3.0
1911	1,265	48	3.8	1,363	56	4.1
1912	....	..	..	....	...	..
1913	....	..	..	1,495	100	6.6
1914	1,339	90	6.7	1,615	99	6.1
1915	1,451	72	5.0	1,639	89	5.4
1916	1,457	68	4.7	1,621	91	5.6
1917	1,491	80	5.3	1,631	118	7.2
1918	1,483	78	5.3	1,639	109	6.7
1919	1,269	84	6.7	1,557	138	8.9
1920	1,299	112	8.9	1,493	151	10.1
1921	1,244	94	7.6	....	...	...
1922	981	81	8.3	1,176	129	10.1

price and quality of the shoe were identical; the one printed in color brought approximately 30 times as many orders. These are extreme instances. Very often, however, in mail-order catalogs color pages bring between 4 and 6 times as many orders.

A national distributer of patterns, after an experience covering 10 years, finds that it is necessary, whenever they advertise a model of a certain pattern in color, to order 10 times as many patterns of this particular style as of those for which the model is advertised in black and white. This company distributes its patterns through approximately 20,-000 retailers. Apparently the difference between color and black and white holds in general advertising as well as in mail-order advertising.

A certain pattern was advertised in a prominent woman's publication in black and white in May, 1918. The same pattern was advertised in color in October, 1919. In one year the black-and-white advertisement brought 418 orders; the advertisement in color brought 2,392 orders in 2½ months.

The Baltimore Bargain House, a wholesale concern specializing in millinery by mail, reports:

Items in color process usually bring in from three to four times the business brought by black-and-white pages. Ribbons were advertised in black and white over fourteen pages of color. The cost of the four pages is approximately the same as were the fourteen pages; approximately double the amount of business is done in color. . . . .[1]

Another large mail order house had two pages devoted to skirts, one in color, the other in black and white. The prices were practically the same and the goods were equally desirable. The color page pulled ten times as much.[2]

The National Cloak & Suit Company spends approximately $3,000,000 a year for catalogs. In a recent catalog 76 pages were in color, costing approximately 61% of the total cost of the catalog. The color pages bring approximately six times as large returns as the black-and-white pages. In 1920 the Butterick combination had $2,400,000 of its space in color, or approximately 25% of the total space. The *Ladies' Home Journal* in 1920 had 473 pages in color, costing $5,203,000, or approximately 25% of the total space. The *Pictorial Review* had 301 pages in color, costing $4,214,000, or approximately 25% of the total space. Fourteen leading publications in 1920 had $30,291,-000 of their space in color. The *Saturday Evening Post* in 1920 had 1,314 pages in color, costing $10,752,000. At the present time approximately 15% to 18% of the space in the leading magazines is in color.

A vulcanizing company in Wisconsin inserted a page in black and white in an automobile journal. The cost of the page was $62.50. In December, 1914, it brought 17 in-

[1] Nichols, G. A., *Printers' Ink*, Dec., 1919.
[2] *Printers' Ink*, June 17, 1920, p. 132.

quiries at a cost of $3.68 per inquiry. In January, 1915, it inserted a page in color in the same journal at a cost of $75. It brought 100 inquiries at 75 cents each. The greater returns in January, as compared with December, may in part, but certainly not entirely, be due to the fact that it was the second insertion.

The Adams Seed Company of Decorah, Iowa, relates the following experience regarding the use of color in its catalog.

The Adams Company found that its special pages pulled in very near the same proportions among different classes of buyers. In one section of the book is shown seed corn, kaffir, corn, grass, millet and other items of exclusive interest to farmers. In another are flowers and bulbs. And then there are garden seeds which are of general interest. The farmer, being practically the only one who would buy seeds strictly for business reasons, might be expected to explore the black and white pages after the fashion that the wholesale catalog houses, with but indifferent success, are trying to impress upon retailers. But the orders coming from farmers were made up in overwhelming proportion of the items on the feature pages.

Orders in the garden seed section, interesting to relate, in addition to being received on the nine-to-one basis just described, came in larger numbers from bankers than any other one class of people. The catalog was sent to a list of 10,000 bankers and a careful check made on the results.[1]

Mr. Benjamin Berfield reports the results of an experiment on the use of color in letters sent to dealers conducted by Barmon Brothers Company, Inc., of Buffalo, N. Y., manufacturers and exporters of house dresses:

The company's mailing list consists of the names of some 30,000 prospective dealers and out of this 12,000 names were chosen for the test. These dealers were divided into groups of 250, and these groups were arranged in four sections governed by geographical boundaries. This was done to eliminate any inaccuracies which might arise from location, climate and seasons.

The same letter was used throughout the entire experiment, the only variation being in the dress offered and the color of stock used. The letters were multigraphed and filled in by hand, a signature cut being used.

[1] *Ibid.*, June, 1922.

TABLE 106
EFFECT OF COLOR ON RETURNS

Letter No.	Quantity	Color of Letter	Cuts	Heading	Color of Return Envelope	Pull
1	1,000	White	No	Yes	White	9%
2	1,000	White	No	Yes	Blue	12
3	1,000	White	Yes	Special	White	18
4	1,000	White	Yes	Special	Blue	22
5	1,000	Corn	No	Special	White	14
6	1,000	Corn	Yes	Special	Blue	26
7	1,000	Green	No	Special	White	16
8	1,000	Green	Yes	Special	Blue	28
9	1,000	Gold	No	Special	White	21
10	1,000	Gold	Yes	Special	Blue	34
11	1,000	Pink	No	Special	White	26
12	1,000	Pink	Yes	Special	Blue	48

Records were kept of the total number of replies, the geographical locations from which they came, the length of time elapsing between the receipt of the first answer and of the last, and other pertinent information.

The results, when tabulated, proved to be surprising. In studying the following tables it is interesting to note the difference in the duration of pull between letter Number 1, on white stock without illustrations, and letter Number 12, on pink stock with illustrations. This is just as surprising as the difference in the pulling power of the two letters.

In the first table two columns need explanation. Each of the letters sent out was embellished with two little cuts of a special folder illustrating what the company calls its Folio line. Under the column "Headings" the word "special" means that the regular company letterhead was not used, but a special head originated for these letters. All the other items on the tables are clear and indicate the nature of this illuminating test.

The tables are reproduced as Tables 106 and 107.

The last table of results intermingles the use of cuts and colors. A part of the letters used a special cut and a part of them did not. Likewise a part of them were in colors and a part in black and white. If we separate these two elements we obtain a tabulation (Table 108) which shows that in the case of the letters which contained no

TABLE 107

DURATION OF PULL

No.	First Week	Second Week	Third Week	Fourth Week	Fifth Week	Total	Total Per Cent
1	18	32	21	11	8	90	9
2	20	37	36	15	15	120	12
3	60	61	34	9	8	178	18
4	54	78	58	21	6	217	22
5	34	53	39	11	2	139	14
6	61	141	43	12	3	260	26
7	86	67	..	6	..	159	16
8	90	164	22	5	2	283	28
9	72	131	5	3	..	211	21
10	65	258	13	2	1	339	34
11	58	193	7	..	2	260	26
12	63	407	8	1	1	480	48

cuts the average return from the letters on white paper was 10.5%, whereas the average return of the letters on colored paper was 19.2%. In the case of the list which used a cut the average return from the letters on white paper was 20% and the average return from the letters on colored paper was 34%.

TABLE 108

COLOR IN RELATION TO RETURNS

Letter No.	No Cut White	No Cut Color	Cut Used White	Cut Used Color
1	9%			
2	12			
3			18	
4			22	
5		14 (corn)		
6				26 (corn)
7		16 (green)		
8				28 (green)
9		21 (gold)		
10				34 (gold)
11		26 (pink)		
12				48 (pink)
Average	10.5%	19.2%	20%	34%

TABLE 109
RETURNS ACCORDING TO COLOR OF RETURN ENVELOPE

Color of Letter Sent and Use of Cut	Color of Return Envelope	
	White	Blue
White and no cut used	9%	12%
White and cut used	18	22
Average	13.5%	17%

At this point the question arises, if color is so much more effective, why should not all advertisements in a publication be in color? The answer is of course that the value of color lies in its contrast effect with black and white pages and in its own inherent artistic and illustrative value. If all advertisements were in color they would necessarily lose their contrast value. In fact as the proportion of color pages in a publication increases their contrast value decreases. A publication can probably not carry over 15 to 20% of its space in color without reducing considerably the effect of contrast.

"PULLING POWER" OF COLOR

A recent writer discusses the additional cost of color printing compared with its additional "pulling power." Although he calculates that a booklet illustrated by the three-color process costs four times as much as the same booklet illustrated in black, he nevertheless concludes that the extra cost is clearly justified. To quote:

Does it possess four times the attention value and sales power of the book illustrated in black only? . . . . The answer is, it does. Excellent proof of this lies in the fact that the big mail-order houses, which figure costs and results down to the fraction of a penny, pay the fourfold cost of color process work without a murmur, use more of it every year, and have found by comparative tests that a cut in color will sometimes sell as high as 15 times as many goods as a black cut.[1]

[1] *Advertising and Selling*, Vol. 19, p. 1196.

Mr. Harvey Conover,[1] of Thomas Cusack Company, states that the label of a cough-drop package was changed from white to a design in red, white, green, and gold. In the former case it was unsuccessful, while in the latter it met with immediate success.

The mail-order houses have perhaps better opportunities for ascertaining the effectiveness of color than almost any other form of business. In response to an inquiry for accurate data the author received the following replies from two well-known firms in Chicago. From one firm:

The value of colored advertising material is pretty well established, although we cannot, from our own business, give you any definite ratio of pulling power as compared with black and white.

Color advertising is one of the many topics in which generalizing is dangerous. If color is an essential feature of the merchandise, then a colored illustration is pretty sure to pay if quality and price are right according to market conditions. The elements entering into this question are numerous enough to make a book. It has been found, for instance, that a single word in red ink increased the pulling power of a certain advertisement exactly one-third. This was plainly due to the contrast afforded and would not be the case if other color printing had been in competition with the same advertisement.

Generally speaking, our experience with colored advertising is, that it has great possibilities for increasing business but must be used with caution on account of the expense and the many other factors involved.

From the other firm:

We have found that color cuts pull a great deal better in practically every instance and their additional cost is fully warranted by the tremendous increase in the business that they draw.

OPINIONS OF ADVERTISERS

A recent inquiry made by *Printers' Ink* among over a dozen leading national advertisers concerning their reasons for using color in advertisements showed the following points as justification for the extra cost of color:

[1] *Printers' Ink*, December 19, 1912, p. 31.

1. Color is more attractive than black and white.
2. Color reproduces the package as it really is.
3. Color emphasizes the trade-mark.
4. Color gives atmosphere.
5. Color will keep the advertisement on the library table.
6. Color is useful when the product itself is in colors.
7. Color has an innate appeal which is worth the price.
8. Color achieves, through judicious combinations, distinctiveness for an advertisement over others in the same issue.
9. Colored advertisements attract a better class of replies.
10. Colored advertisements are advisable for conventional reasons in preferred positions.

USE OF COLOR

Let us turn now to a more detailed consideration of the uses and values of colors. Their chief uses in advertisements may be classified under three heads: artistic value, attention value, and illustrative value. The particular colors which may be most suitable and effective for a given advertisement, label or carton, may be determined by scientific tests such as will be described in the latter part of this chapter. First, however, it will be of value to review briefly the available facts regarding color preferences in general.

Artistic Value of Different Colors. Some interesting studies have recently been made concerning the relative attractiveness of colors. Professor Wissler,[1] at Columbia University, tested the color preference of some 300 men and women and found striking likes and dislikes, as indicated in Table 110.

The author made a test with 292 persons—211 men and

[1] *Correlation of Mental and Physical Tests*, p. 17.

TABLE 110

COLOR PREFERENCES OF A GROUP OF ABOUT 300 MEN
AND WOMEN

	Tests on Men			Tests on Women		
	Preference	Prejudice	Difference	Preference	Prejudice	Difference *
Red	22	7	15	42	8	34
Orange	5	25	—20	8	31	—23
Yellow	2	32	—30	5	8	— 3
Green	7	15	— 8	9	21	—12
Blue	42	12	30	9	23	—14
Violet	19	8	11	19	9	10
White	3	1	2	8	0	8

* Difference between preferences and prejudices. The minus sign means a preponderance of prejudices over preferences.

81 women—using 10 standard Hering colors mounted on a
white background. Each person numbered the colors in
the order of his preference, putting the most agreeable color
first, the next most agreeable color second, etc. Table 111

TABLE 111

COLOR PREFERENCES ACCORDING TO A TEST MADE WITH
211 MEN AND 81 WOMEN

Rank No.	Test with Men			Test with Women		
	69 Men	103 Men	39 Men		64 Women	17 Women
8 Blue	2.4	2.8	2.2	Red	3.3	5.5
1 Red	2.5	3.8	4.4	Blue	4.1	4.5
10 Purple	3.4	4.5	4.6	Greenish Blue	4.8	5.0
9 Violet	4.0	5.3	5.5	Violet	5.2	4.5
5 Green	4.8	5.6	5.9	Green	5.5	5.3
2 Orange	5.5	7.2	6.5	Yellow	6.1	6.3
7 Greenish Blue	6.8	6.6	5.1	Bluish Green	6.3	7.5
6 Bluish Green	7.2	5.3	7.5	Purple	6.5	8.5
4 Yellowish Green	8.8	7.8	8.8	Orange	6.6	8.6
3 Yellow	9.0	9.2	9.6	Yellowish Green 6.7		7.0

indicates the results of the experiment. The smaller the
number of the rank attached, the more highly the color was
preferred.

These two investigations agree fairly closely. Both show

that the most agreeable color for the men is blue, and for the women red, and that the second choice for the men is red, and for the women blue.[1] It will be noticed that red and blue are practically a tie for first choice with the men in the second table.

Jastrow took a color census of 4,500 men and women at the World's Fair in Chicago in 1893.[2] He found that blue is pre-eminently the masculine favorite and red the feminine favorite.

Grant Allen, basing his statement on the reports of missionaries, places the color preference of primitive people in the following order: red, blue, and green.

Winch conducted an experiment on color preference with 2,000 children in London. He found the following order of preference: blue, red, yellow, and green. Yellow decreased in preference with the increase in age and intelligence of the child, while green increased in preference with the increase in age and intelligence of the child. Dr. Kate Gordon likewise made experiments with colors on white background and found the following order of preference: Blue, red, green, yellow.

In view of these facts and their practical bearing upon advertising, it is important to notice the distinction between color preference, or artistic value, and attention value. The advertiser must, of course, use those colors which not only arrest attention but which at the same time are agreeable to the eye, so that the eye may be held upon the advertisement rather than be repelled from it.

ATTENTION VALUE OF COLORS

Gale made some tests to determine, by the rapid exposure method,[3] the pure attention value as distinguished from the artistic value of colors. He exposed various colors for an

---

[1] Or violet in the first table.
[2] Jastrow, J., *Popular Science Monthly*, Vol. L, p. 361.
[3] Gale, H., *Attention Value of Colors*, p. 56.

instant on a white background to determine which ones would be noticed most frequently and most easily. His results are stated in Table 112, which gives the number of times each color was noticed and the percentage of times each color was noticed of the total number of times that all the colors were exposed to the observers:

TABLE 112

ATTENTION VALUE OF COLORS—NUMBER AND PERCENTAGE OF TIMES GIVEN COLORS WERE NOTICED

	Test on 9 Men		Test on 7 Women		Average
Red	88	19.5%	113	32.2%	25.9%
Black	151	33.5	43	12.2	22.9
Green	87	19.3	66	18.8	19.1
Orange	88	19.5	38	10.8	15.2
Blue	24	5.3	38	10.8	8.1
Purple	8	1.7	29	8.2	5.0
Yellow	4	.8	23	6.5	3.7

In this test, the attention value of colors is in the order mentioned in the last column. Red has the greatest attention value, black is next, while purple and yellow have the least. Apparently there are differences between the sexes, but the number of men and women is too small to make a significant comparison. It is interesting to note that red is first in attention value and also first in preference for the women and second for the men, while blue is first in preference for the men and second for the women, but it is considerably farther down the list in attention value.

Dr. J. M. Baldwin reports an experiment conducted with young children in which colored objects were displayed within the children's reach to determine for which ones they would reach most commonly. By this method he found the order of attractiveness of colors to be as follows: red, blue, white, green, and brown.

Red has greater attention value than any other color because it arouses greater physiological activity in the retina of the eye, and possibly because it has long been associated with war and bloodshed. Artists call it a warm color, in contrast with blue as a cold color.

In this connection it is significant to notice that red, next to black, is the most frequently used color in advertisements in which the color is not determined by the natural color of the object illustrated in the advertisement but in which the color is used for its power of attraction. A tabulation of colored advertisements appearing in various magazines showed that 77% used red, 19% brown, 8% blue, 6% orange, 6% green, 6% yellow, and 5% purple.

ILLUSTRATIVE VALUE OF COLORS

In addition to the uses already mentioned, colors also have, as a rule, a very high illustrative value. Thus by means of colors it is possible to represent adequately and correctly the natural appearance of the article—its texture, grain, pattern, outline, quality, etc. The reader obtains thereby a far more realistic impression of the object as it actually appears, and is able to imagine it with much greater facility and clearness. This is especially true of such articles as clothing and rugs. Excellent examples may be seen in almost any high-grade advertising medium.

Furthermore, the use of colors enables the customer to recognize packages, cartons, and products much more easily than does the simple use of a name or trade-mark. Good illustrations of this are the cartons used for foods, canned goods, toilet articles, etc. Recall, for example, the packages, labels, and wrappers of the National Biscuit Company, Colgate & Co., J. H. Williams & Co., Lever Bros. Co., Joseph Campbell Co.

Colors also aid in producing perspective. Red seems nearer than blue at the same distance, and a bright object seems nearer than a dark one. These differences in shades and tints of colors help to create an appearance of perspective and depth in the presentation of objects which makes them seem more realistic and true to life.

There has been much confusion in discussions regarding the use of colors. This has been due primarily to two causes: first, we have not had, until recently, a relatively satisfactory method of designating the precise color that is being considered; and secondly, we have not developed or applied methods of determining or testing what particular color or colors are most suitable for a given situation. Before undertaking to discuss the various methods by which the usefulness of specific colors for particular purposes or advertisements may be determined, let us note briefly the psychological and physiological theories which have been proposed to explain color phenomena.

COLOR THEORY

There is much confusion in discussing color with regard to the number of primary colors and what these colors are. Traditionally we speak of the seven colors of the rainbow. Various theories of color designate three, or four, or five colors as the primary ones. However, the researches on color phenomena along psychological lines have led to the conclusion that there are four primary colors besides black and white. These four colors are red, green, yellow, and blue. This theory, originally proposed by Hering and more recently modified by various students of color, explains probably more satisfactorily than any other theory most of the phenomena that we know regarding color sensations. The second reason for assuming that there are only four primary colors is that with the combination of black and white in varied proportions with one or more of these colors it is possible to produce or match with close approximation any particular color in our environment. This theory of color includes, in the next place, the fact that red and green, and yellow and blue are complementary pairs. Red and green when mixed will produce gray; likewise yellow and blue when mixed produce gray or white. By mixture here is meant a mixture that takes place in the eye as a result of successive or simultaneous impressions of two or more colors coming into the eye, as by rotating two colored disks on a color wheel. These elementary facts regarding color phenomena, and the color theory proposed to explain them, are useful in helping us to understand many of the phenomena of color and also to deal with colors more intelligently and to use them more effectively. Carrying this conception of complementaries further we find, if we arrange the colors of a spectrum in the form of a perimeter on a circumference begun at red and continued through orange, green, yellow, blue, and purple, that any pair of colors at opposite ends of a diagonal drawn through the center are approximately complementary.

The Hering theory of color, more recently modified by Christine Ladd-Franklin, assumes that there are two colored substances in the retina of the eye, a red-green substance and a yellow-blue substance. Whenever the red-green substance is stimulated positively it produces the sensation of red. When it is stimulated negatively or when it is recovering from a stimulation of red it produces green. In the same manner yellow and blue are related to each other. This assumption explains such phenomena or conditions as after-images, color-blindness, color-contrast, and the like. The interested reader should consult the larger treatises on psychology for more complete discussions of color phenomena.

THE MUNSELL SYSTEM OF COLOR NOTATION

In 1905 Professor A. H. Munsell published a plan for designating colors and issued a series of charts on which the various colors with their designations were kept permanently. The basis on which this system of notation was

prepared is as follows. It starts with the three characteristics of color which are:

1. Hue, or the color, as red or blue or yellow;

2. Value, or what psychologists commonly speak of as
brightness, that is, variations in lightness or darkness, ranging from pure black to complete white;

3. Chroma, or what psychologists and physicists commonly speak of as saturation, that is, more or less of the
same color, as, for example, a strong, rich blue as contrasted with a weaker saturation of blue.

The system in the next place divides each characteristic
into a series of 10 steps of approximately equal distances.
Thus, for example, the scale of values extends through a
series of 10 steps from pure black to a complete white,
number 1 being pure black and number 10 being pure
white. Likewise the scale for chroma or saturation extends
through a series of 10 steps from the most saturated tint
of a color to complete absence of that color, number 1
being the weakest tint of a color and number 10 being the
strongest or most saturated shade of that color. On this
principle, then, any given color may be designated by a
symbol which accurately describes it. As, for example,
$B\frac{6}{3}$ means the color blue with a value or brightness of six
and a chroma, or saturation value, of three, number 1
being the palest or least saturated blue, and 10 a very
strong blue. Value 6 means the sixth step from black
to pure white. The symbols used for the various
colors are: R=red, G=green, Y=yellow, B=blue, P=
purple, and N=neutral gray.

The important contribution made by this system of notation is the provision of a means whereby a color may be
accurately identified so that anyone, by use of the charts
prepared on the basis of this notation, is able to know exactly what color is meant by $B\frac{6}{3}$. The colors in the charts

are prepared in such a way that they are practically if not absolutely permanent colors and will not appreciably lose any of their original quality.

In the next place the Munsell system attempts to apply this scheme of notation to practical problems of color combinations, such as in advertisements and designs and wherever color combinations are used for commercial purposes. The central idea in the combinations of colors according to the Munsell system is based on the theory of complementarism which has been known to psychologists and physicists for a long time. The theory is that, in general, colors which are complementary, whether it be two or more, constitute a pleasing combination. Thus, for example, a light yellow combined with a dark blue will produce a neutral gray when mixed on a color wheel. A greenish yellow is complementary to a purple blue, and so on.

TESTS TO DETERMINE THE VALIDITY OF THIS THEORY

Under direction of the author, Mr. T. M. Shepard carried out a series of tests and experiments designed to determine (1) the preferences for single colors in advertisements, (2) the preferences for color combinations in advertisements and (3) to what extent the principle of complementariness is practically valid for advertisements and other commercial uses. Practically all tests on the preferences for colors made thus far have been carried out with color patches apart from any advertisements or objects in connection with which the colors were to be used. Likewise, the theory of complementariness had been tested out experimentally chiefly apart from objects with which they were to be used. The purpose of these experiments was to ascertain to what extent complementary colors in advertisements actually did constitute pleasing combinations.

Method of the Investigation. The investigation was begun by obtaining (1) a set of 10 single-color advertisements,

(2) a set of two-color advertisements, and (3) a set of multicolored advertisements. Two different series of tests were made with these advertisements. The first series of tests was designed to discover the actual relative preference of consumers and artists for the various colors *on* the advertisements. The second series of tests attempted to determine by analysis whether or not the colors used on the advertisements were complementary or to what extent they approximated complementariness.

Let us take first the tests made with the single-color advertisements. The 10 advertisements used were the following:

1. A street-car card of Cluett-Peabody & Company, advertising Arrow Collars. The background was yellow, the lettering black. The colors in terms of the Munsell system and the relative amount of area occupied by each color were as follows:

$$92\% \ Y\frac{8}{9} \text{ and } 8\% \ N\frac{1}{0}$$

2. Wearever water bottle made by the Faultless Rubber Company; *Saturday Evening Post*, Sept. 25, 1920. The colors and the proportions of areas were as follows:

39%—R-5/10	10%—N-4/10
28%—N-8/0	1%—N-1/0
22%—N-9/0	

3. Crystal White Soap advertisement, by Peet Brothers Company; *Ladies' Home Journal*, November, 1916, page 76. For the remaining advertisements the colors and proportions of various colors will not be specified in terms of the Munsell notations. The color will simply be mentioned. In this advertisement it was purple-blue.

4. Listerine Toothpaste, made by the Lambert Pharmacal Company, appearing in the *Butterick Quarterly* in the winter of 1920-21, page 75. Color—greenish yellow.

5. Community Silver, by Oneida Community, Ltd.; back cover *Saturday Evening Post*, October, 1920. Color—yellowish red.

6. Cataract Washer; *Good Housekeeping*, March, 1920, page 109. Color—blue-green.

7. Lexington Automobile; *Saturday Evening Post*, Nov. 27, 1920, page 85. Color—blue.

8. Street-car card, Fisher Business College of Boston. Color—orange.

9. Street-car card, Cambridge Laundry, Cambridge, Massachusetts. Color—violet.

10. Street-car card, London Harness Company of Boston. Color—green.

The relative pleasingness of these colors was determined by the ranking method with 32 men, 25 women, and 25 artists, as observers or judges. The results of this test are shown in Table 113, which gives the median ranks.

TABLE 113

RESULTS OF TESTS ON PREFERENCES FOR VARIOUS COLORS ON THE ADVERTISEMENTS

Test Card Number	Color	32 Men		57 Consumers			
		15 College Men	17 Business Men	Total Men	25 Women	Total Consumers	25 Artists
3	Purple-Blue	4.0	4.0	3.2	4.0	3.5	3.85
7	Blue	4.5	3.6	3.85	4.33	3.89	6.7
5	Yel. Red	5.33	6.0	4.6	4.25	4.33	2.85
6	Blue-Green	4.75	7.33	5.75	5.8	5.66	5.62
2	Red	6.0	7.0	6.0	7.0	6.0	6.5
9	Violet	7.5	6.66	6.75	6.0	6.25	7.5
1	Yellow	7.0	6.33	5.56	7.5	6.75	4.25
10	Green	7.5	6.75	7.0	7.83	7.9	9.66
8	Orange	5.0	6.5	7.8	7.0	7.42	5.5
4	Green. Yellow	7.25	10.0	10.6	9.8	9.9	10.58

A further test was then made by using color patches cut from the same advertisements to determine the relative color preference when the color alone is seen and considered apart from its use in an advertisement. The color patches were approximately an inch and a half square. The results of this test are shown in Table 114.

These results show that there are decided color preferences on the part of consumers, and that there is a substan-

TABLE 114

RESULTS OF TESTS ON PREFERENCES FOR VARIOUS COLORS OFF
THE ADVERTISEMENTS

Test Card No.	Color	32 Men		57 Consumers		
		15 College Men	17 Business Men	Total Men	25 Women	Total 57
2	Red	4.33	3.6	3.85	4.33	4.0
3	Blue	4.5	5.0	4.5	5.0	4.56
4	Orange	5.0	4.0	4.6	5.0	4.56
5	Blue-Green	4.5	5.0	4.85	5.4	5.0
9	Violet	5.0	5.75	5.5	5.33	5.28
7	Green	7.33	4.25	5.5	6.5	5.56
1	Purple-Blue	5.75	7.0	5.85	5.83	5.91
8	Yellow	6.6	8.0	6.88	6.5	6.66
6	Yel. Red	7.0	9.5	8.83	8.55	8.56
10	Green. Yellow	10.0	9.75	9.87	10.22	10.03

tial agreement among the various groups. There is also a
fairly close agreement between the color preferences when
the colors are seen on the advertisement, and when they are
seen off the advertisement in patches. Third, there is a decided disagreement between the preferences of the commercial artists and of the consumers (the 32 men and 25
women). The artists considered yellow and orange to be
the most effective, while the test with the 57 consumers
showed yellow to be distinctly low in preference value. The
artists agreed with the consumers in placing blue relatively
high.

Another test was carried out with the 10 two-color advertisements. The details regarding the proportions of the
various colors in them will not be given. The chief colors,
however, will be mentioned. The 10 advertisements used
were the following:

1. Klenzo Toothpaste; *Saturday Evening Post,* May 8, 1920.
Chief colors: orange and blue.

2. Cutex Manicure; *Pictorial Review,* November, 1920. Chief
colors: green and violet.

3. Steero Bouillon Cubes; *Delineator*, December, 1916. Chief colors: orange and purple (yellow violet).

4. Snider's Catsup; *Ladies' Home Journal*. Chief colors: green and red.

5. Ivory Soap Flakes; back cover *Ladies' Home Journal*. Chief colors: purple and yellow.

6. Michelin tires; *Saturday Evening Post*, Nov. 27, 1920. Chief colors: purple and yellow.

7. Royal Baking Powder; *Peoples' Home Journal*, March, 1920. Chief colors: yellow and red.

8. Street-car card of Hecker's flour. Chief colors: blue and red.

9. Street-car card of Daggett & Ramsdell's cold cream. Chief colors: green and red.

10. Bon Ami; back cover *Good Housekeeping*. Chief colors: green and yellow.

Tests similar to those described above were carried out with the same groups of persons. Table 115 gives the results.

TABLE 115

RESULTS OF TESTS ON COLOR PREFERENCES

Test Card No.	Color	57 Consumers					25 Artists
		32 Men					
		17 Business Men	15 College Men	Total Men	25 Women	Total Consumers	
5	B and Y	5.33	4.0	4.0	5.0	4.5	2.62
8	B and R	4.6	5.0	4.33	5.5	4.6	4.0
6	P and Y	4.0	6.33	5.0	6.0	5.0	6.66
2	V and G	7.0	4.5	6.0	5.6	5.5	5.16
4	R and G	5.0	5.66	5.5	5.5	5.5	5.35
9	R and G	7.0	5.5	6.0	6.0	5.8	10.36
1	B and O	5.0	6.0	6.5	6.75	6.5	7.22
7	R and O	7.0	8.2	7.5	7.5	7.25	6.62
3	P and O	7.66	7.25	7.35	8.14	7.6	6.4
10	G and Y	7.66	8.66	8.25	6.85	7.6	8.0

A similar series of tests was then made with patches taken from these advertisements. Results are shown in Table 116.

TABLE 116

RESULTS OF TESTS ON COLOR PREFERENCES

Test Card No.	Color	15 College Men	32 Men 17 BusinessMen	Total Men	25 Women	Total Consumers 57
7	Vio. and Green	7.33	7.66	7.33	3.33	4.5
4	Blue and Yel.	5.0	4.0	4.33	4.66	4.66
2	Blue and Red	3.5	3.5	3.5	6.66	4.8
1	Purp. and Ora.	6.0	4.0	4.75	6.66	5.37
9	Purp. and Yel.	6.5	7.66	6.8	5.0	5.66
8	Red and Green	7.0	7.0	5.5	6.75	5.89
6	Purp. and Yel.	6.0	5.75	5.83	8.0	6.2
10	Red and Green	5.5	5.5	6.66	6.0	6.37
5	Red and Yel.	6.5	6.25	6.33	8.0	6.87
3	Green and Yel.	9.0	9.6	9.2	7.75	8.66

Here again there are decided preferences for various color combinations. Various groups agree rather closely. In general the consumer preferences seemed to be in favor of combinations made up of colors of low brightness value and strong chroma or saturation. It appears that single color preferences seem to have an important influence upon the color combination. Thus, for example, combinations containing blue in large areas were placed relatively higher than the others, while those containing large amounts of yellow and orange were placed low. A blue and yellow combination seemed to be the outstanding favorite of all combinations. It was followed closely by a blue and red combination. Red and green, purple and orange, and red and orange combinations were ranked consistently among the lowest. Complementary combinations were ranked relatively higher in the list of consumer preferences than non-complementary combinations. There was a fair agreement on these color combinations between commercial artists and consumers.

The next step was to determine the extent to which these colors actually approximated complementariness. Consequently the color areas of the various colors were measured in these advertisements by means of a planimeter and the relative proportions of each color were expressed in percentages of the total area of the advertisement. (For example, see the first two advertisements mentioned on page 598.) These colors were then expressed in terms of the Munsell notation, and color discs, in the proportions in which they occurred in the advertisement, were placed upon a mixing wheel to determine what the resulting color would be. This resulting color was then again designated in terms of the Munsell notation. The colors are given in Table 117 in the order in which they approach neutral gray or complementariness. The ones practically neutral gray are given at the beginning of the table.

TABLE 117

RESULTS OF TESTS ON COLOR PREFERENCES

Test Card No.	Colors	Resultant Color	Consumers' Preference		Artists' Preference	
			Median	Rank	Median	Rank
4	Red and Green	N-6/	5.5	4	5.6	4
5	Blue and Yellow	N-7/	4.5	1	2.6	1
2	Violet and Green	N-7/	5.5	5	5.1	3
10	Green and Yellow	N-8/	7.6	9	8.0	9
6	Purple and Yellow	P-3/1	5.0	3	6.66	7
3	Purple and Orange	RP-6/2	7.6	10	6.4	5
9	Red and Green	GY-7/2	5.8	6	10.3	10
1	Blue and Orange	RP-6/3	6.5	7	7.2	8
7	Red and Orange	YR-6/6	7.2	8	6.62	6
8	Blue and Red	P-4/6	4.6	2	4.0	2

The third series of advertisements consisted of 10 multi-colored advertisements as follows:

1. Modart Corset; *Pictorial Review*, October, 1920. Chief colors: blue, violet and red.

2. Wesson Oil; *Ladies' Home Journal*, November, 1920. Chief colors: blue, yellow, red and green.

3. Bon Ami; *Ladies' Home Journal*. Chief colors: violet, yellow and green.

4. Mavis face powder; *Ladies' Home Journal,* September, 1920. A mixture of a great variety of colors.

5. Cole Motor Car. Chief colors: green, red and blue.

6. Sunkist oranges; *Ladies' Home Journal,* August, 1916. Chief colors: blue and orange.

7. O'Sullivan's Rubber Heels. Street-car card. Chief colors: purple, yellow, red and green.

8. Wrigley's gum. Street-car card. Chief colors: yellow, red and green.

9. Street-car card of Mueller's Spaghetti. Chief colors: green, blue and red.

The preference tests for the colors off the advertisements with the same groups of persons previously mentioned showed the results given in Table 118.

TABLE 118

RESULTS OF TESTS ON COLOR PREFERENCES

| Test Card No. | Colors | 15 College Men | 32 Men | | 25 Women | Total Consumers | 25 Artists |
			17 Business Men	Total			
5	G-B-R	3.0	2.5	2.5	4.5	2.87	5.33
1	B-P-R	5.0	4.75	4.85	3.25	4.12	6.6
6	O-B-G	4.66	4.0	4.17	4.75	4.3	2.75
4	R-G-Y	5.0	5.5	5.0	4.6	4.7	7.6
2	R-Y-G	7.0	5.5	6.14	5.5	5.8	4.0
7	P-Y-R	5.5	7.0	6.17	6.5	6.12	5.66
3	V-Y-G	5.0	7.4	7.0	6.75	6.72	3.62
10	G-B-Br	8.5	7.66	8.0	8.14	7.0	7.33
9	R-B-Y	8.5	9.0	8.6	9.0	8.7	9.3
8	Y-R-G	10.22	10.0	10.0	9.6	9.7	9.0

Next the proportions of the various colors in these advertisements were measured by means of a planimeter and the colors were mixed in those proportions on the color wheel. The mixture yielded colors in terms of the Munsell notation as shown in Table 119.

The results show a fairly decided preference for complementary combinations, and the more nearly balanced or complementary the colors were the more highly they were

TABLE 119

RESULTS OF TESTS ON COLOR PREFERENCES

Test Card No.	Colors	Resultant Color	Consumers' Preference		Artists' Preference	
			Median	Rank	Median	Rank
1	Blue-purple-red	N-6/	4.1	2	6.6	6
2	Red-yellow-green	N-6/	5.8	5	4.0	3
3	Violet-yellow-green	N-8/	6.7	7	3.6	2
5	Green-blue-red	P-3/1 or N-3/1	2.8	1	5.3	4
6	Orange-blue-green	YR-6/	4.3	3	3.7	1
10	Green-blue-brown	Y-7/2	7.0	8	7.3	7
7	Purple-yellow-red	RP-4/3	6.1	6	5.6	5
4	Red-green-yellow	YR-5/5	4.7	4	7.6	8
8	Red-blue-yellow	YR-7/6	9.7	10	9.0	9
9	Yellow-red-green	R-4/6	8.7	9	9.3	10

preferred. The preferences of the artists differ quite materially from the preferences of the consumers. The specific inference is that the consumer, who is ultimately the person to be reached and influenced, is a more reliable index of color preferences than are commercial artists. The difference in the results between the artists and the other men and women may possibly be explained on the ground that the artists had certain preconceived ideas and theories regarding colors which kept them from showing a naive color preference. After all, the ultimate test is the naive preference for colors on the part of the consumer who is to be influenced rather than a theoretically preconceived notion regarding what should and what should not be preferred. The suggestion here then is that when colors are an important matter the particular colors, tints, or shades to be used and their combinations should be determined by means of color tests such as those here outlined. The tests should be carried out with the consumers to whom the advertisement is intended to appeal. Such a procedure will avoid the use of disagreeable, inappropriate and ineffective colors.

XXV

LAYOUT AND TYPOGRAPHY

Importance of layout. 1. Attention elements. Importance of attention factors. Laws of attracting attention: (a) The law of magnitude or intensity. Application of law of magnitude. Increase in size of display type used. The point system of measuring type. Testing the attention value of display type. How large should display lines be? (b) Law of isolation or counter-attraction. Application of the law. (c) Movement—its application to layout. Borders, eye-movement and attention. Increase in use of borders. Rules for the use of borders. Directing the movement of the eyes. (d) The principle of contrast. An experimental test of contrast. Contrast devices. Black and white contrast. Comparative values of mechanical and interest factors in securing attention. 2. Artistic elements. Art for business' sake. Psychological effects. Artistic forms. Classes of forms and outlines. Applications in advertisements. Meaning of balance. The optical center. Location of the main features. The principle of support or stability. Representation of action. Meaning of harmony. Harmony in forms and shapes. Styles of type. 3. Comprehension factors: type and legibility. Four main factors. The type. Type faces commonly used at the present time. Individuality in type. The distribution of letters and words. The effect of background.

By "layout" is meant either (1) a diagram accompanied by the copy and by instructions which set forth either roughly or accurately the manner in which the advertisement is to be constructed, or (2) the arrangement, features and typography of the finished or printed advertisement. The functions of the layout of the finished advertisement may be stated as follows:

1. To secure attention
    (a) To the advertisement as a whole, or
    (b) To important parts of the advertisement
    (c) To direct the attention from part to part in the desired order

2. To convey the message easily and effectively, so that it may be read and grasped with the least effort

3. To be pleasing to look at

606

These functions at once suggest then the chief questions which must be considered in planning an effective layout. They are the following: How may the layout secure the attention most effectively? How may it be constructed so that the advertisement will be grasped and read most easily? How may the layout be made most pleasing and attractive? We shall therefore discuss the problems of layout under these three headings:

The Importance of Layout

There is no better way of fixing the definite responsibility of the layout—the advertisement's structure—in helping copy produce maximum sales than from evidence furnished by mail-order campaigns.

In advertisements that send prospective buyers to the dealer's store it is, of course, next to impossible to determine a layout's value, because advertising of that sort is not usually keyed.

But the moral behind this article applies with even greater force to the latter type of copy than it does to mail-order copy, for in direct mail-order advertising results are easily traceable.

And a correct copy structure has been proved to be far more vital than the average manufacturer might imagine.

A middle-western manufacturer several years ago got himself into a tight place. He had a $10 article. The manufacturing cost was $2.50. He had been getting inquiries at approximately $1.50 each. As he sold a heavy percentage of inquiries—for he had an excellent follow-up selling plan—he secured one order from every three inquiries. That made selling cost, counting advertising literature, about $7.25. Adding to this his overhead, salaries and other like items it brought the cost of getting the article into each consumer's hands almost $7.75 each, leaving a profit on each article of about $2.25. Yet his was an excellent mail-order business, for few of them manage to sell more than 15% of their inquiries.

But his success brought two competitors into the field. They had good copy, and from the instant reduction in his volume of inquiries, he imagined that they were sharing heavily in what had previously been his field exclusively. Their article presented slight advantages that his did not.

His inquiry cost began going up. From $1.50 each, replies began to cost him around $2. Then, when they shot above that mark, he became frightened, for inquiries at $2.25 meant a profitless business and above that amount he would lose money.

He finally took his problem to efficient advertising counsel. They surveyed his literature without comment. He told them it was necessary to cut inquiry cost or he would have to go out of business. How to do it was a puzzle to him.

The advertising counsel was loath to change copy that had been possessed of known productivity. They measured up the copy to all standards they knew and finally decided that that was not the way out.

One bright mind criticised the layout for the copy. Then came a number of layout suggestions—means that would clarify the readability of the advertisement. It was decided to allow the wording of the advertisement to stand and rehabilitate the copy's structure.

The advertisement had a border that overshadowed the headline. This was stripped off entirely. Then instead of the hand-lettered type headline, Cheltenham Bold type was substituted. The headline was set in "reverse" white letters on a black background—thus giving it 50% greater attraction power.

The advertisement was approximately 50 lines by two columns. The first line beneath the headline was 6-point lightface and two columns in width. The first few lines of the advertisement were changed to 8-point blackface—to give the eye an easier task in dropping from the large headline to the smaller lightface type below. It was decided two-column measure was too long for the remaining lines of 6-point type, the eye having reached the end of the line had difficulty finding the next line below, thus, in a measure, destroying interest—it was hard to read. The side borders of the advertisement were left off altogether—giving the type more room. A black bar, that balanced the black background at the top of the advertisement, was placed at the bottom. The illustration faced outward. The experts turned it inward—so it faced the copy—and induced interest in that direction.

It must be remembered that these advertising men were redressing an advertisement that had produced returns, and they were fearful lest by some miscue they might injure its pulling power.

The last touch, however, was to place a black circle around the copy and allow the illustration to break into the circle. This was just below the "reverse" headline and the black background at the top of the advertisement was flush to the top of the circle.

They took the copy and took the competitor's advertising. All three were pasted upon the page of a mail-order paper, for the purpose of gaging the attention value of each. Not a word of the copy was changed.

The new advertisement, though not large, absolutely dominated the page.

The advertiser was a trifle skeptical still, so he utilized the new copy in a few mediums only, at first. It had been out scarcely a day when he felt his problem had been solved. Inquiry cost instantly dropped two-thirds. Where he had been paying between $2 and $2.10 for replies, at that time, he found that he was now getting them for less than 70 cents each.

He was amazed at the increase in the volume of inquiries and could scarcely attribute it to what to his mind was trivial—the layout. In spite of this attitude, however, he immediately substituted the new advertisement in his entire list. The same result followed from every mail-order publication he was using.

It was little short of a miracle to him, and within a short time one competitor dropped out of sight and he bought out the one who managed to hold his own for a while.

The incident demonstrated absolutely the value of correct layouts. I have seen similar cases, but never before one that so vividly portrayed the necessity of giving the advertisement's structure thorough study before dismissing the building of the layout.

The layout has two primary functions: Attraction power and readability—making it easy to read.

In giving the advertisement power to attract the reader's eye as the line of vision enters a page there are various methods of achievement. It can be done with extraordinarily large black bars at the top and bottom; with a heavy black border; with a circle; a curve; anything that will intercept the left-to-right path of vision and carry it to the desired point in the advertisement. White space to the left of the type matter has the same effect.

Setting the headline in "reverse"—white letters on a black background—has 50% greater power to attract the eye than plain black type.

Oftentimes the name of the article advertised is used in the middle of the advertisement. To be optically correct this name, if set in heavy black type, should be two-thirds to three-fourths the length of the advertisement above its base.

That is, in a 100-line, single column advertisement, the center display should be 25 to 33 lines below the topmost point of the copy. Then, if the advertisement be page size, it is directly in line with the reader's natural line of vision. Experts have determined that fact by experiment. It is due to the way the average reader holds a magazine or newspaper.

When the type gets down to 6-point it becomes hard to read if the lines are 5 or 6 inches in length. The type columns should then be "doubled up"—two columns of type instead of one—thus shortening the distance the eye must travel on one plane. This makes reading easy.

If the headline is set in plain type, then it should be surrounded with 1½ to 2 inches of white space, governed, of course, by the advertisement's size, to allow it to stick out from the surrounding type matter.

A line or bar in an advertisement that intercepts the line of vision is always capable of getting attention. A diagonal line across the side of a layout will invariably arrest the eye and carry it to the point desired.

In this class is the copy that ran last winter, I believe, in the resort classified sections of certain magazines and weeklies. It had a crayon check mark on the left-hand side of the copy. The upward stroke of the check mark was diagonal, and it stuck out from the entire page of classified advertisements to the extent that it was the first apparent point of interest to the man who turned to that page. The writer understands that this insignificant five- or six-line classified advertisement produced abnormal returns, due simply to the bit of strategy in laying out the copy.

A circle surrounding the type of an advertisement, with the headline at the top of the circle and breaking into it, is another attraction power that has been used with good returns in various types of copy.

The arrow was a magnet that in the past few years has worked overtime.

In constructing the layout for an advertisement that occupies from three-fourths of a page to a full page there is, of course, no especial necessity of attracting the eye; that is achieved by the fact that the eye has to pass over the advertisement in reaching the next page. Its size guarantees it a reading if there is sufficient force in the copy.

The illustration can be made to induce interest in the copy. Most illustrations are placed on the left-hand side of the advertisement, or in the middle. By turning the illustration so that it faces the type matter, if it is on the left- or right-hand side, the eye is made to travel toward the type.

The average copywriter can intuitively tell whether an advertisement is easy to read; whether the headline type is too strong for the illustration; whether the body type lines are too long;

whether there is too much or too little white space; whether the advertisement dominates the page it is on.

One plan that gives at a glance the verdict as to the attraction power of an advertisement is this: Have the advertisement proofed up on the same paper that it will be printed on in the publication for which it is intended. Then take a typical page of that publication and carefully paste the advertisement upon it. Have it surrounded by other advertisements, if that is the way the copy usually appears.

Then close the paper and in the presence of someone, run over the pages. When you arrive at the page on which the advertisement is pasted, ascertain which advertisement on that page was the first that caught the eye. You will usually get fair judgment, and it is usually a fair test of the layout.

When the selling plan is decided upon; when the layout is finished satisfactorily, then comes the selection of the headlines, which is one of the biggest of tasks. For with plan, layout, and headline selected, the execution of the copy is simple.[1]

ATTENTION ELEMENTS

Importance of Attention Factors. Students of advertising have always realized that the attention factors are highly important. We have, however, not known in an accurate manner to what extent the attention factors are responsible for the total effectiveness of an advertisement. The results presented in Table 64, Chapter XIV, demonstrate that the attention value of an advertisement is approximately twice as important as the actual convincingness of the text itself. This is shown by the fact that the correlation between the relative attention values of various series of advertisements and the final results brought by the advertisements is considerably higher than that for convincingness. The correlation for attention value is about .70.

The first obvious function which every advertisement must perform is that of arresting the attention of the reader. Whatever else an advertisement must do, first of all it must catch the reader's eye. No matter how effective and forceful the text of the advertisement may be, if it remains un-

---

[1] *Printers' Ink,* January 25, 1912, p. 10.

noticed it is wasted. Many an otherwise excellent advertisement is a loss simply because it fails to be noticed. On the other hand, the effectiveness of an advertisement does not lie in its attention value alone; it must have something to offer after the attention has been obtained. But the securing of attention is an indispensable function, and it is this vital point which we are to discuss here.

The author made a tabulation of all firms advertising with full pages in the year 1890 in two standard magazines. These advertisements were then classified into three groups according as their attention values were judged to be good, fair, or poor. Then the advertising sections of the same two magazines for the year 1910 were searched to find which of these firms were still advertising in these magazines. The investigation brought the results shown in the following tabulation.

	Number of Firms Using Full Pages in 1890	Number of These Firms Left in 1910
Attention value good	35	17 or 49%
Attention value fair	30	5 or 17%
Attention value poor	32	5 or 16%

Hence there were approximately three times as many firms whose advertisements had high attention value, who were still advertising in the same mediums 20 years later as there were firms whose advertisements had inferior attention value. While these figures do not absolutely prove the point in favor of the attention-compelling advertisements, they have, nevertheless, considerable weight. There are many obvious reasons, besides inefficient advertising, why a firm might not be advertising in the same mediums 20 years later. The mediums might not have been suitable for its product, or the business might have been discontinued, or the product might have been in demand only temporarily, or the methods of selling might have been changed. Nevertheless, these figures have some corroborating force in favor of the greater efficiency of properly constructed advertisements.

Several factors have tended to make the task of securing attention for a given commodity a more difficult one today than it was 50 years ago when advertising was in its comparative infancy. It is, therefore, all the more important to study thoroughly this aspect of our subject, namely, the methods and principles of reaching the potential customer through effective layout. Among the most important factors which make the problem of securing attention a difficult one today, we may mention the following four:

1. *Hasty Reading, Due to Increase in Number of Mediums.* In the first place, the tremendous volume of printed matter that has literally flooded the land has probably developed a habit of more hasty reading. Half a century ago the typical home had one or two magazines which were read thoroughly from cover to cover. The same home today has perhaps half a dozen magazines which are skimmed more or less superficially. Newspapers, too, were formerly few in number and small in size, and their advertisements therefore had a greater chance of being read. The figures presented in Chapter II show the increase in the number of publications.

2. *Growth in Circulation.* A second factor in the growth of advertising matter is the tremendous increase in the circulation of most of the publications. The following are a few examples. The *Saturday Evening Post* has a circulation of nearly two and a half millions. In 1897 its circulation was only 3,000. *Collier's Weekly* has a circulation of about one million. The *American Magazine* has a circulation of 1,900,000. In 1884 the circulation of the *Ladies' Home Journal* was about 25,000. Today it is about two millions. From 1900 to 1910 the total circulation of the 60 leading national periodicals doubled. In 1922 their combined circulation had again doubled and was about 60 millions. Among newspapers the distribution of some of

the metropolitan dailies is very large. For example, the *Chicago Tribune* has a distribution of over 400,000 copies, the *New York Herald* over 200,000, the *New York Sun* about 200,000, and the *New York Tribune* about 125,000. According to F. Hudson (*Journalism in America*, page 525) the New York papers mentioned here had in 1842 an estimated circulation of 15,000, 20,000 and 9,500 respectively.

3. *Increase in Firms Advertising.* In the third place, there has been a manifold increase in the number of firms using advertising mediums. All are bidding for the reader's attention. Note the data on this point presented in Chapter II.

4. *Increase in Size of Mediums.* In the fourth place, not only have the mediums and their circulation and the number of advertisers greatly increased, but, as a consequence of the latter fact, the total advertising space of all kinds has manifolded even more rapidly.

These conditions are partly offset today by the more general habit of reading advertisements, by the greater confidence which people have in advertising, by the better methods of advertising, by a more thorough understanding of its principles, and by the introduction of classified advertisements which give the small advertiser a better chance. The general public has acquired the habit of reading advertisements and has greater confidence in their reliability. It has acquired this confidence largely as a result of the honesty of nearly all advertising appearing in high-class periodicals. In its early days, advertising dealt largely with patent medicines. There were no standards of discrimination as to the genuineness of the advertisements or the responsibility of the firms back of them. Today the high-grade mediums are almost entirely free from unreliable forms of publicity. This condition has been a powerful factor in making advertising more effective. A fuller discussion of this topic has been presented in Chapter XX.

LAWS OF ATTRACTING ATTENTION

The psychological principles which underlie the conditions of attracting attention are substantially the same whether they apply to attracting attention to advertisements or to any other feature in our environment. These may be conveniently divided into two types:

A. Mechanical, external, or objective factors
    (1) The law of magnitude or intensity
    (2) The law of isolation or counter-attraction
    (3) The law of motion or suggested movement
    (4) The law of contrast

B. Mental, internal, or subjective factors
    (1) The effect of the present mental attitude or "set"
    (2) The effect of previous experience and training
    (3) The effect of inborn or instinctive interests

(a). *The Law of Magnitude or Intensity.* This law, stated in general terms, is that, other things being equal, the duration and the degree of attention depend upon the intensity of the stimulus. A loud sound, a strong light, a large object, or a pungent odor arouses the attention more easily and more surely than a weak sound, a faint light, a small object, or a mild odor. Powerful stimuli impress the sense organs with much greater effect than do weak stimuli. This law of intensity is a broad biological principle deeply ingrained in human nature. A strong stimulus to an animal as well as to man, particularly in primitive conditions of life, means a warning signal and therefore something to be heeded.

To demonstrate the strength of this law, an experiment was performed by exposing for a short interval of time a card upon which 25 words had been printed. Five words, scattered among the rest, were printed in type approximately twice as large as the other 20. This card was exposed to 22 persons, with the following results:

	Large Type	Small Type
Number of words shown	5	20
Total noticed by 22 persons	60	48
Average noticed per person	2.7	2.2
Percentage noticed per person	54%	11%

Thus we see that the words printed in large type had about five times as much attention value as the words printed in small type—54% as compared with 11%.

Application of Law of Magnitude. We will now consider in detail the applications of the law of magnitude or intensity to the use of display type in the construction of advertisements. The chief practical questions are: Is the attention value directly proportional to the size of the type? Is there a limit to the desirable size of type? What is the best size of display type to use in a given advertisement?

That large-type headlines have greater attention value than small-type headlines has been generally recognized as advertising has developed. As evidence of this point let us notice the following two entirely different sets of data.

INCREASE IN SIZE OF DISPLAY TYPE USED

Since the early beginnings of advertising in this country up to recent years, larger and larger display type has been used. If one turns back to the early magazines, one is struck with the small headlines then in use. In order to verify this general impression, the author measured the height of the headlines in the full-page advertisements in two standard magazines (*Scribner's* and *Harper's*) at intervals of 10 years since 1870. The average for each year was computed as shown in Table 120.

It will be noticed from the table that there has been a steady increase in the size of display type. However, it seems that the maximum size of display type for a magazine page was reached at about 1910. This point has been verified by H. D. Kitson, who measured the height of the type

TABLE 120

INCREASE IN SIZE OF DISPLAY TYPE

Year	Average Height
1870	6.6 millimeters or approximately 24-point type
1880	7.2 millimeters or approximately 26-point type
1890	9.7 millimeters or approximately 30-point type
1900	11.3 millimeters or approximately 40-point type
1910	12.4 millimeters or approximately 48-point type

in the headlines in full-page advertisements in *Collier's Weekly* from 1911 to 1920. His results are given in Table 121.

There has been no increase in the height of the type of the average headline since 1910. Headlines larger than 48 points, or possibly 72 points (which rarely occur), would seem out of proportion on an ordinary magazine page held

TABLE 121

INCREASE IN SIZE OF DISPLAY TYPE

Year	Height in Millimeters	Year	Height in Millimeters
1911	13.4	1916	12.7
1912	12.7	1917	13.2
1913	12.2	1918	12.5
1914	12.1	1919	13.6
1915	13.3	1920	13.5

at the natural reading distance. The table also indicates that the most rapid increase took place from 1880 to 1900, the period of most rapid development in American advertising. More firms began to use advertising during this period than during any preceding period of equal length.

The apparent implication seems to be that larger display type, because of its greater attention value, has made advertisements more effective and so has come into more general usage. Like many other psychological principles, this one has unconsciously been worked out through practical experience and observation. Of course the tendency does not absolutely prove the principle. A common usage may sometimes be a common error. But considering that the tendency has been constant for so many years and that other facts point in the same direction, Table 121 furnishes an interesting corroboration of the principle.

About 1886 the American Type Founders Union established what became known as the Point System. Before that time various type sizes were designated by special names, as for example, diamond, pearl, agate, ruby, nonpareil, etc. Type sizes were, therefore, entirely unstandardized as there was no common or uniform method of measuring type or indicating sizes. The point system has as the unit of measure the point. Seventy-two points equal one inch. Thus, for example, 8-point type, set solid, is of such a size that the distance from the bottom of one line of print to the bottom of the next is 8/72 of an inch. Hence, 9 lines of 8 point type occupy one column inch. The designation of size refers to the body of the type, that is to the block of type and not to the face of the type. If the type is not set solid usually 2-point leads are placed between the lines. In this case only 7 lines of 8-point type can occupy one column inch. The agate line is the standard unit for expressing the size of advertising space. It is approximately 5-point type. There are 14 lines of agate type to the inch. The change which the introduction of the point system has made is shown in the following list of equivalent values. The sizes of various kinds of type formerly used are designated according to the point system.

4-point equals Diamond	9-point equals Bourgeois
5-point equals Agate or Pearl	10-point equals Long Primer
5½-point equals Ruby	11-point equals Small Pica
6-point equals Nonpareil	12-point equals Pica
7-point equals Minion	14-point equals English
8-point equals Brevier	18-point equals Great Primer

The size of the letter M pica type, was used, and is still used to a certain extent, as a common unit for designating printed areas. The pica M is 12 points square so that if the width of a column is designated as 13 picas it means that it is 12 times 13 points wide, or 2 1/6 inches.[1]

TESTING THE ATTENTION VALUE OF DISPLAY TYPE

The following set of data is derived from the experimental investigation referred to in chapter XXIV as the magazine test. From these results the accompanying table was prepared to show the number of times each full-page advertisement in which there was no illustration had been noticed. The "all-text" advertisements alone were used because the object was to determine the attention value of the different-sized display lines in advertisements in which the headline was the chief means of arresting the attention. The height of the display type in these advertisements was measured, and the results are given in Table 122.

TABLE 122

ATTENTION VALUE OF DIFFERENT SIZES OF DISPLAY TYPE

Height of Type in the Display Lines	Average Number of Times Each Advertisement Was Noticed
5-7 millimeters	6
8-10 millimeters	11.4
11-13 millimeters	25.5

There is obviously a regular increase in attention value with the increase in the size of the display type. The last figure, 25.5, however, is so very far above the others partly because one of the advertisements in that group was an unusually familiar one.

Harlow Gale[2] made a test on this point several years ago

---

[1] See the Appendix for samples of type.

[2] Gale, H., *Psychological Studies*, pp. 52-54.

TABLE 123

ATTENTION VALUE OF DISPLAY TYPE

	Percentage of the Possible Number of Times the Words Were Noticed		
Height of Type	Men	Women	Average
2 millimeters	8.7	11.6	10.1
4 millimeters	20.2	15.8	18.0
5 millimeters	27.7	27.5	27.6
6 millimeters	43.0	45.0	44.0

by exposing cards on which four words were printed in four different sizes of type. These cards were exposed 10 times each for a fractional part of a second, to each of 15 persons. Table 123 gives the percentage of times each size of type was observed and recalled.

These measurements likewise show a regular increase in attention value with the increase in size. The largest type was three times as high as the smallest type. It was noticed over four times as often.

In order to pursue this problem further from a different point of view the author conducted a test as follows: A chart 22x28 inches, on which had been mounted six pairs of letters of varying sizes, two letters of each size, was prepared. These letters were grouped in a miscellaneous manner so that no two letters of the same size were close together. The two largest letters were 3½ inches high. The remaining sizes were as follows: 1¾ inches, 1¼ inches, ⅞ inch, 11/16 inch, and ½ inch, respectively. This chart was hung on the wall of a classroom before the class entered the room. No reference was made to the chart, as other charts were hung about on various parts of the wall. At the end of a 50-minute class period the chart was taken away and the students were asked to write on a sheet of paper the letters which they had observed on the chart. This test was conducted with a total of 260 students. Table 124 gives the sizes of the letters and the number and percentage of students who remembered the letters of the various sizes:

TABLE 124

ATTENTION VALUE OF DISPLAY TYPE

Height of Letters	Number of Persons Recalling Letters
3.5 inches	143
1.75 inches	50
1.25 inches	38
.87 inches	20
.69 inches	38
.5 inches	51

The results of the comparison of the attention value of the letters and their corresponding sizes are shown in Figure 70. It will be noted that the two graphs run along practically parallel with two exceptions, which indicates that in general the attention value of the letters is closely proportional to the size of the letters. The two exceptions to this are, in the first place, that the two smallest sizes of letters were noticed more frequently than their sizes would lead one to expect. This is explained by the fact that these two sizes were so small that it was somewhat difficult to see them, consequently no doubt a great many persons who looked at the chart tried to discover what the smaller letters were and looked at them somewhat more carefully and longer until they deciphered them, as a result of which they were impressed more fully upon their minds. A second exception is that the attention value tends to increase somewhat more rapidly than the size. If we disregard the two smallest sizes, the remainder of the two curves show that the graph for attention value rises somewhat more rapidly than does the graph for size.

HOW LARGE SHOULD DISPLAY LINES BE?

Our next question is, What shall determine the size of the display type for a given advertisement? The answer depends on several considerations. First, it depends on

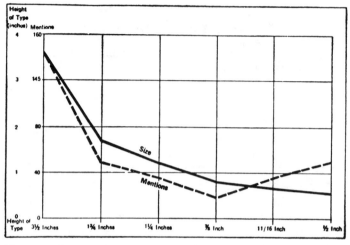

Figure 70: Attention value of different sizes of display type *(See page 621)*

whether the headline is to be the chief means of attracting attention, or whether a large illustration is to be used. If only an insignificant illustration is inserted, the heading should, as a rule, be larger than would be the case if a prominent illustration is used. Again, the size of the headline should in general be proportional to the size of the entire advertisement. Thus, a full-page advertisement may appropriately have a heading as large as 48-point type, or possibly in some instances 72-point type, but such type would appear out of proportion in a one-eighth page space. In so far as it is possible to state any general rule of practice, the headings in common use are between one-tenth and one-twentieth of the height of the advertisement. This will hold only for the ordinary, rectangular shape of advertisement, and even then there are wide deviations.

(b)*Law of Isolation or Counter-Attraction.* The next principle of securing attention has both a positive and a negative application. The demands of the positive phase are satisfied by making one particular feature or set of

Westclox

Baby Ben will slip snugly even into small stockings

BABY BEN does his work with a smile—and gets you up the same way. Not so easy sometimes, either, on those cold, dark mornings when you'd a lot rather stay in bed for another little roll-over nap.

Maybe it's his littleness that gets him so many friends: folks chum up with Baby Ben on sight. But he's a lot more than just cute! Otherwise his friendships wouldn't last.

He's a good timekeeper and a dependable alarm—like all Westclox.

Baby Ben will call you once with a long ring or he'll coax you gently out of bed with intermittent calls—any way you say.

He's just about as big as a minute but he takes every minute seriously —as a good timekeeper should.

That Westclox construction inside his case is what helps him make good. The name, Westclox, on the dial and tag *always* means Westclox patented construction; and honest, faithful timekeeping.

WESTERN CLOCK CO., LA SALLE, ILLINOIS, U.S.A.

Makers of Westclox: Big Ben, Baby Ben, Pocket Ben, Glo-Ben, America, Sleep-Meter, Jack o' Lantern
Parlor, Pirot, Bloom. In Canada, Western Clock Co., Ltd., Peterborough, Ont.

Figure 71: An advertisement that secures attention by the application of the principle of isolation *(See page 624)*

features in an advertisement prominent. The negative phase is fulfilled by avoiding competition among the various devices designed to attract attention. That is, subordinate everything to one main feature. This is what is known as the principle of emphasis or isolation, or the principle of counter-attraction, and may be stated in the following general terms: *Other things being equal the amount and dura-tion of attention* depend upon the absence of counter-attrac-tions. That is, the smaller the number of objects, the greater are the chances that any given object will attract attention. A single person going by your window is more certain of being noticed than the same person in a crowd. One con-spicuous feature on a printed page or on a billboard is more certain of being noticed than a dozen. The experimental demonstration of this law was discussed on page 493 in connection with the length of headlines.

APPLICATION OF THE PRINCIPLE OF ISOLATION OR COUNTER-ATTRACTION

The application of the law of counter-attraction to the construction of a layout may be stated somewhat dog-matically as follows: An advertisement should contain one, and preferably only one, conspicuous feature, which should stand out prominently above the other features as an agency for catching the attention. If there are several prominent features they compete with one another and tend to lessen the attention value of the advertisement as a whole. Elementary as this principle seems, there are, nevertheless, many violations of it, as may be seen from the illustration in Figure 72. This advertisement is weakened by having too many almost equally emphatic features, namely, several dis-play lines, an illustration on the upper left-hand side, and another illustration towards the bottom. This advertise-ment would be much improved if the display lines were made less conspicuous. Compare it with Figures 71 and 73 and notice the excellent emphasis secured in each of these by making only one feature prominent.

This principle of emphasis is more frequently violated in small advertisements than in large ones. The user of small space feels that he ought to say as much as possible in the available space and consequently he leaves little room for a conspicuous heading. In most instances of this kind, the advertisement would be more effective if some of the text were sacrificed to the securing of better display. Observe instances of this tendency shown in Figure 71.

Furthermore, it is often profitable to leave vacant white space, especially if the advertisement is one among many on a page. Its display type will thereby stand out more conspicuously. A striking example of this method is found in Figure 73, on page 626.

Still another violation of the principle of counter-attraction consists of making the subheadings relatively too prominent. Unimportant points are often overemphasized by larger type than the subject-matter demands, and consequently they compete unduly with the main headline. As a general rule, subheadings should not exceed one-third the size of the main display line.

The underlying psychological reason for the avoidance of counter-attractions in an advertisement is the limitation of the field of attention. Strictly speaking, only one thing can be attended to at one time, but four or

Figure 72: A violation of the law of isolation *(See page 624)*

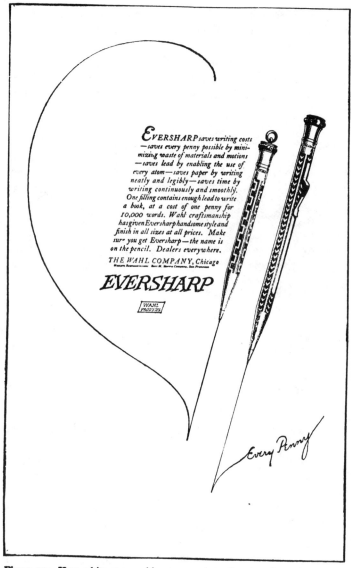

Figure 73: Here white space adds very much to the attention value of the advertisement. *(See page 625)*

five separate parts within this field can be apprenhended simultaneously by the reader. These principles of attention must be kept in mind in the preparation of the layout for advertisements, if the greatest degree of efficiency is to be secured.

(c) *Movement—Its Application to Layout.* It is a well-known psychological law that objects in motion tend to attract the attention more readily than objects at rest. The application of this principle to the layout of an advertisement has obviously two phases. In the first place, suggested movement or action in a picture will tend to have a higher degree of attention value than static pictures and illustrations. In the second place, the principle of motion may be applied to the control of the movements of the eyes themselves. It is a well-known fact, in accordance with this principle, that the eyes tend to follow suggested movement. Thus, for example, a line which points in a certain direction will cause the eyes to move in that direction and will control the attention accordingly. Borders or other lines which are at right angles to the movement of the eyes tend to arrest the movement and cause the eyes either to stop or to follow in the direction of the lines.

BORDERS, EYE-MOVEMENT AND ATTENTION

Borders have four more or less distinct uses: (1) when properly applied they tend to increase the attention value of advertisements; (2) they lend unity, compactness, and individuality; (3) they serve to separate small advertisements on the same page from one another; (4) they may be used to add a decorative and illustrative value to advertisements. Examine the illustrations in this chapter, and observe how these uses are exemplified.

A full-page advertisement is often enhanced by a border, especially if it be a simple one. In the advertisements shown here, observe how the border lends an appearance

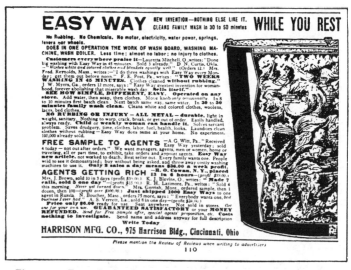

Figure 74. Example showing use of small type in older advertisements
(See page 663)

of unity and completeness not always found in advertisements without borders. For a small advertisement a border is practically indispensable. It is necessary to set it off from the other advertisements on the same page and to give it an individuality of its own.

INCREASE IN USE OF BORDERS

It is noteworthy that borders are a recent element in the construction of advertisements. In the early days they were almost wholly absent from the large advertisements. Of course, the small spaces have always required a means of separation, and consequently some form of border has always been present, although inconspicuous at times. The illustration in Figure 75 shows a half-page of advertisements in which no borders were used; these advertisements formed an undivided mass. The increase in the use of borders is indicated in Table 125, which shows the percent-

Figure 75: Advertisements showing the need of borders. *(See page 628)*

age of full-page advertisements having borders in standard magazines.

TABLE 125

PERCENTAGE OF FULL-PAGE ADVERTISEMENTS POSSESSING BORDERS

Year		Year	
1880	6%	1900	82%
1890	38	1910	77

Kitson reported a tabulation of the proportion of full-page advertisements which had borders, in *Colliers* from 1910 to 1920. He found that the decline indicated in Table 125 from 1900 to 1910 was continued so that at the end of the period only about 40% had borders. This decline may be due in part to the large increase in the use of illustrations and the use of color. Advertisements composed largely or entirely of text still have borders for the most part. Kitson's data are as follows: [1]

TABLE 126

PERCENTAGE OF FULL-PAGE ADVERTISEMENTS HAVING BORDERS

Year		Year	
1910	60%	1916	55%
1911	61	1917	50
1912	53	1918	45
1913	56	1919	38
1914	71	1920	35
1915	67		

ARRESTING EYE-MOVEMENT

Borders increase the attention value by their tendency to arrest eye-movement. The vertical lines of the border run at right angles to the usual horizontal movement of the eyes as they glance from page to page. It is a well-known and easily demonstrated fact that objects, and more particularly crosslines, in the path of the movement of the eyes tend to arrest the eyes. The right-hand section of the horizontal line in Figure 76 looks longer than the left-hand section because the crosslines tend to arrest the eyes as they sweep over the lines, thus requiring more energy and consequently making that part of the line appear longer. The same phenomenon of arrested eye-movement can be shown by taking photographic records of the movements of the eyes.

Now, it is this function which is served by borders and by other lines of the border variety, such as circles, lines, arrows, underscoring bars, contracted borders, and panels. They tend, by mechanical stimulation, to stop the sweep of the eyes. And the point upon which the eyes are

[1] *Journal of Applied Psychology*, March, 1921, p. 10.

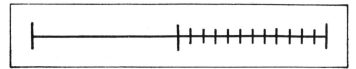

Figure 76: Example illustrating the fact that objects, and more particularly crosslines, in the path of the movement of the eyes tend to arrest the eyes

focused is usually the point upon which the visual attention is centered. If the eye is arrested, the attention also is usually arrested. This is shown by the fact that it is rather difficult for a person to direct his attention to some object off toward the side in the indirect field of vision, while his eyes are focused upon another point. Long established habits have associated the center of vision with the focus of visual attention.

It is this principle of arresting and directing the movement of the eyes which makes such devices as circles, panels, and lines of all sorts, valuable for securing emphasis upon an advertisement or upon some one of its features.

RULES FOR THE USE OF BORDERS

Much care must be exercised in the use of these devices so that they may not be employed unnecessarily or act as counter-attractions.

The size and nature of the border to be used for a given advertisement depend upon the size and nature of the advertisement, and upon the article advertised. As a general rule a plain, simple border is preferable to a fancy, elaborate border. In fact, it is safe to say that an elaborate, ornamental border should not be used unless there are special reasons for it, as in cases, for example, in which it would distinctly enhance the attractiveness or illustrative value of the advertisement. Examples of this are found in commodities in which the artistic or decorative aspect is particularly important. The accompanying illustrations are

Figure 77: Example of advertisement arresting attention by means of borders. *(See page 631)*

examples in point. The elaborate border is apt to attract the eye to itself rather than to the central feature of the advertisement. The border is only a secondary matter and should be so constructed that it will subserve rather than dominate the purpose of the advertisement as a whole.

Figure 78: Example of a border that adds to the artistic value of the advertisement. (*See page 631*)

DIRECTING THE MOVEMENT OF THE EYES

We find, therefore, that in order to direct the attention, it is necessary to know how to direct the movement of the eyes. This is achieved by various means, chiefly by lines, arrows, position of cuts, etc. It is generally observed that the eyes tend to follow along any line of suggested movement. For example, they have a tendency to follow along the direction in which a person is looking or walking.

The implied suggestion is that there is something interesting and important in that direction, and the eyes almost involuntarily follow the suggestion. If you see a person or a group of persons intently gazing in a certain direction you almost invariably turn your eyes in that same direction. The application of this principle can best be understood by examining the illustrations here presented.

It is, of course, an obvious necessity that all suggested eye-movement in an advertisement should be such as to keep the eyes centered upon the advertisement instead of directing it away to some other adjacent one, or off the page. Yet there are frequent violations of this principle; an illustration of this is given in Figure 79. Although these problems of eye-movement concern minute, and apparently unimportant, details in the construction of an advertisement, nevertheless they are worthy of careful attention, for often the strength of an advertisement depends to a considerable extent upon just such details; correctness in detail may make the difference between success and failure.

THE PRINCIPLE OF CONTRAST

Numerous unusual devices for securing attention are being used at the present time which may be grouped together under the principle of contrast, or novelty. This law states that, other things being equal, the duration and degree of attention depend upon the contrast of an object with surrounding objects. A flash of light at night, a man wearing an Indian blanket in a city, a cool gust of wind on a hot July day, a shrill sound in a forest, all compel attention by reason of contrast with their surroundings.

An Experimental Test of Contrast. The force of contrast may be demonstrated in many ways. One method used was to expose before a group of persons, for a brief interval of time, a card containing 25 words—20 printed in black, and 5, scattered among the rest, printed in red. Immediately after the exposure each person recorded the words he had noticed. This test, made with 24 persons, yielded the following results:

	In Black	In Red
Number of words exposed	20.	5.
Total noticed by 24 persons	39.	78.
Average noticed per person	1.6	3.2
Percentage noticed per person	8.2%	64.0%

Hence the words printed in red had approximately eight times as great a chance of being noticed as the words printed in black. And obviously the advertisement which has a really novel and striking feature has far greater power of attracting attention.

Another example of the principle of contrast is to be found in objects or stimuli which change quickly or vary suddenly from their normal behavior. The clock in your room may not be noticed as long as it continues to tick, but as soon as it stops, your attention is at once aroused. The investigator Preyer is reported to have placed a frog in cold water. He then raised the temperature of the water to the boiling point at such a slow rate that the frog made no reaction whatever. The frog was boiled apparently without noticing any uncomfortable increase in temperature. The change was too gradual to attract attention or provoke a response.

Contrast or novelty makes such a strong impression because it has such a deep-seated physiological basis, not only in man, but in the lower animals as well. Any sudden change in the environment requires attention, because it is usually a vital matter, and may endanger the life of the animal. Thus a change in the temperature of the atmosphere stimulates birds to migrate, or else they would perish.

In man, anything novel appeals to the instinct of curiosity and consequently is a strong incentive for closer attention and interest.

CONTRAST DEVICES

Some of the devices based on the law of contrast which are in common use are the following: Black, gray, or colored backgrounds; large amounts of vacant white space; odd shapes, circles, ovals, curves, diagonal lines; bizarre type; unusual illustrations; diagonal or inverted position of cuts; odd borders; unusual arrangements of type and words. Practically all of these devices have been used to advantage under certain conditions. Some are more useful than others. All of them, however, if used frequently, lose their novelty and become commonplace. The strength of the device lies in its newness. The advertiser is forced, therefore, continuously to exercise his ingenuity and originality.

Furthermore, some of the above schemes are accompanied by serious objections. For example, any background other than white makes the advertisement, as a rule, more difficult to read. The same is true of bizarre type, or unusual arrangement of words. A dead-black background often is repulsive to the aesthetic sense. In such cases it is a question of balancing the advantages against the disadvantages, and determining according to the best judgment whether the device can be used effectively. These and other points will be considered in their appropriate connections under other topics.

Black and White Contrast. One of the most common forms of contrast is that of black and white. A dark shade and a light shade close together tend to make each other appear darker and lighter, respectively, than they would appear separately. This fact is an important one to consider in the construction of advertisements and in the combination of adjacent advertisements in a medium. Some advertisements by virtue of their contrast tend to increase the effectiveness of each other, while others tend to weaken each other.

COMPARATIVE VALUE OF MECHANICAL AND INTEREST FACTORS IN SECURING ATTENTION

The factors which are responsible for attracting attention to an advertisement, according to the list described, may be referred to as Mechanical Factors, and Interest or Suggestive Factors. Hollingworth reports a brief study in which he attempted to determine which of these two types of attention factors were the more important in securing the attention of the reader to advertisements. Accordingly he had nine persons—six advertising men and three psychologists—analyze 77 full-page advertisements which appeared in a given issue of *Everybody's Magazine*. Each person was asked to judge whether the attention factors in a given advertisement were mechanical or interest factors. At a previous time, Dr. E. K. Strong had made a test with these same advertisements, in which he had given this issue of *Everybody's* to a group of 137 women who were instructed to read a certain article in this magazine. At the end of one week they returned the magazines and were tested by means of the recognition method in order to determine which of the advertisements they had observed.

Tables 127 and 128 give the results for the 10 advertisements which stood highest and for the 10 which stood lowest in Strong's test as measured by the percentage of women who recognized the advertisements. The numbers for mechanical and interest incentives indicate the number of items of these two classes mentioned by the nine persons as the features which were chiefly responsible for attracting attention to the advertisements.

These results tend to show that the interest factors are possibly more important than the mechanical factors. In the 10 advertisements recognized most frequently by the 137 women the average number of interest factors mentioned by 9 judges was 15 as against 4.1, the average for the mechanical factors. For the poorest 10 advertisements the average was 5.7 for the interest factors and 5.3 for the mechanical factors. In other words the mechanical factors were practically equally common in both the best and the poorest advertisements, while the interest factors were approximately three times as numerous in the 10 best advertisements as in the 10 poorest advertisements. Best and poorest here mean remembered most frequently or least frequently on the part of the 137 women.

Figure 79: Example of advertisement which directs the attention to the adjacent advertisement. The pencil directs the eye movement to Jung's arch braces. *(See page 634)*

ARTISTIC ELEMENTS

Art for Business' Sake. The advertiser is interested in art for business' sake. He believes in constructing his advertisements in accordance with approved principles of artistic arrangement because beautiful advertisements have more pull-

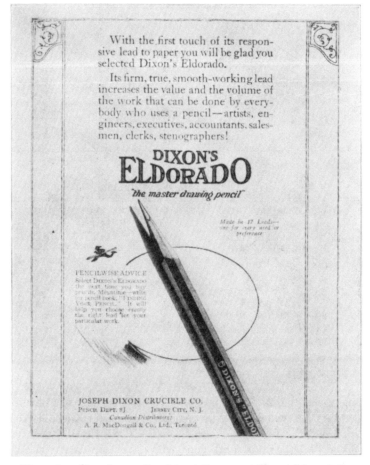

Figure 80: Here the pencil points at the name. The position of the pencil helps to keep the attention on the advertisement.

TABLE 127

THE TEN BEST REMEMBERED

Firm or Commodity Name	Number of Mechanical Incentives Reported	Number of Interest Incentives Reported	Percentage of 137 People Who Remembered
128 Ivory Soap	6	16	8.2
6 Cosmopolitan	1	15	8.0
29 Barbara Worth	1	6	8.0
117 Gillette Razor	8	9	7.0
37 Post Toasties	8	15	7.1
36 Campbell's Soup	6	17	7.1
96 Jap-a-Lac	5	15	6.8
66 Western Electric	2	21	6.6
57 Baldwin Piano	1	18	6.3
60 Mallory Hats	3	18	6.3
Averages	4.1	15	7.2

Percentage Interest Incentives, 78.5

TABLE 128

THE TEN LEAST REMEMBERED

Firm or Commodity Name	Number of Mechanical Incentives Reported	Number of Interest Incentives Reported	Percentage of 137 People Who Remembered
62 Overland Auto	9	4	1.2
55 Genasco	3	13	0.9
64 Wilcox Trucks	6	12	0.9
63 Overland Auto	9	4	0.7
96 Dahlstrom	2	1	0.6
48 Underfeed	3	1	0.2
53 J. M. Asbestos	9	9	0.2
30 Lord and Thomas	4	3	0.2
44 Keystone Watch	3	5	0.0
52 Congoleum	5	5	0.0
Average	5.3	5.7	0.5

Percentage Interest Incentives, 51.8.*

* Hollingworth, p. 129.

ing power than ugly ones. Why? Simply because the beautiful attracts, while the ugly repels. The beautiful holds the interest; the ugly produces disgust. The beautiful secures favorable attention and good-will; the ugly arouses displeasure and ill-will.

All these factors of pleasure and displeasure operate in subtle but telling ways. In order to appreciate more fully their half-hidden, half-unconscious appeals, let us briefly notice, first, the physiological, and, second, the psychological effects of pleasant, as contrasted with unpleasant, stimuli.

Physiological Effects. Several interesting investigations have been made relative to these problems. For example, it has been found that pleasant stimuli, such as agreeable colors, odors, tastes, and tones, tend to facilitate the depth and rate of inspiration, to produce free and energetic action of the heart, to allow the muscles to liberate more energy, and to remove inhibitions to normal nerve action. The popular expressions, to "feel chesty," or "down in the mouth" are more than mere figures of speech. By means of a pneumograph attached to the chest an accurate record of breathing may be obtained, which shows that the chest tends to become slightly larger in the deeper and more regular inhalations. Hence, to feel happy and proud, means to feel "chesty."

Dearborn [1] made a study of the involuntary movements produced by the application of various pleasant and unpleasant stimuli to 19 persons. By means of delicate recording devices he was able to register the slightest movements made with the fingers, hands, feet, or head. He found that under unpleasant stimuli his subjects tended to contract the muscles, while under pleasant stimuli they tended to extend the muscles. His subjects were instructed to sit quietly and passively, so that all responses were purely involuntary and unconscious. The following tabulation gives the flexions and extensions of the muscles under the different forms of stimulation:

	Stimulation Unpleasant	Stimulation Indifferent	Stimulation Pleasant
Flexion	66.6%	49.0%	32.2%
Extension	33.3%	51.0%	67.8%
Ratio	2 to 1	Nearly equal	1 to 2

[1] Dearborn, G. V. N., *Psych. Rev. Monog.* Sup. No. 9 (1899), p. 41.

Figure 87:   Specimen advertisement showing contrast

Hence, under the influence of disagreeable stimuli the chances were two to one that muscles would contract, while under the influence of agreeable stimuli the chances were two to one that the muscles would extend or expand.

By means of a dynomometer the grip exerted with the

hand may be measured accurately. Titchener [1] found the following results, expressed in kilograms, produced under various pleasant and unpleasant stimuli of odor:

Normal	Pleasant	Unpleasant
23.0	26.5 (crabapple blossom)	21.0 (carbon disulphide)
24.0	27.0 (white rose)	22.0 (wood alcohol)
23.0	25.0 (oil of anise)	21.0 (stale cheese)
25.0	26.0 (spirits of camph.)	22.5 (burnt hair)
Average 23.7	26.1	22.5

It is clear that the "pleasant squeeze" is always the strongest, and the "unpleasant" the weakest.

Psychological Effects. The psychological effects of pleasant or unpleasant stimulations are not less striking than the physiological. In fact, many of the above phenomena of reactions depend both on physical and mental conditions. In general, we may say that agreeable external situations or stimuli cause the mind to act more quickly and more normally—associations and thoughts to flow more readily. They make one optimistic and open to conviction. The customer in good spirits is more apt to be influenced in the desired way. He is more easily persuaded; suggestions take effect more quickly.

How radically the view of life may be affected by agreeable or disagreeable situations is well illustrated by the following entry in the diary of an early New England circuit minister:

Wednesday evening. Arrived at the home of Brother Brown late this evening, hungry and tired after a long day in the saddle. Had a bountiful supper of cold pork and beans, warm bread. bacon and eggs, coffee, and rich pastry. I go to rest feeling that my witness is clear; the future is bright; I feel called to a great and glorious work in this place. Brother Brown's family are godly people.

The following entry was made the next morning:

[1] Titchener, E. B., *Experimental Psychology*, Instructor's Manual (Qualitative), p. 169.

Thursday morning. Awakened late this morning after a troubled night. I am very much depressed in soul; the way looks dark; far from feeling called to work among this people, I am beginning to doubt the safety of my own soul; I am afraid the desires of Brother Brown and his family are set too much on carnal things.

The aesthetic elements of pleasure and displeasure play a far more subtle rôle in human affairs than is commonly realized. We like to think of pleasant things. The eyes are held focused upon a beautiful picture. The ears are entranced by a beautiful symphony. So the well-constructed, artistic advertisement attracts and interests in a way that the poorly constructed one is unable to do.

Artistic Forms. Even the most casual observation reveals the fact that certain outlines and forms are much more pleasing than others. For example, you would much prefer having your photograph mounted on a rectangular card to having it mounted on a square card. You prefer a rectangular book to a square one, or a vase with curving outline to one with an angular outline.

All these factors of likes and dislikes in form and proportion, curvature and symmetry, come up in numberless ways in the layout of advertisements, and each contributes its mite of strength or weakness to the effectiveness of the advertisement. Neglect or disregard of these factors is particularly absurd, because it costs no more to have an advertisement planned and constructed correctly than to have it thrown together in any chance manner. Yet an advertisement which is well-constructed is far more valuable than one that is ill-constructed.

It is often said that concerning tastes there can be no disputing, but the student of art knows well that there are certain universally established principles which must be observed in order to achieve successful work and pleasing results. Much advertising consists of blind blundering, but the high-grade advertiser studies the principles and effects of correct, artistic arrangements as thoroughly as the painter or the architect.

The chief types of forms and outlines may be simply classified as follows:

(1) *The Square.* Here we must distinguish between the mathematical and the optical or apparent square. The mathematical square has the exact proportion of one to one, where the sides are exactly equal. Owing to the visual "illusion of the vertical," this form does not look square, but slightly higher than wide. The "illusion of the vertical" refers to the fact that a vertical line appears to be longer than a horizontal line of the same length. The reason is that the eyes are more accustomed to move from side to side than up and down, and, consequently, it requires more energy to look along a vertical than along a horizontal line, and so the vertical line seems the longer. The optical or apparent square is one that looks square but is actually wider than high to compensate for this illusion. The amount of the illusion is approximately 3%; that is, the apparent square must have the proportion of 1 to 1.03. A difference of 3% is small and may seem negligible, but, as a matter of fact, it is far in excess of the smallest difference between lengths recognizable by the average person. The average eye can distinguish as small a difference as 1%.

(2) *The Circle.* Here also the proportion is one to one. This proportion of unity is, in general, a pleasing one. In some instances, as in wall-paper patterns, many illusions of curved lines of various sorts enter, but the effect upon the eye is that of one to one.

(3) *The Double Square,* the sides of which are one to two.

(4) *The "Golden Section"* or rectangle, the proportions

of which are 1 to 1.62, or approximately 5 to 8. This is generally considered to be the most pleasing rectangular form. In mathematics the relation of its sides is known as the mean proportion. That is, the short side of a rectangle is to the long side as the long side is to the sum of the two. The wide prevalence of this proportion in art was discovered about 1855 by Zeising. It had been present all through the history of art, but its mathematical conformity was not recognized until then.

To discuss the reasons offered to explain why this is the most agreeable rectangular form would take us too far afield. Suffice it to point out the two chief lines of evidence for the universal recognition of this formula.

(a) We find that objects in general use approximate the golden proportion, such as books, envelopes, cards, stationery, windows, doors, pictures, etc. This principle has worked itself out unconsciously since the earliest aesthetic feelings of mankind, long before there was any appreciation of mathematical formulae. Back of it all there may be an element of utility, but many objects, such as envelopes and stationery, might as well be square as far as use is concerned. Nevertheless, we prefer the rectangular forms.

(b) The problem has been investigated experimentally.

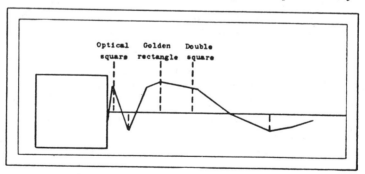

Figure 82: Chart showing results of investigation of impression created by figures running from the perfect square to the double square

Witmer prepared a large number of rectangles varying in proportion from the perfect square up to and beyond the double square. The rectangles usually employed for tests of this kind are alike in width but vary in length. Witmer presented these to his subjects and asked them to indicate which ones they liked and which ones they disliked. His results are shown in Figure 82, page 646. Beginning with the square at the left of the graph and gradually lengthening it out, he found that the mathematical square was not liked; then as it became long enough to take the form of the optical square, it became distinctly pleasing. But as soon as it exceeded the apparent square, it suddenly became displeasing, and later, as it approached the proportion of 1 to 1.62, it became more and more agreeable. The graph reaches a higher point there than it does for the square, which means that the golden proportion is more pleasing than the square. It should also be noted that there is a rather wide range in the neighborhood of the golden proportion in which the proportions are quite pleasing. On the other hand, a slight deviation from the optical square makes it at once disagreeable.

(5) *The Oval.* The most pleasing oval is the one that conforms to the golden ratio, in which the short axis is to the long axis as the relation of 1 to 1.62.

APPLICATIONS IN ADVERTISEMENTS

The external proportions of space in standard mediums, especially in magazines, are, of course, determined, so that the advertiser has little choice, but there are numerous opportunities for exercising discretion in newspaper space, booklets, and particularly in the parts of an advertisement. Furthermore, the magazine and the newspaper page roughly conform to the desirable rectangular form. In the standard magazine the spaces have the following proportions:

The full page, 5½ by 8, or 1 to 1.45.

The horizontal half page, 5½ by 4, or 1 to 1.33.
The vertical quarter page, 2¾ by 4, or 1 to 1.45.
The vertical half page, 2¾ by 8, or 1 to 2.91.
The horizontal quarter page, 5½ by 2, or 1 to 2.7.

Hence it is obvious that the full page and the vertical quarter approach most closely to the proportions of the golden section.

Figure 83:   Example of a well-balanced illustration

Most high-grade booklets have approximately the golden proportion.   Street-car cards, being 11 by 21, approach the proportion of one to two.

Aside from the external form of the advertisement, the question of form must be met in the arrangement of parts, such as the form of cuts, panels, or blocks of text, ovals, etc., and particularly in the handling of the now prevalent long column spaces. See the illustrations and comments. The long column advertisement should be broken up into sections, each of which may have a pleasing form. (Figure 85).

Meaning of Balance. The principles of balance are relatively simple. They may be understood most easily if we consider them in relation to two general fundamental notions, namely, the location of the optical center and the principle of "gravity" or support. Balance, let it be understood, refers to the arrangement of the parts and features of an advertisement so that it gives the appearance of symmetry and stability. An advertisement is said to be balanced when it is not top-heavy, lopsided, irregular, or unsymmetrical in the location of its features.

The Optical Center. By this term we mean that point of a given area which is located apparently at the center of the area. It is located above the actual center by approximately one-tenth of the distance from the lower border to the mathematical center. Thus in the standard magazine page, which is 5½ inches by 8, the mathematical center is four inches from the lower border, but the optical center is about one-tenth of four inches, or about three-eighths of an inch, above the mathematical center. In the illustration on page 650 the shorter line is drawn exactly through the actual center of the rectangle, while the longer one is drawn through the optical center. The first line looks to be too low, and makes the rectangle seem top-heavy. To give the impression of stability and sufficient support, it seems to be necessary to make the lower half slightly larger, in order to seem to maintain the weight of the upper. There are numerous illustrations in which this fact applies. For example, the lower half of the letter S is slightly larger than the upper half. This difference can be more easily observed by turning the letter upside down; also the middle bar in the letter E is slightly above the center.

Location of the Main Feature. Earlier in this chapter it was pointed out that an advertisement ordinarily ought to

Figure 84: Illustration showing both the optical center and the actual center of a rectangle *(See page 649)*

have one prominent display feature, picture or headline, and preferably not more than one. What is the best location for this main display element? Other things being equal, the best positions are as follows, in the order of preference:

(1) At the optical center.

(2) At the upper division point of the "golden proportion." That is, at the point so located that the upper area and the lower area maintain the ratio of 1 to 1.62. See the illustration on page 653.

(3) At the lower division point of the "golden proportion."

(4) Near the extreme top.

(5) Near extreme bottom.

These are the natural points for locating features and the ones which give the most pleasing division of the space. In many instances, specific conditions must be taken into consideration, but all well-constructed advertisements adhere to these positions as closely as the material at hand will permit.

THE PRINCIPLE OF SUPPORT OR STABILITY

An advertisement appears balanced if all its parts seem to be evenly supported at the optical center. Thus, if an advertisement has one heavy cut, it would ordinarily not do to place it to one side without having a feature of equal weight to counter-balance it on the opposite side. It is simply the principle of gravity, if we may call it so, applied to pictorial arrangements. We may best understand the application of this principle in its simplest form by the following diagrammatic illustrations. If we have a weight, say a cut, or a block of heavy type, in one position, it must be placed above the center of support. If it is placed at one side of the space it must be counter-balanced by a weight on the opposite side. The center of horizontal support in an advertisement is the optical center or in a line passing vertically through the optical center. See Figure 86.

If we follow out still further the analogy of gravity, we notice that the principle of leverage also applies. That is, if you have a large, heavy weight on one side, it may be offset by a smaller weight on the opposite side, provided it is placed at a correspondingly greater distance. Or, it may be offset by two smaller weights symmetrically located as shown in Figure 87. Heavy black cuts, or bold black type, or deep colors give the impression of heaviness as contrasted with light gray or bright colors. All these factors have to be estimated according to their apparent weight and then counter-balanced proportionately.

Notice how these principles of balance are beautifully illustrated in Figures 85, 86 and 87. All parts are thoroughly counter-balanced and fully supported at the optical center.

Notice the illustrations of advertisements in this chapter in which the chief possible locations of cuts are pointed out. If one cut only is used, it may be placed in any of the positions pointed out on page 651. If two or more cuts are used, they must be placed so that they will offset each other. Figure 71 shows the main feature of attention at the upper location of the golden proportion, Figures 72 and 77 at the top, Figure 73 at the optical center, and Figure 87 at the bottom.

Figure 85: Example of a well-balanced advertisement

REPRESENTATION OF ACTION

As was said on page 525, movement must be represented in such a manner that the person or animal in action is shown in one of the positions of momentary rest. A per-

Figure 86: An advertisement in which "all parts are thoroughly counter-balanced" *(See page 651)*

son represented as walking would seem unstable if he were
shown with one foot in the air in the act of taking a step.
On the contrary, both feet must be on the ground, as they
are after having completed a step, when they are ready to
take the next one.   The picture in the advertisement on

Figure 87:   Here the principle of symmetry is well illustrated *(See page 652)*

HATCHWAY

BUTTONLESS!

NOT a single button, front or back; not one unnecessary trouble-maker in its entire design; nothing but ease and comfort and freedom from annoyance—that's the

HATCHWAY
NO-BUTTON
UNION SUIT

See these garments at your favorite dealer's today. He can get them for you. It has been a big job to keep dealers stocked up this Spring, but if you have any difficulty in getting just what you want, we will be glad to see that you are supplied. delivery free anywhere in the United States. In ordering, please state size and enclose remittance to our mill at Albany. Send for free catalog illustrating complete line of Hatchway No-Button Union Suits and Hatch One Button Union Suits photographed on live models.

Men's Nainsook Suits, $1, $1.50, $2, $3, $5. (The $5 garment is all silk.)
Boys' Nainsook Suits, $1, $1.25.
Men's Knitted Suits, $1.50, $2, $3, $3.50.
Boys' Knitted Suits, $1, $1.25.

It's difficult to realize, until you actually see this new kind of underwear with your own eyes. See it now at any good store. It is designed to conform perfectly to the lines of your body. It has to be that way without a single button to pull and stretch it into shape.

DEALERS
Write us for samples and swatches if you are interested in stocking Hatchway No-Button Union Suits, or ask to have our representative call. In certain localities exclusive agencies are open to the right kind of merchant.

FULD & HATCH KNITTING CO., Albany, New York
Used. Chatterer Co., Toronto, Canada, Licensed Manufacturers of their lines for Canada.

Figure 88: A good representation of action

this page is a good illustration of how a person should be represented in action.

Meaning of Harmony. By harmony in an advertisement we mean the agreeable combination of the parts and elements— such as borders, type, cuts, shapes, and colors —out of which the advertisement is constructed. Not only should the various parts harmonize in a pleasing manner, but still more fundamental, the structure and appearance of the advertisement as a whole should be in accord with the commodity advertised. There are, for example, c e r t a i n commodities which require particular emphasis upon artistic aspects, while others require the plain, undecorated form of presentation.

To illustrate: an advertisement of millinery should be prepared in an entirely different manner from an advertisement of hardware. The former is made effective by bringing out artistic, dainty, and fashionable aspects, while the latter should give the appearance of strength and durability. Imagine, for example, a barb-wire fence advertised after the manner of fine millinery, or vice-versa. The effect would be utterly incongruous. The advertising of Ivory Soap, at least in recent years, is an excellent example of cleanliness and good taste in the advertisements.

HARMONY IN FORMS AND SHAPES

Similar shapes, forms, or outlines, as a rule, go together better than forms that are distinctly different. Thus curves and curvilinear forms harmonize among themselves; straight lines and rectangular forms go well together.

The Border should harmonize with the nature of the commodity. Some advertisements may be made more effective by a decorative border, particularly those which require emphasis upon artistic qualities.

The Quality and Kind of Paper must be taken account of.

Tone. By tone is meant the appropriate degree of grayness or blackness. Many advertisements contain too much dead black and thus give a depressing effect.

Styles of Type. Besides legibility, the main considerations in selecting the type for an advertisement are:

(a) Fancy or special type should be used only when it adds to the effectiveness of the advertisement, either in giving it distinctiveness or greater aesthetic effect.

(b) As few type faces and sizes as possible should be used. As a rule, not more than two different faces should be allowed, unless they are closely related faces; otherwise the advertisement has a clashing, incongruous appearance.

COMPREHENSION FACTORS: TYPE AND LEGIBILITY

A prominent advertising manager not long ago said: "An advertisement that looks easy to read is read twice as often as one that looks hard to read." Notice the difference between the advertisements in Figures 89, 90 and 91. No observing person would question that there are great differences in the legibility of advertisements. That an advertisement should be easy to read and inviting to the eye is not only desirable, but altogether imperative.

Four Main Factors. What makes one advertisement easy to read and another difficult to read? There are four main factors which affect the legibility of print: (a) The type; (b) the length of the lines in print; (c) the distribution of the lines, words, and letters; (d) the background upon which the text is printed.

Readableness as distinguished from legibility depends upon certain additional factors which combine to arouse the reader's interest, such as the wording, the illustration, the article advertised, etc. But we shall put these matters aside for the present and consider only the legibility of print.

The Type.[1] The two principal characteristics of type which affect its legibility are the style and the size.

(a) *The Style or Face of the Type.*[2] Experiment as well as experience has shown that there is a tremendous difference in the facility with which different type faces may be read. A glance at the illustrations in Figures 90 and 91 will readily demonstrate this difference.

In order to compare the legibility of italic and roman type, the author obtained two pieces of text, alike in all respects except that one was set up in italics and the other in roman.

The test was made with 40 persons by asking each one to read both pieces of text at the rate at which he would naturally read. The time taken by each person for reading

[1] Much of this chapter appeared in an article by the author in *Judicious Advertising*, August, 1911. Reproduced by permission of the publishers.

[2] See Appendix for names and illustrations of the most common type faces in use.

Figure 89: Specimen type faces used for logotypes

these two kinds of print was accurately measured by a stop-watch. The test showed that the italic text was not read as rapidly as the roman text.

Capitals are more difficult to read than lower-case letters. They are stiff, and have more angles and fewer curves. They are also less common, so that the eye is not so fully accustomed to them.

A test like the one just referred to made with 40 persons showed an average reading rate of 5.01 words per second for the lower-case type, but only 4.55 words per second for the capitals. This is a difference of 10% in favor of the lower-case type.

Miss Roethlein made an elaborate series of experiments [1] for the purpose of measuring the relative legibility of different faces of types. Her method was to measure the distance at which the different type faces could be recognized. This method is open to considerable criticism because the

[1] These experiments were made at Clark University.

distance at which letters can be recognized depends so largely upon the size and heaviness of the parts of the let-

Figures 90 and 91: "An advertisement that looks easy to read is read twice as often as one that looks hard to read" *(See page 657)*

ters. Her results, however, are set forth in the following tabulation, in which the reading distance, for lower-case letters in groups, is expressed in centimers. Hence, the larger the number, the greater was the legibility.

News Gothic	166	Scotch Roman	151
Cushing O. S.	163	Bulfinch	150
Century O. S.	162	Caslon	149
Century Expanded	159	Cushing Monotone	144
Cheltenham Wide	159		

From this tabulation it appears that certain faces are more legible than others. Condensed and expanded faces are harder to read than the ordinary widths of type, especially if used in large quantities with little space between the words and lines. Expanded faces, however, are often good for street-car cards because of the oblique angle from which they are generally seen.

A type face constructed on plain, simple lines with relatively few angles and corners is read most easily. The old Roman type face, or some closely related face, comes nearest to these requirements and is generally conceded to be the most legible type face. It is claimed that the angular and difficult character of the German print is, in part, responsible for the prevalence of visual defects among the school children of Germany.

Fancy and unusual types are difficult to read. They contain too many nooks and corners, too many angles and curly-cues. As a general rule, fancy type should be avoided unless there are good reasons for using it. In such cases the advantages may outweigh the disadvantages. In some instances, fancy type adds greatly to the artistic appearance of an advertisement, if it is appropriate and in harmony with the commodity advertised. Or, it may be desirable to use artistic or unique type as a heading or name, which, when used continuously in advertisements of the same article, becomes a mark of recognition very similar to the use of a character, such as the Cream of Wheat chef, or the Gold Dust Twins.

Figure 92: Specimens showing individuality in type faces *(See page 662)*

Type Faces Commonly Used at the Present Time.
Among the numerous type faces that have been designed
by type-founders and designers a relatively small number
are used in actual print. Most of the type faces designed
are used only for exceptional and unusual purposes. At
the present time the most common type faces are Bodoni,
Caslon, and Cheltenham and two or three others. These
are used most commonly because experience and psychological experiment have shown that the small, plain, graceful
type face is, on the whole, the most legible as well as
the most pleasing.

Individuality in Type. Illustrations are the uniform type
used in the advertisements of various firms. See Figure 92.
The same kind of type has been used for a long time in the
advertisements of these concerns and it has acquired considerable accumulative value. Because of this fact, we recognize the advertisements of these firms immediately without
even reading any of the text.

The recent advertisements of Tiffany and Company were
uniformly printed in capitals, and so presented a certain
uniqueness, because text in lower-case type is more common. In some instances, though perhaps rarely, the
greater strain in reading capitals is outweighed by this
contrast effect.

An advertisement whose text is all set up in capitals is
not read with as great facility, and is more apt to be passed
over by the reader.

TABLE 129

PERCENTAGE OF ALL-CAPITAL HEADLINES

1881	85%	1900	43%
1899	69%	1910	43%

In this connection it is also an interesting fact that during the past 40 years there has been a marked decrease in
the use of "all-capital" headlines in advertisements.

Table 129 shows the percentage of full-page advertisements in which the headlines were set up entirely in capitals. It is based on the advertising section of the *Century Magazine*.

Thus, "all-capital" headlines are now only about one-half as prevalent as formerly. A great many scientific principles are gradually being worked out as the standard of advertising and the training of advertising men progress.

(b) *The size of the type,* of course, affects the legibility. Type smaller than 10 point becomes increasingly difficult as it decreases in size. There is rarely or never any reasonable excuse for using fine print in the body text of a large advertisement. Of course, it is a different matter with the very small advertisement.

If one turns back to the early files of magazines, one is struck with the large number of advertisements containing a body text printed in type as small as five and six point. A tabulation was made to show the percentage of full-page advertisements in the *Century Magazine* having the main body text printed in eight-point type or smaller:

1881	85%	1900	18%
1890	38%	1910	5%

Here is an immense drop from 85% to 5% in 30 years —an eloquent testimony against eye-straining type in advertisements.

Length of the Line of Print. On theoretical grounds one might reason that it ought to make no difference in legibility whether the lines are long or short, if only the type itself is plain and sufficiently large. Experiments and even casual observation indicate, however, that the length of the line is an important factor. A line five or six inches in length does not look as inviting to the eye as a shorter one. It seems difficult; it looks involved and tedious. Of course, it depends also upon the size of type used. A long line printed in large type is easier to read than the same line in smaller type.

Figure 93: Rough layout for advertisement in Figure 94   *(See page 669)*

In order to determine approximately what is the most satisfactory length of line, the author made the following tests:

Three pieces of text were set up exactly alike, except that they differed in the length of the lines. In the first text the

In OKLAHOMA CITY
Many important concerns such as Oklahoma City Building and Loan Association, Gloyd-Halliburton are large users of Baker-Vawter loose leaf and filing equipment.

YOUR filing depart-
ment is the memory
of your business. Is it
always alert to give
you instantly the news
as well as the history
of the business?

BAKER-VAWTER COMPANY
General offices, Benton Harbor, Michigan
We serve and sell direct   Our own offices in 55 cities
In Canada – Copeland Chatterson Ltd. Brampton, Ontario

Originators and Manufacturers Loose Leaf and Filing Equipment

Figure 94:   Finished advertisement made up from layout shown on opposite
page   *(See page 669)*

lines were 1½ inches long.   The test was made with 40
persons individually by asking each one to read each piece
of text at his natural rate of reading.   The time taken by
each person to read each piece of text was measured with

a stop-watch. These persons, of course, did not know what the object of the test was, so they were not influenced for or against any one text.

The outcome is set forth in the following tabulation, which gives the average number of words read per second for each kind of text:

Length of line	1½ in.	2¾ in.	5 in.
Average number of words per second	5.25	6.06	5.69

The 2¾-inch text is thus read 16% more rapidly than the 1½-inch text, and 7% more rapidly than the 5-inch text. There is, consequently, a certain *optimum* length of line somewhere in the neighborhood of 3 inches.

If we made further experiments with lines of text graded by small steps from 2½ inches to 3½ inches, we should probably find that there is very little difference within these limits. A very short line is hard to read, just as a very long one is hard to read.

Newspaper and magazine columns usually fall within these limits. The average newspaper line is about 2¼ inches and the average magazine line is about 2½ inches long. The magazine page is, for convenience, split into two columns. Much of the better class of advertising conforms to this idea. For example, the booklets sent out in recent years by Hart, Schaffner & Marx have the lines of print 3¼ inches in length.

The chief reasons why lines of moderate length are more legible than very long or very short lines are as follows:

(1) Fewer fixations of the eye are required. The eyes, in reading, do not move along smoothly, but take successive glimpses at intervals of three to five words. The eyes cannot see distinctly while they are in motion, and consequently they make successive fixations separated by short intervals. This fact can easily be observed by watching in a mirror the eyes of the person who is reading.

(2) In lines of moderate length the subject-matter in adjoining lines is more closely related than in long lines.

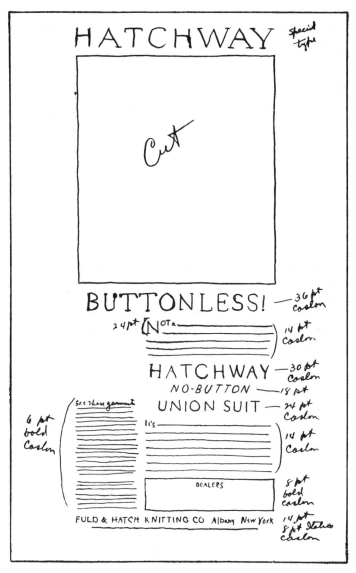

Figure 95: Layout carrying type specifications for advertisement

Thus, the context of the line below the one that is being read is, to a slight extent, apprehended. This facilitates the reading.

(3) In very long lines it is more difficult for the eyes, when shifting from the right end to the left, to find the beginning of the next line.

The difficulty of long lines, in large space advertisements in which much text is used, may be avoided by breaking up the text into columns and short paragraphs as shown in Figure 71.

THE DISTRIBUTION OF LETTERS AND WORDS

Under this head we should include the problems of paragraphing, spacing between lines, etc.

The main criticism to be noted here, however, is directed against unusual arrangements and distributions of letters and words, which often make an advertisement nothing short of an optical puzzle.

Several years ago a "worst-ad contest" was conducted by *Printers' Ink,* for which contributors sent in what they considered the worst advertisement which had come under their observation. The advertisement which won the prize as being the poorest out of the large number submitted had a very conspicuous fault. The words of the text were arranged in step-ladder fashion from the bottom up, making it exceedingly difficult to read. That was not the only criticism, but it was a very important one.

THE EFFECT OF BACKGROUND

The background also affects to a considerable extent the legibility of the text. A white background with black type is, as a rule, the most legible combination. A different kind of background, as, for example, black, gray, or color, has the advantage of being conspicuous by contrast, but it has the disadvantage of reducing facility in reading. No doubt, in many instances the added uniqueness and contrast of unusual backgrounds outweigh the reduced legibility. In such cases, where advantages and disadvantages are balanced against each other, good judgment must decide which is to be used. But it is a very important matter to know what the advantages and the disadvantages are.

In an experiment similar to the ones described, 40 persons were tested for the purpose of determining their natural rate of reading—(a) white type on a dark gray background, and (b) black type on a white background. The difference was very great. The average number of words read per second in (a) was 4.26, whereas, the average number of words read per second in (b) was 6.06. This is a difference of 42% in favor of the black type on white background.

MAKING THE LAYOUT

Figures 93 and 95 illustrate how a layout may be prepared. A complete layout should give detailed specifications just how the advertisement is to be constructed. If the printer understands pretty well what is wanted the instructions of the layout may be less detailed. Figure 94 shows the finished advertisement for the layout of Figure 93.

TRADE-MARKS

MENTION has been made at various points of the five functions of an advertisement. The last of these functions is that of producing a permanent impression in the mind of the consumer or potential consumer. In a word, the psychological value of a trade-mark consists primarily of its memory value as a means of identifying the product.

The term trade-mark includes any mark, design, symbol or word which identifies a product. A trade-name is one kind of trade-mark. Trade "characters," such as the Cream of Wheat chef, are also classed as trade-marks.

There are several reasons why a trade-name is valuable.

1. The use of a name is a simple and convenient method of identifying a commodity. It makes purchasing simpler, both for the buyer and for the seller. Thus, for example, the name Ivory Soap is a far more convenient and more easily recognizable identification of the commodity than the long phrase Procter & Gamble's soap.

2. A name affords protection, both for the manufacturer and for the consumer, against substitution. An article with a definite name and a uniform standard of

production is the same wherever it is purchased. The name insures the customer against the substitution of an inferior article. In short, it is a guarantee of quality.

3. The use of a name in constant association with the article makes possible the increasing accumulative effect of the reputation of the article in the mind of the users. The mere psychological effect of repetition acquires a tremendous momentum for the commodity. A name represents the crystallized result of continued advertising, and of wide use of, and familiarity with, the article. This subtle effect is recognized by firms which place stupendous values upon well-established names and trade-marks.

THE PLACE OF THE TRADE-MARK IN BUSINESS

Probably the five most outstanding developments which have taken place in American advertising are the following: (1) the increase in the size of the average advertisement, mentioned in a preceding chapter; (2) the remarkable improvement in the typographical and pictorial aspects of advertisements; (3) the movement for truth in advertising; (4) the development and use of thoroughgoing methods of research; and (5) the phenomenal growth in the number and reputation of trade-marks. We may obtain the most vivid realization of the place which trademarks occupy in modern business and of the rapidity with which these have appeared in recent years, by noting the recency of many of the trade-marks which are well known at the present time. It is, in a way, surprising when we realize that, while men have always done business and have always needed marks of identification, very few trademarks go back more than a generation. Some of the older ones are given below.

Baker's Chocolate	1780	Gold Dust Twins	1887
Pears Soap (about)	1800	Kodak	1888
Colgate Company	1806	Spearmint Gum	1892
Rogers Brothers	1847	Paris Garters	1895

Durham's Tobacco	1860	Uneeda Biscuit	1898
Quaker Oats	1867	Rubberset	1905
(Transferred to present		Victor (His Master's	
concern in 1907)		Voice)	1901
Keen Kutter	1869	Dutch Boy (Nat'l Lead	
Ivory Soap	1879	Co.)	1907
"Fairy" of Fairy Soap	1885	Kellogg's Cereal	
		Products	1909

The above are only a small percentage of the total number of trade-marks now in use; it is evident, therefore, that the large bulk of them have appeared in the more recent years.

The question naturally arises, Why were not trade-marks established earlier on a large scale? Even the few names that go back more than 50 years were not known the world over as they are today.

At least three important reasons may be given. In the first place, transportation facilities did not develop until the latter part of the nineteenth century. Business on a national scale was impossible until rail and water transportation facilities developed sufficiently to make rapid and regular distribution of goods possible. Trade-marks were therefore not needed so much and did not develop until business men were able to penetrate with their products to distant markets. National trade-marks are highly essential for national business, but national business is impossible without national distributing facilities.

In the second place, there has occurred during this same period of time a shift of the center of manufacture from the home to the factory. When every household was complete in itself, when the necessities of life were manufactured in the home, trade-marks were unnecessary. The goods were made in the home and used in the home.

In the third place, the development of trade-marks on so large a scale has been made possible through modern advertising. Even with the shift of manufacturing from the home to the modern industrial plant, and the enormous expansion of the transportation system, trade-marks would not be known either so widely or so well without advertising. Advertising itself did not assume important and extensive proportions until the facilities for conveying and distributing advertising mediums had developed. Perhaps a more correct statement would be to say that magazines and newspapers did not develop until the revenue derived from advertising made their development possible. Advertising has largely made the magazine and newspaper of today. Through the facilities and the persistence of present-day advertising, the modern trade-mark has become known far and wide.

Further tangible evidence regarding the growth of trademarks in recent decades will be seen in the statistics of registration of trade-marks and brand-names in the United States Patent Office. Table 130 gives the number of trademarks registered year by year since 1870, when the present system was established. The total number of valid trademarks registered up to February, 1922, was 150,310.

The expansion of modern business has necessitated the

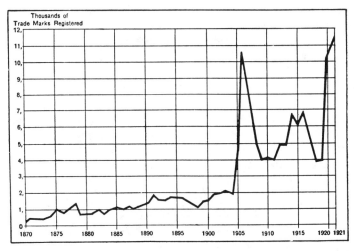

Figure 96: Graph showing increase in number of trade-marks registered each year, 1870-1921

TABLE 130
TRADE-MARKS REGISTERED*

1870	121	1888	1,059	1906	10,568
1871	486	1889	1,229	1907	7,878
1872	491	1890	1,415	1908	5,191
1873	492	1891	1,762	1909	4,184
1874	559	1892	1,737	1910	4,239
1875	1,138	1893	1,677	1911	4,205
1876	959	1894	1,807	1912	5,020
1877	1,216	1895	1,829	1913	5,065
1878	1,455	1896	1,813	1914	6,817
1879	872	1897	1,671	1915	6,262
1880	349	1898	1,238	1916	6,791
1881	834	1899	1,649	1917	5,339
1882	947	1900	1,721	1918	4,061
1883	902	1901	1,928	1919	4,208
1884	1,021	1902	2,006	1920	10,282
1885	1,067	1903	2,186	1921	11,654
1886	1,029	1904	2,158		
1887	1,133	1905	4.490		

* *Official Gazette of U. S. Patent Office*, Feb. 21, 1922, p. 674.

establishment of trade-marks. The function of advertising in this connection has been to teach trade-marks to the people so that they would remember them and use them as a means of identifying products.

THE VALUES OF TRADE-MARKS

In view of the accumulated good-will and prestige which have become associated with many of our present-day trademarks, it is not surprising that almost incredibly high values are often assigned to them. It is, of course, extremely difficult to assign a definite financial value to a trade-mark, and also it must be remembered in attempting to do so that a trademark, as such, cannot be sold apart from its business. Nevertheless the owners of trade-marks have at times assigned specific values to them, and in connection with transfers of businesses and litigations in courts definite values have been necessarily assigned. It will, therefore, be of interest to know the values that have been assigned to typical, well-known trade-marks.

President Green of the National Biscuit Company stated in a public address some 10 years ago that he estimated the trade-mark "Uneeda"—which has been flattered by more than 400 imitations and infringements—as worth to his company more than $1,000,000 a letter, or in excess of $6,000,000 in all. The Gorham Manufacturing Company declared, in a legal suit for the infringement of their Lion and Anchor trade-mark, that this mark was worth between $1,000,000 and $2,000,000. An officer of the Coca-Cola Company placed a valuation of $5,000,000 upon the trade-mark of his firm. In the recent plan to dissolve the American Tobacco Company, the trade-marks were valued at over $45,000,000 out of total assets of $227,000,000. The trade-mark "In-er-seal" used by the National Biscuit Company was said to be valued at $1,000,000. The trade-mark "Royal" for baking powder was valued at $8,000,000.[1]

According to a statement made in 1907, the trade-mark of Mennen's Talcum Powder was estimated at that time to be worth several times as much as the whole business was a decade previously. Today the trade-mark is valued at over $10,000,000. The trade-mark of Walter Baker & Co. has been rated at $1,000,000.

"Characters," while not the same as trade-names, owe their value to the same psychological causes and serve very much the same purpose. Mr. N. K. Fairbanks asserted that $10,000,000 could not buy the Gold Dust Twins and the Fairy Soap Girl. The mark of Onyx hosiery has recently been rated at $1,500,000 by an officer of the firm.

Other well-known trade-marks have been assigned the values as follows: The Quaker Oats trade-mark was valued at $9,000,000. The name Kodak has been valued at many millions. The United Cigar Stores on December 31, 1916, appraised in their annual report trade-mark, trade-names, good-will, brands, etc., at $21,400,000 out of total assets of

[1] *Assoc. Advertising*, Sept., 1919, p. 116.

$44,306,957.[1] It has also been stated that the DeLong Hook & Eye Company have been offered $1,000,000 for the name DeLong, but that they would not take many times that amount.[2] According to an officer of the California Fruit Growers Association, the trade-mark "Sunkist" is valued at at least $2,000,000. The Tobacco Products Corporation, in buying the business of the Schinasi Brothers' "Natural" brand, paid $2,000,000 for the trade-name and good-will alone. This amount was equal to about four years' profits of the business. It also took over the Melachrino brand on the basis of earnings of $300,000 on the name.[3]

Mr. Duke testified on the witness stand that he valued the name "Bull Durham" at between $10,000,000 and $20,000,000. It has been rumored that the R. J. Reynolds Tobacco Co. was offered $10,000,000 for the good-will and name of the Camel cigarette.

Some concerns carry a definite valuation of their brands, trade-marks and good-will, in their financial statements. Some examples of such instances and of the values assigned are the following.[4]

Hart, Schaffner & Marx in 1921	$10,000,000
B. F. Goodrich Co. in 1915	57,798,000
American Tobacco Co. in 1918	54,099,430
P. Lorillard Co. in 1918	21,132,777
Liggett & Myers Tobacco Co. in 1918	40,709,711
Republic Motor Truck Co. in 1920	4,805,936
Pyrene Manufacturing Co. in 1918	1,002,450
United States Light & Heat Co. in 1919	4,608,256
Hoover Steel Ball Co. in 1920	25,457
General Motors Co.	7,934,198
Shredded Wheat Co. in 1923	4,500,000

At this point the question arises: On what basis may any definite value be assigned to a trade-mark? As far as a definite basis may be determined it must necessarily rest upon the magnitude of the business and on the profits involved. A further point often taken into consideration is

[1] *Printers' Ink*, April 19, 1917, p. 129. [2] *Ibid.*, August 21, 1921, p. 116. [3] *Ibid.*, Nov. 25, 1919, p. 117. [4] *Ibid.*, Nov. 11, 1920, p. 109.

that of the amount of money expended in establishing its present standing. Sometimes a concrete estimate is based upon the earnings or profits of the product over a period of four or five years.

The value of trade-marks and names is fundamentally, if not wholly, psychological. It represents the good-will and the esteem existing in the minds of the people for the product to which it applies. "What's in a name?" is strikingly illustrated in an experiment conducted by Colgate & Company with their perfume. Women, in general, state that they prefer foreign perfumes. The experiment was made by using three Colgate perfumes and three imported perfumes, each placed in a plain bottle; then 103 women were asked to make a first, second, and third choice. Before the test was made they were asked to state whether or not they preferred a foreign perfume to a domestic perfume. Sixty-one of the 103 women said they preferred a foreign perfume. The test, however, showed that when they did not know whether a perfume was foreign or domestic, but judged it purely on the basis of quality and general impressions, 63 chose domestic perfumes, and 41 of these 63 women had before expressed a preference for a foreign brand.[1]

The preference of consumers for trade-marked articles was shown in an interesting manner in an investigation conducted by the National Trade Association in response to the following questions:

Question 1. When you go into a store and find two articles of a similar nature for sale at the same price, one of which is a nationally advertised article, which do you purchase? Answer: 87.6% buy the advertised article; 3.6% buy the unadvertised article; and 8.8% were non-committal.

Question 2. When you find two similar articles for sale at different prices, the unadvertised article being priced

[1] *Ibid.,* Aug. 26, 1915, p. 28.

lower than the advertised, which do you buy? Answer: 60.6% buy the advertised article; 24.2% buy the unadvertised article; 15.2% were non-committal.[1]

A conspicuous example of the development of a name for a family of products and of the accumulated momentum which the name adds to each new product as it is launched is the "Rubberset Family." After the name "Rubberset" had been decided upon, the first brush put upon the market was the shaving brush, which met with immediate success, particularly because safety razors were so widely advertised at that time. Later there were added Berset Shaving Cream, Rubberset paint brushes, and Rubberset tooth brushes.

When recently asked as to the extent to which each succeeding member of the Rubberset Family was benefited by the advertising given its predecessors, T. B. Denton, the advertising manager of the company, referred to the tooth brush experience as follows: "Each product has been able to make its start miles ahead of where the one before it was compelled to start its race for public favor. Indeed, this cumulative appreciation on the part of the consumers of what our name stands for got us into trouble when it came to the Rubberset Tooth Brush. We planned initiation of our tooth brush months ahead, and ordered advertising in the March issues. No labor familiar with the manufacturing of tooth brushes being available in Newark, we had to open a school of instruction, and teach our help. Mr. Albright estimated that if we had a million brushes on hand before the advertising started, that would be enough.

We made up the million. But so great has been the demand for Rubberset Tooth Brushes, as the result of what was practically a mere mention of it in the advertising pages, that we are today 2,000 gross behind in our orders from dealers, in spite of the fact that we are making 20 to 30 gross a day, an amount far in excess of what we expected to make. Because of our inability to make deliveries, we have given ourselves no end of

[1] Reported in the *Retailers' Journal*, and quoted by *Printers' Ink*, Dec. 1, 1921, p. 170.

trouble with our long-standing dealers. We have canceled, for the present, what Rubberset Tooth Brush space we had secured, wherever possible. A recent back cover on *Collier's*, which could not be canceled on such short notice, and which had been originally intended for tooth brush advertising alone, was divided up into quarters, and one each given to the shaving brushes, paint brushes, dental cream, and tooth brushes.[1]

Other well-known names for groups of products are the Keen Kutter, Heinz 57 Varieties, Brown-bilt shoes, including Buster Brown, Barbara Brown, and Burton Brown.

On the other hand, there are instances in which the prestige of one old-established name was not so planned as to carry over to a new product of the same firm. How much might not the new product, Crisco, have gained if it could have been given the momentum of Ivory Soap! Perhaps that would not have been desirable because of the difference in these two products. Or, consider how great the advantage would be to the National Biscuit Company if its products had been built up around one "family" name instead of having separate and unrelated names such as "Uneeda," or "Zu Zu," or "Nabisco." These are, however, somewhat tied together through their common trade-mark "In-er-seal."

The development of trade-names and trade-marks has been very rapid in recent years. Numerous manufacturers have devised names and marks for their commodities. "Family" names for large groups of products are now quite common. The following is the experience of the National Enameling and Stamping Company in developing a trade-mark.

To unify the product that is composed of several thousand articles, made up into a dozen or two different lines; to obtain some identifying mark so that each would have its own identity and yet all be related—that was the problem that confronted the National Enameling and Stamping Company.

Labels, names, and designations galore! Trade was for years familiar with the old lines under the diversified and numerous

[1] *Printers' Ink,* June 30, 1910, p. 3.

names, yet as a selling proposition it was simply so much merchandise that happened to be sold by a salesman representing this company. In other words, though there were labels and trade-marks and names, each more or less familiar to the trade because of long continued buying, yet between product, designation, and organization there was no established relationship.

To acquire a better understanding, let's look back a bit and see what we had to work with.

Seven immense factories located at strategic points, both as to labor conditions, raw materials, and shipping of finished products; an organization that covered the entire country; established trade with jobbers and dealers wherever in the United States the merchandise was used, and that meant everywhere. A product that is in daily and constant demand in every household. This product included such lines and items as Royal Granite enameled ware, tin ware, including wash boilers, pie and cake tins, etc., japanned ware, milk cans, dairy pails, Nesco Perfect oil heaters, galvanized ash cans, garbage cans, tubs, pails, fly swatters, and so on, almost ad infinitum.

In the way of tools for use we had, as suggested above, variously shaped and designed labels under almost as many designations as there were items. Some time back the word Nesco had been coined out of the initials of the Company, and, for want of anything else to do, it had been put inside a diamond.

Years ago some clever artist designed a sign which he sold the company for advertising purposes—a window transfer showing a boy who received the appellation "Knight of the Kitchen." Catalogs, of course—a general one and some smaller ones of special lines.

This, then, was the situation when I was delegated to take up the work of creating some effective advertising for the company. Such work is largely evolution—it cannot be developed in a moment nor created out of a session of thinking with the purpose of finding a "big idea" around which to operate.

One of the first steps was to register as trade-mark the word Nesco and its use inside the diamond. This word we embossed into many of the pieces manufactured. Then came the expression, a very necessary one, "Nescoware"—euphonious, easy to remember, and full of meaning. And, because of our almost universal distribution, we were justified in the use of the expression "Nescoware is Everywhere," implying great popularity because of such general use. As new articles were brought out and names and labels were required, we little by little combined some of the ideas in an effective manner.

CLASSES OF TRADE-NAMES

While it is difficult to draw a definite line between various kinds of names, yet there are certain rather obvious distinctions which divide names into a small number of classes.

1. The name of the maker or of the firm is often given to the articles, such as Williams' toilet articles, Colgate's products, Ingersoll Watches and Baker's Cocoa.

2. Geographical names are used, such as Hawaiian Pineapples, Boston Garters, Paris Garters, LaCrosse Plows.

3. High-quality words, such as Perfection, Ideal, Reliable, Gold Medal, Blue Label, Regal, Royal, Peerless, Premier, Monarch, Diamond, Standard, Victor, Gold Dust, Challenge, etc.

4. Artificially coined names without meaning or descriptive implications, such as Nabisco, Kodak, B. V. D., Karo, A. B. C. Auto, "61" Floor Varnish, Phoenix, Necco Sweets. Many of these coined names were produced by combining the initial letters or the initial syllables of the names of the firm. For example, the name Nabisco is derived by combining the first syllables of the name of the firm, National Biscuit Company; Necco is derived by combining the initial letters of the firm name, the New England Confectionery Company; Sampeck is obtained from Samuel W. Peck & Co. Many others are derived from foreign words, for example, Tarvia from the English word tar and the Latin word via (road).

5. Artificially coined names with a descriptive or at least suggestive meaning, such as Holeproof, Innerplayer, Cat's Paw, Nuskin, Cream of Wheat, Ivory, Auto Strop, Shur-on, Kantleek, Uneeda, Milady Chocolates, Underfeed Furnace, Pianola, and Simplex.

These five classes include practically all the varieties of names in use at the present time.

2. THE SELECTION OF A TRADE-MARK

Desirable Characteristics of a Good Trade-Mark. Several important factors enter into the selection or coinage of a new name. 1. A trade-name, above all things, should be simple and short. It takes a long time to speak, and much space to print, a long ponderous name. The psychological effect is stupefying and confusing. When advertising space is expensive, the cost of printing long names is an item worth considering. Compare, for example, Kelly-Springfield Pneumatic Tires with Continental Tires; Barret Specification Roofs with Rubberoid; Mennen's Borated Talcum Powder with Mennen's Talc; Barrington Hall Bakerized Steel-Cut Coffee with Whitehouse; or George Washington Prepared Coffee with Postum.

2. A name should be easy to pronounce and easy to remember. The average reader will have considerable hesitancy in trying to pronounce such names as Caementium, Sanatogen, Olivilo, Clicquot, Aa-A1, Cuticura, Telegathoras, Mentholatum, Koh-I-Noor, Sieger's Angostura Bitters. Compare with these such simple, terse, and easy names as Victor, Kodak, Presto, Mum, Ivory, Jello, Cremo, Lux, Fab.

The experience of a manufacturer of a substitute for coffee is an illustration in point:

Knowing he had a good proposition, the food expert prepared to promulgate the news upon the American public by advertising.

He decided upon the name "Koffee-NO." The "NO" was underlined.

He then set about to capture a share of the coffee business in several middle-western cities. With good illustrations and concise, salesmanlike phraseology, copy was prepared, featuring in big heavy type the "Koffee-NO."

Retailers were stocked fairly well and the jobber's efforts were enlisted.

Then, good-sized advertisements, inaugurating the campaign, appeared in newspapers of the several cities.

The advertiser sat back and waited for returns. Nothing stirred. The campaign apparently was not sending housewives to their grocers for the product. The advertiser was amazed. He had concluded that the proposition was one the public could not fail to recognize as good. The advertising was good and there was no flaw in the plan of distribution. But he had to quit advertising. He called the campaign a failure, yet he had no constructive reason why it failed.

An advertising man in the writer's acquaintance determined to look into the proposition for his personal satisfaction. He had anticipated a hidden defect in the product.

He visited a retail store near his home and asked for "Koffee-NO."

The clerk asked him to repeat the name. He repeated it and then was compelled to give a description of the product.

"Oh, you mean 'Coffeeno,' don't you?" interrogated the clerk, pronouncing the name with the accent on the second syllable, giving it an entirely different pronunciation from the one its maker intended.

He secured the cereal coffee and at home asked his wife to prepare some of it for dinner, which she did.

"Koffee-NO" pleased the advertising man and his wife. They both agreed it was good and determined it was worth using continually in place of coffee.

"By the way, what do you call it?" queried the advertising man of his wife that evening, believing the experience with the retailer might shed some light on the selling difficulties.

"Why, let's see," she replied. "Why, I've forgotten. Just a minute, I'll get the package and see."

"Never mind, it's too difficult to remember. I can see that!" Had the name of this cereal coffee been flashed from a newspaper page at his housewife, it would have been impossible for her to recall it at her grocer's. That sale would have been killed by the intricacy of the product's name.

Which explains the Waterloo of this good product.

The advertising manager for a well-known manufacturer was on intimate terms with the president of the house. The institution, which manufactured household articles, commenced manufacturing a new specialty.

The advertising manager was asked to invent a new name. He was fond of calling the president by the initials of his name. So, after due consideration, he determined upon "J. B." as the cognomen for the specialty—these being the first two initials of the president's name.

Later this advertising manager left his position for one in a larger field. The new advertising manager found "J. B." to be the poorest seller the manufacturer had, and also satisfied himself that it was fully up to the concern's standard of merit.

When he had been with the house a week the letters "J. B." went into the discard and the new man bluntly told the president the reason. He made plain the fact that he was drawing his salary for selling goods, not for nursing vanities.

He gave the article a short, terse, descriptive, easily understandable, easily remembered name.

The trade was notified. The articles that had grown dusty on dealers' shelves were shipped back to the factory and restamped.

Salesmen were instructed never to refer to "J. B "—to absolutely wipe the name from their memories. The original selling energies that had marked the birth of "J. B." were applied to the newly named article.

In three months and a half the article became the second best seller the house had. Sales for that quarter-year leaped to quadruple the number that dealers had made in the previous three months.

Among 5-cent cigars one of the best sellers in this country is the Club Smoker, manufactured by a Chicago concern. One of the main factors in its success has been its easily remembered name.

And the name should be a far more vital point with a cigar manufacturer than with other articles to which the consumer devotes more time in considering the purchase.

Yet cigar manufacturers are probably the worst offenders in the matter of names. One authority charges many ineffectual efforts of cigarmakers to advertise their products to the invariable tendency to christen every star cigar with a Spanish name, or worse, a mixture of Spanish and American.

We are not Spanish people. And naturally it is hard for us to grasp and mentally to hold a Spanish name. So few of us do it.

A cigar store clerk told the writer that fully 50% of the sales in his store are made to men who either ask for a "good Havana cigar" or, pointing to one in the case ask for "one of those."

A certain large system of drug stores issues bulletins from time to time to its clerks, stating how the public pronounces various names for drugs, so that the clerks might be prepared to recognize the things called for. Thus they found that "Todco Cream" was called for as "Tuxedo," and "Cuticura Soap" was asked for as "Keeley Cure Soap."

Many names, not only those of foreign origin, but especially those which are artificially coined, often are grossly deficient in the element of pronunciation. Undoubtedly many names are difficult to popularize and difficult to remember and are often avoided even though remembered, because of their difficult pronunciation. An interesting case in point is that of the Ghirardelli chocolates. Mr. Lyle Ghirardelli, of San Francisco, made the statement that the *h* in his name cost his firm $1,000,000 in business.

It was realized that the thing that had to be done was to get people to go to the store and say "Gearardelly." It was known that most people couldn't pronounce the name, and even in the past phonetic copy had been tried. But it was plain that just phonetic spelling was not enough; it had to be presented in a pleasing, unobtrusive manner which would not affect the sensibilities of the average person who dislikes to be told or have it inferred that he cannot pronounce a name. It was a delicate subject to handle. In the very admirableness of the handling lies the success of the idea.

In the mind of the Ghirardelli Company was the truism that people are sensitive; they do not want to be held up to ridicule, even impersonally; they do not want to be set down and have a lesson preached into their heads; they are independent and must be properly approached; and there was also this idea—the average man likes to laugh at a joke on the other fellow, but not on himself; furthermore, he is perfectly willing to be amused over the stupidity of the other fellow just so long as he realizes that the man who tells the story knows that it is the other fellow who is the butt of the joke. And in an honest adherence to this belief and a proper working out of the copy, based on that idea, the success of the parrot idea in Ghirardelli copy is surely so.

In brief, then, instead of taking a man by the neck, as it were, and explaining to him that Ghirardelli was pronounced in a certain way which he undoubtedly didn't know, they invited, so to speak, the general public to sit down with them when between them they taught a parrot how to say "Gear-ar-delly." And so the first outdoor display, gotten up in all the striking colors of the macaw or Spanish American parrot, was put up. The color scheme of the macaw lent itself wonderfully well to poster art and the pictures stood out as plainly as the proverbial sore thumb. One couldn't help being attracted by the brightly colored illustrations, the warm colors of which, properly blended by an artist who knew human nature and who realized the psychological importance of proper color combinations, insinuated themselves into the unconscious mind of the average consumer.

And then there was the whimsical picture of the little girl who was trying to teach polly to say "Gear-ar-delly" and the polly was slow to learn and so the girl was shaking him by the throat until even some of his feathers were flying out and saying to him: "Say Gear-ar-delly." How could anyone feel that this was a personal thrust at him? But at the same time, the person who stopped to look, and who could hardly help but give the one little glance which was all that was necessary to tell him the message "Say Ghirardelli," knew all about it. For years and years and years he or she had been told that Ghirardelli meant good ground chocolate. This copy told him how to pronounce it and it acted as the little piece of dynamite which broke the dam, and overnight, as it were, people began to "Say Gear-ar-delly" and there was an immediate loosening up of the demand. The key to the situation had been found in the right copy.

Other instances of foreign names which had difficulty in the same respect are Sempre Giovine, Djer-Kiss, and Baume Analgésique Bengué. The last-mentioned company has put considerable emphasis in recent advertisements upon teaching the pronunciation of this name by means of an Anglicized spelling and by using the phrase "Say Ben-Gay," the Anglicized pronunciation of the word Bengué. Likewise, the pronunciation of the name Sempre Giovine has been stressed in advertisements by an English equivalent spelling—Sem-pray Jo-ve-nay.

3. A name should be unique and distinctive, so that it may not be easily imitated or infringed upon. Blue Label Ketchup might be mimicked by the name "Brown Label," or some other colored label. Almost every well-known successful name has been imitated. Note the following illustrations:

Uneeda	Iwanta
Limetta	Limette
Egyptian Deities	Egyptian Prettiest or Daintiest
Peruna	Rupena
Pain Killer	Pain Expeller
Cascarets	Castorets

Apollinaris	Appolinis
Honeymoon	Honeycomb
Moxie	Noxie, Hoxie, Modox, Nonemall, Moxine
Sorosis	Sartoris

Producers of new commodities intended to compete with older commodities of the same class often attempt to adopt names as nearly like the older names as possible without having them identical. The newcomer thereby attempts to rob the old concern of some of its established prestige. It is therefore extremely important to adopt a name at the outset which will be difficult to copy and which may be legally protected. Apropos of this point we may quote from *Real Salesmanship in Print:* [1]

> Another thing to look out for is the danger of substitution. There are a great many lines where substitution by dealers kills from one-half to two-thirds of the trade. Rare is the article which attains big success against such a handicap.
>
> Substitution cannot always be entirely eliminated, but there are ways to minimize it. And it must be reduced to modest proportions before an advertising campaign can be advocated.
>
> This is one of our gravest problems. And it must be solved in the original plans if one is to solve it at all. It is folly to raise crops for others to garner.
>
> Foresight in this matter is an essential. Without it, the most brilliant campaign might result in disaster. In many other cases results have been multiplied by simply taking proper precautions.
>
> Toasted Corn Flakes has succeeded despite substitution. But the Kellogg concern is not getting more than 40% of the trade it created. And fortunes are spent on advertisements aimed merely to defend that percentage.
>
> Suppose the same trade, at the same expense, had been built around a name like Post Toasties. How much more would the trade have been worth?
>
> Suppose the Kodak had been called Eastman's Camera. Suppose Uneeda Biscuit had been named National Soda Crackers. Consider how impregnable are their positions today compared with what they might have been had they overlooked the trademark foundation.

[1] Lord & Thomas, p. 17.

. . . . We can cite numerous instances where a change in name has multiplied the results of the advertising. We know cases where the name has done more for the article than all other selling arguments.

One of our greatest successes of the past six months is due, apparently, mainly to a name we coined. An enormous business, long established, was doubled in four months. And the main element we added, in our estimation, was a name which brought to one maker the trade which had hitherto been divided. . . .

One of our clients makes an evaporated milk.[1]

This milk, in the process of sterilization, is given a slight scalded flavor.

At one time we found that this unnatural flavor killed a large percentage of the trade we created. Users failed to buy again.

This problem, as usual, came up to our strategists. The natural solution would be to explain the flavor. But any explanation which we could devise sounded too much like apology.

Then one man suggested, "Let us call it the Almond Flavor. Let us make it a virtue—an indication of purity—of freedom from germs. Let us tell the buyers to seek for this Almond Flavor—that the milk is not genuine without it."

And we did. We changed the objection into an advantage. This advertiser now is selling close to fifty million cans per year.

4. A name should not be absurd or degrading for the article to which it is applied. On the other hand, a name should rather be suggestive of value and worth. The name "It" as applied to a breakfast food is not the kind of name which would elevate one's conception of the food. Or the name "Smile" as applied to a high-grade $20 hat has a distinctly depreciating effect. There is nothing about the name that would induce a person to buy the hat. It is one of the useful functions of a well-chosen name to add to the desirability of the commodity. The name and picture for "Old Dutch Cleanser" carry an atmosphere of cleanliness and numan interest. The human interest appeal is presented in the name "Quaker Oats" as contrasted with "Oatmeal," or "Ivory Soap" as compared with simply a bar of soap. "Old

[1] *Ibid.,* p. 62.

Dutch Cleanser" is a better name than "Bon Ami." It suggests something about the use and cleanliness of the article. It also is easier to pronounce and easier to remember.

Notice some of the absurd names that have been used:

Asperox, Alamo-Bromo, Alkolo, Bo-alka, Bovax, Americanitis-Flizer, Babeskin, Coeterine, Enurience, Germea, Cow-Oil-Ene, Hekake, Kalone, Kilfyre, Kremette, Kremola, Kis-me (gum), I O U (champagne), Nix-E, Thom-a-Tol, Oxyma, Oxyneura, Oxeta, Tarterlithene, Kodal, E Z 2 Tie (neckwear), Har-in-felt (mattress), Carbolineum, On-Time (yeast), Stainoff, Payo, Powdo, So-Lite (shoes), Keep-shape.

Mapeine (whiskey), Sal-lac, Wonderful Dream (salve), Silk-ilo, Acisilk, Radiumite (razor), Flexo (garter), E Z (stove polish), Rex, Elintcote, Ho-Co (thermos bottle), Hot-a-Co (thermos bottle), Nosmellee, Pantosote, Nufangel.

Names of foods: Cere-Fruto, Malto-Vita, X-cello, Malto Food Flakes, Grandose Flakes, Flaketa, Norka, Eata-Biscuit, Cereola, Dr. Price's Eatabita, Perfo, Graino, Koffa, Carmel-Cereal, Neutrita, Grap-Suga, Flakes, Granola, Maz-all, Coffay-ette, It, Malta Nut, Tarvena, Nulife.

It is an advantage to a name to be suggestive, if not descriptive, of the nature of the article or of some essential feature of it. The name "Holeproof" is excellent in suggesting the innovation in the hosiery business of guaranteeing hosiery for a certain length of time. Other illustrations are "Rubberset," "Shinola," "Auto Strop," "Poros-knit," etc. However, one difficulty with names which are too strongly descriptive is that they cannot be registered. But it is possible to have a prominent suggestive element and still comply with the registration laws.

A good trade-name is probably characterized by the following five important points. To be effective, it should be

1. Easy to pronounce
2. Easy to remember and recognize
3. Pleasing and appropriate to the product for which it stands
4. Suggestive of the product but not overdescriptive
5. Unique and distinctive

CONTESTS FOR SELECTING NAMES

In recent years the realization of the great values which trade-marks and brand-names acquire in the course of the development of a business has emphasized the great desirability of selecting a name or mark which shall satisfy the requirements of a thoroughly useful identification. Consequently much more care has been exercised in recent years when a trade-name is chosen for a product.

In 1911 it was a unique thing for a concern, in choosing a name for a new product, to carry out a contest and choose a name with the help of a group of judges. It was considered an unusual procedure for Procter & Gamble, in selecting their name "Crisco," to conduct a contest in which a prize of $500 was offered for the purpose of securing an appropriate name. Many hundreds of names were submitted and the name Crisco was chosen because the word was short, snappy, simple, easily remembered, because it lent itself to an attractive design, had no descriptive or suggestive qualities whatever, and was entirely fanciful.

One of the largest contests ever conducted for the purpose of selecting a name was that carried out by the American Ever-ready Works in choosing the name "Daylo" for a flash-light. In 1916 this company announced a contest for names in which a prize of $3,000 was offered for the winning name. This contest created such an unusual interest and attracted such wide-spread attention that a total of 540,000 replies were received, including responses from practically all parts of the world. The absolutely impossible names that were submitted is almost unbelievable. Thus, for example, one name submitted was "Torch Tricita." Others were "Killdark," "Nytesun" and the like. In the entire list of replies there were altogether 67,000 names which were considered for the prize. Some names were duplicated approximately a thousand times. The total expenditure for the contest was $140,000. The intended cost of the plan was originally $100,000. This, of course, included more than merely the contest for getting the name, as it was tied up with an extensive plan for displays and special sales with dealers. However, it cost approximately $10,000 in clerical help to handle the returns of the name contest. Four persons had submitted the word "Daylo" and each person was paid the full sum of the prize. In 1921 the name "Daylo," however, was abandoned, because the company believed that it had served its purpose in popularizing the flash-light and that the name "Ever-ready" had become thoroughly associated with it. It was abandoned in favor of such other names as "The Ever-Ready Spot-light," "The Ever-Ready Flash-light," etc.[1] A contest carried out successfully in this way of course accomplishes more than merely the securing of the name. It focuses the attention of a large proportion of the public in a concentrated manner upon the particular product and helps especially in the case of a new product to make it known in a very short period of time.

The name should be elevating and not degrading to a product. It should suggest the worth and desirableness of the product. Thus, Victrola is better than talking machine; Fairy Soap is better than merely a cake of soap; Big Ben, or Junior Tattoo, is better than alarm clock; Sunbrite Cleanser is better than plain scouring powder. It is surprising how frequently names which are obviously depreciating to a product are chosen by the promoters and makers of a product. The Eighteenth Amendment has resulted in the production of a flood of soft drinks. In 1919 some 30 advertising campaigns were under way for various beverages. This has been accompanied by a flood of all sorts of grotesque and bizarre names such as the following: Orange Jooj, Sparkler, Sparkade, Appleju, Fruitex, Cherriport, Grapetone, Dan-de-li-o, Cham-pay, Champtail, Champanet, Fizzo, Fan-Fizz, Min-tu-lip, Minto-Malt, Konsolation, Dry-Town, Whistle, O-Kid-O, Te-To, Flivver, Newfad, Wow, Jazz, Submarine-Chaser, Jewell, A-Cooll-A Vigoro, Vigorone, Zest, Life Staff.[2]

[1] *Printers' Ink*, March 1, 1917, p. 45, and Sept. 15, 1921, p. 28.
[2] *Ibid.*, June 26, 1919, p. 77.

SCIENTIFIC METHODS IN SELECTING A TRADE-MARK

By means of properly devised tests and experiments it is possible to determine with considerable accuracy the relative merits of various possible names which are being considered for a product. We shall outline here two examples of such analyses in selecting a name for a new product or in selecting a new name for an old product. The first instance consists of the problem of selecting a name for an automobile accessory, a product which had been in use for a considerable time and had established a considerable amount of business. The name, however, was difficult to pronounce and had not been found suitable. The plans for selecting a name for this product were carried out as follows:

A contest was announced in which a series of prizes were offered to contestants submitting winning names. This was carried out on a small scale and brought approximately 1,200 different names. This list of 1,200 names was then submitted to 16 judges, composed of 8 psychologists and 8 advertising experts, who were asked to go through the list and check each name which they considered desirable or suitable. These 16 selections were then combined, and 350 names were selected by including all names which had been approved by one or more of the 16 judges. In other words, the names omitted were those which had not been approved by a single judge. The next step was to select out of this list names which had been approved by two or more of the judges. This yielded a total of 164 names. These 164 names were then submitted to a group of 26 men. These men were told that these names were proposed for the particular product in question and that they were to mark each name with a plus sign if it was considered good, with a minus sign if it was considered poor, with a double plus if it was considered very good and with a double minus if it was considered very poor. Indifferent names were to be left unmarked. From this list the 80 highest names were chosen.

These 80 names were then submitted to a test to determine their relevancy to the product. The test was carried out by the "association method." The names were submitted to 22 men who were asked individually to write after each name what it suggested to him, or what first came to his mind when he saw that particular word or name. These reactions were then tabulated to determine how many reactions were relevant or suggested the product in question, and a percentage score was then assigned to each name according to the percentage of relevant associations or reactions given. These results, combined with the preceding rankings, furnished the basis for selecting the 21 highest names. These 21 names were then submitted to 23 men operating garages and automobile repair shops. Each man was asked to select his first 5 choices and to number them from 1 to 5. These rankings were then tabulated and the names were finally arranged in the order of desirability as shown by the tests.

This was a relatively simple procedure and led to the arranging of the highest names in the entire list according to their relative order of value and desirability.

SELECTING A NAME FOR A NEW PRODUCT

The problem in this case consisted in selecting a name for a new food product. Such an undertaking consists essentially of two parts: first, securing a large variety of possible names; and second, carrying out tests to determine which are the best names among those submitted and arranging the small number of best names in the order of greatest desirability.

A contest was carried out to secure a large number of names. An announcement was made in a relatively small amount of space—six inches by two columns. It will be surprising to note how much attention a small amount of space devoted to a contest attracts. The number of replies received was nearly 8,000. The average number of names submitted per contestant was approximately 10, making a total of some 75,000 names. Experience in conducting this contest showed that it is probably not necessary to have so large a number of names submitted. It became evident, as the results were worked over, that probably a fraction of the number of names submitted would have produced the desired result. Probably not more than 2,000 names would be sufficient in most contests to supply all of the raw material in names and to include probably all of the really desirable ones. The individual contestant should be limited to perhaps two or three names.

This list of 75,000 names was examined by 12 judges. Each judge was instructed to examine these names and to select any names that appealed to him individually as desirable possibilities. This produced a selected list of approximately 500 names. This list was then submitted again to the same 12 judges who were asked once more to look over these names carefully and to select a list of from 25 to 35 names appealing to them as really first-class possibilities.

A composite list was then prepared by including all names which were selected by at least 2 of the 12 judges.

This method yielded a total of 64 names. These 64 names were then submitted to more extensive tests and ratings. They were personally submitted to 331 women, the majority of whom were housewives and a small proportion of whom were domestic science students and specialists. The relevancy of these words was determined by submitting them to an association test similar to the one described in connection with the automobile accessory product. The women tested were asked to write after each name—not knowing what the name stood for—what the word suggested or meant to them. The scores assigned were determined according to the proportion of reactions which were relevant. On the basis of these scores a smaller list of 21 names was chosen for a more thorough and careful testing and rating. Five tests were carried out to determine the relative standing of these names with respect to their memory value, pronunciation, pleasingness, relevancy, and general value.

Memory Test. The person being tested was handed the list of names on a sheet of paper face downward. At a signal he was asked to turn over the sheet, and according to instructions previously given him to read each word silently from the top of the list down to the bottom. In order that an equal amount of time might be given to each word the experimenter tapped with a pencil at the rate of once a second to indicate when the person was to pass to the next word. After he had finished, the sheet was immediately turned over again and each person was asked to record all the names that he remembered.

None of the persons were told what the experiment was for; they were not told that they would be asked to remember any of the words, but they were simply told to read them. The purpose of the experiment was to see what words, by their inherent interest and make-up, would appeal to the average person so that he would remember them.

A further point of importance in the technique of this experiment was the splitting up of the list so as to have the words in several different arrangements. The purpose of this was to give all words equal opportunity of being seen in the best positions. It is a common psychological fact that in a series of words or objects of this sort the ones at the beginning or the end of the list have an undue advantage.

The memory test was scored by tabulating the number of times each word was remembered. The scores, as given in Table 131, represent the percentages of persons who remembered each particular word.

Pronunciation. This test consisted in having each person go through the list from top to bottom and make a check mark after each name that caused hesitancy, doubt, or difficulty in pronunciation. This test was then scored by tabulating the number of times each word was reported or checked as causing difficulty. The scores were then expressed in terms of percentage.

Another test for pronunciation was made here, which, however, did not prove to be very satisfactory. The test aimed to determine the speed with which each word could be pronounced. More careful technique than it was possible to apply here would no doubt yield more satisfactory results.

Pleasingness. A name ought to be pleasing irrespective of the product to which it is to apply. This is particularly true if the word is more or less irrelevant. A test was carried out, therefore, to determine the pleasingness of these names. The test was conducted in two different ways. According to the first method the persons tested were not told to what product these names were to be applied. They did not even know for what general kind of product the names were to be used. The persons tested were asked to look at each name and mark it either with a plus or with a minus sign if the name appealed to him as agreeable or as disagreeable. A name was to be marked with a double plus or a double minus if it appealed to the observer as being very agreeable or very disagreeable. If a name seemed to be indifferent, neither agreeable nor disagreeable, it was to be left unmarked. The results of this test were scored and tabulated to show the number of times that each word was marked with a plus, a minus, or a double plus or a double minus.

The test was then repeated in exactly the same manner with another group of women, except that in this case the women were told for what particular product these names were intended to be applied. There was no essential difference in the results of the two methods and therefore they are combined in Table 131.

Relevancy (free association test). The persons tested were not told for what these names were to be used. Each person was given the list of names and asked to write after each word what it suggested to him or what came to his mind when he first saw the word. The results were scored in the same manner as was previously described for a relevancy test. The proportion of reactions which were of a relevant character was determined.

General Rating (choice of first five). In addition to these four tests which were made without the knowledge of what the words were for, except in the case of the one group in the test for pleasingness, each person was finally told what

TABLE 131

RELATIVE STANDING OF 21 NAMES WITH RESPECT TO THEIR
MEMORY VALUE, PRONUNCIATION, PLEASINGNESS,
RELEVANCY, AND GENERAL VALUE

Number of Name	Memory Test 90 Persons	Pronuncia- tion 90 Persons	Pleasing- ness 130 Persons	Relevancy (Free Asso.) 90 Persons	General Rating 130 Persons	Final Score
1	55%	88%	70%	42%	54%	58%
2	38	97	74	34	47	52.5
3	47	96	67	41	39	50
4	26	80	60	68	40	49.5
5	27	76	61	25	29	37.5
6	50	92	54	9	25	33
7	37	92	49	7	10	28
8	28	79	35	33	10	26.5
9	32	94	53	8	7	26
10	48	98	57	0	3	26
11	17	94	57	6	8	25
12	18	84	44	17	6	23.5
13	17	94	39	9	8	23.5
14	32	92	37	4	4	22.5
15	26	88	48	8	2	22
16	15	67	44	13	7	21.5
17	28	96	31	12	1	21.5
18	32	52	42	5	6	21
19	33	90	34	7	1	21
20	17	39	24	32	3	18
21	14	30	21	23	2	15

these names were to be used for and was then asked to select his first five choices and to number them in order from 1 to 5. The names were arranged in various orders for this test so as to avoid giving advantage to the names at the top or bottom of the list. The results of all of these tests were then combined into a final table in which one-half weight was given to the four tests combined and one-half weight to the general rating. The scores for the 21 names are given in Table 131. The names are indicated by numbers from 1 to 21. It is obvious that the names themselves could not be given here.

The figures in the column under Memory are the percentages of persons who remembered the particular name in the test. The figures under Pronunciation are the percentages of persons who had no difficulty in pronouncing the particular names. Under Pleasingness the percentage scores are so adjusted that above 50 means agreeable and below 50 disagreeable. The scores under Relevancy represent the percentages of persons who responded with relevant reactions. Under General Rating the percentages indicate the number of times the particular word was chosen as first.

An examination of these results shows that the difference in the value of the 21 words was very great with regard to each of the characteristics specifically tested. Thus, for example, the memory value varies enormously for the various words. Name Number 1 was rememberd most frequently, with a score of 55, whereas name Number 21 was remembered least frequently, with a score of 14. Similar divergences will be found in each of the other tests. In Relevancy, the words vary all the way from 68% down to zero. The word having the zero score did not suggest even once the particular class of product which it was intended to represent, namely, a food product. Instead it suggested batteries, engines, automobiles, flash-lights, and so on. It did not suggest to anyone a food product. In all other respects, however, this word had a fairly good rating. But it is evident that it would have considerable opposition to overcome in the minds of consumers if it were applied to this particular food product.

The outcome of this entire investigation was that these 21 names were arranged in the order of desirability and appropriateness with a fairly high degree of certainty.

However, in addition to the characteristics of a good trade-mark, which we have just examined, the possibility of registration must be considered. The name selected as best might present difficulty in being registered. A still further consideration is the possibility of using these names in foreign countries. The particular food product here in question was to be sold not only in the United States, but in foreign countries as well. It was therefore necessary to look into the possibility of the meanings of these words in foreign languages. It was found, for example, that one of the words which stood fairly high in the list was associated with disease in a certain European language. For special reasons the concern here in question decided not to choose the name which was at the top of the list, but chose the second and third names, one for distributing the product in packages and the other for distributing it in bulk. The chief significance of this entire investigation for the reader is the demonstration of the possibility of applying scientific procedure to the selection of a name or a trade-mark. A similar plan may be used in choosing the design of a trade-mark other than a name. This experimental procedure insures with a high degree of reliability the selection of the best possible name from among those devised and considered. Such a result is impossible when the choice is made by one or two individuals, no matter how expert they may be. This procedure may seem long and intricate, but its cost is trivial compared to the ultimate value which any trade-mark of consequence will acquire, or compared to the expense incurred if the trade-mark is ill-chosen and unsuitable and hence meets with popular resistance.

3. REGISTRATION AND PROTECTION OF TRADE-MARKS

One point concerning trade-names and marks that is often overlooked is the possibility of registration. Names that have been popularized at considerable cost are discovered, in many instances, to be infringing on some older names. A good illustration in point is the following experience of a candy maker:

There are a number of manufacturers in this country who are using trade-marks that in fact do not belong to them. Sooner or later, just about the time they realize that their marks are worth more than the very plants in which the marked products are produced, they will be compelled to abandon their marks in favor of the rightful prior users. . . .

A Mr. Candy Man some twenty-odd years ago in a large university town began to manufacture chocolate creams which he designated by a certain mark which he thought was original. All at once this candy man woke up to the fact that his special brand of creams had become very popular not only in his own vicinity, but all over the United States. You see, the chocolate creams were good, and some of the thousands of students, after leaving their university—which was located in Mr. Candy Man's town—in addition to sending back for express orders of creams, holiday times and on other special occasions, told their dealers about these fine creams, and custom grew rapidly.

Well, one of the old university boys who happened to be a trade-mark lawyer, upon a visit to his Alma Mater, dropped in to say hello to his old friend, the candy man, who was getting richer every year and prouder of his good creams. The latter, like any man who has a successful trade-mark, lost no time in telling the lawyer about the success of the creams.

The lawyer, being with an old personal friend and thinking of the mark from a trade-mark lawyer's standpoint, emphatically suggested that such a valuable mark be registered and that he would be glad to take care of the matter for a certain fee. Mr. Candy Man enthused and told the lawyer to go ahead, not to make a preliminary search, because Mr. Candy Man was so sure that he was the original user of the mark, but to make application for registration right away.

In brief, the application went to the Patent Office and in due time the examiner came back with a cold refusal to register the mark, rightfully basing his refusal on the grounds that the same identical mark had been registered by a large eastern candy manufacturer some 25 years back—just 5 years before Mr. Candy Man in good faith appropriated the mark. The result was that Mr. Candy Man not only made himself liable in what might have been a serious infringement suit but had to give up that pet mark in favor of the prior user.

Now Mr. Candy Man has the tedious and costly task of building up a reputation of an entirely new mark. This time I am quite sure that he will take his trade-mark lawyer into consultation and select a mark that will be his property forever.

THE PROCESS OF REGISTRATION

A trade-mark may be registered by filing in the Patent Office an application in writing, accompanied by a written declaration to the effect that the applicant believes himself to be the owner of the trade-mark and that no other person or firm has the right to use this trade-mark. The application must also be accompanied by a description or copy of the trade-mark. The Commissioner of Patents then publishes the trade-mark in the official Gazette of the Patent Office. Anyone who believes himself to be injured by the trade-mark may file an opposition to it within 30 days. If no opposition is filed and if it complies with the regulations of the Patent Office the Commissioner issues a certificate of registration.

What Sort of Names Can Be Registered? Mr. W. A. Knight, legal specialist on trade-marks, answers this question thus:

Generally speaking, a trade-mark to be valid must not be the name of a person, name of a place, descriptive of the goods or of the quality of the goods, or old in the class into which the goods fall on which the mark is to be used, according to the arbitrary classification of the Patent Office.

The objection to personal and geographical names is that any other person by the same name living in the same locality might enter upon the production of a line of goods competing with the one already well known. He would have the right to use his own name or the name of his locality in designating the goods, because personal names and geographical names cannot be registered.

Names consisting of words purely descriptive of the article are objectionable because any one else selling that kind of an article would have the right to use the same descriptive name for it. This rule is strictly adhered to by the courts.

For instance, it would hardly seem that the person who adopted this jaw-breaking title, "Ammoniated Bone Superphosphate of Lime," for a fertilizer would either rob his neighbors of a phrase they might wish to use, or sell enough of the stuff to litigate about. But it is a fact that such a trade-mark was held invalid because it presumably only described the fertilizer. Even the refined word "Desiccated," when applied to the sacred New England codfish, will not do alone as a trade-mark, since a good dictionary shows it to be descriptive of a process which anyone else may adopt.

The courts go so far as to hold that words borrowed from foreign languages will not do as trade-marks as, when translated, they merely describe the article. One would certainly think that the original introducer of "Parchesi" had hit upon a capital trade-mark, but since the word is Hindustanese for a game in India, and since others have the right to make and sell the game under its real name, this trade-mark has been held invalid.

Some of these cases are very close and depend largely upon the "personal equation" seated upon the bench. Dr. Dadrian, the originator of "Matzoon," which is the Armenian name for buttermilk fermented by a special process, lost his case against an imitator in the Federal Courts in New York City on the ground that the word, translated, was merely descriptive, while in the New York courts, sitting on the other side of City Hall Park from the Federal Courts, it was held that "Matzoon" was a perfectly valid trade-mark.[1]

Most of the names rejected by the registration office come under the class of descriptive names. Some very close distinctions are made; thus, "Rubberoid," "Nextobeer," and "Kantleek," have been refused registration on the ground of their descriptive character. More recently

[1] *System*, May, 1911, p. 489.

"Crystal Domino" as a name for sugar was refused registration because crystal is descriptive of sugar. For similar reasons "Turknit" (Towel), "Master Craft" (for suits and overcoats), and "Bras-Brite" (for polish) were rejected. There was difficulty in registering "Crisco" because the name "Crispett" was already on the register. "Onyx" as a name for underwear was refused registration because the name was already widely known as a name for hosiery.

Many names have been registered which would now be refused registration. The trade-mark law passed in 1905 provided for the registration without question of any trademark which for 10 years or more prior to 1905 had been in exclusive use by the applicant or his predecessors. Personal and geographical names such as "1847 Rogers Bros.," "Boston Garters," "Elgin" or "Waltham" or "Ingersoll" watches could not be registered today. Names or portraits of deceased celebrities may be registered. The name of a living celebrity may be registered if he gives permission for the use of his name. Statements added to trade-marks must be truthful to be registrable. "Made in Germany" or "Bottled in England" cannot be registered unless the goods were actually made in Germany or bottled in England.

Summarizing, we may say that the best name is a short, fanciful name suggestive of the article as much as possible. Thus, nearly ideal names are "Uneeda," "Nabisco," "Gold Dust," "Regal," or "Holeproof." Personal and geographical names are conservative and dignified, but they cannot be registered and hence may be used by others. High quality names suggest worth and desirability of the goods, but they sometimes sound boastful and egotistical, and often the same name is used by many different firms for many different commodities. Such words as perfection, standard, premier, and peerless, are used for a large variety of articles. There is a Peerless Automobile, a Peerless Cream Separator, a Peerless Bicycle, and a Peerless Beverage.

Fanciful, or artificially coined names, if suggestive, are

on the whole the best, but they usually have the weakness of being more difficult to remember and to popularize. The words "Bon Ami" required much time and money to hammer into the mind of the public. "W. H. Childs, of the Bon Ami Company, now states that he would be willing to give many thousands of dollars if only the name could be changed to any one of a number of other names which his experience has shown him would be far better, without losing the time, money, and effort which have been put into past advertising. 'Bon Ami' is objectionable, for one thing, because the 'Masses' do not know enough French, as a rule, to appreciate its meaning, and hence its appropriateness." [1]

Personal names in general cannot be registered. The theory underlying this principle is that every person has a right to use his own name and to apply it to his product. There are, however, many complicated angles to the problem. It is also a matter of common justice that when a manufacturer has developed a considerable amount of goodwill and reputation for a product known by his name he shall be protected against unfair competition from others who may have the same name and who distribute their goods with the implication that they are those of the better-known manufacturer. Numerous cases of this sort arise from time to time in which persons who have the name of a well-known manufacturer enter upon the manufacture of the same product and utilize their own names. Thus, for example, persons by the name of Pillsbury have thought it desirable to go into the flour business, persons by the name of Ford into the automobile business, or automobile accessories, persons by the name of Baker into the cocoa and chocolate business, persons by the name of Fownes into the glove business, and so on.

An interesting case, in connection with which there was a considerable amount of litigation, was that of the Knabe Piano. The original Knabe interests sold the piano and the

[1] *Printers' Ink,* July 28, 1910.

rights to it to the International Piano Company. Shortly after that, however, the grandsons of the original Knabe decided to manufacture pianos and naturally they wished to apply their own name to their product. The International Company, however, had bought the rights to the original Knabe Company and felt that they were alone entitled to use the name Knabe. In the course of litigation over the question the decision finally was that the grandsons were entitled to use their name in connection with their product, but that they must not use it in any way to confuse the buyer regarding the particular Knabe Piano that he was purchasing. In other words, the grandsons were required to put upon the fall-board of the piano a statement to the effect that this piano was made by William and E. J. Knabe, grandsons of the original Knabe.

In a decision made by the Supreme Court of the United States, A. A. Waterman & Co. were required to put upon the pen the full name Arthur A. Waterman & Co. followed by the words "not connected with G. E. Waterman Company."

Geographical names can ordinarily not be registered, for a reason similar to that which in general forbids the registration of personal names. Any person living in a certain city or locality is entitled to use that as the name of his business. However, names have been allowed by the Patent Office which did not have any geographical significance for the particular product in question. For example, the name Arab was allowed as applied to sardines since sardines are not imported from Arabia, but it was not allowed as applied to dates. The name Occident was allowed for flour, but the name Orient was not allowed, the reason given by the Patent Office being that the word Occident is more general in its meaning than the word Orient, and that the latter refers to a specific portion of the world.

Descriptive names in general are prohibited, for the reason that it would not be just and fair to give exclusive right to one maker to describe his product in a common way. Every manufacturer of the same type of product is entitled to use the English language and describe the product in common terms. The name Auto Strop Razor has had an interesting history in connection with this problem. It was originally allowed registration in this country. During the recent war when the American soldiers were buying Auto Strop razor blades in European countries a considerable amount of business developed for this razor, with the result that the company desired to register the name in Great Britain. The British Registration Office, however, refused to accept it on the ground that it was regarded as descriptive. The company, therefore, has added the word "Valet" as a prefix to the previous name—Valet Auto Strop. It gradually is using this additional name in this country. The word "valet" was first used in smaller type underneath the phrase Auto Strop, but has gradually become more and more prominent and is now of equal prominence.

The word "International" was allowed for the International Harvester Company, but it was not allowed for the International Banking Company, because it was regarded descriptive for the latter but not for the former.

Misspellings of words in this connection do not help the possibility of registering a descriptive name. Likewise a picture which is regarded as a description of the object cannot be registered as a trade-mark for the product. Similarly a slogan to be registered must not be descriptive nor advocate some specific virtue of the article. For example, the statement "An apple a day keeps the doctor away" was registered for the beverage "Appleju," but a statement "A drink of Appleju a day keeps the doctor away" would probably not be allowed registration. The phrase, "Dictate to the Dictaphone" could probably not be registered because it contains the name of the article.

A picture of a portion of roofing manufactured by the Barrett Company was not allowed to be registered because it was a direct pictorial reproduction of the product itself.

The Cooper Underwear Company was granted registration for a group of figures dressed in underwear on the ground that while it showed the product in the picture it was the particular arrangement of the figures which was protected. Persons in underwear, as such, as a trade-mark for underwear could not be registered.

Territorial Protection. As a general principle a trade-mark can be protected only within the territory in which the business is done. Thus, for example, a flour concern in the South was using the same name as a flour concern in the North. When the business of the two concerns began to expand they found themselves overlapping in their territory and the case was decided by granting each one permission to use the same name in its own particular territory in which the reputation for the name had been developed.

Protection Within a Given Field of Products. Closely allied to the preceding principle is the principle that a name may be protected only as applied to products within the same field. For example, the name Mazda for a gas mantle was refused registration because it belongs to the same class of products as electric lamps, to which the name had previously been applied. On the other hand the name Gillette as applied to a water bottle was allowed registration, since it is a product in a different field from that of safety razors, to which the name had previously been applied.

Continuous Use. In order to safeguard the permanent protection of a trade-mark it is necessary to make continuous use of it. If a trade-mark is abandoned for a period of time, another concern may use the mark and popularize it with the probability that the original firm could not use it again if it so desired at a later time. Thus, for example, the Royal Baking Powder is an interesting case in point. The original company ceased business. Shortly afterward another company adopted the name Royal for baking powder. Then later the original company attempted to claim right to the name but found it impossible to do so because it had abandoned it. Many firms in order to demonstrate continuity of usage keep a file of advertisements, reports

TABLE 132

NUMBER OF INFRINGEMENTS OF THE TRADE-MARKS OF THE NATIONAL BISCUIT COMPANY

Trade-Marks	1905	1906	1907	1908	1909	1910	1911	1912	1913	1914
In-er-seal Trade-Mark	58	80	96	108	120	128	133	134	137	145
Uneeda Biscuit	29	35	37	39	42	45	49	51	52	58
Red Label Graham	27	31	35	41	42	42	42	43	43	48
Ribbon Design	22	26	29	29	29	29	29	29	29	35
Mary Ann	22	28	29	30	30	32	33	35	35	37
Social Tea	13	15	17	21	24	24	28	29	31	35
Zu Zu	11	11	12	13	13	13	13	14	15	18
Lemon Snaps Label	6	8	9	12	12	13	13	13	13	13
Oysterettes	6	10	11	12	12	13	15	15	15	19
Jonnie	4	4	4	6	7	7	7	8	8	8
Faust	4	9	10	10	10	10	10	10	10	10
Saratoga Flakes	3	3	6	6	9	10	10	12	12	12
Oatmeal Crackers Label	1	3	5	6	6	7	7	7	7	7
Eagle	..	4	4	5	6	8	8	8	8	8
Royal	2	2	5	6	7	10	12	15	16	21
Five o'Clock	..	..	3	5	5	6	8	10	11	13
Nabisco	..	2	3	3	5	5	8	8	8	8
Premium	..	2	3	6	6	8	9	9	9	10
Sorbetto	..	..	3	3	5	10	10	10	10	10
Cow Design	..	..	3	5	5	12	12	12	13	15
Fig Newtons	..	..	..	..	1	2	3	4	5	10
Dainties	..	..	..	..	1	2	2	2	2	10
Tid-Bits	3	3	3	3	3	3	3	3	3	10
Refillers of Cans and Boxes	2	12	14	26	30	37	55	63	69	72
American Beauty, Crispy, Champion, Cameo, Festino, Golden Rod Kream Klips, Picnin, Pretzelettes, Old Time, Shell, Star, Sea Foam, Taffy, etc., etc.	36	42	57	77	81	90	93	100	110	197
Total by Notice	249	330	398	472	514	566	612	644	674	833
By Injunction	19	32	32	32	32	32	32	32	32	49
	268	362	430	504	546	598	644	676	706	882

and other materials with dates, to indicate at what times these names and marks were used.[1]

Priority of Usage. Whenever there is a conflict between two trade-marks the firm which can demonstrate prior usage is ordinarily allowed protection or registration for the name. For example, the name "Vivo" used by the Mueller Brewing Company of Milwaukee and the name "Bevo" used by the Anheuser Busch Company of St. Louis came into conflict when these firms attempted to register them. Investigation showed that the name "Vivo" had been used since 1905, whereas the name "Bevo" had been used since 1908. The former was therefore granted registration.

Infringements of Names and Marks. Much litigation is constantly in progress over the infringements of names. Many concerns will attempt to use a name or trade-mark very similar to ones already in wide usage and for which a large amount of business has been developed. It will be interesting to note to what extent such practices occur if we turn to the records of the National Biscuit Company. From Table 132 it will be seen that many infringements have been made upon many of their trade names and marks. This table gives a summary, by different years up to 1915, of the abandonments of infringing trade-marks used by other firms.

THE PSYCHOLOGICAL CONFUSION OF NAMES AND MARKS

Confusion of trade-marks is primarily a psychological problem. The problem is to determine to what extent a given trade-mark is confused in the minds of people with other trade-marks. This question has not received the attention which it deserves. It is evidently very difficult for a court to decide to what extent one trademark is an infringement upon another or to what extent it may cause confusion with other trade-marks in the minds of buyers. A significant pioneer study along this line was made by R.

---

[1] *Printers' Ink,* May 6, 1920, p. 62.

TABLE 133—RECOGNITION METHOD

The Original Trade-Mark, the Imitative, the Name of the Article, the Order, and the Recognition Scores in the Uninformed, the Informed, and the Control Groups.

Decision	Trade-Mark Original	Trade-Mark Imitative	Name of Article	Order	Uninformed Per Cent Confused	Informed (Groups — Per Cent Recognized as) Identical	Informed Changed	Informed New	Control Per Cent of Correct Identification of Originals
I	Welcome	Welcome A. Smith	Soap	1	5	.....	80	20	85
I	Our Little Samson	Samsoncalf	Shoes	2	10	.....	50	50	75
N	Golden Charm	Charm	Flour	3	10	5	50	45	80
N	Walkeasy	Waulkwell	Shoes	4	10	.....	100	.....	80
N	Holeproof	Knotair	Hosiery	5	10	10	80	10	95
I	Rubberset	Rubber-vulc	Shaving Brush	6	20	.....	75	25	80
N	Keepclean	Sta-Kleen	Toilet Brushes	7	20	5	70	25	90
I	Yusea	U-C-A	Incandescent Lights	8	20	10	70	20	80
N	Every Day	Everybody's	Soap	9	20	20	70	10	85
N	Union Leader	Union World	Tobacco	10	30	5	60	35	70
I	Kalamazoo Wagon	Kalamazoo Buggy	Company	11	30	10	60	30	95
N	No-To-Bac	Baco-Curo	Medicine	12	30	15	55	30	100
N	Don Carlos	Don Caesar	Olives	13	30	15	60	25	75
N	Royal Irish Linen	Royal Vellum	Writing Paper	14	30	15	65	20	85
I	Uno	Ino	Medicine	15	30	20	60	20	100
I	Liveraid*	Liverine	Medicine	16	30	30	50	20	85
I	Beats-All	Knoxall	Lead Pencil	17	35	.....	65	35	95

	Brand	Imitation	Product						
N	S. B.	B. & S.	Cough Drops	18	35	30	70	.....	80
N	Maraschino	Marceno	Candy	19	35	45	35	20	90
I	Pep-Kola	Pepko	Tonic	20	35	40	45	15	80
N	Ruberoid	RubberO	Roofing	21	40	10	60	30	90
I	Shipmate	Messmate	Galley Stove	22	40	15	50	35	65
N	Pratt's Astral	Standard White Astrak.	Oil	23	40	20	50	30	70
I	Worth	Our Worth	Edge Tools	24.5	40	20	55	25	95
N	Bestyette	Veribest	Raincoat	24.5	40	20	55	25	95
I	Sorosis	Sartoris	Shoes	26	45	5	70	25	90
N	Sozodont	Kalodont	Toothpaste	27	45	5	80	15	85
I	Cyco	Cyco Prize	Carpet Sweeper	28	45	10	55	35	75
N	Ma-Le-Na	Man-a-lin	Medicine	29	45	15	60	25	95
N	Old Country	Our Country	Soap	30	45	20	40	40	75
I	Six Little	Six Big	Tailors	31	45	30	55	25	90
N	Dermacura	Dermakola	Skin Ointment	32	45	30	25	45	90
I	Maisena	Maizharina	Corn Flour	33.5	45	30	40	30	80
N	Bear Lithia Springs	Great Bear Sp	Company	33.5	45	30	40	30	85
I	Mellwood	Mill Wood	Whiskey	35	45	30	45	25	85
I	Seafoam*	Sodafoam	Baking Flour	36	45	35	50	15	60
N	Magic	Magico	Cleanser	37	45	40	30	30	60
I	Amber Bead	Amber	Beer	38	45	40	40	20	75
N	Victor	Victoria	Millinery	39	45	45	35	20	70
I	Capital	Capitol	Coffee	40	45	45	40	15	90
N	Electric	Elec. Light	Flour	41	50	.....	70	30	75
N	Eagle	Gold Eagle	White Lead	42	50	10	45	45	70
I	Green River	Green Ribbon	Whiskey	43	50	15	50	35	95

TABLE 133—RECOGNITION METHOD (Continued)

Decision	Trade-Mark		Name of Article	Uninformed		Groups			Control
	Original	Imitative		Order	Per Cent Confused	Informed			Per Cent of Correct Identification of Originals
						Per Cent Recognized as:			
						Identical	Changed	New	
I	Carbolineum	Creo-Carbolin	Preserving Paint	44	50	20	30	50	80
N	Social Register, Newport	Newport Social Index	Directory	45	50	20	40	40	80
I	German Sweet	Sweet German	Chocolate	46	50	25	50	25	95
N	Henderson	Anderson	Whiskey	47	55	15	55	30	85
I	Mormaja*	Mojava	Coffee	48	55	20	60	20	95
I	Nitro	Nitro-Hunter	Firearms	49	60	10	35	55	100
I	Grenadine	Grenade	Syrup	50	60	25	25	50	100
N	Muresco	Murafresco	Wall Covering	51	65	25	60	15	90
I	Trenton	Trenton Style	Port Roll	52	65	55	10	35	85
I	Johnston's	Johnson's	Chocolates	53	65	75	15	10	75
N	Willoughby Lake	Willoughby Ridge	Scythe-stones	54	70	.....	50	50	70
N	West End	East Ridge	Distilling Co.	55	70	20	55	25	95
I	Cottolene	Cottoleo	Sub. for Lard	56	70	40	35	25	80
I	Dyspepticure	Dyspepticide	Medicine	57	75	35	60	5	95
I	Ceresota	Cressota	Flour	58	80	25	65	10	85
I	Siphon	Siphon System	Refrigerator	59	80	50	30	20	85
I	Nubia	Nubias	Cigarettes	60	85	40	30	30	90

*Through error these words were spelled, and used in the experiments, slightly different from the way in which they occur in the court records: Liverald should be Liveroid, Seafoam should be Sea Foam, and Mormaja should be Momaja.

TABLE 134—RANKING METHOD

The Original Trade-Mark, the Imitative, the Name of the Article, the Order, the Average Grade of Confusion, Its Probable Error and the Recognition Scores.

	Trade-Mark (Original)	Imitative	Name of Article	Order	Relative Position Grade	P.E.	Groups Recognized as: Uninformed Per Cent Confused	Informed Per Cent Recognized as: Identical	Changed	New	Control Per Cent of Correct Iden. of Originals
	Syphon	Black Diamond	Refrigerator—D*	1	.1	.02					
	Fits-U	Ariosa	Eyeglasses—R†	2	.2	.04					
	O-Zell	Lustro	Gelatine—D	3	.2	.04					
	Hammermill Bond	Globe-Wernicke	Paper—R	4	.2	.04					
	Globe Trotter	Certain-teed	Automobile—D	5	.3	.06					
	Everstick	Herringbone	Rubbers—R	6	.7	.12					
	Hensoldt	Buckhead	Prism Binocular—R	7	.7	.11					
	White Rock	Stonetex	Table Water—R	8	1	.11					
N	Holeproof	Knotair	Hosiery	9	2	.21	10	10	80	10	95
N	Royal Irish Linen	Royal Vellum	Writing Paper	10	2.4	.20	30	15	65	20	85
I	Our Little Samson	Sansoncalf	Shoes	11	3.5	.26	10	0	50	50	75
I	Rubberset	Rubber-vulc	Brush	12	3.5	.22	20	0	75	25	80
N	Sozodont	Kalodont	Tooth Paste	13	3.5	.24	45	5	80	15	85
	Beats-All	Knoxall	Lead Pencil	14	4.1	.27	35	0	65	35	96
N	Union Leader	Union World	Tobacco	15	4.2	.24	30	5	60	35	70
I	Six Little	Six Big	Tailors	16	4.3	.26	45	20	55	25	90
N	Bestyette	Veribest	Raincoat	17	4.4	.26	40	20	55	25	95
N	Bear Lithia Springs	Great Bear Spgs	Company	18	4.5	.22	45	30	40	30	85
N	Walkeasy	Waulkwell	Shoes	19	4.6	.26	10	0	100	0	80
I	Sorosis	Sartoris	Shoes	20	4.7	.28	45	5	70	25	90
N	Ma-Le-Na	Man-a-lin	Medicine	21	4.7	.28	45	15	60	25	90
I	Seafoam	Sodafoam	Baking Powder	22	4.7	.22	45	35	50	15	60
I	Carbolineum	Creo-Carbolin	Preserving Paint	23	4.7	.21	50	20	30	50	80
I	Shipmate	Messmate	Galley Stove	24	5.0	.25	40	15	50	35	65

TABLE 134—RANKING METHOD (Continued)

	Trade-Mark		Name of Article	Relative Position			Uninform-ed (Per Cent Confused)	Groups Informed Per Cent Recognized as:			Control Per Cent of Correct Iden. of Originals
	Original	Imitative		Order	Grade	P.E.		Iden-tical	Changed	New	
I	Green River	Green Ribbon	Whiskey	25	5.3	.24	50	15	50	35	95
I	Nitro	Nitro-Hunter	Firearms	26	5.3	.21	60	10	35	55	100
N	Social Register, Newport	Newport Social Index	Directory	27	5.5	.28	50	20	40	40	80
I	Usea	U-C-A	Incandescent Lights	28	5.5	.35	20	10	70	20	80
I	Maizena	Maizharina	Corn Flour	29	5.8	.22	45	30	40	30	80
N	Pep-Kola	Pepko	Tonic	30	6.2	.18	35	40	45	15	80
I	Electric	Elec. Light	Flour	31	6.2	.21	50	40	40	30	75
I	Amber Bead	Amber	Beer	32	6.3	.22	45	40	40	20	75
N	Muresco	Muresco	Wall Covering	33	6.3	.18	65	25	60	15	90
N	Trenton	Trenton Style	Pork Roll	34	6.4	.22	65	55	55	35	85
N	Old Country	Our Country	Soap	35	6.5	.24	45	20	40	40	75
I	Dyspepticure	Dyspepticide	Medicine	36	6.6	.23	75	35	60	5	95
I	Cyco	Cyco Prize	Carpet Sweeper	37	6.7	.21	45	20	55	35	75
I	Uno	Ino	Medicine	38	7.0	.10	30	20	60	20	100
N	S. B.	B. & S.	Cough Drops	39	7.1	.22	35	30	70	20	80
I	Cottoleo	Cottoleo	Sub. for Lard	40	7.1	.21	70	40	35	0	80
N	Worth	Our Worth	Edge Tools	41	7.3	.18	40	55	55	25	85
I	Magic	Magico	Cleanser	42	7.6	.19	45	40	30	30	60
I	Cresota	Cresota	Flour	43	7.9	.15	80	25	65	30	85
I	German Sweet	Sweet German	Chocolate	44	8.0	.14	50	25	50	10	95
I	Nubia	Nubias	Cigarettes	45	8.3	.15	85	40	50	25	90
I	Capital	Capitol	Coffee	46	8.3	.11	45	45	10	30	96
I	Johnson's	Johnson's	Chocolates	47	8.9	.09	65	75	15	10	75
	Drinket	Drinket	Coffee—Id††	48	10.	.00	……	……	……	……	……
	Quickwood	Quickwood	Collars—Id††	49	10.	.00	……	……	……	……	……
	Whiz	Whiz	Stove Polish	50	10.	.00	……	……	……	……	……

*D—Very dissimilar mating.   †R—Random mating.   ††Id—Identical mating.

H. Paynter and was published in the *Archives of Psychology*, Columbia University, January, 1920.

In this investigation 60 pairs of litigated trade-marks or words were used. Sixty of these were originals and 60 were imitations. The investigation was carried out by two different methods: (1) the recognition method; and (2) the ranking method. In the recognition method the 60 pairs were split up into 6 sets of 10 pairs each. Each trade-mark was typed on a card. The person with whom the test was made was asked to look at each of the 20 cards in a set for one second. After he had finished, a set of 40 cards was given to him, composed of the 10 originals and the 10 imitations which he had just seen together with 20 additional words which he had not seen. He was asked to state which of these he had just seen and to indicate his degree of certainty, namely, "absolutely certain," "reasonably certain," "faint idea" or "guess." The test was carried out with three groups of persons: an uninformed group composed of 10 men and 10 women who did not know the purpose of the test; an informed group of 10 men and 10 women who were told the purpose of the test; and a control group of 10 men and 10 women with whom no imitation trademarks were used. A control group was used in order to determine the accuracy of recognition of the original trademarks themselves.

In the ranking method 50 pairs of trade-marks were used. Each pair was written on a separate slip of paper. Thirty-nine of these pairs were trade-marks concerning which there had been litigation. The remaining 11 pairs were made up for the purpose of this experiment. Three pairs were purposely made very dissimilar, 5 were random matings and 3 were identical matings. These 50 slips of paper were given to a person who was asked to sort them into 11 groups according to their similarity. The 11 groups were to be arranged as follows: The first group, called zero group, was to contain those pairs of trade-marks which in the opinion of the persons tested were in no way similar and could not possibly cause confusion. Group Number 10 was to contain those trade-marks which were completely identical. The other groups in between were to contain the remaining trade-marks graded in steps from zero to 10. This method of testing was carried out with 25 men and 25 women. The results of these tests are shown in Tables 133 and 134. Table 133 gives the results of the recognition method, and Table 134 gives the results of the ranking method.

Concerning this table, Paynter says:

One of the first things to be noticed about the table is that all imitations, non-infringements as well as infringements, cause some confusion in the Uninformed group. Furthermore, both in the Uninformed and Informed they do not divide into two groups, but extend over about three-fourths of the entire length of the scale, forming a continuum. These two findings do not support the legal treatment of imitations. Indeed, they present clear proof against the statements made in trade-mark laws, judicial decisions, and legal text-books which consider imitations as falling into only two discreet groups, those likely to deceive and those not likely to deceive. For legislative bodies and courts to think and work on false principles and assumptions in regard to imitations has surely a detrimental effect not only on their own proceedings but also on business and commerce. Confusion, though it be a subjective fact, is also a quantitative one. To handle it correctly it needs to be measured, not merely defined. In ordinary conversation we are usually satisfied in remarking that the weather is hot, warm, cool, etc. But in scientific and industrial laboratories these adjectives become exceedingly vague and are replaced by degrees on the thermometer. By standardizing our notions about degrees of heat, the thermometer permits of greater accuracy in working with them. Clear and quantitative meanings attached to the legal and illegal categories of deception would undoubtedly favor greater accuracy in handling them too.

Let us now see what the highest and lowest scores are for each kind of recognition. In the Uninformed, "Nubia * Nubias" is the most confusing pair of trade-marks, deceiving 17 out of 20 individuals or 85% of the group. The least confusing pair is "Welcome * Welcome A. Smith" with a score of 5%, deceiving only 1 out of 20 individuals. Column 7 shows that in the Informed group seven pairs of trade-marks have 0% scores of confusion. In the Uninformed, one of these, "Welcome * Welcome A. Smith," has 5% of confusion, and another, "Willoughby Lake * Willoughby Ridge," has 70%. For the 0% scores in the Informed this is the largest difference between the confusion of any two in the Uninformed. "Johnson's * Johnston's" with 75% of confusion is the most confusing imitation in the Informed, it being eighth from the top in the Uninformed where its score is 65%. This pair of trade-marks is one of the three which received a higher score of confusion in the Informed than in the Uninformed; these being the only cases where the natural results of more confusion in the Uninformed than in the Informed does not obtain. As the difference is not large in any of the three cases it is quite possible that further experimentation would reverse the advantage. It will be noticed that the scores of confusion in the Informed tend in general to increase with their corresponding ones in the Uninformed. In 52 cases out of 60 the confusion in the Uninformed is higher than in the Informed, and in 5 cases they are equal.

In the column for correct recognition of change, "Walkeasy * Waulkwell" has a 100% or perfect score, and "Trenton-Trenton Style" with 10% stands at the lower limit. The former in the Uninformed confused 10%, and in the Informed 0%; the latter in the Uninformed confused 65%, and in the Informed 55%. An imitation that is easily detected is apt to cause little confusion, and vice versa. In the column for incorrect discriminations, or those imitations recognized as new, the highest score is 55% and the two lowest are each 0%. Two scores at 60% are the lowest for correct identifications of the originals, and 4 perfect ones are the highest. The identifications of the originals are higher in correctness than any other kind of recognition. A comparison of the correct identifications of the originals with the incorrect identifications of the imitations shows that in all but two instances the originals were more often identified as originals than imitations are identified as originals. "Johnston's-Johnson's" in the Informed with 75% are the exceptions. These scores indicate that the imitations look just like the originals and under the experimental conditions are not distinguishable. Each of the 3 most confusing pairs of trade-marks in the Uninformed differ in percentage of identifications from that of their respective originals by only 5%. We may see from these cases the extent to which an imitation may displace its original.

The scoring permitted a difference of no less than 5%. The range in percentage of the various kinds of recognitions varies from 40% of the entire length of the scale (from 60% to 100%) of correct identifications of the originals to 90% of the entire length of the scale (from 10% to 100%) of correct recognitions of change of the imitations; or from four-tenths of the entire range to nine-tenths. In the different ranges there are only a few gaps between any two pairs of trade-marks, and those not very wide. If we had experimented further, or had used more trade-marks of other degrees of deceptive similarity, there is no doubt that all the missing steps would have been filled in. The frequencies of the different percentages of the various recognitions in the 3 groups tend, when plotted, to resemble the normal probability curve, excepting the incorrect identifications in the Informed which are skewed toward the high end.

The following brief table shows the results of nine decisions, in which five were adjudications of infringements in which the use of the imitation was enjoined, and four were adjudications of non-infringements in which injunctions were refused. The following nine cases were selected because no element other than confusion was involved in the decision.

TABLE 135
COURT DECISIONS AND THE AMOUNT OF CONFUSION OF TRADE-MARKS

Decision	Original	Imitation	Recognition Method Per Cent Confused	Ranking Method Average Rank
N	Sozodont	Kalodont	28	3.6
I	Nox-all	Non-X-Ell	28	4.9
I	Club	Chancellor Club	35	2.7
N	Bestyette	Veribest	35	4.1
N	Mother's	Grand-Ma's	38	3.2
I	Au-to-do	Autola	40	4.3
N	Peptenzyme	Pinozyme	43	5.2
I	Green River	Green Ribbon	50	5.7
I	Ceresota	Cressota	63	7.9

The conclusions drawn by Paynter are as follows:

1. Some of the imitations declared to be legal by the courts actually confused more individuals in the recognition experiment

than some imitations declared illegal, and vice versa. The results of the relative position method confirm this. Therefore, some of the judicial decisions were inaccurate and inconsistent.

2. The scores of the imitations of the two supposedly distinct decisions overlap throughout most of their range, so that the decisions do not represent two really different legal or psychological categories.

XXVII

PACKAGES, CARTONS AND LABELS

Purposes served by the package. Elements of the container. 1. Size. 2. Shape. 3. Convenience in use of the container. 4. The label on the container. Methods of selecting containers. Test to determine the size and shape of the container. Results of investigation. Tests for selecting cartons. Appropriateness of labels.

THE package serves two purposes: (1) it serves as a convenient container for a commodity; and (2) it provides a means for remembering the product. In some respects, therefore, its function is similar to that of a trade-mark: it serves as a means of identification. The importance of the package or container may be realized when we note that the custom of selling in standardized packages has increased enormously in the last decade or two, and as a result the container has acquired an important sales value. The selection and design of the package, therefore, both as to shape and external decoration and layout is an important matter. Many products have become successful through the use of an appropriate container; many products have found new outlets by being put up in a new unit, either larger or smaller than the one customarily used. A conspicuous instance of the latter is the new outlet that was developed for raisins through their sale in 5-cent packages. The 5-cent raisin package was first put upon the market by the Associated Raisin Company, in July, 1921. At the end of three months approximately $16,500,000 worth of raisins had been sold in 5-cent packages, or a total of 330,000,000 packages. While this volume did not keep up, the small package nevertheless provided a new outlet through which a considerable amount of raisins are distributed.

The General Electric Company, among many others, has

recently given renewed attention to its packages and labels. It is desirable that the dealer be induced to pay considerable attention to a proper display of packages on his shelves. It is equally important that the packages themselves be attractive and distinctive so that they may have maximum sales value. Recently the General Electric Company has redesigned a considerable number of its containers with satisfactory results. A folder entitled "Wiring Devices That Sell Themselves," issued by the General Electric Company, contains the following statement:

Electrical dealers heretofore have been handicapped in the making of attractive displays because the nature of their goods has often seemed to make it practically impossible to show their wares effectively. Goods packed in plain containers do not lend themselves to advantageous showing. Moreover, formerly there seemed no way of conveying to the eye of the shopper a proper idea of the use to which the article was to be put. Even if the article were removed from its box and displayed, in many cases the general public was not aware of its advantage over older-fashioned appliances. Nor did the ordinary, technical, plain label give any real help in explaining the article's use.

It is possible for the electrical dealer, with the use of these new labeled boxes, to make attractive store and window displays. These products will now sell themselves. The beauty of the package attracts the eyes of the public. The illustrations tell them at once the uses and advantages of the products contained, desire for possession is created, and sale is easily made.

Seven labels were designed and used as an experiment in the revision of the containers. The "G. E. Advertiser," the house organ of the company, makes the following statement regarding the importance of this experiment.

The "G-E Advertiser" takes pride in devoting this issue to the most powerful selling force that has been offered to the electrical trade in many years—a new system of box labels which will automatically and permanently multiply your sales of electrical products.

This is not an experiment, but a settled policy of the General Electric Company. It does not call for extraordinary efforts on the part of the dealer; on the contrary, the various devices will describe their own uses, speak for themselves, literally sell themselves.

Elements of the Container. The chief factors which contribute towards the design, utility and sales value of a container are probably the following:

1. Size. The size of the container depends upon the commodity it is to contain. It is also important to determine, however, what is the most economical and convenient unit in which to distribute the product, that is, whether the container should hold several ounces, one pound, or a very much larger amount.

2. Shape. The shape is determined by the nature of the product and convenience in handling it.

3. Convenience in Use of the Container. When a product is to be used in its container, the factor of convenience is an important one. Toilet articles, for instance, toothpaste, shaving cream, etc.—should be put up in a container that is convenient to use.

4. The Label on the Container. The three important elements in the design of a label are: first, the layout, that is, the pictorial and typographical design; second, the color, and the color scheme; and third, the message of the text.

METHODS OF SELECTING CONTAINERS

Because of the increasing recognition of the importance of the container, manufacturers are beginning to give attention to the careful designing and construction of containers. Some manufacturers are, in fact, beginning to use scientific methods to determine what sort of a container is most useful and has the greatest sales value. In the application of scientific methods to the selection of a container there are in general two types of procedure that may be followed.

The first method aims to secure all possible data that

may be useful in deciding what kind of a container to use. That is, before any attempt is made to design or to prepare a container, all the information that can possibly be secured regarding a desirable container should be obtained. Information regarding the convenience and appropriateness of various types of containers may be obtained in connection with a questionnaire investigation. (Methods of carrying out a questionnaire investigation are outlined in Part II.)

If the container is an important element in a product one or more questions regarding it may easily be inserted in a questionnaire. In the case of a toilet preparation, for instance, a question may be framed that will secure the general opinions of the consumer regarding the desirability of certain conveniences in the container, his objections to various containers and his suggestions for improvements of old containers.

If the second plan of procedure is followed, various kinds —shapes, sizes, etc.—of containers should be prepared and submitted to suitable scientific tests. These tests can be made with a satisfactory degree of reliability, as will be shown by several illustrations cited. Let us take some typical instances in which the particular problems involved were submitted to scientific tests.

TEST TO DETERMINE THE SIZE AND SHAPE OF THE CONTAINER

In many instances the particular size and shape of the container are predetermined by the nature of the product. In many cases, however, they are not so determined. Thus, for example, a container of macaroni or of certain kinds of crackers is determined to a large extent by the shape of the product. On the other hand, in the case of a great many canned goods the shape may be determined by factors other than those of the nature of the product. For example, the factor of apparent size may be an important element.

In the investigation here cited, the problem was to determine for a certain fish product the most suitable size of can in which to sell the product. The price to be charged and the amount of the product to be put into the can had already been determined, for it was decided that this was the most suitable amount to sell in a single retail unit. The problem, therefore, consisted primarily in selecting a container which should have a maximum apparent size for the quantity that was to be put into it. Five cans of various sizes, which will be designated by the letters A, B, C, D, and E, were prepared. Cans A, C, and D were all of standard size, Number 1 American Can Company. The cubical contents were all alike. Can A was the tall form, can C, the flat form, and can D was also tall, but it had a label without a border on the edge. Can B was a larger size, and can E was a smaller size than the other three.

A test was made with these cans to determine their apparent size. The person tested was asked to arrange the cans in the order of apparent size. A similar test was made with a series of four cans, which will be designated as F,

TABLE 136

RESULT OF TEST TO DETERMINE THE APPARENT SIZE OF FIVE LABELED CANS

Can	Averages		Ranks	
	Group 1	Group 2	Group 1	Group 2
A	4.3	7.2	4	4
B	2.1	2.4	1	1
C	3.5	5.5	2	2
D	4.1	6.9	3	3
E	5.5	10.6	5	5

G, H, and I. The difference between the set of five cans and the second set of four cans was simply that the latter contained no labels, whereas the former set did. In this second set cans F and I corresponded to cans A and C in the first set, respectively, while G and H corresponded to cans B and E, respectively.

TABLE 137

RESULT OF TEST TO DETERMINE THE APPARENT SIZE OF
FOUR CANS WITHOUT LABELS

	Averages		Ranks	
Can	Group 1	Group 2	Group 1	Group 2
F	3.9	5.9	3	3
G	1.7	2.8	1	1
H	4.8	7.8	4	4
I	2.6	5.2	2	2

The experiments were carried out with two sets of persons—12 men and 23 women. Each person was asked to rank the cans in the order of apparent size. The results of this investigation were as shown in Tables 136 and 137.

The numbers in these tables are average ranks. The smaller the average rank, the larger was the can indicated. In the first set can B was the largest and can E was the smallest. These two, of course, were distinctly larger and smaller respectively and were used primarily to show that there were cans of actually different sizes in the series.

The interest of the experiment was really centered in cans A, C, and D in the first set and F and I in the second set, since they had the same cubical size and would each hold 10 ounces; the problem was to determine which of these three cans had the largest apparent size. The results showed that there is a distinct difference in apparent size among these particular cans. It will be noticed in the tables that can C and can I, which were identical, except for the presence or absence of the label, appeared to the eye to be the largest. Can C, American Can Company's flat can Number 1, was regarded as larger and as apparently containing more than cans A and D, the American Can Company's standard tall can Number 1. The evident conclusion is that the flat can of the same cubical size is distinctly larger in appearance than the taller ones.

Considering cans C, D, and A of the first series and I

and F of the second series separately, and regarding can C and can I as 100% respectively, we obtain the following relative apparent sizes:

Can	Relative Value
C	100%
D	80
A	76
I	100
F	79

These figures indicate that if can C is assigned a size value of 100, can D is apparently only 80% as large, can A only 76% as large and can F only 79% as large as can I.

It is interesting to note that these data coincide closely. The results of the two experiments with the different sets of cans check up closely and there is also a very close agreement between the two groups of persons tested. It will be noted that the ranks agree perfectly showing that the test results have a high degree of reliability.

TESTS FOR SELECTING CARTONS

The Beech-Nut Packing Company had the problem of selecting a suitable container for its macaroni. The scientific procedure in carrying out tests for this purpose, as reported by Mr. Richard B. Franken,[1] was as follows:

The general shape and size of the carton to be used in this case was determined by the nature of the product. There is, however, a certain variation possible in the length of the package.

Twenty-three cartons were submitted by artists. These divided themselves naturally into four groups, according to size and general design. See illustrations in Figure 97.

Group 1 consisted of four cartons of the same length and size and general design. Each had the oval Beech-Nut trade-mark in the center and the rest of the design blank.

[1] *Printers' Ink Monthly*, December, 1920, p. 55.

Group 2 was composed of seven containers very much shorter than the rest. Groups 3 and 4 were formed in a similar manner.

Three types of tests were made in order to determine the relative values of these cartons from the following three different angles: (1) general appropriateness; (2) color and color combinations; (3) the designs and their arrangements. The experiment was conducted according to the usual ranking method. The entire investigation was conducted after the plan of a tournament. Each of the four groups of cartons was tested separately by each of the three tests mentioned. The experiments were carried out with customers in various retail stores. After a customer had entered the store and made a purchase he was introduced, by the clerk or the proprietor, to the investigator, who was regarded as a representative of the Beech-Nut Packing Company. The investigator then asked the customer to rank the particular group of cartons from the standpoint of general appropriateness as containers for macaroni. After this had been done the customer was asked to reconsider them and rank them again independently from the standpoint of the general design and pleasingness of the color. These three sets of tests were conducted with all four groups of cartons. As a result of these tests the two cartons standing the highest in each group were selected and put into a new group for a final test. This final group was then composed of eight cartons plus two additional ones chosen from among the cartons of competitors. The same three tests were then repeated with these ten cartons. The results are shown in Tables 138 and 139.

From these results it appears that the best carton is X in Group II. This stands first with both men and women and in all three of the tests made. The second best carton is N in Group IV, which stands either second or third in all of the tests made. G-I in Group V was poorest in all of the tests made and G in Group III was the next poorest in all the tests.

TABLE 138

TABLE OF AVERAGES (LOWEST AVERAGE BEST)

		Gen. Appro.		Color		Design		Final Average Women and Men	Final Rank
Set	Pkg.	Women	Men	Women	Men	Women	Men		
I	B	5.67	5.85	5.13	5.35	5.43	5.85	4.14	5
III	E	6.03	4.95	5.93	4.9	5.97	5.85	4.56	6
III	G	8.77	8.35	8.8	8.15	8.23	8.7	5.89	9
V	G-I	8.87	9.05	9.1	9.1	8.87	9.15	6.76	10
V	H	7.2	7.45	7.63	6.15	8.1	7.35	5.54	8
III	I	3.47	3.25	3.47	4.1	3.4	3.15	2.6	3
IV	N	2.33	3.5	3.33	4.2	3.17	3.45	2.42	2
IV	P	6.77	6.25	5.87	6.35	6.37	6.45	4.76	7
II	X	1.8	2.2	2.1	2.5	1.67	1.75	1.48	1
II	Z	4.1	4.15	3.63	4.2	3.73	3.4	2.9	4

An examination of these results makes it evident that it is possible to determine what is the most suitable package with a very satisfactory degree of confidence and reliability. The package chosen by the Beech-Nut Packing Company was the one that stood the highest in the test and is the one in which Beech-Nut Macaroni is distributed at the present time, namely X in Group II of Figure 97. This procedure, of course, does not insure securing the best possible container that may be devised. It does, however, insure the selection of the best container among those that have been devised or designed. Someone may possibly design a bet-

TABLE 139

TABLE OF RANKS (1 BEST, 10 POOREST)

		Gen. Appro.		Color		Design		Final Rank
Set	Pkg.	Women	Men	Women	Men	Women	Men	
I	B	5	6	5	6	5.5	5.5	5
III	E	6	5	7	5	6	5.5	6
III	G	9	9	9	9	9	9	9
V	G-I	10	10	10	10	10	10	10
V	H	8	8	8	7	8	8	8
III	I	3	2	3	2	3	2	3
IV	N	2	3	2	3.5	2	3	2
IV	P	7	7	6	8	7	7	7
II	X	1	1	1	1	1	1	1
II	Z	4	4	4	3.5	4	4	4

ter one than the best one in this series of 23, but whether
or not it is better could be determined by a scientific procedure similar to the one here outlined.

APPROPRIATENESS OF LABELS

The design, layout, and color scheme of the label are
obviously very important both from the standpoint of identification and from the standpoint of sales value. The
method of selecting an appropriate label will be illustrated
in two or three typical cases. W. S. Heller reports an investigation designed to determine the influence of the label
of the package upon the purchaser and also to determine
whether there is any relation between the seeming quality
of the contents (as judged by the appearance of the fruit)
and the attractiveness of the label. For the purpose of
this experiment 12 different brands of canned "yellow
cling peaches" were put up in 2½ lb. tins. All tins were
of the same size; all bore the name of the California Fruit
Canners Association, but they were different in brand,
name, and label. The various brands used are those mentioned in Table 140. These 12 brands were divided into 5
different grades of quality as follows:

	Quality
Extra Special Quality	1
Extra Quality	2
Extra Standard Quality	3
Standard Quality	4
Seconds Quality	5

One test given was designed to determine the relative
value and appropriateness of the labels and cans; another
was designed to determine the quality of the fruit contained in each can, as judged by appearances in a saucer
and not by trial. These tests were made with 50 men and
50 women. In addition to these two tests there was also
a memory test regarding the memory value of the labels on
the cans. The tests were made by the ranking method.

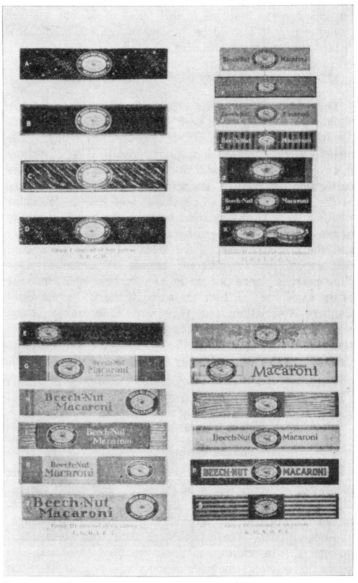

Figure 97: Cartons used in tests by the Beech-Nut Packing Company for the selection of a macaroni container *(See page 726)*

Table 140 gives results of the first test, namely, the relative ranks of the 12 different cans as judged from the appearance of the label and can.

TABLE 140
QUALITY OF FRUIT AND THE LABEL ON THE CAN

Quality	Name of Brand	Men	Women	Men and Women	Memory Men and Women
1	Griffon	5.90	6.52	6.21	26.5%
2	Del Monte	2.78	1.92	2.35	75.5
2	Acme	6.00	5.42	5.71	47.2
2	Oak	7.92	7.78	7.85	51.5
3	Mission	4.10	4.48	4.29	62.6
3	Gold Seal	4.88	4.56	4.72	31.2
3	Sweet Briar	6.44	7.10	6.77	40.5
4	Banquet	7.38	8.78	8.08	65.5
4	Swallow	7.84	8.38	8.11	47.0
4	Bouquet	8.32	8.58	8.45	33.0
5	Ideal	6.06	3.88	4.97	42.0
5	Creole	10.32	10.66	10.49	65.7

The smaller numbers in the table represent the higher ranks.

An examination of this table shows that the men and women agreed very closely in their reactions to these 12 different brands. So far as the relationship between the quality of fruit and the attractiveness of the label and the can is concerned, it will be observed that there is a considerable discrepancy between the two. There is some relationship between them, but there is also quite a large difference in regard to many of them. The Del Monte brand had the most attractive seal and can. The fruit was of a second quality as shown in the first column of the table. The Griffon brand had first quality fruit, but its can and label stood sixth. On the other hand, the Mission and Gold Seal brands stood second and third in respect to the label and can, but contained third quality fruit. Other comparisons may be noted in the table. The coefficient of correlation between the quality of the fruit and the attractiveness of the can and label was .48.

The memory test was conducted by asking the persons,

after they had ranked the cans, to state which of the labels they remembered and what features they remembered about them. The results of this test are given in relative percentage ranks in the last column of Table 140. These figures indicate that the Del Monte label was remembered most frequently, the Creole label next, and the Griffon label was remembered least.

The test made to determine the quality of the fruit as judged by its appearance yielded the following results:

	Men	Women	Men and Women
Quality 1	3.26	2.60	2.93
Quality 2	5.86	5.37	5.61
Quality 3	5.77	5.91	5.84
Quality 4	6.26	7.04	6.65
Quality 5	10.54	10.23	10.39

(The smaller numbers represent the higher ranking.)

This tabulation shows that the quality of the fruit can be judged quite accurately by its appearance. The tabulation shows, however, a large difference in appearance between Quality 1 and Quality 2, and likewise a large difference between Quality 4 and Quality 5. Qualities 2, 3, and 4 are close together in rankings.

A further test was made with regard to five specific elements in the label of the can, namely: (1) the color scheme, (2) simplicity of the label, (3) richness of the label, (4) appropriateness of the label, and (5) pleasingness of the label. The ranking method was used here also and the results are shown in Table 141.

Column one in that table, designated "Uncontrolled Judgment," gives the results of the judgment of the label and can as a whole. These results have already been presented in the fifth column of Table 140. It will be noticed that the results of the "uncontrolled judgment," or composite rank agree fairly well with the results of the rankings of individual elements. It will also be noted that the difference between the best and the poorest is considerably greater in some of the elements. For example, in the case

TABLE 141
TEST RESULTS ON THE VALUE OF LABELS

	Uncontrolled Judgment	Color	Richness	Pleasing- ness	Sim- plicity	Appropriate- ness
Del Monte	2.35	3.32	3.51	3.67	3.27	4.51
Mission	4.29	5.43	4.54	3.81	6.00	5.40
Gold Seal	4.72	5.81	3.97	5.13	6.30	5.05
Ideal	4.97	5.45	5.72	4.86	1.48	5.32
Acme	5.71	5.02	6.06	5.75	2.35	6.00
Griffon	6.21	7.70	4.87	6.64	6.37	6.86
Sweet Briar	6.77	5.75	6.93	6.08	7.10	6.27
Oak	7.65	6.94	7.09	5.43	6.37	7.10
Banquet	8.08	8.64	8.60	10.43	11.37	6.46
Swallow	8.11	6.81	8.18	6.21	10.27	7.67
Bouquet	8.45	8.02	8.21	8.62	9.30	7.73
Creole	10.49	9.02	10.30	11.32	7.72	9.60

of simplicity, the range is very wide, extending from 1.4 to 11.37. On the other hand, the range for appropriateness is considerably narrower, extending from 4.51 to 9.60. The probable explanation of this fact is that the element of simplicity was more definite and could be judged more readily than could a more complex characteristic such as appropriateness.

A similar investigation was made by a distributer of a fish product for the purpose of determining the most appropriate label to use upon a particular size and shape of can which had been previously determined. In this particular experiment 15 labels on cans were used which were especially selected or devised for the purpose. Tests in this case were made to cover 6 characteristics as follows: general appropriateness or atmosphere; color scheme; design; beauty; size; and clearness of type. In this instance the tests were made with 20 persons, all women. As a result of these tests the 5 poorest cans were eliminated and a further test was made with the remaining 10 cans. The results of this final series of tests are shown in Table 142, which gives the final ranks only, and not the median ranks for each individual test.

TABLE 142

TEST RESULTS ON THE VALUE OF LABELS

Cans	General Appropriateness	Color Scheme	Design	Beauty	Size	Clearness of Type
A	3	4.5	6	7	2	6
B	1.	4.5	2	8	7	2
C	4	9	1	10	9	9
D	10	1	7	1	3	5
E	8	7	10	3	1	1
G	9	3	9	2	4	7
H	5	10	3	6	10	3
M	6	8	5	9	5	10
N	7	2	1	5	6	4
O	2	6	4	4	8	2

1 indicates the best, and 10 the poorest, rank.

An examination of this table will show that there is a considerable difference among the various elements in the labels. Thus, for example, label D is last in general appropriateness and seventh in design, but first in color scheme and beauty. This is due in part to the fact that these differences actually exist, but also is in part probably due to the relatively small number of persons with whom the tests were made, namely, 10 in this last test. The preliminary test was made with 20 persons.

Another type of investigation may be cited here, the aim of which is to determine the appropriateness of the slug or name design on a can or label. In the particular instance cited here 18 slugs were devised and photographed. Two tests were made with them, one to determine the clearness or legibility, and the second to determine the general appropriateness for the product in question. The ranking method was used and in the preliminary test a total of 44 persons were tested. On the basis of this preliminary test 12 slugs were selected for a final test which was conducted with a total of 37 persons. It will not be necessary here to give the details of these results, since the general plan and procedure was identical with that used in the tests that have been described. We need only to point out, perhaps, that such tests and investigations have proved themselves to be highly reliable. Such tests can be made with a relatively small expenditure of time and money. If they are carefully made and if all scientific conditions are observed, they will be found to have a very high degree of reliability even though carried out with a relatively small number of persons.

PRINCIPLES OF ADVERTISING

PART V

MEDIUMS

XXVIII

GENERAL CONSIDERATIONS

Placing the advertisement in the proper medium. Classes of mediums:
Relative importance of various classes of mediums. The number of magazines and newspapers. Seasonal fluctuation in advertising space. General
criteria in the selection of mediums. Quantity of circulation. Quality of
circulation. Distribution of circulation. Quality of advertising carried.
Time of issuing. Flexibility. Determining the relative value of various
mediums for a given product.

THE next logical step in the development of advertising
plans, after the copy has been prepared and all attendant
work completed, is the placing of the advertisements in the
proper mediums. They should be placed where they will
reach the particular classes of persons who are the actual
or potential consumers of the product. The discussion of
mediums, therefore, ties up most closely with problems discussed in Part II, namely, the human aspect of the market.
The problem is mainly one of fitting the mediums to the
class of persons who constitute the market. The fundamental problem, therefore, is: How may the advertisement
be brought before the public so that it will receive the maximum favorable attention from the largest number of prospective buyers? This question in turn will necessitate
a study of two subordinate questions: (1) What are the
comparative merits of the various mediums available at the
time? (2) What are the conditions and factors that bear
upon the selection of mediums for a given commodity or
for a given advertising plan?

CLASSES OF MEDIUMS

The various advertising mediums may conveniently be
classified as follows:

(1) Newspapers—daily and weekly;

(2) Magazines and periodicals—including the general magazines, women's publications, trade and professional journals, and agricultural and business publications;

(3) Direct mail mediums—including letters, circulars and catalogs, house organs and the like;

(4) Street-railway cards;

(5) Billboards and outdoor signs;

(6) Novelties—including calendars, blotters, etc.;

(7) Window trims and cut-outs;

(8) Miscellaneous mediums—including directories, theater programs, handbills, and other mediums just recently developed, such as moving-picture films;

(9) Demonstration and sampling might possibly be added.

RELATIVE IMPORTANCE OF VARIOUS CLASSES OF MEDIUMS

The relative importance of the various classes of mediums and the relative extent to which they are used is roughly indicated by the sums of money paid annually for advertising space in them. The following estimates reported in *Printers' Ink,* 1911, show the approximate amounts of money spent annually in the United States for advertising, through the chief mediums.

Newspaper advertising	$250,000,000
Direct mail advertising	100,000,000
Farm and mail order	75,000,000
Magazine advertising	60,000,000
Novelty	30,000,000
Billposting	30,000,000
Outdoor electric signs	25,000,000
Demonstration and sampling	18,000,000
Street-car advertising	$10,000,000
House organs	7,000,000
Distributing	6,000,000
Theater programs	5,000,000
	$616,000,000

Thus we see that about 40% of all advertising is done in the newspapers, about 15% in farm and mail-order journals, and about 10% in magazines. Each type of medium has uses and advantages of its own and may be suited to particular commodities. These points will be discussed in detail later.

A similar estimate made for 1920, during which the expenditures for advertising reached a higher figure than during any previous year, shows the following expenditures in the different mediums:

Newspapers	$600,000,000
Direct advertising	300,000,000
Magazines	150,000,000
Business papers	70,000,000
Novelties	30,000,000
Foreign papers	27,000,000
Directories	20,000,000
Window display	20,000,000
Billposting	20,000,000
Street-car cards	11,000,000
Programs	5,000,000
Motion pictures	5,000,000
	$1,258,000,000

From the figures for 1920 we note substantially the same relative distribution for the various classes. The expenditure in newspapers is 47% of the total expenditure for advertising; this is slightly higher than in 1911. The magazines constitute approximately 12% of the total, as against 10% in 1911.

The Number of Magazines and Newspapers. It will be of interest to note not only the total number of different magazines and newspapers in the United States at the present time, but also the numbers year by year since a fairly accurate record has been kept. Table 143 gives the detailed facts regarding the numbers of the various types of publications since 1871, based upon the *American Newspaper Annual and Directory,* issued by N. W. Ayer & Son.

TABLE 143

NEWSPAPERS AND PERIODICALS PUBLISHED IN THE UNITED STATES AND CANADA

Showing the number of newspapers and periodicals published in the United States and Canada during each year from 1871 to 1922, both inclusive, as reported by the *American Newspaper Directory* (1871 to 1879) and the *American Newspaper Annual and Directory* (1880 to date).

Year	Number of towns in which papers are publ.	Daily	Tri-Weekly	Semi-Weekly	Weekly	Fort-nightly *	Semi-Monthly	Monthly	Bi-Monthly	Quarterly	Misc.	Total
1871	.....	637	118	129	4,642	21	100	715	14	62	...	6,438
1872	.....	570	126	128	5,087	25	93	728	6	57	...	6,922
1873	.....	695	115	111	5,466	29	88	715	12	60	...	7,291
1874	.....	724	105	103	5,869	27	98	785	12	61	...	7,784
1875	.....	774	100	121	6,287	27	108	850	10	71	...	8,348
1876	.....	782	90	135	6,592	35	107	791	1	70	...	8,617
1877	.....	755	79	129	6,564	37	89	701	15	58	...	8,427
Jan. 1878	.....	776	75	135	6,899	36	85	733	36	57	...	8,832
Oct. 1878	.....	782	68	139	7,207	38	92	775	19	54	...	9,174
July 1879	.....	868	73	130	7,534	45	112	853	17	52	...	9,684
1880	4,476	973	74	150	9,221	54	114	997	17	70	5	10,674
1881	4,712	1,021	73	152	8,629	58	125	1,079	16	76	5	11,234
1882	4,982	1,096	63	162	9,014	58	167	1,135	18	88	4	11,805
1883	5,237	1,198	56	165	9,579	56	171	1,248	30	95	7	12,605
1884	5,541	1,274	57	170	10,172	58	206	1,297	21	91	7	13,343
1885	5,884	1,286	53	165	10,706	56	202	1,349	35	97	9	13,958
1886	6,284	1,341	56	170	11,478	54	200	1,475	33	94	7	14,908
1887	6,580	1,481	50	189	12,003	58	206	1,485	31	89	8	15,600
1888	7,005	1,604	49	204	12,774	61	211	1,580	25	89	7	16,604
1889	7,310	1,612	46	202	13,252	73	219	1,715	34	100	12	17,265
1890	7,633	1,753	41	222	14,136	80	274	1,874	36	103	12	18,531

1891	7,753	1,821	42	226	14,424	77	265	1,996	35	113	12	19,011
1892	7,994	1,935	45	236	14,982	80	323	2,337	37	129	11	20,115
1893-4	8,275	1,996	40	253	15,565	66	282	2,372	39	149	12	20,774
1895	8,442	2,085	44	357	15,837	70	272	2,270	34	160	13	21,142
1896	8,589	2,158	52	402	15,895	71	262	2,182	30	157	16	21,225
1897	8,873	2,238	48	473	16,402	79	263	2,235	39	162	16	21,955
1898	8,958	2,246	55	494	16,275	79	281	2,430	43	173	16	22,092
1899	9,055	2,293	59	560	16,376	76	285	2,430	45	170	14	22,308
1900	9,178	2,319	64	559	16,452	69	283	2,469	47	161	13	22,436
1901	9,400	2,334	64	569	16,608	65	286	2,531	49	169	12	22,687
1902	9,600	2,366	59	568	16,724	66	268	2,552	53	171	12	22,839
1903	9,867	2,429	55	611	16,927	59	272	2,632	54	171	11	23,221
1904	10,044	2,457	56	634	16,935	65	285	2,698	53	192	10	23,385
1905	10,233	2,495	59	637	16,981	64	283	2,698	56	187	20	23,480
1906	10,365	2,474	61	627	17,026	55	275	2,814	55	193	15†	23,595
1907	10,620	2,533	62	660	17,132	55	282	2,828	63	186	18	23,819
1908	10,697	2,564	57	642	17,022	59	281	2,817	66	198	20	23,726
1909	10,873	2,584	64	648	17,088	60	281	2,873	76	202	18	23,894
1910	11,049	2,602	63	657	17,120	65	265	3,014	73	210	20	24,089
1911	11,219	2,614	70	661	17,260	63	280	2,977	77	214	19	24,235
1912	11,413	2,610	75	650	17,258	59	287	3,075	77	235	19	24,345
1913	11,529	2,633	73	644	17,285	60	287	3,069	78	234	18	24,381
1914	11,629	2,646	73	649	17,323	70	322	3,106	70	244	24	24,527
1915	11,739	2,661	74	662	17,380	63	314	3,224	72	244	30	24,724
1916	11,692	2,646	77	653	17,156	65	310	3,294	95	263	30	24,589
1917	11,770	2,666	75	635	17,168	72	313	3,476	98	330	35	24,868
1918	11,610	2,604	83	575	16,599	81	304	3,477	28	361	40	24,252
1919	11,189	2,562	79	522	15,735	66	304	3,297	111	360	38	23,074
1920	10,988	2,528	100	526	14,959	74	321	3,390	102	380	48	22,428
1921	10,894	2,503	101	515	14,863	92	334	3,415	109	382	59	22,373
1922	10,780	2,517	94	532	14,633	102	348	3,517	120	410	80	22,353

* Shown as "bi-weekly" 1871 to 1890 and as "fortnightly" thereafter.   † Issue not known for three years.

From this table several interesting facts appear. In the first place, the total number of publications gradually rose to its maximum in 1917. Since then it has somewhat declined, owing to the shortage of paper and the business depression following the World War, so that at the present time there are some 2,000 fewer magazines and newspapers than there were in 1917. In the next place, it is interesting to note that the increase since 1871 has been marked in monthly publications, increasing approximately fivefold, namely, from 715 to 3,517, as against an increase of approximately three and one-half times for all publications combined. Daily newspapers likewise have increased somewhat more rapidly than the rate of increase for all publications combined, the increase being approximately fourfold —from 637 in 1871 to 2,517 in 1922. Another interesting fact is the large proportion of weekly publications. Of the total number of 22,353 publications, 14,633 are weekly publications, probably 12,000 of which are weekly newspapers. The loss in total publications since 1917 is due primarily to the disappearance of the smaller country weeklies. The drop in that case has been from over 17,000 in 1917 to 14,633 in 1922.

SEASONAL FLUCTUATION IN ADVERTISING SPACE

The seasonal fluctuation in the amount of advertising done is very large. Figure 98 shows the variation for four successive years. This fluctuation is similar from year to year. There are two very active periods, reaching their heights in May and November respectively, and two dull seasons, reaching their lowest points in January and August respectively. During these latter months only about half as much advertising is done as during the former months. A similar tabulation made for the newspapers shows a corresponding seasonal fluctuation. These data are shown in the graphs of Figure 99.

GENERAL CRITERIA IN THE SELECTION OF MEDIUMS

Many factors must be considered in choosing avenues through which the printed sales message for a given product may be presented most effectively. This and the succeeding five chapters deal with this problem in detail. As a preliminary step, however, let us examine the general bases on which the merits of a given medium or set of mediums may be evaluated.

QUANTITY OF CIRCULATION

First, the value of a medium depends upon the circulation—upon the number of people who see it. Until recent years, statements of circulation have been utterly unreliable. They were, as a rule, so exaggerated that they had little or no meaning whatever. During the last 10 or 15 years, publishers have adopted a totally different attitude,

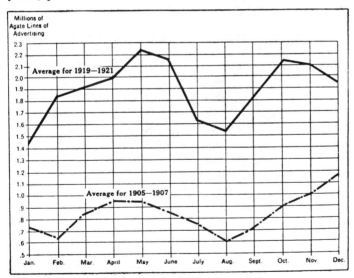

Figure 98: Magazine advertising space—seasonal fluctuation
(See page 744)

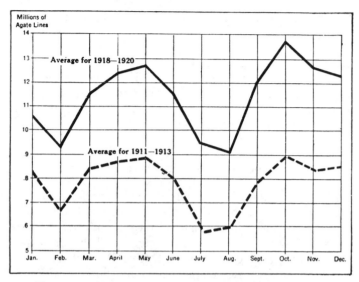

Figure 99: Newspaper advertising space—seasonal fluctuation
(See page 744)

so that today nearly all reputable mediums issue sworn statements of their circulation and distribution. The advertiser is entitled to know just how many people he is apt to reach when he buys space in a medium. He is also entitled to know whether the cost of space in a medium is proportionate to the size of the circulation. Business firms and publishers have therefore come together in the past decade and established a common means by which statements of circulations are expressed. Rates in relation to circulation are now commonly stated in terms of the agate line per million circulation, that is, in terms of the milline. This point is discussed in detail in the next chapter.

QUALITY OF CIRCULATION

Secondly, the value of a medium depends not only upon the quantity but also upon the quality of the circulation, that is, upon the kind or class of people reached. Thus, for

example, the *Atlantic Monthly* and the *Popular Magazine,*
or the *Ladies' Home Journal* and *Comfort,* go to very different classes of people.

The *Atlantic Monthly,* with a guaranteed circulation of
40,000 in 1914, had the following distribution of subscribers:

Lawyers	23%	Bankers	10%
Business men	21	Railroad officials	6
Doctors	12	Farmers	5
Clergymen	12	Miscellaneous	10

The advertiser is entitled to know what share of the circulation of a medium goes to persons who are likely to become customers. He is entitled to know something of the
financial, social, professional, and educational status of the
readers of a medium. For example, a man advertising
a commodity used only by lawyers or by bankers, would
be entitled to know whether *Collier's* or the *Saturday
Evening Post* or some other magazine has a sufficiently
large number of lawyers or bankers among its readers so
that he might with profit advertise in it. Some mediums
are better suited for certain articles than are others. Some
commodities can be advertised successfully only in certain
kinds of mediums. Thus, it would obviously be absurd to
advertise church pews in an engineer's or clothier's magazine.

Distribution of Circulation. Third, it is essential to
know the territory in which a given medium is distributed.
Through the Audit Bureau of Circulation reliable figures
are now available to show the distribution of a publication
by states, and to some extent by cities of various sizes, and
so on. Some publishers give very detailed figures regarding
the distribution of their publications. For example the Curtis Publishing Co. gives the number of *Saturday Evening
Posts* distributed in each city and town of 1,000 people or
more.

Quality of Advertising Carried. Fourth, the value of a

medium depends upon the kind and standard of advertising carried. The confidence which readers have in the truthfulness of an advertisement depends upon the medium in which it appears. Thus, a financial advertisement would appeal very differently in various publications. How much confidence will be commanded by an advertisement—even though it is literally true in every statement—if it is seen side by side with a medical advertisement offering a panacea for all ills or with an advertisement guaranteeing a large permanent income from rubber stock?

Time of Issuing. Fifth, the value of a medium depends, to a certain extent, upon the time and frequency of issuing. In the case of a newspaper, it may be important to consider whether it is a morning or an evening paper; in the case of a magazine, to know whether it appears weekly or monthly.

Flexibility. Sixth, in many instances it is desirable to consider the flexibility of a particular medium. Thus, for example, direct-mail material, newspapers, and certain other mediums allow for considerable flexibility in the use and distribution of advertising material.

DETERMINING THE RELATIVE VALUE OF VARIOUS MEDIUMS FOR A GIVEN PRODUCT

It is, of course, desirable to determine as accurately as possible the suitability of a given medium for a given product or a given advertising plan. In addition to the exercise of judgment on the basis of the general principles, it is desirable to obtain more specific and definite facts about the mediums under consideration. There are two general methods by which such information may be obtained. First, the advertiser may turn to available published material issued by the publishers and promoters of the various types of mediums themselves, to the reports of the Audit Bureau of Circulations, and to the regular available services, such as the Standard Rate and Data Service. This information may be supplemented by a careful inspection of the mediums themselves to determine the general editorial policy and typographical make-up.

Secondly, the advertiser may obtain information from those of the readers and subscribers themselves who are the actual or potential buyers of his particular commodity. That is, specific information regarding the mediums read and the standing and influence which these mediums have with the subscribers may be obtained in connection with questionnaire investigations as outlined in Part II. Very useful information may be obtained in connection with such questionnaire or field surveys. If we turn at this point to typical results obtained in Part II, we may note the kind of information that can be obtained and the manner in which it may be interpreted. For instance, if the investigation is carried out carefully, it will reveal which particular mediums are read and seen most frequently by the particular class of persons who buy the commodity. The results will also show the relative influence and standing of the mediums with the readers and the consumers. These facts, however, cannot be taken at direct face value, but must be considered in relation to the total circulation of a given medium. Thus, for example, a given medium may be read by a considerable proportion of the persons interviewed, but it may not be as large a proportion in relation to its circulation as another medium which may be read by a smaller number of persons interviewed. This and similar problems will be discussed in detail in the chapters following.

XXIX

MAGAZINES

UNDER the heading of magazines and periodicals we usually include general magazines, both monthly and weekly, women's magazines, foreign papers, business, trade, and professional publications. In other words, under the general heading of magazines and periodicals are included all publications, other than daily or weekly newspapers, which appear at regular intervals.

The relative importance of the various classes of publications is indicated to some extent from the number of publications in each class. By referring to Table 143 in the preceding chapter, we will note that from the standpoint of numbers the monthly magazines are the most numerous. In 1920 there were 3,390 monthly publications out of a total of approximately 5,000 magazines and periodicals.

From the standpoint of the amount of advertising carried, a relatively small group of magazines is found to contain the large bulk of the advertising space used. The Curtis Publishing Company has issued from time to time a report entitled *Advertising in National Publications*, which sets forth the amount of national advertising in terms of the cost of the space in 72 publications. (See Figure 100.) An examination of this chart will show that

750

these 72 publications carried in 1920 approximately $132,000,000 worth of advertising space, constituting about 85% of all the paid advertising space in all magazines combined. The total estimate of the advertising space in all of the magazines, as given in the preceding chapter, was placed in 1920 at $150,000,000. In 1921 the same 72 publications carried $95,439,236 advertising out of a total of about $120,000,000 of magazine advertising. The extent to which the advertising space is concentrated in a relatively small number of publications is still further seen in that approximately $110,000,000 worth of advertising space was carried in 1920 by five publications, namely, the *Saturday Evening Post,* the *Literary Digest,* the *Ladies' Home Journal,* the *Pictorial Review,* and the *Woman's Home Companion.* These five publications carried slightly over 50% of all of the advertising space in all magazines combined.

The three Curtis publications, namely, the *Saturday Evening Post,* the *Ladies' Home Journal,* and the *Country Gentlemen,* carried in 1920 approximately $50,000,000 of advertising space, or about 33% of all of the magazine advertising space. In 1921 they carried approximately $38,000,000 of advertising. The four Crowell publications —the *Woman's Home Companion,* the *American Magazine, Collier's,* and *Farm and Fireside*—carried approximately $15,500,000 of advertising space, or about 11% of the total advertising space in magazines.

From the standpoint of the amount of advertising space carried as measured in terms of agate lines, we may note the tabulation which indicates the relative amount of space carried by the leading publications in each of the three or four chief classes of publications. These data are published monthly in *Printers' Ink.*

2. THE CIRCULATION OF MAGAZINES

Statements of Circulation. The development of different kinds of statements of circulations and the reliability of

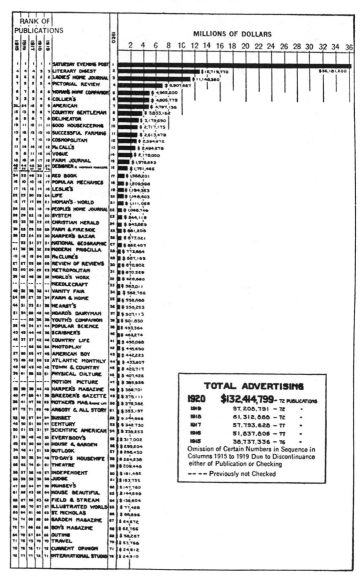

Figure 100:   Total advertising in 72 publications—1920 *(See page 750)*

such statements has in a general way run parallel with the development of advertising and the devising of modern standardized methods. Until within a relatively recent time, statements of circulation consisted largely of voluntary statements made by the publishers without any careful check on the correctness of such statements. Indeed, until within the last decade, during which very substantial progress has been made in the methods of determining reliable circulation statements, it was not far wrong to say that the publisher with the smallest conscience had the largest circulation.

The following types of statements of circulation may be noted:

(a) Publishers' Statements. By this originally was meant simply a statement by the publisher, usually unsworn, that his circulation was so and so much.

(b) Sworn Statements. These were statements made by the publisher and accompanied by an affidavit. These statements, while more satisfactory than unsworn statements, were nevertheless made in various unstandardized ways. While probably in most cases correct, they did, however, differ considerably in regard to just what was included in the statement.

(c) Statements Made to the Post Office Department. Since about 1914 the Post Office Department has required a statement every six months from publishers relative to the circulation and ownership of the publication. These statements have helped to a considerable extent to bring about more reliable statements of circulation. However, there are frequent abuses in connection with these statements, partly due to the lack of facilities and authority on the part of the Post Office Department to penalize in any effective manner misrepresentations made in reports.

(d) Guaranteed Circulation. Under this plan the publisher not only furnishes a reliable statement of circulation,

but he also guarantees that the advertising rate for his publication is based upon a certain minimum circulation and agrees that if the circulation drops below this point during the time of the contract he will refund to the advertiser pro rata for the advertising space used.

(e) A. B. C. Statements. In the latter part of 1913 the Audit Bureau of Circulations was organized. It was put into effective operation in 1914. The work of this bureau came about as the result of several organizations which were interested in the endeavor to develop a generally acceptable means of obtaining reliable, standardized statements of circulation. It was felt that the time was ripe for devising such means and that the advertiser had a right to know what he was buying when he bought space in publications. It was desirable to know not only the total circulation but also something about the various aspects of this circulation, facts which are almost as important as the statement of the total amount of the circulation. In 1913 the Association of American Advertisers, which had been in existence for a considerable number of years prior to that time, went out of existence, and the Association of National Advertisers was formed in New York to work out this problem. At the same time a similar plan was under way in Chicago. These two organizations merged and established the Audit Bureau of Circulations in December, 1913. The first convention was held in the spring of 1914 at which time a complete organization was effected.

About 1870 the only facts generally available regarding circulation were the statements in George P. Rowell's Directory; and since that time, the Ayer Directory was the chief source of information. In order to bring about a somewhat more reliable statement of circulations at that time, Mr. Rowell added a gold mark to the name of the publication if the publisher made an affidavit concerning his circulation. This was accompanied by an offer of $100 to anyone who could disprove the claim made. In more recent years,

Printers' Ink published for a considerable time statements of circulation accompanied by a star which indicated in a similar manner that the circulation had been sworn to, and likewise that a reward of $100 was offered to anyone who could prove that the statement was not correct.

Perhaps the best manner in which to obtain a clear conception of the way in which the Audit Bureau of Circulation operates will be to examine the miniature reproduction of a circulation statement for a magazine, as is shown in Figure 101. In general the A. B. C. reports attempt to answer three main questions: (a) How large is the circulation? (b) Where does it go? and (c) How was it obtained? The Bureau operates by requiring from its publisher members a so-called publisher's statement every six months. The Bureau itself makes an audited report once a year. The content of the two reports is substantially the same.

An examination of the audited report shows the average net paid circulation for each quarter. It indicates also the

---

1. The Atlantic Monthly.	**AUDIT BUREAU OF CIRCULATIONS**
2. Boston.	**CHICAGO**
3. Massachusetts.	**AVERAGE NET PAID**
4. Year Estab. 1857.	3rd quarter 1920 105,043
	4th quarter 1920 111,007
5. Published monthly.	1st quarter 1921 117,396
6. Report for twelve months ending	2nd quarter 1921 108,930
June 30, 1921.	Date Examined November, 1921.

8. Average Distribution for period covered by Paragraph 6 above:

Mail Subscribers (Individual)*	75,942	Correspondents	52
		Advertisers	186
Net Sales through News-dealers	32,955	Advertising Agencies	508
Mail subs. (special)		Exchanges and Complimentary	561
(see Par. 28)	153	Canvassers and Samples	435
		Employees	117
TOTAL NET PAID	109,050	File Copies	2
Term Subscriptions in Bulk	1,382		
Single Issue Sales in Bulk	162		
TOTAL NET PAID			
INC. BULK	110,594	TOTAL DISTRIBUTION	112,455

*See Par. 28.

10. Net Paid Circulation by States based on issue of February, 1921.

STATE	Mail Sub-scribers	News-dealers	STATE	Mail Sub-scribers	News-dealers
Maine	797		Ohio	4,588	
New Hampshire	660		Indiana	1,369	
Vermont.........	475		Illinois	5,528	
Massachusetts	9,445		Michigan	2,467	
Rhode Island	731		Wisconsin	1,910	
Connecticut	2,678		Minnesota	2,102	
N. E. STATES	14,786		Iowa	1,397	
			Missouri	1,312	
New York	14,452		North Dakota	195	
New Jersey	3,711		South Dakota	236	
Pennsylvania	6,348		Nebraska	558	
Delaware	241		Kansas	664	
Maryland	1,321		MID. STATES	22,326	
Dist. of Columbia	1,092				
N. AT. STATES	27,165		Montana	269	
			Wyoming	127	
Virginia	1,116		Colorado	975	
North Carolina	537		New Mexico	128	
South Carolina	349		Arizona	226	
Georgia	501		Utah	240	
Florida	507		Nevada	32	
SO. E. STATES	3,010		Washington	1,003	
			Idaho	198	
Kentucky	582		Oregon	689	
West Virginia	361		California	5,230	
Tennessee	436		WEST. STATES	9,117	
Alabama	391				
Mississippi	206		Unclassified	1,354	
Louisiana	263		UN. STATES	81,446	34,022
Texas	886				
Oklahoma	286		Alaska & U. S. Poss.	551	
Arkansas	277		Canada	1,246	
SO. W. STATES	3,688		Foreign	1,984	
			Miscellaneous*		154
			GRAND TOTAL	85,227	34,176

*Miscellaneous—Sales other than mail subscribers or newsdealers.

12. PERCENTAGES OF SUBSCRIPTION CIRCULATION BASED ON ISSUE OF FEBRUARY, 1921, IN CITIES OF

500,000 and over	21.38%	2,500 to 10,000	13.99%
100,000 to 500,000	18.31	Under 2,500	16.64
25,000 to 100,000	15.82	Unclassified	6.02
10,000 to 25,000	7.84	Total	100.00

TOTAL SUBSCRIPTION CIRCULATION FOR ABOVE ISSUE: 85,227.

The above percentages are based on publisher's analysis of the Feb., 1921, mailing list, which compilation was tested by auditor and found correct.

13. CLASS, INDUSTRY OR FIELD COVERED?
Current events, literature, science, art and politics.

ANALYSIS OF CIRCULATION METHODS
DURING THIS PERIOD

21. 1. SINGLE COPY PRICE: 40c.

   2. REGULAR SUBSCRIPTION RATES:
Prior to Nov. 1, 1920, one year, $4.00; two years, $7.00;
thereafter, one year, $5.00; two years, $9.00.

   3. SPECIAL SUBSCRIPTION OFFERS (INCLUDING TRIAL OR
SHORT TERM RATES):

Prior to Nov. 1, 1920, period of 3 months for 75c.
period of 6 months for $1.50.
period of 9 months for 2.25.
period of 12 months for 3.00.
period of 13 months for 4.00.
After Nov. 1, 1920, period of 3 months for $1.00.
period of 6 months for 2.00.
period of 9 months for 3.00.
period of 12 months for 4.00.
period of 13 months for 5.00.

   4. RATES AT WHICH CLUB RAISERS TAKE SUBSCRIPTIONS FOR
THIS PUBLICATION ALONE:

Prior to Nov. 1, 1920, rate of $3.50 per year in clubs of
two or more.

After Nov. 1, 1920, rate of $4.50 per year in clubs of
two or more.

   5. SPECIAL RATES MADE FOR RENEWALS OR EXTENSIONS:

Subscribers renewing their subscriptions not later than
60 days after expiration were offered for their renewal
subscription with one or more gift subscriptions the
special rate of $3.50 each, previous to Nov. 1, 1920;
thereafter, $4.50 each.

22(a). 1. WERE RETURNS ACCEPTED? Yes.

   2. PERCENTAGE OF NEWSDEALER SALES SOLD ON RETURN-
ABLE BASIS? 99.59%.

   3. PERCENTAGE OF TOTAL NEWSDEALER SALES SOLD ON
NON-RETURNABLE BASIS? 0.41%.

In Par. 8 of this report all returns from newsdealers have
been deducted and only the net sales shown.

(b), (i), (o). Premiums and Contests:

Records show that a book entitled "Literature with a Large L" with an advertised value of $1.00 was given free to subscribers with a six-month subscription (value $2.00) for $2.00 and with yearly subscriptions at the regular rate.

Records also show that a book entitled "Atlantic Year Book" with an advertised value of $1.00 was given free to subscribers with yearly subscriptions at the regular rate.

Records indicate that 9,447 subscriptions were received as a result of the above offer.

Records do not show any contests to have been employed during the period covered by this report.

(c). Canvassers (if Employed State Whether Paid by Salary or Commission or Both):

Records show canvassers were employed on a commission basis.

3. Percentage of Subscriptions Through Canvassers? 9.71%.

(d). Were Subscriptions Received from Club Raisers Paid by Rewards Other Than Cash?

None of record.

(e). Were Clubbing Offers Made of This and Other Publications?

Yes. Records show that a combination consisting of a one-year subscription to this publication and a one-year subscription to one of two other publications published by the same interests with combined advertised subscription rates of from $9.00 to $11.00 were offered to subscribers for from $7.00 to $9.00.

2. Percentage of Subscriptions Received Through Such Offers? 0.51%.

(f). 1. Were Subscriptions Received Through or from Other Publishers? Yes.

2. Percentage of Subscribers Received Through or from Other Publishers? 1.94%.

3. Were Subscriptions Received Through Subscription Agencies? Yes.

4. PERCENTAGE OF SUBSCRIPTIONS RECEIVED THROUGH SUBSCRIPTION AGENCIES? 34.95%.

(g). PERCENTAGE OF MAIL SUBSCRIPTIONS RENEWED?
Actual figures not available.

(h) BULK SALES:

"Term subscriptions in bulk," as shown in Par. 8, amounting to an average of 1,382 copies per issue, represents subscriptions sold to colleges and schools for classroom purposes in lots of from 2 to 600 at from 25c to 33⅓c per copy per issue.

"Single issue sales in bulk," as shown in Par. 8, amounting to a total of 1,946 copies or an average of 162 copies per issue, represent sales to associations, commercial interests and individuals in lots of from 1 to 300 copies at from 20c to 40c per copy, distribution being made by the purchaser.

(j) WERE SUBSCRIPTIONS RECEIVED ON THE INSTALMENT PLAN?
None of record.

(k) 1. WERE SUBSCRIPTIONS ACCEPTED ON TRIAL OR SHORT TERM OFFERS? Yes.

2. WERE THESE SUBSCRIPTIONS STOPPED PROMPTLY AT EXPIRATION? Yes, no exceptions noted.

(p) OTHER SOURCES FROM WHICH SUBSCRIPTIONS WERE RECEIVED?
None of record.

23. PERCENTAGE OF SUBSCRIPTIONS (OTHER THAN INSTALMENT) IN ARREARS? Based on issue of Feb., 1921. Up to three months 8.47%, total 8.47%.

(a) PERCENTAGE OF NEWSDEALER CIRCULATION IN ARREARS? None. Based on issue of June, 1921.

24. ASSOCIATIONS OF WHICH PUBLICATION IS AN OFFICIAL ORGAN? Not the official organ of any association.

27. WAS EACH COPY OF EACH ISSUE UNIFORM AS TO CONTENTS AND QUALITY OF PAPER STOCK? Yes, no exceptions noted.

28. EXPLANATORY:

Included in "Mail subscribers (individual)" shown in Par. 8, there is an average of 240 yearly subscriptions sold to the U. S. War Department at $3.50 per subscription, to be mailed direct by the publisher to education and recreation officers for libraries in different forts, camps, hospitals, etc., on a list of names furnished by the purchaser.

"Mail subscribers (special)" as shown in Par. 8, averaging 153 copies per issue, represent copies served during this audit period on yearly subscriptions received from various commercial and manufacturing interests in lots of from 49 to 120 subscriptions at $3.00 per subscription and which were for the use of their branch offices and managers. Copies were mailed by publisher in individual wrappers direct to names and addresses furnished by the purchasers.

The difference in net paid circulation as shown in this report compared with publisher's statements for the period audited, amounting to an average of 382 copies per issue, is accounted for by deductions made for additional newsdealer returns, publisher having underestimated returns in compiling semi-annual statements.

Net paid circulation for this period by issues follows:

1921		1920	
January	119,838	July	102,320
February	119,403	August	104,891
March	112,949	September	107,919
April	111,266	October	109,897
May	107,715	November	110,832
June	107,811	December	112,294

For comparative purposes we give below the net paid circulation by quarters as shown in audits for the previous three years, as well as the quarterly averages for the period covered by this report.

3rd quarter	1917	64,576	3rd quarter	1919	90,783
4th quarter	1917	72,118	4th quarter	1919	100,204
1st quarter	1918	80,529	1st quarter	1920	109,968
2nd quarter	1918	81,812	2nd quarter	1920	105,077
3rd quarter	1918	80,364	3rd quarter	1920	105,043
4th quarter	1918	88,073	4th quarter	1920	111,007
1st quarter	1919	95,576	1st quarter	1921	117,396
2nd quarter	1919	94,839	2nd quarter	1921	108,930

AUDIT BUREAU OF CIRCULATIONS.

CITY—Boston, Mass.   DATE—November, 1921.
(The Atlantic Monthly, Boston, Mass.,—No. 6501.)

Figure 101: Sample A. B. C. magazine report

amount of circulation which goes to mail subscribers and the amount which goes to news dealers; also the circulation which goes to various miscellaneous organizations such as advertisers, agencies, samples, etc. It also gives the circulation by states, both as distributed through news dealers and to mail subscribers. This phase of the report is very valuable in determining to what extent a publication is actually national in circulation and to what extent it may be concentrated in various parts of the country.

Then under item 12 is given the circulation in cities of various sizes. This part of the information will give a good index as to whether the circulation is primarily in small towns, large cities, or in rural districts.

Item 21 and those following deal with various aspects of the general question as to how the circulation was obtained. This phase of the report deserves careful study with reference to each publication.

The Audit Bureau of Circulation is of great value to advertising because it has made available reliable statements of circulation covering many different phases. In case of error, either intentional or unintentional, the Bureau has established certain rules which it follows. In case of error, a publisher or advertiser member of the Bureau may ask for a re-audit of any publication, if he so desires. If the re-audit is within 3% of the original audit, the expense is borne by the complainant. If it is beyond 3% of the original audit, the expense is borne by the Bureau. If the re-audit proves that the publisher had misrepresented the facts, the expense is borne by the publisher, and this fact is then bulletined to the other members of the Bureau and the publisher is subject to suspension and expulsion from the Bureau.

Up to February 10, 1922, 137 general magazines and periodicals were members of the Bureau, 84 agricultural publications, 247 business publications, and 816 newspapers.

The members of the Bureau comprise the following classes:

Class A—Advertisers: Annual dues $240, payable quarterly in advance.   Members of this class are to receive all reports, data, bulletins, and other service rendered by the Bureau.

Class B—Associate Advertisers: Annual dues $60, payable quarterly in advance.   An Associate Advertiser-Member to receive all reports and other service rendered by the Bureau on any one of the following divisions:

Service 1—Magazines and Periodicals
Service 2—Business Publications
Service 3—Farm Papers
Service 4—Newspapers in New England and North Atlantic States
Service 5—Newspapers in Middle States
Service 6—Newspapers in the Southern and Western States
Service 7—All Canadian Publications
Service 8—Any list of publications not exceeding 50, designated by the advertiser

An Associate Advertiser-Member shall pay $120 for any two, or $180 for any three of the above services.

Class C—Local Advertisers: Annual dues payable in advance based on reports furnished in city where such advertiser is located.

In cities where reports on 10 or more publications are furnished dues shall be $15.   In cities where reports on between 5 and 10 publications are furnished dues shall be $10.   In cities where reports are furnished on less than 5 publications dues shall be $5.

A Local Advertiser-Member to be entitled only to reports and data of newspapers and local periodicals generally circulated in the city where such member is located.   Such reports are for the individual use of the member only.

Class D—Advertising Agents: Annual dues $360, payable quarterly in advance.   Members to receive the same service as Class A members.   An additional charge of 25% of the regular dues will be made for each duplicate service taken, which duplicate service shall be used only for the Agency's own organization.

Class E—Associate Advertising Agents: Annual dues $90, payable quarterly in advance.   An Associate Advertising Agent-Member to have the same rights and to receive any one of the divisions of service provided for Associate Advertiser-Members. An Associate Advertising Member shall pay $180 for any two, or $270 for any three of the above services.   An additional charge of 25% of the regular dues will be made for each duplicate service taken, which duplicate service shall be used only for the agency's own organization.

Class F—Publishers: Annual dues, payable quarterly in advance, based on gross distribution:

MAGAZINES AND PERIODICALS

Service		Rate per Week
1.	500,000 circulation or more	$11.50
2.	250,000 and less than 500,000	10.35
3.	200,000 and less than 250,000	9.20
4.	150,000 and less than 200,000	8.05
5.	100,000 and less than 150,000	6.90
6.	75,000 and less than 100,000	5.75
7.	50,000 and less than 75,000	4.60
8.	25,000 and less than 50,000	2.88
9.	10,000 and less than 25,000	1.73
10.	5,000 and less than 10,000	1.15
11.	Less than 5,000 circulation	1.00

NEWSPAPERS

Service		Rate per Week
12.	200,000 circulation or more	$12.00
13.	150,000 and less than 200,000	10.00
14.	100,000 and less than 150,000	7.00
15.	50,000 and less than 100,000	6.00
16.	25,000 and less than 50,000	4.00
17.	15,000 and less than 25,000	3.00
18.	10,000 and less than 15,000	2.00
19.	5,000 and less than 10,000	1.50
20.	Less than 5,000 circulation	1.00

TOTAL MAGAZINE CIRCULATION

In 1905 the total estimated circulation of the magazines listed in *Ayer's Directory* was approximately 15,122,000; in 1910 it was approximately 25,512,000; in 1915 it was 49,464,000; in 1920 it was approximately 55,000,000. These figures, of course, are subject to the errors and to some extent to the unreliability of the statements of circulation given for individual publications. However, we know with a high degree of reliability the total circulation of all publications for which A. B. C. reports are available.

This covers the large majority of the publications with the large circulations, even though it covers only a relatively small proportion of the total number of magazines.

In April, 1922, the total circulation of the 137 general magazines reported by the A. B. C. was 39,659,097. The total circulation of the 84 agricultural publications reported by the A. B. C. was 12,259,724. The total circulation of the 247 business publications was 1,645,476. It is therefore likely that the above estimates are not very far from being correct, when we consider the large number of publications which are reported by the A. B. C.

From another angle, the American Association of Advertising Agencies has prepared in recent years a chart covering the circulation of 52 magazines. In 1919 the total circulation of these 52 magazines was 25,436,000. On the basis of these figures it is interesting to note the circulation of magazines per family and the variation by states and sections of the country. Based on the circulation of these 52 magazines, the number of magazines per family is 1.06. The variation by states is very wide. Thus, for example, the circulation per family in certain of the states is as follows:

California	1.94	Oregon	1.64
Washington	1.70	Ohio	1.56
Montana	1.96	Colorado	1.54

On the other extreme, we find the following proportions:

Kentucky	.48	South Carolina	.39
Louisiana	.48	Alabama	.37
Arkansas	.41	Mississippi	.29

Table 144 gives the circulation of the magazines listed in the *Standard Rate and Data Service* for February, 1921, showing the percentage of circulation to population, by sections of the country:

These tabulations are represented in Figure 102 and in Figure 103. Figure 102 shows by different shadings the proportion of circulation in the various sections of the United States. Figure 103 shows the relative amounts of circulation

TABLE 144

PERCENTAGE OF MAGAZINE CIRCULATION TO POPULATION, BY SECTIONS OF THE COUNTRY

General Magazines

New England	.33	Southeastern	.09	Middle	.23
North Atlantic	.25	Southwestern	.10	Western	.37

Women's Magazines

New England	.20	Southeastern	.12	Middle	.27
North Atlantic	.17	Southwestern	.16	Western	.22

Agricultural Publications

New England	.06	Southeastern	.19	Middle	.21
North Atlantic	.08	Southwestern	.10	Western	.13

of these three groups in each of the six main divisions of the country. It will be evident that general magazines have the largest proportion of circulation in New England; the women's publications are next; and the agricultural publications are last. In the southeastern section the reverse of the situation is the case. The general magazines have the

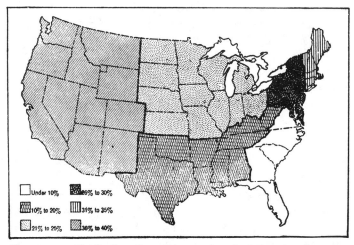

Figure 102: Distribution of general magazine circulation—based on percentage of circulation to population, 1921

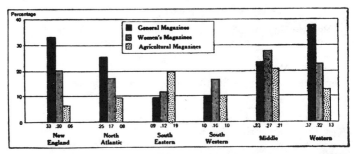

Figure 103: Saturation of magazine circulation in the United States, by geographical division, based upon percentage of circulation to population

smallest circulation, the women's publications are next, and the agricultural publications have the largest circulation. The middle western section of the country has very nearly the same proportion of circulation for each of the three types of publications. In the far West the largest proportion is again general magazines; women's publications are second; and agricultural publications are third.

If we take the total circulation of 55,000,000 as an approximately correct figure, we find that there are between 2 and 2½ magazines per family the country over. We must remember in this connection that a considerable number of families are not magazine-reading families. Possibly not over two-thirds of the families in the country may be regarded as magazine-reading families. On this basis the average number of magazines per family is approximately three and a half.

GROWTH OF CIRCULATION

The increase in the circulation of magazines that have been in existence for a considerable number of years has been very marked. If we take the figures quoted above as a whole, we note that the increase from 1905 to 1920 has been approximately 2½ to 3 fold. Individual publications have grown enormously. Typical illustrations are the following: In 1897 when the *Saturday Evening Post* was taken over by the Curtis Publishing Company it had a circulation of approximately 3,000 copies. At the present time it has a circulation of about 2,250,000. In 1884 the *Ladies' Home Journal* had a circulation of approximately 25,000. At the present time it has a circulation of about 2,000,000. The *Literary Digest* in 1890 had a circulation of about 15,000. In 1921 it had a circulation of about 1,300,000.

The growth in the circulation of agricultural publications has likewise been very rapid. In 1880 the total combined circulation of six farm papers having a general circulation was approximately 290,000. In 1920 eight farm publications with a general circulation, including the six just referred to, had a combined circulation of practically 4,000,000 copies.

DUPLICATION OF CIRCULATION

With this increase in the circulation of magazines there arises constantly the question of the duplication of circulation. From the standpoint of the advertiser this is an important problem. If he wishes to select a limited number of periodicals he is quite likely to want publications which do not have a great deal of overlapping in circulation. On the other hand, if he is desirous of using a considerable number of publications the duplication of circulation is a less important problem.

No reliable figures are available at the present time to indicate the amount of duplication in the circulation of the leading publications. In 1915 an investigation known as the Eastman Investigation, conducted by Frank Seaman, Incorporated, attempted to determine the amount of duplication among 52 leading magazines by an inquiry among 16,000 persons. The results of this research were published in *Advertising and Selling*, January, 1915. The chart there presented shows the number of readers of each magazine and the number and percentage of duplications of each given magazine with every other one of the 52. Thus, for example, the *Century Magazine* duplicated with the *Atlantic Monthly* to the extent of 15% of the readers of the latter. On the other hand, the *Atlantic Monthly* duplicated with the *Century Magazine* to the extent of 8% of its readers. The difference in percentages for these two magazines stated in these two ways is due to the fact that there is a difference in the total circulations of the two magazines. The amount of duplication between some of the magazines is obviously very considerable. Thus, for example, the *Woman's Home Companion* duplicated with 27% of the circulation of *Modern Priscilla*, and with 25% of the circulation of *Christian Herald*, but with only 10% of the circulation of *Country Life*. The *World's Work* duplicated with 20% of the circulation of the *Century Magazine* and with 17% of the circulation of *Outing*, whereas it duplicated with only 1.7% of the circulation of *Home Life* and with 2.4% of the circulation of *Today's Magazine*.

Such figures as these would be extremely valuable if they could be kept reasonably up to date, and if, in view of the fluctuation in circulation of a considerable share of the magazines, they could be obtained by sufficiently reliable methods to be representative of a fair sample of readers of magazines in general. The value of such figures may be illustrated as follows: Suppose the advertiser wishes to use only two weekly publications, because his advertising appropriation is relatively limited. He would probably wish to select two publications which duplicate very little with each other. Two such publications would be the *Saturday Evening Post* or *Colliers* and the *Christian Herald*. Or, if he wishes to select two women's publications which duplicate very little with each other, he might select the *Woman's Home Companion* or the *Delineator*, or the *Ladies' Home Journal*, or *Good Housekeeping* on the one hand and *Home Life* or the *Woman's World* on the other. However, such figures would be valuable only when derived from reliable and up-to-date figures regarding the duplication of circulation.

With regard to the desirability of overlapping when a larger number of mediums are to be used, it is a debatable question whether or not a certain amount of duplication is not a good thing. Theoretically, the question would be that of whether or not the advertiser will derive twice as much benefit or make twice as large an impression on a given group of people when the same advertisement is seen by them in two different publications during the same month or week. It is quite likely that the same advertisement will be seen in the two different publications separated by a sufficient interval to make the impression which it creates a valuable one and to add to the general impression already created.

3. ADVERTISING RATES

Advertising rates are expressed in several different ways. In the first place, rates are commonly expressed in terms of the page or fractional part of a page. Or, again, they are expressed in terms of the agate line. Both of these methods are more or less unsatisfactory in view of the fact that the rate depends upon the amount of space and upon the circulation of the publication. That is, a page rate cannot be compared directly with the page rate of another publication because of the fact that the page may be different in size and that the amount of circulation, likewise, is different for the two publications. The agate line is for the most part a fairly uniform unit of space, and as such it takes account of the one variable, namely, the size of the space, but it does not take account of the variable of circulation. Thus, to say that the agate line rate in the *Saturday Evening Post* is $11 and in the *Century Magazine* $1.50 does not give us a direct comparison as to which of the two rates is actually higher or lower, since we do not take into account the circulation of the two publications.

THE MILLINE

In 1920, Mr. B. H. Jefferson, of Lyon & Healy, proposed, therefore, a new unit in terms of which advertising rates might be expressed in a comparable manner. He proposed the term "milline" rate. By milline is meant a unit of space of one agate line with a circulation of one million readers or subscribers. This term takes into account the two chief variable elements upon which rates depend, namely, the unit of space and the circulation. The unit of space is the agate line and the circulation is always in terms of one million. Thus, the milline rate for the *Saturday Evening Post* with a circulation of 2,108,000 and with an agate line rate of $11 would be $5.21. The milline rate of the *Century Magazine*, on the other hand, with a circulation of 47,000 and an agate line rate of $1.50 would be $31.63. Thus we may compare directly the milline rate for these two publications, and find that the milline rate of the *Century Magazine* is approximately six times as great as that of the *Saturday Evening Post*.

It may be pointed out that the agate line is not an absolutely uniform amount of space, since the width of the column varies somewhat in different publications. While that is true, it will be found upon examining the widths of columns in various publications, including newspapers, that they vary within very narrow limits. Practically, the standard column width is 2¼ inches. If one examines the column width for various publications in the *Standard Rate and Data Service*, one will find that only in extreme instances does it vary, and then only from 2 to 2½ or 2⅝ inches. A very large majority of the publications have a practically uniform column width of 2¼ inches. Newspapers have a practically standard column width of 2¼ inches. Thus it will be seen that while occasionally there occurs a slight variation, the milline basis is practically uniform and standard.

It has been suggested, in view of the fact that the large

majority of publications have a circulation under one million, that it would be more convenient to express these rates in terms of the agate line per one thousand circulation instead of per million circulation. It would be more desirable to do so except for the fact that the rate becomes such a small quantity that it is difficult to conceive it or visualize it. Thus, for example, the line rate per 1,000 circulation for the *New York Times* would be approximately $.001688; for the *Chicago Tribune*, $.001519; for the *Cosmopolitan Magazine*, $.00677; and for the *American Boy*, $.00768. On the other hand, the milline rate for the *New York Times* is $1.68; for the *Chicago Tribune*, $1.51, for the *Cosmopolitan Magazine*, $6.77; and for the *American Boy*, $7.68. The rates expressed in terms of millines, therefore, are more readily understood and are in terms of amounts within the usual range of comprehension.

VARIATION IN MILLINE RATES OF TYPICAL PUBLICATIONS

Typical variations in milline rates among monthly publications are illustrated in the following figures. The milline rate of the *Century Magazine* is $31.63; the milline rate of *Scribner's*, $15.34; of the *Atlantic Monthly*, $16.42. On the other hand, the milline rate of the *American Magazine* is $6.93; of the *Cosmopolitan*, $6.76; of the *Blue Book*, $4.24.

Among weekly publications the milline rate of *Outing* is $13.88; of *Life*, $11.55. On the other hand we find the *Young People's Weekly* with a milline rate of $4.95; the *Pathfinder* with a milline rate of $4.37; and the *Saturday Evening Post* with a milline rate of $5.21. Among the women's publications the milline rate of *Fashion and Art* is $17.71; of the *Woman's Home Companion*, $6.47; of *Good Housekeeping*, $8.78.

In view of these variations, it may be of interest to note what the median milline rates for the various classes of publications are:

		Median Milline Rate
55	Monthly Publications	$11.72
18	Weekly Magazines	7.56
19	Monthly Women's Magazines	6.36
30	Foreign Publications	7.50
185	Business and Trade Publications	50.00

It will be observed that the variation is very large even among the publications of a given class and that there is also a very considerable difference among the median rates of the different classes as a whole. Probably the largest variation among the publications within any given class is to be found among the business and trade publications. Thus, for example, the milline rate of the *Grocers' Magazine*, having a circulation of 3,670, is $565.50, and the milline rate of the *Shoe and Leather Facts*, with a circulation of 4,000, is $1,625. On the other hand, the milline rate of *Building Industry*, having a circulation of 3,500, is $71, and the milline rate of *Machinery*, with a circulation of 24,000, is $10.17.

The question arises here as to the reasons for the large variation in the milline rates. Probably the chief factors which influence the milline rates are (a) circulation, (b) the class of readers, (c) standards and policies and (d) cost of production of the publication. Probably the first two are the chief determining factors, and indirectly the cost of production enters in, for it is affected by circulation.

Let us note the extent to which circulation influences the rates. The low milline rate for women's publications is explained very largely by the fact that the circulations of most of the women's magazines are large. Of the 19 women's publications mentioned in the above table more than half of them have a circulation of over one million. Table 145 shows the relationship between the circulation and rate.

Thus it will be seen that there is an inverse relationship between circulation and milline rates. The smaller the cir-

TABLE 145
RELATIONSHIP BETWEEN CIRCULATION AND RATE

Circulation Weekly Magazines	Number of Magazines	Median Milline Rate
1,000,000 or over	4	$5.72
500,000—999,999		
250,000—499,999	5	7.56
100,000—249,999	5	9.52
0—99,999	4	9.83
Monthly Magazines		
1,000,000 or over	2	6.85
500,000—999,999	1	6.32
250,000—499,999	9	7.26
100,000—249,999	11	10.00
0—99,999	28	17.50

culation the higher the milline rate is. So far as the business and trade publications are concerned, the high median rate of $50 against $6 to $10 for other classes of publications is explained undoubtedly by two main factors, namely, the relatively small circulation, and the limited and specialized class of persons to whom the publication goes. A banker will probably read his banking journal somewhat more carefully than he reads a general publication. A lumberman will be interested in reading his special trade publication probably somewhat more carefully that a general publication. The advertising is directed, therefore, specifically at a fairly uniform class of persons with common interests and common business requirements.

Rates to the average outsider sometimes seem extremely high, particularly in the case of publications with large circulations and with high page rates, although their milline rates are relatively low. To make some specific comparisons, the *Literary Digest* with a page rate of $4,000 and a circulation of 1,300,000 makes, therefore, a charge of approximately 3/10 of one cent per subscriber. In other words, the *Digest* is able to present a full-page advertisement to each subscriber at 3/10 of one cent. If the *Satur-*

day Evening Post has a circulation of about 90,000 in the city of Chicago, it is able to reach each person with a full-page for approximately 3/10 of a cent, or the entire 90,000 persons for about $280. The postage required to reach 90,000 persons would be $900 for one-cent postage alone, and this amount would not include the cost of inclosure and the mechanical process of handling and sending out the mail. Of course, not every subscriber to a publication reads or even sees each full-page advertisement. The best estimates that we are able to make are that probably between 55% and 60% of the readers of a magazine see on the average each full-page advertisement. In other words, then, if every person receiving the one-cent circular saw it, it would be comparable to approximately a little over half of the circulation of the publication; that is, the rate for a given number of readers would have to be nearly doubled in order to make it comparable with the one-cent postage.

PREFERRED POSITIONS

Magazines in general are divided into two groups: the so-called standard magazines and the so-called flat magazines. The standard magazine class comprises those of the standard page size and make-up, such as the *Century, Harper's, Scribner's,* and so on. The flat magazine class comprises those of a larger page, which have the advertising and reading matter intermingled. There has been a decided tendency in recent years in the direction of the flat make-up, as it has been felt that it gives the advertiser a certain advantage because practically all advertising is thus placed next to reading matter. The standard make-up has the reading matter and advertising material in separate sections, the advertising at the front and at the back of the magazine.

In the flat magazines the preferred positions usually are only three in number, namely, the three cover positions ranking in value in the following order: the fourth cover, and the second and third covers which are of equal value.

In the standard magazines the preferred positions vary somewhat, according to the make-up and arrangement of the contents of the magazine. Consequently, some have more and others have fewer preferred positions, but the maximum number of preferred positions arranged approximately in order of value, are as follows:

(1) The fourth cover
(2) The second cover
(3) The third cover
(4) Page facing the second cover
(5) Page facing the third cover
(6) Page facing the beginning of the reading section
(7) Page facing the end of the reading section
(8) Page facing the table of contents

FLAT VERSUS STANDARD MAGAZINES

As already stated, there has been in recent years a decided tendency toward changing the make-up of magazines from the standard to the flat make-up. This tendency began about 1912 to 1915. At that time there was considerable difference of opinion as to whether it was desirable to intermingle the advertising and the reading matter. Professor Münsterberg protested against it on the ground that it was undesirable to intermingle reading and advertising matter, because he believed that the mind of the reader when he is reading a story in a magazine is not in a receptive attitude toward the message of the advertisement appearing on the opposite page. His point of view was expressed as follows:

A very familiar case of magazines is the nowadays widespread habit of mixing reading matter and advertisements on the same page. That tendency developed from the superficial belief of the advertisers that they profit when the story from the front page of the magazine is carried over to the rear part in the midst of the business announcements. They fancy that these advertisement pages might otherwise be neglected, but they overlook the most essential feature of the situation, that the new scheme was entirely unfit to secure the right mental attitude for the reading of their advertisements.

If the old mechanical view of psychology were still in order, it would make no difference whether two columns of advertisements were sandwiched between two columns of a love story or whether all four columns were given over to the story. If the advertisements were well written, they would make the same impression no matter what their surroundings might be. But from the new point of view, it works quite differently. The wish to read a story and to enjoy its contents demands an interest setting which is entirely different from the attitude in which we follow the advertisements, whatever they may be. The one demands the attitude of sympathetic interest by which we lose ourselves in the fate of the hero and heroine; the other appeals to our personal practical needs and to our wish not to waste our money. The two ways of mental behavior are so different that the one almost excludes the other and if we are disposed in the one way, everything which would demand the other practical disposition must fail to impress us.

The craze for the mixing of text and advertising is one of the most curious psychological blunders, and experience can easily prove that the advertiser is at once in his own way if he is lured by this fallacious fashion. The old scheme of separating safely the text pages from the commercial pages was not only more aesthetic and more tasteful, but it was in every way more profitable for the purse of the advertiser. The fear that the casual magazine reader would not find his way to the front and rear pages was in any case unjustified.[1]

Professor Münsterberg's point of view was largely theoretical rather than based on actual comparative facts. It is undoubtedly true that the mental attitude of the reader, if the reader is interested in following a story, is not "set" in a receptive frame of mind for an advertisement of a tooth brush or a vacuum cleaner which may appear near to the story. Nevertheless, the extent to which these two interests compete cannot be determined by introspection alone, but can be determined only by the evidence of objective results and comparative effectiveness of advertisements next to reading matter or in a separate section. While Professor

[1] *Printers' Ink*, Oct. 21, 1915, p. 25.

Münsterberg's point of view has undoubtedly a certain amount of justification, it is quite likely that the attention value and the greater chances of being seen when an advertisement is next to reading matter outweighs the disadvantage of mental attitude suggested by Professor Münsterberg.

Mr. E. E. Calkins took a different point of view from that of Professor Münsterberg, and replied to his statements in the following manner:

From first to last advertisers have paid a great deal of money for position. Position almost invariably means next to reading matter. The shrewdest advertisers, those who have spent the largest appropriations for the longest periods are the most insistent buyers for these double-priced positions. The popularity of the flat shape is very largely due to the fact that it offers the advertiser so many preferred positions. The demand for the few such positions that the old standard form offered, even at appreciated prices, was so great that publishers could not stand the pressure. As the quantity of advertising in the back of the standard magazines increased, the advertiser became more and more discontented. He insisted that his announcements were buried. Is it true that they were interested in the more desirable locations? Was the position on the first advertising page less desirable because it faced reading matter?

Some of the flat publications have carried more advertising than the standards in the palmiest days, but the advertiser does not now claim that he is buried. It was not the amount of advertising carried that worried him; it was the lack of prominence given to his individual advertisement.

It is true that publishers in making up their flat publications have not been guided entirely by considerations of advertising display. The varying length of the articles and stories necessitated their being carried over into the back part of the magazine. It was good editing to present the features of every number to the reader in the front of the book. The desire for a strong caption across the entire page, the exigencies of illustration, the necessity of dressing the pages to the best advantage, all formed a sort of Procrustean bedstead into which the literary matter must be made to fit. To do this each story or article was lopped off when it had filled its allotted space. The remainder was carried over into the pages where the make-up was more elastic, and broken columns could be filled out with short matter that did

not go well in the opening pages. It was argued that once the
reader had become interested he would not mind chasing the
thread of his story on to page 58, even though he had to hurdle
a few page advertisements before he reached the conclusion.

Mr. Calkins then points out that there is a considerable
amount of practical evidence to indicate that positions alongside of reading matter have brought better returns than
positions in separate advertising sections. The following is
given by him as one illustration:

A maker of boilers advertised a Primer of Heating to be sent
free. A three-quarter page space was used in *McClure's Magazine*. During the run of this offer, *McClure's* was rearranged so
that a page of reading alternated with a page of advertisements.
The stories from the front of the book were broken and carried
over into the advertising pages. The heater advertisement faced
such a page. The requests for the Primer immediately increased
1,000%. Results from advertisements, whether in reply to offers
of booklets, or offers of samples, or merchandise requiring money
to be sent, are much greater from the flat publications than from
the standards. Actual tabulations would show this, only com-
putations are difficult as publications vary so greatly in selling
power and circulation. The instance given above is better, because the transformation took place in the same publication and
with the same offer.

Mr. Calkins summarizes his reply to Professor Münsterberg's point of view as follows:

(1) Both the publishers who sell the space and advertisers
who pay for it have recognized the enhanced value of positions
next to reading matter.
(2) Flat publications offering a position next to or facing
reading matter for every advertiser, charging the same price to
all, have had their advertising greatly augmented on this act
alone.
(3) The replies from all keyed advertisements making allowance for difference in short line and pulling power are all in favor
of the next to the reading position.

Shortly after this discussion an investigation was undertaken by Dr. Walter Dill Scott in which he attempted to
ascertain what facts and opinions there were which were

actually based on experience with regard to the relative advantage of a standard as against the flat make-up. Accordingly, he addressed an inquiry to a considerable number of advertisers and advertising agencies. This inquiry consisted essentially of three questions:

(1) Do you know of any evidence (facts and not opinions) that advertising next to reading matter is of greater value to the advertiser than advertising space massed at the two ends of the magazine?

(2) Have you any facts to show the contrary to be true?

(3) Have you data to prove that the matter of location in no way affects the power of the advertisement to influence the reader?

Replies to this inquiry were received from 580 advertisers and from 196 agencies. These results are summarized in Table 146.

TABLE 146

COMPARISON OF STANDARD AND FLAT MAGAZINES

	Facts for Standards	Facts for Flats	Opinions for Standards	Opinions for Flats	Undecided	Total
Advertisers	34 (6%)	60 (10%)	54 (10%)	131 (22%)	301 (52%)	580
Agencies	12 (6%)	27 (14%)	9 (9%)	54 (28%)	99 (51%)	201
Total	46	87	63	185	400	781
Total per cent	6%	11%	8%	24%	52%	

The 196 agencies are here tabulated as 201, as 5 presented data on both sides of the debate.

So far as these results may be regarded as reliable evidence, they seem to indicate that there is a distinct predominence of advantage in favor of the flat make-up. So far as facts are concerned, 11% of the replies gave facts in favor of the flat make-up as against 6% in favor of the standard make-up. So far as opinions are concerned, 24% gave opinions in favor of the flat make-up as against 8% in favor of the standard make-up. However, it must be borne in mind that over half or 52% of the persons responding were undecided in their opinion. Along with these facts one must bear in mind that the class of readers to whom a periodical primarily goes no doubt are a factor to be considered in the comparative advantage of the two types of make-up. It is quite likely that magazines of the type of the *Century* or the *Atlantic Monthly* would lose in favor and standing with a large majority of their readers if the make-up were changed. The flat make-up may be more effective in the case of magazines which have a more general mass circulation. However, our opinions must be checked up by actual facts, as it is impossible to decide a question of this kind by bare opinion.

RATES OF PREFERRED POSITIONS

The preferred positions have, of course, a considerably higher rate as compared with the ordinary positions. It will, therefore, be pertinent to ascertain what the rates for preferred positions are as compared with ordinary positions and also to ascertain to what extent there may be a difference in this regard between the flat and the standard magazines. There is considerable variation among the various magazines with regard to the additional rate for the preferred positions. In some instances the difference is extremely large. For example, the *Century Magazine* has a rate six times as large for the back cover as for an inside page. To illustrate a few typical differences in rates between preferred and non-preferred positions, the examples in Table 147 may be quoted.

If these increases in rates for preferred positions are expressed in percentages with the inside page as 100% we have the following increments, based on an average of 32 magazines:

Inside page rate	100%	Third cover rate	125%
Second cover rate	125	Back cover rate	250

In other words, the average increase in rate of the second or the third cover over an ordinary position is $\frac{1}{4}$, and the

TABLE 147
RATES FOR PREFERRED POSITIONS

Magazines	Inside Page	Second Cover	Third Cover	Back Cover
Century Magazine	$250	$400	$400	$1,500
Munsey's	250	750	750	1,000
Review of Reviews	360	460	460	1,200
Scribners	300	500	450	1,200
Outlook	400	550	550	600
The Nation	200	240	200	240
The Forum	100	125	165	175

increase of the back cover over an ordinary position is 2½ times.

A similar computation made for a group of 41 flat magazines shows the following increments, considering an ordinary inside position as 100%:

Ordinary inside page	100%	Third cover	125%
Second cover	125	Back cover	170

Comparing these results with the increments for the standard magazine, we note that the increase of the second and third cover over the inside position is the same as for the standard magazine. However, the increase of the back cover is not so great as in the case of the standard magazines, being only 70%, as against 150%. The explanation for this is undoubtedly the belief that the inside positions in a flat magazine are not at so great a disadvantage as compared with the back cover as they are in the case of the standard magazines with front and back advertising sections.

THE VALUE OF PREFERRED POSITIONS AS SHOWN BY EXPERIMENTAL AND STATISTICAL EVIDENCE

The value of preferred positions consists largely, perhaps entirely, of their greater attention value; not in better copy or better illustration or greater persuasive power, but simply in the greater amount of attention which they are able to command because of their position.

This greater attention value is due in the first place to the fact that an advertisement in a preferred position is seen by a larger number of persons. Even those people who claim not to read advertisements can hardly escape reading what is printed, for example, on the outside cover page, or on the page facing the first page of reading matter. Secondly, an advertisement in a preferred position, particularly on the outside cover, is seen not only by more people, but it is seen more frequently by the same persons, and, thirdly, it is often the first or the last advertisement seen when looking through a magazine. First and last impressions are made more deeply and more permanently.

The Greater Values of Preferred Positions. In order to determine how much more attention value preferred positions have than others, • the following experiments were made.

A pamphlet was prepared containing six leaves of ordinary magazine size. On the middle of each page was placed a syllable composed of three letters, a vowel and two consonants. The syllables used were lod, zan, mep, dut, rad, hon, vib, lin, fos, dar, hep. One of the syllables was inserted twice, on the third and eighth pages. This was done for a special purpose, as will be pointed out later.

This pamphlet was given to the person being tested, who was told that it contained syllables and that he should turn the leaves of it as he would the leaves of a magazine or book and read each syllable, going through the entire pamphlet only once. He was then asked to lay it aside. A sheet of paper was given him on which he wrote all the syllables he remembered. In this manner 50 persons were tested.

The aim was to find out how many times the syllables on the various pages would be remembered. Since no one could recall all the syllables, and most remembered but four or five, it is obvious that only those would be recalled which had made, for some reason, a deeper impression than the rest.

One question will naturally arise in the mind of the reader: Why would it not be just as well or even better to make the experiment by using full-page advertisements in the form of a pamphlet, letting each person look through these and then report what he remembered. Such an investigation was made at a later time, and the results are stated below. There are, however, several objections to such a plan, for by using advertisements, it is difficult to eliminate all of the factors which influence attention and memory; the problem we wish to solve is the relative importance of position, pure and simple.

For instance, some advertisements might be more familiar and better known than others, and some might be more attractive because of large type or beautiful illustration or striking border. Still others might be remembered more readily because of special interest in the class of articles presented in the advertisements.

All these difficulties were avoided in the use of syllables, for they were all equally meaningless, equally simple, and equally large. The only difference was that they were placed on different pages, and this question of position was the very one which was being investigated.

In order to guard still further against the possibility that certain syllables might have been remembered for some reason other than position, the same 12 syllables were redistributed in a similar pamphlet. If, for example, the syllable *lod* on the first page had been recalled more easily than others, it was placed on a different page in the second pamphlet. Each of these two pamphlets was used with about half of the 50 persons tested.

Now if the outside pages have greater attention value, we should expect the syllables on these pages to be remembered more frequently. How much more attention value they have should be roughly indicated by the greater number of times these syllables were remembered. The investigation gave the following statistics:

Average number of times the syllables on the first and last pages were recalled: 34

Average number of times the syllables on the second and eleventh pages were recalled: 26

Average number of times the syllables on all the other pages were recalled: 17

Total number of syllables recalled: 261

The pure attention value of an outside page would therefore seem to be approximately twice as great as that of an inside page. The ratio of the figures happens to be exactly two to one, 34 and 17.

In the case of a magazine, the attention value of a cover page is no doubt more than twice as much as that of an inside page, for the reason that a magazine lying on a reading table or elsewhere displays constantly one or the other of the cover pages. However, in the present experiment the readers saw the pamphlet only once, and the greater attention value shown here was due entirely to the psychological principle that first and last impressions in a series of impressions are remembered better than others. This is known in psychological terms as the law of primacy (first) and the law of recency (last).

In the case of the magazine we find not only the effect of this law, but also the fact that the outside cover page is seen oftener and by a greater number of people.

Pages 2 and 11 in the pamphlet used correspond to the two inside cover pages of a magazine. Their attention value also is greater than that of the other inside pages, but is of course not as great as that of the outside cover page. The average number of syllables remembered for these two pages was 26, which is about 50% more than the average for the other inside pages.

We might, therefore, represent the relative attention values of an inside page, the second or third cover page, and the last outside cover page by one, one and one-half, and two, respectively.

If, then, it is true that the outside cover page is worth twice as much as an inside page, it should also be true that two inside pages are worth as much as the one outside page. It was the object of the repeated syllable mentioned on page 783, to determine whether or not this is the case. As a matter of fact, it was found that the repeated syllable was remembered 40 times, or just a little oftener than the average for the outside pages. More extensive tests, however, as well as the values placed by publishers on preferred positions, indicate that the outside cover is considerably more than twice as valuable as an inside position and that other preferred positions have proportionate values, because of additional factors which operate in the actual use of periodicals.

THE MAGAZINE TEST

The magazine test described in a previous chapter furnished some valuable data on this question. These results were tabulated to show the number of mentions of the advertisements located in the various preferred and non-preferred positions. Only the full-page spaces were considered in this tabulation, because all advertisements in preferred positions occupied full-page spaces. The final data are set forth in the curve in Figure 104 which is so drawn that the value of the outside cover is placed at 100, and all other positions have proportionate values on the scale of 100. Now, there are two very obvious elements which interfere with the validity of these data: first, the great familiarity of the persons tested with some of the firms and commodities; and secondly, the greater attention value of some advertisements over others. The effect of the first factor was eliminated as far as possible, as previously explained on page 546. The effect of the second factor has been eliminated by smoothening the curve according to the usual statistical methods. Thus, the article advertised on the page facing the last inside cover page was Ivory Soap, and the number of mentions was unduly high. These inequalities are distributed as fairly as possible by the smoothened curve.

The main facts brought out by the graph are as follows: (1) that the outside cover is probably at least three times as valuable as an inside position; (2) that all positions within approximately eight pages from the end of the advertising section have greater value than other inside positions. These values gradually diminish as indicated by the drop of the curve. This advantage does not extend as far into the advertising section if we start at the reading section, counting from either end. (Apparently it extends only over four pages.) The positions facing the first and last pages of reading matter have approximately two-thirds of the value of the outside cover.

At the instigation of the Association of National Advertisers, Dr. E. K. Strong carried out an investigation to determine the relative values of preferred positions as compared with ordinary positions.

The experiment was carried out by using the September, 1911, copy of *Everybody's Magazine.* The investigation was made during February and March of 1912. A copy of this issue was given to about 160 men with the instruc-

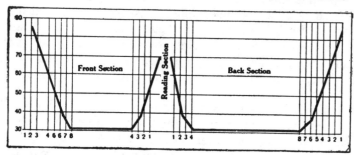

Figure 104: Chart showing result of test to determine relative position values for advertisements in the various sections of a magazine
(See page 785)

tion that they were to read a certain article in it. Only 80 men complied with the request, and at the end of one week they were tested to determine which advertisements they had noticed in the magazine. The test was made by giving each of these men a set of advertisements containing all of the full-page advertisements in this issue of *Everybody's* and an equal number of full-page advertisements which were not in this issue. Each person was asked to look through these advertisements and select those which he remembered having seen in this issue of *Everybody's*.

The test was carried out in the same way with a group of 40 business men and a group of 40 college students. There were 77 full-page advertisements in the magazine apart from the three cover positions. The 80 men tested showed the following results:

27, or 34%, remembered not a single advertisement, or 0% of the ads
12, or 15%, remembered from 1 to 10 advs., or approx. 6% of the ads
12, or 15%, remembered from 11 to 20 advs., or approx. 19% of the ads
7, or 9%, remembered from 21 to 30 advs., or approx. 32% of the ads
6, or 7½%, remembered from 31 to 40 advs., or approx. 45% of the ads
6, or 7½%, remembered from 41 to 50 advs., or approx. 58% of the ads
1, or 1%, remembered from 60 of the ads, or approx. 86% of the ads

A similar test had been made previously by Dr. Strong with 137 women. The results compared as follows with the test with the above men:

	Men	Women
Per cent who did not notice any advertisements	34	45
Per cent who noticed from 1 to 10 advertisements	26	24
Per cent who noticed more than 10 advertisements	40	31

From these data it appears that at least at the time of this experiment approximately between one-third and one-half of the men and women did not notice any of the advertisements in a magazine of standard make-up. Approximately another one-fourth of the persons noticed between 1 and 10 advertisements, and evidently only those which they happened to notice by chance. These were the ones chiefly in preferred positions.

In order to show to what extent these results indicate a difference between the preferred and the non-preferred posi-

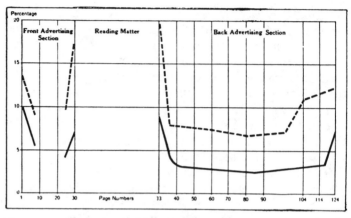

Figure 105: Curve showing the relative attention value of preferred and non-preferred positions in a standard magazine

tions, the data were computed to show the number of times each advertisement was recognized in the test. These results presented in the form of a graph in relation to their positions in the advertising section are shown in Figure 105. In this graph the continuous line represents the result for the 137 women; the broken line shows the result for the 80 men. The broken portion in the front advertising section is due to the fact that it contained no full-page advertisements at the points indicated. The figures along the base line indicate the number of the page in the advertising sections.

The advertisement on the page opposite the second cover was noticed by 10½% of the women and 13½% of the men; the advertisement on the page just after the reading matter, by 9¾% of the women and 19¾% of the men; and the advertisement on the last page opposite the third cover, by 7% of the women and 11½% of the men. Contrasted with these preferred pages, we find but 2¾% of the women and 7% of the men noticing advertisements in the neighborhood of page 88, the center of the back advertising section.

From these results it is evident that there is a certain amount of advantage in positions at the ends of the advertising section in addition to the ones that are recognized as preferred positions. There is some advantage in all of the positions, apparently, within six to ten pages from the ends of the advertising section, that is, from the covers.

TEST CARRIED OUT WITH FLAT MAGAZINES

The author made an investigation with nine different issues of the *Saturday Evening Post* published between the dates of August 8, 1914, and March 28, 1915. This test was carried out by having each person look through one copy of one of these issues. He was instructed to turn all the pages and to look at whatever interested him and to pass over whatever did not interest him. This consumed approximately 20 minutes. At the end of this time the copies of the magazine were laid aside and each person was asked to write down all the advertisements he remembered having seen in this particular issue. These results were then tabulated to show the number of times the advertisements in various positions were recalled. The data are shown in Table 148.

TABLE 148

INVESTIGATION SHOWING RELATIVE VALUE OF PREFERRED POSITIONS

Mentions and Relative Values	Second Cover	Facing Second Cover	Facing Reading Section	Average Mentions of all other full-page ads	Facing Third Cover	Third Cover	Fourth Cover
Number of Mentions	50	45	51	32	37	47	67
Relative values (100 taken as equaling the average mentions of non-preferred positions)	156%	140%	159%	100%	116%	147%	209%

These results indicate that in a flat magazine the fourth cover, as far as these tests go, has more than twice (209%) the value of an ordinary position; the second and third covers have approximately 50% greater value than an ordinary position; the pages facing the second and third covers have in the one case 40% greater value, and in the other 16% greater value respectively.

A similar investigation was carried out by Mr. R. B. Franken with issues of the *Saturday Evening Post*, but by a somewhat different method than the one employed by the author. A copy of the November 8, 1919, issue of the *Saturday Evening Post* was given to each student in a class in New York University with the instruction that a certain article in it was to be read during the course of the following week. At the end of the week the 104 persons in the class were tested. Each was given a set of all of the full-page advertisements together with an equal number of other advertisements mixed in. The results of this investigation yielded the comparative figures for the preferred positions as shown in Table 149.

TABLE 149

VALUES OF POSITIONS IN DIFFERENT PARTS OF A PUBLICATION

Position of Advertisements	Average Value	Per Cent
60 black and white pages (Inside pages)	33.1	100
Pages 1 and 2	87.5	264
First group of 10 pages, 33-51	38.6	116
Second group of 10 pages, 52-85	29.7	90
Third group of 10 pages, 84-144	34.0	103
Fourth group of 10 pages, 147-164	35.0	
Fifth group of 10 pages, 167-184	26.2	
Sixth group of 10 pages, 187-200	31.9	
Center spread	37.0	112
First group of 5 colored pages	46.0	
Second group of 6 colored pages	30.0	
Third group of 6 colored pages	38.0	
Second cover, colored	29.0	
Third cover, colored	38.0	
Fourth cover, colored	93.0	

The numbers in this table indicate the number of times the various advertisements were recognized by 104 persons.

From these results we may note that the average value of a non-preferred position is 33.1. The second and third covers have a value respectively of 29 and 38, while the fourth cover has a value of 93. These results are somewhat affected by the fact that only one issue was used; this did not take into account the individual familiarity or lack of familiarity with the particular commodities advertised in the preferred positions. Furthermore, advertisements as a whole are rather well known to a group of students, which tends to give the advantage, to some extent, to the advertisements in the non-preferred positions.

POSITIONS ON A PAGE

About 1900, Professor Harlow Gale was interested in experimenting with various types of advertising problems, and among others he conducted a set of tests to compare the relative attention values of various positions on a page. In the investigation he used a page the size of the standard magazine page, divided into four horizontal quarters. A word was placed in each quarter; four words only were used, but these four words were interchanged in their positions so as to avoid giving preference to any one position as the result of the peculiarity or preference for the word itself. He used what is known as the rapid exposure method; that is, the entire page was exposed for a brief interval—less than a second—to an observer, who then reported immediately afterwards the words which he had noticed. This experiment was carried out with 8 persons, giving each one 10 exposures. The results were as follows:

Position 1, top horizontal quarter, was seen 38 times or 11.8%
Position 2, second quarter, was seen   166 times or 51.8%
Position 3 was seen   99 times or 20.9%
Position 4, bottom quarter, was seen   17 times or 5.3%

These results are of value only in so far as they indicate the relative advantage because of the focusing of the eyes first on certain portions of the page. They probably indicate that the second quarter secures the greatest attention; that the third quarter stands next in frequency; the top quarter third, and the bottom quarter last. There is, of course, a certain advantage in the position which receives the initial attention of the eye on the page.

Is there any difference in advertising value between the upper and lower halves of a page? Presumably the upper half would be regarded by most advertisers as a better position. If there is a difference it would be of practical interest to determine how much more valuable the upper half is.

This problem was approached by the author by the method of syllables discussed in connection with a previous investigation. Twelve syllables were put in a small pamphlet, one placed in the middle of each half page. This pamphlet was presented to 50 persons who read it through once and then reported what they remembered.

The experiment gave the following result:

Total number of syllables recalled	354
Recalled in the upper half	54%
Recalled in the lower half	46%

The pure attention value of the upper half therefore seems to be about 8% greater. A similar investigation made some time ago showed a difference of 10% in favor of the upper half.[1]

What is the comparative worth of quarter-pages? To answer this question, four syllables were placed on each right-hand page, one in the middle of each quarter. This pamphlet was likewise submitted to 50 persons, the results were as follows:

Total number of syllables recalled:	224
Percentage of mentions for each quarter:	
Upper left quarter	28%
Upper right quarter	33%

[1] *Judicious Advertising*, VI, p. 17.

| Lower left quarter | 16% |
| Lower right quarter | 23% |

Thus, the upper quarters, and particularly the right quarter on the right page, appear to have appreciably greater values than the lower quarters, particularly than the lower left quarter. These differences are, no doubt, mainly due to our habits of eye-movement. We are more inclined to notice the upper features of an object than the lower. We begin to read at the top of the page. We notice a person's face more than his feet. The upper half of letters is more significant than the lower half. It is easier to recognize a word when the upper part of the letters is shown than when the lower part is shown. This may be illustrated by taking a printed word and cutting it in two horizontally.

There is unquestionably a difference in the advertising value of different positions on a page, yet seldom is there a difference in the rate for different positions on a page.

In several of the tests conducted by the author comparisons were made between the upper and lower halves of the pages. Standard magazines were used in which the pages were divided horizontally in this manner into upper and lower halves. One test of this sort was made with the *Cosmopolitan Magazine* for April, 1910. This issue contained 19 upper halves and 13 lower halves. The persons tested were asked to look through the advertising sections and were then asked to report what advertisements they had seen. Results of the test showed that the upper halves were remembered on the average 12.6 times while the lower halves were remembered on the average 11.4 times. This gives an advantage of approximately 10% in favor of the upper half.

Mr. R. B. Franken, in connection with the investigation already referred to, made a comparison between the right- and left-hand pages, in which he obtained the results shown in Table 150.

TABLE 150

COMPARATIVE VALUE OF RIGHT AND LEFT PAGES

	Number of Left-Hand Pages	Left-Hand Average Attention Value	Number of Right-Hand Pages	Right-Hand Average Attention Value		Percentage of Advantage
17 colored pages	7	35.6	10	38.9	Right	9
62 black and white pages	30	33.9	32	35.8	Right	6
20 half-pages	11	24.3	9	22.2	Left	8.5
14 quarter-pages	4	14.0	10	15.8	Right	1.3

From these results it appears that there is relatively little difference between the right- and left-hand pages. What difference there is is slightly in favor of the right-hand page, but the difference is easily within the limits of the error of the experiment.

By similar comparison between upper and lower quarters, Franken arrives at the conclusion that the upper quarter is approximately 25% superior to the lower quarter. In view of this result and the generally recognized fact that the upper half is probably somewhat better than the lower half, a great many of the flat magazines make up their pages so that the halves are not upper and lower horizontal halves, but vertical right and left halves. This has the advantage of giving each half-page an upper as well as a lower portion of the page.

Professor Adams has made a series of comparative tests with a view to determining the relative advantages of various positions on a page. He prepared a series of cards the size of the standard magazine page. Each card was divided into a number of divisions. A letter was placed in each division. Each card was shown for a half-second to the person tested, after which he reported the letters he had seen. This test was carried out with 150 persons. When the page was divided into four divisions representing four quarters, two upper and two lower, the results were as follows in terms of the percentage of attention each quarter received:

Upper left quarter	33%	Lower left quarter	21%
Upper right quarter	28	Lower right quarter	17

From the standpoint of the percentages of times the letter in each of these four positions was seen first, the results were as follows:

Upper left quarter	81%	Lower left quarter	13%
Upper right quarter	4	Lower right quarter	2

The comparison between the upper and lower halves when he divided his page into two halves gave the following results when tabulated from the standpoint of the number of times each half was seen:

Upper half	50.4%	Lower half	49.6%

From the standpoint of the number of times each half was seen first, it yielded the following results:

Upper half	85.5%	Lower half	14.5%

In the next place, Adams prepared a dummy of 26 pages of advertisements composed of 16 one-page advertisements, 12 half-page advertisements, 17 quarter-page advertisements, and 14 one-eighth page advertisements. The test was made by allowing each person to observe each page for a fractional part of a second. The test was carried out with 47 persons. After a person had seen a given page, he was asked to write down what he had observed.

Comparing the full right-hand and full left-hand pages with each other, he found the following comparison:

Items observed on the left-hand page, 937, or 65%
Items observed on the right-hand page, 1,427, or 100%

A similar comparison made from the standpoint of half-pages, showed the following number of items observed in the respective four halves:

Upper left-hand page	608
Upper right-hand page	1,020
Total for the two upper halves	1,628
Lower left-hand page	329
Lower right-hand page	407
Total for the two lower halves	736
Total for left halves	937
Total for right halves	1,427

A tabulation of the data for horizontal quarters on both right- and left-hand pages showed the following results:

	Left Page	Right Page	Total
Top quarter	350	603	953
Second quarter	250	417	657
Third quarter	177	262	439
Fourth quarter	152	145	297
	929	1,427	

These results indicate very much the same situation as has been found in the other experiments reported, namely, that the upper half has the advantage over the lower half, and that the right page has a slight advantage over the left page. So far, however, as the horizontal quarters are concerned, the results do not check up in every detail with those obtained by Gale. Gale found that the second quarter from the top was the most desirable position, whereas, according to Adams' results, the top quarter is the most desirable horizontal quarter. This type of division of the page is now no longer employed by most magazines, since it is generally acknowledged that the vertical quarter is not only the more attractive looking space, but is also more easily used in laying out the features of an advertisement.

THE EFFECT OF THE SIZE OF THE ADVERTISING SECTION UPON THE VALUE OF INDIVIDUAL ADVERTISEMENTS IN IT

Dr. E. K. Strong made an investigation to determine what is the attention and memory value of full-page advertisements in advertising sections of varying sizes. The tests were carried out after the manner of those already reported. Two different methods were used to find which advertisements were remembered. In the one case the test was made immediately after the advertisements had been seen; in the other case the test was made after an interval of one week. The results obtained by the two methods are essentially the same; both show a difference in attention value relative to varying sizes of the advertising sections. The results obtained from the immediate test were as follows:

Attention value of
1 ad in a magazine of	5 ads	83.1%
1 ad in a magazine of	10 ads	81.4
1 ad in a magazine of	25 ads	72.6
1 ad in a magazine of	50 ads	57.2
1 ad in a magazine of	100 ads	50.4
1 ad in a magazine of	150 ads	35.1

Corresponding results for the test made after an interval of one week were as follows:

Attention value of
1 ad in a magazine of	5 pages	14.4%
1 ad in a magazine of	10 pages	14.2
1 ad in a magazine of	25 pages	12.6
1 ad in a magazine of	50 pages	9.9
1 ad in a magazine of	100 pages	8.7
1 ad in a magazine of	150 pages	6.1

The chief difference between the two types of tests is that the percentage of advertisements remembered after an interval of one week is considerably smaller than the percentage remembered immediately after. The relative values, however, are practically identical. The results of this investigation indicate that the individual advertisement loses considerably in attention value when it appears as one among a very large number of advertisements compared to its value when it appears among a smaller number of advertisements.

THE SELECTION OF MEDIUMS

The intelligent selection of magazines requires a careful comparison of the available mediums and an intimate knowledge of the nature and characteristics of the various types of magazines. The information supplied by the reports of the Audit Bureau of Circulation is very important, and furnishes a valuable basis on which to make a selection of mediums. However, the Audit Bureau of Circulation is not in a position to cover certain aspects of a medium, particularly those relating to the editorial policy and the general standing of the publication among its readers, except in so far as that is indicated indirectly by various items of the report. Probably the advertiser will obtain the best direct comparison if he will supplement the A. B. C. reports with such impressions as he himself is able to make from a careful examination of a number of typical issues of a publication.

Buyers of space follow various plans for making as careful comparisons as possible among the various publications before a selection is made. Thus, for example, one advertising agency has devised the following score card plan for evaluating the suitability of a given medium for its particular problem:

SCALE OF POINTS

General: 5

    Appearance, stock, make-up, printing, color, illustrations, etc.   3.0
    Age, financial soundness, general reputation, ethics   2.0

Appeal: 40

    Appeal to women consumers   30.0
    Appeal to men consumers   4.0
    Dealer influence   6.0

Circulation Distribution (A) Territorial: 5

    Per cent eastern   .5
    Per cent southern   2.0
    Per cent central   1.0
    Per cent mountain and coast   1.5

Circulation Distribution (B) Community: 5
Over 10,000 population	1.0
Under 10,000 population	4.0

Circulation Volume: 10
Rate per line per thousand of net paid circulation	6.0
Proportion of market covered	4.0

Circulation Quality (A) Editorial: 5
Fiction, news, features	2.0
Service departments	3.0

Circulation Quality (B) Investigations: 5
Investigations among readers	5.0

Circulation Quality (C) Subscription Methods: 10
Price of subscription	2.0
Percentage of mail subscribers	2.0
Percentage of married women	.5
Percentage renewals.	2.0
Percentage arrears	.5
Percentage instalment subscriptions	.5
Percentage clubs with others	.5
Percentage premiums with subscriptions	.5
Percentage premiums for subscriptions	.5
Percentage bulk circulation	.5

Class of Advertising Carried: 7
High-class mail order	2.0
High-class publicity	2.0
Long-term "repeats"	3.0

Special Considerations: 8
Previous advertising	2.0
Inquiry costs	2.0
Acceptance of size space	4.0

Grand total   100

Taking up these points categorically, some brief comment is in order. The points grouped under "general" are judged on general observation and information. As we have remarked, "appeal" forms the heaviest single factor in selection, and to appeal to women in this case is attached three-fourths of the weight under this head. In fact, this formed the primary consideration for selecting a publication. It will be readily gathered that as a factor it would weigh heavily against, say, a business or other publication appealing almost solely to men. Man, it will be noticed, is accorded a scant 4% of desirability. This is because an investigation by the manufacturer discovered that men buy in a proportion of one male to seven or eight women. For a proposition involving, say, a razor or shaving brush, this proportion of valuation would, obviously, be turned about somewhat.

The item of "dealer influence" under this head was also gauged on information developed by the manufacturer's investigation. Originally this item was allowed 8 points, and "women" 28 points, but a revision was made, allowing the latter 2 more points, and subtracting 2 points from the former. This will illustrate the care exercised to insure the highest possible degree of accuracy in gauging relative values.

Under "circulation distribution (a) territorial," it will be noticed that Southern and Pacific Coast circulation is considered especially desirable. This is because the market for this product, experience proves, is especially favorable in these sections. As for the community circulation distribution, circulation in towns under 10,000 outweighs that in towns above that limit by four to one for the reason that a large percentage of this product is sold in the smaller towns.

Circulation volume shares with circulation quality second position in the batting average, with 10 points to its credit.

"We regard a million of circulation in one medium," said the agent, "as more valuable than a million divided among three, since the rate charged is based on the total, not the non-duplicated circulation."

JUDGING CIRCULATION

Circulation quality, A and B, is judged by scrutiny of editorial matter to discover the class of women readers and by investigations among readers, with the Eastman investigation used as a basis, showing (1) readers in Class A and B homes; (2) times mentioned as the favorite; (3) times mentioned in proportion to total circulation; (4) total homes receiving.

The rest of the card speaks for itself.

"As you will readily see," explains the score-board man, "the big point (already remarked), is the appeal to women, and we have accordingly scored it heavily. The rest of the factors involved have been graded from six points down, according to their importance.

"The next step was to group the publications to be considered into four classes, high-class women's, small-town women's, farm, and general. From this point the procedure is plain. To the publication in each class approaching nearest to perfection on any factor we have given the total number of points allowed to that factor. Using this number as a basis, we computed the standing of the other publications, and graded them accordingly (mathematically where it was possible). When all the candidates were graded, the total of points showed the relative efficiency of each in its class for our proposition. It is well to note that, in scoring the publications considered, we scored straight across the board, totaling neither in whole nor in part until the scoring was complete on every factor.

"The results of this score-card have been gratifying. Our opinions of relative values of publications were confirmed in every group but one, and we are ready to admit that in that one case we had been misled before. The score-card showed just where and how we had been misled.

"The score-card prevents us from overlooking any item, however small. It enables us to keep our sense of proportion. It insures both fair treatment to publications and protection to clients." [1]

Other organizations have worked out variations of similar plans. The advantage of a score-card plan such as is here proposed is perhaps not so much in the final score that is obtained nor in the precise amount of value that is assigned to each particular point, since that is very largely a matter of subjective estimate and judgment rather than objective fact, but rather in the care taken to make certain that all of the essential points regarding the selection of a medium are borne in mind. A score-card serves to bring before the advertiser or the buyer of space the desirable and the undesirable points regarding a medium, as related to a given advertising plan.

[1] *Printer's Ink*, Jan. 18, 1917 p. 37.

XXX

NEWSPAPERS

Number of newspapers in each of the chief divisions. Growth in newspaper advertising. The country weekly: Comparison of newspapers with
magazines. Frequency of issue. Localized circulation. The appeal. Circulation. Growth in newspaper circulation. Distribution of newspaper
circulation. Rates for newspaper space.

IN 1920 there were the following number of newspapers
in each of the chief divisions, according to *Ayer's Newspaper Annual and Directory:*

		Total Circulation
500	morning dailies	12,797,000
1,651	evening dailies	19,109,000
	Total daily	31,906,000
511	Sunday papers	15,926,000
112	Canadian dailies	2,263,000
12,000	weekly newspapers	14,000,000

In April, 1922, the Audit Bureau of Circulations had 816
newspaper members with the following circulations:

	Total Circulation
Morning papers	9,886,389
Evening papers	14,369,298
Total daily	24,255,687
Sunday papers	17,626,571

From the standpoint of the total amount of advertising
space as well as from the standpoint of the expenditure of
money in the various mediums, we note that approximately
47% of all money expended for advertising is devoted to
newspaper space. These figures give an idea of the large

amount of money expended in newspaper advertising as well as of the amount of space used for advertising in newspapers. During 1920 approximately $600,000,000 was spent in newspaper advertising. Of this amount, approximately 10%, or $60,000,000 was expended in the so-called country weeklies.

Furthermore, it will be interesting to note that of the $600,000,000, approximately 75% was expended for retail and local advertising, and 25%, or approximately $150,-000,000, was expended by national advertisers. If we refer to page 741, in Chapter XXVIII, we will note that approximately $150,000,000 is expended for national advertising in the magazines. In other words, national advertisers expend about the same amount in each of the two types of mediums. The total expenditure in newspaper advertising is approximately four times the total expenditure in magazines.

GROWTH IN NEWSPAPER ADVERTISING

An investigation was made by Mr. Robert Armstrong under the direction of the author to determine the growth in newspaper advertising space over a considerable period of years. This study was made by measuring the total amount of advertising space in the issue appearing on the fifteenth of each month in two newspapers, namely, the *New York Tribune* and the *Boston Transcript*. This tabulation was made for seven full years, at intervals of ten years beginning in 1860. The results are shown in Table 151.

These figures indicate a very great increase since 1860 in the amount of advertising space carried. See Figure 3, page 34. Thus, the increase in the *Boston Transcript* advertising is approximately thirteen fold; the increase in the *New York Tribune* is approximately fivefold.

Similar figures for the *New York Times*, but covering a shorter period, indicate likewise a very great increase in

TABLE 151

GROWTH IN THE ADVERTISING SPACE OF TWO NEWSPAPERS
FROM 1860 TO 1918

Year	Boston Transcript	New York Tribune
1860	18,872 agate lines	15,862 agate lines
1870	27,339 agate lines	18,900 agate lines
1880	34,342 agate lines	12,628 agate lines
1890	40,628 agate lines	18,720 agate lines
1900	87,472 agate lines	47,180 agate lines
1910	133,462 agate lines	39,480 agate lines
1918	236,628 agate lines	80,848 agate lines

total advertising space.   The figures are as follows for
typical years:

New York Times

1896	2,227,196 agate lines	1910	7,550,650 agate lines
1900	3,978,620 agate lines	1915	9,682,562 agate lines
1905	5,953,322 agate lines	1920	23,447,395 agate lines

From these figures it will appear that the growth from
1896 to 1920 was approximately tenfold.   However, the
year 1920 was an unusual year, as the volume of advertising was larger than it had ever been before.   Nevertheless, the growth up to 1915 was approximately a fivefold
increase.

THE COUNTRY WEEKLY

Referring to Table 143, page 742, we note that approximately 14,000 publications are classed as weekly newspapers and periodicals.   Of these 14,000, approximately
12,000 are weekly newspapers.   Consequently, in view of
the volume and the type of circulation which they have, they
constitute an important advertising medium embracing a
field probably not covered by any other publication.   From
the standpoint of the advertiser, it is therefore important
to note the manner in which advertising in these weekly
publications is handled.   Most of the country weeklies are
printed in cooperation with a number of large newspaper

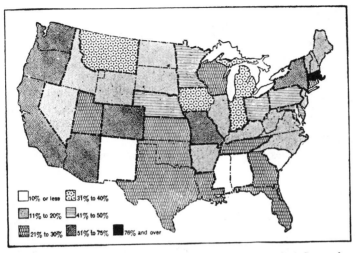

Figure 106: Density of newspaper circulation in the United States, by states—based upon percentage of circulation to population

unions. The average country weekly has eight pages. Of these eight pages four are printed by the newspaper union. The largest of these unions is the one known as the Western Newspaper Union, which in 1921 controlled 4,633 papers, and supplied a certain amount of service to approximately 7,000 additional papers. In addition to this, a smaller number of papers are handled by the Pacific Newspaper Union, and others by the Canadian Newspaper Union.

As an illustration of the manner in which the various newspaper unions cooperate with the local publishers in issuing weekly newspapers, we may observe the general procedure of the Western Newspaper Union. The Western Newspaper Union has a total of 32 printing establishments located in suitable cities over the country, as follows:

Boston	Memphis	Fargo	Wichita
New York	Cincinnati	Sioux Falls	Oklahoma City
Baltimore	Indianapolis	Sioux City	Little Rock
Pittsburgh	Fort Wayne	Des Moines	Dallas
Cleveland	Detroit	Omaha	Houston

Charlotte	Chicago	Lincoln	Denver
Atlanta	Milwaukee	Kansas City	Billings
Birmingham	Minneapolis	St. Louis	Salt Lake City

Each of these shops prints the papers that are supplied for its particular section. For example, Atlanta, Georgia, supplies 73 different local papers. The Western Newspaper Union prints the required number of papers and sends them to the local publisher. He in the meantime has prepared the copy for the remaining four pages, so that when the supply arrives he runs the papers through the press, thus printing the other four pages.

This arrangement is probably an advantage both for the small weekly paper and for the advertiser who is to use this publication. From the standpoint of the paper itself, it makes it possible to provide the readers with higher-grade material and with kinds of material that could not otherwise be secured. The Western Newspaper Union prepares a considerable variety of features in proof form. These are submitted to the local editor, who selects the particular features that he desires and the amount of space that he wishes to devote to each one. According to this arrangement the Union then prints the four pages each week. This makes it possible for the local paper to have a considerable amount of individuality in spite of the fact that the material is prepared elsewhere for a large number of papers at one time. Some of the typical features supplied by the Union are the following: Sporting, special correspondence, short stories, stories about the states, agricultural news, current correspondence from Washington, styles, the Sunday School lessons, and the like. Serial stories by high-grade writers are likewise supplied so that the local editor may choose among them and print each week an instalment of the story.

National and general advertising is placed in the four pages printed by the Union through its own arrangements and agreements. Thus, if an advertiser wishes to use space in these papers issued in cooperation with the Union, he makes a contract with the Union covering either all of the papers or any particular section issued from one of the various shops. The advantage of this arrangement obviously is that the advertiser needs to contract only with one party instead of with each one of the individual publications. It also results in a certain uniformity in the manner in which the advertising is handled. Local advertising is of course handled by the local publisher in each case.

This arrangement with the Union makes it possible to have a lower rate for the general advertising than would be the case if it were handled through each individual local paper. The rate is approximately 8 cents per inch per paper for each insertion. This, however, is subject to a considerable discount in case a large amount of space is used. For example, if a contract of $10,000 is made, a discount of as much as 40% may be made; thus the net rate is brought down to less than 5 cents per inch. On the other hand, the local rate is considerably higher because of the greater expense involved in the composition and the printing.

COMPARISON OF NEWSPAPERS WITH MAGAZINES

There has been at various times a certain amount of antagonism between the magazines and the newspapers as groups of mediums. This is an undesirable as well as unnecessary form of competition, since the two types of mediums are not necessarily competitive, but in most instances are supplementary. As a matter of fact, the relative amount of money expended in the two types of publications has remained very nearly the same. There has been, possibly, a small relative gain on the part of the newspapers.

However, it will be of interest as well as of value, in considering the two types of mediums, to compare them with each other in order to note the essential differences between them. Most of the comparative differences may be centered around three or four main points.

(1) FREQUENCY OF ISSUE

The fact that the newspaper is issued every day, or every week in the case of weekly publications, offers certain possibilities which the monthly magazine does not possess. Thus, for example, it makes possible greater flexibility in the planning and carrying out of the advertising schedule. It is possible to choose the day of the week on which copy may be issued. On some days of the week it may be more desirable to have certain types of copy issued. Possibly advertising of washing machines, soap powder, etc., may be placed more advantageously on Monday, which is considered in many families as wash day. The advertising of fish may be more effective on certain days of the week than on others. Retail store managers may find it to their advantage to advertise sales on certain specific days of the week.

It makes possible the frequent insertion of copy when that is desired for certain purposes. It is also possible to produce the accumulated effect of advertising which may be desirable in connection with certain advertising plans. Thus, for example, the *Encyclopedia Britannica* in 1911 had set May 31 as the date on which the Britannica would be raised in price. This date and the increase in the price were very emphatically impressed on the people by repeated insertions, so that a cumulative effect was produced in an effective manner.

Another element of flexibility, due to the frequency of issue, is timeliness. Magazine copy must be prepared usually six to eight weeks in advance. Quite frequently some conspicuous public event affords a strategic opportunity to tie up advertising. A catastrophe such as a fire or a flood may afford an opportunity for stressing certain commodities. Thus, for example, a fire in Passaic, New

Jersey, some time ago was capitalized by an advertiser of a fire extinguisher, and this advertising resulted in a considerable volume of business. Likewise, any event of public nature, political or otherwise, because of its general interest, affords an idea which can be used effectively in advertising.

(2) LOCALIZED CIRCULATION

The fact that every newspaper—even the large metropolitan daily—circulates in a certain limited range affords to the advertiser certain possibilities and advantages for certain purposes. Advertising may be carried out intensively within a limited area. For example, it may be carried out where there is distribution and not elsewhere, thus avoiding waste of advertising. Or it may be concentrated in those parts of the general territory which are weak and which need strengthening. Or the territory in which business is to be done may be gradually expanded by such localized advertising. This is particularly desirable in the case of a product for which the distribution cannot be secured at once. The advertising may therefore be undertaken within a limited area. It may cover only a certain city and the surrounding territory covered by the papers in that territory. As the business develops, progressive zones may be added until finally the entire country or a large section is covered. Newspaper advertising also permits the handling of various territories according to the seasonal climatic conditions. Thus, for example, the earlier spring season which occurs in the southern part of the United States may require special copy, and may make it possible to advertise certain special commodities in that part of the country. The advertising may be varied progressively as the season advances northward. Price variation may likewise be taken care of through the localized character of newspaper circulation. Try-out campaigns may be handled conveniently by using the newspapers in the local territory selected.

The localized character of the circulation also makes possible the utilization of local interest and happenings. This point is illustrated by a plan carried out by a large public utility interest. This company varied its copy in the different localities by tying it up with the events and historical incidents prominent in each locality. Thus, while the same general appeal was utilized in all sections of the country, the appeal was given a local flavor by tying it up with local events and incidents. Newspaper advertising takes into account the differences which exist among various parts of the country in the distribution and relative frequency of use of various commodities. The distribution of automobiles varies considerably from state to state, from as high as one to 7 or 8 persons to as low as one to 30 to 35 persons. The variation in distribution of electrical appliances is even greater. In one state 79% of the population live in electrically lighted homes; in another, only 8% do.

(3) THE APPEAL

There is little remaining to be said that has not already been pointed out. Variation of appeal is made possible through the two factors above mentioned, namely, frequency of issue, and localization of the circulation. Perhaps one more point should be added here. The one difference between the appeal of a magazine and that of a newspaper is that the newspaper is on the whole much more a mass medium, and is read by a larger proportion of families than are magazines. There are a considerable number of families who are not subscribers to magazines but who do read newspapers.

CIRCULATION

Statements of circulation of newspapers were decidedly unreliable prior to the introduction of the recent methods of requiring more accurate reports. The Audit Bureau of Circulations has extended its activities to cover newspapers as well as magazines. Similar statements for newspapers are therefore prepared by this Bureau. The A. B. C. requires reports to be prepared by the publisher himself twice a year and itself issues an audited report once a year. The general items in the two reports are substantially identical, and are practically identical with those of the magazine reports. The chief difference is that the statement prepared for the newspapers gives the distribution of the circulation territorially in two ways. First, it gives the distribution in the city in which the paper is published, in the suburban territory, and in more distant localities.

Secondly, the geographical distribution is minutely indicated, at least for a large number of the papers. That is, the number of copies distributed in each city in which 25 or more copies are circulated is given in the report, as shown in Figure 107.

It is unnecessary to point out here the distinct value of the information made possible through the A. B. C. reports, and the reliability of this information. The advertiser is entitled to know what he buys when he buys newspaper space. He is able to know much more fully the nature of the space that he buys as a result of these reports that are available.

		Corrected Report—See Par. 17.
AUDIT BUREAU OF CIRCULATIONS		AUDITOR'S REPORT
CENTURY BUILDING, CHICAGO		1. The Chicago Tribune.
		2. Chicago.
		3. Illinois.

		Average Net Paid		4. Year Estab. 1847.
Quarter		Daily	Sunday	5. Published every morning and Sunday.
2nd	1920	420,782	715,440	
3rd	1920	453,257	707,064	6. Report for twelve months ending March 31, 1921.
4th	1920	453,245	757,010	
1st	1921	468,356	818,894	Date Examined May, 1921.

7. Population City (Corporate Limits) 1910 U. S. Census 2,185,283. 1920 census 2,701,705. Population Trading Territory (Total City and Suburban) 3,500,000.

8. Daily Average Distribution for Period Covered by Section 6, Above.

DISTRIBUTION	Morning		Sunday	
[1] City				
[2] Carriers (Regular)				
Dealers and Ind. Carriers				
Street Sales				
Counter Sales				
Mail Subs				
Total City		234,244		373,922
[1] Suburban (Trading Ter.)				
[2] Carriers (Regular)				
Agts., D'rs. and Ind. Carr.	60,578		84,360	
Mail Subs. (incl. R. F. D.)	2,303		72	
Total Suburban		62,881		84,432
Total Local (City and Sub'n)		297,125		458,354
Country				
Agents and Dealers	90,108		84,047	
Mail Subs. (incl. R. F. D.)	61,677		7,201	
Total Country		151,785		291,248
TOTAL NET CASH PAID		448,910		749,602
[3] Bulk Sales (Average)				
Total Net Paid (incl. Bulk)				
TOTAL				
Advertisers	171		118	
Employees	382		460	
Correspondents	9		8	
City Employees				
R. R. and P. O. Employees	116		238	
Total Service Copies		678		824
Advertising Agencies	182		79	
Exchanges				
Complimentary	132		210	
Sample Copies			722	
Office Use and Files	1,198		1,618	
Total Unpaid Copies		1,512		2,629
TOTAL DISTRIBUTION		451,100		753,055

[1] "City" refers to corporate limits unless exception is made as shown in Paragraph 16 (a) "Suburban" is the trading territory, See Par. 16 (b).

[2] A "Regular Carrier" is one whose route lists, showing names and addresses, or addresses only, of subscribers are on file in the publisher's office. An "independent Carrier" is one whose route lists, showing the names and addresses of subscribers, are NOT on file in the publisher's office.

[3] All copies sold in quantity and paid for by other than the recipient, whether annual or term subscriptions, or special one day sales shall be considered bulk sales.

A "Paid Subscriber" is a subscriber served by mail or carrier, who has paid not less than 50% of either the regular advertised subscription price, or newstand price and who is not over six months in arrears; also short term and trial subscriptions not in arrears.

A "Short Term Subscriber" is a subscriber who has paid for a period of less than one year. Copyright, 1914, by Audit Bureau of Circulations. Form N A R 5920

9. NET PRESS RUN FOR THE LAST TWO CALENDAR WEEKS COVERED BY THIS REPORT?

Sun.	886,455		Sun.	863,345
Mon.	482,851		Mon.	488,711
Tues.	485,323		Tues.	487,484
Wed.	486,803		Wed.	486,848
Thur.	489,213		Thur.	487,770
Fri.	499,213		Fri.	484,966
Sat.	484,585		Sat.	480,129

11. Net Press Run by Editions and Time of Issue?

	Morning, 3/31/21		Sunday, 3/27/21	
(a)	9:00 p.m.	62,248	Sat. 3:45 p.m.	81,172
(b)	11:00 p.m.	87,587	Sat. 5:15 p.m.	142,284
(c)	1:15 a.m.	138,175	Sat. 9:00 p.m.	156,848
(d)	3:15 a.m.	197,884	Sun. 12:30 a.m.	432,810
Predate (e)			Fri. 4:30 a.m.	34,280

Morning issue:

(a) and (b) Mail editions for distribution to mail subscribers and country dealers and city street sales in the down-town business section.

(c) Home edition for general distribution in the city and suburbs and to mail subscribers not served with (a) or (b).

(d) Final edition for city and suburban distribution and to mail subscribers not served with (a), (b) or (c).

Sunday issue:

(a) and (b) Bulldog edition for general distribution.

(c) Mail edition for distribution to mail subscribers and country dealers.

(d) Final edition for distribution principally in the city and suburbs.

(d) Predate edition (going to press at 4:30 a.m. Friday) is distributed to country dealers in distant and remote territory.

All editions of the daily and Sunday carry all foreign advertising.

16. Territory Boundaries Are as Follows:

(a) City circulation as shown in Par. 8 is all that within the city corporate limits of Chicago, Ill., and Oak Park, Ill.

(b) Names of Eight Largest Towns and Radius of Area Included in Trading Territory:

Gary, Ind.	Joliet, Ill.
Aurora, Ill.	Chicago Heights, Ill.
Evanston, Ill.	Elgin, Ill.
Waukegan, Ill.	Hammond, Ind.

Suburban circulation is all that within an average radius of 40 miles and includes all of Cook county, Ill., entire central and southern portion of Lake county, Ill., southeastern portion of McHenry county, Ill., all of Du Page county, Ill., entire central and eastern portion of Kane county, Ill., northeastern portion of Kendall county, Ill., all of Will county, Ill., except a small southwestern portion, entire central and northern portion of Lake county, Ind., northwestern portion of Porter county, Ind.

17. DISTRIBUTION OF SUBURBAN AND COUNTRY CIRCULATION IN TOWNS RECEIVING 25 OR MORE COPIES DAILY THROUGH CARRIERS, DEALERS, AGENTS AND MAIL.

Dealers, gross; mail, net.

LIST OF TOWNS RECEIVING 25 OR MORE COPIES DAILY AS OF MARCH 14, 1921, AND SUNDAY AS OF MARCH 13, 1921

Town	Daily			Sunday		
	Dealer	Mail	Total	Dealer	Mail	Total
ILLINOIS						
Abingdon	45	48	93	276		276
Albion	24	24	48	41		41
Alden				25		25
Aledo	30	215	245	205		205
Alexis	18	44	62	68		68
Allerton		28	28	25		25
Alpha				27		27
Algonquin	30	9	39	60	2	62
Etc., through the complete list						
MANITOBA						
Winnipeg	98	16	114	228	5	233
ONTARIO						
Kitchener				30		30
Toronto	35	30	65	49	14	63
SASKATCHEWAN						
Regina				34	2	36
Totals	141,907	40,304	182,211	397,382	2,875	400,257

ANALYSIS OF CIRCULATION METHODS
DURING THIS PERIOD

21. REGULAR SUBSCRIPTION RATES?

	By Mail per Year	By Mail per Month	By Carrier per Year	By Carrier per Month	By Carrier per Week
Morning and Sunday	$15.00	$2.00	$12.00	$1.00	
Morning only	7.50	1.00	7.80	.65	
Sunday only	7.50	1.00	4.20	.35	

Above rates are in effect in zones 1, 2, 3 and 4.

In zones 5, 6, 7 and 8 the rates are daily and Sunday $19.50, daily only $12.00, Sunday only $7.50.

SPECIAL SUBSCRIPTION OFFERS (INCLUDING TRIAL AND SHORT TERM RATES)? None of record.

SINGLE COPY PRICE? Morning 2c, Sunday in Chicago and suburbs 7c, elsewhere 10c.

22(a) WERE RETURNS ACCEPTED?

Publisher's stated policy as to returns was city, suburban and country non-returnable for the entire period covered by this report with the exception of newsdealers in Milwaukee, Toledo and New York City who had a limited return privilege.

The actual returns together with allowances for late, non-delivered and unsold copies for the period covered by this report were found to have been: from city dealers, morning, 1.5%, Sunday, 00.5%; from suburban dealers, morning, 00.4%, Sunday, 1.31%; from country dealers, morning, 00.48%, Sunday 00.13%.

These percentages are based on the gross draw and have been properly deducted therefrom, leaving net paid circulation as shown in Par. 8.

(b), (g), (h), (l), (m) PREMIUMS, CONTESTS, ETC.

Records do not show any premiums to have been used during the period covered by this report.

Records show popularity contest was employed between the dates of Nov. 28th and Dec. 12, 1920, to ascertain the most popular motion picture actor and actress. Coupons appearing in the paper were cut out and filled in with the name of the actor or actress selected and forwarded to the publication to determine the winners.

Records also show a Beauty Contest was employed between the dates of Jan. 30, 1921, and Apr. 9, 1921, in which cash prizes amounting to $20,200.00 were to be awarded to the successful contestants. All contestants sent in their photographs and had their pictures published in the paper, the winners being selected by three judges appointed by the publication.

Records also show University Scholarship Contest employed between the dates of March 5, 1921, and Aug. 21, 1921, in which scholarships to five Universities are to be awarded to the successful contestants. The prizes consist of five 4-year scholarships in any of five Universities to be awarded to the contestants sending in the largest number of subscriptions, all other contestants (excepting the above) turning in 250 or more subscriptions are to be awarded a one-year scholarship in any of five Universities. Non-winners of scholarship prizes to receive 50c on each subscription turned in. As this contest does not close until Aug. 21, 1921, subscriptions received as a result of same cannot be ascertained at this time.

(c) CANVASSERS (IF EMPLOYED STATE WHETHER PAID BY SALARY OR COMMISSION OR BOTH)?

Records show canvassers were employed in city and country on salary basis.

(d) WERE SUBSCRIPTIONS RECEIVED FROM CLUB RAISERS PAID BY REWARDS OTHER THAN CASH?

None of record.

(e) WERE CLUBBING OFFERS MADE OF THIS AND OTHER PUBLICATIONS? None of record.

WERE SUBSCRIPTIONS RECEIVED THROUGH OR FROM OTHER PUBLISHERS? Yes.

(f) BULK SALES.

None of record.

(n) OTHER SOURCES FROM WHICH SUBSCRIPTIONS WERE RECEIVED?

Postmasters.

23. CONDITION OF COLLECTIONS AS AT (state date) Mail, April 27, 1921; All Others, Dec. 31, 1920

	CITY					SUBURBAN			COUNTRY	
	Reg. Carr'r	Dealer and Ind. Carr'r	Total	Street	Car's.	Deal's	Mail	Deal's	Mail
Paid in Advance			91.75			.60	100	.60	98
Paid on Delivery			.12						
Paid Weekly			7.57						
Paid Semi-Monthly									
Paid Monthly			.53			98.85		98.85	
Paid Quarterly									
Arrears under 6 mos.			.03			.55		.55	2
Total	100%	100%	100%	100%	100%	100%	100%	100%	100%

28. EXPLANATORY:

The average net paid circulation as reported by publisher in statements to the Bureau has been substantiated by this audit.

Records show for the period covered by this report the wholesale rates were as follows:

City distributers paid from $1.00 to $1.40 per hundred copies
daily and from $4.50 to $5.50 per hundred copies Sunday.

Suburban and country dealers paid from $1.00 to $2.50 per
hundred copies daily and from $4.50 to $7.75 Sunday.

All distributers were on a non-returnable basis except dealers
in Milwaukee, Toledo and New York City who had a limited
return privilege.

For comparative purposes we give below the net paid circulation by quarters as shown in audits for the previous three years,
as well as the quarterly averages for the period covered by this
report.

		Daily	Sunday			Daily	Sunday
2nd quarter	1917	388,437	640,044	2nd quarter	1919	412,649	668,386
3rd quarter	1917	373,919	588,251	3rd quarter	1919	436,456	664,605
4th quarter	1917	362,777	601,340	4th quarter	1919	421,277	715,377
1st quarter	1918	372,492	608,919	1st quarter	1920	420,202	749,836
2nd quarter	1918	393,229	650,305	2nd quarter	1920	420,782	715,440
3rd quarter	1918	422,432	615,738	3rd quarter	1920	453,257	707,064
4th quarter	1918	435,008	688,699	4th quarter	1920	453,245	757,010
1st quarter	1919	412,935	698,554	1st quarter	1921	468,356	818,894

City—Chicago, Ill.

Date—May, 1921.

                                AUDIT BUREAU OF CIRCULATIONS.

Figure 107: Sample A. B. C. newspaper report

GROWTH IN NEWSPAPER CIRCULATION

As reliable data concerning total circulation extending
back over a considerable number of years are not available,
an accurate picture of the growth of circulation cannot be
obtained. This is due in large measure to the unreliability
of the circulation figures that were available up to about 10
years ago. It will be of interest, however, to note the
growth in circulation in recent years of a number of typical
papers. For example, in 1912 the Chicago dailies had a
total combined circulation of approximately 1,100,000; in
1920 they had a total combined circulation of approximately
1,732,000. The *Boston Post,* one of the large daily papers,
is an illustration of growth from a relatively small circula-

tion to a very large circulation in a short period of time. In 1900 the circulation of the *Boston Post* was 20,000; in 1921 it was approximately 420,000. The *New York Times* has likewise had a very phenomenal growth, as may be seen from the following figures:

	Average Circulation		Average Circulation
1896	21,516	1910	191,981
1900	82,106	1915	318,274
1905	120,710	1920	342,553

It has been stated above that the total combined circulation of daily newspapers is approximately 32,000,000. This makes approximately one daily newspaper to three inhabitants. It is interesting to note the variation of newspaper circulation by states and sections of the country. A tabulation was prepared by Mr. T. M. Shepard under the direction of the author on this question. The total circulation in each state of the daily papers listed in the *Standard Rate and Data Service*, February, 1921, was ascertained. These figures were then expressed in terms of the percentage of newspaper circulation to population; that is, in Table 152, Massachusetts, which has a total circulation of 3,206,000 and a population of 3,852,000 is in the lead with a percentage of 83. The percentage ratios for the various states in order are given in the table.

This tabulation is, of course, based not on the complete newspaper circulation but on approximately two-thirds of the total newspaper circulation. This, however, probably does not introduce any serious error so far as the relative rankings of the various states are concerned. One point which no doubt to some extent affects the results is the fact that daily papers published in certain large cities are distributed over a considerable area, although they may be actually credited only to the circulation of that one state. There is a certain amount of overlapping among the various adjoining states. Thus, for example, the Chicago daily

TABLE 152

PERCENTAGE OF NEWSPAPER CIRCULATION TO POPULATION

Massachusetts	83	California	56
Missouri	67	Illinois	55
Oregon	58	Arizona	53
New York	57	Washington	52
Colorado	50	Georgia	21
Minnesota	47	Florida	20
Maryland	46	Maine	19
Pennsylvania	45	New Jersey	18
Ohio	43	Kentucky	18
Nebraska	42	Nevada	18
Michigan	39	Virginia	17
Rhode Island	39	Idaho	17
Iowa	37	West Virginia	14
Montana	32	Wyoming	14
Connecticut	30	Vermont	13
Utah	30	South Dakota	13
Texas	26	North Dakota	13
Louisiana	26	New Hampshire	12
Tennessee	25	North Carolina	12
Indiana	23	Arkansas	11
Kansas	23	Alabama	10
Delaware	23	South Carolina	9
Wisconsin	21	New Mexico	8
Oklahoma	21	Mississippi	3

papers have a certain amount of circulation in Wisconsin, Iowa, Indiana, and Michigan. This weakness may be off-set by the fact that Iowa papers published along the Mississippi River circulate also on the Illinois side. The same point would occur in the case of papers published in Minneapolis. It undoubtedly introduces a certain amount of error, however, such as in the case of the large Boston dailies having a circulation all over New England. Computation based on the *Standard Rate and Data Service* would credit this circulation only to Massachusetts. This undoubtedly explains in part why Massachusetts stands so high.

Distribution of Newspaper Circulation. A tabulation was made to ascertain the average amount of circulation of a newspaper in the city in which it is published, the average amount of circulation in suburban territory, and finally the average amount of circulation in the country at large. For this tabulation two papers in each state were selected by chance. The proportion of circulation in each of these three divisions was ascertained. The tabulation for these 98 papers showed that an average of 54% of the circulation is in the city, 26% in the suburbs, and 20% in the country at large.

OVERLAPPING OF NEWSPAPER CIRCULATION

An investigation was carried out in the City of Boston to ascertain the amount of overlapping of newspaper circulation among readers of the various papers. A total of over 5,000 persons were questioned regarding the newspapers which they read. These inquiries were made of customers in a store, after they had made a purchase. The sales clerk

TABLE 153

PERCENTAGE OF DUPLICATION OF BOSTON NEWSPAPERS

Based on the papers read by 5,000 customers of a store. The figures are valid only for the one store and not for all readers of these papers or for another store.

Distribution of Papers			Percentage			
Papers			American		C. S. M.	
	Number of Mentions	Per Cent of Total	No.	Per Cent	No.	Per Cent
American	732	7.6			6	.82
Christian Science Monitor	76	.8	6	7.9		
Globe	2,498	25.8	346	13.9	19	.76
Herald	1,547	16	80	5.2	22	1.4
Post	2,382	24.6	375	15.7	12	.5
Record	199	2.1	27	13.6	3	1.5
Transcript	1,156	12	64	5.5	16	1.4
Traveler	1,073	11.1	126	11.7	11	1

The two columns under each paper show, first, the actual number of duplications and, second, the percentage of duplication with the paper mentioned at the left on the same line. The first column at the left shows

asked the customer what newspapers he or she read. The results of this investigation are given in Table 153.

RATES FOR NEWSPAPER SPACE

Perhaps the best conception of the nature of advertising rates may be obtained by an examination of typical advertising rate cards. The two cards shown in Figures 108 and 109 illustrate the rates for the *Boston Globe* and the *Boston Post*.

Compared with magazine rates, it will be observed that there are a larger number of detailed statements of rates for various types of positions and commodities advertised. For example, in the rate card of the *Boston Globe*, the most highly preferred position is of course on the first page. Then this varies according to the commodity advertised. Thus, political advertising on the first page has a rate of $2.50 as compared with other advertising on the first page, for which the rate is $1.50. The base rate for run-of-paper position is 45 cents per line.

TABLE 153 *(Continued)*
PERCENTAGE OF DUPLICATION OF BOSTON NEWSPAPERS

Based on the papers read by 5,000 customers of a store. The figures are valid only for the one store and not for all readers of these papers or for another store.

of Duplication

Globe		Herald		Post		Record		Transcript		Traveler	
No.	Per Cent	No.	Per Cent	No.	Per Cent	No.	Per Cent	No.	Per Cent	No.	Per Cent
346	47.3	80	10.9	375	51.2	27	3.7	64	8.7	126	17.3
19	25	22	29	12	16	3	3.9	16	21	11	14.5
		369	14.8	1,059	42.4	83	3.3	328	13.1	400	16
369	23.9			321	20.7	85	5.5	595	38.5	297	19.2
1,059	44.5	321	13.5			62	2.6	263	11	448	18.8
83	41.5	85	42.7	62	31.2			39	19.6	46	23.1
328	28.4	595	51.5	263	22.8	39	3.4			187	i6.2
400	37.3	297	27.7	448	41.8	46	4.3	187	17.4		

the number of customers reading each paper, and the next column shows the percentage of that number of the total.

THE BOSTON POST
Boston, Mass.
Published Daily, Weekday Mornings, Sunday Mornings

RATE CARD No. 3
Issued June 10, 1920   Effective July 1, 1920

1—GENERAL ADVERTISING PER AGATE LINE:

a. Base Rate   Daily $0.60
                          Sunday   .55

b. No time discount.

c. No space discount.

d. Next to Reading   15% extra
Following and next Reading   25% extra
Specified Pages, 2 or 3, at publisher's option   50% extra
Specified Pages, 4 or 5, at publisher's option   25% extra
Editorial Page   25% extra
Sporting Page   25% extra
No advertisements of less than 42 lines accepted for "full position"; "next to reading" 20 lines.

e. Minimum depth for 2-column advertisements, 28 lines; 3-column, 42 lines; 4-column, 56 lines; 5-column, 70 lines; 6-7-8 columns, 84 lines.

f. Contracts not made for more than one year.

Orders for one or more insertions, carrying indefinite printed clauses, shall not be considered as contracts for space or rates.

"Till Forbid" orders are subject to change in rate without notice.

The receipt of orders shall be construed by the publisher as acceptance of all conditions of the current rate card.

Advertisements, set as imitation readers, must be marked "Advertisement" at top.

All Contracts and circulation guarantees conditional on strikes, fires, war, inability to obtain raw materials, or any cause not subject to the control of the publisher.

All rate cards of prior date void after July 1, 1920.

2—CLASSIFICATIONS: Daily   Sunday
a. First Page $2.00 $2.00

Last Page	.65	
Outside Pages of Sections		.60
Financial	.60	.60
Oil and Mining	.75	.75
Amusements, Excursions, etc.	.60	.60
Automobiles and Accessories	.60	.55
Political, First Page	3.00	3.00
Political, Last Page	1.50	1.50
Political, r. o. p.	1.00	1.00
Publications	.60	.55

b. "Position" not sold on first page.

ADVERTISEMENTS IN COLORS IN THE SUNDAY POST:

Quarter Page	$ 400.00
Half Page	700.00
Full Page	1,350.00

Space in Color Section printed in black, per agate
line.   Inside pages .60   Back pages .65

CLASSIFIED ADVERTISEMENTS

Rate per Agate Line, Display and Solid—Count Six
Words to a Line on Wants.

All classifications not noted herewith	Daily	$0.45
	Sunday	.35
Advertisements out of proper classification		.60
Information wanted		.60
Real Estate	Daily	.45
	Sunday	.35
Situations wanted	Daily	.30
	Sunday	.25
Legislative and other Hearings		.45
Corporation or Legal Notices, Proposals, etc.		.45
Church, Sunday Services		.25
Births, Marriages, Deaths, 4 lines or less, $1.00;		
each additional line		.25

3—READING NOTICES:

a. Accepted for inside pages only. Nonpareil, count lines,
$2.50. Heading $2.50 per agate line.

b. Must be marked "advt." at bottom.

4—COMMISSION AND CASH DISCOUNT:

a. Agency Commission 15%.

b. Cash discount 2% for payment by 20th of the month.

5—MECHANICAL REQUIREMENTS:

a. Width of column, 12½ pica ems or 29 agate lines.

b. Depth of column 296 lines, or 21⅛ inches.

c. Eight columns to page.

d. Center double page space—21 inches deep, 35 ½ inches wide.

e. Full page contains 2,368 agate lines.

Color Section—columns 296 lines deep—7 columns to the page i. e.: page is 21⅛ inches deep, 15 inches wide.

f. Copy required three weeks prior to publication on color advertising.

g. Half tone screen required, 65.

h. Can use mats. Prefer unmounted electros.

Can make cuts from photographs or line drawings.

Figure 108: Sample rate card for a newspaper

Preferred positions are not in general as specifically and uniformly agreed upon among newspapers as they are among magazines. This is partly due to the fact that the newspaper has a variety of features, and also to the fact that it is composed of several sections, so that there may be first pages on a number of sections.

The rate card of the *Boston Post* is somewhat simpler than that of the *Globe.* In addition to locations on certain pages or opposite certain departments, other special positions are recognized, such as next-to-reading-matter, or following-reading-matter. Among these special positions the most highly preferred position on a page is what is known as a "full" position. By "full" position is meant a space at the top of the page bounded on both sides and at the bottom by reading matter. Obviously this is the most desirable position on a page.

Classified rates are stated in great detail by most of the larger newspapers, and cover a large variety of classifications. As an illustration, note the classified rates for the *Boston Daily Globe:*

Boston Sunday Globe

General Business

Per single col., agate line, each day

First Page	$2.00
Editorial Page	.70
Main Section and First Page of 2nd Section	.70
Table Gossip, opp. Table Gossip, opp. Editorial, Household and Other Outside Section Pages	.55
Latest Publications (Run of Paper)	.55
Railroads	.55
Remedies, Medicines, etc., Main News Section, and 1st Page of 2d Section (25% extra for position)	.75
Remedies, Medicines, etc. (Run of Paper) (25% extra for position)	.55
Political (First Page)	3.00
Political (Run of Paper)	.75
Run of Paper	.55
Financial	.50
Automobile	.50
Amusements (Run of Paper)	.60
Toilet Preparations, Main News Sections, and First Page of 2d Section	.70
Toilet Preparation, Run of Paper	.55
Reading Notices ⎰ First Page—Advt.	4.00
Nonpareil ⎱ Any Other Page—Advt.	2.50

Color Section Rates

Advts. in color, per agate line (minimum ⅛ page)	1.00
Advts. in black on color pages, per agate line	.75
Advts. in black on other pages, per agate line	.60

Color advts. must be released three weeks in advance of publication.

Boston Daily Globe

Morning and Evening

Per single col., agate line, each day

First Page	$1.50
Editorial Page	.50
Last Page	.45
Inside Pages, except Editorial	.45
Latest Publications (Run of Paper)	.45
Political (First Page)	2.50

Political (Run of Paper)	.75
Railroads	.45
Remedies, Medicines, etc. (Run of Paper) (25% extra for position)	.50
Run of Paper	.45
Financial	.50
Automobile	.45
Amusements (Run of Paper)	.60
Toilet Preparations	.45
Reading Notices ⎰First Page—Advt.	4.00
Nonpareil ⎱Any Other Page—Advt.	2.50

SUNDAY MAGAZINE RATES

Run of paper (on any page except the 1st) .60

These rates are flat and there are no extra charges or discounts of any name or nature.

Width of column	2 inches
Length of column, 235 agate lines	
Columns to a page	5
Agate lines to the inch	14

Copy must be released two weeks in advance of date of publication.

NO DISCOUNTS OF ANY KIND OR CHARACTER

Reading Matter, Cuts and Extra Large Type Must Be Acceptable to the Publisher.

BOSTON DAILY GLOBE RATES—WANT CLASSIFICATIONS

In Effect April 15, 1921
No Discount for Cash or Repeated Insertions

Rate per Agate Line

	Solid	Display		Solid	Display
Agents, etc.	40c	40c	Auctions—Real Estate	35c	40c
Rate for "Agents," "Partners," Outside "Salesmen" or "Saleswomen" ordered under Male or Female Help is 50c solid, 50c display.			Auction Sales	35c	40c
			Automobile Insurance	40c	40c
			Automobiles (Used Cars)	35c	35c
			Autumn Resorts	35c	40c
			Billiards and Pool	40c	40c
			Board and Rooms	30c	35c
Antiques and Curios	40c	40c	Business Chances	35c	40c
Apartments and Tenements	35c	40c	Business Notices	40c	40c
			Business Personals	40c	40c
Auctions—Automobiles	35c	35c	Carpet and Vacuum Cleaners	40c	40c
Auctions—Horses and Carriages	35c	40c	Cash Registers	40c	40c

Church Services	25c	25c	Photographs, Cameras,		
City of Boston	35c	35c	etc.	35c	40c
Clothing	40c	40c	Poultry, Pigeons, etc.	35c	40c
Copartnership Notices	35c	35c	Proposals	40c	40c
Coastwise Steamship Lines	40c	40c	Real Estate for Exchange	35c	40c
Detective Agencies	45c	45c	Real Estate Mortgages	35c	40c
Diamonds, Jewelry, etc.	45c	45c	Refrigerators, etc.	35c	40c
Dogs, Cats, Pets, etc.	35c	40c	Safes	35c	35c
Dramatic	40c	40c	Schools, Colleges, etc.	40c	40c
Dressmaking, Millinery,			Sewing Machines	35c	40c
etc.	40c	40c	Showcases, Desks, etc.	35c	40c
Farm and Garden	35c	40c	Situations Wanted—		
Financial	50c	50c	Female	20c	30c
For Adoption	40c	40c	Situations Wanted—Male	20c	30c
For Sale	35c	40c	Situations Wanted (Emp.		
Furniture, etc.	35c	40c	Agencies)	40c	40c
Hearings	35c	40c	Spirit Meetings	40c	40c
Heating and Cooking	35c	40c	Sporting Goods	40c	40c
Help Wanted (Female)	35c	40c	Storage	40c	40c
Help Wanted (Male)	35c	40c	Stores, Offices, etc.	35c	40c
Help Wanted (Emp.			Summer Cottages	35c	40c
Agencies)	40c	40c	Summer Home Supplies	40c	40c
Horses, Carriages, etc.	35c	40c	Summer Resorts	35c	40c
Hotels	45c	45c	Sunday Meetings	25c	25c
Houses to Let and			The Ballroom	40c	40c
Wanted	35c	40c	Toilet and Invalid Articles,		
Information Wanted	35c	40c	etc.	40c	40c
Legal Notices	30c	30c	Tours and Travel	40c	40c
Legislative Hearings	35c	40c	Typewriters, etc.	35c	40c
Live Stock	35c	40c	Wall Papers	35c	40c
Lost, Found, etc.	40c	40c	Wanted	40c	40c
Machinery and Tools	35c	40c	Winter Resorts	35c	40c
Mail Order Business	40c	40c	Yachts, Boats, etc.	35c	40c
Meetings	40c	40c	Advts. out of classification	50c	50c
Miscellaneous	40c	40c			
Money to Loan	50c	50c	On Advertisements which do not		
Motor Trucking	35c	35c	properly come under classification,		
Railroads	50c	50c	50c will be charged in all instances		
Real Estate	35c	40c	except where the net rate is higher.		
Motorcycles, Bicycles, etc.	35c	35c	This applies especially to ads under		
Music	35c	35c	"Auction," "Help Wanted," "Real		
Musical Instruments	35c	40c	Estate," etc.		
Notices	35c	40c	No Want Ad Taken for Less Than		
Ocean Steamship Lines	40c	40c	2 Lines		
Parcel Post	40c	40c	No Advertisement with a Border		
Patents	40c	40c	Taken for Less Than 10 Lines		

Figure 109: Sample rate card of classified advertising in a newspaper

The differences shown in rates for various types of business in the classified space are probably to quite an extent due to traditional development and to some extent due to the ability of the advertiser to pay. For example, rates

No Want Ad Taken for Less Than

for "Situations Wanted" are 20 cents, as compared with "Money to Loan," 50 cents, or hotel advertising, 45 cents.

In this connection it will be of interest to compare the milline rate of newspapers with that of magazines. Table 154 shows the relationship between circulation of newspapers and the milline rate. This table was based upon the newspapers listed in the *Standard Rate and Data Service* for February, 1921:

TABLE 154

MILLINE RATES FOR NEWSPAPERS

Circulation	Number of Papers	Average Milline Rate
100,000 and over	47	$ 2.25
25,000 to 99,999	122	3.17
1,000 to 24,999	419	9.43
0 to 999	21	26.19
All morning dailies	136	6.57
All evening dailies	473	8.67

It is evident from these figures that there is an inverse relationship between the milline rate and the size of the circulation. The same fact was found to be true in the case of the magazines. Thus the milline rate of papers with a circulation of less than one thousand is approximately 12 times that of papers whose circulation is one hundred thousand and over.

It will also be noted that the milline rate for evening papers is slightly higher than that for morning papers. This is probably due to two factors. In the first place, evening papers include a considerably larger number of small publications. Only the larger publishers are in a position to issue morning papers. This factor may account for most if not all of the difference between the average milline rates for the two types of papers. A second factor which may play a minor part, however, is that evening papers may be regarded as being read somewhat more thoroughly, and for that reason may be able to obtain a somewhat higher rate.

XXXI

DIRECT MAIL MATERIAL

The growth of direct mail advertising. Classes of direct mail material. A comparison of mail material with other mediums. 1. Directness; 2. Elasticity; 3. Personal element. Uses of direct mail material. Results of direct mail advertising. How to carry out direct mail advertising effectively.

In the figures presented in Chapter XXVIII it was shown that in 1920 approximately $300,000,000 was expended for various forms of direct mail advertising. This is approximately 25% of the total expenditure for advertising. At the same ratio, with the expenditure of $1,000,000,000 in 1922, some $250,000,000 was expended for direct mail advertising. This indicates something of the enormous volume of this particular advertising medium alone. Compared with other items, it will be noted that it is second to newspapers in the total expenditure for advertising; it is approximately half of the amount expended for newspaper advertising.

Aside from the actual expenditure for this form of advertising, the importance of direct mail material is further indicated by the fact that it has become a constantly increasing element in sales activities. Sales letters, circulars, and catalogs have been playing an increasing part in sales plans. Historically, this type of medium has increased rapidly with the introduction of means by which direct mail material could be easily and conveniently prepared. The universal use of typewriters and the wide use of duplicating machines have enormously increased the volume of this class of advertising. Another reason for its growth is that by means of direct mail advertising it is possible to reach, in a fairly selected manner, the particular classes of customers or prospects who may be interested in the particular product in question. In other words, by a careful selection of the individuals to whom direct mail material is addressed, it is possible to reduce the waste circulation to a minimum. The increase in directories—telephone, commercial, fraternal, social, and the like—in recent years has stimulated the use of direct mail material because of the many possible types of addresses this has made readily available.

Mr. Robert Ramsay addressed an inquiry to a large number of national advertisers regarding the relative amounts of expenditure for direct advertising as compared with advertising in general mediums, and found that in the case of these firms the proportions were approximately $33\frac{1}{3}\%$ for direct advertising and $66\frac{2}{3}\%$ for advertising in general mediums. This inquiry included responses from such firms as Armstrong Linoleum, Buick Automobile, Glidden's Varnish, Hupmobile, Haynes Automobile, Morris & Ricker Gloves, Pyrene, Purina Mills, U. S. Cartridge Company, and others.[1]

CLASSES OF DIRECT MAIL MATERIAL

We may classify the numerous and varied types of direct mail material into the following groups, arranged approximately in the order of importance:

1. Letters. This includes personal sales letters, form letters, printed letters, and various types of miscellaneous material bearing a resemblance in general form and appeal to letters.
   2. Catalogs
   3. Booklets and circulars
   4. House organs
   5. Mailing cards
   6. Broadsides
   7. Enclosures

[1] *Postage*, April and May, 1918, pp. 8, 9, 17, and 30.

8. Package inserts
9. Folders
10. Poster stamps
11. Miscellaneous, including blotters, coupons, photographs, novelties, samples, etc.
12. Portfolios
13. Almanacs

A word of explanation may be necessary in connection with several of the above classifications. Most of them are obvious. By a mailing card is meant a small-sized piece of cardboard or stiff paper which may be larger than an ordinary folder or enclosure, but which is not as difficult to fold as a regular folder.

By a broadside is meant a large printed sheet which may be as large as 25x38 inches and which is folded, often in rather special ways, to a much smaller size, so that it may be mailed individually, either with or without a special envelope. Its purpose, usually, is to make a rather striking impression, either at the beginning or at the end of a series of direct mailings.

By a poster stamp obviously is meant any form of sticker or label which contains some brief advertising message, and is attached to packages and articles, and sometimes to large pieces of mail.

By enclosures are meant various forms of printed material which are enclosed in letters mailed, usually, for other purposes. For example, they are special printed material enclosed with monthly bills or other regular material or letters. Sometimes they are also called stuffers.

By package insert is meant a piece of advertising material, such as a card, a slip or bill which is inserted in a package and is aimed directly at the dealer or the consumer.

By a portfolio is meant the portfolio of an advertising campaign giving the complete campaign in proof form, which may be sent out directly, in most instances to dealers. in some instance to wholesalers, and in individual instances also to consumers. Its purpose is to present to the retailer the plan of the advertising which the manufacturer proposes to carry out for a particular product which he wishes the dealer to carry, or which the dealer is carrying.

It is, perhaps, unnecessary to point out that by a house organ is meant a publication issued by an individual firm or house, usually at regular intervals, and mailed either to its employees or to its regular customers, or to prospective customers. The purpose is to keep the particular group informed of happenings relative to the product and to the organization in whose interest it is issued. House organs are on the border line between regular periodical mediums and miscellaneous direct mail material. As most house organs are issued at regular intervals like any periodical, they may carry advertising other than that which relates directly to the concern which is issuing it. However, house organs may be said to belong in direct mail classification rather than among magazines and periodicals, since their primary purpose is to serve specifically the interests of the concerns issuing them.

The circulation of some house organs is extremely large, running, in some instances, into many thousands, and sometimes over a million circulation. Almost every organization of any size issues a publication of this sort.

Catalogs are used in very large numbers, particularly by concerns which do a great deal of direct mail-order business. The larger mail-order houses issue literally millions of catalogs each year. For example, several of the larger mail-order houses issue a large catalog twice a year, with a total distribution of from four to six million copies for each issue. In addition to these large catalogs, numerous smaller catalogs for special departments, or special occasions, are sent out.

A COMPARISON OF MAIL MATERIAL WITH OTHER MEDIUMS

Direct mail material has certain advantages and serves certain purposes which are not possessed or cannot be served by other types of mediums. As pointed out before, there is frequently an unnecessary antagonism among the different types of mediums and among firms or persons interested in the various mediums. Persons interested in direct mail advertising will point out that it is the most economical form of advertising. Publishers of newspapers, in their turn, will point out that newspaper advertising is the most economical form. The same is true of magazines and other types of mediums. It is obvious, of course, that probably no type of medium can literally claim that it is the most economical form of advertising in general. The fact is that each form of advertising serves a purpose which can probably not well be served by any other medium, and that for that particular purpose it is probably the most suitable and the most economical.

We may, therefore, point out the specific functions of direct mail advertising. Its peculiar characteristics and advantages are the following:

1. Directness. Direct mail advertising is, probably, more direct, as its name states, than most other forms of advertising, particularly if it is properly used. When the list of names is properly selected, it will go most directly to the particular customers or prospects who are most likely to be interested in buying that particular commodity. Waste distribution may, therefore, be reduced to a minimum in a way which is probably not possible in any other general medium, such as magazines or newspapers or street-car cards or billboards. The effectiveness of direct mail material, however, depends precisely upon the care and accuracy with which a list of names is prepared.

2. Elasticity. Direct mail advertising lends itself to a great deal of adjustment, variation, and individual control, both as to timeliness and with regard to the appeal which may be made. The material may be sent at a time and in a succession which will be most appropriate and most effective for a given territory and a given distribution of customers.

Timeliness may be controlled very accurately by means of direct mail material. It may be made to reach the prospect at a time when he will be most ready to give it attention and to consider the proposition presented. Mr. C. W. Hurd reports that one advertiser had mailed a form letter to several hundred persons in New York City so that it would reach them in the morning mail. A very small number of replies was received. It was then decided to change the mailing so as to reach the prospects in the afternoon delivery when there would probably be less mail received and when the attention to it might be greater. A list of prospects was made up in the same manner as for the morning delivery. The results from the afternoon delivery were reported to be approximately 10 times as large.[1]

3. The Personal Element. In the case of sales letters, personal, direct mail advertising may be adapted to the individual to almost the same degree as the personal salesman is able to adjust his sales argument to the particular customer with whom he is dealing.

USES OF DIRECT MAIL MATERIAL

The chief functions of direct mail material may be classified as follows:

1. To sell directly by mail. This is illustrated in the case of mail-order houses and mail-order departments of manufacturers and retailers. In this case all of the selling is done by the mail material.

2. To serve as a supplement to general advertising done in other mediums, as magazines and newspapers. A large proportion of general advertisers supplement their newspaper and magazine advertising with some form of direct mail material.

3. To prepare the way for the salesman before he calls.

4. To follow up a call of the salesman; to present addi-

[1] *Printers' Ink,* April 22, 1915.

tional selling arguments or to keep alive the interest which may have been created where a sale has not actually been produced by the salesman. This may be continued at intervals until the next call of the salesman if no sale is produced in the meantime. This may also serve to emphasize in particular certain important points or arguments which may have been presented either by the salesman or by other forms of advertising.

5. To make special efforts or drives in selected sections of the territory covered by the concern. A given section of a territory may be new, or may not be yielding as much business as it is expected to yield; various forms of direct mail material may be employed in that particular section to stimulate sales.

6. To meet unexpected changes and conditions which may result from certain events, happenings or weather conditions. In this respect its flexibility is similar to that of newspapers, whose advertising may be modified to meet such changing conditions.

7. To distribute samples. Samples of a product may be distributed directly through the mails and may be accompanied by various forms of printed advertising material.

RESULTS OF DIRECT MAIL ADVERTISING

The usefulness of direct mail material in connection with the work of salesmen may be illustrated in the case of a certain large concern which had been receiving but one order for seven calls of the salesman, *without* the use of direct mail material. A change was made so that three letters were sent by the firm prior to the salesman's call. The result of this was that during the next year one sale was made for every five calls of the salesman.

Much is said at times regarding the waste of material sent out directly through the mails, the impression being that much of it, if not actually all of it, is thrown into the waste-basket without any consideration on the part of the recipient. However, it will be of interest to know the results obtained where direct mail material has been suitably used and handled properly and effectively.

Much direct mail material was used in connection with the many war activities, particularly in the solicitation of funds. A striking example of its effective use was reported at the Indianapolis Convention of the Associated Advertising Clubs in 1920. A single letter, in mimeographed form, was sent out to four million persons at a total cost of $200,-000. The returns were keyed. The letter was prepared by the Staff of the *Literary Digest* and was as follows: [1]

Dear Friend:

Another little child has shriveled up and died!

The mother, creeping back, gaunt and cold, from the desert, has put down the thin little bones with those that strew the road, so—many—miles, and has sunk beside them, never to rise again.

Only a little child, and a mother, out on the bleak Armenian road—but what is that Vision hovering there—and what is that Voice the cold winds bear to the ears of our souls—"I was hungry, and ye gave me no meat—I was naked and ye clothed me not?"

Today—yes, today—while we are preparing our gifts for Christmas—many more of these little children—not a hundred, nor a thousand, but two hundred and fifty thousand of them—are still wandering uncared for and alone in that dead land, "their weazened skins clinging in fear to their rattling bones," and they are crying out with gasping breath, "I am hungry! I am hungry! I am hungry!"

Now the children and the mothers in Armenia are dreading the winter. "Just human remnants, they are, not protected, many of them, from the elements by even the dignity of rags."

But we can feed and clothe those perishing ones—some of them —before it is too late. Herbert Hoover cables from the Caucasus: "It is impossible that the loss of 20,000 lives can at this day be prevented, but the remaining 500,000 can possibly be saved." They need not starve, and freeze, and die, if we will save them. Open now your heart and purse. They need not die! Give ye them to eat!

[1] Ramsay, *Effective Direct Advertising,* p. 457.

Today nearly eight hundred thousand destitute Armenians—His people—need food and clothing. He took little children in His arms and blessed them. Today will you take one, or more, of these sad, cold, hungry little children of Armenia into your arms and heart, in His name, and give them food, and warmth, and life?

"Inasmuch as ye have done it unto one of the least of these, my brethren, ye have done it unto me."

The pledge card for your Christmas gift to Him is here in this letter.

Faithfully yours,

WM. H. TAFT,
HENRY MORGANTHAU,
ALEXANDER J. HEMPHILL,
for the Executive Committee.

The total subscriptions obtained by this one letter were $1,200,000.

The Addressograph Company of Chicago sent out, shortly after the war, a broadside entitled: "The Value of Being Prepared." This broadside was sent to 25,612 individuals at a cost of $1,135, and brought 517 inquiries, which, followed up by salesmen, produced, in six months, a total of $20,000 worth of sales.[1]

A Pittsburgh firm selling electric coal-mining machinery mailed 676 letters to prospects, offering small centrifugal pumps. The results, within three weeks, were 21 replies, 5 inquiries for pumps, and 3 sales. The net profit on the 3 sales was $470. The cost of the advertising was $48.27. It is worthy of note that the 21 replies, 5 inquiries, and 3 sales were all new business, and that the 3 orders were closed entirely by mail.[2]

A broadside of 8 pages printed in colors was sent to 110,000 hardware dealers, drug stores and department stores. The purpose of this broadside was to urge the dealer to bear Gillette safety razors in mind, and to have him order, and agree to use, window display material. A return post-card was enclosed. The total replies received were 30,000, or approximately 30% of the dealers to whom it was sent.

[1] *Ibid.*, p. 460.   [2] *Mailbag*, September, 1920.

The broadside was also sent to jobbers, of whom 85% replied.[1]

The Van Sicklen Company, Elgin, Illinois, sent out two 4-page pieces with a return unstamped postal card asking for a catalog. The product made by this company is known as the Chronometric Tachometer. The pieces were sent to a selected list of 1,900 engineers. The results were 275 returns, of which 21 were sales, and a considerable number of the others were prospects.[2]

The *Atlantic Monthly* has carried on at regular intervals solicitation by mail for subscribers. This soliciting is done, usually, by means of a so-called Almanac, together with other folders and circular letters. Mr. MacGregor Jenkins, publisher of *Atlantic Monthly*, recently stated: "Our circulation today is 81,032, of which 49,000 are subscribers. That makes a gain of 27,800 subscribers since we started our direct advertising campaign in 1912."[3]

The *Literary Digest* carries on its subscription campaigns entirely by advertising, which is done in part by advertising in newspapers and street cars, and in part by means of direct mail material. A recent statement given out by the *Literary Digest* was as follows:

Our investment is $750,000 a year in 400 newspapers. Our yearly investment in street cars for cards is $300,000. The most important feature of the plan is not so evident. It is a part of our main campaign, the object of which is not only to secure new subscribers but to increase the national prestige of the *Literary Digest*. There are approximately 9,000,000 (1918 figures) telephone subscribers in the United States. Three times a year we write 6,000,000 of the best of them a personal letter telling them about the editorial features of the publication and soliciting their subscriptions. In the larger cities we send these letters under first-class postage. . . . Our newspaper work this last year has, of course, made this direct-by-mail work more productive. We find that each kind of advertising we do helps the others

[1] *Printers' Ink*, Jan. 4, 1917. [2] *Printer's Ink Monthly*, January, 1920.

[3] *Direct Advertising*, Vol 4, No. 1.

and they all dovetail in together as do the various forms of advertising done by national advertisers. . . . I wish to emphasize this fact, that every subscriber to the *Digest* comes to us through printers' ink of some kind. We have no solicitors, and no subscription is secured because of friendship or because of a salesman's strong personality.

Wm. J. Moxley, Inc., Chicago, carried on a campaign consisting of several broadsides and letters sent out for the purpose of securing new dealers. The company succeeded in obtaining 6,815 dealers in 90 days. This plan is described in the *Mailbag* [1] as follows:

THREE DEALER BROADSIDES

These were 14 x 21 inches in size, printed in two colors, from illustrations made from photographs posed by live models. The broadsides were folded to 10½ x 4¾ before mailing.

Number one approached the dealer from a basis of asking his advice, the headline being, "Will You Help Us Answer This Important Question?" The question being, "Shall we advertise in the big magazines or spend the money with you?" The latter referred to a series of three illustrated letters which would be sent direct to the dealer's prospects at the manufacturer's expense.

Number two. "A Profitable Partnership." This broadside approached the very important subject that no dealer was interested merely in the amount of business but also in the PROFITS he could make.

Number three. ". . . . and then he dictated this letter." This piece brought in the outside viewpoint, showing a letter from a dealer's customer to the manufacturer, taking up the advantages of the average dealer handling the product.

FOUR "NEW ACCOUNT" LETTERS

The purpose of these was to keep continually sold the dealer who had already been sold on the product.

Number one was written on the regular stationery of the company signed by "Director of Sales," and with imprinted department heading: "Office of Director of Sales." The letter was to secure the cooperation of the dealer until actual buying demand would keep the cooperation alive.

Number two, mailed two days after, was on the personal (baro-

nial style) stationery of the president. The president congratu-
lated the dealer, having just heard the news from the director of
sales.

Number three was a four-page letterhead printed in two colors
from "Director of Advertising." This played up the advertising
cooperation.

Number four, another four-page letterhead from the "Manager
of Production," sold the dealer on the quality and uniformity of
product.

All these letters were carefully procèssed and filled-in to match
with dealers' names, and each was signed with a pen-and-ink
signature.

Three "Dealer-to-Consumer" Letters

The preceding were selling the dealer. The following were
serving him by selling the consumer.

Number one, featuring food value and recipes, was mailed in
a No. 9 envelope (penny-saver). It was four-page in style, and
was printed in colors on a heavy folding enamel stock. The object was to get the housewife addressed to try one pound of the
oleomargarine.

Number two, likewise a four-page letter, was the dealer's recommendation, and laid especial stress on the wholesomeness of
the product.

Number three was a one-page letter giving the dealer's argument for customers and his guarantee.

Instances of results obtained from direct mail advertising might be multiplied indefinitely. Not all direct mail
advertising campaigns are, of course, effective or successful. The important thing to bear in mind here is that they
are effective when they are properly planned, properly coordinated with other activities, and used in cases where direct mail material may reasonably be expected to bring
returns. The fallacious inference which is sometimes made
from a citation of rather glowing results is that all advertising, whether it be direct mail or any other form, is uniformly
and highly effective and that anything may be accomplished
by it. There are failures here as there are in other types
of business activities. The value of citing successful cases

lies in analyzing them to ascertain the methods employed and the factors which contributed toward the results.

A careful analysis of the problems involved in direct mail advertising shows rather plainly that they are substantially the same as those occurring in any other form of advertising. A detailed study and analysis of direct mail advertising may therefore be considered from the point of view of the five fundamental problems outlined in Chapter I, viz:

1. To whom may the product be sold?
2. By what appeals may it be sold?
3. How may the appeals be presented most effectively?
4. The mediums in this case would be the direct mail mediums.
5. What is a reasonable expenditure for direct mail material for the particular situation in question?

If direct mail advertising is a part of the larger general advertising plans of a concern, and if the advertiser has therefore made a careful study of the fundamental facts and data necessary for making his plans intelligently, he will have at hand most of the information necessary for the carrying out of his direct mail plans in a proper way. If, however, the direct mail advertising is his sole form of advertising, then obviously it will be necessary for him to carry out the required research for obtaining definite information regarding the four fundamental problems outlined.

The first question, To whom may the product be sold? if properly analyzed and investigated, will provide information on the basis of which to prepare a suitable list of the prospects to whom to send the mail material. A detailed study of this problem will show where the market lies, who the prospects are, and how they may be reached.

In order that direct mail material may be used as economically as possible, it is highly important to prepare the mailing list in the most careful manner, and to keep it as accurate and up-to-date as possible. Changes in addresses are very frequent and direct mail advertisers often make the mistake of not paying sufficient attention to keeping a proper list and keeping it accurate and up-to-date. Often mailing lists are not only months, but several years, out of date. It has been pointed out by users of mail material that a list ought to be revised at regular intervals, possibly as often as every three or six months. Firms which send out a considerable amount of direct mail material at regular intervals often send out a special inquiry, usually a return postal card, asking the recipient to state whether or not his address is correct, and whether or not he is interested in receiving continuously the particular pieces of mail being sent to him.

It is stated by persons who regularly use mailing lists that over 20% of the addresses of families change every year; that somewhere between 15% and 20% of addresses of dealers change; and that in some of the trades changes of addresses run over 30%. Mr. F. C. Drew reports in *Postage*, May, 1918, a direct mail campaign which failed primarily because of a defective mailing list. The product, the price, and the terms of sale were satisfactory from every point of view. The product was a device sold to power-plant owners. "The campaign was a fizzle." "A post-mortem investigation developed that the client's mailing list which he considered good and so represented to us, was 85% useless! Eighty-five per cent of the names on it owned and operated power plants of a type which not only did not require, but could not use his device!" [1]

Names for mailing lists may be obtained from a great variety of sources: directories of various types, such as city and telephone directories; government records, such as city, county, and state records of various kinds; permits and licenses, such as building permits, automobile licenses,

[1] Ramsay, p. 115.

tax lists, etc.; membership lists of various kinds of fraternal, business and trade organizations; labor records; press items, such as social columns, local news items regarding real estate transfers, removals, changes of business, organization of new firms; the names of advertisers in various mediums; and, finally, there are the lists constructed from the inquiries received in response to general advertising in magazines and newspapers. Lists of names may also be obtained from such miscellaneous sources as investigators, delivery persons, mail carriers, school records, and the like.

The second large problem, that of the appeals, may be handled in a scientific way by methods outlined and discussed in the earlier chapters of this book. The methods there outlined are for the most part directly applicable to the handling of corresponding problems presented here. Special investigations, either by questionnaires or special tests, or other methods of securing information may be devised as the need suggests.

The third problem, the presentation of the appeal, although in the main similar to that found in other forms of advertising, presents here certain individual problems. The question is, How are the appeals and the material decided upon to be presented in the most effective manner? This large problem resolves itself into the five subdivisions already named in Part IV. The functions of an individual piece of advertising are as follows:

1. To secure attention
2. To arouse interest
3. To produce conviction
4. To produce a response
5. To impress the memory

The solution of these problems may be handled for the most part by methods similar to those outlined in Part IV. Tests may be devised as outlined.

In addition, however, direct mail material has certain supplementary problems, such as the number of pieces of direct material which should be sent to accomplish a certain purpose, the intervals which should elapse between successive mailings, and the like. There is probably no general practice regarding the number of pieces sent out or the intervals at which the various pieces are mailed. This problem is necessarily controlled by the purpose to be accomplished, by the particular product advertised, and by circumstances surrounding it, such as the coordination of salesmen, the coordination with other forms of advertising, the speed with which results must be accomplished, and so on. We find that many firms follow up their first mailing by two additional mailings, and that probably the most frequent number is three in addition to the first mailing. Beyond that, the number of firms sending out as many as five and six mailings gradually decreases.

Probably the best way to determine how many pieces should be sent out and the intervals that should be allowed to elapse between successive mailings is to keep experience records. Any concern should, as far as possible, keep a careful record of the mailings and the returns obtained thereby, so that it may decide from its own experience what is the economical limit in this regard.

Some individual instances may be of interest. The follow-up sometimes varies anywhere from one to an indefinite number of mailings. The Gibson Mandolin-Guitar Company, whose campaign was one of the prize-winners in the Direct Advertising Contest of 1919, has a series of eight follow-up pieces. The National City Company of New York has a follow-up continuing during a period of six months, in connection with inquiries about bonds.[1] An insurance agent found that four follow-up letters brought the best results in selling insurance.[2] A common practice with many firms is to follow up as many as five to seven times, at intervals of ten days or two weeks. Quite frequently the interval becomes longer for later follow-ups.

In this connection a citation in some detail of the num-

[1] *Advertising and Selling*, July 12, 1919. [2] *Mailbag*, May, 1917, p. 10.

ber of letters sent and the returns obtained by each successive letter may be of interest. Shryer tabulated the results of successive follow-up letters sent out in his campaign for the American Collection Service, as follows:

Order of Letters	Number Mailed	Number of Sales	Amount Cash	Percentage
First	28,576	368	$7,844	.012
Second	27,623	443	8,882	.015
Third	27,202	303	5,736	.011
Fourth	26,966	288	5,166	.0106
Fifth	21,962	233	3,512	.0106
Sixth	12,101	161	2,282	.018
Seventh	10,140	137	2,109	.013
Eighth	8,558	38	460	.0046
Ninth	1,205	4	57	.0033

The tabulation continues to the twenty-first letter, where the returns decreased to practically nothing.

A similar record was kept of returns for the follow-up letters sent out during a campaign for a kitchen device.

Order of Letters	Number Mailed	Number of Sales	Amount Cash	Percentage
First	4,109	166	$2,522.35	.04
Second	4,821	83	1,209.80	.017
Third	5,700	78	1,188.76	.013
Fourth	9,577	145	2,283.44	.015
Fifth	7,286	66	1,005.25	.009
Sixth	8,051	71	978.10	.008
Seventh	3,127	7	102.50	.002
Eighth	823	7	85.00	.008

It is not necessary to point out the decreasing returns due to repeated appeals. The same tendency of any series of appeals proves the fallacy of the theory that repeated stimuli cause a final surrender of the individual. Some are prone to be influenced by repeated appeals. Otherwise, it would not pay to appeal more than once to any one. The point of the matter is this: The strongest appeal is the first, other things being equal. As appeals are repeated, fewer and fewer respond. This certainly is a law. If it is a law, there is no such thing as cumulative value in publications.[1]

[1] Shryer, W. A. *Analytical Advertising.*

Quite the opposite inference may be drawn from these tables. They do not disprove cumulative value even in these follow-up letters themselves. Of course, it is obvious that the percentage of returns gradually decreases. That is necessarily expected, because the possibilities are gradually being exhausted. The very fact that succeeding letters brought any returns at all shows that repeated stimuli had an effect, otherwise all those who would be influenced to respond should have responded to the very first letter.

It will be of interest to consider here the data presented regarding the rate of forgetting, discussed on page 561. The inference to be drawn from it is that mailings should be made at shorter intervals at the beginning and at longer intervals later.

The question of whether it is more effective to send out direct mail material under one- or two-cent postage is often raised. Which is the more effective can probably not be determined as a matter of general principle, but will depend upon the individual business and circumstances surrounding it. Probably the most satisfactory method of determining this point is by means of a test campaign carried out on a limited scale in which the same piece should be sent to two comparable lists, using one-cent postage in the one case and two-cent postage in the other. A great deal obviously depends upon the manner in which the mail material is prepared. Mr. A. J. Reiss, of the Sherwin-Williams Company, stated at the Cleveland Direct Advertising Convention:

We use the penny saver envelopes (a patented envelope giving the appearance of a sealed envelope, but open to inspection at the end, and mailable at third-class rate) with the green (one cent) stamp. We had formerly used the two-cent stamp, but we found by actual test that the one-cent stamp gave us just as good results.[1]

Mr. W. A. Hersey, of Robert H. Ingersoll & Brother, re-

[1] *Marketing*, March, 1920.

ported that they had sent out 2,500 pieces as first-class mail, the enclosure offering a stock-keeping system for jewelers. Later on 2,500 pieces were sent out as third-class mail to a list of substantially the same character and possibilities. There was no difference in the results. The first-class mailing brought one more reply than the third class.[1]

The problem of making the address as personal as possible is often discussed in the same connection. Mr. Charles W. Hoyt reported at the Toronto Convention of Associated Advertising Clubs that a thousand letters were sent out as first-class mail in which the names were carefully filled in, and one thousand letters were sent out under one-cent postage, in which the names were not filled in. The former brought 14% replies, the latter 2%. The letter advertised a book. Mr. O. C. Harn, of the National Lead Company, speaking at the same convention, reported a test covering three lists of 5,000 names each. To one list an original printed circular was sent; to the second list a filled-in letter was sent; and to the third a non-filled-in letter was sent. Mr. Harn reported that the printed circular produced the largest percentage of returns.[2]

The principles of securing attention and interest and producing conviction, outlined in the chapters in Part IV, are directly applicable, and can be used with very little adaptation or modification. Scientific methods of testing various elements, by the laboratory method or other means as outlined, may be applied here equally well for determining the relative values of letters, circulars or booklets.

One point that ought to be further emphasized is the great negligence in the handling of inquiries produced by advertising. The value of inquiries depends to a very large extent upon the manner in which they are handled, upon the follow-up that is sent, and the promptness and care with which inquiries are taken care of. The negligence found in many concerns is illustrated in the case of a certain business man who had spent a considerable amount

[1] Ramsay, p. 418. [2] Ibid., p. 228.

of money in advertising, but who found that his office had allowed inquiries to pile up to so great an extent while he had been away for a few days that he was unable to do anything else until he had cleared them away. The correspondence coming into the average business office frequently contains many hidden leads which, when carefully followed up, produce profitable business. There is often much loss from delay in answering inquiries. Answers must be made promptly and appropriately. Strike while the iron is hot, is a proper maxim to bear in mind in this connection. It is an all too common practice among business concerns to attend to everything else before looking after inquiries.

XXXII

STREET-CAR CARDS

Street-railway cards as an advertising medium. The number of street cars in the United States. Control of space. Proportion of passengers looking at cards.

THE placard, as an advertising medium, has assumed general importance only in recent years, and is still regarded by many as a form of advertising merely subsidiary to the magazine or the newspaper. There are, however, several prominent national advertisers who have built up their business primarily through the street-railway cards. This is particularly true of food products, toilet articles, and many local commodities. The Heinz "57 varieties" were popularized largely through street cars and billboards.

Some of the distinctive features of street-railway cards are:

1. So far as attention value goes, every card has an equal chance with every other card, as all spaces are of the same size. The small advertiser, therefore, cannot be overshadowed by the large advertiser, as may be the case in a magazine or newspaper. Furthermore, there is little or no difference in positions. All have practically an equally advantageous location. The only exception is in rare instances where cards are placed over the doors.

2. Car placards have been free from objectionable advertising. The advertiser in street cars is not exposed to the danger of being placed in juxtaposition to a fraudulent or deceptive advertisement. The cards are so constantly before the people that common sentiment has kept the objectionable advertiser out of the street cars.

3. The seeing of placards requires a minimum of effort.

They appeal entirely to the passive attention of the reader. While this may have its drawbacks, it has the advantage of reaching people who may pay little attention to advertisements in the newspaper or magazine. Every passenger in a street car has the cards before his eyes. He becomes familiar with them unconsciously, as the following incident shows. A certain woman claimed that she paid no attention whatever to the cards on the street car line on which she had traveled for years; yet, upon being questioned, she showed familiarity with practically every product advertised in those cars.

4. Street-railway cards are practically a universal medium reaching all classes of people who live in cities. Probably a fair estimate is that 85% to 90% of all adults in cities ride on street cars with some regularity. Street car advertising is particularly effective in reaching the lower classes of people, classes who are little influenced by newspapers and not at all by magazines. The placard, like the billboard, reaches the masses.

5. The street-car cards are usually the last advertisements seen by shoppers. They consequently afford excellent opportunity to present the commodities that are bought on a shopping trip, such as foods, household articles, toilet articles, wearing apparel, etc. Placards serve as the last reminders.

6. Cards are read repeatedly and in a leisurely mood. Professor Scott has pointed out that the things with which we spend much time unconsciously assume much importance in our minds.

The passengers on street railways have but little to distract their attention. They go over the same road so frequently that the streets passed through cease to be interesting. Since newspapers and magazines cannot be easily read, the cards have but few rivals for attention. Even those who have but little interest in the advertisements find that they glance at the cards frequently and that the eyes rest on a single card for a considerable length of time. . . . The goods which through their advertisements have occupied our minds for long periods of time assume in our minds an importance which is often far in excess of anything which would have been anticipated by one who is not familiar with the peculiar power here described. In estimating the relative values of two competing lines of goods, I assume that my judgment is based on the goods themselves as they are presented to my reason. I am not aware of the fact that I am prejudiced in favor of the goods that have occupied my mind the longest periods of time.[1]

TABLE 155
NUMBER OF STREET CARS IN THE UNITED STATES

New England States		Southern States	
Connecticut	1,869	Alabama	427
Maine	538	Arkansas	240
Massachusetts	6,411	Florida	305
New Hampshire	290	Georgia	677
Rhode Island	1,082	Louisiana	654
Vermont	127	Mississippi	116
Total	9,317	North Carolina	187
		Tennessee	741
Eastern States		Total	3,670
Delaware	225		
District of Columbia	1,124	Western States	
Maryland	2,050	Arizona	52
New Jersey	3,171	California	3,661
New York	17,762	Colorado	444
Pennsylvania	7,419	Idaho	37
Virginia	775	Kansas	369
West Virginia	632	Montana	119
Total	33,158	Nebraska	583
		Nevada	9
Central States		New Mexico	16
Illinois	5,815	North Dakota	37
Indiana	1,867	Oklahoma	292
Iowa	941	Oregon	731
Kentucky	1,013	South Dakota	33
Michigan	2,792	Utah	214
Minnesota	1,377	Washington	1,129
Missouri	2,667	Wyoming	15
Ohio	5,165	Total	9,038
Wisconsin	902		
Total	22,539	Grand Total	77,772

[1] Scott, *Psychology of Advertising*, p. 224.

THE NUMBER OF STREET CARS IN THE UNITED STATES

According to the *Electrical Railway Directory* for 1920, there are in the various states of the country the numbers of street cars as shown in Table 155.

The largest number of street cars in any one state is, of course, in New York (17,762); the second largest is in Pennsylvania (7,419); Massachusetts is third (6,411); and Illinois is fourth (5,815). At the other extreme the smallest number of cars in Nevada (9), Wyoming (15), and New Mexico (16). The total number of cars in the United States in 1910 was approximately 50,000. Thus, there has been a very large increase during the past 10 years.

The average street car has 30 card positions. This makes a total for the entire country of approximately 2,331,660 cards.

Facts concerning the number of passengers carried are of interest. Thus, for example, in New York City in 1919 a total of 2,079,942,604 passengers were carried, or 570 passengers carried each day by each car.

CONTROL OF SPACE

The development of the use of cards in street cars is relatively recent and has come about chiefly since the general use of the electric street car. The first attempt to handle systematically the sale of space in street cars was in the early '70s in New York City. It is said that the first man to secure the rights to place cards in street cars was W. J. Carleton, a conductor on the Third Avenue Line in New York City, about 1875. He began by tacking up signs in his car for some of his patrons. In 1886 he came to Boston and made contracts for inserting cards. At that time there were no standard cards and there were no general contracts. This arrangement finally extended to a number of other cities so that in the late '80s arrangements were made by W. J. Carleton and George Kissam for the control of about 4,000 cars in New York, Boston, and Chicago.

About 1890 the Randall Card Rack was devised which permitted the use of standardized cards and made possible a more frequent change of copy.

In the early '90s Artemus Ward (trading as Ward and Gow) organized a syndicate of contractors in 10 large cities and undertook to sell space on a standardized basis. This did not succeed well in view of the fact that the various contractors quite frequently cut the rates. This syndicate was then abandoned and a little later there was developed the Street Railways Advertising Company.

The result of this growth has been that we have at the present time in all cars of the country uniform standardized cards the dimensions of which are 11 x 21 inches. Practically all of the street-car space of the country is under the control of the following firms:

The Eastern Advertising Company of Boston, controlling all of New England, about 9,000 cars.

Artemus Ward (Ward & Gow), controlling the New York subways and elevated lines (about 4,000 cars).

The Philadelphia Rapid Transit Co., controlling the cars in Philadelphia, about 2,700.

The Chicago Elevated Car Co.

The Broadway Home Boro Car Advertising Company, controlling the Brooklyn street cars.

The Street Railways Advertising Company, which controls the remainder of the country with the exception of some small scattered places. This company also controls street-car cards in Latin American countries.

Through these organizations it is possible to contract for space in cities all over the country.

RATES

On the whole, rates are fairly uniform throughout the country, although there are some differences on certain lines, particularly in the large cities. In general, the rates are in the neighborhood of 65 to 75 cents per card per car per month. The obvious reason for the uniformity of rates is, of course, that any one card can be seen by approximately the same number of passengers at a given moment as any other card in any car.

Space in street cars is usually contracted for according to the proportion of cars used in a given city or on a given line. Thus, for example, a full run means one card in every car on the line or in the entire system. A half-run means a card in every other car. Contracts are usually made for periods of six months or a year; but quite frequently they are made for several years. The concentration of cards within a short period of time or the distribution of them over a long period of time is obviously determined by the conditions and the purpose of the campaign. Where a steady use of car space is contemplated, it is usually considered better to have a half-run for a year than a full-run for six months. Rates vary somewhat from city to city and in the larger cities from route to route. In New York City the rates on some routes are as high as $2.50 to $3 per single card per month. The average in New York City is $1.25 per card per month.

There is a tendency to change the basis of rates to so much per 1,000 passengers per month. On this basis at the present time the rate is approximately 6 to 9 cents per 1,000 passengers per month. For a full showing, that is, for a card in every car in the United States, it costs approximately $50,000 per month.

PROPORTION OF PASSENGERS LOOKING AT CARDS

In 1913 Dr. E. K. Strong prepared a report for the Association of National Advertisers which was designed to determine the proportion of passengers in street cars of various types who were looking at the cards in the cars. The inquiry was carried out by several investigators, who observed the passengers on certain lines, and determined the propor-

tion who were reading newspapers or other material and
the proportion who were looking at the cards. The results
are briefly summarized in Table 156. This table is based
on the observation of passengers between two successive
stations, a length of ride of approximately two minutes.
Approximately one-half to one-fourth of the car was considered or observed at one time.

TABLE 156

PERCENTAGE OF PASSENGERS OBSERVING CARDS DURING A
PORTION OF THE TRIP

Subway	Sitting	Standing
Men observed	6,621	866
Per cent reading	41%	22%
Per cent looking at cards	15%	15%
Women observed	3,602	192
Per cent reading	13%	7%
Per cent looking at cards	21%	26%

When passengers were observed during the entire trip
the results shown in Table 157 were obtained.

The general results may be summarized as follows: There
were approximately three times as many men reading newspapers, books, etc., as there were women.

The percentage of persons reading newspapers, etc., decreased as the day advanced, except in the case of persons
who were standing, and during the evening rush period.

Fifty to seventy-five per cent more women looked at the
street-car cards than did men.

The percentage of both the men and the women who
were seated and looking at cards was approximately constant during the day, namely, 15% of the men and 20%
of the women.

A much larger proportion of persons observed the cards
between the first two stations of their ride. This was probably due to self-consciousness on the part of the passengers
when they came in to find a seat. In order to avoid the gaze

TABLE 157

PERCENTAGE OF PASSENGERS OBSERVING CARDS DURING THE
ENTIRE TRIP

Subway	
Men observed	319
Per cent looking at ads during the trip	37%
Women observed	375
Per cent looking at ads during the trip	53%
Surface Line—Seats lengthwise	
Per cent of men looking at ads	23%
Per cent of women looking at ads	35%
Surface Line—Seats crosswise	
Per cent of men looking at ads	1%
Per cent of women looking at ads	5%
Elevated Lines—Seats mostly crosswise	
Per cent of men looking at ads	8%
Per cent of women looking at ads	10%

of other passengers, the person turned to the advertisements.

The extent to which passengers observe cards is influenced (a) by the opportunity to look outside of the car, and (b) by the position of the seats, whether lengthwise or crosswise of the car. The results showed definitely that the largest number of persons observe advertisements in subway cars where they are unable to look out of the window, and in cars where the seats are lengthwise instead of crosswise. Thus, in the case of passengers observed continuously among those riding in subways, 35% of the men and 53% of the women looked at the advertisements. In the case of the elevated cars with the seats mostly crosswise, 8% of the men and 10% of the women looked at the advertisements. In the case of surface cars with seats crosswise, 1% of the men and 5% of the women looked at the advertisements. As a general observation, also, it was found that the uneducated laboring classes looked very much less at advertisements than did the other passengers.

Most of them apparently did not look at the advertisements nor read anything, even when riding alone for a long distance.

A similar investigation was undertaken by the author in the Boston street-car system. The method followed was

TABLE 158

PERCENTAGE OF PASSENGERS OBSERVING CARDS

Subway	Sitting	Standing
Men observed	426	50
Per cent reading papers, etc.	24%	4%
Per cent looking at ads	28%	34%
Women observed	348	
Per cent reading papers, etc.	11%	
Per cent looking at ads	28%	
Surface Cars—Seats crosswise		
Men observed	201	
Per cent reading papers, etc.	19%	
Per cent looking at ads	26%	
Women observed	144	
Per cent reading papers, etc.	5%	
Per cent looking at ads	22%	
Surface Cars—Seats lengthwise		
Men observed	66	56
Per cent reading papers, etc.	24%	20%
Per cent looking at ads	17%	25%
Women observed	96	
Per cent reading papers, etc.	10%	
Per cent looking at ads	36%	

substantially the same as that used by Strong. The results are summarized in Table 158.

These results corroborate in general the findings obtained by Strong. A larger proportion of passengers read the cards in the subway trains where there is no opportunity to look out of the windows. Likewise, there is a slight tendency for a somewhat larger proportion of passengers to read cards in cars when the seats are lengthwise than when they are crosswise, although this difference is not as marked as in the case of Strong's results.

XXXIII

POSTERS AND MISCELLANEOUS MEDIUMS

The three kinds of outdoor advertising mediums. Sizes of boards and posters. Rates. Censorship. Electrical signs. The motion picture film as an advertising medium. Radio broadcasting.

THERE are three kinds of outdoor advertising mediums: billboards, painted signs, and electrical signs. It is estimated by the Poster Advertising Association that there are approximately 26,000 billboards in the United States, located in or controlled from 7,000 cities and towns.

The control of outdoor advertising is in charge of a large number of local poster plants which are associated in what is known as the Poster Advertising Association. There are approximately 8,000 local plants represented in this association. The association has done much to standardize the business methods and the requirements of billboards. Another function of the association is to check up the space used to see that contracts made with advertisers are fulfilled. There is a plant affiliated with the Poster Advertising Association in practically every city of 5,000 or over.

In 1910 the association classified all billboards into three groups, as follows:

Class A—Rendering "excellent service; highly recommended."

Class B—Rendering "good service; meeting association requirements."

Class C—"Not up to association requirements."

In 1912 the association abolished Class C as being unprofitable and unbusinesslike, and established Class AA, which consists of paneled steel boards and "such framing of posters that each appears like a picture." The association has requirements as to the location of the boards and the number of feet of poster space in relation to population in each town. It has also specified the construction of the boards in considerable detail, covering such matters as thickness of posts, and the like. Each board must be capped with the name of the owner. Quite recently illuminated boards have been constructed. In and about the larger cities there are a great many illuminated boards, some of them using reflectors.

SIZES OF BOARDS AND POSTERS

The standard sheet or poster is 28 x 42 inches, which includes a margin of white space around the edges. The boards are standardized so that they are 4 sheets high and anywhere from 1 to 6 posters wide; that is, a single board may contain from 4, 8, 12, 16, up to as many as 20 or 24 sheets or posters. The board is always just 4 posters high. Thus, an 8-sheet poster is a board which is 4 sheets high and 2 sheets wide and would be 106 x 80 inches; a 16-sheet poster board is 106 x 160 inches; etc.

Rates. The rates for poster space vary considerably and are fixed by each plant. They are stated in terms of so much per sheet of 28 x 42 inches per month of four weeks. What is known as a "full" showing would consist of an eight-sheet space on each board in a given community. To illustrate the variation of rates in relation to population, we may quote the figures in Table 159.[1]

From these figures it will appear that the rates vary with the size of the city, increasing as the size of the city increases. The basis for this is obviously that a board in a larger city is seen by a larger number of persons. Usually a discount of 5% is allowed for a three months' contract and 10% for a six months' contract. Contracts are usually made for three-quarters, one-half, or one-quarter showings.

[1] *Poster Advertising*, p. 49.

TABLE 159

RATES FOR POSTERS

City	Population	No. of Posters	Rate per Sheet per Month	Cost per Stand	Total Cost per Month
Scottesdale, Pa.	5,456	7	$0.10	$0.80	$ 5.40
Wheeling, W. Va.	41,641	70	.12	.96	67.20
Dayton, Ohio	116,577	150	.16	1.28	192.00
Pittsburgh, Pa.	533,905	525	.18	1.44	756.00
Chicago, Ill.	2,185,283	800	.20	1.60	1,280.00

Rarely is a contract made for a full showing. A half-showing would mean a poster on every other board in a community. The cost of a full showing for the United States would be approximately $197,000 per month and would require about 26,000 poster sheets.

CENSORSHIP

The association has a regular inspection service for the various boards to see that they are maintained according to standard specifications and that contracts are properly fulfilled. It may be pointed out here that billboard advertising has been for the most part free from objectionable advertising. This is probably due to the fact that a billboard is so much in the public eye that objectionable features come readily to the attention of the public and general sentiment would be very distinctly against the persistence of questionable features and methods.

Very extensive use was made of posters during the World War. Approximately $1,500,000 worth of posting was done. Much of it, as was true in the case of newspaper advertising, was contributed by local business concerns or individuals. Numerous posters were used in the various Liberty Loan drives; they were used not only on the billboards themselves but particularly in windows and other conspicuous places. Approximately 2,000,000 posters were distributed in connection with the first Liberty Loan drive; 7,000,000 were used in connection with the second; 9,000,000 in connection with the third; and 10,000,000 in connection with the fourth. Some 50,000 of these were 24-sheet posters. Many advertisers have made a very conspicuous use of posters. Thus, for example, the Royal Typewriter Company made very effective use of billboards in connection with New York elevated and subway stations. The copy consisted largely of a picture of the typewriter and a statement of the price, which attracted considerable attention at the time because of a lower price. Among other extensive users of billboards may be mentioned Gold Medal Flour, Wrigley's Gum, Dodge Automobiles.

There has been at times considerable opposition on the part of the public to billboards. There is no doubt some justification for this opposition, as in cases when boards are placed in positions where they detract from the natural scenery and beauty of the surroundings. Certain cities have regulations which specify that billboards must not be erected within certain distances, say 300 feet, of public parks and boulevards. Where there is a distinct opposition to the presence of a billboard in a certain location, it is, of course, poor advertising to maintain its presence. Thus, for example, a manufacturer of chocolate erected a billboard at a certain point on the Hudson River. The community objected to it, and so the company decided to remove this board.

Various civic and welfare organizations are at times active in prohibiting the erection of billboards in localities where they will interfere with the natural beauties of the environment. Thus, for example, the District of Columbia prohibits the use of billboards on the ground that it is a matter of public welfare. St. Louis has passed an ordinance for the safe construction of billboards. The ordinance designates their position and requires them to be built free of other structures, so that the risk of fire will be minimized, and also requires a high clear space under them to lessen the danger of their becoming a nuisance. In 1911 an ordinance was passed in Chicago, prohibiting boards on the roofs of buildings and requiring a majority consent for erecting them in residential districts. This matter of majority consent was taken to the United States Supreme Court by the billboard interests concerned. The Supreme Court upheld the provision of this ordinance. The value of billboards as advertising mediums has undoubtedly been demonstrated for certain products. As far as the public point of view is concerned, restrictions should probably be established and enforced, prohibiting the presence of billboards where they will mar the natural attractiveness of the environment and where the sentiment of the community is distinctly against them.

ELECTRICAL SIGNS

Electrical signs are a form of advertising much in use in the larger cities. There are, however, probably not as many conspicuous, specially constructed signs on tops of buildings or other high scaffolding as the public is likely to believe. There is a certain illusion of numbers and size due to the intense and ever-present impression made upon the observer. New York City, which has more electrical signs than any other city in the country, has a total of some 28 or 30 large electrical signs, that is, signs other than ordinary signs above entrances to buildings and places of business. The largest and most elaborate electrical sign in the world is the Wrigley sign at Times Square, New York. It is 200 feet long, 50 feet high and contains 15,000 electric bulbs. It costs approximately $100,000 a year to maintain it.

THE MOTION PICTURE FILM AS AN ADVERTISING MEDIUM

With the development of each new form of mass communication there always develops the possibility of using such a means for advertising purposes, for disseminating information and appeals for specific products. With the development of moving pictures naturally the use of films for advertising and informational purposes has arisen. They are coming into more and more rapid use in connection with industries, particularly for the purpose of illustrating and exhibiting various manufacturing processes. As such they have very distinct possibilities for accomplishment not possessed by other types of mediums. In a certain sense the moving picture film is a powerful medium, as it has attention in a way that perhaps no other medium is able to obtain. A typical film relating to industrial products is shown in a moving picture house for a period of 15 minutes, during which it receives the close attention of the spectators in a darkened room. Many industries have prepared films in recent years to exhibit the process of manufacture of their products, activities in and about their plants, and similar facts of interest. A reel is usually 1,000 feet in length and is known as a unit; it may be exhibited in about 15 minutes. This passes through the projecting machine at the rate of approximately one foot per second. The constant movement of the picture is an added stimulus to attention, as any moving object attracts greater attention than a static object. The film may be exhibited at any time in any place or numerous places wherever it may be desired. In that respect it has a certain flexibility which is not possessed by other mediums, with the possible exception of direct mail.

At the present time, there are no standard rates or practices developed. Films prepared by industries are shown quite commonly in theaters and before various organizations, such as churches, lodges, societies, chambers of commerce, and special clubs of business concerns. Thus, for example, a film prepared by one of the large paper manufacturers is used by the salesmen to exhibit to groups of printers, who are gotten together for the purpose and who are large buyers of paper.

The moving picture film is being used for an increasing

variety of purposes. Thus, for example, a bond house, in raising half a million dollars in New York City, employed the use of a film to illustrate the value of savings and investment in safe securities. This film was shown in a series of 50 theaters in New York City and proved to be a very effective means of selling the bonds in question. In fact, it resulted in the withdrawal of savings from various banks to such an extent that the savings banks asked for a change in some of the titles of the films. In connection with this campaign printed circulars were distributed and order coupons were printed in the theater programs, which brought in literally thousands of requests for further information and actual orders for bonds.

A manufacturer of tools and dies used a film in connection with his products and found it effective in like manner. A bakery prepared a film showing the processes and sanitary conditions surrounding the baking of its bread and showed the film in surrounding cities. This proved very interesting. The bakery stated that the film was one of the most effective forms of advertising which it had used. There is something real and appealing about the actual visualization of a process and of its surroundings. As it is instructive and interesting to the public personally to see a plant or a manufacturing process in operation, so the moving picture film brings the visual impression and active process to the people directly without making it necessary for them to go to the plant.

In preparing a film, it is important to decide definitely what purpose the film is intended to serve. This purpose will necessarily be the guiding factor in determining what should or should not be included in a picture. There is always a temptation to include material which is not directly pertinent to the subject.

"Sky writing" by means of airplanes may develop as another form of advertising with the growth of flying. At the present time it is reported that the terms are $500 for each word which remains visible for 10 minutes.

RADIO BROADCASTING

The development of radio broadcasting is presenting another possibility of mass communication which probably will be utilized for advertising purposes. It is too early to predict what its possibilities may be or how successfully it may be utilized.

PRINCIPLES OF ADVERTISING

PART VI

SPECIAL FIELDS OF ADVERTISING

XXXIV

NATIONAL ADVERTISING

The first step in planning a national advertising campaign. The policy. The appropriation for advertising. The advertising agency and the advertising manager. Coordination of advertising with sales plans and sales functions. Cooperation of the manufacturer with the dealer.

IN a sense, all of our discussion thus far may be regarded as an analysis of national advertising, since the methods presented, step by step, have attempted to show how advertising plans may be intelligently prepared and executed, for any field of advertising. The purpose of this chapter is, therefore, merely to coordinate the various steps in a unified plan or campaign and to point out the means by which such a plan may be carried out.

THE POLICY

The first important step in planning a national advertising campaign is to determine in broad outlines the general policy according to which the plans are to be governed. In a broad sense the advertising policy should state the general point of view, the purpose of the advertising plan, the general method by which it is to be carried out, and the coordination of the advertising plan with the general sales and business plans of the organization as a whole. A point to be borne in mind here is that the advertising plans should not be carried out as an independent undertaking, but should be made an integral part of the policy and plan of the entire business. The advertising done by a firm is the firm's representative in the eyes of the public and the public very largely judges a firm, its policies and practices by the advertising which the firm puts out. A policy, of course, states merely in a broad way the point of view, the plans to be carried out, and the methods to be used. It is a question as to how far the policy may state in detail the exact method of carrying out the plans. Obviously it is not the function of a policy to state in minute detail the actual execution of the plans. This will develop in connection with the fuller preparation of the plans. The policy should also determine the proportionate amount of money to be expended for advertising at different seasons of the year. Should the expenditure of money for advertising be relatively greater during the dull seasons and less during the more active seasons, or should it be directly proportionate to the business activities at all seasons? Should it be relatively greater during active seasons and less during dull seasons, or should it be uniform throughout the year irrespective of either seasonal or business fluctuations?

THE APPROPRIATION

Detailed figures have been presented in Chapter III regarding the expenditures for advertising by a considerable number of different firms. These average expenditures for various lines of business serve as a rough guide in determining the amount of the appropriation. However, the problem requires that an analysis be made of the most suitable basis upon which the advertising appropriation may be determined. There are various methods in use by various firms for determining the appropriation. In a recent discussion of this subject, J. A. Murphy has outlined 11 different bases upon which to determine the appropriation. Briefly they are as follows: [1]

(1) Setting aside a certain amount of money for advertising as an investment in good-will. This evidently does not suggest a definite basis on which the amount may be determined.

(2) Taking a certain percentage of the sales, either the sales for the past year or the anticipated sales for the coming year.

---

[1] *Printers' Ink,* Dec. 9, 1920, p. 3; and Dec. 16, 1920, p. 41.

(3) Making an assessment on a certain unit of the product, either the number of units sold in the previous year or the number anticipated for the following year.

(4) Putting all the money that can possibly be obtained into advertising as an investment in future sales.

(5) A budget system.

(6) Finding out how much advertising it takes to get a new user or a new dealer for a given product and then appropriating the required amount of money to secure the number of dealers or users desired.

(7) Investing in advertising to buy inquiries or direct sales. This is the usual mail-order method.

(8) Ascertaining the minimum job to be accomplished by the campaign and then deciding upon the mediums and the size of space necessary to accomplish the task.

(9) Appropriating a certain percentage of the previous year's profits.

(10) Determining the amount in the light of what competitors are spending.

(11) A combination of a percentage of sales and a budget system.

MacMartin [1] suggested a similar series of considerations on which the appropriation might be determined, some of which coincide with the ones just mentioned:

(1) An investment in good-will and insurance of business already established

(2) Amount per unit of expected sales

(3) Based on the available capital

(4) Setting aside a certain amount per possible purchaser

(5) Cost per inquiry

(6) Business desired

(7) Based on the profits of previous year

(8) Based on the amount spent the previous year

(9) Based on the difference between selling expense and price plus a reasonable profit

In the last analysis all of these methods may be reduced to two chief bases on which the advertising appropriation may be best determined. One method is to determine the

---

[1] *Advertising Campaigns.*

amount in relation to either business done or business anticipated or desired, that is, a percentage basis. The second method requires a budget plan, and the setting aside of a certain total amount for publicity purposes. Probably the most satisfactory basis is a combination of these two methods, using the first method as the chief basis. It is obviously impossible to plan any advertising appropriation on a sound basis without definitely taking into account the total amount of business done or anticipated. The combination of the two methods makes it possible to keep the advertising appropriation more or less flexible. When the amount is determined purely on the basis of the percentage of sales, the policy becomes ironclad and is not able to meet unexpected situations and is not capable of adjustment on the basis of the fluctuations of business. The result is that often too little is appropriated after a year of dull business, or more than is necessary when the year's business has been unusually prosperous. A certain amount of flexibility is desirable, and the combination of a budget system with a percentage basis, with the latter as primary consideration, will as a rule result in the most satisfactory arrangement. The percentage figured will depend upon various circumstances, but will in most instances lie within the limits indicated in Chapter III, that is, between 1% and 4% or 5% of the net sales.

The ratio or percentage basis of determining the appropriation should probably be the fundamental basis and should then be modified by the following considerations:

a. By anticipated business conditions
b. By the aim set for the coming period
c. By what competitors are doing
d. By the profits of the previous year
e. By the location of the business (This applies particularly to a retail business.)
f. By the newness of the product in the market

THE ADVERTISING AGENCY AND THE ADVERTISING MANAGER

Since practically all national advertising is handled through agencies, it is well to consider the function which the agency serves and the manner in which the advertising is handled through an agency. About the middle of the last century, when advertising agencies first developed, their primary function was to act as space brokers. Gradually their functions expanded and their services became more uniform and standardized until at the present time the highest type of agency service approximates impartial, fairminded counsel rendered on a professional basis. To be sure that is not the uniform practice by any means, but in its best form agency service approximates this goal. The functions which an agency performs have therefore expanded very considerably beyond that of merely contracting for space. In the first place, an agency makes a careful investigation of the problems presented; it has a properly organized research department with facilities for carrying out in a thoroughly adequate manner all investigations necessary. It has also a production department which prepares the plans and the copy as based upon the results of the research work. It has an art department which either prepares or arranges for the preparation of the art work. It has a space department the members of which are specialists in facts about mediums and the most suitable purchase of space; and it has a checking department to see that the advertisements have been inserted in the various mediums contracted for and that the contracts are carried out.

The remuneration of agency service is at the present time on the commission basis; that is, a certain percentage is paid by the publisher to the agency on the basis of the amount of space contracted for. This, by common agreement, is at the present time 15% of the cost of the space. Thus, for example, if a given campaign involves an expenditure of $100,000 for advertising space, the commission received by the agency from the publisher will be 15%, or $15,000. In practical operation, it means that the advertiser pays $100,000 for the space to the agency and the agency pays the various mediums 15% below that sum, or $85,000. There has been considerable controversy regarding this basis of remuneration. Certain advertising interests feel that this is not a just basis of payment, that the payment of service rendered by an agency should be on a fee basis paid by the client or advertiser to whom the service is rendered. The present commission system is a traditional one and has developed out of the original function of the agency, which was that of selling the space for the publisher. At the present time, the best type of agency service is not merely selling space, but primarily that of rendering fair-minded and reliable advice and the preparation of advertising plans accordingly. In other words, it is primarily a service to the client or advertiser.

The relation between the advertising manager of the client and the advertising agency varies greatly with the persons concerned. The advertising managers or advertising departments of some firms take a dominating part in determining the details of an advertising campaign and use the agency primarily as a means of making contracts for the space. In other instances the reverse is true; the advertising manager may play only a perfunctory part and leave the preparation of the advertising plans to the agency practically from beginning to end. Which of the two is the more desirable it is difficult to say. In general it will depend upon the equipment and professional status of the agency. The agency necessarily accumulates a wider range of experience and information and has at hand more completely equipped facilities for research and for carrying out plans than has ordinarily the advertising department of a client. On the other hand, it is always desirable for the advertising manager to be thoroughly familiar with what is being done and to cooperate in the closest manner with the activities of the agency.

The first step to be taken by the agency in the establishment of its relations with the advertiser should consist of a thorough study of the client's problem. Each agency employs its own general plan whereby this preliminary information may be obtained. This varies all the way from a purely haphazard inquiry to a rather complete and thorough study made according to a plan uniformly applied to all new clients. A careful study should undoubtedly be made; more effective plans would unquestionably result if a thorough study were made in each instance according to a well thought out analytical plan. We shall, therefore, propose the following program of facts and information which the agency should obtain, in so far as this is applicable in each case. This program will furnish the general basis upon which to form the detailed plans for an advertising campaign. It will reveal the points for which actual investigations and research should be carried out. An analysis according to this program will give the agency a fairly complete conception of the business and problems of the new client. Probably very few if any advertisers are in a position to supply the information on each one of the points involved in this program, Figure 110, which starts on the next page. The preliminary survey called for by this plan often serves as a useful self-examination for a firm, irrespective of its use in relation to proposed advertising efforts.

A careful checking up of the information available from the company itself by means of this plan will show where the loopholes are, and on what points further information must be obtained. In other words, this will serve as a point of departure for the making of actual plans for further research and for the preparation of the final advertising campaign. The representatives of the agency should go through this program of inquiry with the various representatives or departments of the client's business to obtain as full information as possible. Then the agency in conference with the client can plan further necessary research.

I *The Business*
   1. Name of firm or company;
   2. Address, including branch offices;
   3. Location of plant or plants;
   4. Names of chief officials;
   5. Names of officials with whom to deal regarding sales and advertising;
   6. Organization plan of the company;
   7. Origin and history of the business—including growth and important changes;
   8. Present capitalization;
   9. Financial status—balance sheet;
   10. Volume of business each year for past five or more years;
   11. Number of leading companies in the industry;
   12. Relative standing of the company in the industry as a whole—domestic and foreign;
   13. History of the industry;
   14. General trend of the industry as a whole;
   15. Legal regulations or restrictions of the industry;
   16. Associations for the promotion of the industry;
   17. Outstanding policies of the company;
   18. Ability to meet foreign competition.

II *The Product and Its Production*
   1. The trade-mark or name of the product;
   2. Other products made by the company;
   3. What raw materials go into the product?
   4. Source of the raw material;
   5. Restrictions or difficulties in securing the raw material;
   6. The process of manufacturing the product;
   7. Special skilled workmanship;
   8. Research on which manufacture is based;
   9. Patents on the process;
   10. Patents on the product;

11. History of the process;
12. How long has product been made?
13. Average life of product;
14. Cost of manufacturing the product;
15. What is present output?
16. Output each year for past five or more years;
17. Is product guaranteed? If so, what is the nature of the guarantee?
18. Methods of inspecting and testing the product;
19. Weak points in the product;
20. How does product compare with competing products?
21. Special features of the product;
22. Complete list of uses of the product;
23. Efficiency and thoroughness in accomplishing its uses;
24. Ease of using or operating the article;
25. Repair service.

III *The Distribution*
1. Channels of distribution;
2. Number of distributers of the product—wholesalers and retailers;
3. Are they exclusive jobbers or retailers?
4. What proportion of total dealers are handling the product?
5. Geographical location of distributers;
6. Classes of retailers who sell the product;
7. Terms and arrangements with distributers—jobbers' and retailers' profits;
8. Credit policy;
9. Units or quantities in which product is sold;
10. Jobbers' attitude toward product;
11. Retailers' attitude;
12. Rate of retail turnover.

IV *Consumption and the Consumer*

1. Total consumption of this class of product;
2. Percentage of this company's product of total;
3. Consumption per capita, per family or other unit;
4. Is total consumption increasing, remaining constant, or decreasing?
5. Is consumption seasonal? What is best season and poorest season?
6. How much difference is there between best and poorest season?
7. What class of persons are the consumers?
8. How many are there now?
9. Where do they live? Distribution by states, cities, etc.
10. How many potential consumers are there?
11. Within what range of income are the potential buyers?
12. How does the consumer buy this product?
13. What appeals to him about the product?
14. What criticisms are made of the product?
15. How frequent are complaints?
16. What manufacturers, businesses, or organizations use the product?
17. What special conditions, if any, affect the demand?
18. Limitations on the consumption of the product;
19. How often do consumers buy or re-order the product?
20. Testimonials from consumers;
21. Testimonials from authorities.

V *Sales Methods and Policies*
1. The sales policy;
2. Number of salesmen;
3. Territorial or trade assignments of the salesmen;
4. Organization scheme of the sales force;
5. Selection of salesmen;
6. Training of salesmen;

7. Supervision of salesmen;
8. Compensation of salesmen;
9. Do you have sales inventories?
10. Quotas, contests;
11. How often do the salesmen cover the retail trade?
12. Chief sales arguments;
13. Cost of selling—percentage of net sales;
14. What are chief difficulties in the sale of the product?
15. Retail price and range of retail price in different sections of the country;
16. Demonstrations;
17. Is product sold under company's brand, under jobbers' private brands, or under both?
18. Is product sold in bulk? If so, what proportion?
19. Chief sales arguments and methods used by competitors;
20. How does price of product compare with that of competing brands?

VI *Advertising*
1. The advertising policy;
2. What has been the direct aim of the advertising?
3. The appropriation—amount and percentage of net sales;
4. How is the appropriation determined?
5. Relative expenditures in different classes of mediums—magazines, newspapers, direct mail material, etc.;
6. What are the relative expenditures for trade and consumer advertising?
7. Advertising schedule of past year or season;
8. Material and help furnished to dealers;
9. Chief appeals that have been used;
10. What other appeals might be used—make a complete list;
11. Advertising done by the retailers;

12. Advantages or disadvantages of the trade-mark;
13. Is it registered?
14. How was the trade-mark selected?
15. The label and package: design, size, shape;
16. Have you done any sampling? If so, how and where?
17. History of the company's advertising;
18. Do you issue a house organ? If so, how often?
19. How are sales and advertising plans coordinated?
20. What records, if any, are available regarding the results of past advertising?
21. Are there any test records of individual advertisements?
22. Has a questionnaire field survey ever been made for the product? If so, how was it made and what were the essential results?

Figure 110: Program of facts and information for the planning of an advertising campaign by an agency

COORDINATION OF ADVERTISING WITH SALES PLANS AND SALES FUNCTIONS

Too much emphasis cannot be laid upon the need for proper coordination of all advertising and sales activities, in order to get results. Both advertising and sales activities have failed often because of the lack of coordination. There is at times a tendency for each department to carry on its activities independently. Questions which arise in relation to advertising naturally concern also the distribution of the product in relation to advertising plans. Shall the product be distributed before advertising begins or shall the advertising be started first with the expectation that a demand will be created and distribution may be made afterwards? Shall distribution and advertising begin simultaneously? Various methods are followed. For example, the manufacturer of a toothpaste employing practically no salesmen started to advertise and continued advertising until so great a demand was created that the retailers were ready to carry the toothpaste in stock. This may be an expensive method of procedure, since it requires a considerable expenditure for advertising before an impression is created sufficiently large to produce an actual consumer demand. According to another method, the product is distributed first, the dealers stocked with it, and then the advertising is begun to help the retailer in the sale of the goods. The third plan, which is probably on the whole the most efficient, provides that the advertising and the distributing shall begin more or less simultaneously. In this case rather complete advertising plans are made, the space contracted for, and the advertisements shown in portfolio form to the retailers upon whom the salesman calls. These portfolios are a valuable aid to the salesmen in getting the retailers to stock the goods; they are a proof to the retailers that definite advertising plans are under way, and that these will be carried out according to a certain definite schedule of dates and mediums.

COOPERATION OF THE MANUFACTURER WITH THE DEALER

The next step in the successful carrying out of national advertising and sales plans is to establish proper cooperation with the dealer, to secure his assistance in both advertising and sales efforts. There has grown up a practice of supplying the retailer with a certain amount of advertising material, such as direct mail material, booklets, circulars, folders, and window-display material; and it has been the custom either to furnish this free to the retailer, or to arrange with him to pay for it on a cooperative basis. The United Drug Company, for example, has worked out a successful plan whereby the dealer purchases from the company the material that he desires and expects to use. The disadvantage of supplying the retailer with free dealer-help material is that usually in that case he will be oversupplied and may not be particularly aggressive in making use of it. Much of it is therefore wasted. If, on the other hand, the dealer must decide for himself just what he wishes to use and pay for, he will be much more careful to obtain only what he really wants and will see that it is actually used.

Another form of dealer cooperation relates to the use of space in local newspapers. In 1920 and 1921 the Hoover Suction Sweeper Company prepared a portfolio of advertising plans, showing different amounts of space which might be used. The portfolio was sent to the dealer who then ordered the particular size of advertisement and the number of different advertisements, that he wished to run. Similar plans have been followed by a number of firms in recent years. The space is then usually paid for cooperatively by the dealer and the manufacturer. A plan similar to this is carried out by Bird & Son in the advertising of roofing materials and other products. Recently a study was made by the Association of National Advertisers of the question of dealer cooperation. Results were obtained as shown in Figure 111.

Question No. 1. Demand of the dealer for local newspaper advertising as against general magazine advertising, or supplementary thereto.

Number of replies covering some 20 different industries	150
Dealer demands local newspaper advertising	21
Dealer requests local newspaper advertising	68
Number of firms acceding to dealers' request	84
Number refusing dealers' request	5
Number of firms using local newspaper advertising	81
Number of firms not using local newspaper advertising	69

Question No. 2. Division of cost of newspaper advertising with the dealer.

Number of replies	150
Number of firms who urge dealers to use local space	30
Number of firms who do not urge dealers to use local space	1

Number of firms paying all cost of local space used by dealers	15
Number paying part of cost of local space	33
Number paying none	83
Number furnishing electros free for dealers' use	131

Charging the dealer for helps:

Number of firms replying	281

Number of firms charging dealers for booklets:

Yes	14
No	236
Sometimes	10
Do not use	21

Number of firms charging dealers for signs:

Yes	22
No	237
Sometimes	9
Do not use	13

Number of firms charging dealers for window trims:

Yes	16
No	228
Sometimes	6
Do not use	31

Number of firms charging dealers for electros:

Yes	13
No	247
Sometimes	6
Do not use	15

Envelope stuffers furnished free:

Yes	215
No	45
Do not use	19

Figure 111: Answers to questionnaire on dealer cooperation in advertising

If the manufacturer wishes to make dealer help effective and to keep it from being wasted or stored in basements instead of being used or sent out he must secure proper cooperation and interest from the dealer. It may be of interest to note how the matter is handled by typical firms. The following is an account of the plan carried out successfully by Sherwin-Williams Company:

The main link in the campaign is the tie-up plan. Realizing that it is asking too much of dealers to tie up with the national advertising plan without the necessary means of doing it, the company is putting out a series of complete Tie-Up Envelopes to the dealers. The envelopes go out two or three weeks ahead of each advertisement in the series and contain a broadside illustrating and explaining the complete tie-up for the campaign, window poster, window display, mailing card, newspaper electro and lantern slides. There is a coupon at the bottom of each broadside which enables the dealer to order the specific features which he wants to tie up with the coming advertisement.

But, in order to catch all of the dealers, and not just the ones who return the coupons, there is a window poster and a set of periodical advertisement proofs enclosed in the original envelope so that anything he sends for on the coupon is an additional tie-up, and there is no chance of his having nothing to display in his window and store at the particular period when the advertising appears.

A Sign for Use Inside the Store

An enameled iron sign with clips hanging from it was sent to all of the agents prior to the first mailing, and they are asked to hang the proofs from this sign as they come along. The sign is of such permanent character as to make a good indoor agency sign when used alone and a better one when used as directed for hanging the proofs and posters.

In the magazine advertising, six main products are specially featured, and the six tie-up campaigns are sent out to the dealers simultaneously with the appearance of the double-spreads on these six particular products.

When the consumer sees the national advertising and then sees the same illustration on the poster in the dealer's window, then gets a reminder on the mailing card, then sees the same illustration in the dealer's newspaper advertising, what is the result? He buys the product advertised and is a good prospect for further advertising and tie-ups on the other products in the line. It is not just a national plan, for fully 50% of the plan is devoted to the localized tie-up helps which appeal to the dealer and enable him to identify his store locally as the Sherwin-Williams agency.

Each envelope contains a broadside, a window poster and ad proofs. These envelopes are all mailed from Cleveland to the agency list. The return coupons, however, are imprinted and come back to the local sales promotion department, where they are taken care of, and from which point are sent the requested window displays, electros, lantern slides, mailing cards, and other tie-up features.

The results from the first August tie-up mailing are interesting in that they indicate quite a preference on the part of the dealer for having something in the original envelope which enables him to put in a tie-up window and display without the necessity of returning the coupon. This also "bridges the gap" between its receipt and the appearance of the advertisement.

The results further indicate that about 95% of the coupons which were returned came from the livest agents. On former campaigns it has been our experience, as well as that of many other advertisers, that where something is offered for nothing on a coupon a large bulk of the returns come from more or less average dealers or customers, and many times the better dealer overlooked sending in the coupon. Not so with this campaign, and the results can possibly be taken as a tribute to the results from long and continued national advertising which have encouraged these dealers to see the possibilities of putting a little of their own energy along with this work to get the local tie-up benefit.

Another interesting thing was the preponderance of orders for the three-column six-inch newspaper electrotype—this being by far the most popular size of all those offered. The principal other size was four-column eight-inch, but the three-column six-inch electros outpulled the other about ten to one, perhaps indicating an average space which most of these live dealers were running regularly under contract in their local papers.

We offered a quantity of mailing cards a little larger than the ordinary post-card, and printed on the back in color with the same design as the national advertisement. Multigraphed above the illustration was a personal message from the dealer, and a place left for the dealer to sign his own name in pen and ink. The dealer was to put his own postage on the cards. The results from the coupon show a big demand for this card, with the result that the estimated quantities ran far short and for the second campaign there will have to be an additional 50,000 or 100,000 of these cards printed to take care of the demand.

This is an indication of the dealer's preference for some personal message to his customers which he can sign. If it is already prepared for him so he just has to sign the card, he is perfectly willing to spend his time picking out his own list and putting his own postage on the card. An extra supply of the broadsides was printed for going after prospective dealers, and this is an effective feature because it shows the prospect the actual tie-up and dealer work being done for the established trade.

In order to get the greatest specific sales benefit from the particular products featured in the series, a classification card system was devised with tabs, and the sales promotion department can use the extra supply of the tie-up envelopes very effectively in trying to bring Class C dealers into Class B and Class B dealers into Class A, as well as in getting a more uniform distribution of the product through special promoting effort.

The tie-up campaign is explained to the salesmen in a little monthly organ called "The Sales and Advertising Chat," pocket size, with front and back envelope pockets containing the advance proofs and the advance broadside. This goes to the salesman just before the dealer envelope goes out, so he is familiar with it, and he also gets the first mailing of the dealer envelope, which he in turn uses as a part of his sales outfit.

The strength of the campaign is almost entirely in the persistent and constant tie-up repetition of the national design and copy with the local features, and in this way much of the waste is eliminated and a considerable additional circulation is secured.[1]

---

[1] *Printers' Ink,* Sept. 16, 1920, pp. 49 and 50.

XXXV

RETAIL ADVERTISING [1]

The function of retail advertising. The magnitude of retail advertising. Proportion of expenditure for various types of retail advertising. The fundamental problems of retail advertising. The advertising policy of a retail store. Retail advertising copy. Attention. Interest. Belief and conviction. Memory and continuity in advertisements. Retail copy service. Research methods in retail advertising. Outside investigation. Inside investigation.

ADVERTISING is probably more necessary to the retailer than to the manufacturer or wholesaler. The manufacturer or wholesaler is able to send his salesmen out to his various customers to sell in large quantities. The retailer, however, is not in a position to send out his sales force directly to see the prospective customers—he must wait for his customers to come into his store. For this reason the function of retail advertising is to a great extent to bring customers into the store.

THE MAGNITUDE OF RETAIL ADVERTISING

While it is practically impossible to arrive at an accurate estimate of the volume of retail advertising done at the present time, it will be of some interest to make as close an estimate as possible. Approximately 70% to 75% of newspaper advertising is local retail advertising, and approximately 25% to 30% is so-called foreign or national advertising. Taking the figures for 1920—approximately $600,-000,000 expended for newspaper advertising—we arrive at an estimate of approximately $400,000,000 to $450,000,000 for retail advertising. This proportion, 70% to 75%, is based on individual papers. Thus, for example, the three

[1] A part of the material in this chapter was obtained with the assistance of C. J. O'Connor, a former student under the author's direction.

Milwaukee papers, the *Journal,* the *Wisconsin News,* and the *Sentinel,* carried, in 1920, 74.6% local advertising, and 25.4% foreign or outside advertising.

Similar figures for the New York papers are as follows for the month of November, 1920:

	Morning Papers	Evening Papers	Sunday Papers
Local display advertising	62%	70%	70%
Local non-display advertising	17	13	14
Foreign advertising	21	17	16

It is probable that the proportion of foreign advertising is greater in smaller cities than in larger cities and for that reason the estimate of 70% to 75% is probably correct for the average metropolitan newspaper.

PROPORTION OF EXPENDITURE FOR VARIOUS TYPES OF RETAIL ADVERTISING

The statistical department of the *New York Evening Post* has tabulated for some years the lineage of newspaper advertising space carried in over 100 leading newspapers in some 20 cities. The expenditure for various types of retail advertising may be illustrated by the New York papers for November, 1920, which include 7 morning papers, 10 evening papers, and 10 Sunday papers. Table 160 gives the percentage of the total lineage used by each class of products.

An inspection of this table will show that the largest single item is the expenditure for advertising dry goods, being 21% in morning papers, 38% in evening papers, and 32% in Sunday papers, or an average of 30%. Women's specialty shops come next, and men's furnishing shops are likewise a fairly large item, although much smaller than dry goods. Among the other large items are financial advertising, real estate, steamships and travel, and amusements. The remaining items are relatively small.

TABLE 160
PROPORTION OF EXPENDITURES FOR VARIOUS TYPES OF RETAIL
ADVERTISING

Types of Advertising	Morning Papers	Evening Papers	Sunday Papers
Amusements	3.8%	3.3%	4.4%
Art	.2	.1	.3
Auction sales	1.9	.1	.9
Automobile display	2.5	1.9	3.8
Boots and shoes	1.2	1.4	.9
Building material	.1	.1	.2
Candy and gum	.6	1.0	.2
Charity and religious	.8	1.4	.3
Dancing	.2	1.1	.1
Deaths, etc.	.7	.3	.4
Druggist preparations	1.7	1.1	2.0
Dry goods	21.0	38.0	32.0
Financial	7.0	3.5	1.5
Foodstuffs	1.3	4.0	1.0
Furniture	3.9	3.0	8.0
Hotels and resorts	.6	1.0	.4
Jewelry	.6	.6	.6
Legal	.9	2.7	
Men's furnishings	5.4	5.2	1.2
Musical instruction	.1	.1	.2
Musical instruments	1.7	2.2	2.6
Miscellaneous display	6.8	5.2	6.2
Miscellaneous non-display	3.8	4.8	3.2
Newspapers	.1	.1	
Office appliances	.4		
Proprietary medicine	1.0	2.1	.7
Public service	.2	.3	.1
Periodical magazines	.5	.1	.4
Publishers	1.7	.5	2.5
Railroads	.5	.2	
Real estate	7.0	4.0	8.0
Resorts	.6	.2	.5
Steamship and travel	4.8	1.0	1.4
Schools and colleges	.5	.1	.6
Tobacco	.8	1.1	
Wants	9.5	1.5	6.5
Non-intoxicating beverages	.3	.2	.4
Women's specialty shops	5.2	6.0	8.0

In the case of the Milwaukee papers, 27% of all the newspaper advertising is devoted to department stores, 5.9% to women's wear, and 2.9% to men's wear.

THE FUNDAMENTAL PROBLEMS OF RETAIL ADVERTISING

The fundamental problems of retail advertising are in general the same as those of any other field of advertising. The purpose of retail advertising, as of any other form of advertising, is to sell or to help sell. Consequently, the four or five fundamental problems of the retailer are the same as those outlined in the first chapter of this book.

The following paragraphs summarize, therefore, the chief problems of retail advertising. (1) To whom may his commodities be sold? To what class or classes of people does the particular store appeal or aim to appeal? In Chapters VI and IX various phases of these questions have been discussed in detail. The retail advertiser, like the national advertiser, usually does not have the necessary detailed facts that he should have about his customers or possible customers in order to plan intelligently his advertising activities. The extent to which this is true is fully illustrated by the data presented in Chapters VI and IX, which concern the distribution of the customers in a certain boys' department of a store in a middle-western city.

(2) By what appeals may the various commodities be sold? This question, with its many subdivisions, is as important to the retailer as it is to the national advertiser. In some respects the retailer's problem is even more complicated than the national advertiser's, because the retailer handles so many different types of commodities. The national advertiser, on the other hand, deals with a much more limited variety of products in each particular case.

(3) How may the appeals be presented most effectively? This question is no more complicated perhaps for the retailer than it is for the national advertiser. The psychological factors involved in the most effective presentation

of appeals are in general similar to those involved in the presentation of national appeals. There are, however, certain variations and differences which must be observed by the retailer. The physical and mechanical phases of the execution of advertising copy are, of course, very similar to those of any other form of advertising.

(4) By what mediums may the appeals be presented most effectively? Here the problems are again very similar to those of the national advertiser. The chief difference is, however, that the retailer must have a more detailed knowledge of the class of readers of each particular newspaper in his locality in order properly to connect the advertising with the particular class of people who are the chief buyers in his store. The retailer, in other words, must have more minute and more definite information than is ordinarily needed by the national advertiser regarding newspapers in various cities.

(5) What is a proper expenditure for accomplishing the proposed aims? More detailed data regarding the methods of handling the various phases of these five fundamental questions will be presented in this chapter. Illustrations will be given of methods of investigation by which the retail advertiser may determine with a reasonable degree of certainty questions of importance to him. A preliminary and in some respects a more fundamental problem which must be considered here is that of the advertising policy of a given retail store.

THE ADVERTISING POLICY OF A RETAIL STORE

In some respects the policy upon which advertising plans and methods are based is the most fundamental thing to be determined with respect to retail advertising. A detailed statement of policy would mean, of course, a complete answer to each of the many questions arising out of the four or five fundamental problems already stated. However, in brief terms the policy of advertising may be said to be a statement of the guiding principles according to which the plans shall be carried out.

It is a very desirable and a very useful thing for a retail store to decide as a matter of executive action what its fundamental policy shall be. Indeed, it is desirable to prepare such a policy in written form so that it may be definitely agreed upon by the executives of a store and referred to as the guiding conception for the advertising manager who carries out the plans in detail. It is a rare exception for a retail store even of large size to have a written policy, but it is undoubtedly a desirable thing. Such a stated policy will in general attempt to answer three questions; namely, What are you going to do? Second, Why? and third, How? Unless a general policy is agreed upon by the executives of a retail store, there is apt many times to be considerable deviation and uncertainty as how to carry out the specific plans. In the broad sense, of course, the advertising policy is not a thing apart from the general policy of the store as a whole, since the advertising is not only tied up with the store, but is, indeed, the store's representative to the public at large and to its customers specifically.

One of the questions which an advertising policy should answer is to what extent the advertising manager is subordinate to, or whether he should be co-ordinate, with the other large divisions of the business. Whether or not he should be subordinate, for example, to the merchandising department or whether he should be co-ordinate with the merchandising department depends to some extent upon the purpose of the advertising plans. In general, it is desirable for the advertising department to be on an independent and co-ordinate basis with the other large departments of the store, for the reason that the advertising department must assume large responsibilities, and should consequently have large powers. The difference in the point of view often held by these two departments is another reason why they should be on a par rather than the one subordinate to the other. For example, the merchandising department is often more specifically interested in the particular merchandise which the store has on hand, and may take the point of view that the purpose of advertising is to sell those goods which may be difficult to sell or which may not have been bought as wisely and discriminately as they should have been bought. The advertising department, however, represents more nearly the point of view of the customer and the public.

This problem of organization leads, therefore, to the question as to what should be advertised. There are two general, and possibly opposing, points of view in regard to this question. Shall the chief purpose of the advertising be to advertise those goods which are difficult to sell, for which there has been little call in general, the goods which people have not wanted? Or shall the advertising be directed primarily toward selling the goods for which there is a large demand and the sale of which, therefore, may be stimulated still further by advertising?

Undoubtedly, a great deal of money expended for retail advertising is devoted to the former type of procedure, in which case the purpose of the advertising seems to be primarily to advertise special clearance sales, left-overs, markdowns, and so on. The wise investment of the advertising appropriation may no doubt be gained by devoting it almost entirely, or at least largely, to the stimulation of sales of the new goods in season and of goods that appeal most strongly to the public or in which people will be most readily interested. The reason for this obviously is that the attempt to sell goods in which the public is not interested is a difficult, up-hill task, and undoubtedly means the expenditure of a considerable amount of money without producing commensurate results. Only a small share of the advertising appropriation should ordinarily be devoted to the sale of left-overs, those things which the people have not wanted and have left on the shelves of the store.

Another important point to be determined by the policy is the question of where and to whom to advertise—the kind or class of people to whom a store intends to appeal. If we may think of people roughly as divided into three classes from the standpoint of buying power and social status, namely, high, medium, and low, a store should determine to which class or classes it aims to appeal. It has been said that no store can successfully appeal to all three classes; that it can probably appeal only to two, either the high and medium classes, or the medium and lower classes. The importance of this general question may be seen if we understand that the advertising must necessarily be prepared to accord with the particular class or classes to whom the store appeals. Frequently a store appealing primarily to the highest class or the medium class will carry out its advertising as though it were directed to the lowest class.

The next problem is that of the appropriation to be set aside for advertising and for how long in advance such an appropriation should be determined. Ordinarily the advertising appropriation should be determined for at least six months or a year in advance. This should necessarily be sufficiently flexible to allow for emergencies. The basis upon which the appropriation is made and the common practice with regard to the amount of money appropriated by various types of retailers has been discussed in Chapter III. In general, it will be sufficient to say at this point that the most common expenditure for retail advertising is in the neighborhood of 2%. It may range actually from nothing in the case of very small retailers up to as high as 8% or 10% on the part of other retailers. An appropriation as small as 1% or less may in many instances be too small to get the total proportion of the business to which a given store may be entitled. On the other hand, an appropriation which runs as high as 6%, 8%, or 10% is undoubtedly too large, certainly in the case of a store which is well established. The practice on the part of a good many retail stores is to limit the amount of money expended for newspaper advertising to not over 1% to 2% and to limit the total expenditure for advertising, including other forms of publicity, such as window display and decorations, to 4% or 5%. Many stores regard a safe limit of advertising expenditures to be about 2% of the total sales for newspaper space and about 4% for all forms of publicity, including window display. They also specify that the advertising expenditure for specific articles shall not exceed about 10% of the sales of these articles.

Probably a definite percentage of sales will serve as the most suitable basis for determining the amount of appropriation. However, this may well be combined with a budget plan by which a certain definite amount will be determined upon so that emergencies and unforeseen fluctuations in the volume of business may properly be met. Thus, for example, in the case of a business slump it may be desirable to spend a slightly larger amount than a direct uniform percentage would permit. Or, again, in times of unusual volumes of business the appropriation may be reduced below the specified percentage. Thus, for example, when a store may have a very large volume of business during the pre-holiday season and the customers in the store are more numerous than can well be taken care of, it may be wise to reduce the amount of expenditure or to stop advertising entirely for a week or 10 days.

The appropriation set aside for window display would ordinarily include the various expenditures directly or indirectly involved such as light, power, special fixtures, rental for the space of the windows, and so on. Thus, for example, it is a practice on the part of some large stores to charge a certain amount for the window rental to various departments and to deduct this from the rent of the store.

Another question of general policy is the question of when to advertise. Should the advertising be done every day, on Sundays, in the morning, or in the evening papers? Should most of it be done in the height of the season, or during the dull season? Roughly, in the case of most retailers the fluctuation between the best month and the dullest month in the year is approximately 2 to 1. That is, approximately twice as much business is done during the best month as during the poorest month, and in general the amount of advertising done will run along in a parallel manner, except in so far as it should be modified on account of other circumstances. In general, probably more is derived from the advertising investment if a larger amount is expended during the busiest periods and a correspondingly smaller amount during the duller periods. One large store, however, eliminates practically all of its advertising during a period of about 10 days prior to the holiday season, during which time the store is overcrowded with shoppers. With reference to advertising on Sundays or week days, it may be noted that it is the policy of certain large stores not to advertise on Sunday at all. It is the practice of most stores, however, to do more than the usual amount of advertising on Sunday. Along with the question of mediums, it is a problem of policy to determine what types of goods shall be advertised in each of the various mediums or newspapers in a city in which there are several newspapers available.

Another question of policy is the determination of the general style of the advertising, what the main appeals should be, price, quality, institutionality; whether or not illustrations shall be used, and whether the text shall be full, descriptive, and wordy. An examination of the advertising of several large retailers will show that there are certain typical practices followed by many retailers. Thus, for example, Altmans in New York and Stearns in Boston use no illustrations.

RETAIL ADVERTISING COPY

In order to prepare copy for retail advertising and to judge it, one must have certain criteria or standards prepared both on the basis of the policy which has been decided upon and also on the basis of the fundamental principles of appeals to human nature. What shall these criteria be? Naturally, that which may be good advertising for one firm may not necessarily be good advertising for another firm and in another type of situation. From the foregoing discussion of the problems of policy it will be seen that certain fundamental criteria will evolve out of the nature of the policy which has been decided upon. Aside from this consideration, there are certain fundamental criteria by which retail copy may be evaluated. It will be unnecessary to go into detail here in discussing these criteria, since they are fundamentally the same as for any type of advertising. An individual advertisement or a series of advertisements may be prepared and judged on the basis of the functions which an advertisement is intended to accomplish. These have been previously pointed out and are the following: (1) to secure attention, (2) to secure interest, (3) to produce belief and conviction, (4) to produce a response, and (5) to impress the memory.

ATTENTION

So far as attention is concerned, the same general principles and specific conditions regarding the technique and execution of the advertising layout will apply here which have been discussed previously. One problem, however, which is different in the case of retail advertising is that of the use of space. Shall the retail advertiser use all of his space in one block or shall he split it up and use it in several different units? This problem arises particularly in the case of retailers who handle a large variety of commodities, which however is true more or less of practically every retailer. Is it better to split up the space or to use it in one unit? The practice on the part of various retailers has been to follow both methods, and probably successfully. So far as a tendency may be recognized at the present time, it is apparently in the direction of splitting up the space and using it in units, according to the commodity or department of commodities which may be associated together. There are advantages obviously in both methods. In favor of the use of space in one unit it may be stated that a small retailer is able to give an impression of size and dominance which he cannot give by splitting up his space into a number of relatively small units. Furthermore, the single unit also saves the space otherwise needed to repeat the signature and name either at the top or at the bottom. On the other hand, the splitting up of the space into smaller units, particularly in the case of a large retailer who uses a considerable amount of space, makes it possible to group together in one place as a unit by itself, constructed as an independent advertisement, items which are naturally associated. This avoids the miscellaneous compilation of a great variety of irrelevant and miscellaneous articles. The purchaser may be interested in gloves or dresses but may not be interested in hardware or fur coats at that moment.

As a general conclusion, we may venture the statement that for the small retailer it may be desirable to use space more generally in one unit, whereas for the large retailer it may be to his advantage to divide the space into separate units. So far as the statistical evidence presented in Chapter XXIII on the relative attention value of large and small space is concerned, it is likely that there is not as much difference in favor of the large space in the case of newspaper advertising as in the case of magazine advertising; and therefore this question will be decided more on the basis of other factors.

INTEREST

As in all advertising, the important means of securing the attention of the reader are the interest incentives consisting of the display lines and the illustrations. The headline is the sorting device for selecting the readers which the advertisements attract. Thus, for example, the headline,

"Women's Silk Dresses at $19.50," will attract one class of buyers. On the other hand, the woman who is interested in buying a hundred-dollar dress will not be interested in reading any further about this offering. The headline serves as a sifting device somewhat analogous to a grading device for sorting oranges according to size. The headline, if properly constructed, should attract the customer who will naturally be interested in that particular commodity.

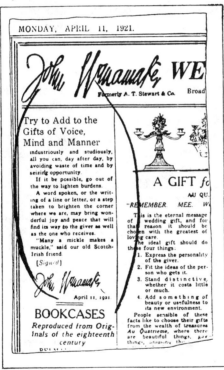

Figure 112:   One way of developing the sustained interest of the reader in the store as an institution

One point in which retail advertising is somewhat different from other types of advertising is in the utilization of the news element.   While any form of advertising may use the news element to advantage, it is more valuable perhaps in the case of retail advertising than in other types of advertising. The retail advertisement should, of course, always give the firm name a fair amount of display, since the purchaser is at once interested in seeing this or that particular store's advertising. The name of the particular firm is as much a matter of interest as is the individual commodity. A national advertiser must present his commodity; the retail advertiser is in part interested in presenting his own merits as an institution. However, aside from this consideration, specific news is one of the chief appeals which the retailer may use. Why? In the first place, news is one of the chief stimuli to interest and curiosity. Curiosity is an inborn instinct to which news appeals and as such it goes back to fundamental motives in human nature. In primitive days something new stimulated curiosity as a matter of the survival of the fittest. Among primitive tribes news was a matter of life and death. The approaching of a tribe was news, and meant that they had better prepare to meet the enemy. The chief of the tribe returned from a fishing or gaming trip with a new supply of food. This was news. The frost had killed the crop of fruit or berries upon which they depended for their existence. That was news. Life today, as well as in primitive conditions, depends on changing processes, on news. The one who knows it early and fully has a better advantage of meeting the situation accordingly, as in primitive conditions he had a better chance of surviving. In modern civilized conditions, life is very little different from this standpoint. It is for this reason that news furnishes an excellent appeal to use in retail advertising.

In the second place, the psychological attitude of the reader of the newspaper is the news attitude. His mind is set for news. He is reading the news of the day; consequently, his mind is ready to receive news from any source. He is in an attitude to receive the news about a store or a business or a commodity. On the principle that when you are afraid of a thief at night, every sound is the sound of a thief, so the eye in looking through a newspaper sees what is dominating the mind. It is looking for news.

Figure 113: Example of an advertisement using news to develop the interest of the reader

In an investigation conducted some years ago by Professor W. D. Scott in connection with the Chicago newspapers, he found that 80% of the 4,000 men interviewed who read the Chicago newspapers did so because of the news. It is evident, then, that the advertisements in newspapers compete with the news of the day. Consequently, they must be as interesting as the news itself in order to compete successfully. Many women read the paper to see what the stores have to offer and are as much, if not more, interested in the news of the stores as they are in the news of the day. A considerable number of women look first for the advertisements and afterwards for the news. It is said that at one time a strike in the printing plants of the newspapers of a large city eliminated all of the department store advertising. The circulation was said to have decreased very considerably on that account.

The headline is the point where the advertiser makes his first contact with the reader. It is, therefore, imperative that a contact be made and that the right contact be made. The news should be specific. It is not enough to present general news about spring or Easter or some commodity in general—it must be specific news. You catch one kind of fish with one kind of bait and another kind with a different kind of bait. Of course in some cases a store may have developed such standing and general interest in the community that anything which it presents will be read by the customers, and general news in such a case may be effective; but as a rule, specific news will catch the interest of the reader more directly and more surely.

BELIEF AND CONVICTION

What will produce belief and conviction in the case of national or other forms of advertising will also produce belief and conviction in retail advertising. There are two basic essentials. The first is an adequate and appropriate description of the goods. This is necessary in order that the reader may visualize them and obtain as clear a conception as possible. Such a description must be specific, correct, and complete. The mail-order houses have learned to produce effective descriptions. They have learned that since their only contact with the customer is through the printed page, the statements must be accurate, specific, and complete. Otherwise, the customer will not have a correct conception of the goods. This will necessarily result in the

return of a large percentage of goods. The retail advertiser may learn this lesson from the mail-order advertiser.
It is a matter of dollars and cents to the mail-order advertisers to make as many sales as possible, naturally, but it
is also a matter of dollars and cents to avoid having goods
returned because of faulty descriptions and impressions.

Figure 114: Example of an advertisement that gives appropriate description and illustration of the goods advertised

Secondly, in order to produce belief and conviction it is as necessary in retail as in any form of advertising to make absolutely truthful and believable statements. We shall not discuss this point in detail here because it has been fully discussed in a preceding chapter. Perhaps a distinction ought to be made between the terms "truthful" and "believable," because a considerable amount of advertising is truthful but it is not all believable. There are two main reasons for this: first, the truth is often couched in such terms that it does not seem plausible or believable; second, although certain statements may actually be literally truthful, they are often not believed by the public-at-large because of the deceptions which have been so generally practiced with regard to these statements by retailers. Thus, for example, a retailer may announce through the mail a special so-called private sale to a limited number of his customers. Many customers may not believe that it is actually a limited sale announced to them only. Or a product may be announced at a considerable reduction in price, literally true, but the public may not believe it because of the deception and unreliability that is so often practiced in connection with price reductions.

In general there are two main rules—in addition to those already discussed in a previous chapter—which should be borne in mind in order to produce absolutely truthful and believable copy. First, avoid grandiose, exaggerated statements; instead make the statements specific, relevant, and to the point. Second, avoid, in general, comparative prices. While there are two sides to this question—for, as previously pointed out, comparative prices are justifiable in many instances,—yet the fact that they are abused so many times makes them unbelievable for the most part to a considerable share of the public. For this reason, many of the better merchants are avoiding their use. If comparative prices are literally true and if they have not been abused so that the public will not believe them, they are, under special conditions when justified, extremely strong appeals. If the public absolutely believed these comparative price statements there are probably few appeals that would be stronger than the comparative price appeal. It is an appeal to the desire for economy, which is an expression of the instinct of possession, one of the strongest instincts in human nature. One example of evasion of statement in quoting comparative prices is the use of such a phrase as "made to sell at $30; our price, $17.50." If a commodity was made to sell at $30, why should it not then be sold at that price? When that is really true, some impression ought to be given to the reader that there is a genuine reason for this reduction in price.

The question may be asked here: Why is the comparative price appeal so much used and why is it so effective with so large a proportion of the people? In spite of the deception practiced by retailers and in spite of the disbelief on the part of a large share of the public, the statement may be made that its effectiveness is no doubt due to a large extent, particularly with the lower-grade stores, to the general credulity of human nature.

MEMORY AND CONTINUITY IN ADVERTISEMENTS

Every retailer wishes to have his name and products remembered; he also wishes to make it possible for the reader to identify his advertisements as he becomes a steady reader and customer. To accomplish these ends it is desirable to establish certain elements of uniformity and continuity which may be recognized as the individual features of the advertising of a particular retailer. Individuality acquired through such features is a distinct advantage. Such marks of individuality may be the uniformity of the name display and the logotype; uniform borders and a type of border layout for basement advertising different from that used for upstairs advertising; or a uniform layout and border for certain departments. A uniform style of phraseology is often used also as a mark of individuality.

The advertising prepared by many retailers is in accord neither with the standing which they have in a community nor with the merchandise that they carry. The results of an investigation made under the writer's direction in Madison, Wisconsin, illustrate this point. Ten advertisements of women's coats and suits were obtained from 10 different retail establishments and were submitted to a test by 100 women. These 10 advertisements were made up in two identical sets. In one set the names of the stores were omitted. In the other they were retained. The 10 advertisements without the names were submitted to each woman individually. She was asked to look them over carefully and to rank them in the order in which they appealed to her as good places for buying a suit or coat. The same advertisements but with the names present in the advertisements were then submitted to the women, who were again asked to examine them and to rank them. The results are set forth in Table 161.

TABLE 161

EFFECT OF REPUTATION OF A STORE UPON ITS ADVERTISING

Ads	Rank of Ad When Name of Firm Was Not Known	Ads	Rank of Ad When Name of Firm Was Known
A	1	D	1
B	2	C	2
C	3	I	3
D	4	E	4
E	5	A	5
F	6	H	6
G	7	B	7
H	8	F	8
I	9	K	9
J	10	G	10
K	11	J	11

The advertisement of store B was second in the estimation of the 100 women when the name of the store was not known to them, but it was seventh when the name was known. On the other hand, store I had a poor advertisement but its reputation is very good. When the name was not known advertisement I was ninth; when the name was known it ranked third.

Retail Copy Service. Some advertising organizations make a business of supplying retail copy to various types of merchants. This copy is usually supplied for specific kinds of retailers, as, for example, men's furnishings, boys' departments, shoes, and the like. The advantage of such service is that the small retailer is able to have better copy than he himself is able to prepare, unless he is unusual and gives considerable thought to it. On the other hand, the disadvantage of copy service of this sort is that the copy is necessarily designed to apply to any retail store, and is thus devoid of local touch and of the conditions that suit the particular individual store.

RESEARCH METHODS IN RETAIL ADVERTISING

It will be of value to illustrate a number of typical problems which arise in any retail store and the manner in which fairly definite answers may be obtained to them. The investigations which are reported here are presented merely to illustrate methods of approach rather than to present the actual data obtained. The facts were obtained as a result of one rather fundamental question regarding which the store desired definite information. This question was: "Does the — store distribute its advertising to the best advantage in the various papers?" The store was doing a considerable amount of business in the city of Boston and surrounding territory and had been using approximately the same amount of space in all of the leading dailies.

This question led to related problems and consequently a plan was prepared for making as thorough an investigation as possible of various aspects of retail advertising relative to this store. In general the investigation was divided into two main sections: (1) that carried on outside the store and (2) that carried on inside the store. The investigation inside the store was divided into two subdivisions, namely: (1) the upstairs store, and (2) the basement store.

OUTSIDE INVESTIGATION

It was decided to undertake certain inquiries which could be handled most satisfactorily by interviewing customers scattered more or less by chance over the metropolitan district of the city. Consequently a plan was adopted for making personal interviews and the set of questions shown in Figure 115 was used.

Fifty women scattered over all parts of the metropolitan district of the city were interviewed personally by means of this questionnaire. The women were very much interested in this inquiry and showed a very helpful attitude in supplying information in a careful, straight-forward manner. Seventy per cent of the women were married, and 30% were unmarried. Only in rare instances was the attitude unsatisfactory. Any unsatisfactory responses thus obtained were discarded in the tabulations. The following results were based on 50 interviews. No mention was made in connection with these interviews of the particular store for which this investigation was being made.

Question 1—What newspapers do you read?

Paper	Per Cent of Readers	Paper	Per Cent of Readers
Post	25.2	Transcript	11.2
Globe	23.1	American	9.8
Herald	26.1	Record	2.1
Traveler	12.6	Monitor	0.

Name   Occupation

Address   If married, husband's occupation

1. What newspapers do you read?
    American   Post   Traveler   Record
    Globe   Herald   Transcript Christian Science Monitor

2. Do you make it a point to read the newspaper advertise-
    ments before going shopping?
    Always   Usually   Rarely   Never

3. To what extent do you have confidence in department store
    advertising?

4. Do you take any stock in bargain sale advertising?

5. Do you believe in comparative price advertising?

6. Mention the stores in whose advertising you have confidence.
    (Number them in order, 1, 2, 3, beginning with the store
    in which you have most confidence.)

7. What newspaper advertising do you read most?
    Morning   Evening   Sunday

8. Below are listed various appeals in retail advertising. Please
    rank them in the order in which they appeal to you.
    Price   New Merchandise
    Quality   Complete stock of merchan-
    Style   dise every day
    Durability   Prices guaranteed
    Reliability of the firm Satisfaction or money re-
                               funded

9. Do you trade regularly at any stores?

10. Why do you trade at these stores?

11. How do these two statements strike you? (Two moderate-
    sized advertisements were presented each stating the gen-
    eral policy of the particular store.)

12. Do you read these news items? (A typical sample adver-
    tisement was shown which contained in one column a
    variety of news items about the store.)
    All of them   Considerable   None

13. This part of the investigation consisted in having the per-
    son rank in order of appeal 10 typical retail store adver-
    tisements.

Figure 115: Consumer investigation regarding retail advertising

Although the results of this questionnaire were based on only 50 women, information was obtained on a number of the same questions in the investigation conducted within the store.   The returns from these questions showed a very close agreement with the results obtained from the 50 questionnaires.

Question 2—Do you make it a point to read newspaper advertisements before going shopping?

Always	52%	Likely	14%
Usually	32	Never	2

It is interesting to note that the percentage of women who either "always" or "usually" read the newspaper advertisements before they go shopping is fairly high.   The results on this point will be verified from the larger returns obtained inside the store.   Apparently the women have quite generally established the habit of looking at the advertisements before going shopping.

Question 3—To what extent do you have confidence in Department Store advertising?

The answers to this question were reported verbatim as they were given and were divided into four classes as follows:

Complete confidence	20%	Fair confidence	36%
Much confidence	34	No confidence	10

The considerable proportion of women who have only fair confidence in department store advertising is large enough to be a matter of some concern.   When combined with the proportion of women who state they have no confidence in retail store advertising, we have a total of 46%, or nearly half.   The lack of confidence is due, undoubtedly, to the failure of the merchants to represent their goods in a thoroughly reliable and dependable manner.   The 10% of the women who expressed themselves as having no confidence in department store advertising stated that they seldom found what was advertised and a number of them definitely stated that they did not believe the advertising to be honest.

Question 4—Do you take any stock in bargain sale advertising?

Yes	34%	Very little	12%
At times	22	No	28
Some stores	4		

The answers to this question were likewise recorded in the exact words in which they were given by the women interviewed. These figures show to what extent there is a lack of confidence in bargain sale advertising. Only one-third of the women have confidence or a very distinctly qualified confidence. A large number of the women who answered that they took little or no stock in bargain sale advertising gave such reasons as these: "When I get there, the merchandise is all gone," or "The goods on sale are always odd lots or out sizes." The trouble with these cases is that the bargain sale appeal has been and is being constantly abused. Either the stores have not had sufficient merchandise to satisfy the demand for it or they have not told the truth about the merchandise which they have so advertised.

Question 5—Do you believe in comparative price advertising?

Yes, 38%; No, 28%; Depends on store, 34%.

The returns to this question again show the abuse of comparative prices and the substantial lack of confidence in comparative prices as they are ordinarily used. Relatively speaking only somewhat more than one-third of the women have confidence in comparative price statements. Slightly less than two-thirds either have none or have very limited confidence. The wording of comparative price statements is undoubtedly important. Such phrases as "Was so much; now selling for so much," and "Value, so much;

selling price, so much," should not be used because of their triteness. New and original phrases with a sincere tone, backed up by a reliable policy will greatly remedy the disrepute into which comparative prices have fallen.

Question 6—Mention the stores in the advertising of which you have confidence.

The answers to this question will be omitted for obvious reasons.

Question 7—What newspaper advertising do you read most?

Morning, 42.2%; Evening, 31.1%; Sunday, 26.7%.

Question 8—Relative rank of appeals. The following table gives the median rank of each appeal. The highest rank is given at the top and the lowest at the bottom.

Quality	2.32
Price	3.3
Style	3.7
Reliability of firm	4.2
Durability	5.2
Satisfaction or money refunded	6.2
Price guaranteed	7.8
New merchandise	7.7
Complete stock of merchandise	8.9

These results obviously show that quality of merchandise is a fundamental consideration in the minds of people; price is second; style, third; reliability of firm, fourth. The other appeals are relatively unimportant. This point is of interest in view of the fact that the price appeal has been made more conspicuous on the part of a considerable proportion of retailers. The purchaser is not interested in price as such, but he is always interested in merchandise at a certain price. It is a consideration of the two together that is the important thing. As one examines retail advertising one obtains the impression that the price is the important thing rather than the merchandise. In a great deal of retail advertising the price is displayed more conspicuously even than the name of the merchandise. Incidentally, it may be pointed out here that the result of the first group of 25 women agreed very closely with the results of the second group of 25 women. The correlation between the two was .93.

Question 9—Do you trade regularly at any stores?

Yes, 80%; No, 20%.

It is evident that a decided majority of women have developed the custom of trading regularly at certain stores. This, of course, does not mean that 80% of the women trade only at one store, but that they trade regularly at certain stores. The results here emphasize the value of developing in customers the habit of returning regularly to the same store.

Question 10—Why do you trade regularly at these stores?

The answers were recorded verbatim, and were then classified as follows:

Complete satisfaction with merchandise	32%
Reliability of firm	16
Quality of merchandise	14
Exchange goods and adjustment service	10
Obliging sales clerks	6
Firm stands back of merchandise	6
Complete stocks of merchandise	4
Like management	4
Better values	4
Like store in general	2
Delivery service	2

Question 11—How do these two statements strike you?

Blank Company—The Mercantile Heart of New England
To the Best of Our
Knowledge and Belief
Our Entire Stock of Merchandise
Is Marked at Replacement Value and It
Will be Kept on This Basis.

(In fact, hundreds of items are just now even less than replacement value)

We believe the public should buy their needs freely for the next few months under these circumstances, as nearly all manufacturers with whom we do business tell us that their prices will be no lower, and some may be higher by May or June.

Note: Handling many hundreds of thousands of different articles as we do, it is quite possible that there may be a few lines where the manufacturer's price has been recently reduced and we have not as yet been informed of the fact. We would thank our patrons or any other persons to call the attention of either department managers or their assistants or the executive management to any such case, when upon investigation adjustment will immediately be made.

Blank Company

Blank Company—The Mercantile Heart of New England

One of the most important principles upon which this business has been built is

Complete Stocks of
Desirable, Dependable Merchandise
In Every Department—Every Day in the Year

The largest and most complete assortments in New England— including the highest grade and most exclusive varieties— both foreign and domestic

From This Policy We Shall Never Depart

We remind the public of this fact, in case some may have been misled by the unusual amount of markdown and special-sale merchandise we have been obliged to offer the past few months on account of the unusual market conditions.

You can usually find what you are looking for here without looking elsewhere.

Blank Company

The answers were recorded again in the words given by the women interviewed. They were divided into two groups, favorable and unfavorable, as follows:

Favorable		*Unfavorable*	
Very good advertising	46%	Untrue	14%
Sounds reasonable	12	Not interested in them	12
Believes in them	8	Does not mean anything	8

The salient fact is the large number of women who considered this good advertising and the relatively small number who thought the statements were untrue. More women criticized the statement, "complete stocks of merchandise," than the statement, "to the best of our knowledge and belief our merchandise is marked at replacement value." Some women did not believe that any store had complete stocks of merchandise every day. A number of others did not understand what was meant by "replacement value." This illustrates the advisability of couching the ideas in advertisements in such language that they will be clear to the average reader.

Question 12—Do you read these news items? (Some samples of news items such as are printed along the side of the advertisements of the firm were shown to determine what was the attitude of the women towards these news items.) The answers are classified as follows:

Read all of them   46%   Read none of them   12%
Read a considerable part   42%

These answers refer to the items in any one day's announcements rather than to all of the announcements from day to day. The comments regarding them were very favorable, and the extent to which women read these items was further indicated by the fact that over 80% of the women interviewed recognized these items and associated them with the particular firm which issued them.

Question 13—The next question consisted of a series of tests with a set of ten advertisements. These ten advertisements represented a variety of types of retail advertisements. Five of these were from the firm whose problems were being studied; the remaining five were from four other retailers dealing in similar goods. The women were asked to read these advertisements over and to obtain a clear impression of them and then to rank them in the order in which they appealed to them as effective and convincing advertisements. In making this test, all marks of identification were removed from the advertisements; that is, the names and other features identifying certain advertisements in the minds of people were removed. This was done for the purpose of obtaining as objective a rating of the advertisements as possible, unaffected by the general reputation of the firms concerned. The results are very interesting for the particular firms involved. Of the five advertisements of the firm here in question, one stood at the top of the list of ten as being the most appealing advertisement; two were at the bottom of the list as being the least effective advertisements. Advertisement "H," reproduced in Figure 117, was the first one; and advertisement "D" (not from the same firm), shown in Figure 116, was the second one in the list of ten as indicated by the tests.

The reason why advertisements "H" and "D" stood high is not only because of their general attention value, but also because of the interest and appealing copy which they contain. The headlines are good; they have a strong news appeal; the layout is attractive; and the principal features are well displayed. The headline, "early showing of new misses' dresses for all occasions," is a good display line. It immediately attracts the attention of the women who are interested in this type of goods and also eliminates those who are not interested in it. The advertisement is simple and attractive, and sets forth one item to good advantage.

The results of this ranking were tabulated separately for the first 25 women and for the second group of 25 women. It will be noted here that the two groups agreed very closely, with a correlation of .76. This corroborates in general the point previously made, that a good set of tests with a small group of even 25 persons gives ordinarily a fairly reliable measure.

A large number of the women interviewed commented on the advertisements; in fact, they were encouraged by the investigators to do so. Many said that department store advertising lacks the news element and that it is not well illustrated. Likewise, a large number of the women said that they liked a great deal of news and good descriptions of the merchandise as well as good illustrations of the merchandise.

Figure 116: Specimen of an advertisement with principal features well displayed *(See page 916)*

Perhaps the chief importance of this portion of the investigation is that it demonstrates to the retailer the value of making, at intervals of a year or two, an investigation of this sort. The investigation will at times perhaps need to be more limited than the one here indicated and at times more extensive. There is a very distinct value in an investigation carefully carried out in this manner. The retailer

EARLY SHOWING
of
NEW MISSES' DRESSES
FOR ALL OCCASIONS

The sketch on the left shows an After-noon Dress of the season's most favored material, Canton Crepe, trimmed with rows of fagoting which reveal Leghorn underdress. The neck and bodice are also trimmed in the Leghorn shade **59.50**

Dresses trimmed with lace were never more popular than they are this year. Shown on the figure sketched above is a ı ın for Afternoon or Evening wear of ɛɑ ₁ with an overskirt of lace to match. Folds of satin give a bouffant effect at the hips. Gray and brown **45.00**

Figure 117: Example of display in a retail advertisement *(See page 916)*

were present it would unconsciously tend to warp the re-
is able to obtain reactions which will be extremely valuable
to him and which he cannot obtain in any other way. The
important point, however, that should be emphasized here,
is that such an investigation must be carried out in a manner to avoid bias and prejudice in favor of the firm for
which the investigation is being conducted. If such bias

sults, making them appear too favorable for the firm in question. The investigation will be most successful if carried out either by someone who is not connected with the firm itself or by someone who knows how to conduct such an investigation impersonally and fairly. No reference should be made to the store concerned, and the questions should be put to the customer in such a manner that she will not be influenced to answer in favor of any particular store.

INSIDE INVESTIGATION

The second portion of the investigation was made inside the store. The purpose was to obtain further information on a larger scale concerning three or four of the points covered in the outside investigation. The chief points of inquiry were mediums and the extent to which the advertising is read prior to purchasing. Consequently, a brief questionnaire containing the three questions reproduced in Figure 118 was printed. The salespersons asked the customer these questions after a purchase had been made.

In obtaining answers to these questions several departments were selected each day, a part of which had been advertised for that day and a part not. Each salesperson in that department was provided for that day with a supply of these questionnaires. The salespersons were instructed to ask these questions as far as possible of every other person or every fourth or fifth person who came to purchase from them. The purpose of this was to obtain as fair a chance distribution of customers as possible. This was probably not strictly observed, but the purpose of the instructions was to impress upon the salespersons that a chance cross-section should be made. The investigation was conducted over a period of 10 days, from March 9 to March 19, 1921. A total of 5,325 customers were interviewed in this way, and 5,298 questionnaires were secured

Dept. No.   No. of Sales Person   Date   Name of Customer
Address

(1) Would you object to telling me whether or not you saw this article advertised?   (The word "article" referred to whatever had been purchased.)

Yes   No

The salesperson would then explain as follows: The reason I inquire is because the   Company wishes me to ask if you would mind answering, if you have not already done so today, two other questions regarding the value of this firm's advertising to you. (Note: If the customer should inquire why these questions were being asked, you should answer, "We are trying to place our advertising announcements where they will result to the best advantage of our customers and of ourselves.")

(2) Do you read the newspaper advertisements before you go shopping?

Practically always   Usually   Rarely   Never

(3) What daily paper or papers do you read regularly?

American   Post
Christian Science Monitor   Record
Globe   Transcript
Herald   Traveler

After a customer has left, fill in the following from your sales slip, provided the article purchased was one she saw advertised:

Article purchased   Amount   Cash   Charge

Figure 118: Investigation of retail advertising by interviewing customers

filled in satisfactorily. They were used in the following tabulation. The results for the upstairs division of the store and for the basement division were kept separate. The number of customers interviewed in the upstairs division was 3,895; in the basement, 1,403.

A very useful part of this investigation was the securing of the names and addresses of the customers. These were carefully tabulated geographically to ascertain the distribution of the customers over the metropolitan and surrounding territory. This distribution is of very distinct value. Any retail store of considerable size will find information thereby obtained worth while.

Question 1—Would you object to telling me whether or not you saw this article advertised?

The question was put in this particular form in order to avoid any antagonism or ill-will that might result from conducting such an investigation on a large scale. It is evident that, unless care is taken, such an inquiry, even though it may be very brief, might arouse the antagonism of the customers and produce a considerable amount of ill-will. However, it is believed that this was entirely avoided by the manner in which the questions were put and by the instructions which were given to the salespersons. The results of the first question were as follows:

	Yes	No		Yes	No
Upstairs	14.1%	85.9%	Basement	40.5%	59.5%

The proportion of persons in the upstairs division who stated that they had seen the particular article which they had purchased advertised is relatively small. However, this percentage is considerably larger, practically three times larger, in the basement. This is partly due to a sale which was being advertised in the basement during a part of this period. However, there is no doubt a difference in the two types of customers. The customers in the upstairs store probably do more general shopping from department to department than is the case with the basement customers. The figures probably indicate, also, that the advertising is successful in bringing customers into the store, as a result of which they go about from department to department in addition to the one in which they may be interested or which they may have seen advertised the day or morning before.

A comparison was made between the departments advertised and those not advertised. The results for the upstairs store only were tabulated from this point of view and were as follows:

	Yes	No
Articles bought which customers had seen advertised	18.9%	81.1%

There is a noticeably larger proportion of Yes's in the departments which had specifically been advertised. The proportion of customers who responded with "Yes" on various days varied quite considerably, being as high as 36% on one day and as low as 9% on another day. Likewise, the percentage varied considerably by departments, being as high as 90% in some departments and as low as zero in other departments on various days.

Question 2—Do you read newspaper advertising before you go shopping?

	Upstairs	Basement	Average	50 Outside Women
Always	37. %	56.7%	46.8%	52%
Usually	38.5	31.5	35.0	32
Rarely	16.5	8.8	12.6	14
Never	7.9	2.7	5.3	2

These results are interesting as showing the extent to which women read the advertisements before they go shopping. The basement returns are somewhat larger than the upstairs returns, which is probably due in part to the special sale advertised in the basement during part of this period. It is also in part due probably to the somewhat greater bargain interest which the basement customers have.

A point of considerable interest from a statistical point of view is the remarkably close agreement between the results of the 50 outside customers and the 5,298 customers inside the store. While there are differences, the results are substantially the same.

Question 3—What daily paper or papers do you read regularly?

	Upstairs	Basement	Average	50 Outside Customers
Globe	24.1%	30.7%	25.8%	23.1%
Post	22.3	31.7	24.6	25.2
Herald	18.7	8.1	16.	16.1
Transcript	14.3	5.1	12.	11.2
Traveler	11.9	9.2	11.1	12.6

American	5.7	13.2	7.6	9.8
Record	2.2	1.4	2.1	2.1
Monitor	.8	.7	.8	o.

The purpose of this series of facts was to relate them to the amount of advertising space carried in the various papers. Consequently, the figures regarding the amount of space used in each of the papers were obtained together with the circulation of each paper and were compared with the proportion of the customers who read each particular paper. These figures, given in Table 162, are significant only for a given store and for a given period of time.

These figures show some striking facts regarding the use of space, the circulation, and customer readers. In the first place, it will be noted that the amount of space used is substantially the same in five papers. Considerably less is used in the *Transcript,* and only a very small amount of space is used in the other papers. A comparison of the space used and the reader customers in relation to circulation will show, for example, that the *American,* which carried nearly as much space as the other four large papers has 21.8% of the total circulation of all of those papers combined. There were only 5.7% of the upstairs customers

TABLE 162

CORRELATION OF NUMBER OF CUSTOMERS, READERS OF
NEWSPAPERS AND ADVERTISING SPACE FOR A
GIVEN STORE AND A GIVEN TIME

	Column Inches	Per Cent of Total Space Used	Circula-tion	Per Cent of Total Circu-lation	Customer Readers Basement	Customer Readers Upstairs
Post	416	17.2	422,000	30.7	22.3	31.7
American	387	15.9	301,000	21.8	5.7	13.2
Globe	419	17.4	285,000	20.7	24.1	30.7
Traveler	424	17.6	140,000	10.2	11.9	9.2
Herald	424	17.6	110,000	8.0	18.7	8.1
Record	99	4.0	43,000	3.1	2.2	1.
Monitor	16	.7	42,000	3.1	.8	.7
Transcript	232	9.6	33,000	2.4	14.3	5.1

among the readers and 13.2% among the basement customers. It is evident that the *American* had a larger proportion of space than the number of readers among the customers would warrant in relation to the other papers. Furthermore, it had a larger proportion of readers among the basement customers than among the upstairs customers. The *Herald*, on the other hand, had a much larger proportion of readers among the upstairs customers than among the basement customers, 18.7% as against 8.1%. The *Post* had a considerable number of readers both among the upstairs and the basement customers, but the proportion of readers among the basement customers was distinctly larger. In other words, an examination of the table will show that certain papers would be used more profitably as a medium for basement advertising and others more profitably for upstairs advertising.

Facts are distinctly valuable from the standpoint of an intelligent distribution of the advertising appropriation among the various mediums. Important details will readily be discovered when the facts are studied specifically from the standpoint of a given store.

XXXVI

FOREIGN ADVERTISING

World commerce. Problems. The human aspect of the market. The appeals and their presentation—the copy. May copy prepared in English be directly translated into the language of the foreign country? Mediums. A bird's-eye view of advertising in various countries: Cuba, Chile, Peru, Argentina, Uruguay, Brazil, Japan, China, The Philippines. Brief outline of an international campaign.

FIFTY years ago in this country national business and national advertising were practically non-existent. Even 20 or 25 years ago advertising in the United States was, to quite an extent, local. During the last two decades it has assumed larger national proportions. In a similar sense, world commerce is just beginning to develop today. While there has been international commerce for centuries, it has, however, not developed to the extent that the manufacturers have gone directly to the consumers in foreign countries and appealed to them, either through printed publicity or otherwise. Great Britain is probably in advance of any other country in world commerce and in thinking in terms of world trade and international advertising and sales activities. America is a newer country and has been struggling primarily with its own resources and has not felt the need of expanding its outlets into other countries. America, however, is at the threshold of expansion into world markets. It is for these reasons, therefore, that foreign advertising is becoming an important field. In 1918 foreign advertising was, for the first time, discussed at the meeting of the Export Trade Council.

Problems. Fundamentally, advertising is the same in foreign countries as it is in the United States, and in that sense the fundamental problems are the same as they are for domestic advertising. We may, therefore, conveniently refer to these five fundamental problems in dealing with foreign advertising. The chief, and perhaps the only, point of difference in their application and solution in foreign countries is that they must be solved in somewhat different ways to meet the peculiar conditions, customs, habits, and methods of doing business in each particular country. Take, for example, the advertising of safety razors in various foreign countries. The five fundamental problems are substantially the same as they would be for a study of advertising in this country; the only difference is that the particular conditions and methods of solution would be different for each country. But it is just as important to have the correct answer to each of the five problems in a foreign country as it is in this country. These five problems, it will be recalled, are:

1. To whom may the product be sold?
2. By what appeals may it be sold?
3. How may these appeals be presented most effectively?
4. In what mediums may they be presented?
5. What may reasonably be expended for advertising the product?

A complete and satisfactory answer to these five questions, in any particular country in which the advertiser is interested, would serve as an intelligent basis for planning his advertising activities. Let us briefly consider these five questions in order.

THE HUMAN ASPECT OF THE MARKET

It is, to begin with, very essential that the market conditions be carefully studied in a foreign country. A thorough study of the human, as well as of the more strictly economic phases of the market for a given product in a foreign country would avoid a great many of the mistakes which are at present being made by many foreign advertisers.

Thus, for example, an artist preparing a picture for a safety razor to be advertised in India drew a picture of a person of low caste sitting on the curbstone of the street shaving himself with this particular safety razor. A study of conditions prevailing in India with regard to the persons using safety razors would have avoided such an incongruity. Or, an advertiser of canned milk featured the use of the milk in coffee and tea in China. He overlooked the important fact that the Chinese do not drink coffee and that they drink their tea without milk or cream. The chief use for canned milk in China is for children and invalids. A manufacturer of toilet goods had developed a good market for talcum powder, cold cream, and toothpaste among Chinese women. He later attempted to market a shampoo preparation; in this it was important for him to know that while Chinese women dress their hair elaborately, they seldom wash it. It was therefore necessary to prepare extensive educational advertising and demonstration. Numerous angles of this sort, which may make the success or failure of an advertising plan in a foreign country, should be discovered in advance so that the plans may be made accordingly. A careful study of the human aspect of the market is therefore obviously necessary.

The methods of study of this problem are essentially the same as those suggested in the chapters in Part II. General statistical facts may be gathered from available sources, but it is highly desirable to make a study corresponding to the questionnaire-field survey such as is made in this country. There is, of course, greater difficulty in carrying out such a study in a foreign country at long distance. But a careful, systematic study, when the expenditures and plans are of large proportions, would unquestionably be an economic investment. Advertisers often base advertising plans upon the observations of travelers who have observed people and conditions in foreign countries, but these observations are so often based purely on exceptional and peculiarly outstanding circumstances that they do not at all represent the real facts or normal conditions in the large majority of instances. It is safer to rely upon carefully conducted investigations. In other words, the scientific point of view in making a study of market conditions is essential.

THE APPEALS AND THEIR PRESENTATION—THE COPY

The statement is frequently made that human nature is the same everywhere. Fundamentally this is true; the essential motives, instincts and constituents of human nature are, no doubt, largely the same all over the world. The difference, however, is in their exterior manifestations, in the habits that are developed and in the ways of satisfying the needs and desires in various parts of the world. The inborn make-up is very much the same, but acquired habits and customs differ materially. Thus, for example, the instincts and desires connected with eating are fundamentally the same in all human beings, but the ways in which the instincts and desires of food-getting are satisfied vary enormously. The utensils differ, the habits of eating differ, the foods differ, their preparation differs, and numerous other details differ. It is these differences that the advertiser must carefully learn before he ventures into a foreign field.

The modes of presentation of a given appeal necessarily differ. For example, the variation in literacy in various countries differs enormously. Thus, in a country in which illiteracy is very high the pictorial presentation is highly important. Likewise, the use of the trade-mark, while important in any country, is perhaps still more important in a country in which illiteracy is high. Thus, for example, in China the illiterate coolie will notice, remember and identify trade-marks and buy goods by trade-mark identification. The trade-mark in such instances should carefully take into account the pictorial make-up. A picture, perhaps, rather than a word, will serve more suitably as a brand of identification.

MAY COPY PREPARED IN ENGLISH BE DIRECTLY TRANSLATED INTO THE LANGUAGE OF THE FOREIGN COUNTRY?

Much discussion has centered around this point and probably the answer to this question, in the light of the experiences of American advertisers in foreign countries, would be that the copy prepared in English may be used in a general way as a basis for the appeals and the presentation to be prepared, but that the copy should not be translated directly into the language of a foreign country. The better plan to follow is to take the English copy as a guide and to have a person who is either a native of a given foreign country or thoroughly familiar with the conditions in that foreign country prepare the copy in the particular foreign language. The reason for this conclusion is that a literal translation will often overlook idiomatic expressions in a foreign language, the omission of which may often make an advertisement either ridiculous or ineffective. Dialects in various sections of the country may differ very materially. This point is illustrated by the following: "The Spanish word for child is 'nino' or 'nina' and is so used in Cuba. In Chile the word for child is 'guagua,' while in Argentina it is 'nena.' 'Nino' might be understood in all these countries, but it would not make the instant appeal the local word would." [1]

Another point to be considered in various countries is the question of colloquialism as against a dignified style. A considerable amount of colloquial copy is used in this country. Observers relate that similar copy would not be effective in foreign countries. Thus, for example, Mr. Sanger observes with regard to Chile and Latin-American countries generally the following: "Moreover, a free-and-easy, colloquial, friendly and sometimes intimate copy much in favor in certain types of American advertising, and particularly in 'gingery' sales letters, not only would not be understood, but would be misunderstood and indeed would

[1] J. W. Sanger, *Advertising Methods in Cuba*, p. 23.

affront Latin Americans, who would regard it as rather impudent. The advertising of 'Prince Albert' tobacco would mystify, and probably offend Latin Americans, and at its best would certainly fail to convince, whereas the quiet, dignified handling of 'Fatima' cigarettes would probably meet with a welcome response. Not that the Latin American is averse to novelties. On the contrary he is more susceptible to their appeal than we are and more easily attracted by a simple moving display in a window, or an ingenious souvenir, or a novel illustration." [1]

MEDIUMS

Facts about mediums must necessarily be obtained for each country separately. Just as no one could intelligently select mediums in this country, even if he has lived here all his life, without a careful study, so it would be still more impossible to select mediums in a foreign country without obtaining the facts about them. This is a more difficult task in most foreign countries than in America, because the facts are not so readily available. Mediums are not as well standardized as in this country; there is no source of information corresponding to the American Audit Bureau of Circulations from which accurate information can be obtained regarding circulations. The relative importance of various types of mediums varies in different countries. Thus, for example, in Japan the newspapers and magazines are among the leading types of mediums, whereas in China probably the most outstanding and most successful medium is the poster or billboard. In the Philippines direct-mail material is perhaps the most useful medium. In most Latin American countries the newspaper is the chief advertising medium. In Great Britain the newspapers occupy a relatively more important place even than they do in America. National advertising is carried on in the newspapers in Great Britain more than in the maga-

[1] J. W. Sanger, "Special Agents Series," No. 185, p. 231.

zines. In the United States national advertising is carried on practically equally in magazines and newspapers.

A BIRD'S-EYE VIEW OF ADVERTISING IN VARIOUS COUNTRIES

A useful series of studies of advertising in Latin American countries and in oriental countries was made by J. W. Sanger, trade commissioner, and reported in the Department of Commerce Bulletins. "Special Agents Series": No. 178, *Advertising Methods in Cuba;* No. 183, *Advertising Methods in Chile, Peru and Bolivia;* No. 190, *Advertising Methods in Argentina, Uruguay and Brazil;* No. 209, *Advertising Methods in Japan, China and the Philippines.* A brief survey presented here is based primarily on these reports.

Cuba. Cuba is regarded as a good experimental field for the American advertiser who is planning to extend his markets in Latin America. It is a compact country, and is, for the most part, typical of Latin American countries.

Cuban business has little of the "touch-and-go" character of the "speeding up" so common in American business. Fixed prices are the exception, not the rule, and the few merchants who have adopted the principle are confused with the less scrupulous ones, because both hang up in their windows and stores the lure of the legend "Fixed prices here." In general, the price asked merely indicates the price the shopkeeper would like to receive, and the price actually paid depends entirely upon the patience and shrewdness of the shopper.

No weeklies or monthlies of general circulation are published in Cuba, such as Americans are accustomed to, and consequently the Cubans are without the well-illustrated educational and informative news articles and advertisements that play so large a part in our lives. American magazines circulate in Cuba, but in only a limited way; they reach a negligible portion of the Cuban public. The daily newspapers published in Havana are, practically speaking, the only island-wide media for news and advertising. They carry mostly Cuban advertising, somewhat crudely conceived and not always notable for good taste or information. What little American advertising appears in their pages is largely that of proprietary medicines, which are finding a good market in the island. There has been little or no advertising of American goods along the lines that have made it successful in this country nor even along modified lines to meet Cuban requirements. Little attempt has been made to merchandise American goods in Cuba, accompanied by and coordinated with advertising. Few well-known American trade-marks are known there. No goods are asked for by name and brand, nor are prices shown and advertised. The bulk of export trade-paper advertising is essentially dealer advertising, and the consumer does not enter into the advertiser's consideration. Thus the merchant is almost entirely in control of the situation and has the first and last word as to what will be sold and how much it will sell for. The dealer is not merely one factor in the merchandising triangle but an absolutely dominating power unobstructed by the wholesome influence of the consumer.

It is perhaps not without significance to the American advertiser that neither England nor Germany, the two exporting nations most vigorous in the prosecution of foreign trade, have ever directly used advertising to support their sales work. It is true that their representatives in both the importing and the retail field have used it in a conventional way, but neither directly nor indirectly has advertising played an important part in the conquest of new fields with these countries, which have called to their aid every other effective means of sales promotion.

The leading retail merchants of Havana are almost unanimously of the opinion that the retail "bargain" methods of the United States would be useless in Cuba. They give as their reason that the native women are not careful or close buyers and have little knowledge of prices or qualities. Neither do they buy for the future, but only for today's needs, so that the offer of say, 7 bars of 5-cent soap for 25 cents would awaken little response, for the naive reason that "no family could use 7 bars of soap at once." Another factor of importance is that the Cuban woman is not the head of her home in the same sense as is the American woman, who buys shrewdly and wisely within the limits of her particular province. The Cuban woman, on the other hand, because of the cheapness of servants and for other reasons, delegates the buying of all food and similar supplies to the cook, who usually cannot read or write. As one well-to-do Cuban told the writer, "In common with most Cuban families of our class, we allow our cook a fixed amount per day on which to 'feed' the family." Therefore, the cook becomes a singularly important factor to the manufacturer of food products who wishes to call advertising to his assistance. It is quite likely that he will have to adjust his advertising to an intelligence to which primary colors and simple trade-marks make some of the few possible appeals. Inasmuch as Cuba imported about $80,000,000 worth of foodstuffs in 1916-17 (about one-third of its total imports), a considerable portion of which is or can be packaged and advertised, this matter is of prime importance.[1]

The various mediums used besides newspapers and magazines, are, of course, direct-mail material, catalogs, and directories in larger cities, such as Havana. The chief newspapers are published in Havana; although each small town has its own local paper, they are not strong nor of great importance. The Havana papers are sold on the streets of Santiago within 36 hours after publication. In practically all Latin American countries there is a considerable misuse of the news type of advertisement which appears as news, but is really advertising material, for there is no requirement that reading notices shall be labelled with the word "advertisement" as is the case in the United States.

A well-known Cuban who has spent many years in both the United States and Europe said to the writer, "We Cubans do not think constructively in the Anglo-Saxon sense but enjoy enjoying our emotions. We love color and life in everything, and we demonstrate it in the bright colors of our automobiles and in the spots of pink, terra cotta, and blue in our older houses." His opinion, and it was substantially supported by many others, has a distinct bearing upon the "copy appeal" necessary in Cuba. Carried to its logical conclusion, the evidence of these witnesses and the writer's observation both tend to indicate that "reason why" copy, common in the United States, finds little response in Cuba except in the advertising of articles of a distinctly technical nature.

With few exceptions, Cuban women are not newspaper readers, and save for the social columns of their newspapers and magazines and the style illustrations in American fashion magazines, reading as it is known among American women plays but a small part in their lives. Taking no active part in home, club, civic, or national affairs, which have been influential factors in broadening the American woman's outlook, the Cuban woman has cre-

[1] J. W. Sanger, *Advertising Methods in Cuba*, pp. 10 and 11.

ated little demand for national magazines of the types that circulate in every corner of the United States.

The necessity for giving the fullest consideration to climate and social conditions in gaging the advertising appeal is sometimes overlooked by American advertisers. The writer observed one advertisement of an American cleaning fluid or wax, in which the illustration pictured the man of the house and his wife deeply interested in the work of cleaning their car. In Cuba all cleaning, without exception, is done by the chauffeur or in a public garage. Even the cheapest automobiles are driven by chauffeurs, and the owner exerts no appreciable influence as to the kind of cleaning fluid or polishing wax used. He is the opposite of the American who has a turn for mechanics and who does not object even to cleaning his own car at times.

Another advertisement of a well-known American proprietary medicine, widely advertised as a preventive of colds, showed the danger of cold weather and its attendant sickness by picturing two children in a snowstorm. Cuba is in the tropics and snow has never fallen there.[1]

Chile. Approximately 50% of the population is literate. Chile contains approximately 400 publications, including newspapers and magazines of all kinds. Approximately 15 dailies and weeklies are of importance.

Properly speaking, neither "reason-why" nor "institutional" advertising has ever been tried in Chile to any extent. As has been commented before, Chile is in its infancy as far as original or distinctive advertising is concerned, and thus far "general publicity" carries the burden. There is a general prejudice against "reason-why" copy, though the objectors could give no reason for their opposition other than that "it wouldn't work." Modified to suit Chilean conditions, there is no good reason why it should not find a place, though perhaps a lesser one than it does with us. The same thing is true of "institutional" advertising. The old-established houses are there; they believe in advertising and use it, but as the experimental stage is just beginning in Chile, as there are few advertising men there to prepare such copy and make a test of it, and as there are few full campaigns from the United States, both these types of appeal will have to wait their turn until a demand for more original copy is made by advertisers.[2]

[1] *Ibid.*, pp. 21 and 22.

[2] J. W. Sanger, *Advertising Methods in Chile, Peru and Bolivia*, pp. 22 and 23.

Peru. Daily newspapers are here the chief medium, and circulation statements are rather uncertain. One paper which was said to have a circulation of 50,000 was found to have actually a circulation of only 20,000. Only approximately 20% of the population of Peru is literate.

As must be evident from the foregoing account of advertising methods and conditions in Peru, the writer does not regard that country as a promising field for the advertiser. The many and varied difficulties may be summed up as follows: (1) The low average of literacy, the general poverty, and the correspondingly low consumption of imports per capita; (2) the lack of any generally influential media, with the possible exceptions of the newspapers and motion pictures, the detailed difficulties in the use of which have been explained; (3) the lack of an evident ability to cooperate even to the extent of actively desiring foreign advertising on the part of the leading publications, the reasons for which are also given in detail; (4) the lack of local channels, such as advertising agencies or similar services, giving local points of contact and acting in an intermediary and advisory capacity.

That an advertising investment is not recommended to the manufacturer desirous of entering the Peruvian market does not mean that these markets are not proving a profitable field for certain classes of American goods. Every year sees more American goods used and there is prospect of continued yearly increases. And so, for the benefit of the manufacturer who is determined to test the value of this market, the following methods of entering it are named in the order of their importance:

(1) By resident American agents, or, better still, by branch houses wherever the expense is warranted;

(2) By traveling salesmen;

(3) By using local houses as agencies;

(4) By correspondence;

(5) Through export commission houses. This last method, while it may possibly produce more immediate sales, is the least satisfactory for the manufacturer who desires to insure an increasing market for his own goods.

Peru is potentially one of the richest countries in South America, and it is proving a profitable field for a variety of American products. But for the manufacturer who wishes to call advertising to his aid in the solution of his marketing problems there, it is a country for the future, not the present.[1]

Argentina. Argentina uses a considerable amount of consumer advertising as against trade advertising in other countries. In 1917 there were some 500 regular publications, newspapers and magazines. We are told that the most widely advertised commodity is the "43" cigarette, for which it is said that $645,000 is spent a year in advertising. American advertisements, such as Edison products, cameras, etc., are seen in Argentina.

Argentine newspapers and weekly publications are, all in all, better than those of any other Latin American country and offer the advertiser an admirable medium for reaching all classes of consumers. The best of these publications are concentrated in Buenos Aires and circulate throughout the Republic. More information is available today regarding their rates than has been obtainable for many years past, and local rates for foreign advertising may now be secured provided payment is made promptly. The Argentine trade journals, however, like those of other Latin American countries, are almost negligible in widespread influence if not in numbers. The trade, as such, will still have to be reached through direct selling, export trade papers, catalogs, and other methods formerly in vogue.

Other local media, such as street cars and billboards, are poorly organized and poorly utilized, and will continue to be of much less value than similar media in the United States until they are more effectively organized and given more uniformity and stability, and until better display methods are adopted. An encouraging sign is seen in the presence of many advertising agencies in Buenos Aires. However useful they may have been in some cases, their equipment and training show no signs of an ability to keep pace with the highly developed demands of modern American merchandising practice. In this respect the most hopeful sign is the increasing interest manifested by American advertising agencies in South America, and it is believed that with more encouragement they will come to occupy the same valuable position in relation to foreign advertising as they now enjoy in the domestic field. Highly skilled services such as they render in the United States are needed to parallel and support the

[1] *Ibid.*, p. 49.

expanding sales plans now being contemplated by many American manufacturers abroad.

A judicious and profitable use may be made of motion pictures and other aids to selling. The dealer has been ignored too much by both European and American exporters. He will not change overnight, because his traditions and training are along European lines, but helpful suggestions from American advertisers based on an understanding of his problems, practical "dealer helps" and consumer advertising will work wonders in changing his outlook and his attitude.[1]

Uruguay. Of Uruguay's publications only those issued in Montevideo are of interest to the American advertiser. There is less concentrated influence to be found in its newspapers than in Buenos Aires, and it may be found necessary to use a greater proportion of them, though not necessarily at a greater cost, to achieve the same relative results. They are more keenly partisan and political than the Argentine dailies, somewhat more insular, and not so well organized in a business way. Uniform advertising rates do not obtain except possibly in a few of the leading ones. Once the basis for the local rate is understood, it is possible for foreign advertisers to obtain this rate, provided they will pay their bills promptly. Buenos Aires newspapers have no appreciable circulation in Uruguay, but Argentine weekly publications circulate widely there.

Except two farm papers, there are no publications of consequence in Uruguay aside from its newspapers. There are no significant trade journals, and the importer and merchant will still have to be reached by direct-selling methods, export trade papers, catalogs, correspondence, and such other similar methods as have been found to be useful.

Outdoor and street-car advertising in Montevideo is widely used, but it is of decidedly secondary importance in any campaign and will remain so until its display methods are much improved. Basically, it is a sound medium, but it cannot be properly utilized by the American advertiser today because of the general methods of handling it and other obstacles that attend its use.

Aside from their possible use for the placing and checking of copy, the Montevideo advertising agencies will be of little value to the American advertiser. He will find a better solution by using the American advertising agencies that are awakening to the importance of this field and are making plans for eventually

[1] J. W. Sanger, *Advertising Methods in Argentina, Uruguay, and Brazil,* pp. 54 and 55.

rendering a service such as they extend to advertisers in domestic markets.[1]

Brazil. The language in practically all Latin American countries is Spanish, but in Brazil the official commercial language is Portuguese. Eighty to eighty-five per cent of its population cannot read or write. Approximately 800 publications of various kinds are published.

Japan. Depending on the viewpoint of the inquirer, one can answer either "Yes" or "No" to the question, "Is Japanese advertising and merchandising modern?" If the questioner has in mind only the American 1920 standard, then Japanese practice is several decades behind us. If, on the other hand, some sort of an average standard of the rest of the civilized business world is the comparison in mind, then Japan measures up amazingly well. Speaking from the advertising standpoint, both as to the mediums available and the methods of using them, Japan is immeasurably ahead of any other Asiatic country and would compare favorably not only with a leading South American country like Argentina, but with most of the advanced countries of Western Europe as well.

The country can boast of many daily newspapers, of which about 200 are of some importance. Approximately 1,500 magazines are issued in Tokyo, and, while most of them are negligible, the better ones cover the entire field of human interest, ranging down from serious reviews to comics. There are the crude beginnings of outdoor advertising—mostly posters in railway stations and signs on telegraph poles. There is some street-car advertising, not well organized or executed, but at least making a start. There are a good many electric signs. There are excellent printing and lithographing establishments. There are many advertising agencies, mostly Japanese, operating largely on a brokerage basis; while paying scant attention to "service," they have at least broken the ground. And there are a considerable number of Japanese advertisers whose appropriations reach rather imposing figures. Above all other considerations, there is a general consciousness of advertising, by and large, and it is a distinct factor in Japanese business today. Though it is often mawkish or badly done, and is unorganized for the most part, the Japanese have passed beyond the "patent-medicine" stage in advertising practice.

[1] *Ibid.,* p. 69.

The largest single advertiser, when all mediums are taken into consideration, is a manufacturer of a sort of pellet called "Juntan," which would seem to correspond in its use somewhat to our chewing gum. The largest single advertiser (and probably group of advertisers also) in newspapers and magazines is a manufacturer of toilet goods.

As showing the kind and quantity of Japanese newspaper advertising, the following statement, prepared by a very large Osaka daily, at the writer's suggestion, is interesting, the figures at the right indicating lines (nine to an inch) of display advertising carried by this one newspaper during January, 1920:

Toilet goods	52,669	Foods	9,334
Patent medicines	72,617	Machinery	8,576
Books and magazines	41,281	Clothing	3,300
Financial statements	2,690	Stocks and bonds	19,326
Hospitals	2,697	Government notices	7,467
Shipping notices	9,413	Miscellaneous	37,984
Death notices	5,306		
Stocks and promotion	66,451	Total	351,520
Liquors and soft drinks	12,394		

A surprisingly large group of advertisers in newspapers are book and magazine publishers, not only on account of the widespread literacy (it is estimated that only 10% of the people are illiterate), but also because of the eagerness and avidity with which the people at large have in recent years taken to reading. In this connection it is interesting to note, since universal compulsory education became a fact in Japan, that all students are compelled to learn to read English. Unfortunately, they are not taught to speak it even as well as they read it; the teachers themselves are Japanese, and they, like the rest of their countrymen, show no great facility in pronouncing the English language. With these facts in mind, one's surprise is lessened upon finding few Japanese, among the masses of the people, who even attempt to speak English.[1]

Ninety per cent of the population of Japan is literate, which is very high. It has some 1,500 magazines and about 900 newspapers, of which 200 are of chief importance. Half a dozen dailies and a number of magazines are published in English. The circulation of the newspapers is

[1] J. W. Sanger, *Advertising Methods in Japan, China and the Philippines,* pp. 15 and 16.

fairly large; about a dozen have circulations of between 100,000 and 500,000.

China. In China the illiteracy is very high; approximately only 10% are literate. However, in spite of that

Figure 119: Specimen of a Chinese advertisement

fact the advertising of trade-marks is probably an important feature.

It is true that the coolie who earns 20 to 30 cents a day complains not of the high cost of living but that "rice is dear," for the reason that rice is almost the only thing that he buys every day and he measures all costs by what is most familiar to him. Yet that same coolie is buying cigarettes made from American tobacco, and he is buying American kerosene—things unknown to him 20 years ago—simply because they have appealed to his taste or his need, and because they have been presented to him attractively, in small packages, within his means, and their "chops" (trade-marks) have been made known to him through advertising. There are hundreds of items such as these whose sales can be expanded indefinitely within the space of a few years as China's industrial life grows, simply because people are there to produce or consume in unlimited quantities.

It is true that less than 10% of the Chinese are literate, and that only 1% of them are enrolled in schools, as compared with 20% in the United States. But even the illiterate coolie can read a few characters on a shop front or label and has been taught to buy his oil and cigarettes by advertised trade-marks, and the 1% of Chinese in schools means that 4,000,000 children are receiving a rudimentary education such as very few Chinese children enjoyed a few years ago.

In walking through almost any Chinese city, one's first impression is that it is a huge bazaar with the outstanding features of banners, flags, and signs, and that the buildings are of quite secondary importance. One suspects, too—and closer inspection confirms the suspicion—that these thousands of highly decorated flags and banners carry advertisements of one kind or another. And so they do, even if no more than the name of the shop. Gaudily colored posters, consisting of a simple picture and a few Chinese characters, cover walls and fences, and indeed are found in every place where "sniping" can be done. Posters of one kind or another constitute the single most widely used and most important advertising medium in China. It is with primitive, easy-to-understand methods such as these, as well as with parades and gifts of puzzles, calendars, or kites, all bearing advertisements, that the advertiser reaches the common people of China. Even some of the junk and sampans on the Yangtze River have advertisements painted on their sails. The ancient custom of itinerant story-tellers going from place to place still obtains here, and they, instead of the "movies," furnish the only relief from the humdrum life that the country people know. But even these story-tellers have been turned to advantage by the advertisers, and many of them may be heard weaving into their tales the stories of new brands of cigarettes or kerosene or whatever the advertiser has paid them to tell about.

The American who wants to reach the masses of China with his product must completely readjust his entire idea of what advertising is, since the crude poster and still cruder "ballyhoo" methods (all of which will be discussed in detail in other sections of this book) must form the backbone of his campaigns.

For selling higher-class articles, there are of course other means to be used in conjunction with or separate from these outdoor methods. There are, for example, the mails, which are invaluable as a means of reaching those who can read; they are particularly important because any written message is regarded as almost sacred by the Chinese and is never thrown away.

As to publications: Ten years ago there were a scant handful, despite the invention and use of movable types in China 500 years before their invention in Europe. Today there are some 400 publications of one kind or another. They include certain dailies and weeklies in the English language, published by British or American interests and intended almost wholly for the European and American residents and for the comparatively few Chinese who prefer to get their news in a foreign language. Most of these 400 publications are, however, Chinese dailies. They come and go with startling frequency, and while many of them are little more than political organs of ambitious Chinese politicians (and as such lead a precarious life), there are a good many excellent ones. The best of these vernacular dailies, some of which were established 30 years or more ago, are published in Shanghai, and the leaders each have bona fide circulations in excess of the total of all the English-language dailies in China. A few of the English-language and a score or more of the Chinese-language publications are under Japanese control or direction.

Advertising is not nearly so well organized in China as it is in Japan, and with its present development it would be impossible to arrange for it or place it from the United States except through some kind of intermediary in China. There are a number of advertising agencies there, both Chinese and foreign; one particularly capable agency under American direction is located in Shanghai.

Before the war the Germans and Japanese were the most aggressive advertisers in China. Indeed, the Germans continued their general publicity efforts (despite the fact that they had no goods to sell) until 1917, when the Chinese Government ordered them stopped; the Japanese were extremely active with both newspaper and poster advertising until the boycott of May, 1919, closed all Chinese publication channels to them. The British have never done much advertising to the Chinese consumer, and the French have done even less. American advertising until very recently was largely limited to the efforts of a few houses with active sales organizations in the field, which were supported by consumer advertising; during 1919 and 1920 a considerable number of new American advertisers began modest campaigns on a "try-out" basis.

The largest single advertiser in China is the British-American Tobacco Co., known familiarly as the "B. A. T." Under British management, its advertising is in the hands of Americans; its yearly publicity and sales-promotion expenditures reach about $1,800,000 Mex., of which less than 10% is expended in newspapers and other publications, the remainder being devoted to posters, calendars, premiums, displays for dealers, etc. They have their own poster plant, and out-door advertising constitutes the backbone of their appeal to the Chinese masses. They make and sell but one product—cigarettes—and as regards the marketing of one article, their large and efficient publicity department in Shanghai is better acquainted with the avenues and uses of advertising than any organization in China. A few of the large general import houses in Shanghai have their own advertising departments, but no one of them seems to have delved deeply into the problem of using advertising as a means of reaching China "from top to bottom" with a variety of products.[1]

While illiteracy is very high, and while the circulation of newspapers is relatively small, only 10,000 to 30,000 as a maximum, this condition is in part offset by the fact that the Chinese have a very high regard for the printed word. Learning to write is a difficult process and consequently the Chinese people have acquired a high respect for writing and reading ability. In the second place this condition is in part offset by the fact that newspapers are passed on from one person to the next, so that a paper with a circulation of a given amount will have actually several times as many readers. Oftentimes a paper will be in the hands of one family from seven to eight o'clock and then a boy will call for it and pass it on to someone else from eight to nine, and so on. Space is measured in Chinese newspapers not in terms of columns, but in terms of square inches. Mr. Sanger points out that he does not believe the common rumor spread in other countries regarding super-

[1] J. W. Sanger, *Advertising Methods in Japan, China and the Philippines*, pp. 56, 57, and 58.

stition about colors among Chinese people to be true. He believes that there is very little basis for feeling that the Chinese will be offended by using a wrong color in advertising

About 40 different Chinese of both sexes and of different classes were asked to suggest colors for a certain hypothetical label. Every imaginable combination of colors was suggested, and without any evidence that any of them in any combination were "tabu," the composite Chinese opinion really forced the conclusion that any or all colors were good so long as the general effect was striking and somewhat vivid.[1]

There is, apparently, considerable uncertainty in advertising, due to the evils of the "sniping" of billboard space.

Any coolie with enough money to buy a pot of paste and a brush can become a billposter, and painted signs, fences, walls, and any other surfaces are subject to his "sniping." So reprehensible have these abuses become in large treaty ports like Shanghai that as many as 12 gangs of coolies have been known to successively cover up the preceding gangs' posters within 24 hours, with the result that none of the 12 postings had any value whatsoever. Even where these conditions do not obtain and where the circumstances are more favorable, it is estimated that the life of a poster does not exceed three days.[2]

Advertising interests in Shanghai are at work to raise the standards. The Advertising Club of China, which is affiliated with the Advertising Clubs of the World, is attempting to reorganize the entire business and put it on a more reliable and substantial basis.

The Philippines. In the Philippines, English is the official and leading commercial language. However, in order to reach the people by advertising it will ordinarily be necessary to use at least two, if not three, languages, namely, English, Spanish, and Tagalog, which is a dialect.

Mention has already been made of the variety of tongues spoken in the Philippines, all of which are represented in one way or another by newspapers, weeklies, or monthlies. Aside

[1] *Ibid.*, p. 71.   [2] *Ibid.*, p. 79.

from an English-language weekly, which is the most influential publication in the islands, most of the publications of any consequence are daily newspapers. There are some in English, in Spanish and in Tagalog; others in English with Spanish sections or editorials, and Spanish newspapers with dialect sections; there are dailies in seven other dialects besides Tagalog, as well as newspapers in Moro and in Chinese. Their policies and their value as advertising mediums vary as widely as the languages in which they appear; they range all the way from clean-cut, free-spoken, honest, independent organs to newspapers at the far end of the scale. There are also periodicals devoted to education, farming, and other special interests.

To one familiar with the publications of any Latin American country, the publication situation in the Philippines, while somewhat more confused as the result of the many dialects spoken there, presents many points of similarity.

The bulk of the newspaper advertising is placed locally; a small percentage of it is sent directly from the United States, but practically none from any other countries. The rates charged foreign advertisers are considerably higher than those paid by local ones, even when there is a Manila distributer of the article advertised; when the space is contracted for locally, even if paid for by the American manufacturer, the local rates prevail. It should be said, however, that, except in three or possibly four papers, no fixed rates obtain, though rate cards are published. It is difficult to see how it would be possible to carry on intelligently and economically a comprehensive campaign in many Philippine mediums from the United States, because of its much higher cost under such circumstances, and the fact that 13 languages would be required; this difficulty would, of course, be somewhat lessened in a more restricted campaign where only English and possibly a few Spanish publications were used.

Of the two largest advertisers in the islands, the Pacific Commercial Co. spends about $175,000 annually in advertising, and the Manila Trading & Supply Co. about $50,000. Both of these are American import houses; manufacturers whom they represent usually share in the advertising expenditures.

There are a number of small, local service agencies in Manila operating as advertising agencies, but their work is almost wholly with local retailers and others—probably because of the dominance of the large import houses which prepare and place most of the foreign advertising, representing products for which they have the exclusive sales agencies.

Direct-by-mail methods, including letters, booklets, folders, and other printed matter, together with house-to-house distribu-

Figure 121: Specimen French advertisements

tion of handbills, have proved to be the most important single means of reaching both dealers and consumers, this condition being due to the fact that the great majority of those who can read some language or dialect do not regularly read newspapers.

As regards outdoor advertising, it may be said that posting is not done at all, on account of the heavy rains which make the use of paper impracticable. Painted signs, however, are used in Manila, the organization controlling this medium being affiliated with the Poster Advertising Association of the United States. Many of these boards are excellently situated and are electrically lighted for night display.

Street-car advertising is done to some extent in Manila, where the cards in the cars appear in three languages—English, Spanish, and Tagalog.[1]

There are some 106 newspapers and periodicals in the Philippines, published in 13 different languages and dialects. It is estimated that after duplicates of readers are eliminated, there are approximately 125,000 readers of

[1] *Ibid.*, pp. 90 and 91.

newspapers out of a total population of 10,000,000. Trademarks are substantially as well protected as they are in the United States.

BRIEF OUTLINE OF AN INTERNATIONAL CAMPAIGN

Recently a campaign was prepared to cover a large share of the world market. This was a campaign for a mechanical pencil. The advertisements appeared in 27 countries and were issued in 9 different languages. A fact of interest is that mediums nearly all over the world now have certain uniform standards of size and publication methods. In placing the advertisements of this product in 47 cities in 27 countries, it was found that only three newspapers had a different column width. There has been a remarkable standardization in this respect since the World War. These three newspapers were in Amsterdam, each one of which had its own column and space measure. Except for Great Britain, the appeal used in a large number of foreign countries was pictorial, more so than in the United States. Twelve hundred pieces of copy were prepared, all of them illustrated.

An illustration of a campaign in a foreign country was the advertising of an electric lamp in Cuba. This campaign was based upon the appeal of selling the idea of light. Consequently it was founded upon the conception of stressing the usefulness and attractiveness of well-lighted rooms and places of business and factories. Each advertisement contained a prominent picture setting forth this conception. The advertisements were placed in 30 newspapers and 12 magazines, and comprised some 12 pieces of magazine copy and 64 pieces of newspaper copy. The illustrations were drawn by a Cuban artist. The campaign covered the principal cities in Cuba. The effect of this campaign was an increase of 25% in the sale of this particular brand of electric lamp during a period of 9 months.

XXXVII

FINANCIAL ADVERTISING

Growth of financial advertising. The responsibility of financial institutions to the public. Determining the appropriation for financial advertising. Chief problems of financial advertising. Sample investigation for advertising securities. Consultation on purchase of securities. Monthly sales of spurious and doubtful stocks. Banks buying securities for themselves or for their customers. Bank sales made from securities held or through purchase for a customer. To what extent are banks active in buying securities for their customers? Reasons why banks buy for customers. The relative importance of safety, yield and marketability. The extent to which investors seek banker's advice regarding the purchase of securities. The bank's advice to investors. How far bank's advice extends regarding the purchase of securities. Relative importance of five factors or appeals regarding the desirability of securities. The bank's attitude regarding the use of advertising for high-grade securities in the local papers. The appeals and their presentation—copy. Mediums. Results of financial advertising.

Most financial houses and banks have been slow to accept advertising as a means of promoting their business. This has been due partly to the fact that in its early history advertising was used by and associated to quite an extent with questionable products and types of business and was characterized by questionable methods in many instances. However, this condition has been greatly improved so that in recent years financial houses and banks of the highest rank have turned to advertising in considerable numbers. Consequently at the present time a large amount of financial advertising is carried by our best mediums. For example, according to the tabulation made by the *New York Evening Post*, the New York newspapers carried in November, 1920, the following percentages of space devoted to financial advertising.

Morning Newspapers	7.0%
Evening Newspapers	3.5
Sunday Newspapers	1.5

Investment houses have in recent years used many varied forms of advertising, including magazines, newspapers, and particularly direct mail material.

THE RESPONSIBILITY OF FINANCIAL INSTITUTIONS TO THE PUBLIC

It is the duty of financial houses to aid in directing the investments of the community into the right channels. Financial houses have here a real duty and responsibility. The instinct of possession and economy is so strong in human nature that large sums of money are annually invested in worthless securities and stocks purely because of the lure of receiving large returns. The persons who are robbed of their savings in this manner are wholly uninformed and ignorant regarding the possibilities of reliable investments and should be educated by the financial houses to discriminate between sound and unsound investments. The questionable, fly-by-night investment schemes have utilized the most efficient methods of advertising for a long period of time. There is no reason why high-grade financial houses should not attempt to use, in a thoroughly legitimate manner, not necessarily the same methods but appropriate methods to educate the public in a more discriminating use of their money and in putting it where it will be of service to the community and to themselves. An editorial in a prominent magazine recently put the matter as follows:

What is known as big business—and moderate-sized business as well—had better get over its dignity and apply to the great financially unsophisticated public for funds with the same skilled human appeals as are employed by the fakers and swindlers.

The reputable, standard concern with stock to sell or bankers of good standing who have securities to sell are mortally afraid of being undignified. Their advertising must be cold and devoid of human interest or else they shiver from fear of criticism. There are signs of a change on the part of a few distributers of high-grade securities. But the great majority of concerns do not know how to get down to human levels in selling their bonds and shares.

A most attractive little booklet explaining in the simplest terms the elementary facts which the investor should know recently came to the writer's attention. It was well gotten up and calculated to sell. The only drawback was the fact that the promoter behind the concern had a long prison record. The reputable concern is afraid of being too interesting lest he be associated with those of no standing. But why can he not steal their thunder? The big industries of the country—packers, railroads, steel makers, textile mills, and the like—are engaged in a vital work. Why should they be afraid to appeal to the public at large and by means which the public understands?

The great corporations of the country are telling the stories of their business operations to the public in advertisements which all can understand. There is no reason why just as large a public should not participate in their profits through being bondholders and stockholders.[1]

The possibilities of selling high-grade investments to the American public were never realized until the War Liberty Loan Bond Campaigns were put through. Conservative estimates had placed the number of bond investors at 500,000. However, during the war approximately 25,000,000 persons bought Liberty Bonds. Probably not all of these would under ordinary circumstances be buyers of bonds. Nevertheless, a very large percentage of them are in a position to do so and no doubt ought to invest their money in sound stocks, bonds or savings. It is of course difficult if not impossible to estimate the amount of money put into fraudulent, risky and unsound investments. Conservative estimates place it at $500,000,000 a year.

Effective use has also been made of proper publicity methods in connection with the sale of public utility bonds and securities. The possibilities of using advertising in this field, however, have not been realized since little careful study of its problems has been made.

[1] *Saturday Evening Post,* July 3, 1920.

DETERMINING THE APPROPRIATION FOR FINANCIAL ADVERTISING

Because the use of advertising in an extensive manner for investments and banking houses is such a recent development there are no standard bases on which appropriations may be determined. A rule observed by some of the larger banking houses is that the appropriation should not go beyond 2/10 of 1% of the total deposits, and preferably it should be kept below that point. The trust division of the American Bankers Association has recently inaugurated a cooperative publicity program. Each member bank or company contributes 1/100 of 1% of its capital, surplus and undivided profits. The minimum assessment is $25.

During 1920-21 the Savings Banks Association in the state of New York carried out in large space a state-wide advertising campaign on a cooperative basis. The purpose of this campaign was twofold—(1) to increase depositors and (2) to counteract certain misconceptions regarding the use of savings by the banks for the purpose of speculation and enrichment of the wealthy. The campaign was, therefore, largely of an educational nature. It was found that in spite of the fact that the state of New York had a large number of savings depositors, a very large proportion did not have savings accounts because of this misconception. Out of a total population of 10,500,000 in the state of New York, approximately 3,700,000 had savings accounts. Mr. G. M. McLaughlin, State Superintendent of Banks, was particularly interested in having an educational campaign of this sort conducted to dispel the misconception surrounding the savings banks. He stated his point of view as follows:

I believe that if your Association will lift this veil of mystery and lay the plain truth about our savings banks before the people of the state, especially the 3,700,000 people who are depositors in your member banks, the result would be greater public confidence, which is so important during this period of general readjustment; and furthermore, you will prove to them that the savings banks can be relied upon as their faithful and efficient allies. This, in my estimation, will be a definite stride for a better public understanding of savings banks.

The campaign was prepared and carried out in newspapers and magazines, street cars and in picture films. The story of thrift and the importance of saving were set forth in an interesting manner. The campaign was financed by having each member bank contribute 1/100 of 1% of its total resources. The campaign was planned for one year. While the state of New York had a large sum of money in savings banks, with an average of $203.96 per depositor, it nevertheless was considerably behind the neighboring states of Connecticut with $301.02 per account and Massachusetts with an average of $308.59 per account.

The nature of the copy for the campaign may be illustrated by the first two advertisements. The first one which consisted in part of an extract from a letter from Mr. McLaughlin was as follows:

WHO GETS THE EARNINGS OF THE SAVINGS BANKS?

The law provides:

Deposits must be invested in non-speculative securities.

A reserve fund must be maintained to protect deposits.

Only depositors may participate in the earnings from investments.

The savings banks are organized with no shares of stock.

The second piece of copy was written as part of a reply to Mr. McLaughlin's letter by Mr. J. J. Pulleyn, president of the Emigrant Industrial Savings Banks and head of the Savings Bank Association.

Every member of this association agrees with you that the time has come when the veil of mystery should be lifted from the banking business. We bankers did not realize how little the public really knew about their own great savings bank system until we were confronted with published statements which gave the impression that mutual savings banks have stockholders who share in the profits of the banks; that savings banks invest the depositor's money in speculative securities; that dormant accounts eventually find their way into the bankers' pockets, and a number of other statements derogatory to mutual savings banks which obviously were based on misinformation.[1]

CHIEF PROBLEMS OF FINANCIAL ADVERTISING

As previously mentioned, a logical procedure in the study and preparation of plans for advertising in any special field is to consider the numerous problems that arise in relation to the five fundamental problems outlined in the first chapter, namely: the human aspect of the market; the appeals; the presentation of the appeals; the mediums; and the expenditure for advertising. We may, therefore, profitably examine a typical piece of research carried out in connection with one particular type of financial advertising, namely, securities.

Sample Investigation for Advertising Securities. The investigation to be cited here was made in a middle-western state and was designed to obtain information relative to the purchase and advertising of sound investments on

TABLE 163

OFFICERS BUYING SECURITIES FOR A BANK

Who Buys for Banks	Over 10 Million (16 Reports)	3 to 10 Million (30 Reports)	1 to 3 Million (30 Reports)	Less Than 1 Million (23 Reports)
President	31.3%	50.0%	43.6%	30.4%
Vice-President	31.3	23.3	12.8	8.7
Secretary	6.3	6.7	10.3	8.7
Treasurer	12.5	3.3	5.1	
Cashier	12.5	20.0	46.2	65.2
Manager Bond Department	25.0	6.7		
Other officer or employee		3.3	2.6	8.7

[1] *Printers' Ink,* Dec. 30, 1920, p. 94.

the part of banks and to obtain definite information to assist in guiding the investments made by customers of local banks.   For this purpose a carefully prepared set of 50 questions was used.   Responses to these questions were obtained by personal interview with officers in 109 banks, ranging in size from banks with deposits of less than $1,000,000 up to banks with deposits of over $10,000,000. The officers interviewed were for the most part cashiers, presidents, vice-presidents, secretaries, and in the case of the larger banks the manager of the bond department.   In response to the question—Who Buys for the Bank?—the distribution of responses in Table 163 was received.

Consultation on Purchase of Securities.   The tabulation below shows the extent to which consultations are held by the officers of a bank:

	No. Banks Reporting	Per Cent of All Reports
Invariably hold consultation	81	75.0
Sometimes hold consultation	13	12.0
Rarely hold consultation	4	3.7
Never hold consultation	10	9.3

MONTHLY SALES OF SPURIOUS AND DOUBTFUL STOCKS

Of the 100 bankers who responded to this question 56% stated that they had no basis of knowing the expenditure for worthless speculative stocks in their respective communities.   The 44 remaining bankers who responded estimated all the way from $500 to $150,000 per annum, with an average of $28,000.   This evidently is largely a guess, as no one has available any definite basis for an answer to this question, but it illustrates the extent to which every community is drained of its savings by speculative and worthless schemes.

Banks Buying Securities for Themselves or for Their Customers.   Ninety-four banks reported on this point as follows in relation to the size of the bank:

Over 10 million—13 banks—   40.7% for customers.
                            59.2% for own account.
3 to 10 million—24 banks—   22.8% for customers.
                            77.2% for own account.
1 to 3 million—37 banks—   35.0% for customers.
                            65.0% for own account.
Less than 1 million—20 banks—25.6% for customers.
                            74.4% for own account.
Average for all banks—   30.7% for customers.
                            69.3% for own account.

BANK SALES MADE FROM SECURITIES HELD OR THROUGH PURCHASE FOR A CUSTOMER

Ninety-two banks reported on this question as follows:

Over 10 million—15 banks—44.3% bought for customer.
                        55.7% securities held by bank.
3 to 10 million—24 banks—62.3% bought for customer.
                        37.7% securities held by bank.
1 to 3 million—34 banks— 58.2% bought for customers.
                        41.8% securities held by banks.
Less than 1 million—   68.2% bought for customers.
                        31.8% securities held by bank.
Average for all banks—   59.1% bought from investment
                             houses for customers.
                        40.9% sales of securities held
                             by bank.

It is evident from these figures that the proportion of securities sold to customers which were held by the bank increases with the size of the bank.

TO WHAT EXTENT ARE BANKS ACTIVE IN BUYING SECURITIES FOR THEIR CUSTOMERS?

The 109 banks interviewed showed the following conditions regarding this question:

Regularly buy for customers	28.4%
Sometimes buy for customers	17.4
Rarely buy for customers	22.9
Never buy for customers	31.2

Analyzing this question further in relation to the size of the banks we have the figures given in Table 164.

TABLE 164

EFFORTS MADE BY BANKS IN BUYING SECURITIES FOR CUSTOMERS

Size of Bank	Act as Dealer	Sometimes Act as Dealer	Rarely Act as Dealer	Never Act as Dealer
Over 10 million (16 banks)	62.5%	12.5%	12.5%	12.5%
3 to 10 million (50 banks)	3.3	13.3	30.0	23.3
1 to 3 million (39 banks)	23.1	25.6	20.5	30.8
Less than 1 million (24 banks)	8.3	12.5	25.0	54.2

From these figures it appears that the proportion of banks actively buying for customers increases very decidedly with the size of the bank.

Reasons Why Banks Buy for Customers. The responses to this question could not well be presented in statistical form. The chief reasons given by those who actively bought for customers were that they regarded it as a service to depositors, that it was profitable to do so, that there was an income to the bank from it, and that it brought new people to the bank. The chief reasons given by the banks who did not buy for their customers (which were in all only a small percentage of the total number of banks) were that they did not believe it to be the proper function of the bank to do so, that it places the bank in a wrong position—this is stated particularly by smaller banks —that the bank is not in position to give full information regarding the type of investment, etc., that it lowers the bank's deposits and requires special machinery for handling securities.

The Relative Importance of Safety, Yield and Marketabil-

ity. These were mentioned in order of importance as follows by the banks interviewed:

	Safety	Market-ability	Yield
With Respect to Corporations and Firms	57.8%	22.4%	19.8%
Large Individual Investors	63.8	15.3	20.9
Small Individual Investors	63.6	13.7	22.7

THE EXTENT TO WHICH INVESTORS SEEK BANKER'S ADVICE
REGARDING THE PURCHASE OF SECURITIES

Consult Bank	No. Banks Reporting	Per Cent of All Reports
Almost entirely	9	8.3
A great deal	37	33.9
Considerable	32	29.4
Very little	29	26.6
Not at all	1	0.9
Does not know	1	0.9

The Bank's Advice to Investors. The purpose of this question was to determine to what extent banks considered it their legitimate function to advise inquiring investors regarding the purchase of securities.

HOW FAR BANK'S ADVICE EXTENDS REGARDING THE
PURCHASE OF SECURITIES

	No. Banks Reporting	Per Cent of All Reports
Decidedly bank's function	76	69.7%
Probably bank's function	23	21.1
Doubtful as to bank's function	4	3.4
Not bank's function	6	5.5

The results of this question are presented in Table 165 in relation to size of the bank.

Relative Importance of Five Factors or Appeals Regarding the Desirability of Securities. The five appeals were ranked

TABLE 165

NATURE OF ADVICE TO CUSTOMERS

Bank's Advice	Very Large Over 10 Million (16 Reps.)	Large 3 to 10 Million (30 Reps.)	Medium 1 to 3 Million (37 Reps.)	Small Less Than 1 Million (23 Reps.)
Confined to advising investor what not to purchase	6.3%	23.3%	16.2%	17.4%
Extends to recommendation of general class of securities to be bought	68.7	53.3	48.7	52.2
Extends to recommendation of the specific securities to be bought	25.0	23.3	35.1	30.4

in order from one to five and the final ranks were determined from these rankings. Each first was counted 100, each second ranked 50, each third ranked 35, each fourth ranked 25, each fifth ranked 20. This resulted in the following relative values:

1. Kind of Security   72.1
2. Kind of Business Behind Security   54.8
3. Assets—Total and Quick   37.1
4. Name of Investment House Offering
   Security   36.6

THE BANK'S ATTITUDE REGARDING THE USE OF ADVERTISING
FOR HIGH-GRADE SECURITIES IN THE LOCAL PAPERS

If such advertising of securities were accompanied with the statement—"You may send your order through your own bank," or "Consult your banker regarding these securities," or a similar statement, the results of the group of 109 bankers were as follows:

Very favorable	20.2%	Unfavorable	16.5%
Favorable	42.2	Do not know	0.9
Passive	17.4	Will not state	2.8

The Appeals and Their Presentation—Copy. Until recently the advertising of most high-grade banks and financial houses has been overdignified and ultra-conservative. The banker should take the same point of view in the preparation of his advertising material as is taken by any high-grade form of business; namely, he should take the point of view that he has something to sell and that he is entitled to present his services and his facilities in the same manner as any other business which has something meritorious to offer and does so in a fair and honorable manner. The chief weaknesses, therefore, of the usual financial advertising have been:

(a) It is too formal. The usual bank advertisement has consisted of merely an announcement of its officers and board of directors and its capital and assets and deposits. It has taken the point of view that its function is to accept business rather than to invite or seek business.

(b) It has been too indirect and irrelevant. Where financial advertising has attempted to do more than merely present its business card it has often become too indirect and irrelevant; it has set forth in booklets and in advertisements merely general things in relation to business or the community in which it was located. Booklets of this sort are a valuable form of publicity only if they tie up definitely with the financial institution which issues it.

(c) There has been a lack of really convincing appeals and of effective methods of presentation. Until within 10 years there has been no real effort to study the psychology of bank advertising, or to determine what appeals may be effective and convincing and interesting to the reader, or to employ the skill used by questionable types of business.

(d) There has been too much institutional advertising, too much use of booklets and advertisements which have dealt largely with the banking business as a whole in a very distant and impersonal manner. While a certain amount of advertising of this sort is undoubtedly interesting and effective to some extent, it does not directly proceed to the point of presenting specifically the merits and advantages of the particular institution which is issuing it.

A very fertile source of financial advertising material will be found along the lines of information specifically relevant to the particular services which a given financial house has to offer. The banks and investment houses have an abundant opportunity for the use of educational copy to instruct the average investor and bank depositor regarding the most elementary facts and practices relative to investments. The average person is wholly ignorant as to what is meant by bonds and stocks, debentures, preferred and common stock, accrued interest, mortgages, municipal bonds, public utility bonds, the difference between bank service and trust service, and the like. He is wholly ignorant as to what constitutes a sound investment, or reasonable return combined with safety. This unquestionably explains, to a very large extent, the ease with which the average small investor is led to part with his hard-earned savings and to give them to a glib-tongued salesman or send them in response to an enticing advertisement for questionable investments. That the great need is more general information has been shown by the activities of the Better Business Commissions along these lines. For example, the Better Business Commission in the city of Cleveland undertook recently a campaign to drive out questionable types of investments and the persons engaged in promoting them; the method used was a simple presentation of the facts regarding the various investments, their possibilities and their lack of soundness. This proved very effective. A good slogan is "Investigate before investing."

There is no reason whatever why a high-grade banking or investment house should not study most carefully the methods by which the attention and interest of the customer may be secured, how he may be convinced, how he may be made to act and to remember permanently the impressions made, just as is done by other lines of business in the preparation of high-grade advertising plans. The banker has no material commodity to sell, but he has service and professional advice to offer. In general it might be said that no bank has any special superiority or advantages to offer over any other bank or investment house, except in so far as it exercises discrimination and judgment and presents careful and reliable information regarding the investments and services which it offers. Service is as truly a commodity as is any material product presented for sale, and the superior advantages to be found in one bank as compared with another are as great as are the differences in quality and value among varying material products.

Progress, however, has been made, and particularly so during the past 10 years. It will be of interest in this connection to note an advertisement issued on October 9, 1799, in the *Mercantile Advertiser* of New York City, as follows:

The office of discount and deposit will open for the transaction of business for the present, at ten o'clock in the forenoon and continue open until three o'clock in the afternoon, when the business of the day will be closed. Henry Remsen, Cashier.

This advertisement was issued by the Manhattan Company, now The Bank of Manhattan Company of New York City. On May 9, 1921, the same company issued the following advertisement in the *New York Times*, which illustrates to some extent a change in the point of view during the period of 122 years.

Few organizations responsible for a product of such international fame as the Steinway Piano can point to a continuous active family management, as can Steinway and Sons, since the founding in 1853. The early Walker Street factory (here shown) was but the promise of the present large plant in Long Island City. Steinway & Sons is one of the old and honored accounts of the bank.

This illustrates the attempt to set forth something specific, to mention an individual depositor who has made use of this particular bank for a long term of years.

During the last few years there has been a distinct improvement in the direction of making financial advertising more specific, direct and appealing. Illustrations were practically unknown before 1915. At the present time highgrade financial houses use illustrations freely in their advertisements as well as in booklets and folders regarding specific offerings.

What is needed in financial advertising is the application of the same methods of scientific field investigation and copy testing as have been outlined in Chapters XIII and XIV. Such methods would make it possible to determine what appeals and modes of presentation are most effective.

MEDIUMS

The mediums used most satisfactorily by banking houses are in general the same as those used by any other type of business. Possibly somewhat greater use can be made and is being made of direct mail material, particularly in connection with investments. The advertisements in magazines and newspapers are primarily for the purpose of building prestige and good-will and of securing more specific inquiries regarding definite offerings of securities. This inquiry constitutes merely the first step in the selling of securities. This is then followed up in a typical instance by further direct mail material and by calls of salesmen. It may be of interest to note in somewhat more detail the plan followed by one or more investment houses.

Let us assume that in this case $100,000 worth of bonds of $1,000 denominations are to be sold. Advertisements are inserted in newspapers and possibly magazines, calling particular attention to this issue. The copy used is specific and to the point, and the purpose of it is primarily to secure an inquiry from the reader. Seldom will a client be sold through the newspaper advertising as such, but the main object is to locate potential prospective investors.

The first essential in using the direct mail materials is to follow up these prospects brought by the general advertising. Another opening for direct mail materials is through the use of a list of names which the company may have available in its file. It is highly important that the list should be up-to-date and contain possibilities. Ordinarily an issue of $100,000 worth of bonds can be sold with a list of 10,000 names. The particular company in question here follows the plan of sending out three letters after the inquiry has been brought by a newspaper advertisement.

1. A letter to precede the call of the salesman
2. A letter to follow the call of the salesman
3. A letter in case the prospect has not been sold

The copy ordinarily is drawn up so that it does not give the customer a chance to say No or Yes. The assumption is that the customer is interested and that he may be sold later on. In a crude way patent medicine advertising has shown skill in the use of appeals by assuming that the reader has a pain in his back and that he needs a remedy for it. The same principle in modified form holds here.

Many banks issue numerous booklets covering a great variety of topics of general interest. Thus, for example, the Old Colony Trust Company of Boston has issued in recent years booklets on "The League of Nations," "Safeguarding Your Family's Future," "Income and Excess Profits Taxes for 1919," "The War Revenue Act 1919," "The Transportation Act 1920," "Concerning Trusts and Wills," "The Lodge-Lowell Debate on the League of Nations," "Investors Who Know," "The Massachusetts Corporation Tax," "Your Financial Requirements and How We Can Meet Them," "The Services of This Company as Your Agent," "The Massachusetts Income Tax," "The Certification of Municipal Bonds," "War Loans of the United States," "New England Old and New," and so forth. In addition to these, it issues booklets regarding specific bond offerings from time to time. It also issues a house organ or news letter.

Figure 120: Specimen financial advertisements

To illustrate further methods employed by an individual bond house, particularly with regard to the use of sales letters, we may quote the methods used by S. W. Straus & Company. Four letters are issued in this particular series. The first letter is designed to emphasize the importance of knowledge about investments and the need of expert advice on the subject. The letter reads as follows:

Could you draw the plans for a building, or would you consult an architect?

Do you understand law, or do you consult a lawyer?

Unless you happen to be an architect or a lawyer, you would employ either when needed. You realize that no one man can be proficient in every business and profession.

The point I am trying to bring out is this: Why do the majority of men feel competent to invest their money without consulting a bank or investment house? I have often wondered.

I suppose it is because it is so easy to buy securities. Brokers are in every community, and scarcely a week goes by that you are not offered an opportunity to put your money into something.

Even if you have the knowledge necessary to make a thorough investigation of the proposition offered—have you the time? Most of us are so busy making a living in our own particular business that we have not the time to spare. It's easier to take someone's word.

Just ponder a moment—isn't this haphazard and unscientific?

It would cost you a large fee to get the opinion of a big lawyer on the point of law and still you would not hesitate when a large sum of money was involved. The money you are to invest is just as precious. You can consult with the big Institution of S. W. Straus & Co. and it will cost you nothing and perhaps save you a loss.

Please feel free to write us. We welcome inquiries.

The second letter, sent about a week later, is intended to bring out the firm's dependability and the safety of the bonds offered:

Recently we sent you our booklet describing the Straus Plan. We trust that you found it interesting.

Doubtless the first question that came to your mind, was— are these bonds as safe and secure as they seem to be? Each individual forms his opinion according to his past experience, and something tested and tried to another might seem untried and new to you.

The best proof of the safety of the mortgage bonds offered by this house, is the fact that no investor has ever lost a dollar nor waited one day for his interest during the 39 years of our existence. Now, there must be a reason for this and that reason is: the soundness of the Straus Plan which safeguards the mortgages that we underwrite.

Generations have proved that no form of investment is more secure than a first mortgage on a piece of well-located property, improved with a high-grade building.

Our loans are selected with great care as it is only the exceptional loan that can measure up to standards demanded by us. The fact that banks buy these bonds for their own investment is a very high recommendation.

Nearly every one whom you know has made investments that have not turned out well. If you and your relatives had put all your savings in first mortgage bonds underwritten by this house, none of you would have lost a dollar but would have received 6% interest every year. Just think what this means.

Read the enclosed circular carefully. Wouldn't you like to own some of these bonds? You will find an order blank enclosed.

This letter quite often brings results in the way of actual sales, but its chief purpose is to secure a response from the prospect. The third letter is intended to emphasize the idea of service in the following manner:

When we sell a mortgage bond to you the transaction is not complete—in fact it has only begun. The property covering your particular bond is carefully watched and inspected at regular periods. We see that the interest is paid promptly and that the taxes are paid, insurance kept in force, and so on.

If you buy a ten-year bond from us you may rest assured that we will collect the interest that is due all through these ten years and that the principal will be waiting for you at the expiration of that period without a day's delay. We are constantly guarding your investments.

Our prompt payments and our record of Thirty-nine Years Without Loss to Any Investor have been made possible by the operation of the Straus Plan. This has been conceded by prominent financiers to be the greatest safeguard that has been devised this age to protect investors. This plan is clearly explained in the book which we sent you.

Nothing could be simpler or more effective than the operation of the Straus Plan for safeguarding first mortgage investments. Briefly described we demand that the mortgagor reduce his loan approximately 5% each year. Namely, that a principal payment of one-twelfth of the yearly amount due be paid each month, so you can clearly see that at the end of each six months, the accumulated interest is ready for the bondholders as well as the sum that is to pay a portion of the principal. This plan of reducing the loan strengthens it by increasing the margin of safety.

After careful consideration we trust that you will decide to make an investment through us. You will find an order blank enclosed.

Awaiting your instructions, we are, etc.

The company has found that this service letter brings the largest number of returns. This is then followed up after about two weeks by the fourth letter which is intended to bring the prospect to a final decision. This also has brought excellent returns and the persons who do not respond are dropped from the list. The letter is as follows:

We have written you a number of letters and we are wondering if the booklets that were sent reached you safely. We would like very much to hear from you.

Is there any question that you would like to ask? Or, if there is any point not clear, it would be a pleasure to explain to you.

In these days of uncertainty, there is one form of investment which stands above all in safety and desirability, and that is, First Mortgage Bonds safeguarded under the Straus Plan. If you heard of an individual who had made investments for 39 years and had never lost a dollar you would think it remarkable. That is our record.

We want to be of service to you, Mr. . . . ., but, of course, it is pretty difficult to do so by letter, unless you write us frankly.

I am enclosing a stamped envelope for your convenience, and will certainly appreciate hearing from you.

Assuring you of our interest in serving you, and awaiting an early reply, we are.

RESULTS OF FINANCIAL ADVERTISING

Tangible results are being produced where the plans are carried out in an efficient, interesting and thorough-going manner. It will be pertinent here to refer to the experience of the Canada Trust Company.

Coming back to our advertising—since 1914 the guaranteed investment department of the Canada Trust Company has shown an increase of 220%. We attribute this mainly to staff cooperation and direct-by-mail advertising. These splendid results, achieved in a period that began with the war, have proved to us beyond all question the necessity of thoroughly educating the prospect. From the beginning of this campaign the officers of the company felt that direct-by-mail advertising was the best method of conducting the necessary education of the public, and, as the results began to show, the direct-by-mail method was quickly applied to other departments with correspondingly good results.

We used three forms of approach—folders, booklets, and letters. It was realized that some different and greater force than that possessed by the average booklet or letter must be used to produce results in the minds of the class of prospect we had to work upon and to produce results of the nature we were after.

A series of well-written, well-printed folders containing a facsimile reproduction of the bond and coupons was prepared. In passing I might say that it has been abundantly proved that the main reason for the unusual success of these folders was that we showed fac-similes of the bond and coupon. As a matter of fact, we have consistently tried to embody in our advertising matter the sound merchandising and advertising maxim of Arthur Brisbane, "A good picture is worth a million words." A good many prospects actually came into our offices holding in their hands the identical folders or letters that we had mailed them.

It is trite to say that 80% of goods are sold through the eye. Financial advertising is among the hardest, is perhaps the hardest to illustrate pertinently, but the financial prospect is just as susceptible to the pulling power of a "right" illustration as the purchaser of a piano, a cake of soap, a typewriter, or an automobile.[1]

The Hibernia Bank & Trust Company of New Orleans

[1] *Printers' Ink*, July, 1917, p. 96.

has obtained excellent results from its publicity activities. It has organized a department for new business which in combination with the publicity department has been largely responsible for the unusual increase in its business. Within a period of two years the deposits were increased from $24,000,000 to $50,000,000, the total resources from $30,000,000 to $70,000,000, and this in view of the fact that the bank had been in business for 48 years. The expenditure for the advertising department, including all overhead, is approximately 1/10 of 1% on current deposits. Mr. F. W. Ellsworth, vice-president in charge of publicity, describes their methods as follows:

Publicity Department. Our advertising is handled by a distinct department which nevertheless works very closely with the new business and credit departments.

Our advertising plans include:

(a) A comprehensive, specific, continuous campaign for savings accounts, and the gain in this branch of our business during the past 12 months has been approximately 30%.

We use almost continuous display in the newspapers and street cars, painted bulletins, pay envelopes, occasional letter inserts, Christmas club advertising and, last but not least, we maintain small branch offices for savings at several of the large industrial plants.

Also in cooperation with all of the other New Orleans banks, we maintain a school savings system which is meeting with remarkable success. The system has been in use for only two seasons, but already there are even 100% schools in New Orleans, which means that in each case of these schools every one of the pupils has a bona-fide savings account in some one of the New Orleans banks.

(b) We advertise at seasonable intervals for our safe deposit department, and generally choose months just prior to vacation time, which seems to produce the best results. Our advertising for this department is confined almost exclusively to newspapers and pamphlets and folders distributed from our counters.

(c) The advertising for our foreign trade department is also handled by our publicity department under the direction of the foreign trade department. This includes newspaper space, special cards and folders sent to foreign trade houses, all of which is followed up very intimately by personal calls from both our foreign trade and new business departments.

(d) Our fiduciary and trust department advertising includes the use of newspaper space and booklets on fiduciary subjects, such as the appointment of a trust company as agent, trustee, executor; the translation into plain English of some of the trust laws of the state, etc. This form of advertising necessarily must be followed up by personal contact.

(e) Out-of-town bank and commercial business is appealed to through the financial and trade papers and special copy is prepared for this form of publicity. We use about 20 of the leading financial and trade papers, more especially those that circulate in the southern states.

(f) Commercial Business. It is very seldom that we advertise specifically for commercial business, as most of the accounts of this character are obtained by direct personal invitation either from our new business department solicitors or from the solicitation of the officials of the bank.

The advertising that we use, which perhaps appeals more to the commercial people than any other, is what we call good-will advertising. This can best be illustrated by describing a series of advertisements which appeared recently in the New Orleans street cars. The series was known as "Big Industries of our City." Each of the advertisements dealt exclusively with some one industry, and said nothing whatever about the facilities of the bank except that our name appeared at the bottom of each advertisement. The first of these showed a picture of our grain elevator and gave facts about its construction, capacity, cost and the number of employees. The second treated the American Sugar Refining in the same way. The third pictured the new building of the Hibernia Bank & Trust Company, and the fourth described our cotton warehouse, which is the largest in the world. Subsequent cards will continue this series.

Other good-will advertising which has been published by the bank has featured large conventions which have visited our city; the completion and dedication of prominent buildings, the revival of river transportation by the Government, etc. "Of course, any institution," concluded Mr. Ellsworth, "that conducts a systematic, continuous campaign for new business sometimes likes to stop and take stock to determine whether the effort is justified by results.

"Well, we have a thoroughly organized new business department, a cooperating credit department, publicity department, research department and central file department; all independent of, yet cooperating intimately with, each other for the major purpose of helping the bank grow. With the exception of the credit department, all of these activities have been established only since the spring of 1918. At that time our deposits were approximately $24,000,000. Today our normal deposits are in excess $50,000,000. In 1918 our total resources were something over $30,000,000. Today they are approximately $70,000,000. Some of this gain can be attributed to the natural development of business which has occurred everywhere during the past two years, but the fact that our gain is considerably more than the average would seem to indicate that our policy of continuous, concentrated effort along advertising and new business lines pays—and pays well." [1]

Mr. J. W. Carr, of the People's State Bank of Indianapolis, reports in the *Mailbag* the use of direct advertising material to secure 500 new savings accounts. This campaign was carried on prior to July 4. Three letters were used. The first one offered an American flag for every new savings account of $1 or more. The second letter was sent to a list of small bond buyers and the third letter was sent to those already depositors in the savings department. The letter asked them to tell their friends about this offer. They used a list of 2,700 names, from which they hoped to obtain 300 accounts. They had planned to use a second letter after the first mailing, but it was found to be unnecessary. Mr. Carr states:

We were most agreeably surprised. The first three days after our letters were in the mails we reached the 300 mark. We had to put on extra new account clerks. We kept people waiting in line to open account. We decided to set a limit of 500 accounts by July 4—four days away. . . . At 12 o'clock on the day set to end the campaign—our closing hour was two—the five-hundredth flag went across the new account desk and before the closing hour another 40 persons had deposited money but had been promised flag delivery later. The initial deposits averaged approximately $40. [2]

An interesting piece of successful advertising which was em-

[1] *Ibid.*, Dec. 23, 1920, pp. 78. 79.   [2] Ramsay, p. 516.

ployed in one of our campaigns to persuade public utility customers to become security holders in the business, was the following letter on the stationery of the Denver Gas and Electric Light Company, which was distributed in sealed and addressed envelopes to every name on the books:

A Personal Message
To Every Customer of Our Service

"You are invited to become financially interested in this company.

"The gas and electric business is remarkably staple. The earnings of this company are but little diminished by business depressions, nor much inflated in periods of unusual prosperity. It is a business that keeps a very even course throughout all conditions. It therefore fulfils exactly the requirements for permanent and safe investment.

"This company is now bringing out an issue of $1,500,000 of Preferred Stock, which will be sold to retire certain of the company's Bonds, and to provide money required for gas and electric improvements necessitated by the ever-growing city of Denver.

"Instead of allowing the sale of all this stock to eastern bankers (who have offered to buy the entire issue), I have decided to take a hand in the business myself to see that the company's customers may, if they want to, become partners in the business.

"The stock is a well-protected, safe and sane investment, which will pay you over 6% per year in monthly dividends and, in my judgment, it will never give you any worry over the safety of your money.

"I am recommending it to all my friends.

"Yours very truly,
"Wm. J. Barker,
"Vice-President and Gen'l Manager."

The letter was also run in the advertising columns of the newspapers in generous space alongside of an orthodox financial advertisement setting forth the usual particulars of a new offering.

This letter brought genuine prospective investors into the office in such numbers that for about three weeks it was not necessary to seek any by personal solicitation. On one day the purchasers who called in response to this advertisement paid nearly $35,000 in gold coin in making their settlements!

Following the activities produced by this means, a definite plan of personal solicitation was pursued which extended to approximately 5,000 interviews. New stockholders of the company were acquired in that city as a result of this campaign to the extent of about 500, of which more than half had never before owned securities in any corporation. Hundreds of others became interested also in the securities of the holding company, Cities Service Company, as a result of continued sales efforts on all the security issues of the organization.[1]

Another piece of advertising copy we have employed with exceptionally satisfactory results, particularly in newspapers and magazines, where it was used, not as a part of a customer ownership campaign, but rather as a means of obtaining inquiries from investors generally, is as follows:

Permanent
Monthly Income
of $25
can be obtained for
about $3,000
by the purchase of
50 shares Preferred Stock of
Cities Service Company
One of the largest and strongest companies in this country operating public
utility and petroleum properties.
Inquiries Invited.

This offering of a permanent monthly income at a definite and reasonable price has never failed to produce serious inquiries in large numbers, many of which were turned into sales by correspondence or personal interview, and its good effects seem but little influenced by market conditions or by seasons.[2]

Another illustration of the effective use of direct mail material for selling investments is the following instance. Early in 1923 a large Boston trust company sent a letter and a circular describing a high-grade preferred stock to 1,000 names in one of the New England states. The company maintains salesmen in all of the New England states except one. The 1,000 persons addressed resided in this state. Within three weeks this mailing sold 180 shares of stock. One week later another letter and circular offering another preferred stock was sent to the same 1,000 persons. This mailing sold 200 shares.

[1] *Printers' Ink*, Sept. 25, 1919, p. 93.   [2] *Ibid.*, p. 95.

APPENDIX

6 Point Cheltenham Bold
The most ancient materials used for recording events were bricks, tiles, shells, and

8 Point Cheltenham Bold
The most ancient materials used for recording events were bricks, tiles,

10 Point Cheltenham Bold
The most ancient materials used for recording events were

12 Point Cheltenham Bold
The most ancient materials used for recording

14 Point Cheltenham Bold
The most ancient materials used for record

18 Point Cheltenham Bold
The most ancient materials used

24 Point Cheltenham Bold
The most ancient materials

30 Point Cheltenham Bold
The most ancient mat

36 Point Cheltenham Bold
The most ancient

42 Point Cheltenham Bold
The most ancie

48 Point Cheltenham Bold
The most anc

6 Point Cheltenham Bold Extended

The most ancient materials used for recording events were bricks,

8 Point Cheltenham Bold Extended

The most ancient materials used for recording events

10 Point Cheltenham Bold Extended

The most ancient materials used for record

12 Point Cheltenham Bold Extended

The most ancient materials used for

14 Point Cheltenham Bold Extended

The most ancient materials used

18 Point Cheltenham Bold Extended

The most ancient materia

24 Point Cheltenham Bold Extended

The most ancient m

30 Point Cheltenham Bold Extended

The most ancien

36 Point Cheltenham Bold Extended

The most anc

42 Point Cheltenham Bold Extended

The most a

48 Point Cheltenham Bold Extended

The most

6 Point Cheltenham Bold Condensed
The most ancient materials used for recording events were bricks, tiles, shells, and tablets of stones

8 Point Cheltenham Bold Condensed
The most ancient materials used for recording events were bricks, tiles, shells, and

10 Point Cheltenham Bold Condensed
The most ancient materials used for recording events were bricks,

12 Point Cheltenham Bold Condensed
The most ancient materials used for recording events were

14 Point Cheltenham Bold Condensed
The most ancient materials used for recording event

18 Point Cheltenham Bold Condensed
The most ancient materials used for recor

24 Point Cheltenham Bold Condensed
The most ancient materials used

30 Point Cheltenham Bold Condensed
The most ancient materials

36 Point Cheltenham Bold Condensed
The most ancient mat

42 Point Cheltenham Bold Condensed
The most ancient m

48 Point Cheltenham Bold Condensed
The most ancient

6 Point Cheltenham Bold Italic

The most ancient materials used for recording events were bricks, tiles, shells

8 Point Cheltenham Bold Italic

The most ancient materials used for recording events were bricks, tiles,

10 Point Cheltenham Bold Italic

The most ancient materials used for recording events

12 Point Cheltenham Bold Italic

The most ancient materials used for recording

14 Point Cheltenham Bold Italic

The most ancient materials used for reco

18 Point Cheltenham Bold Italic

The most ancient materials used

24 Point Cheltenham Bold Italic

The most ancient material

30 Point Cheltenham Bold Italic

The most ancient ma

36 Point Cheltenham Bold Italic

The most ancient

42 Point Cheltenham Bold Italic

The most anci

6 Point Cheltenham Bold Condensed Italic
The most ancient materials used for recording events were bricks, tiles, shells, and tablets of stones

8 Point Cheltenham Bold Condensed Italic
The most ancient materials used for recording events were bricks, tiles, shells, and

10 Point Cheltenham Bold Condensed Italic
The most ancient materials used for recording events were bricks,

12 Point Cheltenham Bold Condensed Italic
The most ancient materials used for recording events were

14 Point Cheltenham Bold Condensed Italic
The most ancient materials used for recording even

18 Point Cheltenham Bold Condensed Italic
The most ancient materials used for reco

24 Point Cheltenham Bold Condensed Italic
The most ancient materials used

30 Point Cheltenham Bold Condensed Italic
The most ancient material

36 Point Cheltenham Bold Condensed Italic
The most ancient mat

42 Point Cheltenham Bold Condensed Italic
The most ancient

48 Point Cheltenham Bold Condensed Italic
The most ancien

6 Point Cheltenham Old Style
The most ancient materials used for recording events were bricks, tiles, shells, and tablets of stones.　The

8 Point Cheltenham Old Style
The most ancient materials used for recording events were bricks, tiles, shells, and tablet

10 Point Cheltenham Old Style
The most ancient materials used for recording events were bricks, tiles,

12 Point Cheltenham Old Style
The most ancient materials used for recording events were

14 Point Cheltenham Old Style
The most ancient materials used for recording events

18 Point Cheltenham Old Style
The most ancient materials used for re

24 Point Cheltenham Old Style
The most ancient materials used

30 Point Cheltenham Old Style
The most ancient materials

36 Point Cheltenham Old Style
The most ancient mat

6 Point Cheltenham Old Style Italic
The most ancient materials used for recording events were bricks, tiles, shells, and tablets of stone

8 Point Cheltenham Old Style Italic
The most ancient materials used for recording events were bricks, tiles, shells, and

10 Point Cheltenham Old Style Italic
The most ancient materials used for recording events were bricks, tiles,

12 Point Cheltenham Old Style Italic
The most ancient materials used for recording events were

14 Point Cheltenham Old Style Italic
The most ancient materials used for recording eve

18 Point Cheltenham Old Style Italic
The most ancient materials used for rec

24 Point Cheltenham Old Style Italic
The most ancient materials usea

24 Point Bodoni Bold Caps

ONE CAMERA BOOKLET

24 Point Bodoni Bold Caps and Lower Case

Compositors Study Weather

24 Point Cheltenham Bold Caps

LIEUTENANT EXPLAINS

24 Point Cheltenham Bold Caps and Lower Case

Weather Signals Recruits

24 Point Cloister Bold Caps

IMPROVED ENTHUSIASM

24 Point Cloister Bold Caps and Lower Case

Complete Course of Printing

24 Point Scotch Roman Caps

MODERN TEACHER

24 Point Scotch Roman Caps and Lower Case

Secured Precious Jewels

24 Point Caslon Bold Caps

RETURNING HOME

24 Point Caslon Bold Caps and Lower Case

Experienced Physicians

INDEX

INDEX

Titles in This Series

9.
C. Samuel Craig and Avijit Ghosh, editors. The Development of Media Models in Advertising: An Anthology of Classic Articles. 1985

10.
C. Samuel Craig and Brian Sternthal, editors. Repetition Effects Over the Years: An Anthology of Classic Articles. 1985

11.
John K. Crippen. Successful Direct-Mail Methods. 1936

12.
Ernest Dichter. The Strategy of Desire. 1960

13.
Ben Duffy. Advertising Media and Markets. 1939

14.
Warren Benson Dygert. Radio as an Advertising Medium. 1939

15.
Francis Reed Eldridge. Advertising and Selling Abroad. 1930

16.
J. George Frederick, editor. Masters of Advertising Copy: Principles and Practice of Copy Writing According to its Leading Practitioners. 1925

17.
George French. Advertising: The Social and Economic Problem. 1915

18.
Max A. Geller. Advertising at the Crossroads: Federal Regulation vs. Voluntary Controls. 1952

19.
Avijit Ghosh and C. Samuel Craig. The Relationship of Advertising Expenditures to Sales: An Anthology of Classic Articles. 1985

20.
Albert E. Haase. The Advertising Appropriation, How to Determine It and How to Administer It. 1931

21.
S. Roland Hall. The Advertising Handbook, 1921

22.
S. Roland Hall. Retail Advertising and Selling. 1924

23.
Harry Levi Hollingworth. Advertising and Selling: Principles of Appeal and Response. 1913

24.
Floyd Y. Keeler and Albert E. Haase. The Advertising Agency, Procedure and Practice. 1927

25.
H. J. Kenner. The Fight for Truth in Advertising. 1936

26.
Otto Kleppner. Advertising Procedure. 1925

27.
Harden Bryant Leachman. The Early Advertising Scene. 1949

28.
E. St. Elmo Lewis. Financial Advertising, for Commercial and Savings Banks, Trust, Title Insurance, and Safe Deposit Companies, Investment Houses. 1908

29.
R. Bigelow Lockwood. Industrial Advertising Copy. 1929

30.
D. B. Lucas and C. E. Benson. Psychology for Advertisers. 1930

31.
Darrell B. Lucas and Steuart H. Britt. Measuring Advertising Effectiveness. 1963

32.
Papers of the American Association of Advertising Agencies. 1927

33.
Printer's Ink. Fifty Years 1888–1938. 1938

34.
Jason Rogers. Building Newspaper Advertising. 1919

35.
George Presbury Rowell. Forty Years an Advertising Agent, 1865–1905. 1906

36.
Walter Dill Scott. The Theory of Advertising: A Simple Exposition of the Principles of Psychology in Their Relation to Successful Advertising. 1903

37.
Daniel Starch. Principles of Advertising. 1923

38.
Harry Tipper, George Burton Hotchkiss, Harry L. Hollingworth, and Frank Alvah Parsons. Advertising, Its Principles and Practices. 1915

39.
Roland S. Vaile. Economics of Advertising. 1927

40.
Helen Woodward. Through Many Windows. 1926